A User's Guide to Trade Marks and Passing Off

A USER'S GUIDE TO TRADE MARKS AND PASSING OFF

Second edition

Julian Gyngell

LLB, Dip IPL, AITMA
Solicitor, Bird & Bird

Allan Poulter

LLB (Hons), RTMA
Solicitor, Marks & Clerk

Butterworths
London, Edinburgh, Dublin
1998

United Kingdom	Butterworths a Division of Reed Elsevier (UK) Ltd, Halsbury House, 35 Chancery Lane, LONDON WC2A 1EL and 4 Hill Street, EDINBURGH EH2 3JZ
Australia	Butterworths, SYDNEY, ADELAIDE, BRISBANE, CANBERRA, MELBOURNE and PERTH
Canada	Butterworths Canada Ltd, TORONTO and VANCOUVER
Ireland	Butterworth (Ireland) Ltd, DUBLIN
Malaysia	Malayan Law Journal Sdn Bhd, KUALA LUMPUR
New Zealand	Butterworths of New Zealand Ltd, WELLINGTON and AUCKLAND
Singapore	Butterworths Asia, SINGAPORE
South Africa	Butterworths Publishers (Pty) Ltd, DURBAN
USA	Michie, CHARLOTTESVILLE, Virginia

A CIP Catalogue record for this book is available from the British Library.

First edition 1995

ISBN 0 406 89594 5

Typeset by B & J Whitcombe, Nr Diss, Norfolk, IP22 2LP
Printed by Redwood Books Ltd, Trowbridge, Wilts

Visit us at our website: http://www.butterworths.co.uk

Foreword

It gives me great pleasure to have this opportunity to add a few words at the beginning of the second edition of *A User's Guide to Trade Marks and Passing Off*. After all, the last time that I had the opportunity to comment upon the works of Messrs Gyngell and Poulter was in 1985, when both the authors were among my first postgraduate intellectual property students at Queen Mary's College (as it then was). It is rewarding to think that that course contributed to bringing Julian and Allan together – even though, for the next five years, they went their separate ways: Julian to Sydney to practise as a solicitor, Allan to Hong-Kong at the Bar. As we all know, the IP world, although growing, is still small enough that their paths were bound to cross again, and a 'partnership' between the authors was subsequently forged at the 1993 ITMA Christmas Lunch. The fruits of that partnership now include two editions of this *User's Guide* as well as editing the guide to the Community Trade Mark (published by INTA).

I would like to think that it was the course at QMC that has given them the taste for writing about their chosen field of intellectual property law. Perhaps, however, it was the Christmas Lunch! Either way, the authors have manfully tackled the numerous issues which in just three years have already been the subject of considerable judicial interpretation and academic comment. Readers will find in the chapters which follow a comprehensive analysis which has been carefully crafted to give a well-balanced picture of both the technical/legal as well as the practical/commercial issues. This is therefore a book which should be read by the experienced trade mark professional as it should be by students of intellectual property law, marketing consultants and in-house legal advisors – there is something for everyone: *Treat* on infringement and registrability; *Wagamama* on comparing marks; *Barclays/Advanta* and *Vodafone* on comparative advertising; *Prince* on groundless threats; *Penguin* and *Puffin* brand wars; *Sabel v Puma* in the ECJ and on competition law in general; *Spice Girls* and *Elvis* on merchandising rights; *Series 5* on principles for interlocutory injunctions; *Babewatch*, *Wet Wet Wet* and so many more, not least *Philips v Remington* decided only just before last Christmas.

This second edition is particularly well timed because, although there are still many questions outstanding, there is already so much material arising from or concerning the enactment of the 1994 Act. I am grateful to my former students that they have now reduced that material into a manageable and easy to read book.

Professor Jim Lahore
Herchel Smith Professor of
Intellectual Property Law
Queen Mary & Westfield College
London University

February 1998

Preface

Introduction The Trade Marks Act 1994 has now been in force since 31 October 1994 and our second edition states the law in the United Kingdom governing trade marks as at 31 October 1997.

This edition expands significantly upon the first edition in a number of important areas:

1. Cases decided since the first edition (most importantly under the 1994 Act but some under the 1938 Act) are commented upon in the appropriate chapters.
2. Practice and procedure in the Registry which has developed (and has been published recently in the Work Manual) is commented upon, particularly in Chapters 2 and 3.
3. Relevant aspects of United Kingdom and European Community competition laws, so far as they relate to trade marks, have been built into the appropriate sections, particularly in the context of licensing and defences to infringement.
4. A new chapter on the tort of passing off is added.
5. A new chapter summarising the tort of trade libel (in the context of trade marks) is added.
6. Specialist sections have been incorporated within existing chapters dealing with commercial issues such as comparative advertising, Internet domain names, counterfeiting, the so-called 'brand wars', franchising, character merchandising, tax issues and trade marks as security interests.
7. The chapter relating to the Community Trade Mark has been totally rewritten because the Office for Harmonisation in the

Internal Market (better known as the Community Trade Mark Office or CTMO) has, since 1 April 1996, been open for business in Alicante, Spain. Originally, we wrote this chapter as the Introduction to the INTA publication on the CTMO and INTA's kind permission to reproduce this chapter (with minor adaptations) is gratefully acknowledged.

8 Finally, the chapter relating to the Madrid Protocol has been updated now that the Protocol has come into force in the United Kingdom.

The scope of the treatment of each topic is governed by the fact that this publication remains a user's guide to and commentary on trade mark law and practice in the United Kingdom. The emphasis is, therefore, to state the present law as concisely as possible and then to comment upon the practical and commercial implications for trade mark owners and practitioners.

At the end of the Preface to the first edition we noted that we were awaiting with interest the decisions of the courts in cases arising under the 1994 Act. There have been approximately 35 such decisions, and their Lordships Laddie and Jacob (in particular) have already contributed significantly to trade mark jurisprudence in this country. Each of these decisions is commented upon (or at least referenced) in the appropriate chapters which follow. (Note, however, that Jacob J's decision in *Philips v Remington* was handed down too late for us to comment in detail on each of the issues arising in that case. References to the case are incorporated where relevant, but readers may wish to refer also to two recent articles by Gougé (1998) 12 WIPR 53 and Miles (1998) TW Feb, p 12 for a more complete analysis. The case is also the subject of an appeal.) Of course, the overwhelming majority of decisions under the 1994 Act emanate from the Registry and, where appropriate, we have also commented upon or referenced the more important of those decisions.

Interpretation of the 1994 Act Based on the decisions to date, one can already derive some guidance as to how, in general terms, the courts are likely to interpret and apply the provisions of the 1994 Act. The following comments of Jacob J in the *Treat* case make it clear that the Directive will be used to assist in, if not dictate, the proper interpretation of the 1994 Act, whereas *Hansard* will be of less (if any) importance:

'I have some difficulty with the reference to what was said in

> Parliament. The language [of s 9 of the 1994 Act] is taken directly from Article 5 of the Directive and must be intended to have the same meaning. *Pepper v Hart* ([1993] AC 593) allows reference to *Hansard* to find out the meaning of Parliament . . . But in the case of a provision intended to implement a Directive I cannot think that the *Pepper* principle can apply. The intention of Parliament is to implement whatever the Directive means.'

Jacob J goes on to discount the relevance of the White Paper for the same reasons (in so far as the 1994 Act purports to implement the Directive).

We also know from Laddie J's judgment in *Wagamama* that British courts should pay regard to the interpretation and application of analogous or parallel provisions of the trade mark laws of other Member States of the EU. However, Laddie J goes on to warn that:

> 'it would not be right for an English court to follow the route adopted by the courts of another Member State if it is firmly of a different view simply because the other court expressed the view first. The scope of European legislation is too important to be decided on a first past the post basis.'

Since none of the arguments put to Laddie J in that case as to the correct construction of the 1994 Act was acceptable, he considered that it was necessary for him to approach the interpretation of the 1994 Act from first principles. In so doing he concluded (after quoting from various ECJ decisions) that the primary function of a trade mark is to indicate the origin of goods or services, a conclusion which finds support in the preamble to the Directive, which states:

> 'Whereas the protection afforded by the registered trade mark, the function of which is in particular to guarantee the trade mark as an indication of origin . . .'

That the 'indication of origin' or 'badge of origin' principle remains sound and intact under the 1994 Act is of fundamental importance to the interpretation and application of the entire 1994 Act, not least the important practical and commercial provisions relating to registrability, infringement, assignment and licensing. For example, in the *Wagamama* case itself, Laddie J expressly refused to extend trade mark infringement to situations where the effect would be to:

> '. . . create a new type of monopoly not related to the proprietor's trade but in the trade mark itself. Such a monopoly would be likened to a quasi-copyright in the mark.'

Again, in the case of comparative advertising, Laddie J in the *Barclays* case refused to allow the proviso to s 10(6) to strangle the clear object and intent of that section to allow comparative advertising (which, after all, should not offend against the 'indication/badge of origin' principle, because all the advertiser should be doing is using the proprietor's mark in relation to the proprietor's goods or services).

It will therefore be interesting to see whether the more relaxed rules under the 1994 Act relating to the assignment and licensing of trade marks will, indirectly, contribute to a higher incidence of applications under s 46 (revocation) on the grounds that the mark in question has become generic or liable to mislead the public or, even more fundamentally, because it has lost its distinctive character and therefore no longer indicates the origin of the goods in question. With the greater freedom to assign and license trade marks comes the inherent danger that proprietors will lose control of their marks, which will then cease to function as an 'indication/badge of origin'. If this happens, then the mark will lose its distinctive character and it will be liable to be revoked, notwithstanding that the proprietor has not failed to comply with any statutory 'rules' relating to the licensing of his mark.

To conclude, readers may be encouraged by the observations of Walker J in the *Penguin/Puffin* case where, in the introduction to his judgment, he states that although passing off and trade mark infringement cases are 'the subject of a great deal of learning . . . their basic idea is quite simple'. He goes on to express that 'idea' in the form of a 'basic common principle' as follows:

> 'a trader may not sell his goods under false pretences either by deceptively passing them off as the goods of another trader so as to take unfair advantage of his reputation in his goods, or by using a trade sign the same as, or confusingly similar to, a registered trade mark.'

The purpose of this book is to examine the various ways in which the courts have applied the 'basic common principle' referred to by Walker J and, as will be seen, although the principle may easily be stated, the facts of each case may sometimes make it difficult to apply.

Structure of this edition The first edition focused exclusively on the 1994 Act. In this second edition we have divided the book into two parts.

Part 1 deals with legislation which is relevant to trade marks, most importantly the Trade Marks Act 1994.

Part 2 deals with the common law torts of passing off and trade libel (also known as malicious or injurious falsehood).

Acknowledgements Once again, our thanks go to our partners and colleagues at Bird & Bird and Marks & Clerk who have assisted in the writing of this book. In particular, the following people should be singled out for their special contribution: Katharine Stephens (for her invaluable reports of trade mark cases written for the CIPA Journal), Simon Topping (of Bird & Bird's Brussels office, for editing the sections relating to competition law), Susan Lewis (for her guidance in relation to the tax issues) and Clarke Graham (of Marks & Clerk's Alicante office, for reviewing the chapter on the Community trade mark). But, most of all, we thank the heroes at the keyboard, Lucie Newman and Susan Sartoretti.

To Kate and Una, Alasdair, James, Sarah, Olivia-Mòr and Marcus.

JMG
Bird & Bird
London

AMP
Marks & Clerk
London

Contents

Table of statutes

References in the right-hand column are to para numbers. Where a para number is printed in **bold**, this indicates that the Statute is set out in part or in full.

South Africa

Table of statutory instruments

References in the right-hand column are to para numbers. Where a para number is printed in **bold**, this indicates that the statutory instrument is set out in part or in full.

Table of European legislation

References in the right-hand column are to para numbers. Where a para number is printed in **bold**, this indicates that the regulation is set out in part or in full.

Table of cases

Decisions of the European Court of Justice are listed below numerically. These decisions are also included in the preceding alphabetical list.

Glossary of terms

Abbreviation	Full title/citation
Comparative Advertising Directive	Directive 97/55/EC of 6 October 1997 amending Directive 84/450/EEC concerning misleading advertising so as to include comparative advertising
Counterfeit Goods Regulation	Council Regulation (EC) No 3295/94
CTMO	The Office for Harmonisation in the Internal Market, known as the Community Trade Mark Office
Directive	Council Directive No 89/104/EEC of 21 December 1988 to Approximate the Laws of the Member States relating to Trade Marks
EC Treaty	The Treaty establishing the European Community: 'The Treaty of Rome'
Implementing Regulation	Commission Regulation (EC) No 2868/95 of 13 December 1995

Abbreviation – *contd*	**Full title/citation** – *contd*
Journal	The Trade Marks Journal, published by the Registrar in accordance with s 81 and r 65
Mathys Report	British Trade Marks Law and Practice of May 1974, Cmnd 5601
Nice Agreement	The Nice Agreement concerning the International Classification of Goods and Services for the purpose of the Registration of Marks of 15 June 1957 (current version: 6th edition, Cmnd 6898)
Official Journal	The Official Journal of the European Communities
Paris Convention	The Paris Convention for the Protection of Industrial Property, of 20 March 1883 (as revised and amended)
Protocol	The Madrid Protocol Relating to the International Registration of Marks of 27 June 1989
Register	The Register of trade marks maintained by the Registrar
Registrar	The Comptroller-General of Patents, Designs and Trade Marks
Registry	The Patent Office
Regulation	Council Regulation (EC) No 40/94 of 20 December 1993 on the Community Trade Mark
Rules	The Trade Marks Rules 1994, SI 1994/2583

Abbreviation – *contd*	**Full title/citation** – *contd*
TRIPS	The Agreement on Trade-Related Aspects of Intellectual Property Rights, signed in April 1994 as an annex to the Agreement establishing the World Trade Organisation
White Paper	Reform of Trade Marks Law, September 1990, Department of Trade and Industry, Cm 1203
Work Manual	Trade Mark Registry Work Manual
1938 Act	Trade Marks Act 1938, c 22
1994 Act	Trade Marks Act 1994, c 26

Part 1 Statutory provisions

Part 1 of this book (Chapters 1 to 17) considers the law relating to trade marks under the Trade Marks Act 1994.

Part 2 (Chapters 18 and 19) looks at the common law actions of passing off and trade libel.

1 Trade marks

1.01 Introduction The 1994 Act, although primarily directed at the subject of registered trade marks, contains provisions relating to:
(a) unregistered trade marks;
(b) well-known trade marks;
(c) certification marks;
(d) collective marks;
(e) Community trade marks;
(f) international trade marks; as well as
(g) registered trade marks.
The marks referred to in (a) and (b) above are considered in paragraphs 1.10 and 1.11; the marks referred to in (c)–(f) are dealt with individually in Chapters 11–14 respectively; while registered trade marks are the subject of Chapters 2 through to 10. Furthermore, in addition to the categories of marks referred to above, it is relevant to consider company names, business names and Internet domain names, because such names may not be covered by a registration under the 1994 Act. The 1994 Act does not specifically refer to these names but, in certain circumstances, they may be treated as unregistered trade marks for the purposes of the 1994 Act and, accordingly, they are considered in paragraph 1.12. But, before all this, it is necessary first to examine the definition of 'trade mark' in s 1(1) of the 1994 Act.

1.02 Trade mark: the statutory definition, s 1(1) The key definition in the 1994 Act as to what constitutes a 'trade mark' is found in s 1(1) which provides that a trade mark is any 'sign'[1] which is both:

(a) capable of being represented graphically; and
(b) capable of distinguishing goods or services of one undertaking from those of other undertakings.

By way of example, the section goes on to state that a trade mark may consist of:

> '. . . words (including personal names), designs, letters, numerals or the shape of goods or their packaging.'

This is not an exhaustive list; nor is it a deeming provision – words, designs etc are not deemed to be trade marks as such. They are certainly 'signs' but, in order to be trade marks, they must also be capable of being represented graphically and be capable of distinguishing goods or services. The list is, therefore, merely illustrative and any sign which satisfies the two limbs of the definition in s 1(1) is a trade mark for the purposes of the 1994 Act. It is a feature of the 1994 Act that, apart from the two requirements set out in the definition, there is no statutory limit to the categories of signs which may fall within the definition of 'trade mark'. Of course, the fact that a sign is a trade mark for the purposes of s 1(1) does not necessarily mean that it is registrable; the question of registrability is considered in Chapter 2.

It should also be noted that the term 'trade mark' is used in the 1994 Act to embrace marks which are used in relation to both goods and services; there is no such thing as a 'service mark' as such, only a trade mark registered in relation to services.

This chapter first looks as what constitutes a 'sign' and then considers individually the two limbs of the definition of 'trade mark'.

1.03 A 'sign' The word 'sign' is not defined in the 1994 Act. It has been taken directly from Article 2 of the Directive. Dictionary definitions are somewhat unhelpful except in so far as they confirm that the word 'sign' has a wide meaning that will embrace at least all those things which would have been a 'mark' for the purposes of s 68(1) of the 1938 Act.[2] The Chambers Concise Dictionary includes within its definition of the word 'sign':

> '. . . a signal; a mark with a meaning; a symbol; an emblem; a device; an indication . . .'

1 As to the meaning of which, see paragraph 1.03.
2 ie a device, brand, heading, label, ticket, name, signature, word, letter, numeral, or any combination thereof.

It is clear, also, that a 'sign' will include certain things which may not have been a 'mark' under the 1938 Act. In the Explanatory Memorandum to the Regulation the Commission states (in relation to the corresponding definition of a Community trade mark):

> 'No type of sign is automatically excluded from registration . . .'

This approach is confirmed in the White Paper[3] which states that:

> '. . . the word "sign" is intended to be interpreted broadly. It does not exclude the possibility of a combination of colours or even a single colour, or sounds being considered to be a trade mark.'

The TRIPS Agreement follows suit, it states that:

> '. . . signs, in particular words including personal names, letters, numerals, figurative elements and combinations of colours as well as any combination of such signs, shall be eligible for registration . . .'[4]

Consistent with the clear intention of the Directive, the Registry has rightly adopted a broad interpretation of the word 'sign'[5] and this is evidenced by the fact that 'non-traditional' marks such as colours, sounds and smells have been registered under the 1994 Act.

Colours The 1994 Act neither excludes nor makes specific provision for colours. Therefore, any application for the registration of a trade mark which contains or consists of a colour will be examined on its own merits.

Of course, the 1938 Act did not exclude a colour or colours from being regarded as a trade mark. For example, the distinctive appearance of a pharmaceutical capsule which was half coloured and half transparent containing multi-coloured pellets was held to be capable of registration by the House of Lords in *Smith Kline & French Laboratories Ltd v Sterling-Winthrop Group Ltd.*[6] This has been confirmed in a later *Smith Kline & French* case where the colour pale green was adopted for pharmaceutical preparations (albeit that the application was rejected on other grounds).[7]

Colours and colour combinations clearly play an important role in distinguishing products in the market place. Indeed, in certain

3 Paragraph 2.08.
4 Article 15.
5 Chapter 6 of the Work Manual; see also *Philips Electronics NV v Remington Consumer Products* (22 December 1997, unreported) (Jacob J).
6 [1976] RPC 511.
7 *Smith Kline & French Laboratories Ltd's Cimetidine Trade Mark* [1991] RPC 17.

product ranges, competing traders are basing entire advertising campaigns around the colour element of their trade marks. However, courts have a natural reluctance to grant a monopoly in respect of a colour because this may exhaust the colours available to competitors. Examples of 'colour' marks which have been accepted by the Registrar since the 1994 Act came into force are:

(a) the colour turquoise as applied to the visible surfaces of the goods and the frontage of bank premises, in the name of Barclays Bank plc; and
(b) the colour turquoise applied to the packaging or labelling of various pharmaceutical preparations, in the name of Reckitt & Colman Products Ltd.

Sounds Like colours, the 1994 Act neither excludes nor makes specific provision for sounds and an application for registration of a sound mark will therefore be examined on its own merits. There may be a problem with representing a sound graphically, although the use of musical notation has been accepted by the Registry.[8] Examples of 'sound' marks which have been accepted since the 1994 Act came into force are:

(a) the sound of a dog barking registered for paints, varnishes etc in the name of Imperial Chemical Industries plc; and
(b) the Direct Line jingle – depicted in musical notation.

Smells Again, although there may be difficulties in representing smells graphically, where this can be achieved there is nothing to preclude smell marks being considered for registration. Examples of 'smell' marks which have been accepted under the 1994 Act are:

(a) the strong smell of bitter beer applied to flights for darts; and
(b) a floral fragrance/smell reminiscent of roses as applied to tyres.

Phrases and slogans Phrases and slogans were registrable in principle under the 1938 Act.[9] Problems sometimes arose under the 1938 Act where the phrase or slogan was either a descriptive statement or was not being used as a trade mark in the sense required by s 68(1), that is, it was not being used for the purpose of indicating the necessary connection in the course of trade. Although the elements of s 68(1) do not expressly appear in s 1(1) of the 1994

8 See paragraph 1.04.
9 See for example: *'I Can't Believe It's Yoghurt' Trade Mark* [1992] RPC 533.

Act, it is clear that these issues may still be relevant in determining whether the sign is capable of distinguishing the applicant's goods or services, and thus the only issue is whether the phrase or slogan is capable of distinguishing the applicant's goods or services.[10]

Surnames Section 1(1) itself specifically includes 'personal names' within the list of examples of trade marks.[11] Even the most common surname is capable of distinguishing, and therefore it is right that surnames should be a category of 'signs' which can function as trade marks. For example, the trade mark SMITH'S undeniably distinguishes the crisps of a particular manufacturer from those of its competitors.

The shape of goods or their packaging In the *Coca-Cola* case,[12] Lord Templeman stated that the word 'mark', both in its normal meaning and in its statutory definition, was apt only to describe something which distinguished the applicant's goods rather than the goods themselves. Accordingly, it was held that the Coca-Cola bottle could not be a 'mark' for the purposes of s 68(1) of the 1938 Act. Section 1(1) of the 1994 Act makes it clear that a trade mark can consist of the shape of goods or their packaging and therefore there is no requirement that a 'sign' must consist of something which is separate from the goods themselves. Not surprisingly, a new application was filed for the shape of the Coca-Cola bottle under the 1994 Act and this has now proceeded to registration.

Get-up The wording of s 1(1) makes it clear that trade marks can consist of packaging and hence the get-up of goods is prima facie registrable. The issue is whether get-up or trade dress which is not packaging can be a trade mark. Examples of such matter will include the decor of a restaurant or retail outlet, in particular franchising operations. Strictly, any get-up or trade dress which satisfies the requirements of the two limbs of s 1(1) will be a trade mark for the purposes of the 1994 Act.

The key difference between the 1938 Act and the 1994 Act, however, lies not so much in the introduction of the new concept of a 'sign' per se but in the new definition of 'trade mark' which

10 As to which, see paragraph 1.05.

11 As to the registrability of surnames see Chapter 2.

12 *Coca Cola Trade Marks* [1986] FSR 472, [1986] RPC 421; see also *Re James's Trade Mark* (1886) 33 Ch D 392.

involves satisfying the criteria set out in the two limbs of s 1(1). These criteria are discussed in paragraphs 1.04 and 1.05.

1.04 Capable of being represented graphically, s 1(1) The first limb of the definition of 'trade mark' requires the sign to be capable of graphical representation. Essentially, this is a practical requirement which arises from the need to be able to record and publish the mark as well as to search the Register. The Work Manual[13] sets out three criteria for determining if a sign is graphically represented:

(a) it must be defined with sufficient precision so that infringement rights can be determined;
(b) the graphical representation must be able to stand in place of the trade mark, without the need for supporting samples etc; and
(c) it must be reasonably practicable for persons inspecting the Register, or reading the trade marks journals, to understand from the graphical representation what the trade mark is.[14]

In the case of applications for two-dimensional word and device marks these criteria will necessarily be satisfied. However, applicants seeking to register sounds, smells or three-dimensional signs (and any intangible/non-visual signs) will have to find a way to represent their signs graphically to the satisfaction of the Registrar. For example, certain sounds may be capable of being represented in musical notation and shapes can be represented by one or more photographs or series of drawings, but care should be taken to ensure that the sign is depicted clearly.[15] Alternatively, each could be described in words. Smells may be capable of being represented using a methodology which uses a standard list of terms to characterise sensory perceptions; this is the so-called 'sensory evaluation'.[16] Again, words may also in some cases be sufficient to describe the smell.[17]

The requirement of graphic representation means that the Registry

13 Chapter 6, paragraph 2.2.

14 See also *Claydon Architectural Metalwork Ltd's Application* (6 August 1996, unreported) (R G Evans).

15 For an example of a case where the Registrar refused to accept an application because the photographic representation of the three-dimensional mark did not enable it to be identified, see *Kraft Jacobs Suchard Ltd's Application* (15 November 1996, unreported) (A James).

16 For a more detailed analysis of this methodology see D Lyons 'Sound, Smells and Signs' [1994] 12 EIPR 540.

17 See examples given in paragraph 1.03 above.

will not accept, nor will it be sufficient for an applicant to deposit, either three-dimensional objects, recordings of sounds or specimens embodying smells. The White Paper noted that it would be an unreasonable burden on the public and Registry alike if sound recordings or other specimens were to be filed, and it may be noted that the Rules do not provide for a deposit system.[18]

1.05 Capable of distinguishing goods or services of one undertaking from those of other undertakings, s 1(1) The second limb of the definition of 'trade mark' is of fundamental importance because it embodies the principle that a trade mark must serve to distinguish the goods or services to which it is applied.

The Explanatory Memorandum to the Regulation states that the purpose of these words is to focus attention on the question whether:

> '. . . the relevant sign is capable of performing the basic function of a trade mark. That function, in economic and legal terms, is to indicate the origin of goods or services and to distinguish them from those of other undertakings.'

The wording of the second limb will be recognised as being not dissimilar to that used in s 10(1) of the 1938 Act (the old Part B test for registrability) in so far as the phrase 'capable of distinguishing' appears in each. The phrase in the 1994 Act should not, however, be read in the same way as it was under the 1938 Act, where it was interpreted to mean that the mark had to be capable in fact and in law of distinguishing the applicant's goods or services. This is because s 10(1) was understood in the light of:

(a) the definition of 'trade mark' in s 68(1) of the 1938 Act; and
(b) the provisions of s 10(2) of the 1938 Act, which required the court to have regard to the extent to which the trade mark was 'inherently capable of distinguishing' the applicant's goods or services.

These two provisions of the 1938 Act were read together in such a way as to result in the conclusion that a trade mark was not 'capable of distinguishing' unless it was inherently capable of distinguishing the applicant's goods or services both in fact and in law. The reasoning was as follows:

(a) s 68(1) required that a trade mark must indicate a connection in the course of trade between the goods or services and the applicant (or a registered user);

18 White Paper paragraph 1.25.

(b) public policy required that certain descriptive words should be available for all traders to use;
(c) by virtue of their prima facie descriptiveness and by virtue of the public policy consideration referred to in (b), certain words could therefore never indicate the necessary connection in the course of trade (and therefore could never be trade marks for the purposes of the 1938 Act); and
(d) thus, the requirement in s 10(2) that the court should have regard to the extent to which the mark was 'inherently capable of distinguishing' was not fulfilled merely by showing distinctiveness in fact because distinctiveness in fact, of itself, did not necessarily overcome the public policy considerations.

Accordingly, the phrase 'inherently capable of distinguishing' was interpreted as requiring the trade mark to be inherently capable of distinguishing in law the applicant's goods; the reference to 'in law' meant that a mark could not be a trade mark if it was of such a nature that the law required the mark to be available for use by all traders.

The justification for reading in the requirement that the mark be 'inherently capable in fact and in law of distinguishing' was therefore based on two sections of the 1938 Act which do not appear in any form in the 1994 Act. It would, therefore, be inconsistent with the remainder of the 1994 Act for the requirement in s 1(1) to be read as requiring anything other than distinctiveness in fact, that is, that the sign must be capable of distinguishing in fact the applicant's goods or services from those of other undertakings. This proposition is consistent with the decision of Jacob J in the *Treat* case where he stated that:

> 'if a mark on its face is non-distinctive (and ordinary, descriptive and laudatory words fall into this class) but is shown to have a distinctive character in fact then it must be "capable of distinguishing". Under section 10 of the old Act, for a mark to be registrable in Part B, it had to be capable of distinguishing but the Pickwickian position was that some marks, even though 100% distinctive in fact, were not regarded as capable of distinguishing within the meaning of that provision. I do not think the Directive and the 1994 Act take this more limited meaning over.'[19]

19 *British Sugar plc v James Robertson and Sons Ltd* [1996] RPC 281 at 305; see also *Philips Electronics NV v Remington Consumer Products* (22 December 1997, unreported).

1.06 Goods or services, s 1(1) Although amendments in 1986 brought service marks within the scope of the 1938 Act,[20] the 1994 Act takes the opportunity to simplify the position and to have, as far as possible, the same provisions governing marks for services as those for goods. The term 'trade mark' is thus used in relation to both goods and services.

Retail services Under the 1938 Act it was not possible to register a service mark for retail services. This was the practical effect of the Court of Appeal's decision in *Dee Corpn plc*.[1] In that case it was held that a service has to be charged for separately and that retail services are merely ancillary to the function of trading in goods. This decision was based on the definition of 'service mark' in s 68(1) of the 1938 Act which required that the provision of a service had to be for money or money's worth. There is no such requirement in s 1(1) of the 1994 Act: indeed the word 'service' is not defined at all. Accordingly, a sign which is used in relation to retail services (or any other service which does not involve a charge) should qualify as a trade mark provided that the two limbs of s 1(1) are otherwise satisfied. However, the remaining concern is that the Court of Appeal also held that the specification of 'retail services' was too indefinite to provide an identifiable description of the applicant's services for the purposes of registration. This must still be the case, and hence an application drafted in this way may still be refused.[2] Indeed, it remains the Registry's practice not to register marks for 'retail services'. However, the Registry's position is currently that applications filed in respect of 'retail services' are, at the request of the applicant, being suspended until this question has been determined by the courts.

1.07 Undertakings, s 1(1) The definition in s 1(1) does not refer to the applicant's goods or services: it refers to the goods or services of 'undertakings'. The word 'undertakings' is not defined in the 1994 Act. It is taken from the Directive and, assuming that it is therefore to be interpreted so as not to be inconsistent with Community law, it will embrace any legal or natural person including companies, partnerships, trade associations, co-operatives,

20 Trade Marks (Amendment) Act 1984.
1 [1990] RPC 159.
2 As to which, see Chapter 2.

individuals, state-owned corporations, regional and local authorities and statutory bodies[3] engaged in an economic activity, regardless of its legal status or the way in which it is financed and whether or not it is profit making.[4]

The EEA Treaty[5] defines an undertaking as 'any entity carrying out activities of a commercial or economic nature'.

It has further been held that undertakings engaged in the supply of services are 'undertakings' for the purposes of Article 85(1) of the EC Treaty, as are undertakings engaged in the supply of goods.[6]

1.08 Comparison with s 68(1) of the 1938 Act The definition of 'trade mark' in s 68(1) of the 1938 Act required the mark to be:

> '. . . used or proposed to be used . . . for the purpose of indicating, or so as to indicate, a connection in the course of trade . . .'

The definition in s 1(1) makes no reference to the purpose for which the sign is used in order for it to be a trade mark. This is relevant when one considers, in particular, the licensing of trade marks,[7] because it was this requirement in s 68(1) that led to the House of Lords deciding (reluctantly in the case of Lord Bridge) in the *Holly Hobbie* case[8] that the applicant was 'trafficking' in his trade mark: ie, because he was not using his trade mark for the purpose specified in s 68(1), and hence the registration of the applicant's licensees as registered users was refused under s 28(6) of the 1938 Act. Although attention will be focused, quite rightly, on the fact that s 28(6) has been repealed and not replaced in the 1994 Act, it is submitted that an even more important factor is the omission from within the definition of 'trade mark' in s 1(1) of any reference to the requirement that a sign must be used so as to indicate a trade connection with the proprietor. The omission of this requirement means that the commercial exploitation of signs through character merchandising, franchising and other licensing operations which may amount to treating the sign as a commodity will not, of itself,

3 See the cases cited in Bellamy and Child *Common Market Law of Competition*, 4th Edition, Chapter 2.

4 Case C-41/90 *Höfner and Elser v Macrotron GmbH* [1991] ECR I-1979, [1993] 4 CMLR 306; Case T-61/89 *Dansk Pelsdyravlerforening v Commission* [1992] ECR II-1931.

5 The Treaty on a European Economic Area signed on 2 May 1992.

6 eg: Case 155/73 *Italian State v Sacchi* [1974] ECR 409, [1974] 2 CMLR 177.

7 As to which, see Chapter 10.

8 [1984] FSR 199.

mean that the sign cannot be considered to be a trade mark. However, there is no doubt that even under the 1994 Act the primary function of a trade mark is to indicate the source or origin of goods or services. A sign may not be registrable (indeed, the sign may not even be a 'trade mark' as defined in s 1(1)) if it is not capable of distinguishing the applicant's goods or services. It will not so distinguish if by virtue of the nature of the marks, the goods applied for, and the relevant trade, the public does not treat the sign as an indication of origin but rather as a commodity in its own right.[9]

Used or proposed to be used – use in a trade mark sense Cases on a number of different issues decided under the 1938 Act referred to the concept of a trade mark being used 'in a trade mark sense'. This was a reference to the trade mark being used in accordance with and for the purposes described in s 68(1). For example, in the *Nerit* case,[10] the token use of the mark was held not to be use in a trade mark sense and hence not only was the mark struck off for non-use under s 26 of the 1938 Act, but it was also held that the mark was not a trade mark for the purposes of s 68(1).

It is quite clear that the concept of use in a trade mark sense no longer forms any part of the definition of 'trade mark' .The concept does re-surface in the context of infringement cases under s 10, non-use cases under s 46(1)(a) or (b) and revocation cases under s 46(1)(d).[11]

1.09 Comment The Mathys Report recommended that trade mark legislation should clearly exclude the registration of the colour or the shape of goods or the shape of containers, or smells or sounds.[12] Mathys submitted that to permit the registration of such matter was contrary to public policy in that no one trader should be granted a perpetual monopoly of an arbitrarily selected characteristic or feature, whether inherent or applied. It followed from this recommendation that there was no amendment to the definition of 'mark' in the 1938 Act[13] and thus the *Coca-Cola* case[14] was decided as it was.

9 This issue is discussed in more detail in the context of registrability in Chapter 2 paragraph 2.03.
10 *Imperial Group Ltd v Philip Morris & Co Ltd* [1982] FSR 72.
11 See Chapters 6 and 5 respectively.
12 Paragraph 64.
13 ie s 68(1).
14 Supra, paragraph 1.03, note 12.

The statement of principle expressed in the Mathys Report has not been rejected as such. Section 3(3)(a) provides that a trade mark may not be registered if it is contrary to public policy. But the overriding objective of the 1994 Act is to recognise the fact that:

(a) certain signs (which may not have qualified for registration under earlier trade mark legislation) are nonetheless recognised by consumers as distinctive of the goods or services of a particular trader; and
(b) the registration of such signs merely recognises the de facto monopoly in respect of the use of such signs which, for example, may be enforceable by way of an action for passing off.

There is also an argument that signs which could be protected under other intellectual property legislation should expressly be excluded from trade mark registration. Once again, the 1994 Act, consistent with the objective stated above, seeks only to test whether the sign in fact functions in the market place as a trade mark and, if so, it is prima facie a trade mark and registrable unless there are express grounds for refusal.[15]

The 1994 statutory definition of 'trade mark' is therefore intended to serve the needs of commerce and to be open-ended so as to be capable of adapting to changes in trading practices. This pragmatic approach is in marked contrast to the 1938 Act (and its predecessors) and to the attitude of the courts in interpreting and applying the old law. In the past, marks have been denied registration on technical, formalistic grounds when the fact of the matter was that the mark in question was distinctive of the applicant's goods or services and would only have been used by a third party who wanted to trade-off or appropriate the benefit of that distinctiveness.

1.10 Unregistered trade marks Although s 2(2) asserts that no proceedings lie either to prevent or recover damages for the infringement of an unregistered trade mark, the 1994 Act does in fact indirectly recognise unregistered trade marks for certain purposes. It is not the intention to review in detail in this chapter the relevant sections relating to unregistered trade marks. However, it is worth noting briefly the circumstances in which an unregistered trade mark is relevant for the purposes of the 1994 Act.

15 As to which, see Chapter 2 and *Philips Electronics NV v Remington Consumer Products*, supra.

Passing off, s 2(2) In the first place, s 2(2) itself confirms that nothing in the 1994 Act affects the law relating to passing off.[16]

Impediment to registration, s 5 Secondly, in the context of registrability, a trade mark application may be refused on the basis of either:

(a) a conflict with an 'earlier trade mark' which, pursuant to s 6, will include unregistered trade marks which are either:
   (i) well known; or
   (ii) the subject of an earlier filed application; or
(b) if the use of the mark applied for is liable to be prevented in the United Kingdom by virtue of any rule of law protecting unregistered trade marks or signs used in the course of trade.[17]

A mark registered contrary to s 5 is liable to be declared invalid.[18]

Defence to infringement, s 11(3) Thirdly, in the context of defences to infringement, the use of an 'earlier right' in a particular locality, which applies only in that locality, does not infringe a later registered trade mark.[19] For the purpose of this defence 'an earlier right' means an unregistered trade mark or other sign which has been continuously used since before both the use and registration of the registered trade mark. Accordingly, provided that the proprietor of the unregistered trade mark can show that his trade mark is an 'earlier right' for the purpose of s 11(3), he can continue to use his trade mark notwithstanding that such use would otherwise infringe the registered trade mark.

Acts of agents and representatives, s 60 The 1994 Act, in accordance with Article 6*septies* of the Paris Convention, introduces new rights and remedies for the benefit of proprietors in a Convention country of marks (whether registered or unregistered).[20]

Specifically, the proprietor of the mark has the following options open to him in the event that his agent or representative applies for the registration of the mark in the United Kingdom:[1]

(a) to oppose the application, in which case the registration will be refused;[2]

16 See Chapter 18.
17 Section 5, as to which, see Chapter 2.
18 Section 47(2), as to which, see Chapter 5.
19 Section 11(3), as to which, see Chapter 7.
20 Section 60; a Convention country means a country, other than the United Kingdom, which is a member of the Paris Convention: s 55(1).
1 Subject to the provisions set out in s 60(5) and (6).

(b) to apply for a declaration that any subsequent registration of the mark is invalid;[3]
(c) to apply for the rectification of the Register so as to substitute his name as the proprietor of the registered trade mark;[4] and
(d) to obtain an injunction to restrain the unauthorised use of the mark by the agent or representative.[5]

Well-known trade marks Finally, an unregistered trade mark may also be so well known that it is entitled to the special protection which the 1994 Act confers on such marks in accordance with Article 6*bis* of the Paris Convention. These marks are the subject of the next two paragraphs.

1.11 Well-known trade marks, s 56 The 1994 Act, in accordance with Article 6*bis* of the Paris Convention, confers certain rights and remedies on the proprietor of a well-known trade mark.

Section 56 provides that, for the purposes of the 1994 Act, a reference to a trade mark which is entitled to protection under the Paris Convention as a well-known trade mark is to be construed as a reference to a mark which is:

> '... well known in the United Kingdom as being the mark of a person who:
> (a) is a national of a Convention country; or
> (b) is domiciled in, or has a real and effective industrial or commercial establishment in a Convention country,
>
> whether or not that person carries on business, or has any goodwill, in the United Kingdom.'

Convention country It is important to note that the definition of 'Convention country' in s 55(1)(b) limits the category of relevant well-known trade marks for the purposes of s 56 to those which are owned by persons who are nationals of or domiciled in a Convention country, the definition of which specifically excludes the United Kingdom. Proprietors of well-known marks who are nationals of or domiciled in the United Kingdom will either have to register their marks or rely upon the tort of passing off. The

2 Section 60(2), as to which, see paragraph 4.05.
3 Section 60(3)(a), as to which, see paragraph 5.18.
4 Section 60(3)(b), as to which, see paragraph 5.18.
5 Section 60(4), as to which, see paragraph 8.18.

remedy/injunction under s 56(2) is not available to such persons (unless they happen also to be nationals of or domiciled in a Convention country).

Meaning of 'well known' The first issue which must be considered is what is required in order for a mark to be considered to be 'well known' for the purpose of s 56. There has been considerable speculation as to what the answer to this question might be[6] and readers seeking a detailed review of the laws relating to famous and well-known marks both in the United Kingdom and many of the important jurisdictions of the world should refer to *Famous and Well-Known Marks* by Frederick Mostert.[7]

Mr Mostert has analysed the various criteria adopted in numerous jurisdictions and has provided guidelines to assist trade mark authorities (and thus practitioners and trade mark owners) in identifying 'famous' or 'well-known' marks. The relevant factors which he has identified are as follows:

(a) the degree of recognition of the mark;
(b) the extent to which the mark is used and the duration of such use;
(c) the extent and duration of advertising and publicity accorded to the mark;
(d) the extent to which the mark is recognised, used, advertised, registered, and enforced geographically or, if applicable, other relevant factors that may determine the mark's geographical reach locally, regionally, and worldwide;
(e) the degree of the inherent or acquired distinctiveness of the mark;
(f) the degree of exclusivity of the mark and the nature and extent of use of the same or a similar mark by third parties;
(g) the nature of the goods or services and the channels of trade for the goods or services which bear the mark;
(h) the degree to which the reputation of the mark symbolises quality goods; and

6 See for example: MacDonald, Cook and Barr 'Trade Mark Filing Strategies and Pitfalls', Managing Intellectual Property, October 1991.

7 Published by Butterworths 1997. For further reading see David Tatham OBE 'Well-Known Trade Marks', the Intellectual Property Institute 1997; Michael Blakeney 'Well-Known Marks' [1994] 11 EIPR 481; Basile Catomeris 'The Riddle of Well-Known Marks and Other Goodwill Carriers' Trademark World, December/January 1995/6, p 20.

(i) the extent of the commercial value attributed to the mark.

Of course, the question as to whether a mark is well known is essentially one of fact. The problem is to assess in advance the extent to which a mark must be known before it can be said to be 'well known'. Perhaps light can be thrown on this issue by looking at those sections of the 1994 Act where well-known trade marks will or may be relevant.

To start with, s 56(2) provides that the proprietor of a well-known trade mark can obtain an injunction to restrain the use of his well-known mark by third parties in the United Kingdom. However, an injunction will only be available if his well-known trade mark is used:

(a) in relation to goods or services which are identical with or similar to the goods or services for which the mark is well known; and
(b) where such use by the third party is likely to deceive or cause confusion.

Accordingly, the injunction available to the proprietor of a well-known mark under s 56(2) is certainly no broader (and arguably is narrower) than the injunction which would be available to the proprietor of a registered trade mark pursuant to s 10(2).[8]

In any event, the injunction under s 56(2) will never be available in the circumstances described in s 10(3) (that is, where a third party uses his trade mark in relation to goods or services which are *not* similar to those for which the mark is protected). What can one deduce from this? It could be argued that, because the injunction is only available in limited circumstances (limited as compared with s 10(2) and (3)), the level of notoriety required should not be set too high.

On the other hand, the moderate level of protection afforded by s 56(2) is not necessarily indicative of the level of notoriety that will be required in order to establish that a mark is well known. Instead, one could argue that, because the 1994 Act is conferring certain protection on foreign proprietors' trade marks, which may be unregistered in the United Kingdom, it is right that such protection should be limited only to those marks with a very high level of notoriety.

Evidence In certain countries, arbitrary levels of notoriety have been adopted for the purposes of determining whether a mark is well known. This often takes the form of a stipulation as to a certain

8 As to infringement under s 10(2), see Chapter 6.

percentage market recognition of the mark in question. In practice, arbitrary levels are unsatisfactory. If such an approach is adopted, then issues will arise as to what evidence will need to be submitted to the court, for example:

(a) Will it only be necessary to establish a certain level of notoriety in the particular trade or service sector in which the trade mark is used and, if so, what level of market awareness will be required?

(b) Will it also be necessary to establish a certain level of notoriety outside the relevant trade or service sector and, if so, what level of market awareness will be required?

(c) Will it also be necessary to establish a general public awareness of the mark in question and, if so, what level of awareness?

(d) What will constitute a sufficiently representative sample? Presumably this can be answered by statisticians, although it may be difficult to define in advance, given the numerous variables such as: how many people will need to be surveyed/ give evidence, the extent to which those persons must be representative of the various geographical regions of the United Kingdom, as well as the various cultures, age groups, and even standards of education, not to mention gender.

Furthermore, will it be necessary to establish that the notoriety has subsisted for any particular length of time, or will it be sufficient that the mark is well known as at any given date? All these matters suggest that proving that a trade mark is well known may be a logistical nightmare. Having said this, of course, in the majority of cases the notoriety of the mark may almost be a matter of judicial notice. Unfortunately, one cannot necessarily rely on judicial notice; in the Transvaal Provisional Division of the Supreme Court of South Africa, Southwood J held that the trade mark MCDONALD'S registered in respect of hamburgers was not a well-known trade mark in South Africa and ordered McDonald's Corporation's portfolio of trade marks to be cancelled on the grounds of non-use.[9] On appeal this decision was rightly overturned. The Court of Appeal concluded that the purpose of s 35 of the South African Trade Marks Act 1993, which is substantially identical to s 56 of the 1994 Act, was to make it sufficient for a plaintiff to show that his mark enjoys a reputation in

9 Combined cases 19719/93, 16493/94 and 11700/93; cited with approval in *Philips Electronics NV v Remington Consumer Products* (22 December 1997, unreported) (Jacob J).

the country where relief is sought. Unlike the common law of passing off, it was not necessary that the plaintiff should have conducted business in that country or that he should enjoy goodwill there. Furthermore, the Court of Appeal found that, in order to come within s 35, the foreign trade mark proprietor must show that a substantial number of the class of persons who would have an interest in the goods or services of the foreign trade mark proprietor (ie potential customers) would know the foreign trade mark and would be confused by its use in relation to the relevant goods/services of the third party. The survey evidence which was accepted by the Court of Appeal showed that about 80 per cent of the relevant target sector of the population covered by the survey knew the trade mark MCDONALD'S as being the mark of a foreign company. This market survey evidence was held to be admissible and to have probative value.[10]

Conclusion The question as to whether a trade mark is well known is very much at large. Ultimately, the courts will have the pleasure of determining the meaning of 'well known' in the context of a trade mark as well as the nature and extent of the evidence that will be required to establish that a mark is well known.

Assuming, however, that it can be established that a mark is well known, the 1994 Act confers certain rights and remedies on its proprietor and these are mentioned briefly below.

Impediment to registration, ss 5 and 6 In the first place, a well-known trade mark is deemed to be an 'earlier trade mark' for the purposes of s 5[11] and thus can be the basis on which the registration of a later conflicting identical or similar trade mark can be refused,[12] provided that the well-known mark was well known as at the date of the application for the registration of the later trade mark. A mark registered contrary to this provision can be declared invalid.[13]

Defence to infringement Section 11 does not provide expressly that a registered trade mark will not be infringed by the use of an earlier well-known mark. However, it may be the case that a mark which is well known for the purposes of the 1994 Act (see s 56(1))

10 Case No 547/95, 27 August 1996; for a more detailed case comment see O H Dean 'McDonald's trade mark : Ex Africa Semper aliquid novi' [1996] 12 EIPR 683.

11 Section 6(1)(c).

12 As to which, see Chapter 2.

13 Section 47(2), as to which, see Chapter 5.

will also come within the meaning of the phrase 'earlier right' for the purposes of the defence set out in s 11(3). The difficulty with s 11(3) is that it is only available where the use of the earlier right is in a 'particular locality' and where the earlier right 'applies only in that locality'. It must be assumed that the whole of the United Kingdom can be a 'locality' for the purposes of s 11(3) as, although such a conclusion strains the ordinary meaning of 'locality', the alternative conclusion would be perverse and would almost necessarily exclude well-known marks from the ambit of s 11(3) because, of their nature, they are likely to 'apply' throughout the United Kingdom.

There is also a second difficulty in so far as s 11(3) is only available where the use of the earlier right is 'protected by virtue of any rule of law (in particular the law of passing off)'. A well-known mark need not necessarily be protected by virtue of any rule of law (whether passing off or otherwise) because the definition in s 56(1) is wide enough to include well-known marks of proprietors who do not carry on business and/or who do not have any goodwill in the United Kingdom: it is questionable whether the well-known mark of such a person is indeed entitled to any protection by virtue of any rule of law. Certainly, there must be a very real question as to whether the law of passing off will provide such protection.[14] The counter argument which may be available to the proprietor of the well-known mark is that s 56(2), which confers the right on the proprietor to obtain an injunction, provides the necessary protection for the purposes of s 11(3) and, in that case, the proprietor of the well-known mark will have the same defence available to him as is available to the proprietor of any other 'earlier right'.[15]

Remedies, ss 56(2) and 60 The proprietor of a well-known mark is entitled to restrain by injunction the use in the United Kingdom of a trade mark which is identical with or similar to his well-known mark, provided that the mark is being used in relation to identical or similar goods or services and where such use is likely to cause confusion.[16]

The proprietor of the well-known mark may also be entitled to the benefit of the special rights and remedies set out in s 60 vis-à-vis the acts of his agents and representatives, provided that he is the

14 See Chapter 18.
15 As to which, see Chapter 7.
16 Section 56(2), as to which, see Chapter 8, paragraph 8.15.

proprietor of the well-known mark in a Convention country[17] (there being no inconsistency for the proprietor of a well-known mark to be entitled to the benefits of both ss 56 and 60). Of course, the unauthorised use of a well-known mark by a third party may also constitute infringement under s 10 (if the well-known mark is registered under the 1994 Act) and/or passing off where the elements of that tort are satisfied (as to which, see Chapter 18). The remedies available for each of these causes of action are discussed in Chapter 8 and, in the context of passing off, Chapter 18.

1.12 Company names, business names and Internet domain names Such names can operate as trade marks for the purposes of the 1994 Act, whether as registered or unregistered trade marks. However, the purpose of this paragraph is to describe their function and purpose in the context of their status as either company, business or domain names (as the case may be) and to distinguish such names from trade marks.

Company names A company carrying on business in Great Britain must comply with the requirements of the Companies Act 1985 concerning the choice and use of company names.

Choice of name A company cannot register a name which:

(a) is the same as a name already on the index of company names maintained by the Registrar of Companies; or
(b) is offensive or unlawful in the opinion of the Secretary of State.

Further, the approval of the Secretary of State is required to use a name which:

(a) suggests a connection with the government or a local authority; or
(b) contains sensitive words specified in the Company and Business Names Regulations 1981 (as amended).

Other statutes impose restrictions on the use of names which may suggest that the company is carrying on a certain type of business (eg banking), or which may imply the possession of certain professional qualifications. Similarly, the use of names suggesting an association with certain charities (eg the 'Red Cross') is also prohibited.

The company's name must be specified in its memorandum of association and it is by this name that the company is incorporated.

17 As to which, see the summary in paragraph 1.11 at page 16.

Subject to a very limited exemption, the final words of the name of a registered company must be either 'limited' (or its abbreviation 'ltd'), or if it is a public company 'public limited company' (or its abbreviation 'plc').

Changing a company's name – voluntary A company may change its name at any time by a special resolution of its shareholders provided that the new name complies with all the requirements specified above for the selection of the original name. On the payment of a small fee, the Registrar of Companies will issue an altered certificate of incorporation, and notice of this issue must be published in the London Gazette. The new name will only be effective from the date of issue of the altered certificate of incorporation on change of name.

Changing a company's name – compulsory The Registrar may require a company to change its name within 12 months of its incorporation if, in the Registrar's view, the name is deceptively similar to that of another registered company.

Changes may also be required by the Registrar if misleading information was provided for the purposes of registration, or the name gives such a misleading indication of the nature of the goods or services provided that the public is likely to be harmed.[18]

Publicity to be given to a company name A company must comply with the following requirements for the disclosure and publicity of the company name, to ensure that it is apparent to those dealing with the company that it is a limited liability company.

(a) The company name must be fixed in a conspicuous position and in easily legible letters outside every office or place where the company does business.
(b) The company's name must be mentioned in legible characters in all:
    (i) business letters of the company;
    (ii) notices and other official publications;
    (iii) bills of exchange, promissory notes, endorsements, cheques and orders for money or goods purporting to be signed on behalf of the company; and
    (iv) bills of parcels, invoices, receipts and letters of credit.

18 See *Association of Certified Public Accountants of Britain v Secretary of State for Trade and Industry*, [1998] 1 WLR 164 (Jacob J).

(c) If the company has a company seal, then the company's name should be engraved in legible characters on the seal. There is no obligation on the company to have a seal.

Failure to comply with the requirements is an offence on the part of the company and officers responsible, each of whom is liable, on conviction, to a fine and a daily default fine for continued breach.

Passing off and trade mark infringement A company name must be registered on the Companies Registry index and this should prevent another company being registered with the same name. However, registration of a company name as required by the Companies Act confers no proprietary rights on the company (its directors or shareholders) which can be enforced against a third party who uses a similar or identical name. Instead, the use of a company name by a third party may constitute either:

(a) infringement under s 10 of the 1994 Act if the company name is also registered as a trade mark; and
(b) passing off if the company can establish the various elements of the tort (as to which, see Chapter 18).

Furthermore, when choosing a company name, it is advisable to check both the Companies Registry index and the Trade Marks Register to ensure that a name has not already been registered and to minimise the likelihood of potential infringement.

Business names A company carrying on business in Great Britain under a name other than its company (or corporate) name must comply with the provisions of the Business Names Act 1985 ('BNA'). The BNA restricts names which can be used and requires that publicity is given to the correct corporate or company name. Further, a company must also ensure that it complies with the requirements of the Companies Act 1985 for the use of the company name.

Choice of name Similar requirements apply to the choice of a business name as apply to the selection of a corporate name.

A company cannot use a business name which suggests a connection with the government or any local authority, and must obtain the permission of the Secretary of State to use certain sensitive words specified in the Company and Business Names Regulations 1981 (as amended).

The choice and use of a business name can be ratified by the company's board of directors and does not need the approval of the shareholders.

Publicity to be given to a business name The publicity requirements are governed by s 4 of the BNA. The primary purpose of these requirements is to ensure that the limited liability of the members remains apparent.

A company using a business name must state its corporate name and an address in Great Britain for the effective service of documents, in legible form, on all:

(a) business letters;
(b) written orders for goods and services to be supplied to the business;
(c) invoices issued in the course of business;
(d) receipts issued in the course of business; and
(e) written demands for the payment of business debts.

Additionally, a notice stating the same information (corporate name and address for service) must be displayed in a prominent position, and so that it can be easily read, in any premises where the business is carried on and to which customers or suppliers have access.

Further, any person with whom anything is done or discussed in the course of business must be provided with written notice of such information if requested.

Failure to comply with these requirements is an offence on the part of the company and, potentially, officers responsible. Further, a company may be prevented from enforcing a contract into which it has entered in breach of these requirements.

Passing off and trade mark infringement Advice should be sought when selecting a business name to minimise the risk of a passing off or trade mark infringement action. Unlike a corporate name, there is no longer any requirement to register a business name and there is, therefore, no formal and comprehensive index of business names which can be checked. However, it is advisable to check both the Companies Registry index and the Trade Marks Register to ensure that the chosen name has not already been registered.

Unincorporated businesses and partnerships There is no provision for the registration of the name of an unincorporated business or partnership. The names of such business or partnership may need to be recorded with professional or trade associations, but any such recordal or registration does not give the owner of the name any proprietary rights in the name. Accordingly, the owner will have to obtain a trade mark registration of its name and/or rely on its common law rights.

Domain names In order to 'link up' with the Internet, you need a computer with a physical connection to the Internet. Such a connection will usually be obtained through a commercial organisation called an Internet Service Provider ('ISP'). Once physically connected, your computer can 'communicate' with other computers linked to the Internet by a series of interconnected networks. However, for the Internet to function properly each connected computer must have a unique textual address.

On the Internet each machine is assigned a unique number: its 'Internet Protocol Address' or 'IP Address', analogous to a telephone number. Historically, Internet users had to key in these numbers in order to communicate. In the 1980s the Domain Name System (DNS) was devised to facilitate a user's ability to remember unique addresses. Under the DNS, a computer is assigned a unique IP Address (consisting of numbers) and a domain name made up of a series of alphanumeric characters followed by suffixes such as '.com.' The domain name is translated into the numerical IP Address by the DNS.

The network is divided into a series of top-level domains ('TLDs'). Some of the most popular generic TLDs are: '.com' which identifies the user as commercial, '.org' for non-commercial or non-profit entities, and '.net' for network service providers. These TLDs are allocated by Network Solutions Inc ('NSI') under licence from InterNIC, and are the domains predominantly used in the USA; however, as they have no geographic reference, international companies have sought to register domain names with these suffixes. Each country has its own domain registries to allocate TLDs which in general have a geographic reference (for example '.uk', '.jp', '.us') followed by a second-level domain which identifies the entity. For example, in the United Kingdom there is 'co.uk', and also 'plc.uk' and 'ltd.uk'. Domain names with the '.uk' suffix are allocated by Nominet.

With multiple TLDs it is possible for 'ABC.com' and 'ABC.co.uk' to be registered by two completely unconnected organisations. Also, registration of a domain name for 'Apple' will not preclude registrations for 'Apples', 'the apples' etc. Currently there is no easy way of monitoring registration of domain names with different geographical suffixes throughout the world. It is easy to see that, with the huge growth of the Internet and the importance of commercial organisations being 'connected' to the Internet as part of their global marketing strategy, there exists potential for disputes arising when an organisation discovers that its preferred domain name has already been allocated to another entity.

Applying to register a domain name is a relatively simple procedure. In the United Kingdom applications for domain names for either a web site or an e-mail address can be made directly to Nominet or via a service provider. The registration bodies have historically allocated domain names on a 'first-come-first-served' basis. In June 1997 the High Court, in the first case concerning Nominet's policy, ruled that the first-come-first-served policy is the legal basis on which Nominet is entitled to allocate the UK domain names.[19]

There are currently no requirements on registration bodies to conduct trade mark searches or to take other measures prior to registration. In mid-1995, in response to an increase in disputes, NSI altered the 'first-come-first-served' policy by requiring an applicant to make certain declarations as to intended use and representations that the use did not infringe any third party rights. A new applicant is also required to give NSI an indemnity in relation to any use of the domain. In the event of a dispute, NSI will not adjudicate the dispute, but it may suspend use of the domain name pending resolution of the dispute by the parties or a court.

In essence, a domain name, like a company name:

(a) gives the owner of the name no proprietary rights in the name which can be enforced against a third party who uses an identical or similar name; but

(b) the use of the domain name may constitute an infringement of a third party's registered trade mark and/or constitute passing off.[20]

19 *Pitman Training Ltd v Nominet UK* [1997] FSR 797.

20 As to which, see Chapters 6 and 18 respectively.

2 Registrable trade marks

2.01 Approach taken by the 1994 Act In contrast to the 1938 Act, the 1994 Act stipulates only that which cannot be registered as a trade mark, rather than setting down mandatory criteria for registrability. Accordingly, all trade marks[1] are prima facie registrable unless there are express grounds for refusal. It is these grounds which are the subject of this chapter and they fall under four headings:

(a) absolute grounds for refusal: s 3;
(b) relative grounds for refusal: ss 5 and 6 (subject to honest concurrent use: s 7);
(c) specially protected emblems and other signs: ss 4 and 57 to 59;[2] and
(d) the failure to comply with the formalities of s 32 and the Rules.[3]

Absolute grounds for refusal

The *absolute* grounds for refusal of registration are found in s 3; they relate to an aspect of the sign or mark applied for which renders it inherently incompatible with the grant of a statutory monopoly, ie the sign or mark is descriptive, not distinctive, and/or

1 As defined in s 1(1): see Chapter 1.
2 As to which, see Chapter 15.
3 In particular, r 11 and see Chapter 3.

should otherwise remain available in the public domain. By contrast, the *relative* grounds for refusal are concerned with protecting the prior conflicting rights and interests of other trade mark proprietors and (to a lesser extent) the interests of the public in not having similar marks used in relation to the same or similar goods or services.

2.02 Signs which do not satisfy the requirements of s 1(1), s 3(1)(a) Logically, if a sign does not fall within the definition of a 'trade mark' then it cannot be registered: only a sign which is a 'trade mark' as defined in s 1(1) can be registered.[4]

Section 3(1)(a) is the only ground for refusal of registration under s 3 to which the proviso at the end of s 3(1) does not apply.[5] The proviso allows the registration of certain trade marks which would otherwise be refused provided that they have in fact acquired a distinctive character. The fact that this proviso does not apply where the sign in question does not meet the definition of a 'trade mark' would appear to imply that, in certain circumstances, a sign can be refused registration even if it has in fact acquired a distinctive character (ie the requirement of the proviso) as a result of the use made of it. However, this misses the point that where any sign can be shown in fact to have acquired the requisite distinctive character (ie the requirement of the proviso) then, by virtue thereof, it will necessarily satisfy the requirement in the definition that the sign be 'capable of distinguishing' the applicant's goods or services. (It would then only remain to be determined whether the sign is capable of being represented graphically.) This conclusion depends upon the validity of the argument advanced in Chapter 1 (and apparently confirmed by Jacob J in *Treat*), that distinctiveness in fact will always satisfy the second limb of the definition of 'trade mark' set out in s 1(1).[6] In effect, therefore, it is submitted that an objection raised under s 3(1)(a) is easier for the applicant to overcome because the applicant need only show that the sign is 'capable of distinguishing'; whereas, in order to rely upon the proviso to overcome an objection raised under s 3(1)(b)–(d), the

4 Section 3(1)(a); as to which, see Chapter 1.
5 As to the proviso, see paragraph 2.06.
6 *British Sugar plc v James Robertson and Sons Ltd* [1996] RPC 281 at 305; but some marks may be incapable of distinguishing: *Philips Electronics NV v Remington Consumer Products* (22 December 1997, unreported) (Jacob J).

applicant has to show that the trade mark has in fact acquired a distinctive character.[7]

An issue which does not appear to have been raised in the cases to date (perhaps because there can only be one answer) is whether the ground for refusal under s 3(1)(a) should be considered in the context of the particular goods or services the subject of the application. That it should not be so considered may be arguable because s 1(1) sets out a definition of general application and the meaning of 'trade mark' is therefore drafted in the abstract, ie the test under s 1(1) is simply whether the sign is capable of distinguishing the goods or services of one undertaking from those of other undertakings, not whether the sign is capable of distinguishing the applicant's *particular* goods/services from those of other undertakings. Accordingly, it is tempting to suggest that the definition in s 1(1) should only exclude (and, therefore, the ground for refusal under s 3(1)(a) should only apply in relation to) those signs which are wholly laudatory (eg 'best') and which are necessarily incapable of distinguishing any category or class of goods or services. However, this is not the correct way to construe the definition in s 1(1), nor is it the correct way to apply s 3(1) because:

(a) it overlooks the fundamental principle that the function of a trade mark is to indicate the origin of the goods or services in relation to which it is used;[8]
(b) it would be inconsistent with the argument referred to above to the effect that it is proper to have regard to evidence of distinctiveness in fact when assessing whether a sign is 'capable of distinguishing' for the purposes of s 1(1); and
(c) in any event, s 3 is concerned with registrability and one can only register a trade mark in relation to the specified goods and/or services for which the mark is used (or proposed to be used).

7 This would appear to be consistent with the attitude of the courts: for example see the analysis of Jacob J in the *Treat* case [1996] RPC 281 at 305, and see also: *Alamo Rent-a-Car's Application*, O/4/96 (5 January 1996, unreported) (C Barrett) where the slogan WE SET THE HIRE STANDARD was rejected, not under s 3(1)(a) because it was acknowledged that the slogan was 'capable of distinguishing', but under s 3(1)(c) because the word 'HIRE' was a punning allusion to the word 'higher', a laudatory epithet.

8 See for example Laddie J's comments in *Wagamama* [1995] FSR 713, where he confirms that the 'indication of origin' or 'badge of origin' principle remains sound and intact under the 1994 Act.

2.03 Trade marks devoid of distinctive character, s 3(1)(b) Although certain signs will fall within the definition of a trade mark if they are capable of distinguishing the applicant's goods or services, that of itself does not necessarily mean that the trade mark is registrable.

As already stated, the requirement in s 1(1) may be satisfied by proving that the sign has in fact become distinctive through use, because a sign which is in fact distinctive must logically be capable of distinguishing the applicant's goods or services. However, s 3(1)(b) provides that a trade mark (ie a sign capable of distinguishing) shall not be registered if it is 'devoid of any distinctive character' (subject to the proviso discussed in paragraph 2.06). This would seem to require that the trade mark must be more than merely capable of distinguishing and that it must also possess some 'distinctive character'. This is reminiscent of the requirement of inherent distinctiveness under the 1938 Act. Jacob J in the *Treat* case[9] asks the question: 'what does *devoid of any distinctive character* mean?' and he answers his own question thus:

> 'I think the phrase requires consideration of the mark on its own, assuming no use. Is it the sort of word (or other sign) which cannot do the job of distinguishing without first educating the public that it is a trade mark? A meaningless word or a word inappropriate for the goods concerned ("North Pole" for bananas) can clearly do. But a common laudatory word such as "treat" is, absent use and recognition as a trade mark in itself (I hesitate to borrow the word from the old Act but the idea is much the same) devoid of any distinctive inherent character.'

The Work Manual[10] states that the Registrar considers the following types of signs to be devoid of any distinctive character:

(a) two letters (or up to four numerals);
(b) surnames common in the United Kingdom;
(c) shapes which have nothing distinctive about them (whether two-dimensional or three-dimensional); and
(d) signs prohibited from registration under s 3(1)(c) or (d) combined with other non-distinctive matter.

By way of example, a prima facie descriptive sign (eg a lemon-shaped

9 *British Sugar plc v James Robertson and Sons Ltd* [1996] RPC 281 at 306; see also *Philips Electronics NV v Remington Consumer Products*, supra.
10 Work Manual, Chapter 6, paragraph 4.2.

container for lemon juice or the word 'treat' for dessert sauces and syrups) could satisfy the threshold requirement in s 1(1) of being capable of distinguishing goods, and it will be the acquired distinctiveness in fact which establishes that the sign is so capable. However, such a trade mark may nonetheless be devoid of any 'distinctive character' and thus liable to be refused registration under s 3(1)(b).[11] Of course, it would then be open to the applicant to seek to rely upon the proviso by submitting evidence that the trade mark has in fact acquired a distinctive character as a result of the use made of it prior to the date of application. In the *AD2000* case[12] it was argued that, having accepted that the mark was capable of distinguishing (for the purposes of s 1(1)), it was therefore not open to find that it was devoid of any distinctive character. This argument is difficult to fault at first sight: how can a mark be said to be devoid of distinctive character when it has already been found to be capable of distinguishing? Surely its capacity to distinguish must result from some distinctive characteristic? The answer is that it is now recognised that the capacity to distinguish (for the purposes of s 1(1)) and the distinctive character required (for the purposes of the proviso to s 3(1)) in order for a mark to be registered can, in theory, be acquired solely through use and not by virtue of any inherent feature or component of the mark (which is what s 3(1)(b) is concerned with). Jacob J recognises this in the *Treat* case,[13] saying:

> 'of course the power of advertising may be able to turn almost anything (save a pure description) into a trade mark . . .'

In dismissing the applicant's argument in the *AD2000* case, Mr Hobbs QC said that:

> '. . . the essence of the objection to registration under s 3(1)(b) is immaturity: the sign in question is not incapable of distinguishing goods or services of one undertaking from those of other undertakings, but it is not distinctive by nature and has not become distinctive by nurture.'

Thus, an applicant should overcome an objection raised under s 3(1)(b) if his trade mark is endowed by 'nature and/or nurture' with the capacity to communicate the fact that the goods or services with reference to which it is used are those of the applicant. If the

11 As was the case with the TREAT mark [1996] RPC 281.
12 *AD2000 Trade Mark* [1997] RPC 168.
13 [1996] RPC 281 at 306.

applicant relies on the 'nature' of the trade mark, then he overcomes s 3(1)(b) without relying on the proviso; if he relies on his 'nurture' of the trade mark then he must plead the proviso.

'Devoid' There is a further issue arising out of the use of the word 'devoid'. 'Devoid' can be defined as meaning 'destitute, free, empty'. Applying this definition to the phrase 'distinctive character' one could argue a narrow application of s 3(1)(b) such that a trade mark will only be excluded from registration on this ground if there is a complete absence of any element which may serve to distinguish. The corollary to this proposition is that this ground for refusal cannot apply if the trade mark incorporates any distinctive element, notwithstanding that the remainder of the mark may lack any distinctive quality.

Alternatively, a broader interpretation could be taken, that is, that a trade mark will be refused registration on this ground if, when considered as a whole, it lacks any distinctive character. The incorporation of a distinctive element may or may not give it that character. However, it is difficult to conceive of a trade mark which incorporates a distinctive element and yet (subject to the de minimis rule) can be said to be *devoid* of any distinctive character. The Work Manual suggests that the narrow interpretation will be applied. It states that all factors have to be considered but that:

> 'it is likely that any trade mark which contains a distinctive element will be registrable (prima facie) unless the distinctive element is de minimis or, where words are involved, an otherwise distinctive word takes on a descriptive significance when combined with other words in the mark.'

It is submitted that this is the better interpretation because the broader interpretation sits uneasily with the policy of the 1994 Act of allowing the registration of trade marks which are recognised by consumers as being distinctive of the applicant's goods or services. It should not matter, therefore, that such recognition derives from a mere element of the mark or, indeed, from a combination of non-distinctive elements if the combination results in the mark as a whole being distinctive.

Fencing off the English language If the narrow interpretation is correct, a trade mark will only be refused registration under s 3(1)(b) if it is devoid of any element which will enable it to be recognised as such in the marketplace. Or, to express the test in a more commercial way: does the mark contain elements, or a combination of elements, which are unlikely to be required for use by other traders? If the answer to this question is 'yes', then one can argue that the mark cannot be said to be *devoid of any distinctive character*.[14] Mr Laddie QC (as he then was when sitting as an Appointed Person) in the *Profitmaker* case[15] was most concerned to protect the liberties of competitors. He said:

> 'the fact that honest traders have a number of alternative ways of describing a product . . . is no answer to the criticism of the mark. If it were, then all those alternative ways could, on the same argument, also be the subject of registered trade marks. The honest trader should not need to consult the register to ensure that common descriptive or laudatory words, or not unusual combinations of them, have been monopolised by others.'

Merchandising marks Another reason why a trade mark may be held to be devoid of distinctive character is because the distinctiveness which is required is not assessed in a vacuum. A mark (particularly a device) may be highly recognisable but, nonetheless, not distinctive because it does not connote the origin of the goods or services. That is, in the words of Laddie J:

> 'It is a particular type of distinctiveness, namely the ability to distinguish the proprietor's goods from the same or similar goods marketed by someone else.'[16]

Based on this general proposition, Laddie J went on to hold that the ELVIS PRESLEY trade mark (although highly recognisable) did not so distinguish the applicant's goods, because members of the

14 This was the approach taken in *Thank You Candy Co Ltd's Application*, O/141/95 (19 October 1995, unreported) (I Peggie) where the Hearing Officer held that the mark THANK YOU was one which other traders may wish to use and the comments of Lord Parker in *W and G Du Cros Co Ltd's Application* (1913) 30 RPC 660 at 672 were considered to be still applicable under the 1994 Act, namely:

> 'It is apparent from the history of trade marks in this country that both the legislature and the courts have always shown a natural disinclination to allow any person to obtain by registration under the Trade Marks Act a monopoly in what others may legitimately desire to use.'

This passage was also cited in *Interprawl SA's Application* (29 January 1997, unreported) (C Barrett) and in *Procter & Gamble Ltd's Application*, O/35/96 (27 February 1996, unreported) (V Douglas).

15 *Profitmaker Trade Mark* [1994] RPC 613.

16 *Elvis Presley Trade Marks* [1997] RPC 543, a case decided under the 1938 Act.

public purchase ELVIS merchandise simply because it carries the name or likeness of the former entertainer and not because they believe that it comes from a particular source. Importantly, Elvis Presley's fame did not add to the distinctiveness of the mark itself. Instead, the question of registrability (distinctiveness) has to be assessed at the date of the application and must be answered by reference to the particular mark, the particular goods applied for, and the nature of the trade into which they are sold. On the facts of the *Elvis Presley* case, Laddie J concluded that there was no reason to believe that current merchandising practice led the public to assume in all cases that products bearing the name or likeness of a famous personality would come from that person himself. The lesson for those involved in character merchandising is that trade marks which consist of names, likenesses or images of famous people or characters should be registered before the person or character has become so well known or popular that the public will buy the product in question simply because it carries the name, likeness or image of that person or character, and not because it comes from a particular source. The ultimate question is whether the goods applied for are of their nature likely to be connected with the person or character such that the name, likeness or image indicates the origin of the goods. Alternatively, is the use of the name, likeness or image simply supplying a demand for that name, likeness or image regardless of the origin of the goods?

Surnames Unlike the 1938 Act,[17] the 1994 Act does not expressly make reference to the registrability of surnames. However, it could be argued that surnames should be denied registration on the ground that a surname is either:

(a) incapable of distinguishing the applicant's goods or services and hence is not a trade mark; or
(b) is devoid of any distinctive character.

As stated in Chapter 1, there should be no issue as to whether a surname is a trade mark, as even a very common name is, in theory, *capable of distinguishing*. However, for the purpose of s 3(1)(b), a case-by-case analysis will need to be carried out in order to decide whether the surname in question can be said to be 'devoid of any distinctive character'. Under s 9(1)(d) of the 1938 Act, the Registrar

17 1938 Act, s 9(1)(d).

adopted the practice of refusing registration if the surname applied for occurred more than a given number of times in the telephone directory. It is suggested that such a practice is no longer valid, as the issue is not whether the mark applied for is a surname but, rather, whether the mark applied for is 'devoid of any distinctive character'. The fact that a surname occurs any given number of times in a telephone directory must be insufficient evidence in itself that the mark applied for is necessarily devoid of any distinctive character, because one must have regard to the surname in question and to the particular goods or services. Indeed, it must be arguable that in simply applying an arbitrary rule the Registrar may be failing to carry out his statutory duty under s 37(1) to examine in each case whether an application satisfies the requirements of the 1994 Act. If so, any refusal to accept an application which is based simply on the application of the Registry's 'rule' in relation to its definition of a 'common surname' could be reviewed judicially and an order for mandamus sought, requiring the Registrar to consider the application on its individual merits. This argument finds support in the comments of Mr Hobbs QC in the *Eurolamb* case[18] where he said that:

> 'the combined effect of subsections (4) and (5) of section 37 is to eliminate the discretion which the Registrar previously had with regard to registration under the 1938 Act and to put him in the position of having to make a judgment, yes or no, upon the materials before him as to the registrability of a mark put forward for registration.'

Of course, this proposition works both ways, and the mere fact that a surname occurs rarely in a telephone directory should not necessarily preclude the Registrar from refusing the application if the surname is devoid of distinctive character. The Work Manual confirms that the Registry still adopts a prima facie position in relation to surnames which are common in the United Kingdom (that is, names which occur more than 100 times in the London telephone directory). The Registry will treat such names as devoid of any distinctive character.[19]

Geographical names An objection to a word which is a geographical name will usually be taken under s 3(1)(c) (which

18 *Eurolamb Trade Mark* [1997] RPC 279.
19 Work Manual, Chapter 6, paragraphs 4.2 and 8.

specifically refers to designations of geographical origin). However, logically, a geographical name may also be devoid of distinctive character. As with surnames, this involves a case-by-case analysis.

The situation may also arise that a trade mark which is a geographical name will not fall foul of s 3(1)(c) because it clearly does not serve to designate the geographical origin of the goods but the name may nonetheless be devoid of distinctive character. This apparently was the case in the application for COTE D'OR, where the objection under s 3(1)(c) was waived, but the application was still refused because the name was devoid of distinctive character.[20] One would have thought that a geographical name which does not designate the geographical origin of the goods must prima facie have some distinctive character; certainly, the choice of such a geographical name does not prevent competitors from using other non-descriptive geographical names, and therefore public policy does not require that the mark be refused registration (unless, paradoxically, the use of the geographical name other than to indicate the true geographical origin of the goods is deceptive, in which case an objection under s 3(3)(b) could be raised). In the *Cote d'Or* case no evidence was submitted, and therefore the applicant could not rely on the proviso to s 3(1). However, where an objection under s 3(1)(c) has already been waived, one suspects that it would not require substantial evidence in order to establish that the mark has by nature or nurture a distinctive character so as to overcome an objection under s 3(1)(b).

Stylised descriptive marks Where an otherwise unregistrable mark is depicted in a stylised form or with a graphical background, it will remain a question of fact as to whether the stylisation or graphics give the mark the requisite element of distinctiveness. A practice direction was published by the Registry on 30 July 1997 in relation to this issue following a decision of the twenty-fourth German Appeal Senate which talked of the stylisation providing a 'surplus' to the otherwise descriptive nature of the words. In essence, the practice direction states that where a descriptive word is applied for in a stylised form or with a graphical background, the Registrar will consider:

(a) how strongly the meaning of the word(s) points away from the sign being a trade mark (ie how descriptive it is); and

20 *Kraft Jacobs Suchard Ltd's Application*, O/176/96 (15 November 1996, unreported) (A James).

(b) how strongly the stylisation or graphical background points towards the sign being a trade mark.[1]

2.04 Descriptive trade marks, s 3(1)(c) Section 3(1)(c) provides that the following shall not be registered:

> 'trade marks which consist exclusively of signs or indications which may serve, in trade, to designate the kind, quality, quantity, intended purpose, value, geographical origin, the time of production of goods or of rendering of services, or other characteristics of goods or services.'

There are several words and phrases in this subsection which require comment.

Exclusively The use of the word 'exclusively' may limit the application of this ground for refusal because, arguably, any trade mark which is otherwise registrable may not be refused registration under this subsection provided that it merely incorporates at least a single element (subject to the de minimis rule) which does not fall within the ground for refusal. Some support for this proposition is found in the decision of the Hearing Officer in the P.R.E.P.A.R.E. application[2] where the objection under s 3(1)(c) was not upheld because, despite the fact that the word 'prepare' was descriptive, the full stops between the letters meant that the mark did not consist 'exclusively' of a sign falling within s 3(1)(c).

May serve to designate The use of the word 'may' in the phrase 'may serve . . . to designate' is ambiguous, as it could suggest that the Registrar is to exercise some degree of discretion enabling him to speculate as to what a trade mark may serve to designate in the future. Alternatively, and more likely, the phrase 'may serve' should be construed simply as embodying the principle which has always been at the heart of trade mark jurisprudence (and which has been affirmed in the Directive and the 1994 Act), namely, that all traders should be entitled freely to describe or 'designate' relevant characteristics of their goods or services.[3] It has previously been held that no one trader should be able to 'fence off' any section of the

1 See the Journal No 6186, page xiii.

2 *Freemantle's Application*, O/195/96 (18 December 1996, unreported) (J Smith).

3 Jacob J held that the word 'treat' fell within s 3(1)(c) but he did not consider in detail the meaning of the individual words and phrases of this subsection: [1996] RPC 281 at 306.

English language which another trader legitimately may wish to use so as to describe his goods or services. This remains the case under the 1994 Act.[4] In the *AD 2000* case,[5] Mr Hobbs QC thought that s 3(1)(c) (like s 11(2)(b)) denied protection to signs which served only to designate the characteristics referred to in the subsection, on the basis that such signs should be available to other traders. He based this on his analysis of the historical purpose of protecting trade marks, that is, to guarantee the trade mark as an indication of origin. A trade mark which serves to designate a characteristic or feature of the goods or services themselves, and not their origin, is therefore the very antithesis of the purpose of giving protection to trade marks, and accordingly s 3(1)(c) prevents such marks from being registered. The phrase 'may serve to designate' therefore focuses attention on the range of marks which competitors may legitimately wish to use to describe their own goods or services.

Designate The word 'designate' means: 'to show or to indicate; to be a name or label for', according to the Chambers Concise Dictionary. Thus, as is the case in practice, s 3(1)(c) prevents the registration of marks which are merely one of a number of alternative words which could be used to 'indicate' the characteristics referred to. That is, the word 'exclusively' does not apply to the word 'designate'. However, it is submitted that a trade mark which merely alludes to the descriptive matters referred to in s 3(1)(c) should not be refused registration, because such a mark does not deprive competitors of the opportunity to use the appropriate descriptive term(s) to designate the relevant characteristics of their goods or services.

In trade The phrase 'in trade' is not limited expressly to the trade in the goods or services the subject of the application. However, one would expect this section to be construed so that trade marks will not be refused registration unless they are apt descriptions or designations of characteristics of the goods or services covered by the application. It must be right that a trade mark, although it may be descriptive of certain goods or services, may legitimately be used and registered in respect of other goods or services without impinging upon another trader's ability to describe the characteristics of his goods or services.

4 See the cases cited in paragraph 2.03, note 14.
5 *AD 2000 Trade Mark* [1997] RPC 168.

Characteristics of goods or services The Work Manual gives a number of examples of signs or indications which the Registrar considers to fall within the relevant characteristics listed in s 3(1)(c). These include the following:

'Kind':	JUMBO, MINI, PERSONAL (for computers), VERTICAL (for blinds).
'Quality':	GOOD or BEST.
'Quantity':	Numbers of four digits or less.
'Intended purpose':	Any reference to use, or the consequence of providing a service.
'Value':	References to worth, merit or importance, eg: WORTH THEIR WEIGHT IN GOLD.
'Geographical origin':	The trade mark must serve to designate geographical origin if it is to be caught by s 3(1)(c); the mere fact that the mark is a geographical name is insufficient of itself; geographical names as well as devices which are associated with particular places, eg tartan and Scotland, are treated as indicating geographical origin. Note: although trade marks (words and devices) which consist of indications of geographical origin may be refused registration under this section, it may be possible to register such marks as collective marks and/or certification marks pursuant to ss 49 or 50 of the 1994 Act.[6]
'Time':	24 HOUR SERVICE, EIGHT TIL LATE
'Other characteristics':	Representations of the goods or services, descriptions of subject matter, descriptions of get up.
'Phonetics':	Misspellings and phonetic equivalents of otherwise objectionable words will require evidence of factual distinctiveness.

6 See Sch 1, para 3(1) in relation to collective marks, which is dealt with in Chapter 12, and see Sch 2, para 3(1) in relation to certification marks, which is dealt with in Chapter 11. Note also Council Regulation on the Protection of Geographical Indications and Designation of Origin for Agricultural Products and Foodstuffs No 2081/92 and Commission Regulation No 2037/93 which lays down rules of application of Council Regulation No 2081/92.

The Work Manual goes on to set out the Registry's very detailed and wide-ranging guidelines as to what the Registrar considers to be registrable and unregistrable for the purposes of s 3(1)(c). Of course, the Work Manual is not the law as such, but applicants and their advisers should have regard to the provisions of Chapter 6 of the Work Manual in order to anticipate the Registry's likely attitude to any given application. In some circumstances, a minor amendment either to the mark itself and/or to the statement of goods or services may avoid or reduce the scope of the Registry's objections.

2.05 Generic marks, s 3(1)(d) Section 3(1)(d) provides that the following shall not be registered:

> 'trade marks which consist exclusively of signs or indications which have become customary in the current language or in the bona fide and established practices of the trade.'

The comments in paragraph 2.04 above in relation to the word 'exclusively' apply equally to its use within this subsection. The remaining wording of this subsection, however, raises further issues of interpretation and application.

Signs or indications which have become customary The use of the word 'become' would suggest that the use or meaning of the sign or indication must have gone through some form of 'metamorphosis' or at least that its use or meaning must have changed in some form or to some degree. This would perhaps require an analysis of the etymon of a word mark and/or its use in society over a relevant period of time. However, there is no requirement that there be a causal link between the applicant's use of his mark and it becoming 'customary' in the manner referred to in s 3(1)(d). This must be right because the question of registrability should not depend upon the applicant's conduct but on the state of the market place as it happens to be at the time of applying for the mark (of course, the opposite is true in the context of revocation under s 46(1)(c), where the proprietor's acts or inactivity are relevant).

The phrase 'customary in the current language' raises a further problem as to whether it is qualified by the words 'of the trade' which appear at the end of the section. One would hope that this phrase is so qualified, so that this ground for refusal will not catch trade marks which have simply become customary in the English language per se rather than customary in the language of the relevant trade. In the *Treat* case,[7] Jacob J thought that the word 'treat' probably falls within s 3(1)(d) but he did not consider in detail the meaning of the individual words and phrases of this subsection. Mr Hobbs QC in the *AD 2000* case[8] commented in relation to the general purpose of s 3(1)(d) as follows:

> 'Section 3(1)(d) prohibits the registration of signs which satisfy the requirements of section 1(1), but nonetheless "consist exclusively of signs or indications which have become customary in the current language or in the bona fide and established practices of the trade". Signs and indications of that kind are common to the trade and available for use by all who choose to use them so long as no misrepresentation is thereby conveyed as to the provenance of the goods or services in respect of which they are used.'

The clear intention of this subsection is to prevent the registration of signs which have come to be used descriptively or generically (albeit that, in the past, the sign may have been distinctive). This is because a sign which has become generic can no longer function in the relevant market as a trade mark because it no longer indicates the origin of the goods or services. The language used, however, raises questions as to what enquiries will be made and what evidence will be admissible to establish that a sign or indication has become either:

(a) customary in the current language [of the trade]; or
(b) customary in the bona fide and established practices of the trade.

It will be a question of fact in each case whether either of these grounds for refusal is made out.

Use guidelines The way in which the proprietor uses and applies his mark (and polices the use by third parties) may either increase or reduce the chances that his particular mark will become 'customary' (for the purposes of s 3(1)(c)) or a 'common name' (for the purposes of revocation under s 46(1)(c)); paragraph 5.10 in Chapter 5 sets out a number of best practice guidelines as to how proprietors should use their trade mark(s).

7 [1996] RPC 281.
8 [1997] RPC 168.

2.06 The proviso, s 3(1) Subsections 3(1)(b),(c) and (d) are qualified by the proviso that:

> '. . . a trade mark shall not be refused registration by virtue of paragraph (b) (c) or (d) above if, before the date of application for registration, it has in fact acquired a distinctive character as a result of the use made of it.'

This represents a fundamental departure from the 1938 Act (and its predecessors) relating to the registration of trade marks. Although it was possible to register a distinctive mark under s 9(1) of the 1938 Act, that entitlement was subject to the definition in s 9(2) which provided that 'distinctive' meant 'adapted . . . to distinguish . . .' and, accordingly, distinctiveness in fact was not necessarily sufficient.[9] However, under the 1994 Act, if an applicant can establish that the mark applied for has, before the date of application, acquired a distinctive character as a result of the use made of the mark, then the mark will proceed to registration as long as it is not caught by any of the other grounds for refusal which are not subject to the proviso.[10]

The proviso effectively overturns earlier decisions of the courts refusing registration of marks in certain circumstances even where it had been shown that the mark in question was, in fact, 100 per cent distinctive of the applicant's goods.[11]

The proviso embodies the now accepted proposition that a trade mark which is in fact recognised as designating the origin of goods or services should not be denied registration. Note, however, that the proviso only comes to the assistance of an applicant seeking registration of a trade mark which has acquired a 'distinctive character' as opposed simply to having become distinctive. Perhaps this is a distinction without a difference? It is difficult to imagine that a trade mark could have acquired distinctiveness and yet be without a 'distinctive character', but the possibility must exist. The meaning of the phrase 'distinctive character' is considered in paragraph 2.03 above in the context of whether a trade mark is devoid of distinctive character. However, it is worth setting out here the specific comments of Jacob J[12] and Mr Hobbs QC[13] in relation to the

9 See the discussion of this issue in Chapter 1, paragraph 1.05.
10 ie ss 3(1)(a), 3(2)–(6), 4 and 5.
11 See *'York' Trade Mark* [1984] RPC 231.
12 [1996] RPC 281 at 302 and 306; see also *Philips Electronics NV v Remington Consumer Products*, supra.
13 [1997] RPC 168 at 175.

meaning of the phrase 'distinctive character' in the context of the proviso. Jacob J said:

> '. . . the question of factual distinctive character is one of degree. The proviso really means "has the mark acquired a sufficiently distinctive character that the mark has really become a trade mark". In the case of common or apt descriptive or laudatory words compelling evidence is needed to establish this. And in particular mere evidence of extensive use is unlikely to be enough on its own.'

Earlier, Jacob J had warned that:

> 'It is precisely because a common laudatory word is naturally capable of application to the goods of any trader that one must be careful before concluding that merely its use, however substantial, has displaced its common meaning and has come to denote the mark of a particular trader.'

Mr Hobbs QC said:

> 'The expression "distinctive character" is not defined in the Act or the Directive. However, the requirements of the expression as used in section 3(1) of the Act are not difficult to discern. For the purposes of that section, a sign possesses a distinctive character if and when it is endowed by nature and/or nurture with the capacity to communicate the fact that the goods or services with reference to which it is used recurrently are those of one and the same undertaking.'

Evidence It is a question of fact in each case as to whether a mark has acquired a distinctive character. However, the Work Manual[14] gives the following guidance as to what the Registrar will look for when considering this question:

(a) the evidence will usually include sales figures, geographical area of sales, promotional/advertising activity, presentation of exhibits showing the actual use of the mark;
(b) evidence should be given in the form of a statutory declaration or a sworn affidavit;
(c) use for a minimum of five years is a rough guide, but the Registrar accepts that use for a shorter period supported by evidence of extensive use/advertising (especially television advertising) may suffice; and

14 Work Manual, Chapter 6, paragraph 13.

(d) the inherent strength of the objection raised under s 3(1)(b)–(d) will be a factor in the level of evidence of factual distinctiveness required.

Following Jacob J's comments in the *Treat* case (to the effect that, in the case of common, descriptive or laudatory words, 'compelling' evidence is needed and that 'mere evidence of extensive use is unlikely to be enough on its own'), the Registrar is adopting a relatively strict approach in such cases by requiring applicants to adduce independent evidence of factual distinctiveness, rather than merely evidence of use per se (no matter how extensive).

2.06A Further observations It is worth noting three arguments which applicants have, on a number of occasions, sought to advance in order to overcome objections raised under one or other of the paragraphs of s 3(1). The arguments have each been rejected for reasons which suggest that it may be very difficult to convince the Registrar to the contrary in the future. They are:

(a) That an identical or similar mark already appears on the Register and that this constitutes some sort of 'precedent' which the Registrar is bound by – sometimes referred to as the 'precedent' argument. This has been rejected because each mark has to be considered on its own merit and the state of the Register is, in principle, irrelevant to the fate of each application. In the *Treat* case, Jacob J observed that:

> 'in particular . . . the state of the Register does not tell you what is actually happening out in the market and in any event one has no idea what the circumstances were which led the Registrar to put the mark concerned on the Register.'[15]

(b) The fact that a potential defendant in the future may arguably have a defence under s 11 (which contains various provisions designed to protect the legitimate interests of honest traders) has been held to be irrelevant because the first line of defence must be to refuse registration to marks which are excluded from registration under the provisions of s 3.[16]

(c) The fact that an analogy can be drawn to a mark which has been held to be registrable under similar provisions in other EU

15 *British Sugar plc v James Robertson and Sons Ltd* [1996] RPC 281; see also *AD 2000 Trade Mark* [1997] RPC 168 and *Eurolamb Trade Mark* [1997] RPC 279.

16 *AD 2000 Trade Mark* [1997] RPC 168.

jurisdictions which have implemented the Directive is not considered persuasive because:

> 'it is a different mark for different goods in a different country and cannot have a bearing on rules for consideration in the United Kingdom.'[17]

That is, words may have different meanings in different countries and Registries have different practices in terms of conducting (or not conducting) searches for prior conflicting marks.

2.06B Further reading There have been a number of cases decided under one or more of the paragraphs of s 3(1) which are examples or illustrations of the statements of principle which are set out in paragraphs 2.02 to 2.06 above. A selection of these cases is as follows:[18]

1 An application for a three-dimensional red, green, white and yellow bottle was held devoid of distinctive character and descriptive.[19]

2 An application for XPRESSLINK for electro-technical apparatus was held devoid of distinctive character and descriptive.[20]

3 An application for the surname MACMILLAN'S was refused in accordance with the Registry's practice because it occurred more than 100 times in the London telephone directory.[1]

4 An application for EUROLAMB was refused as its obvious meaning was 'European lamb' which was devoid of distinctive character and descriptive.[2]

17 *Eurolamb Trade Mark* [1997] RPC 279 at 286; *Zweckform Buro-Produkte GmbH's Application*, O/143/96 (8 October 1996, unreported) (M Needleman); *Coffea SA's Application*, O/158/96 (1 November 1996, unreported) (M Needleman); this is not necessarily British xenophobia: for a similar decision in Spain, see *Renault v Audi* in the Supreme Court of Madrid, 26 October 1993, noted in [1996] EIPR D-207.

18 For a review of some of the more important cases, see A Inglis 'Registrability and Enforcement of Inherently Non-Distinctive Trade Marks in the United Kingdom' [1997] 3 EIPR 138.

19 *Procter & Gamble Ltd's Application*, O/35/96 (27 February 1996, unreported) (V Douglas).

20 *Siemens Aktiengesellschaft's Application*, O/4O/96 (6 March 1996, unreported) (I Peggie).

1 *Hilborough Mill Foods Ltd's Application*, O/46/96 (21 March 1996, unreported) (W Tennant).

2 *Eurolamb Trade Mark* [1997] RPC 279.

5 An application for FACETOFACE was held to be descriptive of video-conferencing facilities and therefore devoid of distinctive character.[3]

6 A method of improving the aesthetic appearance of the applicant's goods was held devoid of distinctive character and descriptive of their character.[4]

7 An application for OFFICE PACK was refused in accordance with Registry practice in relation to the use of the word 'pack' for packaging material.[5]

8 An application to register the word CYBERPUB was rejected for restaurant services (etc); in coming to the conclusion that CYBER was descriptive of Internet and/or Web facilities, the Hearing Officer referred to various definitions of words incorporating the prefix 'cyber'.[6]

9 Three stylised coffee beans on a bed of leaves was refused for coffee as being devoid of distinctive character.[7]

10 An application for J3LEARNING was refused as it consisted of a single letter, a single number and a descriptive word, the combination not being sufficiently distinctive.[8]

11 PASTELLINE was considered descriptive of goods in pastel colours.[9]

12 THANK YOU was considered to have no distinctive character because it was a term which other traders may legitimately wish to use.[10]

2.07 Signs consisting exclusively of shapes, s 3(2) The 1994 Act specifically provides (in s 1(1)) that a trade mark may consist of

3 *Large, Smith and Walford Partnership's Application*, O/50/96 (29 March 1996, unreported) (W Tennant).

4 *Claydon Architectural Metalwork Ltd's Application*, O/114/96 (7 August 1996, unreported) (R Evans).

5 *Henkel Kommanditgesellschaft Auf Aktien's Application*, O/120/96 (15 August 1996, unreported) (G Miller).

6 *Ind Coope (Oxford and West) Ltd's Application*, O/139/96 (26 September 1996, unreported) (R A Jones); for a similar decision with respect to the mark OPEN CAD, see *Lectra Systemes' Application*, O/157/96 (1 November 1996, unreported) (M Needleman).

7 *Coffea SA's Application*, O/158/96 (1 November 1996, unreported) (M Needleman).

8 *J3LEARNING Corpn's Application*, O/160/96 (1 November 1996, unreported) (M Needleman).

9 *British Steel plc's Application*, O/5/96 (11 January 1996, unreported) (R Evans).

10 *Thank You Candy Co Ltd's Application*, O/141/95 (19 October 1995, unreported) (I Peggie).

'the shape of goods or their packaging', but signs which consist exclusively of certain shapes are excluded from registration. These excluded signs fall into three categories of shapes and are discussed in paragraphs 2.08 to 2.10.

Shapes Although a shape can be either two-dimensional or three-dimensional, the goods themselves can only be three-dimensional and therefore it is only three-dimensional shapes which can be caught by s 3(2). Importantly, it should be noted that s 3(2) does not outlaw the registration of shapes per se, only those shapes which specifically fall within the three categories identified in paragraphs (a), (b) and (c).

Exclusively The same comment needs to be made as has already been made in relation to s 3(1)(c) and (d), namely, that this ground for refusal of registration only applies where the sign consists 'exclusively' of an excluded shape.[11] Thus, one should be able to overcome an objection raised pursuant to s 3(2) simply by ensuring that the trade mark applied for incorporates elements or features (which are not merely de minimis) in addition to an excluded shape.

Public policy The prohibition against the registration of certain shapes is based on public policy considerations and, in particular, to preserve free trade. The drafting of s 3(2) is lifted directly from Article 3(1)(e) of the Directive and gives effect to the concern that indefinitely renewable quasi-monopolistic rights should not be granted in respect of functional material and that to do otherwise would give the owner an abnormal advantage or impose on his competitors unjustifiable restrictions and burdens.[12]

11 See paragraph 2.04 above.

12 For a consideration of the position under Benelux trade mark law, see B Strowel 'Benelux: A Guide to the Validity of Three-Dimensional Trade Marks in Europe' [1995] 3 EIPR 154, in which the author argues that : 'the Directive is so closely inspired by Benelux trade mark law that its provisions on the grounds for refusal of three-dimensional trade marks must be interpreted in light of the Benelux case law.' That the Directive and the 1994 Act are similar to the Benelux Trade Marks Act 1971 (certainly in the context of the registrability of shapes) is not disputed, but it must be questionable as to whether the 1994 Act, on this issue or any other, will necessarily be interpreted by reference to Benelux trade mark law: see Laddie J in *Wagamama Ltd v City Centre Restaurants plc* [1995] FSR 713. Laddie J's approach finds support from the Advocate General and the ECJ in *Sabel BV v Puma AG* [1997] ETMR 283; see also A K Sanders 'Some Frequently Asked Questions about the 1994 UK Trade Marks Act' [1995] 2 EIPR 67.

2.08 Shapes which result from the nature of the goods themselves, s 3(2)(a) Section 3(2)(a) provides that a sign shall not be registered as a trade mark if it consists exclusively of:

> 'the shape which results from the nature of the goods themselves.'

This provision recognises the legitimate concern that the potentially perpetual monopoly afforded by a trade mark registration should not extend to a shape which results from the nature of the goods themselves. This raises two issues relevant to the application of this ground for refusal:

(a) Must the shape be dictated by the nature of the goods in the sense that, by virtue of the nature of the goods, the shape is the only shape which can obtain? and

(b) What elements or features of the goods will be considered to be part of their 'nature'?

Having regard to the purpose of this section, one would expect it to apply only to those shapes which are dictated necessarily by the nature of the goods, and that 'nature' in this context would include those elements or features which affect the shape of the goods. Rarely, if ever, would an aesthetic feature of a product be such that it would necessarily result from the nature of the goods, whereas the function, intended purpose or composition of a product may dictate the shape of that product. Thus, although the definition of a trade mark includes '. . . the shape of goods or their packaging', a trade mark will not be registrable to the extent that the trade mark applied for, being the shape of the goods themselves, results from a function, intended purpose or composition of the goods for which registration is sought. Accordingly, Coca-Cola's application under the 1994 Act to register the shape of its distinctive bottle (its earlier application was refused under the 1938 Act[13]) was not refused registration under this subsection as its shape has no relationship to the function, intended purpose, composition or other nature of the soft drink which it contains.

An example given in the Work Manual is of a toothbrush, which has to have a handle and bristles which are more or less in line, and therefore an application to register the shape of a toothbrush which incorporates a handle and bristles in line (with no other distinctive

13 *Coca-Cola Trade Mark* [1986] FSR 472, HL.

features) will be refused because such a shape results exclusively from its intended purpose.[14]

2.09 Shape of goods which is necessary to obtain a technical result, s 3(2)(b) Section 3(2)(b) provides that a sign shall not be registered as a trade mark if it consists exclusively of:

'the shape of goods which is necessary to obtain a technical result.'

This is a further specific example of the general proposition stated in paragraph 2.07 above. If a shape serves a functional or utilitarian purpose, then other traders should not be prevented (at least under trade mark law) from achieving the same technical result.[15] An important practical example would be, in the computer industry, the shape of porting devices which must be of a certain configuration in order to enable computer equipment manufactured by various companies to communicate with each other.

Necessary Where a wide range of shapes can perform the same function, then any particular shape cannot be said to be 'necessary' to obtain the result. In *Philips v Remington* Jacob J stated the test to be: 'in substance does the shape solely achieve a technical result?' As a result of applying that test, His Lordship held that the shape of Philips's three-headed razor was necessary to obtain a technical result, even though, strictly speaking, there are other shapes which could produce the same result.

2.10 The shape which gives substantial value to the goods, s 3(2)(c) Section 3(2)(c) provides that a sign shall not be registered as a trade mark if it consists exclusively of:

'the shape which gives substantial value to the goods.'

The scope of this section is arguably too broad. After all, many trade marks add value to the goods or services in relation to which they are used. Jacob J specifically recognises this concern in *Philips v Remington* and says that one must not take this exclusion too literally. His Lordship states that s 3(2)(c) should only apply to shapes which exclusively add value to the goods (design or functional appearance) and one can (should) disregard any value attributable to a trade mark function (ie source identification). The example is given of the Rolls-Royce grille which adds value to a

14 Work Manual, Chapter 6, paragraph 2.8.
15 This may be subject to patent or other intellectual property right protection.

Rolls-Royce. But it does so primarily because it signifies Rolls-Royce and not because of its inherent shape. This must be right, because to deny registration to a sign merely because it adds substantial value to the goods is not consistent with the principle which underlies subsections 3(2)(a) and (b).

Substantial value One needs to consider the circumstances in which the shape of the product gives substantial value to that product. What comes within the concept of a shape giving substantial value? The White Paper suggests that a shape will be of substantial value if it serves a utilitarian purpose, whether by making the product itself superior in performance or more attractive to the eye or by facilitating its manufacture, distribution or storage. No doubt there are other categories but, as always, the onus will be on the Registrar to establish that the shape does give substantial value to the product. The following questions can be posed but it is difficult to provide definitive answers:

(a) Will a shape which makes a product more marketable be held to 'give substantial value' to that product?
(b) Will a trade mark only 'give substantial value' if the goods themselves are worth more as a result of the shape?
(c) Can it be the case that products, for which shape is irrelevant or of minor importance to the purchaser, can ever be given substantial value by the adoption of a particular shape?

An objection under s 3(2)(c) has been upheld where the applicant sought to register 'tubes with distorted portions' so as to produce a fence-like structure, because this was considered to be a method of improving the aesthetic appearance of the applicant's fencing and hence would give 'substantial value' to the goods.[16]

Benelux law The Benelux Court of Justice (BCJ) looked at the equivalent provisions of Benelux trade mark law (where the test is whether the shape gives 'essential' value) and stated that:

> 'It depends on the nature of the products in question; if the product is of such nature that its aspect and its shape determines strongly its trade value, the answer must be affirmative; in the opposite case, the answer must be negative.'[17] (Unofficial translation.)

16 *Claydon Architectural Metalwork Ltd's Application*, O/114/96 (7 August 1996, unreported) (R Evans); see also *Philips Electronics NV v Remington Consumer Products*, supra.

17 *Adidas*, Case 83/4, Benelux Court of Justice, 23 December 1985.

In another case, the BCJ considered the same issue again and said:

> 'The fact that the distinctive shape of a product affects its essential value should only preclude protection as a trade mark if the product is of such a nature that its aspect and its form, because of their beauty or their originality, determine largely the commercial value of the product, with, however, the reservation that the influence on the commercial value which would not result from the aesthetic attraction of its shape but from the advertising effect attached to its goodwill as a distinctive sign, must be excluded.'[18] (Unofficial translation.)

2.11 Comment on s 3(2) It should be noted that there is no proviso which qualifies the grounds for refusal in respect of signs consisting of shapes which is equivalent to the proviso to s 3(1). Thus, it is irrelevant that an applicant can show that a shape, which is caught by s 3(2), has in fact acquired a distinctive character as a result of the use made of the shape. This is a derogation from the general principle adopted in the Directive and embodied elsewhere in the 1994 Act that a sign which in fact functions as a trade mark should not be denied registration. It could be argued that the question of registrability should be determined by asking whether the shape serves to distinguish the applicant's goods from rival products and, if it does, then the mark should be registered, except only where such registration would effectively confer a monopoly in the product itself. This argument is consistent with the principle that the specific object of a trade mark is to guarantee to its owner the right to use the mark for the first marketing of his products and to protect his products from competitors who attempt to benefit from the goodwill in the mark.

2.12 Contrary to public policy or to accepted principles of morality, s 3(3)(a) Section 3(3)(a) of the 1994 Act provides that a trade mark shall not be registered:

> 'if it is contrary to public policy or to accepted principles of morality.'

This section is akin to s 11 of the 1938 Act but arguably is wider in so far as s 11 was restricted to certain specified grounds of public policy, whereas s 3(3)(a) embraces all grounds of public policy.

18 *Burberrys I*, Benelux Court of Justice, 14 April 1989.

Public policy, undoubtedly, was the basis of the old s 11 but was not specifically mentioned. The express reference to public policy in the 1994 Act potentially opens up a much wider enquiry. It will be for the courts to determine the scope of public policy and the principles of morality applicable in relation to the registration of trade marks. There is no reason to think that the principles governing decisions under the old s 11 will not continue to be applied and, as was stated by Greene MR in relation to the old s 11, it is to be remembered that the section is one which exists 'not merely for the benefit of traders but for the benefit of the public at large'.[19]

One would also have thought that it would be contrary to public policy to register a mark which was contrary to accepted principles of morality and, therefore, the second limb of s 3(3)(a) may be considered to be merely illustrative. In addition, the fact that s 3(3)(a) embraces all grounds of public policy would suggest that there will be a substantial overlap with s 3(3)(b), which is discussed below.

2.13 Deception of the public, s 3(3)(b) Section 3(3)(b) of the 1994 Act provides that a trade mark shall not be registered if it is:

> 'of such a nature as to deceive the public (for instance as to the nature, quality or geographical origin of the goods or service).'

The examples provided in s 3(3)(b) are clearly not exhaustive and this provision will cover any other feature or characteristic of the goods or services, including their function or intended purpose or any of the other attributes referred to in s 3(1)(c).

As with all other grounds for refusal, the relevant time of deception would appear to be the date of the decision whether or not to register and not the date of application. This follows from the wording 'shall not be registered' which is used throughout ss 3, 4 and 5.

This subsection is substantially similar to the first limb of s 11 of the 1938 Act, although it is limited to trade marks which of their nature deceive the public and does not apply to trade marks which merely cause confusion. As stated above, one would have thought that deceiving the public (and, indeed, confusing the public) would be contrary to public policy and therefore the trade mark would also be refused under s 3(3)(a).

There may also be an overlap to some extent with the relative

19 *Livron* (1937) 54 RPC 161.

grounds for refusal[20] in so far as a mark which is identical with or similar to an earlier trade mark could deceive the public as to the origin of the goods or services.

The point could also be taken that this subsection can be construed so as to require actual deception and not merely the likelihood of deception. Such an argument derives from the omission of the word 'likely' (which appeared in the old s 11). Accordingly, if this is right, and if there is no evidence of actual deception, the trade mark should not be refused under s 3(3)(b). Alternatively, the fact that the enquiry under s 3(3)(b) focuses on the 'nature' of the trade mark can be construed as giving the Registrar and the courts the right to take into account, if not actually assess, the likelihood of deception, and the Registrar's current practice is to make such an assessment.

Examples The Work Manual gives a number of examples of marks which will be considered to be deceptive, although it confirms also that an objection will only be raised under s 3(3)(b) if, in the examiner's view, there is any real potential for deception of the public. Importantly, the Registrar considers that the market itself can be relied upon to prevent many uses of a trade mark which would be deceptive. The example given is the mark HARTLEY'S STRAWBERRY JAM; the Registrar's practice will be to proceed on the basis that there is no realistic possibility that the applicant would use the mark on anything other than strawberry jam. If, in fact, the applicant were to use the mark on another product, then it will of course be open to revocation under s 46(1)(d). The examples of deception given in the Work Manual are as follows:[1]

(a) using names or devices indicating a geographical origin which has a reputation for the particular goods or services but where the goods or services do not in fact originate from that geographical area; and
(b) using names or devices indicating a particular desirable quality of goods or services but where the goods or services do not in fact have that quality.

2.14 Trade marks the use of which is prohibited by law, s 3(4) Section 3(4) of the 1994 Act provides that a trade mark

20 See s 5 and paragraphs 2.17–2.27.
1 Work Manual, Chapter 6, paragraph 11.

shall not be registered if or to the extent that:

> 'its use is prohibited in the United Kingdom by any enactment or rule of law or by any provision of Community law.'

Thus, the prohibition referred to in s 3(4) must relate to the use of the trade mark in the United Kingdom and the use of the mark may be prohibited by any of the following:

(a) any enactment;
(b) any rule of law; or
(c) any provision of Community law.

Section 3(4) should be distinguished from s 5(4).[2] Section 3(4) is an absolute ground for refusal where the use of the trade mark applied for is actually prohibited in the United Kingdom by one or more of the aforementioned laws. Section 5(4) is a relative ground for refusal and applies where the law confers a right on a third party who, in reliance upon such right, may be able to prevent the use of the mark applied for (eg the common law of passing off, which does not prohibit the use of trade marks and which is therefore irrelevant for the purposes of s 3(4), but which does enable a third party to enjoin such use in certain circumstances).

The application of s 3(4) is, therefore, more limited than s 5(4) because there are only relatively few laws which actually prohibit the use of a trade mark per se, as opposed to laws which confer rights on third parties which may be enforced to prevent the use of the applicant's trade mark. Examples of the former are the Trade Descriptions Act 1968, the Olympic Symbol etc (Protection) Act 1995 and Council Regulation No 2081/92 on the protection of geographical indications and designations of origin for agricultural products and food stuffs.

2.15 Specially protected emblems, ss 3(5) and 4 Section 3(5) of the 1994 Act provides that a trade mark shall not be registered in the cases specified or referred to in s 4.[3] Section 3(5) adds nothing to s 4 itself other than to make it clear that s 4 is an absolute ground for refusal as distinct from a relative ground.

2.16 Bad faith, s 3(6) The 1994 Act provides that a trade mark shall not be registered if or to the extent that the application is made in bad faith.[4]

2 See paragraphs 2.24–2.26.
3 See Chapter 15.

What will constitute 'bad faith'? Section 3(6) will certainly embrace the situation where an application has been made without any bona fide intention to use the mark, because this would mean that the statement provided pursuant to s 32(3) would be untruthful.[5] In *Nerit*,[6] it was stated that merely having an ulterior motive was not necessarily inconsistent with the requisite bona fide intention to use. However, for the purpose of s 3(6) of the 1994 Act, one could argue that an 'ulterior motive' may, in the circumstances of a particular case, constitute bad faith even though the statement provided pursuant to s 32(3) was not untrue. The fact that the section contemplates limited or partial bad faith (that is, by incorporating the phrase 'or to the extent that' the application is made in bad faith), would suggest that an 'ulterior motive' which evidences bad faith will not be saved by any other bona fide motive.

The position is more difficult to assess where the applicant's specification of goods or services is simply broader than the actual goods or services for which the trade mark is used or proposed to be used. This issue has been considered (albeit in passing) in at least two cases which have come before the courts.[7] In *Mercury*, Laddie J observed that:

> '. . . there is a strong argument that a registration of a mark simply for "computer software" will normally be too wide . . . in my view it is thoroughly undesirable that a trader who is interested in one limited area of computer software should, by registration, obtain a statutory monopoly of indefinite duration covering all types of software, including those which are far removed from his own area of trading interest.'

Mercury was not a decision under the 1994 Act and the observation

4 Section 3(6).

5 In this respect cases decided under s 26(1) of the 1938 Act in relation to the phrase 'bona fide' will provide some guidance as to what may be considered to be 'bad faith'. In *Electrolux Ltd v Electrix Ltd* (1954) 71 RPC 23 it was held that the phrase 'bona fide' meant 'genuine, judged by commercial standards'. See also *Concord TM* [1987] FSR 209.

6 *Imperial Group Ltd v Philip Morris & Co Ltd* [1982] FSR 72.

7 *Mercury Communications Ltd v Mercury Interactive (UK) Ltd* [1995] FSR 850 and *Road Tech Computer Systems Ltd v Unison Software (UK) Ltd* [1996] FSR 805. See also *Avnet Inc v Isoact Ltd* [1998] FSR 16, Ch D, where Jacob J comments (in strong terms) to the effect that retail services should not be registrable under a 'side wind' of 'advertising and promotion services' when the real commercial activity is the sale of goods.

was made in the course of dismissing an application for summary judgment. However, *Road Tech* was a decision under the 1994 Act and Walker J cited (with apparent acceptance) the words of Laddie J set out above. Walker J went on to consider the various arguments put to him by the parties, but then said:

> 'On the whole I get little assistance from these linguistic arguments. Nor have I been able to derive much assistance from purposive arguments, which might be expected to be very important here . . . Counsel have not been able to refer me to any material which shows the legislative purpose behind the Directive's references to bad faith.'

It would appear that the Registrar is prepared to impute dishonest intent or 'bad faith' in the case of overly broad specifications of goods; for example, an application for 'electrical apparatus' was rejected on the ground that this specification was so broad that there was substantial doubt as to whether the applicant genuinely intended to use the mark in respect of all products falling within the specification. The Hearing Officer, echoing the words of Walker J and Laddie J, stated that: 'it is undesirable that a trader interested in a particular area of electrical goods should be able to obtain a statutory monopoly of indefinite duration among all types of electrical goods including those far removed from his trading sphere.'[8]

Under the 1938 Act, the Court of Appeal considered that the words 'bona fide' had two different meanings, a narrow one in s 8 and a wider one in s 26.[9] Thus, the application for, and artificial use of, a 'ghost' mark was not in good faith but the Court of Appeal did not regard it as dishonest. The question remains, therefore, whether the phrase 'bad faith' in s 3(6) of the 1994 Act requires dishonesty, or is it sufficient that the application is not made in good faith? In the end, Walker J does not provide a definitive interpretation of s 3(6) holding only that the plaintiff's case on s 3(6) was not so strong and clear as to entitle it to summary judgment.

Another example of bad faith would be the situation specifically provided for in s 60 where an unauthorised application is made by a person who is an agent or representative of the proprietor of the trade mark.[10]

8 *ICI Acrylic Inc's Application*, O/83/96 (31 May 1996, unreported) (P Jane Best).
9 *Imperial Group Ltd v Philip Morris & Co Ltd* [1982] FSR 72 at 79, 84 and 91.
10 See Chapter 8.

An interesting issue is whether an unauthorised application to register a trade mark used by another undertaking exclusively outside of the United Kingdom would constitute an application made in bad faith. The argument could proceed on the basis that the applicant was at least engaging in a sharp practice and/or was not the rightful proprietor of the trade mark.[11] Against this is the fact that trade marks are registered on a territorial basis and thus (subject to the recognition of well-known marks) one could argue that the only test should be whether the applicant is the first person in the United Kingdom to use and apply to register the sign as a trade mark for the relevant goods or services. Kerly[12] canvasses this issue and suggests that United Kingdom trade mark law should be more cognisant of the rights of the owners of foreign trade marks. To a certain extent, under the 1994 Act, such rights have been recognised in so far as protection is afforded to 'well known' trade marks in accordance with Article 6*bis* of the Paris Convention.

What must be beyond dispute is that applications involving an element of fraud or any breach of duty such as may exist in any confidential, fiduciary, employer/employee or other similar relationship must constitute bad faith. So also it must be bad faith to apply to register a mark in breach of a contractual obligation contained, for example, in a distribution/marketing agreement, and/or where the use of the mark would infringe a third party's intellectual property rights.[13]

Registry practice As a general proposition, the Work Manual states that the Registrar considers bad faith to mean that the application was made 'dishonestly' (thus, the Registrar takes the narrow interpretation: the application must be dishonest and not merely not in good faith).[14]

The Work Manual refers to bad faith in the context of licensees who wrongly apply for the registration of their licensor's mark, but it states that Examiners will not decide the merits of the competing claims of the parties in such situations and will therefore not raise an objection under s 3(6) in these circumstances. It will be a matter for

11 *Karo Step Trade Mark* [1977] RPC 255.
12 *Kerly's Law of Trade Marks and Trade Names*, 12th Edition, paragraph 4.03.
13 See, for example, in the context of copyright: *Karo Step Trade Mark*, supra and *Oscar Trade Mark* [1979] RPC 173.
14 Work Manual, Chapter 6, paragraph 18.

the licensor/owner to file a notice of opposition if the licensee's application is accepted by the Registrar.

However, the Examiner will raise an objection under s 3(6) if he believes that the applicant's specification of goods or services is broader than the actual goods or services in respect of which the applicant uses or intends to use the mark.

Further examples of when the issue of bad faith will be considered by the Registrar, include:

(a) when the sign applied for incorporates the name, picture or portrait of a famous individual;
(b) when the sign incorporates a representation of a famous painting, where the examiner knows that the painting is owned by a third party; and
(c) when the sign appears to be a 'ghost' mark, but it will be rare for the examiner to be aware of this situation.

An example of a Registry decision on s 3(6) is the opposition filed in relation to the application for SANAPRAV. The opponent succeeded because it was able to show that the application was made in bad faith as the applicant was unlikely to be a legal entity and, therefore, could not have intended to use and did not intend to use the mark.[15]

Relative grounds for refusal

The first part of this chapter has been concerned with the absolute grounds for refusal (set out in s 3) which relate to the characteristics of the mark itself. In contrast, the relative grounds for refusal (set out in s 5) are based on protecting the prior conflicting rights of the proprietors of 'earlier trade marks' or other 'earlier rights'. The relative grounds are dealt with in the second part of this chapter under headings corresponding to the five subsections of s 5.

It should be noted that each of the relative grounds for refusal, whether based on earlier trade marks or earlier rights, can be overcome by:

(a) the applicant obtaining the consent from the proprietor(s) of the earlier mark(s)/earlier right(s), the subject of which is considered in paragraph 2.27; or
(b) the applicant establishing honest concurrent use of his mark in

15 *SANAPRAV*, O/57/97 (27 March 1997, unreported) (M Knight).

accordance with the provisions set out in s 7, the subject of which is considered in paragraph 2.28.

Finally, it should also be noted that the relative grounds for refusal set out in s 5(1), (2) and (3) are substantially the same as the circumstances in which a registered trade mark will be infringed under s 10(1), (2) and (3). Accordingly, the same general principles will apply in interpreting each of these corresponding subsections. Of course, the onus is different in each case: the onus is on the party asserting that there are grounds for refusing the registration of the mark under s 5, whereas the onus is on the party alleging infringement under s 10. Many of the cases decided under the 1994 Act to date have been decided either in the context of registrability (s 5) or in the context of infringement (s 10). In this chapter, reference is made to cases decided under s 10 where the decision establishes a principle which will also be useful in interpreting and applying s 5. However, as subsections 5(1), (2) and (3) are all based on a conflict with an 'earlier trade mark', it is first necessary to consider the meaning of this phrase, which is defined in s 6 (see paragraph 2.17). The phrase 'earlier right' is only relevant in the context of subsection 5(4) and therefore is dealt with only in that context in paragraphs 2.24 and 2.25.

2.17 Earlier trade mark, s 6(1) The phrase 'earlier trade mark' is defined in s 6(1) as follows:

'(a) a registered trade mark, international trade mark (UK)[16] or Community trade mark[17] which has a date of application for registration earlier than that of the trade mark in question, taking account (where appropriate) of the priorities claimed in respect of the trade marks;

(b) a Community trade mark which has a valid claim to seniority from an earlier registered trade mark or international trade mark (UK); or

(c) a trade mark which at the date of application for registration of the trade mark in question or (where appropriate) of the priority claimed in respect of the application, was entitled to protection under the Paris Convention as a well-known trade mark.'[18]

16 See Chapter 14.
17 See Chapter 13.
18 For the meaning of 'well-known trade mark' see paragraph 1.11.

Unregistered marks In addition, an earlier trade mark will also include an unregistered trade mark in respect of which an application for registration has been made provided that it would, if registered, be an earlier trade mark by virtue of s 6(1)(a) or (b).[19] However, if the mark ultimately is not registered, then it will not constitute an 'earlier trade mark'. The effect of s 6(2) is, therefore, that an unregistered mark (for which an application has been filed) may prevent the registration of another mark which is the subject of a later filed application. Indeed, s 6(2) allows the Registrar (and the proprietor of the earlier mark in opposition proceedings), for the purposes of comparing the two marks, to proceed on the basis that the earlier mark applied for is in fact registered. This means that, even in respect of the period between the date of the application and the date of registration of the earlier mark:

(a) the Registrar may maintain an objection under s 5(1), (2) or (3) based on the earlier filed pending application; and
(b) the proprietor of an earlier filed pending application may rely on the mark the subject of that application to file a notice of opposition on the ground that his mark is also deemed to be an 'earlier trade mark'.

Any objection or opposition based on the mark the subject of the earlier application will, however, be conditional upon the earlier application proceeding to registration and, if it does not, then that objection/opposition will automatically fail. In practice, where the Registrar raises an objection based on a prior application, the applicant may seek to have the examination of his mark suspended until the fate of the earlier application has been determined (unless, of course, the later applicant can otherwise overcome the objection).

Expired registrations Another matter which needs to be borne in mind is s 6(3) which provides that an earlier trade mark, falling within s 6(1)(a) or (b), whose registration expires will continue to be taken into account for a period of *one* year after such expiry for the purpose of determining the registrability of a later mark – unless the Registrar is satisfied that there was no bona fide use of the earlier trade mark during the *two*-year period preceding the expiry of the registration.

It is curious that the Registrar must be satisfied that there was no bona fide use of the earlier trade mark in order for him to disregard it

19 Section 6(2).

in determining the registrability of a later mark. The ground on which the registration of a trade mark may be revoked under s 46 for non-use requires that the trade mark has not been put to 'genuine use' and therefore one would have thought that the tests should be phrased consistently. However, in practice, it is assumed that the two phrases must mean the same thing. Secondly, for the purposes of s 46, it will be sufficient if the trade mark in question has been used by the proprietor or 'with his consent'. Section 6(3) does not specify who must use the mark but, presumably, consistent with s 46, it will be sufficient that the use has been either by the proprietor or with his consent, provided only that the use is bona fide.

2.18 Identical marks/identical goods or services, s 5(1) Section 5(1) of the 1994 Act prohibits the registration of a trade mark if it is:

> 'identical with an earlier trade mark and the goods or services for which the trade mark is applied for are identical with the goods or services for which the earlier trade mark is protected.'

This ground for refusal of registration is not remarkable but its extension to all earlier trade marks is one of the features of the 1994 Act in so far as, under the 1938 Act, registration could only be refused under s 12(1) on the basis of a prior conflicting trade mark which was registered under the 1938 Act (or its predecessors). By contrast, as stated in the preceding paragraph 2.17, an 'earlier trade mark' now includes international marks and Community trade marks (which are not registered under the 1994 Act) as well as well-known trade marks, which need not be registered at all.

Identical The meaning of the word 'identical' is unequivocal and any variance (subject to the de minimis rule) between the earlier trade mark and the mark applied for, and/or between the relevant goods or services, should necessarily result in a finding that the marks or the goods or services (as the case may be) are not identical.[20] In such circumstances, the Registrar may still be able to refuse to register the mark under either s 5(2) or s 5(3), but this would also involve showing that there exists a likelihood of

20 This would appear to be the position adopted by the Hearing Officer in *Large Smith and Walford Partnerships' Application*, O/50/96 (29 March 1996, unreported), where the application for the word FACETOFACE was considered to be 'virtually identical' to the previous registration of the trade mark FACE TO FACE.

confusion as a result of the requisite similarity (in the case of s 5(2)) or that the conditions attaching to s 5(3) are satisfied. Whereas, if a trade mark is identical with an earlier trade mark and if the application is made in respect of identical goods or services, then there is no need for the Registrar to establish the likelihood of confusion, nor that the conditions attaching to s 5(3) have been satisfied, before refusing an application under s 5(1).

Non-visual marks There may be practical difficulties in comparing certain trade marks such as non-visual marks. For example, would the registration of a series of musical notes be refused if an earlier sound trade mark comprised the same notes but played on a different instrument and at a different tempo so that aurally there was no identity? This may prove problematical where the registration of non-visual marks takes the form of a written description of the mark.[1]

Variation in typefaces In the *Wet Wet Wet* case,[2] Lord McCluskey found on the facts that the defendant's use of the three words 'Wet Wet Wet' in a different typeface to that of the registration was nonetheless the use of an identical mark. This finding is consistent with the de minimus rule (and the essential feature test) but one cannot derive a general rule from this case – it will be a question of fact and degree as to whether a particular typeface is sufficiently different not to be identical for the purpose of ss 5 and 10.

Use of the word 'protected' The drafting of s 5(1) requires a comparison between:

(a) the goods or services for which the trade mark is applied for; and
(b) the goods or services for which the 'earlier trade mark' is protected.

The use of the word 'protected', rather than the word 'registered', results from the fact that the definition of 'earlier trade mark' in s 6 embraces trade marks which are not necessarily registered, viz well-known trade marks. However, there will be problems in determining the scope of the goods or services for which the 'earlier trade mark' is protected. In the case of trade marks which are registered, one can safely say that the goods or services for which the 'earlier trade mark'

1 See examples in Chapter 1, paragraph 1.04.
2 *Bravado Merchandising Services Ltd v Mainstream Publishing (Edinburgh) Ltd* [1996] FSR 205 at 209.

is (validly) registered are within the scope of the protection, but so are many other goods or services if one takes into account the fact that, under s 10(2) and 10(3), the registered proprietor of a trade mark can sue for infringement in respect of merely similar goods or services and even in respect of goods or services which are not similar to those for which the trade mark is registered. Of course, both s 10(2) and 10(3) require the proprietor to establish other matters but, in principle, it must be right that the category of goods or services for which an 'earlier trade mark' is 'protected' is very difficult to determine without an enquiry as to whether the registered proprietor would have a good cause of action under either s 10(2) or s 10(3). This could lead to the absurd result that the applicant's mark could be refused under s 5(1) albeit that, in fact, the applicants' goods or services are merely similar to, or even dissimilar to, the goods or services covered by the proprietor's registration. This may be an absurd result under s 5(1) but, of course, if the use of the word 'protected' leads to this result it is no more and no less than the result which would obtain under s 5(2) or s 5(3) as they mirror the provisions of s 10(2) and s 10(3) respectively.

Difficult issues arise, however, when the broader interpretations or applications of the word 'protected' are considered. As stated above, the word 'protected' was used because not all 'earlier trade marks' are registered. Accordingly, although the potential scope of an infringement action under s 10 is one test of the scope of 'protection' for the purposes of s 5(1), there is no express requirement in s 5(1) to restrict oneself to the protection conferred by the 1994 Act. Unless the courts construe the word 'protected' as meaning 'protected under the 1994 Act', one has to embark on an enquiry as to the scope of protection conferred by other areas of the law (common law and statute) in respect of trade marks. Of course, the full scope of the meaning of the word 'protected' for the purposes of s 5(1) is unlikely to be explored at the examination stage of an application. However, the party opposing an application which has been accepted, or the party seeking a declaration of invalidity under s 47, may wish to do so, but it is unlikely that they would be able to obtain a result which could not be achieved in any event under either s 5(2), (3) or (4).

Form or substance In comparing the goods or services for which a trade mark is applied for with the goods or services for which the 'earlier trade mark' is protected, one does not look only at the actual specifications of those goods and services. If one were only to look at the actual specifications, then the applicant for the later mark could avoid s 5 simply by drafting his specification of goods or services in such a way that the wording is not 'identical' to that of the earlier specification. For example, by using synonyms or other linguistic techniques, the language of the two specifications may be anything but identical whereas, in substance, the goods or services in question could in truth be the same. Instead, the test must be one of substance rather than form. Any other conclusion would frustrate the purpose of s 5 and would be inconsistent with the approach adopted by Jacob J in the *Treat* case where, in considering whether the defendant's 'spread' was a 'dessert sauce', his Lordship said:

> 'When it comes to construing a word used in a trade mark specification, one is concerned with how the product is, as a practical matter, regarded for the purposes of trade. After all a trade mark specification is concerned with use in trade.'[3]

In deciding that the spread was not identical to a dessert sauce (for the purposes of s 10(1) in an infringement action), Jacob J rejected the argument that the fact that the spread could be used as a dessert sauce made it a dessert sauce and therefore made it identical to the goods or services covered by the plaintiff's registration.

Jacob J went on in the *Treat* case to hold that the defendant's goods could not be identical to those of the plaintiff because the defendant's goods fell within Class 29 and the plaintiff's registration was expressly limited to the goods 'included in Class 30'. Accordingly, Jacob J found there to be a necessary lack of identity.[4] However, the wording of s 10(1) differs from s 5(1) in that the former is specifically limited to the goods or services covered by the

3 *British Sugar plc v James Robertson and Sons Ltd* [1996] RPC 281 at 289. See also the analogous comments of his Lordship in *Avnet Inc v Isoact Ltd* [1998] FSR 16, Ch D, where Jacob J comments in relation to the proper construction of a statement of services saying that such statements should be 'scrutinised carefully' and 'confined to the substance . . . the core of the possible meanings attributable to the rather general phrase [advertising and promotional services]'.

4 See also the analogous comments of his Lordship in *Avnet Inc v Isoact Ltd*, supra, where Jacob J again focused on the effect of the words 'included in Class 35' and stated that one has to look at the Registry's practice to find out whether the Registrar, at the time of registration, included the particular service within that class. In that case the issue was whether the defendant was providing services which could be characterised as 'advertising and promotion services . . . included in Class 35'. It was held that the defendant's services could not be so characterised because, amongst other things, the defendant's services fell within Class 42.

plaintiff's 'registration', whereas s 5(1) (as stated above) covers the goods or services for which the earlier trade mark is 'protected' – which would include similar and even dissimilar goods or services if the proprietor of the 'earlier trade mark' could show that his mark was 'protected' for such goods or services under s 10(2) or 10(3). The fact that the applicant's mark may fall within a different class of goods or services to that of the 'earlier trade mark' should not, therefore, result in a necessary finding that the goods or services are not identical (for example, some goods are variously classified by reference to the material from which they are made and this distinction alone should not lead to the necessary conclusion that they are not identical). Of course, the fact that the goods or services are not in the same class will often be an indication that there is some relevant difference in the nature of the goods or services in question. However, to paraphrase the words of Jacob J quoted above, the real test must be whether the difference is such that as a practical matter the goods or services in question cannot be regarded for the purposes of trade as identical.

In the *Wet Wet Wet* case,[5] Lord McCluskey held that the word 'identical' (in the context of s 10(1)) referred to the general character of the goods because the goods referred to in a trade mark certificate have no distinguishing identity, ie if the registration includes 'books', then the identity required must relate to their character as books; the books themselves cannot be 'identical' as such because the books referred to in the certificate have no distinguishing identity. Likewise, in the *Wagamama* case,[6] the defendant's restaurant services were treated as being identical to the plaintiff's registration for restaurant services and notwithstanding that the defendant's restaurant provided Indian style food whereas the plaintiff's restaurant provided Japanese style food.

2.19 Identical marks/similar goods or services, s 5(2)(a); similar marks/identical goods or services; similar marks/similar goods or services, s 5(2)(b)

Scope and effect Section 5(2) contains further grounds for the refusal of an application for registration where either the trade marks

5 *Bravado Merchandising Services Ltd v Mainstream Publishing (Edinburgh) Ltd* [1996] FSR 205.

6 *Wagamama Ltd v City Centre Restaurants plc* [1995] FSR 713.

in question and/or the relevant goods or services are not 'identical' for the purposes of s 5(1). Section 5(2) will apply where either:

(a) (i) the trade mark applied for is *identical* with an earlier trade mark; and
(ii) registration is sought in respect of goods or services which are *similar* to those for which the earlier trade mark is protected;

or

(b) (i) the trade mark applied for is *similar* to an earlier trade mark; and
(ii) registration is sought in respect of goods or services which are *identical* with those for which the earlier trade mark is protected;

or

(c) (i) the trade mark applied for is *similar* to an earlier trade mark; and
(ii) registration is sought in respect of goods or services which are *similar* to those for which the earlier trade mark is protected,

and

(d) in each case, because of the identity/similarity of the trade marks and the goods or services in question, there exists a likelihood of confusion on the part of the public, which includes the likelihood of association with the earlier trade mark.

The scope of s 5(2) is somewhat broader than the corresponding s 12(1) of the 1938 Act in so far as s 5(2) can apply where the mark applied for is either identical with or similar to any 'earlier trade mark', the definition of which embraces not only registered trade marks (which were the extent of the former enquiry under s 12(1)) but also international trade marks (UK), Community trade marks and well-known trade marks.[7]

Issues The issues to be considered in relation to this section are as follows:

(a) In what circumstances will a trade mark be considered to be 'identical' with an earlier trade mark?
(b) In what circumstances will goods or services be considered to be 'identical' with each other?
(c) What are the rules of comparison which will be applied in determining whether a trade mark is 'similar' to an earlier trade mark?

7 See paragraph 2.17 and s 6.

(d) What are the rules of comparison which will be applied in determining whether the relevant goods or services are 'similar' to each other?
(e) What is the meaning and effect of the phrase 'likelihood of confusion on the part of the public, which includes the likelihood of association with the earlier trade mark'?

The first two issues have already been considered in the context of s 5(1) in paragraph 2.18 above. Issues (c), (d) and (e) are dealt with separately in turn in paragraphs 2.20 to 2.22 below. It is important to treat these issues separately because the final question as to whether there exists a likelihood of confusion/likelihood of association will only arise once the identity/similarity of the trade marks and of the respective goods or services in question has been established. Evidence of confusion/association may, at best, be indicative of or consistent with the conclusion that the marks and/or the goods or services in question are similar, but such evidence is not determinative of the issue. In the *Treat* case, Jacob J warns that one should consider separately the two distinct issues:

(a) the question whether goods or services are similar; and
(b) the question whether there exists a likelihood of confusion/likelihood of association.[8]

For example, although the unauthorised use of a trade mark (particularly a well-known trade mark) may cause confusion in fact, the question as to whether the applicant's/defendant's goods or services are similar to those covered by the proprietor's/plaintiff's registration for the purposes of s 5(2) and s 10(2) must be divorced from the question of confusion/association. To proceed otherwise would give a well-known trade mark far greater protection under ss 5(2) and 10(2) than would be the case for trade marks which are not so well known: in essence, the notoriety of a trade mark must not affect the issue as to whether the goods or services in question are similar.

2.20 Rules of comparison: similarity of trade marks, s 5(2)
The corresponding provision of the 1938 Act prohibited the registration of a trade mark which 'nearly resembles' someone else's registered trade mark.[9]

8 See the *Treat* case [1996] RPC 281 at 294.
9 Section 12(1); provided that the relevant goods or services were also the same or of the same description etc.

The change of wording from 'nearly resembles' to 'similar' was to reflect the wording of Article 4(1)(b) of the Directive and there is no substantive change in the law. However, although there are certain general principles which can be derived from cases decided under earlier trade mark legislation, the bottom line is that, in the words of Lord Cranworth:[10]

> 'What degree of resemblance [similarity] is necessary . . . is from the nature of things incapable of definition a priori.'

The case law suggests that the following broad principles apply:

(a) one has to have regard to the mark as a whole and one should not divide the mark up and seek to distinguish a portion of it from a portion of the other mark;[11]

(b) one has to have regard to the 'idea of the mark', the main idea left on the mind albeit that, when placed side by side, the two marks might have differences – in practice, this means that marks which are either phonetically, visually or 'conceptually' similar (and albeit that they may be dissimilar in other respects) may be held to be similar; so may word marks be held to be similar to device marks if the word(s) in question are descriptive of the device in question; so may word marks be held to be similar to sound marks if the word(s) in question are onomatopoeic of the sound in question;[12]

(c) one should take account of the public's imperfect recollection of trade marks and remember also that the two marks in question will not always be seen by the public side by side;[13]

(d) having regard to (b) and (c) above, the courts and the Registrar have consistently stressed the importance of the first syllable of the marks in question and therefore a distinguishing second or last syllable may not prevent a finding of similarity[14] – but the

10 *Seixo v Provezende* (1866) 1 Ch App 192.

11 *William Bailey Ltd's Application 'Erectico'* (1935) 52 RPC 136. See also *ICI Acrylic Inc's Application*, O/83/96 (31 May 1996, unreported) (P Jane Best) where the applicant unsuccessfully argued that his mark PORTFOLIO was not similar to the earlier mark HIPORTFOLIO.

12 The Advocate General and the ECJ in *Sabel BV v Puma AG* [1997] ETMR 283 referred to what was called 'conceptual' similarity of the marks in question, that is, where the two marks convey the same idea; see the examples cited in paragraphs 17.08 and 17.09 of *Kerly's Law of Trade Marks and Trade Names*, 12th Edition (including the Supplement).

13 *Sandow Ltd's Application* (1914) 31 RPC 196, see Sargant J at 205.

14 See the examples cited in paragraph 17.13 of *Kerly's Law of Trade Marks and Trade Names*, 12th Edition.

converse is not necessarily the case: the lack of identity between the first syllable of the two marks will not necessarily prevent a finding of overall similarity;[15]

(e) the marks should be compared as they would be seen in actual use and not only in the form as they appear on the Register;[16] and

(f) in all other respects, consider all the circumstances of the trade in which the marks in question are used or to be used.[17]

There is no reason to believe that these principles should not be applied when comparing two marks to determine whether they are 'similar' for the purposes of s 5(2) or for the purposes of s 10(2) in the context of infringement. Indeed, these principles would appear to be the basis of Laddie J's observations in *Wagamama* where he stated (in the context of an infringement case) that:

> 'a judge brings to the assessment of marks his own, perhaps idiosyncratic, pronunciation and view or understanding of them. Although the issue of infringement is one eventually for the judge alone, in assessing the marks he must bear in mind the impact the marks make or are likely to make on the minds of those persons who are likely to be customers for goods or services under the marks. Not all customers are the same. It is therefore sometimes of assistance for the court to hear evidence from witnesses who will help him to assess the variety of ways in which members of the target market will pronounce the marks and what, to them, will be the visual or phonetic impact of the marks. When considering infringement it is also necessary to bear in mind the possible impact of imperfect recollection on the part of members of the target market.'[18]

As already stated, each case will always be decided on its own facts. Although it is easy to state the six principles set out above, it is sometimes difficult to apply them consistently. For example, the situation where the applicant appends his 'house mark' to a brand name because the brand name alone would be objectionable under s 5. On one view, the mark applied for should be viewed as a whole

15 As was the case in WAGAMAMA and RAJAMAMA where the identity was in the second syllable: *Wagamama Ltd v City Centre Restaurants plc* [1995] FSR 713.

16 *June* (1941) 58 RPC 147; *Ovax* (1946) 63 RPC 97.

17 See the definitive statement of Parker J in *Pianotist Co's Application (Pianola)* (1906) 23 RPC 774 at 777.

18 *Wagamama Ltd v City Centre Restaurants plc* [1995] FSR 713 at 732.

and one should not divide it up and focus on the house mark element so as to come to a finding that the mark is not similar to an earlier trade mark which does not contain the house mark element but is otherwise identical or similar. In fact, there is no rule or principle which applies in this situation other than the very broad (and therefore unhelpful) statement that it will be a question of fact whether the house mark element of a composite mark sufficiently distinguishes the mark as a whole from the earlier trade mark. The Hearing Officer thought not (on the facts) in the case where the applicant, Inmarsat, added its house mark INMARSAT so as to form the composite mark INMARSAT MESSENGER. The Hearing Officer thought that, in the circumstances, the composite mark was still similar to the earlier trade mark MESSENGER.[19] Compare this with the *Treat* case where Jacob J also disregarded the addition of the defendant's house mark and held that the defendant's use of the mark TREAT as part of the composite mark ROBERTSON'S TOFFEE TREAT was identical to the plaintiff's registration for TREAT. The first two words (ROBERTSON'S TOFFEE) were regarded as added matter and it did not matter in what capacity TREAT was used. (However, in that case, the fact that both marks in question were used in conjunction with their respective house marks led the judge to believe that it was unlikely that there could be any confusion between the two marks because the public would focus on the house marks and treat the words TOFFEE TREAT as essentially descriptive.)

Another example of a form or means of comparing marks is where the court will focus on what it regards as the 'essential features' of an earlier trade mark and compare these features with the mark applied for. In the *European* newspaper case[20] it was held (under s 10(2)) that the title of the defendant's newspaper EUROPEAN VOICE was not similar to the plaintiff's device mark which consisted of the words THE EUROPEAN in a stylised form together with a representation of a dove holding a copy of a newspaper in its beak. The judge based his decision on the fact that the 'essential features' of the two marks were not similar because the essential feature of the plaintiff's mark was the device element. The

19 *International Mobile Satellite Organisation (Inmarsat)'s Application*, O/51/96 (28 March 1996, unreported) (W Tenannt).

20 *European Ltd v Economist Newspapers Ltd* [1996] FSR 431, confirmed on appeal, unreported.

word EUROPEAN was considered to be, in essence, descriptive and therefore not part of the essential features of the plaintiff's trade mark.

Effect of disclaimer The fact that the proprietor of the earlier mark may have disclaimed exclusive use of part of his trade mark does not affect the comparison of the two marks in question. That is, in considering whether the applicant's mark is 'similar' to the earlier mark, it does not matter that the applicant's mark may not infringe the earlier registration (by virtue of the disclaimer). Neither, of course, will a disclaimer be relevant in considering the issue of confusion (which is dealt with in paragraph 2.22 below).

Examples The following marks have been considered under the 1994 Act for the purposes of deciding whether they are identical or similar. This is not an exhaustive list and only includes those cases which are illustrative of the problems encountered by the Registry and the courts (and hence by trade mark owners and their advisers).

1 In *Wet Wet Wet*, the defendant's use of the identical words but in a different typeface was held to be use of an identical sign (where the essential features of the registered mark were the three words, and the typeface was purely incidental).
2 In the *Baywatch* case, BABEWATCH was assessed to be similar to BAYWATCH (but the goods were not similar).
3 FACETOFACE was described as being 'virtually identical' (which presumably means 'similar') to FACE TO FACE.
4 PORTFOLIO was considered to be similar to HIPORTFOLIO.
5 In the *Shepherd Neame* case, the mark SHEPHERDS was considered similar to and likely to be 'confusingly associated' with SHEPHERD NEAME.
6 In the *Lilt* case, the mark TILT was so similar to LILT that Laddie J granted an injunction.
7 JUDI TOE was rejected because it was similar to JUDY COLLECTION and JUDY BOUTIQUE.
8 In *Treat*, the defendant's mark ROBERTSON'S TOFFEE TREAT was considered to be identical to TREAT because Jacob J disregarded the house mark element as merely 'added matter'.
9 In the *European* newspaper case, the defendant's use of the word EUROPEAN did not infringe the plaintiff's registration of its device incorporating the word EUROPEAN because it was

not similar to the essential features of the plaintiff's mark which incorporated a distinctive device.

10 NUMBER FIVE VIRGINIA BLEND was considered similar to GOLDEN VIRGINIA.

11 ZN and Zn were considered to be similar to ZINC because they represent the chemical symbol for Zinc; Walker J went on to say (obiter) that SINC and SYNC would also be sufficiently similar to constitute infringement. (Does this mean that a registration for GOLD would be infringed by the use of the letters Au or AU?)[1]

2.21 Rules of comparison: similarity of goods or services, s 5(2) The corresponding provision of the 1938 Act prohibited the registration of a trade mark in respect of goods or services which were 'of the same description' or which were 'associated' with the goods or services covered by someone else's registration.[2] Section 5(2) requires that the goods or services be 'similar'. Once again, the change in the wording is merely to reflect that adopted in Article 4(1)(b) of the Directive.

It can be argued that, if anything, the requirement of similarity will more easily be satisfied than the old requirement that the goods or services be of the same description. That is, two products or services can be characterised as 'similar' even though one would not necessarily apply the same description to them.[3] It must therefore be right that a visual similarity, functional similarity or any other similarity as to the characteristics of the goods or services in question will always be prima facie relevant even though, from case to case, similarities may be weighted differently.

Jacob J has confirmed in the *Treat* case[4] that the considerations which the court must have in mind are similar to those arising under the 1938 Act in relation to 'goods of the same description'. This is

1 *Sir Terence Conran v Mean Fiddler Holdings Ltd* [1997] FSR 856.

2 Section 12(1); provided that the trade marks in question were identical or nearly resembled each other etc.

3 Of course, this does not mean that goods or services will be found to be similar just because (to take an extreme example) the particular goods or services in question happen to be of a similar colour. There will thus be numerous similarities which, of themselves, will be irrelevant for the purposes of s 5(2) but which may add to or even detract from the overall impression of similarity when considered in the light of other characteristics of the goods or services.

4 [1996] RPC 281 at 296.

because the purpose of the old law and that of the new law is consistent, that is, 'to prevent marks from conflicting not only for their respective actual goods [or services] but for a penumbra also'. However, having said that, he considers that the well-known test previously laid down under the 1938 Act in *Jellinek*[5] needs to be elaborated upon in order to take account of present day marketing methods. The factors which Jacob J considers to be relevant in deciding whether the goods or services in question are similar are as follows:

'(a) the respective uses of the respective goods or services;
(b) the respective users of the respective goods or services;
(c) the physical nature of the goods or acts of service;
(d) the respective trade channels through which the goods or services reach the market;
(e) in the case of self-serve consumer items, where in practice they are respectively found or likely to be found in supermarkets and in particular whether they are, or are likely to be, found on the same or different shelves; and
(f) the extent to which the respective goods or services are competitive. This enquiry may take into account how those in trade classify goods, for instance whether market research companies, who of course act for industry, put the goods or services in the same or different sectors.'[6]

On the facts of the *Treat* case, Jacob J held that the defendant's spread was not similar to the goods covered by the plaintiff's registration (ie dessert sauces and syrups). Jacob J went on to observe that (given that the marks were identical):

'if spreads are similar goods [to dessert sauces and syrups] then British Sugar have gained a monopoly of such a word in the £190 million per annum sector of the market of which their product is not even a member in addition to the ice-cream topping sector. Moreover the monopoly would not stop there. Other goods would also probably be similar: desserts for instance. I cannot think that the Council and Commission intended such formidable monopolies to be created so readily when they made the Directive. It goes far beyond that which is

5 *Jellinek's Application* (1946) 63 RPC 59, per Romer J, approved by the House of Lords in *Daiquiri Rum Trade Mark* [1969] RPC 600 at 620; see also *Floradix Trade Mark* [1974] RPC 583.
6 [1996] RPC 281at 296–7.

needed to protect the word as a badge of trade origin for syrups and dessert sauces.'[7]

This suggests that, at least in the context of infringement, the courts will not be interpreting the word 'similar' in a broad manner and will look to the scope of protection required in order to give effect to the principle that the statutory monopoly should only extend to guaranteeing the specific function of a trade mark, namely, to operate as a badge of origin in respect of the goods or services for which it is used and, conversely, that the monopoly will not be allowed unduly to fetter the legitimate activities of competitors.

As stated above, Jacob J was considering the boundaries of the meaning of the word 'similar' in the context of an infringement case where s 10 requires a comparison between the defendant's goods and the goods set out in the plaintiff's registration. In the context of registrability, under s 5, it may be arguable that the word 'similar' may have a slightly wider application, if only because s 5 requires a comparison between the applicant's specification of goods and the goods for which the earlier trade mark is 'protected'. The use of the word 'protected' in s 5(1) has already been considered in paragraph 2.18; Jacob J noted the difference between s 10(2) and s 5(2) but did not express any final opinion, stating only that:

> 'Whether that [ie the use of the word protected in s 5(2)] means the registrar should consider two lots of similarity (ie what goods are similar to those of the prior registration, because it *protects* use of the mark for such goods, and what goods are similar to the specification of the application) is also to be left for another day.'[8]

Examples The following goods and services have been considered under the 1994 Act for the purpose of deciding whether they are identical or similar. This is not an exhaustive list and only includes those cases which are illustrative of the problems encountered by the Registry and the courts (and hence by trade mark owners and their advisers).

1 In *Wagamama*, it was assumed that the defendant's restaurant services were similar (if not identical) to the plaintiff's registration for restaurant services and notwithstanding that the

7 Ibid at 297.
8 At 296.

defendant's restaurant provided Indian style food while the plaintiff's restaurant provided Japanese style food.

2 In the *Wet Wet Wet* case, the point was made that the comparison is between the goods as commonly described using generic terminology; thus, in that case, the requisite identity was that both products were books and the subject matter of the books did not need to be identical because the books specified in the registration had no distinguishing identity (ie their subject matter was not specified in the registration and therefore it was not relevant).

3 In *Baywatch*, it was held to be arguable that television programmes with an adult content are not similar goods or services to video tapes and video discs featuring music, action-adventure, comedy, animation, sports or exercise.

4 In the *Treat* case, spreads were not considered similar to dessert sauces and syrups.

5 In *Facetoface*, apparatus for recording, transmission, reception etc of sound messages, data, hardware, software, firmware etc, all in use for video conferencing, was held similar to audio cassettes (because of the use of the generic word 'apparatus').

6 In *Judy Collection*, footwear, parts and fittings therefor, was considered similar (if not identical) to articles of clothing for women and girls, parts and fittings for all the aforementioned goods, all included in Class 25; as 'clothing' included 'footwear'.

7 In the *Portfolio* case, the applicant's broad specification of goods: 'electric apparatus' meant that it almost inevitably was similar to the prior registration for computer programs, cassettes and cartridges.

8 In the *Inmarsat* case, it was observed that: 'where the goods or services at issue can be traded in or provided by the same company, the one complementing the other, eg paging services and radio paging apparatus and instruments, the goods and services will be similar . . .'

9 In the *Virgin* case, the defendant's jeans were treated as being similar (if not identical) to the plaintiff's registration for articles of outerwear.

10 In the *Golden Virginia* case, pipe tobacco was considered identical to hand-rolling tobacco.

11 In the *Avnet* case, the defendant's services of allocating its customers an e-mail address and webpage, thereby enabling its

customers to advertise on the Internet, was not identical to the plaintiff's registration for services covering 'advertising and promotion services . . . in class 35'. Furthermore, the mere fact that the defendant itself advertised its own services on the Internet did not fall within the plaintiff's registration.

2.22 Likelihood of confusion/likelihood of association, s 5(2)
If registration is to be refused under s 5(2) it is necessary that, as a result of the identity/similarity of the trade marks and of the respective goods or services, there must exist:

> 'a likelihood of confusion on the part of the public, which includes the likelihood of association with the earlier trade mark.'

This wording, taken directly from Article 4(1)(b) of the Directive, raises the question as to what is meant by the phrases 'likelihood of confusion' and 'likelihood of association'. The latter phrase can be interpreted:

(a) in a narrow or 'classic' sense, to refer to the situation where the public mistakenly believe that the marks in question (or the goods or services supplied under the marks) are associated with the proprietor, perhaps only by virtue of some commercial link, but a link which nonetheless suggests that the proprietor is in some way associated with or responsible for the goods or services ('association as to origin'); or
(b) in a broad or 'strict' sense, akin to the Benelux law, so as to extend to the situation where the use of the mark in question simply calls to mind the proprietor's mark and notwithstanding that the public would not mistake the origin of the relevant goods or services ('non-origin association' or 'association in the strict sense').

These issues would appear to have been resolved, at least for the time being, by the decisions of Laddie J in the *Wagamama* case[9] and the ECJ in *Sabel v Puma*.[10] Both Laddie J and the ECJ concluded that it is not sufficient merely to establish a likelihood of association in the broad sense (non-origin association) and that it will always be necessary to establish a likelihood of confusion in the classic sense (confusion as to origin). On the facts of the *Wagamama* case,

9 *Wagamama Ltd v City Centre Restaurants plc* [1995] FSR 713.
10 *Sabel BV v Puma AG*, Case C-251/95 [1998] ETMR 1, ECJ.

Laddie J was satisfied that members of the public had made an association as to origin in the sense that they thought that the defendant's RAJAMAMA restaurant might be connected with the plaintiff's WAGAMAMA restaurant. Laddie J's decision was cited in the opinion of the Advocate General in the *Sabel v Puma* case[11] where the Advocate General approved of and built upon the comments of Laddie J. In the opinion of the Advocate General, the phrase 'likelihood of association' means that the concept of 'likelihood of confusion' will extend beyond confusion evidenced by a consumer mistaking one mark for the other, and will embrace confusion evidenced by the mistaken assumption that there is an organisational or economic link between the undertakings supplying the goods or services under the marks in question.

Laddie J based his decision (that a broader interpretation of s 10(2) had to be rejected) on the proposition that, to extend the scope of infringement to non-origin association, would be to create a new type of monopoly not related to the proprietor's trade mark, but in the trade mark itself. As there was little or no commercial justification for such an extension, such a change in the law would, according to Laddie J, have to have been stated in 'clear and unambiguous words in the Directive so that traders throughout the EU could be able to appreciate that their legislators had created a new broad monopoly'. The Advocate General expressly cites this passage and takes the point one step further by recognising that most member states have not embraced the concept of non-origin association for the purposes of their trade mark law. Accordingly, he agrees that the Community legislature cannot be assumed (without clear wording) to have attempted to embrace such a concept, especially as this would militate against free trade.

Sabel v Puma in the ECJ The ECJ's decision in *Sabel v Puma*[12] sets out the conflicting interpretations of Article 4(1)(b) of the Directive (s 5(2) of the 1994 Act). The opposing views of the parties in that case were put forward by, on the one hand, the governments of Belgium, Luxembourg and the Netherlands and, on the other hand, by the European Commission and the United Kingdom Government. According to the former three governments, the

11 *Sabel BV v Puma AG* [1997] ETMR 283.
12 Supra.

relevant likelihood of association may arise in three sets of circumstances:

(a) where the public confuses the sign and the mark in question (likelihood of direct confusion);

(b) where the public makes a connection between the proprietor of the sign and the proprietor of the mark, and confuses those proprietors (likelihood of indirect confusion or association); and

(c) where the public considers the sign to be similar to the mark and the perception of the sign calls to mind the memory of the mark, although the two marks are not confused (likelihood of association in the strict sense).

It was the third set of circumstances described in (c) above which was contested by the Commission and the United Kingdom Government. The ECJ held that:

> '. . . the concept of likelihood of association is not an alternative to that of likelihood of confusion, but serves to define its scope. The terms of the provision itself [Article 4(1)(b)] exclude its application where there is no likelihood of confusion on the part of the public.'

The ECJ noted that the tenth recital in the preamble to the Directive provides that:

> '. . . the likelihood of confusion . . . constitutes the specific condition for such protection.'

It is worth quoting further from the ECJ's decision in relation to how the courts should assess the likelihood of confusion:

> '. . . the appreciation of the likelihood of confusion depends on numerous elements and, in particular, on the recognition of the trade mark on the market, of the association which can be made with the used or registered sign, of the degree of similarity between the trade mark and the sign and between the goods or services identified. The likelihood of confusion must therefore be appreciated globally, taking into account all factors relevant to the circumstances of the case.
>
> That global appreciation of the visual, aural or conceptual similarity of the marks in question, must be based on the overall impression given by the marks, bearing in mind, in particular, their distinctive and dominant components.'

The ECJ went on to observe that the more distinctive the registered mark, the greater will be the likelihood of confusion and that it was not impossible that the 'conceptual similarity' resulting from the fact that the two marks in question use images with analogous semantic content may give rise to a likelihood of confusion where the registered mark has a particularly distinctive character, either per se or because of the reputation it enjoys with the public. However, where the registered mark is not especially well known to the public and consists of an image with little imaginative content (described in this case as the idea of a 'bounding feline'), the mere fact that the two marks are conceptually similar is not sufficient to give rise to a likelihood of confusion. Thus, the ECJ held that the mere association which the public might make between two trade marks as a result of their analogous semantic content is not in itself a sufficient ground for concluding that there is a likelihood of confusion within the meaning of Article 4(1)(b).

Normal and fair manner of use In the *Origins* case,[13] in the context of infringement, Jacob J held that in order to determine whether, as a result of the defendant's use of its sign there exists a 'likelihood of confusion', it was proper for the court to assume that the plaintiff's mark is used in a normal and fair manner in relation to the goods for which it is registered and then to assess the likelihood of confusion in relation to the way in which the defendant uses his sign, discounting any external added matter or circumstances. It is assumed that this principle applies (albeit with some modification) to the question of registrability under s 5(2). That is, it is proper for the Registrar to assume that the earlier trade mark is used in a normal and fair manner in relation to the goods or services for which it is protected and then to assess the likelihood of confusion assuming that the mark applied for is also used (or to be used) in a normal and fair manner in relation to the goods or services for which registration is sought. Of course, the more similar the marks and the goods or services in question, the more likely it is that the Registrar will consider that the requisite likelihood of confusion exists.

Addition of added matter, use of house marks It has already been noted that it is a question of fact as to whether a composite mark which incorporates a registered trade mark will be considered to be

13 *Origins Natural Resources Inc v Origin Clothing Ltd* [1995] FSR 280; see also the *Treat* case [1996] RPC 281 (where Jacob J follows his decision in *Origins* and confirms that the correct comparison is of the defendant's *sign* with the plaintiff's *mark*).

sufficiently different to the registered mark so as not to be considered to be identical or similar for the purpose of ss 5 and 10. The use of a house mark in conjunction with a mark which may otherwise be considered to be identical or similar is one such example.[14] However, as the comparison of the two marks and of the related goods or services are completely separate issues to the question of likelihood of confusion, it may be that the marks in question and/or the goods or services in question may be held to be similar (or even identical) and yet, because of either the incorporation of added matter, the use of a house mark and/or any other manner of use, the court may consider that there is no likelihood of confusion.[15]

Evidence of confusion There are various ways in which a party may seek to adduce evidence of relevant confusion for the purposes of ss 5(2) and 10(2). The admissibility and probative value of such evidence differs from case to case. Examples of the sort of evidence which has been led include:
(a) evidence of employees within the plaintiff's office;
(b) evidence of people working within the trade; and
(c) survey evidence of the public in general.
The way in which the courts have dealt with this evidence ranges from (a) outright rejection of the evidence, (b) admitting it, but giving it little weight, through to (c) relying on it to support a decision. Examples of relevant cases decided under the 1994 Act include:

- the *European* newspaper case,[16] where the evidence was either rejected or not considered to be of probative value;
- the *Opus* case,[17] where the process of conducting a survey was described as being a 'heavily booby-trapped road' – this case should be read carefully if only to learn how not to conduct a survey; and
- the *Baywatch* case,[18] where the lack of any evidence of confusion, although not determinative of the issue, was considered to be 'a factor of very great significance in the context of an application for an interlocutory injunction' – it was made clear that

14 As to which see paragraph 2.20.
15 As was the case in *Treat*, supra.
16 *European Ltd v Economist Newspapers Ltd*, supra.
17 *BASF plc v CEP (UK) plc* (1996) 19(4) IPD 9.
18 *Baywatch Production Co Inc v Home Video Channel* [1997] FSR 22.

speculation would not suffice to fill the gap in the absence of evidence of actual confusion.

Further reading The question as to the meaning and application of the phrases 'likelihood of confusion' and 'likelihood of association' has, not surprisingly, been the subject of considerable comment in legal circles. For further reading on the subject we have set out in the footnote below a list of articles to which readers may wish to refer (noting always that they were all written before the ECJ decision in *Sabel v Puma*).[19]

2.23 Trade marks with a reputation in the United Kingdom, s 5(3) Section 5(3) provides a new ground for refusing to register a trade mark where the applicant's trade mark might dilute or otherwise take unfair advantage of or be detrimental to the character or repute of an earlier trade mark.[20] Section 5(3), like s 5(2), applies where the applicant's trade mark is either identical with or similar to an earlier trade mark. However, unlike s 5(2), s 5(3) will apply where the applicant seeks to register his trade mark for goods or services which are *not* similar to those for which the earlier trade mark is protected.

The application of the section is limited to the situation where:

(a) the earlier trade mark has a reputation in the United Kingdom; and

(b) the use of the applicant's mark without due cause would either:
   (i) take unfair advantage of, or
   (ii) be detrimental to,

   either the distinctive character or the repute of the earlier trade mark.

The elements of s 5(3) are considered below.

Scope of protection The first question to consider is the range of goods or services which fall within the scope of the protection of the

19 See, for example, Paul Harris 'Wagamama – Confusion Still Reigns in the UK' Trademark World, October 1995, p 12; Charles Gielen 'Likelihood of Association: What Does it Mean?' Trademark World, February 1996, p 20; Paul Harris 'UK Trade Mark Law: Are You Confused?' [1995] 12 EIPR 601; Anselm Kamperman Sanders 'The Wagamama Decision: back to the dark ages of trade mark law' [1996] 1 EIPR 3; Anselm Kamperman Sanders 'The Return to Wagamama' [1996] 10 EIPR 521; Peter Prescott 'Think before you Waga Finger' [1996] 6 EIPR 317; Peter Prescott QC 'Has the Benelux Trade Mark Law been Written into the Directive?' [1997] 3 EIPR 99.

20 As to the meaning of 'earlier trade mark', see s 6 and paragraph 2.17.

earlier trade mark, as s 5(3) is only relevant where the goods or services covered by the application are outside the scope of that protection, that is, where they are not similar.

The scope of protection of any given earlier trade mark will need to be assessed in the circumstances of each case. For example, the goods or services for which a registered trade mark will be protected are:

(a) those goods or services set out in the specification; as well as
(b) similar goods or services (under s 10(2)); and even
(c) dissimilar goods or services (under s 10(3)),

provided that the various conditions attaching to those two subsections are established.

This leads to the potential conundrum that a mark registered in respect of, say, cameras may also be 'protected' (under s 10(3)) in respect of dissimilar goods such as footwear (provided that the mark otherwise satisfies the requirements of s 10(3): in particular, it must be a mark with a sufficient reputation in the UK). In such circumstances, an applicant seeking to register the same or similar mark for footwear should not, therefore, on a strict reading of s 5, be refused registration under either:

(1) s 5(1), because that section only applies where the goods are identical, and cameras and footwear are not identical; nor
(2) s 5(2), because that section only applies where the goods are similar, and cameras and footwear are not similar; nor
(3) s 5(3), because that section only applies where the goods are dissimilar and, in this example, the footwear (although dissimilar to cameras per se) will fall within the category of goods for which the earlier trade mark is protected because, by virtue of s 10(3), the mark registered for cameras is also 'protected' for 'footwear'; of course, if this is right on a strict reading of s 5(3), then the argument must come full circle and, because the earlier trade mark is 'protected' under s 10(3) in relation to footwear then, under either s 5(1) or s 5(2) (depending on whether the applicant's mark is either identical with or similar to the earlier trade mark), the mark should be refused registration because the goods applied for are similar (if not identical) to those for which the earlier trade mark is protected by virtue of s 10(3).[1]

1 It is hoped that this bizarre situation will be resolved by the courts in a purposive way: Jacob J, however, ducked the question in the *Treat* case and 'left it for another day', supra at 296.

Although this is a somewhat academic exercise, it must nonetheless be carried out in order to determine whether s 5(2) or s 5(3) is to apply (if at all). No doubt the two grounds will usually be relied upon in the alternative by those concerned.

It may be even more difficult to assess the scope of protection in the case of an earlier trade mark which is a well-known trade mark, especially where it is unregistered and therefore its scope of 'protection' is wholly uncertain.

A reputation in the United Kingdom This ground for refusal (as with infringement under s 10(3)) is only applicable where there is an earlier trade mark (or a registered trade mark in the case of s 10(3)) which has 'a reputation' in the United Kingdom. This limitation is rightly imposed because the definition of earlier trade mark in s 6 embraces trade marks which may, in fact, have no reputation in the United Kingdom; even a registered trade mark may have no reputation in the United Kingdom. One assumes, however, that a trade mark which qualifies as a well-known trade mark under s 56 will necessarily have 'a reputation' for the purposes of s 5(3). The requirement of 'a reputation in the United Kingdom' is therefore included in order to limit the category of relevant earlier trade marks.

The 1994 Act does not specify either the nature or extent of the 'reputation' which the earlier trade mark must possess in the United Kingdom. In practice, if the nature and extent of the reputation is not real and substantive, then registration is unlikely to be refused under s 5(3) (and infringement is unlikely to occur under s 10(3)) because the applicant's mark would not take unfair advantage of nor be detrimental to the character or the repute of the earlier trade mark. But one assumes that the requisite reputation need not necessarily extend to the goods or services applied for, as it is possible for the use of the applicant's trade mark either to take unfair advantage of or be detrimental to the distinctive character or the repute of the earlier trade mark, even though the actual reputation of the earlier trade mark does not extend to those goods or services.

It follows from the above that there should be no requirement to establish actual confusion or even the likelihood of confusion resulting from the use of the applicant's mark. Of course, evidence of such confusion must be persuasive that the use of the applicant's mark would either take unfair advantage of or be detrimental to the distinctive character or the repute of the earlier trade mark. However, the absence of confusion (or the absence of evidence of confusion) should not result in a necessary finding that the use of the applicant's mark would not take unfair advantage of nor be detrimental to the distinctive character or repute of the earlier trade mark. This, however, was not the view of either Knox J in the *Opus* case[2] or Mr Crystal QC in the *Baywatch* case.[3] In each of those cases (decided under s 10(3)), the plaintiff's respective submissions in support of infringement were rejected due to the absence of any likelihood of confusion. Knox J gave his decision on an application for an interlocutory injunction and expressly refrained from expressing a definitive view on what the exact scope of s 10(3) should be. However, Mr Crystal QC adopted the approach of Knox J and, in an ex tempore judgment, stated that:

> 'the use of the concept of similarity in section 10(3)(a) introduces in my judgment the ingredient of a likelihood of confusion on the part of the public into section 10(3). Section 10(2) protection is given in relation to similar goods or services where, because of the similarity, there exists a likelihood of confusion on the part of the public. It would, it seems to me, be illogical for section 10(3) to give a greater protection in relation to non-similar goods or services by dispensing with the ingredient of a likelihood of confusion than the protection afforded to similar goods under section 10(2).'

If correct, this is an unfortunate restriction on what trade mark owners (and their advisers) had hoped and expected to be the purpose of the protection afforded by s 10(3) (and, by analogy, s 5(3)). That purpose was to prevent the dilution of the value of the trade mark, provided that the trade mark had the necessary 'reputation'. To say that confusion is a necessary ingredient means that an advantage can only be 'unfair' or that there can only be 'detriment' if there is confusion (or, at least, that taking unfair advantage of, or causing detriment to, the proprietor's mark will only be relevant in the context of ss 5(3) and 10(3) where confusion results). As stated above, it is unnecessary and undesirable that one should limit the relevant advantage and the relevant detriment to situations involving confusion. The authors would respectfully

2 *BASF plc v CEP (UK) plc* (1996) 19(4) IPD 9.
3 *Baywatch Production Co Inc v Home Video Channel* [1997] FSR 22 at 30.

adopt the reasoning of the Advocate General and the ECJ in *Sabel v Puma*.[4] The Advocate General considered the need for confusion in the context of Article 4(4)(a) of the Directive (being the Article on which s 5(3) of the 1994 Act is based) and, in his opinion:

> '. . . it is obvious that Article 4(4)(a) simply provides a different test from that of confusion, by requiring it to be shown that the use of the later mark would take unfair advantage of, or be detrimental to, the earlier mark, and that that test is appropriate to the specific purpose of the provisions, which is to protect marks with a reputation.'

Further support for the submission that confusion is not a necessary ingredient of s 5(3) or s 10(3) is to be found in the obiter comment of Jacob J in the *Treat* case where he stated that:

> 'The construction of this phrase [ie the conditions set out at the end of sections 5(3) and 10(3)] I leave for another day. I only note that it might cater for the case where the goods were vastly different but the marks the same or similar and the proprietor could show that the repute of his mark was likely to be affected. The sort of circumstances of the Dutch case of *Claeryn/Klarein*[5] (mark for gin infringed by identical sounding mark for detergent, damage to the gin mark image), may fall within this kind of infringement, even though they do not fall within section 10(2) because there is no likelihood of confusion as to trade origin . . .'[6]

Without due cause The phrase 'without due cause' qualifies the whole of s 5(3). This would suggest that there may be circumstances in which the applicant's trade mark will not be refused registration under s 5(3) even though its use might either take unfair advantage of, or be detrimental to, the distinctive character or the repute of the earlier trade mark. It is difficult to foresee such circumstances arising other than perhaps:

(a) in the event that such use is authorised by the proprietor of the earlier trade mark;

4 *Sabel BV v Puma AG* [1997] ETMR 283 (Advocate General); Case C-251/95 [1998] ETMR 1, ECJ.

5 Benelux Court of Justice, 1 March 1975 NJ 1975, 472.

6 *British Sugar plc v James Robertson and Sons Ltd* [1996] RPC 281 at 295; see also the strong criticism of the *Baywatch* decision by Ray Black in 'Baywatch: Sour Grapes or Justice' [1997] 2 EIPR 39 and by Stephen James in 'The Baywatch v Babewatch case: Has the English Court boobed again?' Trademark World, January 1997, p 21.

(b) where the applicant is relying upon honest concurrent use; or
(c) where the applicant is in a position to claim proprietorship of the mark in the United Kingdom in relation to the relevant goods or services.

Unfair advantage of/or detrimental to The fact that a trade mark can be refused registration because it takes 'unfair advantage of' an earlier trade mark (all other requirements being satisfied), and the fact that the same phrase appears in s 10(3) in the context of infringement, arguably suggests that, for the first time in the United Kingdom, the concept of unfair competition (well known in other jurisdictions) has been introduced, albeit in the limited circumstances prescribed in ss 5(3) and 10(3). This submission needs to be read in light of the *Opus* case and the *Baywatch* case referred to above. However, for the reasons stated, it is to be hoped that ss 5(3) and 10(3) are applicable in circumstances where there is no confusion nor even a likelihood of confusion and that these sections will be applied more broadly. If this is right, then one needs to consider what should be the appropriate scope of that broader application.

The phrase 'take unfair advantage of' would appear to be directed at the situation where the use of the applicant's mark would benefit from the reputation attaching to the earlier trade mark, whereas the phrase 'detrimental to' must involve some form of diminution in, or damage to, the value of the reputation attaching to the earlier trade mark.

Perhaps some guidance as to the meaning of these phrases can be found in decisions in passing off cases where the likelihood of damage was in issue. For example, there is authority for the proposition that any unauthorised appropriation of, or profit from, another's business goodwill or professional reputation will be detrimental to the character or repute of an earlier trade mark in so far as it deprives the proprietor of the earlier trade mark of the opportunity fully to exploit his trade mark himself (for example, by expanding into new products or businesses, or by licensing others to do so).[7] Alternatively, it is likely to be detrimental to both the character and the repute of the earlier trade mark for a similar trade mark to be used on goods of a quality which is inferior to that

7 *Lego Systems A/S v Lego M Lemelstritch* [1983] FSR 155 and see also *Mirage Studios v Counter Feat Clothing Co Ltd* [1991] FSR 145.

associated with the earlier trade mark, even if those inferior goods are not similar to those in respect of which the earlier mark has built up its reputation (this will depend on the notoriety and reputation of the earlier mark and the specific goods concerned).

Thus, even though s 5(3) only applies where the applicant seeks to register a mark for goods or services outside the scope of the protection of the relevant earlier trade mark, there is no conceptual problem in the proposition that the use of a later mark can either benefit from and/or damage the distinctive character or the reputation of an earlier trade mark even though that character or repute does not extend to the specific goods or services which are the subject of the application. In any event, the greater the 'reputation' of the earlier trade mark in the United Kingdom, the more likely it must be that either or both of these requirements will be established.

Section 10(6) The wording of the proviso to s 10(6) incorporates the phrase 'takes unfair advantage of, or is detrimental to, the distinctive character or the trade mark'. It is tempting to assume that the phrase must have the same meaning in both s 10(6) and s 5(3) (and in ss 10(3) and 11(2)). This, however, is not necessarily the case. In the *Barclays* case,[8] Laddie J stated that:

> 'It is difficult to formulate any construction of the proviso to section 10(6) which affords every word in it a distinct function and which also is consistent with sections 10(3) and 11(2). In my view it is necessary to face up to the difficulties of drafting and to consider section 10(6) alone without deciding whether precisely the same construction of the wording used is appropriate for the other subsections.

2.24 Unregistered trade marks and signs, s 5(4)(a) The applicant's trade mark will not be registered if, or to the extent that, its use in the United Kingdom is liable to be prevented by virtue of any rule of law which protects unregistered trade marks or other signs used in the course of trade.[9] Section 5(4)(a) specifically cites the law of passing off as an example.

There have been two decisions of the Registrar under this subsection; in each case, the applicant was seeking a declaration of invalidity relying on s 5(4) but, unfortunately, neither proprietor

8 *Barclays Bank plc v RBS Advanta* [1996] RPC 307 at 315.
9 See s 5(4)(a).

filed any evidence in support of his registration and, accordingly, the marks were declared invalid on the basis that the applicant in each case had established, prima facie, that he was the rightful owner of the mark in question and passing off by the respondent.[10]

Unregistered trade marks or signs may also be 'works' for the purposes of the Copyright, Designs and Patents Act 1988 and thus may be protected by copyright, breach of which could also enable the owner to prevent the use of the trade mark. The law of copyright would not generally be described as a rule of law which protects unregistered trade marks, but this is academic because s 5(4)(b) specifically refers to the law of copyright, as to which see the following paragraph.

In practice, the problem with this ground for refusal is that it begs the question in each case as to whether the law of passing off (or other 'rule of law') would be available to prevent the use of the applicant's mark; the principle that such marks should be refused registration is, however, incontrovertible.

2.25 Other 'earlier rights', s 5(4)(b) The applicant's trade mark will be refused registration if, or to the extent that, its use in the United Kingdom is liable to be prevented by virtue of any other 'earlier right' (not being an earlier trade mark for the purposes of s 5(1)–(3) nor a rule of law protecting unregistered trade marks or signs under s 5(4)(a).

Section 5(4)(b) specifically cites the law of copyright, design right and registered designs but will include any other earlier right which could be relied upon to prevent the use of the trade mark in the United Kingdom. As with s 5(4)(a), the problem with this ground for refusal is that one has to determine whether the 'earlier right' would prevent the use of the applicant's mark. Would, for example, the use of the applicant's mark in a manner which was contrary to the terms of a licence or other contractual obligation be caught by the subsection? Arguably, a contractual right (in the sense of a chose in action to enforce the terms of the licence/contract) should be an 'earlier right' which could prevent the use of the applicant's mark.

10 See *Hima Laya Natural Cosmetics BV's Application* (31 December 1995, unreported) (M Knight) and *Precious Moments Inc's Application*, O/134/96 (13 September 1996, unreported) (M Knight).

2.26 Comment on s 5(4) The grounds for refusal specified in s 5(4) raise the possibility of the Registrar having to interpret rules of law, decide questions of fact and examine rights conferred by statute and the common law beyond the scope of his normal remit.

Of course, any conflict with such earlier rights is more likely to be raised in opposition proceedings and applications for declarations of invalidity rather than by the Registrar on examination. This will not avoid the problem, however, as all opposition proceedings must initially be brought before the Registrar, and applications for a declaration of invalidity may be brought before the Registrar, who will therefore be called upon to decide these issues even if they are not raised on examination.

2.27 Consent, s 5(5) It should be noted that all objections to registration based on the relative grounds for refusal contained within s 5 can be overcome by obtaining the consent of the proprietor of the earlier trade mark or, in the case of s 5(4)(b), the proprietor of the earlier right. This reflects the shift in policy away from seeking to protect the public from being confused or misled by the use of similar trade marks towards being more concerned with the relative rights and interests of trade mark owners themselves. Thus, whereas under the 1938 Act a letter of consent from the proprietor of a cited registration could be ignored by the Registrar on the grounds of protecting the public interest, the Registrar must, under the 1994 Act, withdraw any citations of earlier trade marks or other earlier rights if the proprietor of the earlier trade mark or earlier right consents to the registration of the applicant's mark. Where the proprietor of an earlier trade mark or earlier right is approached by an applicant who is seeking his consent to registration it will be for the proprietor to determine the consequences of providing that consent and to take such action as he may consider appropriate to maintain the value and distinctiveness of his trade mark or right.

Letters of consent The Work Manual sets out the minimum requirements of the Registrar in relation to accepting a letter of consent. The basic principles to bear in mind are that the consent must be given by the owner of the cited mark, that the application being consented to is clearly identified, and that it is clear that consent to registration (and not just use) of the mark is being given. The Work Manual states that the Registrar's requirements are that:

(a) certified copies of the original letter of consent may be accepted;

(b) letters of consent should preferably be on company headed paper – the consent should always include the details of the person giving the consent (ie name, position, the name of the company and the letter should be signed by the person named);
(c) the application in respect of which consent is being given must be identified – the application number(s) is/are sufficient and it is not essential to include the trade mark – nor is it necessary to identify the earlier trade marks owned by the person giving consent;
(d) if the specification is not referred to, it will be assumed that the specification applied for is acceptable to those giving the consent – however, if a specification is referred to and it is narrower than the one filed, then the application will only be accepted in respect of the goods and services to which the consent specifically refers and applies; and
(e) letters of consent must be in English or, if in a foreign language, must be accompanied by a certified translation.

In the case of technical citations and obtaining consent between companies in the same ownership, the Registrar now accepts a simplified procedure as follows:

(a) a general letter of consent may be provided between the two companies setting out the relationship between the two companies and confirming that they are prepared to consent to any trade mark applications made by the other party; and
(b) on each occasion that a copy of the general letter of consent is filed, the applicant (or his agent) must supply a covering letter certifying that the general consent is still valid.[11]

2.28 Honest concurrent use, s 7 Even if the applicant cannot, or chooses not to, overcome any objections raised by the Registrar under s 5, he may instead seek to rely on the honest concurrent use of his mark. The first issue to consider is the meaning of the phrase 'honest concurrent use'.

Honest concurrent use Section 7(3) states that 'honest concurrent use' means such use in the United Kingdom, by the applicant or with his consent, as would formerly have amounted to honest concurrent use for the purposes of s 12(2) of the 1938 Act. Many of the cases under s 12(2) of the 1938 Act focus on the matters which

11 Work Manual, Chapter 6, paragraph 25.2.

the tribunal had to take into account in exercising its discretion under s 12(2) once honest concurrent use had been established. The Registrar does not have a discretion under s 7 of the 1994 Act once honest concurrent use has been established and therefore these cases on discretion are no longer relevant. (In saying this, we have considered but rejected the possibility that the definition of 'honest concurrent use' in s 7(3), in as much as it points to s 12(2) of the 1938 Act, seeks to embrace the discretionary element of s 12(2). It is submitted that it is only the factual enquiry as to what constitutes honest concurrent use for the purposes of s 12(2) that is relevant for the purposes of s 7(3).)

The two issues which arose under s 12(2) of the 1938 Act (and which are now relevant in considering s 7 of the 1994 Act) were:
(a) whether the use was honest; and
(b) whether the period of use was sufficient.

As to honesty, one factor which may negate honesty is where the applicant has knowledge of the registration of the earlier trade mark, but use in the genuine belief that the use of the mark will not cause confusion is 'honest'.[12]

As to the period of use, it is submitted that 'concurrent' requires only that the applicant must have used his mark concurrently either with the period of registration of the earlier trade mark and/or with the period of use of the earlier trade mark; this is how Jacob J approached the question in *Origins*.[13] In that case it was argued that, by reference to s 12(2) of the 1938 Act and the decision in *L'Amy*,[14] both marks had to be in concurrent use side by side. Side by side use may have been a factor under the 1938 Act in so far as such use was relevant in assessing the likelihood of confusion, which was one of the matters for the tribunal to consider in exercising its discretion under s 12(2). As stated, s 7 of the 1994 Act does not give the Registrar any discretion and therefore side by side use, as well as other matters which were relevant to the exercise of his former discretion, should not affect the meaning of the phrase 'honest concurrent use' for the purposes of s 7. (Indeed, in the *Origins* case, Jacob J doubted whether *L'Amy* was decided correctly in any event, because it would lead to the situation where the proprietor of the

12 *Pirie* (1932) 49 RPC 195 at 206, 211 and 216; *Bali Trade Mark (No 2)* [1978] FSR 193 at 220; see also *Parkington* (1946) 63 RPC 171.
13 *Origins Natural Resources Inc v Origin Clothing Ltd* [1995] FSR 280 at 287.
14 *L'Amy Trade Mark* [1983] RPC 137.

earlier trade mark would be in a better position if he had not used his mark because there would be no opportunity for a side by side comparison.)

The fact that the Registrar retains no discretion and that confusion and/or the likelihood of confusion is not an issue under s 7 of the 1994 Act means that the Registrar's practice of requiring a specific period of concurrent use (in the Work Manual the period of 'five years' good use' is specified[15]) is, at least, doubtful. The only reason why the Registrar looked at the period of concurrent use under s 12(2) was so that he could be satisfied that there was no confusion or likelihood of confusion through the use of the applicant's mark. This is no longer the issue: the test is simply concurrence with either the period of registration and/or the period of use of the earlier trade mark.

Use by the applicant or with his consent The definition in s 7(3) requires that the relevant use be by the applicant or with his consent. This would suggest that use by a predecessor in title must be excluded (unless one gives a very broad meaning to the word 'consent', so that the consent can apply retrospectively and possibly in relation to use of the mark of which the applicant was not even aware!). It is submitted that there is no reason in principle to exclude use by a former proprietor; s 12(2) of the 1938 Act did not exclude such use. However, the wording of s 7(3) is unequivocal and this suggests that an amendment is required.

Evidence of honest concurrent use In order to rely on s 7, the applicant should ideally produce the following evidence:

(a) exhibits must show that the mark applied for has been used as applied for;
(b) the specification of goods or services must be limited to those goods or services for which use is shown; and
(c) where relevant, a history of changes of ownership of the mark applied for should be produced (the Work Manual states that this is not strictly necessary as it is the continuity of the use which is the relevant consideration, not to whom the mark belonged – however, as stated above, although this statement is correct in logic and is consistent with the law under the 1938

15 Work Manual, Chapter 6, paragraph 26, although it is recognised that this period is not a rule of law and may be increased or decreased depending on the circumstances of the case.

Act, the history of the proprietorship of the mark may be relevant because the relevant use must be by the actual applicant or with his consent).

Effect of honest concurrent use If the applicant can show to the satisfaction of the Registrar that there has been honest concurrent use of his trade mark, then the Registrar is required not to refuse the application on the basis of the earlier trade mark/earlier right in respect of which honest concurrent use has been shown[16] *unless* an objection under s 5 is raised in opposition proceedings by the proprietor of the earlier trade mark or other earlier right in question.[17]

The proviso The proviso (commencing with the word 'unless') was described as a 'slightly awkward' formulation in the *Road Tech* case[18] where it was confirmed that, in the absence of any discretion conferred on the Registrar, refusal is mandatory under s 7(2) if the proprietor of the earlier trade mark or other earlier right objects. This means that the recognition of honest concurrent use is somewhat emasculated: once the proprietor of the earlier trade mark raises an objection, the Registrar is bound to refuse the application under s 5 and the concept of honest concurrent use thereafter becomes irrelevant in deciding the registrability of the applicant's mark (and for any other purpose under the 1994 Act). Under s 12(2) of the 1938 Act (albeit that the Registrar retained a discretion to refuse registration even where the applicant established honest concurrent use), the Registrar was able to grant registration based on the applicant's honest concurrent use notwithstanding that the proprietor of the earlier trade mark objected. Now, the discretion is removed and so is the whole concept of honest concurrent use simply because the proprietor of the earlier trade mark/earlier right objects under s 5. Having raised the objection, the Registrar is bound to refuse registration and therefore the success of the opposition proceedings is a foregone conclusion as the opponent (the proprietor of the earlier trade mark/earlier right) is required neither to prove his case under s 5 nor to disprove either the honesty and/or the concurrency of the applicant's use. Can this be right? It seems to be the only interpretation based on the wording of s 7, but does this not

16 Section 7(1) and (2).
17 Section 7(2).
18 *Road Tech Computer Systems Ltd v Unison Software (UK) Ltd* [1996] FSR 805 at 813.

mean that s 7 should be further amended? The practical lesson for applicants is that when seeking to overcome an objection based on an earlier trade mark/earlier right, it would be prudent not simply to rely on honest concurrent use, but also to try to overcome the objection on its merits.

Section 8 order Finally, it should be noted that the Secretary of State will eventually have the power to order that a trade mark is not to be refused registration by the Registrar under the relative grounds for refusal unless an objection under s 5 is specifically raised in opposition proceedings by the proprietor of the earlier trade mark or other earlier right.[19] However, the Secretary of State may not make such an order until 1 April 2006 at the earliest.[20]

19 Section 8(1).
20 Section 8(5); being the 10th anniversary of the day on which applications for Community Trade Marks could have been filed under the Regulation.

3 Practice and procedure

3.01 Introduction Having considered in Chapters 1 and 2 those trade marks which are registrable under the 1994 Act, this chapter examines:

(a) the formal procedure for applying for registration;
(b) the examination and registration procedure;
(c) the procedure for hearings before the Registrar;
(d) appeals from the Registrar; and
(e) certain specific matters relevant to trade mark proceedings in the court.

This first involves describing the administrative framework which exists within the Registry,[1] all of which is dealt with in Pt III of the 1994 Act.

As this chapter relates substantially to matters of procedure, it is worth noting at the outset that any irregularity in procedure before the Registrar or in the Registry can always be rectified on such terms as the Registrar directs.[2] Furthermore, in the case of an irregularity or prospective irregularity which consists of a failure to comply with any times or periods specified either by the 1994 Act or in the Rules and

1 ie the Trade Marks Registry at the Patent Office: r 2(1); referred to in the Rules as 'the Office'.

2 Rule 60(1); an example of the application of this rule is where the Registry overlooked the fact that a Notice of Opposition had been filed and wrongly issued a Certificate of Registration. The 'proprietor' was ordered to return the Certificate and it was directed that the opposition should be heard on its merits: see 'Errors by the Patent Office and Trade Mark Registry – Two Recent Cases' (1996) 19 IPN No 8, August 1996.

where the failure is attributable wholly or in part to an error, default or omission on the part of the Registry or the Registrar, the Registrar can alter the time or period in question in such a way as he thinks fit.[3]

3.02 The Registry The Registry has its Head Office in Newport, Gwent[4] but retains a London office.[5]

There is a video link between the London and Newport offices and hearings can be conducted using this facility; inter partes hearings are more usually conducted in either London or Newport.

For management purposes the Registry is divided into four departments:
(1) examination practice;
(2) opposition, registration and post registration;
(3) information technology; and
(4) new legislation and quality management.

The Manchester Branch; the Cutlers' Company In the past, the Registry maintained a branch in Manchester at which applications relating to textile goods could be filed. Similarly, applications for metal goods could have been filed by traders in the Sheffield area through the Cutlers' Company. The Mathys Report recommended that these filing facilities should be discontinued as they no longer served a useful purpose.[6] These recommendations were implemented by the 1994 Act and therefore all filings must now be lodged with the Registry in either London or Newport.[7] The Registry is open for business during normal business hours on business days which have been promulgated by directions given under s 80.[8]

3.03 The Registrar, s 62 The Registrar is the Comptroller General of Patents, Designs and Trade Marks.[9]

3 Rule 60(2); see also paragraph 3.03 and rr 61 and 62.
4 Cardiff Road, Newport, Gwent, NP9 1RH; Telephone: (0645) 500505, Fax: (01633) 813600.
5 25 Southampton Buildings, London, WC2A 1AY; Telephone: (0171) 412 7919, Fax: (0171) 412 7480.
6 Mathys Report paragraphs 213 and 218.
7 For the purposes of the transitional provisions, the old Sheffield Register will be treated as part of the Register kept under the 1938 Act and applications made to the Cutlers' Company which were pending as at 31 October 1994 are treated as if they had been made to the Registrar: Sch 3, para 20.
8 See the Journal No 6049 dated 31 October 1994.
9 Section 62.

Maintenance of the Register The Registrar is responsible for maintaining the Register of Trade Marks[10] and in this regard he has certain delegated powers and duties.[11] However, the Registrar and his officers will not be liable in respect of the exercise of his powers and the performance of his duties in so far as they are authorised by the 1994 Act.[12]

Examination, s 37(1) Apart from maintaining the Register, the Registrar's primary function is to examine applications for the registration of trade marks as required by s 37(1).[13]

Discretion as to time limits, r 62 Subject to the exceptions referred to below, any time or period which is prescribed in the Rules or specified by the Registrar can be extended by the Registrar as he thinks fit.[14] A person wanting to apply for an extension must do so to the Registrar[15] prior to the expiration of the time or period in question.[16]

However, the Registrar does have a discretion to grant an extension even after the time or period has expired.[17] If a request for an extension is made after the expiration of the relevant time or period, the Registrar may extend the period if he is satisfied with the applicant's explanation for the delay in requesting the extension and provided that the Registrar is satisfied that any such extension would not disadvantage any other person or party affected by the extension.[18]

There are thus two tests which the Registrar will apply before he grants an extension of time depending on whether the application for the extension is made prior to or after the expiry of the time or period in question. If the application is made prior to the expiry, then the time or period may be extended:

(a) as the Registrar 'thinks fit'; and

10 Section 63(1); see also s 71 in relation to the Registrar's annual report.
11 eg s 66(1): the power to require the use of specified forms for the registration of a trade mark; s 67(1): the duty to provide certain information concerning applications and registered trade marks.
12 Section 70(2) and (3).
13 See paragraphs 3.24 et seq.
14 Rule 62(1); see also r 61 as to the effect of interruptions caused by postal services or in the Registry.
15 Using Form TM 9.
16 Rule 62(4).
17 Rule 62(5).
18 Rule 62(5).

(b) on such terms as he may direct.

Whereas, if the application is made after the expiry, then the extension will only be granted:

(a) if the Registrar is 'satisfied with the explanation for the delay'; and

(b) provided that it appears to him that the extension will not disadvantage any other person or party.

It may be that the two tests will, in practice, be applied in much the same way. That is, the Registrar may only think it fit to grant an extension under the first test if the two limbs of the second test are satisfied. Certainly, there is evidence that the Registry was taking a tough stance with parties seeking extensions under r 114 of the 1986 Rules[19] and this policy continues to be applied under the Rules (notwithstanding the fact that the first test could arguably be applied more liberally than the second). The Registrar must be provided with detailed and compelling reasons for an extension. The Work Manual notes that reasons such as 'awaiting client's instructions' and 'client's are considering their next act' will not be accepted.[20]

Where the Registrar does extend any time or period, then any other person or party affected by the extension will be notified accordingly.[1]

In certain circumstances, the period within which a party to any proceedings before the Registrar must file evidence will begin upon the expiry of a preceding period in which the other party to the proceedings had to file his evidence. In the event that the latter party notifies the Registrar that he does not intend to file any such evidence, the Registrar may then direct that the relevant period within which the former party must file his evidence is to begin on such a date as he will notify to each of the parties to the proceedings.[2]

Exceptions, r 62(3) The only instances in which the Registrar cannot extend the time or periods prescribed in the Rules are:

(a) the two month period which one has in order to file an address for service: r 10(6);

(b) the two month period which one has in order to correct deficiencies in an application: r 11;

19 See for example *R v Registrar of Trade Marks, ex p SAW Co SA* [1996] RPC 507.
20 See the Direction published in the Journal on 15 October 1997, No 6197.
1 Rule 62(1).
2 Rule 62(6).

(c) the three month period which one has in order to file an opposition to registration: r 13(1);
(d) the three month period which one has in order to file a counter statement to an opposition to registration: r 13(2) (note that the Registrar takes the view that the three month period specified in r 31(3) within which one has to file a counter statement to an application for revocation or a declaration of invalidity is also not extensible[3]);
(e) the six month period for late renewal applications to be made: r 29; and
(f) the six month period for applying for the restoration of a removed registration:[4] r 30.

Filing of documentation, rr 63 and 66 Rules require from time to time the filing of applications, notices and other documents by sending them by post or hand delivery. However, the Registrar is also given a discretion to permit all such documents to be filed by electronic means, subject to any terms or conditions which the Registrar may specify.[5] It is clearly intended that the Registry, one day, will offer the facility for filing documents electronically and this will considerably improve the filing procedure. At present, the Registry permits documents to be filed by facsimile but not by e-mail or any other electronic means.

On a different but related subject, it may be noted that where a document (or part thereof) which is not in English is sent to the Registrar, the Registrar is entitled to require an English translation to be furnished which must be verified to the satisfaction of the Registrar as corresponding to the original text.[6] The Registrar retains a discretion to refuse to accept any translation which in his opinion is inaccurate and to require another verified translation of the document to be furnished.[7]

Forms, directions and fees, ss 66 and 79 Many of the procedural matters in which the Registrar is involved relating to the registration of trade marks can only be initiated if the proper TM Form is used.[8]

3 *Principles Retail Ltd's Application* (1996) 19(8) IPD 15 (M Knight).
4 Rule 62(3).
5 Rule 63.
6 Rule 66(1).
7 Rule 66(2).
8 Or a replica or such other form as is acceptable to the Registrar: r 3(2).

Section 66 permits the Registrar to require the use of such TM Forms as he may direct for any purpose relating to the registration of a trade mark or any other proceeding before the Registrar.

All TM Forms together with the Registrar's directions as to their use are published in the Journal;[9] and a list of TM Forms can be found in Schedule 3 to this book.

In most instances a fee is also payable in conjunction with the filing of the TM Form which is prescribed in rules made pursuant to s 79.[10]

The Trade Marks Journal, s 81 and r 65 The 1994 Act provides for the continuation of the practice of the Registrar of publishing a journal containing:

(1) particulars of applications for the registration of trade marks, together with a representation of the mark itself;
(2) information as is required to be published by the Rules; and
(3) such other information relating to trade marks as the Registrar thinks fit.[11] (This now includes information relating to applications made under the Protocol.)

The journal is called 'The Trade Marks Journal' and is published weekly.

Appearance in court, s 74 In certain proceedings before the court,[12] the Registrar is entitled to appear and be heard and must appear if directed to do so by the court.[13]

3.04 The Register, s 63 The Register is maintained by the Registrar[14] and references in the 1994 Act and in this book to 'registration' mean registration in the Register. The Register need not be kept in a documentary form[15] and this again confirms that it is the clear intention that the Register will one day be open for electronic filings of applications, notices and other documents.[16]

9 Rule 3(1); see the supplement to the Journal dated 19 February 1997 (No 6163).
10 Rule 4; the current fees are set out in the Trade Marks (Fees) Rules 1996 (SI 1996/1942) and appear in Schedule 3 to this book.
11 Section 81; r 65.
12 As to which, see s 74(1).
13 Section 74(1); unless directed by the court he may choose to submit a written statement in accordance with s 74(2); see also paragraph 3.51.
14 Section 63(1).
15 Rule 32; see also r 36(2).
16 As to which, see r 63 and paragraphs 3.02 and 3.03.

The Registrar enters in the Register details of:
(a) registered trade marks;[17]
(b) prescribed particulars of registrable transactions affecting a registered trade mark;[18] and
(c) such other matters relating to registered trade marks as may be prescribed,[19] for example, any disclaimer or limitation affecting the registration,[20] but no notice of any trust (express, implied or constructive) will be entered.[1]

There is no division of the Register under the 1994 Act into Part A and Part B. All registered trade marks are therefore in one unified Register. There is also no requirement, and therefore no procedure, for trade marks registered under the 1994 Act to be:
(a) 'associated' with another registered trade mark;[2] nor
(b) registered subject to a condition.[3]

Accordingly, such matters cannot be entered in the 1994 Register.

Inspection of the Register The Register is available for public inspection[4] at the Registry during its hours of business.[5] Furthermore, copies or extracts of entries in the Register can be obtained from the Registrar on request.[6] This right of inspection will not be affected if the Register is kept in an electronic form.[7]

Amendments to the Register, s 64(4) and r 38 Substantive amendments to any entry in the Register are dealt with elsewhere in this book.[8] For present purposes it may be noted that certain details

17 The Rules specify the particulars of each trade mark which will be entered in the Register: see r 33; trade marks registered under the 1938 Act as at 31 October 1994 (whether in Part A or in Part B) have been transferred to the 1994 Register and have effect as if registered under the 1994 Act: Sch 3, para 2(1); but the fact that such marks may have been 'associated' with other marks or were registered subject to a condition has ceased to be relevant: Sch 3, paras 2(3), 3(1) and 10(3).
18 See s 25(1) and r 34; see also Chapter 10.
19 Section 63(2)(c).
20 Section 13 and r 24.
1 The Registrar is not affected by notice of any such trust: s 26(1).
2 ie there is no equivalent to s 23(2) of the 1938 Act.
3 ie there is no exact equivalent to s 14 of the 1938 Act.
4 Section 63(3)(a) and r 36(1).
5 The Registry's business hours are specified by the Registrar pursuant to s 80 and are published in the Journal (No 6049 dated 31 October 1994) pursuant to r 64.
6 Section 63(3)(b); the request must be made using Form TM 31R: r 37.
7 Rule 36(2).
8 See Chapter 5 as to revocation and invalidity.

not relating to substance can always be changed on request; thus:

(a) the proprietor of a registered trade mark or a licensee (or any person having an interest in or charge on a registered trade mark which has been registered under r 34) can notify the Registrar[9] of any change in his name or address;[10] and
(b) anyone who has furnished an address for service pursuant to r 10 can change that address.[11]

Rectification or correction of the Register, s 64 and r 31 Errors or omissions in the Register can be rectified or corrected pursuant to s 64. Rectification under s 64 does not relate to matters affecting the validity of the registration of the trade mark: these matters are covered by ss 46 and 47.[12] Thus, rectification must relate only to errors or omissions which do not affect the validity of the registration. An example of such an error being rectified is where the Registry wrongly recorded a change of name of a registered proprietor.[13]

The effect of any rectification of the Register is that the error or omission in question is deemed never to have been made.[14] The Registrar or the court may, however, direct otherwise if the circumstances of the case so require.

Application for rectification, s 64(2) and r 31 An application for rectification can be made by 'any person having a sufficient interest' and may be made either to the Registrar or to the court.[15] However, if proceedings concerning the trade mark in question are already pending in the court, then the application for the declaration must be made to the court.[16] If the application is made to the Registrar, then he may at any stage of the proceedings refer the application to the court.[17]

An application for rectification under s 64 which is made to the

9 Using Form TM 21.
10 Section 64(4) and r 38(1).
11 Using Form TM 33: r 38(2).
12 See Chapter 5.
13 *Henkel Corpn's Applications* (27 August 1996, unreported) (M J Tuck).
14 Section 64(3).
15 Section 64(1) and (2); the phrase 'sufficient interest' was considered in *Henkel Corporation's Applications* (27 August 1996, unreported) (M J Tuck).
16 Section 64(2)(a).
17 Section 64(2)(b).
18 Using Form TM 26.

Registrar[18] must be submitted together with a statement of the grounds on which the application is made.[19]

Where the application is made other than by the proprietor, the Registrar will send a copy of the application together with the statement of grounds to the proprietor.[20] The proprietor then has three months from the date on which the Registrar sends the application to him within which to file a counter statement[1] and the Registrar will send a copy of the counter statement to the party seeking rectification.

Thereafter, the provisions of r 13 will apply to the proceedings in the same way as if the proceedings were in respect of an opposition to the registration of a trade mark.[2]

Intervention in rectification proceedings, r 31(5) There is also the option for any person, other than the registered proprietor, who claims to have an interest in the rectification proceedings to apply to the Registrar[3] for leave to intervene. The intervener must state the nature of his interest and the Registrar may either refuse leave to intervene or grant leave upon appropriate terms or conditions as he thinks fit, which may include an undertaking as to costs.[4] As always, the parties are entitled to request a hearing in relation to the issue as to whether leave to intervene should be either refused or granted.

If the application for leave to intervene is granted, the intervener will be treated as a party for the purposes of the application for rectification and the provisions of r 13 will apply to the intervener, subject only to any terms or conditions which the Registrar has imposed in respect of the intervention.[5]

Registrar's decision When the Registrar has made a decision either in relation to the application for rectification and/or the application to intervene, he will send to the applicant, the proprietor and the intervener (if any) written notice of his decision, including the reasons for his decision.[6] In the event that there is any appeal from

19 Rule 31(1).
20 Rule 31(2).
1 Using Form TM 8. The three month time limit for filing the counter-statement cannot be extended: *Principles Retail Ltd's Application*, (1996) 19(8) IPD 15 (M Knight).
2 Rule 31(4); subject to r 31(2), (6) and (7).
3 Using Form TM 27.
4 Rule 31(5).
5 Rule 31(6).
6 Rule 31(7).

the Registrar's decision, then the date when the notice of his decision is sent to the parties will be taken to be the date of his decision.

Transitional provisions, Schedule 3 An application by a registered proprietor under s 34 of the 1938 Act for the rectification or correction of the 1938 Register which was pending as at 31 October 1994 will be dealt with under the old law and any consequent rectification/correction will be entered in the 1994 Register.[7]

Removal of matter from the Register, s 64(5) and r 39 The Registrar is given the power to remove from the Register any matter which appears to him to have ceased to have effect.[8] The Rules set out the procedure for the Registrar to follow before removing any matter from the Register. Accordingly, where it appears to the Registrar that any matter in the Register has ceased to have effect he must, before removing it, first notify in writing any person who may be affected by its removal. The person concerned can then submit written representations of any objections which he has to the removal of the matter.[9] If the person concerned chooses to make written representations, he must do so within three months of the date of the Registrar's notice and the Registrar will give him the opportunity to be heard if he so requests.[10] The Registrar may then only remove the matter in question if either:

(a) there has not been a response to the Registrar's notice; or
(b) where representations have been made, the Registrar remains of the view after considering the representations that the matter nonetheless has ceased to have effect.[11]

The application procedure

3.05 The application for registration, s 32 and r 5 The formalities governing the filing of applications for registration are set out in s 32 of the 1994 Act and in r 5.

7 Schedule 3, para 18(1).
8 Section 64(5); this relates to matter which was entered in the Register in error and thus rectification is effected by removing such matter.
9 Rule 39(1); the Registrar will also publish his intention to remove the matter where he considers it appropriate.
10 Rule 39(2); where the Registrar has published his intention to remove the matter, then third parties can file a notice of opposition using Form TM 7; in either case, r 13 will apply.
11 Rule 39(3) and (4).

The application must be made to the Registrar[12] and lodged at the Registry.

The application must contain the particulars set out in s 32(2), being:

(a) a request for registration of the trade mark;
(b) the name and address of the applicant;
(c) a statement of the goods or services in relation to which it is sought to register the trade mark as well as a specification of the class in Schedule 4 of the Rules to which it relates;[13] and
(d) a representation of the trade mark.

If the mark is described in words, then the description must be sufficiently precise to enable anyone reading the application to gain a clear understanding of the mark. Although s 32(2)(d) refers to a 'representation' not to a 'graphical representation' of the mark (as is required under s 1(1)), the Registrar takes the view that the omission of the adjective 'graphical' is of no consequence and therefore the application must contain a graphical representation of the mark.[14]

Supplying these particulars is of more than procedural importance because it dictates the date on which the proprietor's exclusive rights take effect under s 9. This is because it is not until everything required by s 32(2) has been furnished to the Registrar that the application is given its 'date of filing'.[15] The date of filing of an application for registration is also deemed to be the date of registration,[16] assuming, of course, that the application proceeds to registration. The proprietor's exclusive rights will then take effect from the date of registration.[17] Thus, somewhat unnecessarily, three phrases are used in the 1994 Act to refer to the same date:

(a) the 'date of filing of the application': being the date on which everything is furnished to the Registrar in accordance with s 32(2);[18]

12 Section 32(1); using Form TM 3.
13 As to which, see paragraph 3.08. NB: the need to file separate applications for separate classes is no longer necessary and it is now possible to file multi-class applications, see paragraph 3.09.
14 *Claydon Architectural Metalwork Ltd's Application* (6 August 1996, unreported) (R G Evans).
15 Section 33(1).
16 Section 40(3).
17 Section 9(3).
18 Section 33(1).

(b) the 'date of application for registration': which is deemed to be the 'date of filing of the application' (see (a) above);[19] and
(c) the 'date of registration', which is deemed to be the date of filing of the application for registration (see (a) and (b) above).[20]

3.06 Address for service, r 10 Every applicant must file an address for service in the United Kingdom.[1] The address for service must be filed together with the application itself.[2]

Anything sent to the applicant at his address for service is deemed to be 'properly sent' for any purpose under the 1994 Act or the Rules.[3]

If an applicant fails to file an address for service, the Registrar will treat the application as having been abandoned.[4] Alternatively, the Registrar is entitled to treat the applicant's trade or business address as his address for service, provided that it is in the United Kingdom.[5]

Upon the registration of a trade mark, the applicant's address for service becomes the address for service of the registered proprietor.[6]

3.07 Fees, r 5 As one would expect, the application is subject to the payment of certain fees:
(a) the prescribed application fee; and
(b) such other class fees as may be appropriate.[7]
The trade mark will not be registered unless such fees are paid within the prescribed period and, in default, the application is deemed to be withdrawn.[8] There is no 'prescribed period' as such, but r 5 states that the application is 'subject to' the payment of the fees. Most trade mark agents have a deposit account which operates in accordance with the Registry's terms and conditions. The fees are

19 Section 33(2).
20 Section 40(3).
1 Rule 10(1)(a). For an example of a case in which a proprietor had provided no address for service, see *Softa Trade Mark* [1996] RPC 457; accordingly (by virtue of r 10(6)(c)) the proprietor could take no part in the invalidation proceedings and his mark was accordingly declared invalid.
2 ie on Form TM 3: r 10(3).
3 Rule 10(4).
4 Rule 10(6)(a).
5 Rule 10(4).
6 Rule 10(2).
7 Section 32(4) and r 5. The current fees are set out in the Trade Marks (Fees) Rules 1996 (SI 1996/1942).
8 Section 40(2); see also r 11(b).

drawn down from this account, thus avoiding any failure or delay in paying the fees. If, however, the fees are not paid, then this will be a deficiency in the application for the purposes of r 11 and the Registrar will notify the applicant. If the applicant does not pay the fees within two months of the date of the notice then the application is treated as abandoned.[9]

3.08 Statement of use, s 32(3) The application must be supported by a statement that the trade mark is being used by the applicant (or with his consent) in relation to the goods or services for which he is seeking registration. Alternatively, the application will have to be supported by a statement that the applicant has a bona fide intention that the trade mark will be so used.[10]

It is significant that, where the applicant does not himself intend to use the trade mark, it is sufficient if the trade mark is used (or it is intended that it will be used) by a third party merely with the applicant's consent. It is therefore not even strictly necessary, for the purpose of complying with this requirement, for the third party user to have a formal licence, let alone for the user to be recorded as a registered user (for which there is indeed no procedure under the 1994 Act). Of course, any formal licence will be a registrable transaction for the purpose of s 25(2) and it will almost invariably be preferable for the owner to enter into a formal licence with any third party user rather than relying simply on a bare consent.[11]

A false statement as to use/intended use will constitute bad faith for the purpose of s 3(6) and thus would constitute an absolute ground for refusal of registration.[12] Indeed, a statement which is broader than the actual goods or services supplied or provided by the applicant may result in the application being rejected pursuant to s 3(6). Certainly, the Registrar's practice is to raise an objection under s 3(6) if he suspects that the applicant has no intention of

9 Rule 11(b).

10 Section 32(3); the bona fide intention of the applicant has been considered in *Road Tech Computer Systems Ltd v Unison Software (UK) Ltd* [1996] FSR 805; see also *Mercury Communications Ltd v Mercury Interactive (UK) Ltd* [1995] FSR 850 (obiter of Laddie J concerning the wide specification of goods chosen by the applicant) and *Avnet Inc v Isoact Ltd* [1998] FSR 16, Ch D, where Jacob J makes strong obiter comments concerning misdescribing retail services as 'advertising and promotional services'.

11 See Chapter 10.

12 It may also be an offence under s 94(1).

using the mark in connection with all the goods/services described in the specification.[13] This practice finds support in the *Road Tech* case and the *Mercury* case.[14]

3.09 Multi-class application, r 8 One of the important practical advantages under the 1994 Act is the procedure allowing an applicant to file a single multi-class application without having to lodge separate applications for each class,[15] but separate class fees will still be payable.[16]

Where a multi-class application is filed, the relevant statement of goods and/or services has to:

(a) list the relevant classes in consecutive numerical order; and

(b) group the goods and/or services by reference to the numbers of the classes as specified.[17]

Adding a class, r 8(3) It has already been noted that a multi-class application must include a statement of the goods and services grouped by reference to the numbers of the classes in relation to which it is sought to register the trade mark. If any goods or services are incorrectly grouped, in the sense that they are grouped by reference to the wrong class numbers, then those wrongly grouped goods/services will need to be re-grouped under the correct class number. This will not be a problem if the original application already includes other goods or services which fall within the correct class number. But if the incorrectly grouped goods or services do not fall within any class to which the original application relates, then the applicant will have to apply for the addition to his application of the appropriate class(es),[18] which will be subject to the payment of additional class fees as may be appropriate.[19]

3.10 Correction of a deficiency in the application, r 11 It is possible for the applicant to correct certain procedural irregularities relating to his application. Rule 11 applies in the situation where the

13 See the Work Manual, Chapter 6, paragraph 19.1.

14 Supra, see note 10, page 108.

15 Rule 8.

16 Rule 5. The fees payable have recently been reduced: see the Trade Marks (Fees) Rules 1996 (SI 1996/1942).

17 Rule 8(2).

18 Using Form TM 3A.

19 Rule 8(3).

Registrar considers that the application fails to comply with any of the requirements set out in:

(a) s 32(2), (3) or (4), concerning the requirements as to the application itself;

(b) r 5, also concerning the requirements as to the application itself; and

(c) r 8(2), concerning the requirements as to the specification of class(es).

If the applicant has failed to comply with any of these requirements, the Registrar will notify the applicant accordingly and the applicant then has two months within which to remedy the deficiency so as to meet each of the requirements. If the applicant fails to remedy the deficiency it will be treated:

(a) as never having been made in the case of a deficiency under s 32(2); or

(b) as abandoned, in the case of any other deficiency covered by r 11.[20]

3.11 Division of an application, s 41(1)(a) and r 19 At any time before registration[1] the applicant may request the Registrar[2] to divide his application into two or more separate applications (referred to as 'divisional applications'). Requests for a division will have to specify the goods or services to which each divisional application will apply, and thereafter each divisional application is treated as a separate application for registration, although the original filing date will be retained.[3]

This is a procedure which was not available under the 1938 Act, although UK patent applications, and trade mark applications in many other countries, have been divisible for many years. It is most useful where an objection is raised by the Registrar, or an opposition is filed by a third party, which relates to only some of the goods or services covered by the applicant's original application. In order to side-step the objection/opposition the applicant may be able to divide his application so that he can obtain registration in respect of those goods or services which are not the subject of the

20 Rule 11(a) and (b).

1 Thus, even after acceptance, but see r 19(2).

2 Using Form TM 12 and upon payment of the prescribed fee. The current fees are set out in the Trade Marks (Fees) Rules 1996 (SI 1996/1942).

3 Rule 20(1).

objection or opposition.[4] Previously, any objection/opposition would have delayed an application until all were overcome (which could have been years), or the applicant would either have had to remove elements of his mark or limit the specification of his goods or services. If the applicant had wished to persevere in an attempt to obtain registration for either the elements of the mark or the goods or services removed, he would have had to file a fresh application with a new and later filing date. It may now be possible to avoid this situation by dividing up the original application in order that the unobjectionable parts of the application can proceed without delay and so that the objectionable parts do not lose their priority date (assuming, of course, that the objection/opposition can be overcome).

3.12 Merger of an application, s 41(1)(b) and r 2 An applicant who has made separate applications for the registration of a trade mark may, at any time before preparations for the publication of any of his original applications have been completed by the Registry, request the Registrar[5] to merge the separate applications into a single application.[6]

The stipulation as to the time by which a request to merge can be made may lead to some uncertainty. For example, how will the applicant know when all the 'preparations' (whatever they may consist of) have been completed? The stipulation is also different to that specified (unambiguously) in r 19 for the purpose of requesting the division of an application.[7]

That aside, the request to merge may only be made in respect of applications which:

(a) are in respect of the same trade mark;
(b) bear the same date of application; and
(c) are, at the time of the request, in the name of the same applicant.

4 Provided that he does so prior to the publication of the application, as otherwise any such objection/opposition to the original application will be taken to apply to each divisional application: r 19(2).

5 Using Form TM 17 (which should be sent to the Examination Unit at the Registry which holds the highest relevant application number) and upon payment of the prescribed fee. The current fees are set out in the Trade Marks (Fees) Rules 1996 (SI 1996/1942).

6 Rule 20(1).

7 As to which, see paragraph 3.11.

If the Registrar is satisfied that these conditions are present, then he has no discretion and must comply with the applicant's request.[8]

This is a procedure which was not available under the 1938 Act. It is most useful in reducing renewal fees where the applicant can merge two or more applications[9] into one, thus resulting in one registration and hence one renewal fee in the future. The merger of applications also simplifies the administration of large trade mark portfolios.

3.13 Series applications, s 41(1)(c) and r 21 A 'series of trade marks' is defined as a collection of trade marks which resemble each other in their material particulars and which differ only as to matters of a non-distinctive character. Any such differences between the marks must not substantially affect the overall identity of the trade mark.[10]

This definition embodies the same concept of a series of marks as was provided for in s 21(2) of the 1938 Act, although the actual wording of the 1994 Act is more general in that it does not attempt to specify the 'matters of a non-distinctive character' which are allowed to differ between the trade marks in the series. However, in the absence of any wording in the 1994 Act to suggest otherwise, it is assumed that the Registrar's practice under the 1938 Act in relation to applications for a series of trade marks will continue unchanged.[11] The Work Manual states that if the marks are very similar both visually and phonetically, they will generally qualify as a series, but marks which meet only one of these tests will not qualify as a series.[12] The ability to apply for a series of marks is common where the applicant's range of products utilises a trade mark which consists of a common distinctive element in combination with material which describes the specific product in question.

The procedure for applying for the registration of a series of trade marks is the same as applying for a single trade mark,[13] except that a

8 Rule 20(2).
9 Or, indeed, registrations: see paragraph 3.37.
10 Section 41(2).
11 Trade marks registered as a series under the 1938 Act as at 31 October 1994 (whether in Part A or Part B) have been transferred to the 1994 Register and have effect as if registered under the 1994 Act: Sch 3, para 2(2).
12 Work Manual, Chapter 6, paragraph 28.2.
13 ie the application is made on Form TM 3 and the fee is the same. The current fees are set out in the Trade Marks (Fees) Rules 1996 (SI 1996/1942).

representation of each trade mark in the series must be incorporated in the application.[14]

In order to overcome an objection to the registration of the series the applicant may:

(a) at any time before preparations for publication of the application have been completed, request the Registrar[15] to divide the application into separate applications in respect of one or more marks in the series;[16] and/or

(b) at any time request the Registrar to delete a mark in the series.[17]

3.14 Classification of goods and services, s 34 and r 7 All goods and services are classified according to the system embodied in the Nice Agreement. There are 34 goods classes and 8 service classes, making 42 in total. On 20 November 1996 a notice was published in the Journal (No 6152) providing details of changes to the Nice classification system following a session of the Committee of Experts which was set up pursuant to the Nice Agreement. These changes came into force on 1 January 1997 and have been reflected in Sch 4 to the Rules which appears in the Appendix to this book. (The notice also reported proposals agreed by the Committee of Experts to create additional classes, although, as yet, these proposals have not been implemented.) Applicants filing multi-class applications must specify which classes their goods or services fall within.[18] Any question as to which is the proper class will be decided by the Registrar.[19] The Registrar will give informal guidance to prospective applicants and their agents (over the telephone or in writing) as to the correct class of goods or services.[20]

The Nice classification system is found in Sch 4 of the Rules and replaces the old classification system which is found in Sch 3 of the Rules. Rule 7 confirms that trade marks which were registered prior to 27 July 1938 are classified in accordance with Sch 3 of the Rules, except where the specification of goods has already been converted to Sch 4 of the Rules under either the 1938 Act or r 40.

14 Rule 21(1).
15 Using Form TM 12.
16 Rule 21(2) subject to compliance with s 41(2); and any such division is subject to the payment of additional application and divisional fees: r 21(4).
17 Rule 21(3); the Registrar has no discretion in relation to such a request.
18 Rule 8(2).
19 Section 34(2); there is no appeal from the Registrar's decision.
20 Telephone: (01633) 814667 or 814425.

For trade marks registered on or after 27 July 1938 (and any prior registrations which have been converted under the 1938 Act) the goods and services are classified in accordance with Sch 4.

3.15 Re-classification of goods, s 65 and r 4 The Registrar may on his own initiative amend an entry in the Register for the purpose of re-classifying the specification of any registered trade mark either:

(a) from Sch 3 to Sch 4; or

(b) so as to reflect any amendment to Sch 4 itself,[1]

provided that the re-classification does not extend the rights conferred by the original registration. This re-classification process may become of some practical importance given the recent changes to the Nice classification system referred to in paragraph 3.14 above.

If, however, compliance with the proviso would involve undue complexity and where the extension would not be substantial and would not adversely affect the rights of any person, then the re-classification can proceed even though it may involve extending the proprietor's rights.[2] The Registrar began the re-classification of Sch 3 registrations prior to the commencement of the 1994 Act.

Notification and objection, r 40 The Registrar must first notify the proprietor of the proposed re-classification[3] and the proprietor is given the opportunity to object in writing within three months.[4] Thereafter, if the proprietor does not object, the proposed re-classification will be published in the Journal[5] and thereafter can only be opposed by a third party.[6]

If the proprietor does object to the Registrar's proposed re-classification, the Registrar will consider those objections and will then publish his proposals either as originally notified to the proprietor or as amended in light of the proprietor's objection.[7]

Opposition, r 41 Specific provision is made in the Rules for third parties to oppose the proposed re-classification which will no doubt

1 Rule 40(1); pursuant to s 65(1) and (2).
2 Section 65(3).
3 Rule 40(2).
4 Rule 40(2)(a).
5 Rule 40(2)(b) and see r 40(3).
6 Section 65(5); r 41.
7 Rule 40(4); the Registrar's decision is final and there is no right of appeal.

be exercised where the third party's rights are affected adversely by the re-classification.[8]

A third party notice of opposition to the re-classification must be made within three months of the publication of the Registrar's proposals.[9] The notice must state the grounds of opposition and, in particular, how the re-classification would be contrary to s 65(3), that is, why it would extend the proprietor's rights conferred by the original registration and why the extension adversely affects the rights of the third party.[10] If a notice of opposition is not filed within the three month period (or if the opposition has been determined) the Registrar will then carry out the re-classification as proposed; his decision in this regard is final and is not subject to appeal.[11]

Amendment by the proprietor Section 65(4) enables the Rules to empower the Registrar to require the proprietor himself to file a proposal for the amendment of the classification of his own trade mark. However, the Rules at present do not so provide.

Transitional provisions, Schedule 3 Trade marks registered under the 1938 Act may not conform to the classification system prescribed by s 34 of the 1994 Act, that is, the Nice classification system.[12]

The Registrar may exercise his powers under r 40 in order to bring any such 'old law' registrations into line with the Nice system.[13] This is particularly relevant in the case of old law registrations which were classified according to the pre-1938 classification system set out in Sch 3 to the Trade Marks and Service Marks Rules 1986.

3.16 Claim to priority: Convention application, s 35 and r 6

In ordinary circumstances the crucial date for the purpose of assessing the registrability of the applicant's trade mark and for determining when the proprietor's exclusive rights will have effect is the actual date of filing the application for registration.

8 See r 41.
9 Using Form TM 7 and upon payment of any prescribed fee. The current fees are set out in the Trade Marks (Fees) Rules 1996 (SI 1996/1942).
10 Rule 41(1); as to the opposition procedure see r 41(2).
11 Rule 41(3).
12 See paragraph 3.14.
13 Schedule 3, para 12.

However, there are two bases on which an applicant may be able to claim a right to priority, that is, the right to rely on an earlier date than the actual filing of the application.[14] The first arises by virtue of an earlier application filed in a Convention country (as to which, see below); the second will arise if an Order in Council is made by Her Majesty conferring a right to priority in respect of applications filed in certain overseas territories with which the United Kingdom has entered into a convention for the reciprocal protection of trade marks (as to which, see paragraph 3.17).

Convention applications In accordance with the Paris Convention, an applicant who has duly filed[15] an application in a Convention country[16] (or his successor in title) has a right to priority for the purposes of registering his trade mark under the 1994 Act in the United Kingdom. The right to priority lasts only for a period of six months from the date of filing of the first Convention application and the applicant's subsequent United Kingdom application must be in respect of some or all of the same goods or services as the first Convention application.[17]

Particulars The right to priority must be claimed in accordance with the Rules.[18] Rule 6(1) prescribes that either:

(a) particulars of the claim must be made at the time of the filing of the United Kingdom application indicating the relevant Convention country (or countries) and the date(s) of filing in that country; or
(b) the application must be accompanied by a certificate of the type referred to in r 6(2).

14 Strictly, there were three bases, as an application which was filed prior to 31 October 1994 for the protection of a trade mark in a relevant country within the meaning of s 39A of the 1938 Act can also confer a right to priority for the purposes of registering the same trade mark under the 1994 Act: see Schedule 3, paragraph 14. A right to priority based on a s 39A application had to have been claimed within six months of that application and therefore this right of priority has not been available since 30 April 1995.
15 See s 35(3) which refers to and defines a 'regular national filing' as giving rise to the right of priority.
16 ie a country other than the United Kingdom which is a party to the Paris Convention: s 55(1)(b).
17 Section 35(1); it matters not that the Convention application may have been made before the commencement of the 1994 Act: Sch 3, para 13.
18 Section 35(5).

Certificate Rule 6(2) requires the filing of a certificate issued by the registering or other competent authority of the relevant Convention country certifying or verifying:

(a) the date of the filing of the first Convention application;
(b) the country of registering or competent authority;
(c) a representation of the mark; and
(d) the goods or services covered by the Convention application.

The certificate must be filed either with the application itself or within three months of the application being filed.

Effect of claim to priority If the right to priority conferred by s 35(1) is claimed validly by the applicant in accordance with the Rules, the relevant date for the purposes of establishing which rights take precedence will be the date of filing of the first Convention application.[19] In certain circumstances a subsequent Convention application will be treated as the first Convention application where, for example, the first Convention application is withdrawn, abandoned or refused.[20] The reference to rights taking 'precedence' reflects the potential existence of competing rights and will be relevant in determining questions of registrability under s 5. However, a claim to priority does not backdate the deemed date of registration, which will remain the actual date of filing of the application in the United Kingdom.

Registrability of applicant's mark If the right to priority is validly claimed as described above, the question of the registrability of the applicant's trade mark will not be affected by any use of the mark in the United Kingdom in the period between the date of the first Convention application and the date of his subsequent corresponding United Kingdom application. That is, the applicant cannot rely on any use of his trade mark in this period in support of his application.[1] If the registrability of the applicant's trade mark is to be assessed as at the date of filing of the applicant's first Convention application, then it is right that the applicant should have to show that his mark is entitled to registration in the United Kingdom as of the earlier date without relying on use subsequent to the filing of the Convention application.

19 Section 35(2)(a).
20 See s 34(4).
1 Section 35(2)(b).

3.17 Claim to priority: reciprocal protection, s 36 and r 6 The second basis on which an applicant may be able to claim a right to priority is in respect of an earlier application filed in:

(a) any of the Channel Islands or a colony; or
(b) any other country or territory with which the United Kingdom has entered into a convention for the reciprocal protection of trade marks.[2]

Section 36 empowers Her Majesty by Order in Council to confer a right to priority on a person who has filed an application for protection of his trade mark in one of the countries, territories or colonies referred to above. To date, there have been two Orders made pursuant to s 36. The Trade Marks (Claims to Priority from Relevant Countries) Order 1994[3] provides that applications filed in the countries listed in the Schedule to the Order will confer priority in respect of an application for the registration of the trade mark in the United Kingdom.[4] Articles 4 to 7 of the 1994 Order make provisions corresponding to subss (2), (4) (5) and (6) of s 35.

As is the case under s 35, the right to priority is only available for the purpose of registering in the United Kingdom the same trade mark for some or all of the same goods or services as has already been registered in the relevant country, territory or colony. No period is specified in s 36 within which the right must be claimed, but it may be assumed that it is likely to be six months or such other period as may be stated in the relevant convention; certainly, the Order referred to above provides for a six month period.

3.18 Withdrawal of an application, s 39(1) Should an applicant not wish to pursue his application for any reason he may withdraw it at any time.[5] In the event that his application has already

2 Section 36(1).
3 Made on 2 November 1994 and in force on 5 December 1994: SI 1994 No 2803 as amended by the Trade Marks (Claims to Priority from Relevant Countries) (Amendment) Order 1995 (SI 1995/2997) which supplements the schedule of relevant countries to which the earlier Order extends.
4 The relevant countries are Antigua and Barbuda, Bahrain, Belize, Bolivia, Botswana, Brunei Darussalam, Columbia, Djibouti, Dominica, Ecuador, Guatemala, Hong Kong, India, Jamaica, Kuwait, Macau, Maldives, Mozambique, Myanmar, Namibia, Nicaragua, Pakistan, Sierra Leone, Thailand.
5 Section 39(1).

been accepted and advertised at the date of the withdrawal, then the Registrar will publish an appropriate notice in the Journal.

A withdrawn application cannot be restored.

3.19 Disclaimers and limitations, s 13 and r 24 An applicant faced with objections raised by the Registrar or a third party opposition (or even for his own reasons) may voluntarily:

(a) disclaim any right to the exclusive use of any specified element of his trade mark; or

(b) agree that the rights conferred by any consequent registration will be subject to a specified territorial or other limitation.[6]

In the event that the application is accepted and the trade mark proceeds to registration, the exclusive rights conferred by registration[7] will be restricted by the terms of the disclaimer and/or the limitation.[8]

However, the position would appear to be that the existence of a disclaimer in respect of any element of the mark as registered will not be relevant in considering whether the use of the disclaimed element constitutes use of that mark: in the *Ford Werke* case, Lloyd Jacob J stated that a disclaimer does not affect the significance which a mark conveys to consumers when used in the course of trade and therefore the use of disclaimed material can be taken into account in considering whether the mark as registered has been used (particularly for the purpose of defending a non-use action under s 46).[9]

All disclaimers and limitations will be entered in the Register and published in the Journal.[10] This provision allowing for voluntary disclaimers is to be distinguished from s 14 of the 1938 Act which enabled the Registrar to require disclaimers in respect of non-distinctive matter as a condition of registration. The 1994 Act does not empower the Registrar to require or even request disclaimers or limitations.[11]

3.20 Restrictions on an application, s 39 In addition, or as an alternative to volunteering a disclaimer or limitation, an applicant

6 Section 13(1).
7 ie pursuant to s 9.
8 Section 13(1).
9 *Ford-Werke's Application* (1955) 72 RPC 191 and see *Safeway Stores plc's Application* (31 October 1996, unreported) (M Knight).
10 Rule 24.
11 See also Chapter 7 in relation to the implication of disclaimers and limitations under the 1994 Act with respect to infringement actions.

may at any time restrict the goods or services covered by his application.[12] In the event that his application has already been accepted and advertised at the date of the restriction, then the Registrar will publish an appropriate notice in the Journal.

3.21 Amending an application, s 39(2) and r 17 Apart from the option of withdrawing his application or restricting the goods or services covered by his application, an applicant may, in respect of limited matters, apply to amend his application.[13]

Permitted amendments Amendments to an application may only be made in order to correct:
(a) the name or address of the applicant;
(b) errors of wording or of copying; or
(c) obvious mistakes,
and provided that the correction does not substantially affect the identity of the trade mark or extend the goods or services covered by the original application.[14]

Thus, for example, the applicant cannot submit samples or photographs of his product nor variants of the representation of his mark, if this amounts to amending the mark applied for.[15] However, it is submitted that such steps should be allowed if for the purpose only of providing a clearer depiction of the mark in question. Subject to the limited right to amend an application provided for in s 39(2), the Registrar is restricted in his examination of the mark to the material lodged with the original application.

An amendment which is made after the application has been accepted and published and which affects either the representation of the trade mark or the goods or services covered by the original application will be open to opposition by any person claiming to be affected by the amendment.[16] In any event, the application as amended will be published by the Registrar to show the amendment.[17]

12 Section 39(1).
13 Section 39(2); the application to amend should be made using Form TM 21; r 17.
14 Section 39(2).
15 *Kraft Jacob Suchard Ltd's Application* (15 November 1996, unreported) (A James).
16 Section 39(3); r 18.
17 Rule 18(1).

Comparison with 1938 Act s 17(7) Section 39(2) is more limited than the right of amendment provided for in the 1938 Act. Section 17(7) of the 1938 Act gave the Registrar the discretion to allow the applicant to amend his application upon 'such terms as the Registrar . . . may think fit'. When read in conjunction with r 121[18] the Registrar's former discretion could have extended to allowing an amendment of any drawing or other representation of the trade mark.

3.22 Opposition to an amendment, s 39(3) and r 18(2) and (3) Any person claiming to be affected by an amendment to an application which affects either:

(a) the representation of the trade mark; or
(b) the goods or services covered by the original application,

may give notice of opposition to the proposed amendment.

The procedure for giving notice of opposition and the grounds of opposition are dealt with in Chapter 4.

3.23 Conversion of a 1938 Act application, Schedule 3 and r 68 An application for the registration of a trade mark under the 1938 Act, which was pending on 31 October 1994, will be dealt with under the old law and if the mark proceeds to registration it will be treated for the purposes of the transitional provisions as an existing registered mark.[19]

However, in the case of a pending application under the 1938 Act which had not been advertised[20] by 31 October 1994, the applicant was entitled to give notice to the Registrar requesting to have the registrability of his trade mark determined in accordance with the provisions of the 1994 Act.[1] If an applicant wished to convert his pending application, then he had to give notice to the Registrar[2] within six months of the commencement of the 1994 Act, that is, the request should have been made on or before 30 April 1995.[3]

If a request had been made for the conversion of a pending application, the applicant cannot reverse his decision. The effect of

18 Trade Marks and Service Marks Rules 1986, SI 1986/1319.
19 Schedule 3, para 10(1).
20 ie under s 18 of the 1938 Act.
1 Schedule 3, para 11(1).
2 Using Form TM 15 set out in Sch 2 to the Rules; r 68.
3 Schedule 3, para 11(2).

making a request for conversion is that the original application is treated as if it had been made immediately after the commencement of the 1994 Act, ie 31 October 1994.[4]

The examination and registration procedure

3.24 Examination, s 37 Applications for the registration of a trade mark will be examined by the Registrar to determine whether the requirements of the 1994 Act are satisfied.[5] The Registrar will, if requested, provide a preliminary opinion as to the registrability of a mark under the 1994 Act.[6] The Registrar will consider the application as lodged by the applicant; further samples or variants of the representation of the mark which are submitted after the application has been filed are only admissible in the limited circumstances provided for under s 39(2).[7]

The relevant requirements of the 1994 Act can be listed conveniently as follows:

(a) that the application is in respect of a 'trade mark', as defined in s 1(1);[8]

(b) that there are no absolute or relative grounds for refusing registration under ss 3, 4 or 5;[9]

(c) that the formalities specified in s 32 and in the Rules have been complied with;[10] and

(d) that any claim to priority is valid in accordance with s 35 or s 36.[11]

Accordingly the Registrar must, inter alia, carry out a search to determine whether there is a conflict with earlier trade marks.[12] As the phrase 'earlier trade marks' is defined[13] to include marks which may not be registered, viz well-known trade marks protected (but

4 Schedule 3, para 11(3).
5 Section 37(1); these requirements will include any imposed by the Rules.
6 Contact the Search and Advisory Service at the Registry; Telephone: (01633) 811010, Fax: (01633) 811020.
7 *Kraft Jacobs Suchard Ltd's Application* (15 November 1996, unreported) (A James). See paragraph 3.21 above.
8 As to which, see Chapter 1.
9 As to which, see Chapters 2 and 15.
10 As to which, see this chapter.
11 As to which, see paragraphs 3.16 and 3.17.
12 Section 37(2).
13 Section 6.

not necessarily registered) under the Paris Convention, this task may prove difficult to fulfil in practice, although the search need only be carried out to the extent to which the Registrar considers necessary. Indeed, the Registry's practice is to cite only those earlier trade marks which constitute grounds for refusal under subss 5(1) and (2).[14] It will therefore be a matter for proprietors of other earlier trade marks either to make observations and/or to file a notice of opposition to protect their interests.[15]

If the requirements for registration are met, the Registrar must accept the application.[16] He has no overriding discretion to refuse registration. The application will then be published in the Journal and will be open to third party oppositions for three months.[17]

3.25 Representations by the applicant, s 37(3) If the Registrar takes the view that the requirements for registration are not met, he must inform the applicant of his objections and give him an opportunity (within a period specified by the Registrar) either to make representations (either in writing or at an oral hearing) or to amend his application[18] so as to comply with the requirements.[19]

If the applicant's representations fail to overcome the objections raised by the Registrar or if he does not amend his application so as to meet the requirements within the specified period, the Registrar will have no option but to refuse the application.[20]

3.26 Disclaimers and limitations, s 13 and r 24 It should be recalled at this point that an applicant faced with objections raised by the Registrar may voluntarily:

(a) disclaim any right to the exclusive use of any specified element of his trade mark; or

(b) agree that the rights conferred by any consequent registration will be subject to a specified territorial or other limitation.[1]

14 Work Manual, Chapter 6, paragraph 21.
15 As to which, see Chapter 4.
16 Section 37(5).
17 See Chapter 4.
18 ie pursuant to and only in the limited circumstances provided for in s 39(2), as to which see paragraph 3.21.
19 Section 37(3).
20 Section 37(4).
1 Section 13(1) and see paragraph 3.19.

3.27 Publication (advertisement), s 38(1) and r 12 If the Registrar accepts the application for registration, he will publish the application in the Journal.[2] This is to give interested third parties the opportunity to oppose the registration of the trade mark[3] and, accordingly, the advertisement is only valid if it correctly depicts the applicant's mark. If the advertisement does not depict the essential features of the mark in question, then the application will have to be re-advertised.[4]

There is no equivalent procedure to that under the proviso to s 18(1) of the 1938 Act whereby the Registrar could have advertised an application prior to acceptance. This is because the proviso to s 18(1) related only to a trade mark accepted pursuant to s 9(1)(e) of the 1938 Act for which there is no equivalent section in the 1994 Act.

3.28 Notice of opposition, s 38(2) and r 13 Following publication of the application in the Journal, any person may, within three months[5] of the date on which the application was published, give notice of opposition to the registration of the trade mark.[6]

The procedure for giving notice of opposition and the grounds of opposition are dealt with in Chapter 4.

3.29 Observations, s 38(3) and r 15 Any person, at any time after the date of publication but before the registration of the trade mark, may make observations in writing to the Registrar as to whether the trade mark should be registered.[7]

The procedure for making observations and the subject matter of such observations are dealt with in Chapter 4.

3.30 Freedom of information, s 67 and rr 42–45 The 1994 Act provides for confidentiality to be maintained by the Registrar prior to the publication of an application (subject to four exceptions) and thereafter for freedom of information following publication.

2 Section 38(1) and r 12.
3 As to which, see paragraph 3.28.
4 For an example of such a situation where the mark CREOLA was advertised as CREOIA, see *R v Patent Office, ex p Chocoladefabriken Lindt and Sprungli AG* (5 December 1996, unreported) (Laddie J).
5 This period cannot be extended, unlike the equivalent one month period under the 1938 Act.
6 Section 38(2) and r 13(1).
7 Section 38(3).

Confidentiality prior to publication Prior to the publication of an application the Registrar must keep confidential all documents and information constituting or relating to the application,[8] except:

(a) the application itself[9] (and any amendments made to it);
(b) any particulars of a registrable transaction given to the Registrar under r 35;[10]
(c) in the case of a person who has received notice that an application for registration of a trade mark has been made and that the applicant will, if the application is granted, rely on the subsequent registration of the trade mark to bring proceedings against that person in respect of that person's conduct after publication of the application. In such circumstances, the person receiving the notice may make a request under s 67(1) (which otherwise is applicable only once an application has been advertised) to inspect any documents held by the Registrar relating to the relevant application as though the application had already been published;[11] or
(d) with the applicant's consent.[12]

Freedom of information, s 67(1) and r 44 Upon publication of an application, the Registrar is obliged to provide to any member of the public who so requests[13] any information held by the Registrar relating to that application and/or the registration resulting from the application. Furthermore, the public are also entitled to inspect for themselves any documents held by the Registrar relating to that application and/or registration.[14]

The Registrar's obligation as stated above is only qualified to the extent that he need not provide access to the public to any document which he requires in order to complete the registration procedure or any of his other tasks.[15]

Any requests for information pursuant to s 67(1) must comply with the Rules, which are quite specific in terms of which documents

8 Section 67(2).
9 Rule 43.
10 Rule 43.
11 Section 67(3).
12 Section 67(2)(b).
13 Using Form TM 31C.
14 Section 67(1) and r 44(1); as to the opening hours of the Registry, see the Journal No 6049 dated 31 October 1994.
15 Rule 44(2).

will not be made available: see r 44(3) and (4). Furthermore, there is no appeal from a decision of the Registrar made under r 44(4).[16]

Direction as to confidentiality, r 45 A person filing a document at the Registry may, at the time of filing or within fourteen days afterwards, request that the document be treated as confidential. Reasons for claiming confidentiality must be stated and the Registrar is given a discretion to direct that the document (or part of it) should be treated as confidential. If the Registrar makes such a direction, then the document will not be open to public inspection[17] without the consent of the Registrar.[18] In any event, while the question of confidentiality is being determined by the Registrar, the document in question will not be open to public inspection. A direction as to confidentiality can also be made unilaterally by the Registrar in respect of documents issued by the Registry.[19]

A direction as to confidentiality can only be withdrawn by the Registrar after consulting with the person who made the original request under r 45(1), unless such a consultation is not reasonably practical.[20]

3.31 Registration, s 4 Where an application has been accepted by the Registrar pursuant to s 37(5) and either:

(a) no notice of opposition has been given within three months of the date of publication of the application; or
(b) all opposition proceedings have been withdrawn or dismissed,

the Registrar must register the trade mark,[1] except only where it appears to him that the application was accepted in error.[2] In this regard, the exception only applies where matters have come to the

16 Rule 44(5).
17 Rule 45(1).
18 Rule 45(2).
19 Rule 45(4).
20 Rule 45(3).
1 Provided that any prescribed registration fee is paid within the prescribed period: s 40(2).
2 Section 40(1). See also *R v Patent Office, ex p Chocoladefabriken Lindt and Sprungli AG* (5 December 1996, unreported) (Laddie J), which confirms that registration does not automatically follow upon the expiration of the three month opposition period. Indeed, until such time as the mark is put on the Register, the Registrar is entitled to take notice of any information drawn to his attention. However, if the Registrar fails to act with due expedition in registering a mark the applicant may apply for an order of mandamus so as to compel him to do so.

Registrar's notice since he accepted the application, which would include information received by way of written observations made pursuant to s 38(3).[3]

If the Registrar decides at this stage that the application was accepted in error, then the applicant will be given the opportunity to make representations or to amend his application in accordance with s 37(3).[4]

Transitional provisions, Schedule 3 Trade marks registered under the 1938 Act as at 31 October 1994 (whether in Part A or Part B) have been transferred to the 1994 Register and have effect as if registered under the 1994 Act.[5]

3.32 Date of registration, s 40(3) The effective date of registration is the date of filing of the application for registration,[6] which is the date on which everything required by s 32(2) is furnished to the Registrar.[7]

The date of registration is crucial because it is from that date that the proprietor's exclusive rights in his trade mark have effect.[8]

3.33 Advertisement of registration, s 40(4) and r 16 On the registration of a trade mark the Registrar will publish the registration, specifying the date upon which the trade mark was entered in the Register.[9] This is purely a formality for the record. The date on which the trade mark is entered in the Register is not the date from which the proprietor's exclusive rights have effect,[10] but it may be significant, for example, in relation to assigning and licensing trade marks.[11]

Upon registration of the mark the Registrar will issue the Certificate of Registration to the proprietor.[12]

3 As to which, see paragraph 3.29.
4 As to which, see paragraph 3.25.
5 Schedule 3, para 2(1); but the fact that such marks may have been 'associated' with other marks or were registered subject to a condition will cease to be relevant: Sch 3, paras 2(3), 3(1) and 10(3).
6 Section 40(3).
7 Section 33(1).
8 Section 9(3).
9 Section 40(4) and r 16.
10 See paragraph 3.32.
11 See Chapter 10.
12 Section 40(4).

3.34 Duration of registration, s 42 The period of registration is ten years. This period applies both to the initial period and to any renewal of the registration.[13] This replaces the respective periods of seven years and fourteen years under the 1938 Act and brings the United Kingdom into line with the majority of its trading partners.[14]

3.35 Renewal of registration, s 43 and rr 27–29 The registration of a trade mark may be renewed at the request of the proprietor. The request can only be made within six months prior to the expiry of the registration.[15] To this end, not earlier than six months and not later than one month before the expiration of the registration the Registrar will notify the proprietor that his registration is approaching expiration.[16]

The trade mark will only be renewed if the prescribed renewal fee is paid.[17] Both the request for renewal and the payment of the fee must be made before the registration expires[18] but the renewal will only take effect from the expiry of the previous registration[19] and will be published accordingly.[20]

If the period of registration expires and the renewal fee has not been paid, the Registrar will advertise that fact in the Journal.[1]

Six months' grace A six month 'grace period' following the expiration of the registration may assist a tardy proprietor. Provided that a request for renewal[2] is filed within the grace period together with both the renewal fee and an additional renewal fee, the Registrar will nonetheless renew the registration without removing the trade mark from the Register.[3]

If renewal is not effected either prior to the expiry of the

13 Section 42.
14 All registrations under the 1938 Act (including registrations in consequence of an application filed under the 1938 Act) will continue to remain in force until the end of their respective seven or fourteen year periods and will thereafter be renewed for ten year periods: Sch 3, para 15.
15 Section 43(1) and r 28; using Form TM 11.
16 Section 43(2) and r 27.
17 Section 43(1); the current fees are set out in the Trade Marks (Fees) Rules 1996 (SI 1996/1942).
18 Section 43(3).
19 Section 43(4).
20 Section 43(6).
1 Rule 29(1).
2 Using Form TM 11.
3 Section 43(3) and r 29(3).

registration or within the grace period, the Registrar will remove the trade mark from the Register.[4] Even so, the proprietor may still be able to restore his registration.[5]

Registration after renewal, r 29(4) In some cases, particularly those where there has been a third party opposition, the applicant's trade mark may not find its way onto the Register until more than ten years after the date on which the application for registration was filed. Because the rights conferred by registration date back to the date of the filing of the application, one may therefore encounter the situation of a trade mark not being put on the Register until after the date when the registration will have become due for renewal. In such circumstances the proprietor must pay a renewal fee within six months of the date on which the trade mark is actually entered in the Register.[6] Provided that the renewal fee is paid within six months of the actual date of registration, the registration will be renewed notwithstanding the fact that the payment of the renewal fee may have been more than six months after the renewal date calculated by reference to the filing date.

3.36 Restoration of registration, s 43(5) and r 30 In the event that the trade mark is not renewed[7] and it is accordingly removed,[8] it is nonetheless possible, in certain circumstances, to restore the registration.

Rule 30(1) sets out the conditions applying to restoration. An application for restoration must be filed[9] within six months of the date of removal (which will be before the publication of the removal) and must be accompanied by the appropriate renewal and restoration fees. The Registrar has a discretion to restore a removed trade mark to the Register and renew the registration if, in the circumstances of the failure to renew, he is satisfied that restoration would be just.[10]

4 Section 43(5) and r 29(2); the Registrar will publish any removal of a trade mark from the Register: r 29(5) and s 43(6).
5 As to which, see paragraph 3.36.
6 Rule 29(4).
7 ie in accordance with s 43 and rr 28 or 29.
8 ie pursuant to s 43(5) and r 29(2).
9 Using Form TM 13.
10 All restorations will be published, showing the date of restoration: s 43(6) and r 30(2).

There was no time limit for restoration under the 1938 Act and it was possible in certain circumstances to obtain the restoration of a registration long after the period of six months from the date of removal.[11] It is now increasingly important for the Register accurately to reflect all trade mark registrations because applications, not only under the 1994 Act but also for Community trade marks and under the Madrid Protocol, may be examined in the light of the United Kingdom Register.

3.37 Merger of a registration, s 41 and r 20(3)–(6) A proprietor of two or more registrations of a trade mark can request the Registrar[12] to merge each of his registrations into one single registration. The practical and commercial reasons for making such a request are to reduce the costs of renewing multiple registrations and managing large trade mark portfolios. The only requirement is that the registrations must be in respect of the same trade mark. If so, the Registrar has no discretion and must comply with the proprietor's request.[13]

Of course, any disclaimer or limitation[14] relating to a trade mark to be merged will apply also to the merged registration.[15]

The date of registration of the merged registrations will be the latest date of registration of the previously separate registrations; of course, this is only relevant where the previously separate registrations bear different dates.[16]

Particulars relating to the grant of any licence or any security interest which relates to a trade mark which is to be merged will be entered in the Register in relation to the merged registration.[17]

3.38 Alteration of a registered trade mark, s 44 and r 25 The proprietor of a registered trade mark can request the Registrar[18] to alter his trade mark provided that the alteration:

(a) is limited to altering the proprietor's name or address which must appear in the trade mark itself; and

11 Rule 68 of the Trade Marks and Service Marks Rules 1986, SI 1986/1319.
12 Using Form TM 17.
13 Rule 20(3).
14 As to which, see paragraph 3.19.
15 Rule 20(4).
16 Rule 20(6).
17 Rule 20(5).
18 Using Form TM 25.

(b) does not substantially affect the identity of the mark.[19]

Any other requested alteration will be refused.[20]

The permitted grounds for altering a registered trade mark under the 1994 Act are narrower than the corresponding provision of the 1938 Act.[1] Under the 1938 Act, alterations were allowed even in respect of essential particulars of the trade mark (including adding to or altering the trade mark in any manner) so long as the identity of the trade mark was not substantially affected.[2]

A request for alteration pursuant to s 44(2) may need to be supported by evidence as to the circumstances in which the application is made.[3]

All permitted alterations will be published in the Journal[4] so as to allow third parties the opportunity to oppose the alteration.

Opposition to an alteration, r 25(3) Any person claiming to be affected by the alteration may file with the Registrar a notice of opposition[5] to the alteration. The procedure for giving notice of opposition and the grounds of opposition are dealt with in Chapter 4.

3.39 Surrender of registrations, s 45 and r 26 The proprietor of a trade mark may surrender his trade mark in respect of some or all of the goods or services for which it is registered.[6]

A proprietor who wishes to surrender his trade mark as above must notify the Registrar using:

(a) Form TM 22, if the surrender is in respect of all the goods or services for which the mark is registered; or
(b) Form TM 23, if the surrender is in respect of some only of those goods or services.[7]

The proprietor's notice will only be effective if he:

(a) supplies the name and address of any person having a registered

19 Section 44(2).
20 Section 44(1).
1 ie s 35.
2 The transitional provisions of the 1994 Act permit all applications under s 35 of the 1938 Act for the alteration of a registered trade mark which were pending as at 31 October 1994 to be dealt with under the old law and any consequent alteration will be entered in the 1994 Register: Sch 3, para 16.
3 Rule 25(1).
4 Rule 25(2).
5 Using Form TM 7.
6 Section 45(1).
7 Rule 26(1).

interest in the mark (such as a licensee or a co-proprietor); and

(b) certifies that any such person:
   (i) has been given not less than three months' notice of the proprietor's intention to surrender his trade mark; or
   (ii) is not affected or, if affected, consents to the proprietor's surrender.[8]

Upon the surrender taking effect, the Registrar will make the appropriate entry in the Register and publish the surrender in the Journal[9] which, in the case of a surrender in respect of all goods or services for which the trade mark is registered, presumably means that the trade mark will be removed from the Register.[10]

Proceedings before the Registrar

3.40 Powers of the Registrar, s 69(b) and (c) and r 52 The Registrar has all the powers of an Official Referee of the Supreme Court in relation to the examination of witnesses on oath and the discovery and production of documents.[11] (The powers of Official Referees are set out in general terms in the Rules of the Supreme Court (RSC) in Ord 36, r 4.) Accordingly, the rules which apply to the attendance of witnesses before an Official Referee will apply to the attendance of witnesses before the Registrar.[12] That is, witnesses may be subpoenaed and it will be a contempt of court for any witness not to attend in accordance with the subpoena. Similarly, the Registrar has to apply the same principles as an Official Referee in ordering the discovery of documents, that is, discovery will only be ordered in respect of those documents relevant to the matter in dispute and which are necessary to dispose fairly of the proceedings.[13]

3.41 Natural justice, r 48 The Rules require the Registrar to give any party to any proceedings before him an opportunity to be heard before he takes any decision on any matter under the 1994

8 Rule 26(2).
9 Rule 26(3).
10 ie pursuant to and in accordance with the procedure in r 39.
11 Rule 52(1).
12 Rule 52(2).
13 *Lifesavers Trade Mark* [1997] RPC 563, a case on the exercise of the Registrar's discretion as to ordering the discovery of documents.

Act which is or may be adverse to that party.[14] The Registrar must indeed give such a party at least 14 days' notice of when the hearing will take place.[15]

3.42 Evidence in proceedings before the Registrar, s 69(a) and rr 49–51 Evidence in proceedings before the Registrar may be given either:

(a) by filing a statutory declaration or an affidavit;[16] or

(b) orally, either in lieu of or in addition to a statutory declaration and/or an affidavit.[17]

In either case, the Registrar must, unless he otherwise directs, allow any witness to be cross-examined on his statutory declaration, affidavit or oral evidence.[18]

The Rules stipulate precisely how a statutory declaration or an affidavit must be made and subscribed and the Work Manual (in Chapter 15, paragraph 6.10) sets out pro forma examples of the formal requirements, which are now reproduced in Schedule 4 to this book.[19] In the United Kingdom this must be before a Justice of the Peace or a Commissioner or other officer authorised by law to administer an oath for the purpose of legal proceedings.[20] Separate provisions deal with the situation outside the United Kingdom.[1]

In addition to such evidence the Registrar may, at any stage of proceedings before him, direct that certain other documents, information or evidence as he may require must be filed within a time limit which he will specify.[2]

It has been confirmed that proceedings in the Registry are civil proceedings as defined by s 18 of the Civil Evidence Act 1968. Accordingly, the rules as to the admissibility of hearsay evidence in civil proceedings (which are contained in that Act) apply such that

14 Rule 48(1).
15 Rule 48(2); unless the party consents to shorter notice.
16 Rule 49(1).
17 Rule 49(2).
18 Rule 49(2).
19 Rule 50(1). In *Principles Retail Ltd's Application* (1996) 19(8) IPD 15 (M Knight), the proprietor's unsworn, unsigned statutory declaration was not admitted as evidence.
20 Rule 50(1); and see r 50(2).
1 See r 50(1)(b) and (c); and see r 50(2).
2 Rule 51. In *Stoves Ltd's Application* (15 October 1996, unreported) (M Knight), r 51 was relied on as giving the Registrar the necessary power to allow a proprietor to rejoin proceedings from which he had voluntarily withdrawn.

hearsay evidence is not admissible except in accordance with that Act: first hand hearsay is admissible, while second hand or remote hearsay is inadmissible.[3] A practice direction has been issued in relation to this subject: see the Journal No 6083 dated 12 July 1995 and the Work Manual in Chapter 15, paragraph 6.9.

3.43 Hearings before the Registrar, rr 53 and 56 All hearings before the Registrar of any dispute between two or more parties relating to an application for the registration of a trade mark or a registered trade mark will be in public, unless the Registrar directs otherwise following a consultation with the parties.[4]

Following any hearing before the Registrar, including any proceedings based on written submissions, the Registrar will send notice of his decision in writing to each party.[5] If the notice of the Registrar's decision does not include a statement of his reasons, then any party may, within one month of notice of the Registrar's decision being sent to him, request[6] the Registrar to state in writing the grounds for his decision.[7] In which case, the date on which the Registrar's written statement is sent becomes the effective date of his decision for the purpose of any appeal.[8]

3.44 Costs, s 68(1) and (2) and r 54 The Registrar has the power to award costs to any party in any proceedings before him under the 1994 Act. Any award for costs is within the discretion of the Registrar as he may consider reasonable. The costs normally awarded by the Registrar are, where appropriate and relevant, based on a scale which has been drawn up by the Registrar; it is fair to say that the level of costs recoverable under this scale rarely match the actual costs incurred by the parties and, in many cases, are substantially less. The Registrar may furthermore direct how and by what parties the costs are to be paid.[9]

In the exercise of the Registrar's discretion he might have regard to whether proceedings could have been avoided if reasonable notice had first been given to the applicant or to the registered proprietor

3 *St Trudo Trade Mark* [1995] FSR 345.
4 Rule 53(1).
5 Rule 56(1).
6 Using Form TM 5.
7 Rule 56(2).
8 Rule 56(2); and see paragraph 3.46 in relation to appeals.
9 Rule 54.

(as the case may be) before any notice of opposition or application for revocation, declaration of invalidity or rectification was filed.

The Registrar's costs order can be enforced in the same way as an order of the High Court.[10]

3.45 Security for costs, s 68(3) and r 55 The Registrar has the power to require any person who is a party to any proceedings before him under the 1994 Act to give security for costs in relation to those proceedings. Furthermore, the Registrar may also require security to be given for the costs of any appeal from his decision.[11]

If the party who is directed to give security does not comply with the direction the Registrar may treat the party in default as having withdrawn his application, opposition, objection or intervention (as the case may be).[12]

Note that in cases where an order for security for costs is sought against a party which is a national and resident in a state which is party to the Brussels Convention, the Registrar will need to be convinced that there is likely to be substantial difficulty in enforcing an ordinary award of costs before he will issue an order for security for costs.[13]

Appeals

3.46 Appeals from the Registrar, s 76 and r 57 An appeal lies from any decision of the Registrar under the 1994 Act.[14] In this regard, a 'decision' of the Registrar will include any act of the Registrar in the exercise of any discretion vested in him by the 1994 Act or the Rules.[15]

10 Section 68(2)(a); in Scotland, the order is enforced in the same way as a decree for expenses granted by the Court of Session: s 68(2)(b).

11 Rule 55(1).

12 Rule 55(2); so may an appointed person under s 76 in the case of an appeal.

13 This follows from the case of *Fitzgerald v Williams* [1996] QB 657, where the Court of Appeal held that an English court should never exercise its discretion under Ord 23, r 1 of the Supreme Court Rules, to order security to be given by an individual plaintiff who is a national of and resident in another member state which is a party to the Brussels Convention, at any rate in the absence of cogent evidence of 'substantial difficulty' in enforcing a judgment in that other member state.

14 Section 76; except as provided in the Rules, for example, from a decision of the Registrar made under rr 40 or 41 (dealing with the re-classification of goods).

15 Section 76(1).

The appeal must be made either:

(a) to the High Court;[16] or

(b) to an 'Appointed Person'.[17]

3.47 Appeals to Appointed Persons, ss 76 and 77 and rr 57 and 59 All appeals to an 'Appointed Person'[18] must be sent by the appellant to the Registrar (not to the Appointed Person) within one month of the date of the Registrar's decision which is the subject of the appeal.[19] That date will be the date on which the Registrar's statement of the grounds for his decision is sent to the appellant.[20] The notice of appeal must be accompanied by a written statement of the grounds for the appeal and the appellant's case in support of his appeal.[1]

The Registrar will then send the notice of appeal and the appellant's statement of grounds to the Appointed Person[2] as well as to any other party to the decision from which the appeal is made.[3]

An appeal to an Appointed Person (which is not referred to the Court)[4] will be heard and determined by the Appointed Person and his decision is final.[5] The hearing of the appeal by the Appointed Person is governed by r 59. The Appointed Person must give at least fourteen days' notice[6] of the time and place appointed for the hearing of the appeal[7] and the notice must be sent:

(a) where no person other than the appellant was a party to the proceedings which are the subject of the appeal, to the Registrar and the appellant; or

(b) in all other cases, to the Registrar and to each person who was a party to the original proceedings.[8]

16 Section 75(a); in Scotland, the Court of Session: s 75(b).
17 Section 76(2), as to which, see paragraph 3.47.
18 ie a person appointed by the Lord Chancellor to hear and decide appeals under the 1994 Act: s 77(1); see also the rules of eligibility and terms of appointment of appointed persons: s 77(2) and (3).
19 Rule 57(1).
20 Rule 56(2).
1 Rule 57(1).
2 Rule 57(2).
3 Rule 57(3).
4 As to which, see paragraph 3.48.
5 Section 76(4).
6 Rule 59(2).
7 Rule 59(1).
8 Rule 59(1).

The rules of evidence,[9] the powers of the Registrar,[10] the conduct of the hearings,[11] and the provisions as to costs and security for costs[12] will apply to all appeals to an Appointed Person as they apply to proceedings before the Registrar.[13]

After hearing the appeal, the Appointed Person will then send a copy of his decision with a statement of his reasons to the Registrar, and to each person who is a party to the proceedings before him.[14]

In *Eurolamb*,[15] Mr Hobbs QC, sitting as an Appointed Person, in dismissing an appeal against a decision of the Registrar, made no order as to costs and commented that:

> '... the normal position under the 1938 Act was to regard these hearings as a continuation of the ex parte procedure. I would be loathe, except in rather unusual circumstances to change that practice. I think it is necessary that this Tribunal should be regarded as a user friendly Tribunal.'

Further evidence on appeal An appeal to an Appointed Person should be treated in the same way as an appeal to the court, that is, it will be a rehearing. This means that further evidence may be admitted in certain circumstances and in the exercise of the court's discretion.[16]

3.48 Referral of the appeal to the High Court, s 76(3) and r 57 An appeal to an Appointed Person may be referred by him to the High Court if:

(a) it appears to the Appointed Person that a point of general legal importance is involved;[17]

(b) the Registrar requests that the appeal be referred to the High Court;[18] or

(c) a specific request is made by any party to the proceedings before the Registrar in which the decision appealed against was made.[19]

9 Section 69 and rr 49–51; as to which, see paragraph 3.42.
10 Rules 51 and 52; as to which, see paragraphs 3.40 and 3.42.
11 Rule 53; as to which, see paragraph 3.43.
12 Section 68 and rr 54 and 55; as to which, see paragraphs 3.44 and 3.45.
13 Rule 59(2).
14 Rule 59(3).
15 *Eurolamb Trade Mark* [1997] RPC 279.
16 See paragraph 3.49 below for further consideration of this issue.
17 Section 76(3)(a) and see r 58(5) and (6).
18 Section 76(3)(b) and see r 58(1)(a), (2) and (4).
19 Section 76(3)(c) and see r 58(1)(b), (3) and (4).

However, before referring any appeal to the High Court, the Appointed Person must give the appellant and any other party to the appeal an opportunity to make representations as to whether the appeal should be referred to the court.[20]

Proceedings in the High Court

3.49 Practice and procedure The practice and procedure of the High Court is governed by the Rules of the Supreme Court ('RSC') and RSC Ord 100 deals specifically with proceedings relating to matters arising under the 1938 Act and/or the 1994 Act. Order 100 has been totally replaced pursuant to RSC (Amendment No 3) 1995[1] following the coming into force of the 1994 Act although, on the whole, the old practice under the 1938 Act has been retained (subject to a few exceptions, as to which see RSC Ord 100, Explanatory Note 100/A). In essence, appeals to the High Court from a decision of the Registrar are governed by Ord 100, r 3 (and Ord 55 in general). Parties to proceedings in the High Court will need to refer to and follow precisely these Orders and further guidance can be derived from the Explanatory Notes at the end of Ord 100.

Further evidence on appeal The hearing of an appeal by the High Court is a rehearing and therefore further evidence, not available or submitted to the Registrar, may be admitted in the exercise of the court's discretion. In the *Swiss Miss* case, Laddie J considered the following factors (at least) to be relevant in any case in the exercise of his discretion:[2]

(i) Whether the evidence could have been filled earlier and, if so, how much earlier.
(ii) If it could have been, what explanation for the late filing has been offered to explain the delay.
(iii) The nature of the mark.
(iv) The nature of the objections to it.

20 Section 76(3).
1 SI 1995/3316.
2 *Hunt-Wesson Inc's Trade Mark Application* [1996] RPC 233 at 242: see also *Elle Trade Marks* [1997] FSR 529, where Lloyd J states that relevant factors going to discretion were the circumstances in which the evidence was not given to the Registrar and the degree of substance of the evidence [1954] 1 WLR 1489.

(v) The potential significance of the new evidence.
(vi) Whether or not the other side will be significantly prejudiced by the admission of the evidence in a way which cannot be compensated, eg by an order for costs.
(vii) The desirability of avoiding multiplicity of proceedings.
(viii) The public interest in not admitting onto the register invalid marks.

Regard should also be had to Laddie J's observations in relation to the practice of inviting the Registrar to comment upon the new evidence. Laddie J observed that in the *Oxon Italia* case[3] it was suggested that the Registrar should be asked to consider whether the new evidence raised any, and if so, what point of public interest which had not been raised at the hearing. Although acknowledging that the Registrar has a right to appear at the hearing and make submissions if he wishes to do so, Laddie J thought that the practice of inviting the Registrar to write a letter as suggested in *Oxon Italia* was of little value and in his view it should no longer be followed. Of course, any further appeal from the High Court to the Court of Appeal will be governed by the stricter rule in *Ladd v Marshall* which sets out three conditions which must be met before new evidence will be allowed in. They are:

(a) it must be shown that the evidence could not have been obtained with reasonable diligence for use at the trial;
(b) the evidence must be such that, if given, it would probably have an important influence on the result of the case, though it need not be decisive; and
(c) the evidence must be credible.[4]

3.50 Certificate of validity, s 73 If the validity of a registered trade mark is contested in proceedings before the court and it is found that the trade mark is registered validly, the court may issue a certificate of validity.[5]

In the event that a certificate of validity has been issued by the court and, in subsequent proceedings:

(a) the validity of the registration is again challenged; and
(b) the proprietor once again obtains a final order or judgment in his favour,

3 *Oxon Italia SpA's Trade Mark application* [1981] FSR 408.
4 [1954] 1 WLR 1489.
5 Section 73(1).

the proprietor will be entitled to his costs as between solicitor and client, unless the court directs otherwise.[6]

Whether or not a certificate of validity has been issued, in all legal proceedings relating to a registered trade mark the registration of the trade mark is of itself prima facie evidence of the validity of the registration and of any subsequent assignment or transmission of the registration.[7]

3.51 Appearance of the Registrar, s 74 In proceedings before the court involving an application for:

(a) the revocation of the registration of a trade mark;
(b) a declaration of invalidity; or
(c) the rectification of the Register,

the Registrar will be entitled to appear and be heard, and indeed must appear if he is so directed by the court.[8]

Alternatively, the Registrar may, instead of appearing, submit to the court a signed statement giving particulars of:

(a) any proceedings before him in relation to the matter in issue;
(b) the grounds of any decision given by him affecting that matter;
(c) the practice of the Patent Office in like cases; or
(d) such other matters as are relevant to the issues and within the Registrar's knowledge as he thinks fit.[9]

The Registrar's statement will become part of the evidence in the proceedings before the court.[10]

3.52 Transitional provisions, Schedule 3 Schedule 3 of the 1994 Act contains the transitional provisions. Many of the transitional provisions relate to matters which have been dealt with in this chapter and references have been included in the text or in footnotes.

By way of a summary, the more important transitional provisions which affect practice and procedure are:

(a) trade marks registered under the 1938 Act as at 31 October

6 Section 73(2); however, this does not extend to the costs of an appeal in any such proceedings.
7 Section 72.
8 Section 74(1).
9 Section 74(2); the Registrar may not exercise this option if he is directed otherwise by the court.
10 Section 74(2).

1994 (whether in Part A or Part B) have been transferred to the 1994 Register and have effect as if registered under the 1994 Act;[11]

(b) trade marks registered under the 1938 Act will continue to be registered:
   (i) subject to any former disclaimer or limitation;[12] and
   (ii) where relevant, as a series;[13]

(c) trade marks registered under the 1938 Act will not continue to be registered:
   (i) subject to any former condition(s) of registration;[14] nor
   (ii) where relevant, as an associated mark;[15]

(d) the rights of co-proprietors of a 1938 Act registration are governed by s 23 of the 1994 Act;[16]

(e) applications pending under the 1938 Act as at 31 October 1994 but which had not been advertised could have been converted into applications under the 1994 Act if the conversion had been requested on or before 30 April 1995;[17]

(f) applications pending under the 1938 Act which had been advertised under s 18 of the 1938 Act will be dealt with under the old law;[18] and

(g) registrations under the 1938 Act will continue in force until the end of their seven or fourteen year periods (as the case may be). On renewal they will be registered for ten year periods.[19]

11 Schedule 3, para 2(1).
12 Schedule 3, para 3(2).
13 Schedule 3, para 2(2).
14 Schedule 3, para 3(1).
15 Schedule 3, para 2(3).
16 Schedule 3, para 7.
17 Schedule 3, para 11.
18 Schedule 3, para 10.
19 Schedule 3, para 15.

4 Oppositions and observations

4.01 Approach taken by the 1994 Act When an application for registration of a trade mark has been accepted by the Registrar, he will publish the application in the Journal. Following publication, there are two options open to a third party who believes that there are grounds for refusing the registration of the trade mark, namely filing a formal opposition and/or making informal observations.

Opposition One option is to give a formal notice of opposition to the Registrar pursuant to s 38(2).

The giving of a notice of opposition is dealt with in the first part of this chapter, which also deals with analogous oppositions relating to:

(a) applications by agents or representatives;
(b) amendments of an application;
(c) alterations of a registered trade mark; and
(d) applications for collective or certification marks.

Observations A second option enables any person to send written observations to the Registrar stating why he believes the trade mark should not be registered.[1] The making of observations is dealt with in the second part of this chapter.

1 Section 38(3).

Opposition

4.02 Opposition procedure, s 38(2) and r 13

Notice of opposition Any person may, within three months of the date on which an application is published, give notice of opposition to the registration of the trade mark.[2] The notice of opposition has to include a statement of the grounds of opposition, a copy of which will be sent by the Registrar to the applicant.[3]

Importantly, the three month time limit cannot be extended,[4] unlike the former one month time limit under the 1938 Act which did not limit either the number or length of extensions that could be obtained with the Registrar's consent.[5]

Counter-statement Following receipt of the notice of opposition, an applicant who wishes to pursue his application will have to file a counter-statement at the Registry[6] within three months of the date on which the notice of opposition was sent by the Registrar. Strictly, the applicant need not file a counter-statement if he is sufficiently confident that the opposition as filed cannot succeed in any event. The Registrar will send a copy of any counter-statement to the person opposing the application.

The three month period cannot be extended,[7] unlike the corresponding two month period for filing a counter-statement under the 1938 Act.[8]

Opponent's evidence Upon receiving the counter-statement, the person opposing the application must, within three months of the

2 Using Form TM 7. This is also the procedure for applications for registration made under the 1938 Act which are advertised after 31 October 1994: r 67. Note that the three month time limit only commences if the mark applied for has been properly published in the Journal – if it has not been properly published and has to be re-published, then the three month time limit will start on the day of the second publication: *R v Patent Office, ex p Chocoladefabriken Lindt and Sprungli AG* (5 December 1996, unreported) (Laddie J).

3 Section 38(2) and r 13(1).

4 Rule 62(3).

5 Trade Marks and Service Marks Rules 1986, r 114.

6 Rule 13(2); the counter-statement should be accompanied by the required notice of counter-statement using Form TM 8.

7 See note 3 above.

8 Trade Marks and Service Marks Rules 1986, SI 1986/1319, r 48.

date on which the counter-statement was sent by the Registrar, file the evidence he may wish to rely upon in support of his opposition. The evidence must be by way of affidavit or statutory declaration and copies of any evidence filed must be sent by the opponent to the applicant.[9] Unlike the periods for filing notices of opposition and counter-statements, the time for filing evidence in support of the opposition (or other evidence in opposition proceedings) can be extended by the Registrar.[10]

If the person opposing the application does not file any evidence then, unless the Registrar directs otherwise, the opposition will be deemed to have been abandoned.[11]

Applicant's evidence Where either:

(a) evidence is filed in support of the opposition; or
(b) the Registrar has directed that no evidence in support of the opposition is required,

the applicant, if he wishes to file any evidence, must do so within three months of the date on which either a copy of the opponent's evidence or a copy of the direction of the Registrar is sent to him. This evidence must be filed by way of affidavit or statutory declaration and a copy of the evidence must be sent by the applicant to the opponent.[12] The three month time limit for filing this evidence may be extended.[13]

Reply evidence The opponent may file evidence in reply to the applicant's evidence within three months of the date on which a copy of the applicant's evidence is sent to the opponent. This evidence, by way of affidavit or statutory declaration filed at the Registry, must be confined to matters which are strictly in reply to the applicant's evidence. A copy of the reply evidence, if any, must

9 Rule 13(3); compare this with the six month period for filing evidence in support of an opposition under the 1938 Act. As to the making and subscribing of affidavits and statutory declarations, see r 50.

10 Rule 62(1). Note that the Registrar must be provided with detailed and compelling reasons for an extension. The Work Manual states that a reason such as 'awaiting client's instructions' or 'clients are considering their next action' will not be accepted. This practice follows the decision in the *Swiss Army Brands* case [1996] RPC 507.

11 Rule 13(4).

12 Rule 13(5); again, compare this with the six month period for filing evidence by the applicant under the 1938 Act.

13 Rule 62(1). See also the comments in note 12 above.

be sent by the opponent to the applicant.[14] The three month time limit for filing reply evidence may be extended.[15]

Additional evidence No further evidence may be filed in the opposition proceedings unless the Registrar, at his discretion, gives leave to either party at any time to file evidence upon such terms as the Registrar thinks fit.[16] This gives the Registrar a general discretion to allow additional evidence to be filed by either party at any time prior to the determination of the opposition proceedings.

Hearing Once all the evidence accepted by the Registrar has been filed, the Registrar will, if a hearing is requested by either party to the opposition proceedings, send to the parties notice of the date for a hearing.[17] There is no prescribed time limit within which such a notice must be sent, nor as to when the hearing must take place.

If no hearing is requested by either party to an opposition, then the Registrar will determine the matter on the evidence filed without a hearing.

Decision of the Registrar Where, following an opposition, the Registrar has made a decision on the acceptability of an application for registration, he will send a written notice of his decision to the applicant and the opponent stating the reasons for his decision.[18]

Appeal For the purpose of any appeal against the Registrar's decision in opposition proceedings the date of the decision will be taken to be the date when notice of the decision is sent to the applicant or, as the case may be, the person opposing the application.[19]

4.03 Who may oppose, s 38(2) Section 38(2) provides that 'any person' may give notice of opposition to the registration of a trade mark.[20] There is nothing in the drafting of this section which expressly requires the opponent to have any specific interest in the

14 Rule 13(6); under the 1938 Act there was a six month extendible period for filing reply evidence.
15 Rule 62(1). See also the comments in note 12 above.
16 Rule 13(7); the terms may include an order as to costs pursuant to s 68(1) and r 54.
17 Rule 13(8).
18 Rule 14(1).
19 Rule 14(2) and see Chapter 3 in respect of the appeal procedure.
20 This is identical to s 18(2) of the 1938 Act.

registration of the mark which he is opposing. This is also the situation with ss 46 and 47 where applications for revocation and declarations for invalidity may also be made by 'any person'. Contrast this with s 21 of the 1994 Act (Groundless Threats) and s 32 of the 1938 Act (Rectification) which specifically require that the applicant must be a 'person aggrieved' by the registration in question. There was a considerable body of case law under the old s 32 as to the necessary standing or interest which the applicant had to show in order to be 'aggrieved'. It must be right that the phrase 'any person' does not require the opponent to be a 'person aggrieved'; it may be, however, that some lesser interest or standing is required. It is difficult (if not impossible) to read into the phrase 'any person' any implied limitation to, or restriction of, the category of persons who may bring opposition proceedings, and perhaps the only limitation in practice will be the financial implications of commencing an opposition. In any event, an opponent is certainly not confined to basing his opposition on an interference with his earlier rights and may also rely on the absolute grounds for refusal.

Proprietor of an earlier trade mark Whatever doubt may exist as to the category of persons who have standing to bring opposition proceedings, the proprietor of an earlier trade mark/earlier right which has been cited by the Registrar during the examination process must prima facie fall within that category. Furthermore, in the situation where the Registrar has waived a citation of an earlier trade mark/earlier right following the submission by the applicant of evidence of honest concurrent use, the mere raising of an objection by the proprietor of that mark/right to the application will mean that the applicant's honest concurrent use will count for nothing. The consequence of this is that if the application had only been accepted by virtue of the applicant's honest concurrent use (ie by virtue of ss 7(1) and (2)), it would appear that the Registrar will have no option but to reject the application without any further consideration of the merits.[1]

4.04 Grounds of opposition The grounds of opposition most likely to be relied upon by an opponent will be any of the following,

1 *Road Tech Computer Systems Ltd v Unison Software (UK) Ltd* [1996] FSR 805.

namely that the trade mark applied for:

(a) is not a sign which is both:
   (i) capable of being represented graphically; and
   (ii) capable of distinguishing the applicant's goods or services from those of other undertakings;[2]

(b) is devoid of any distinctive character;[3]

(c) consists exclusively of signs or indications which may serve in trade to designate the kind, quality, quantity, intended purpose, value, geographical origin, the time of production of goods or of rendering of services, or other characteristics of goods or services;[4]

(d) consists exclusively of signs or indications which have become customary in the current language or in the bona fide and established practices of the trade;[5]

(e) consists exclusively of either:
   (i) the shape which results from the nature of the goods themselves;
   (ii) the shape of goods which is necessary to obtain a technical result; or
   (iii) the shape which gives substantial value to the goods;[6]

(f) is contrary to public policy or to accepted principles of morality;[7]

(g) is of such a nature as to deceive the public (for instance as to the nature, quality or geographical origin of the goods or services);[8]

(h) cannot be used because its use is prohibited in the United Kingdom by any enactment or rule of law or by any provision of Community law;[9]

(i) is a specially protected emblem for the purposes of s 4;[10]

(j) was applied for in bad faith;[11]

(k) is identical with an 'earlier trade mark' as defined in s 6 and the goods or services for which the trade mark is applied for are identical with the goods or services for which the earlier trade

2 See paragraph 2.02 and Chapter 1.
3 See paragraph 2.03.
4 See paragraph 2.04.
5 See paragraph 2.05.
6 See paragraphs 2.07 and 2.11.
7 See paragraph 2.12.
8 See paragraph 2.13.
9 See paragraph 2.14.
10 See paragraph 2.15 and Chapter 15.
11 See paragraph 2.16.

mark is protected;[12]

(l) is identical with an earlier trade mark and is to be registered for goods or services similar to those for which the earlier trade mark is protected and there exists a likelihood of confusion on the part of the public, which includes the likelihood of association with the earlier trade mark;[13]

(m) is similar to an earlier trade mark and is to be registered for goods or services identical with or similar to those for which the earlier trade mark is protected and there exists a likelihood of confusion on the part of the public, which includes the likelihood of association with the earlier trade mark;[14]

(n) is identical with or similar to an earlier trade mark and, although it is to be registered for goods or services which are not similar to those for which the earlier trade mark is registered, would nevertheless take unfair advantage of, or be detrimental to, the distinctive character or the repute of the earlier trade mark for the purposes of s 5(3);[15]

(o) is liable to be prevented from being used by virtue of any rule of law protecting an unregistered trade mark or other sign used in the course of trade or any other earlier right;[16]

(p) is not being used by the applicant or with his consent in relation to the goods or services covered by the application, and the applicant does not have a bona fide intention that the mark should be so used;[17]

(q) was not applied for in accordance with the procedural requirements of s 32 and r 11.[18]

4.05 Opposition to applications by agents or representatives, s 60 Where an application for the registration of a trade mark is made by a person who is the agent or the representative of a person who is the proprietor of the trade mark in a Convention country,[19] the application will be refused if the proprietor opposes

12 See paragraph 2.18.
13 See paragraphs 2.19–2.22.
14 Ibid.
15 See paragraph 2.23.
16 See paragraphs 2.24–2.26.
17 As an example of an application being made in 'bad faith' see paragraph 2.16.
18 See Chapter 3.
19 ie a country other than the United Kingdom which is a party to the Paris Convention; see Sch 1.

the application[20] unless, or to the extent that, the agent or the representative justifies his action.[1]

This provision reflects Article 6*septies* of the Paris Convention and will involve the potentially complicated issue of whether the person claiming to be the proprietor can establish proprietorship of the mark in a Convention country. This will necessarily require the Registrar or courts to consider and determine questions of foreign trade mark law. Presumably, the production of a certificate of registration of the relevant trade mark in a Convention country will be prima facie evidence of proprietorship. However, it must remain open to the agent or representative to challenge the validity of the foreign registration or to put the question of proprietorship in issue generally. This determination under foreign law may be more difficult where the proprietor is seeking to rely upon his proprietorship of an unregistered mark in a Convention country.

Neither Article 6*septies* nor s 60(2) makes it clear whether an opposition under this section is to be treated in the same way as a notice of opposition under s 38, or whether this is a sui generis remedy. Section 60(1) suggests that the proprietor's right to oppose the application arises immediately upon the application for registration being filed by his representative or agent. This is inconsistent with s 38 in so far as a notice of opposition under that section can only be given after the publication of the application following its acceptance by the Registrar.[2]

Furthermore, the Rules do not make express reference to a proprietor opposing an application pursuant to s 60(2). This suggests that the proprietor of the mark whose agent or representative has filed an application merely needs to notify the Registrar of his opposition to the application and the Registrar will be obliged to refuse to register the trade mark unless, thereafter, he is satisfied that the agent or representative is justified in making the application for registration. In the *Road Tech* case,[3] the court had to consider the honest concurrent use provisions in s 7 and concluded that the Registrar had no option but to refuse to register

20 Section 60(1) and (2).
1 Section 60(5).
2 Section 38(1) and (2).
3 *Road Tech Computer Systems Ltd v Unison Software (UK) Ltd* [1996] FSR 805 at 813, as to which, see paragraph 2.28.

the mark in question simply because the proprietor of the earlier trade mark/earlier right lodged an objection. By analogy, it is submitted that the clear wording of s 60(2) is to be applied in the same way as s 7(2) and therefore the Registrar has no option but to refuse to register the mark in question upon receiving notice of the proprietor's opposition.

From a procedural point of view it is not clear whether the proprietor of the mark becomes a party to any proceedings by virtue of his opposition to the application. On the above analysis, he does not. Therefore, the procedure would be as follows:

(a) the agent or representative files the application for registration;
(b) the person claiming to be the proprietor of the mark opposes the application;
(c) the Registrar has no option but to refuse to register the mark; and
(d) the agent or representative may seek to justify the filing of the application, for example, on the ground that the person claiming to be the proprietor of the trade mark is not in fact the proprietor of the mark in a Convention country or perhaps that the proprietor authorised the making of the application.

The complication arises because it is not clear whether the proprietor who opposes the application actually instigates formal opposition proceedings governed by r 13. If not, the question of whether the agent or representative can justify his action may have to be determined in the absence of the person claiming to be the proprietor. Presumably, however, he will be given the opportunity to comment on the grounds sought to be relied upon by his agent or representative by way of justification.

4.06 Opposition to amendment of an application, s 39(3) and r 18(2) Section 39(2) provides for the amendment of an application for the registration of a trade mark provided that the correction does not either substantially affect the identity of the trade mark or extend the goods or services covered by the original application.

Where the amendment is made after publication of the original application, the amendment will be published in the Journal. Thereafter, any person claiming to be affected by an amendment which affects the representation of the trade mark may give notice of opposition to the amendment. The notice of opposition must be sent to the Registrar within one month of the date on which the application as amended was published in the Journal.[4] The notice of opposition must include a statement of the grounds of objection and, in particular, a statement as to why the amendment is contrary to s 39(2).[5] This, in essence, means a statement as to how the amendment substantially affects the identity of the trade mark or as to how the goods or services covered by the original application have been extended. Accordingly, someone opposing an amendment cannot rely on the more general grounds of opposition which would be available in proceedings relating to the opposition to the registration of a trade mark under s 38(2) and r 13. However, the proceedings relating to the opposition to the amendment are the same as the opposition proceedings relating to the registration of a trade mark generally.[6]

4.07 Opposition to alteration of a registered trade mark, s 44(3) and r 25(3) Section 44(2) provides for the alteration of a registered trade mark where the mark includes the proprietor's name or address and provided that the alteration is limited to that name or address and does not substantially affect the identity of the mark.

The alteration will be published by the Registrar in the Journal. Thereafter, any person claiming to be affected by the alteration can give notice of opposition to the alteration which must include a statement of the grounds of opposition.[7] This, in essence, means a statement as to how the alteration either affects elements of the trade mark other than the proprietor's name or address or as to how it affects the identity of the mark. Accordingly, someone opposing an alteration cannot rely on the general grounds of opposition which would be available in proceedings under s 38(2).

The notice of opposition must be sent to the Registrar[8] within three months of the date on which the alteration was published in the Journal. The Registrar will send a copy of the statement of the grounds of opposition to the applicant and thereafter the procedure

4 Using Form TM 7.
5 Rule 18(2).
6 ie r 13 applies; r 18(3) and therefore the three month period in which the notice of opposition must be given cannot be extended: r 62(3).
7 Rule 25(3).
8 Rule 25(3); using form TM 7.

will be the same as the opposition procedure relating to the registration of a trade mark.[9]

4.08 Opposition to applications for collective and certification marks, Schedules 1 and 2 The procedure for opposing an application for the registration of a collective mark or a certification mark is the same as for opposing an ordinary trade mark application. The available grounds of opposition are also the same.[10] In addition, the opposition may relate specifically to the regulations governing the use of a collective mark[11] and a certification mark,[12] including opposition to any amendment of the regulations.[13]

4.09 Opposition following division of an application, s 41(1) and r 19(2) Rule 19 provides for the division of an application into two or more separate applications, referred to as 'divisional applications'. Each divisional application will be treated by the Registrar as a separate application for registration. Therefore, where the division of the application is made after the acceptance and publication of the original application, it should be borne in mind that any opposition to the original application will be taken to apply to each divisional application.[14]

Observations

4.10 Observation procedure, s 38(3) and r 15 Following the acceptance and publication of an application[15] any person may, at any time before the registration of the trade mark, send written observations to the Registrar as to why he believes the trade mark should not be registered.[16] The Registrar will send a copy of any documents containing the observations to the applicant.[17]

9 See r 13(2)–(6) and paragraph 4.02; and therefore the three month period for giving notice of opposition cannot be extended.
10 Subject to adjustments which need to be taken into account: see Chapters 11 and 12.
11 Schedule 1, para 8.
12 Schedule 2, para 9.
13 See r 23(4).
14 Rule 19(2).
15 Pursuant to ss 37(5) and 38(1).
16 Section 38(3).
17 Rule 15.

Neither the 1994 Act nor the Rules specify what is to happen next.[18] However, where an application has been accepted, the Registrar may still refuse to register the trade mark if it appears to him, having regard to matters coming to his notice since he accepted the application, that it was wrongly accepted.[19] Therefore, the Registrar could refuse to register the trade mark if he receives written observations after accepting the application which persuade him to conclude that the application was accepted by him in error.

In any event, the person making the observations will not become a party to any proceedings before the Registrar.[20] If the person making the observations wishes to become a party, then he must formally give notice of opposition to the registration under s 38(2).[1]

4.11 Who may make observations, s 38(3) As in the case of opposition proceedings, s 38(3) provides that 'any person' may make observations to the Registrar.[2]

4.12 Subject matter of observations As with opposition proceedings, neither the 1994 Act nor the Rules specify or limit the subject matter of the observations. The wording of s 38(3) would suggest that any issue relevant to the question of whether a trade mark should be registered could be the proper subject of written observations. This would include any of the grounds of opposition referred to in paragraph 4.04 above.

4.13 Observations in relation to collective and certification marks, Schedules 1 and 2 The procedure for making observations concerning the registration of a certification mark or a collective mark is the same as for making observations concerning the registration of an ordinary trade mark, as is the subject matter for such observations.[3] In addition, written observations may be made relating specifically to the regulations governing the use of a

18 The Registrar has not issued a Practice Direction. However, practitioners should refer to ITMA Information No 5, November 1996, which contains a statement of the Registrar's intended practice in relation to post-advertisement observations.
19 Section 40(1).
20 Section 38(3).
1 See paragraphs 4.02–4.04 above.
2 As to the meaning of 'any person' see paragraph 4.03 above.
3 Subject to adjustments which need to be taken into account: see Chapters 11 and 12.

collective mark[4] or a certification mark,[5] or to any amendment of such regulations.[6]

4.14 Observations following the division of an application, r 19(2) Where an application is divided, any observations made to the Registrar in respect of the original application shall be taken to apply to each divisional application.[7]

Comment

4.15 Comparison with Community trade mark system The Community trade mark system limits the grounds for giving notice of opposition to objections based on the 'relative grounds' for refusal.[8] Furthermore, only the owner of the earlier trade mark or other earlier right may bring an opposition under the Community system. However, any party is able to submit observations concerning absolute grounds,[9] but the person making such observations will not become a party to any proceedings. Accordingly, the opposition and observation procedure under the 1994 Act is wider than is available under the Community system in so far as:

(a) an opposition under the 1994 Act is not restricted to the relative grounds for refusal and can be brought by a person who is not the proprietor of an earlier trade mark or earlier right; and
(b) observations are not restricted under the 1994 Act to the absolute grounds.

The White Paper indicates that consideration was given to aligning the United Kingdom opposition procedure with that of the Community system in terms of the grounds which can be raised in an opposition. However, there was a consensus in favour of continuing to allow any ground of objection to be raised in opposition proceedings and the 1994 Act was drafted accordingly.[10]

4 Schedule 1, para 8.
5 Schedule 2, para 9.
6 Rule 23(3).
7 See paragraph 4.09.
8 ie the grounds equivalent to s 5 of the 1994 Act.
9 ie the grounds equivalent to ss 3 and 4 of the 1994 Act.
10 Paragraph 4.18 of the White Paper.

5 Revocation and invalidity

5.01 Approach taken by the 1994 Act The 1994 Act provides for a registered trade mark either to be revoked or declared invalid in certain prescribed circumstances.

Revocation, s 46 In essence, the grounds for revocation under s 46 are:

(a) non-use of the trade mark for five years;[1]
(b) where the trade mark has become a common name in the trade;[2] or
(c) where the trade mark has become liable to mislead the public.[3]

Invalidity, s 47 In addition, or as an alternative to revocation, the grounds for invalidity under s 47 are:

(a) where the trade mark was registered contrary to the provisions of s 3;[4] or
(b) where the trade mark was registered contrary to the provisions of s 5.[5]

The practical distinction between revocation and invalidity is that the grounds for revocation relate to matters occurring after the registration of a trade mark, whereas the grounds for invalidity are based on matters which affect the original registration itself.

1 See paragraphs 5.02–5.09.
2 See paragraph 5.10.
3 See paragraph 5.11.
4 See paragraph 5.16.
5 See paragraph 5.17

Each of these grounds for revocation and invalidity will now be considered in turn. However, it should be noted that both revocation and invalidity are discretionary orders under the 1994 Act and therefore equitable principles governing the exercise of discretionary powers will be applicable. This follows from the use of the word 'may' in the opening words of ss 46(1) and 47(1). The existence of a discretion has been confirmed in relation to revocation proceedings in *Invermont*[6] but there is an argument that no such discretion exists (or that it should not exist) because Article 3(1) of the Directive is a mandatory provision and lists eight grounds upon which marks 'shall not be registered or if registered shall be liable to be declared invalid'. On the basis of this wording Messrs Kitchen QC and Mellor argue that s 47 should have been phrased in terms of 'shall be declared invalid'.[7] However, the Hearing Officer in *Invermont* thought that the word 'liable' in Articles 4 and 12 of the Directive implies a discretionary power and also that it was undesirable that the word 'may' should be given different meanings in different parts of the 1994 Act.

Revocation

5.02 Non-use, s 46(1)(a) and (b) The registration of a trade mark may be revoked for non-use if either:

(a) within five years following the date of the completion of the registration procedure the trade mark has not been put to genuine use in the United Kingdom, either by the proprietor or with his consent, in relation to the goods or services covered by the registration; or

(b) there has been genuine use for the purposes of (a) above but such use has since been suspended for an uninterrupted period of five years,

provided also that, in each case, the proprietor cannot give proper reasons for the non-use.

In determining whether a trade mark is liable to be revoked for non-use it will be necessary to consider in particular a number of key phrases which appear in s 46; some are similar to those which

6 *Invermont Trade Mark* [1997] RPC 125.
7 The Trade Marks Act 1994.

appeared in the corresponding s 26 of the 1938 Act, some are not.[8] These phrases are discussed in paragraphs 5.03 to 5.05.

5.03 Calculation of non-use period Section 46 removes any doubt concerning the date from which the five year non-use period commences. Under the 1938 Act it had been decided that the non-use period was measured from the date when the mark was actually put on the Register,[9] and not from the effective date of registration which would have been the original filing date. This decision is reflected in Article 10(1) of the Directive which has been adopted in s 46(1)(a).

5.04 Genuine use The 1994 Act sets out three specific instances of what constitutes 'use'. The first two instances apply only for the purposes of s 46(1), whereas the third is of general application. These three instances are considered first, followed by a consideration of the meaning of 'genuine use' for the purposes of s 46(1).

Use In the first place, the proprietor of a trade mark can rely on any use of his trade mark even though the mark actually used differs from the precise form in which it is registered, provided that the differences do not alter the distinctive character of the mark as registered.[10] In *ELLE Trade Marks*[11] the use of the word ELLE alone without the device incorporated in the registered mark was held to alter the distinctive character of the mark in a significant and substantial way.

Secondly, the concept of 'use in the United Kingdom' will include affixing the trade mark in the United Kingdom to goods or to their packaging notwithstanding that the goods are intended only for export.[12] Furthermore, in the *ELLE* case, the use of the proprietor's trade mark in advertisements appearing in foreign editions of its magazine was held to be 'use in the United Kingdom' because the products in question were advertised as being for sale in the United Kingdom. This was described by Lloyd J as being 'fairly near the borderline'.

8 As to pending applications for revocation under s 26 of the 1938 Act, see paragraph 5.15.
9 *Bon Martin Trade Mark* [1989] RPC 537.
10 Section 46(2).
11 [1997] FSR 529.
12 Section 46(2)

Thirdly, it must be remembered that all references in the 1994 Act to the use of a trade mark will include use otherwise than by means of a graphic representation of the trade mark.[13] Thus, the proprietor can rely on any non-visual use, such as oral use, of his trade mark to defend a non-use action (provided, of course, that such use is 'genuine').

Genuine use Although the 1994 Act specifies these three instances of what will constitute 'use' for the purposes of s 46, the Act does not give any guidance as to what must be established in order to obtain the revocation of a trade mark on the grounds of a lack of 'genuine use'. Certainly, the proprietor has the onus of showing what actual use has in fact been made of his trade mark,[14] but the onus remains on the party seeking revocation to prove that that use has not been 'genuine' or that such use is merely de minimis.

The corresponding provision of the 1938 Act was s 26(1)(b) which required the party seeking revocation to establish that there had been no 'bona fide use' of the trade mark. The White Paper asserts that the change to the use of the word 'genuine' in the present law amounts only to a clarification rather than a substantive change.[15] In *Electrix*,[16] it was held that 'bona fide' meant genuine, judged by commercial standards. It must be likely that the test of 'genuine use' will be interpreted by the courts consistently with their interpretation of bona fide use under the 1938 Act. Thus, issues raised by mere isolated instances of use, de minimis use, ghost marks and the stockpiling of trade marks will need to be considered in the context of the facts of each case in order to determine whether the use has been genuine.[17] In the *Rainbow* case,[18] the Hearing Officer refused an application for revocation under s 46(1)(a) and (b) on the basis that the proprietor had made sufficient use of his mark, albeit that the only evidence of such use was in the form of a price list and an invoice, each dated earlier than the relevant five year period before the application for revocation. In relation to the price list the Hearing Officer accepted that the list was effective until

13 Section 103(2).
14 Section 100.
15 Paragraph 4.29.
16 (1954) 71 RPC 23.
17 See, for example, cases under the 1938 Act: *Imperial Group Ltd v Philip Morris & Co Ltd* [1982] FSR 72 and *Huggars Trade Mark* [1979] FSR 310.
18 *Kaytee Products Inc's Application* (6 December 1996, unreported) (M Knight).

withdrawn or replaced and therefore constituted evidence of use of the mark even after the date of the list.

One should also bear in mind the relevance of the concept embedded in the definition of 'trade mark' in the 1938 Act. The definition of 'trade mark' in s 68(1) of the 1938 Act included the express requirement that the mark be used for the 'purpose of indicating, or so as to indicate, a connection in the course of trade' between the goods and the proprietor or a registered user. Accordingly, the decisions under the 1938 Act started with the premise that a mark which was being used for any other purpose could not be a 'trade mark' for the purposes of the 1938 Act. Thus, Lawton LJ in *Nerit*[19] considered that he was entitled to look at the purpose for which the trade mark had been used and concluded that the proprietor's use of NERIT was not 'bona fide use' because it had the 'unreal qualities of the ghost mark'. Furthermore, his Lordship stated that, even if the trade mark did in fact indicate a connection between the proprietor and his goods, where that connection was incidental to the purpose for which it was used, this would also not constitute bona fide use of the trade mark. Put another way, Shaw LJ in the *Nerit* case, referred to the 'philosophical concept' of a trade mark as being something which derives from the use of words or marks in relation to a course of trade in goods giving rise to a goodwill connecting the trader with the goods by reason of the trade mark. His Lordship reasoned that where there is no such course of trading there could be no interest to be protected.[20] The court in *Nerit* thought that ghost marks were not merely outside the scope of the 1938 Act but were directly contrary to its 'spirit and intent'. That is, because ghost marks are not registered for the purpose of building up goodwill and so as to indicate a connection in the course of trade, they could not be trade marks.

The definition of 'trade mark' in the 1994 Act, makes no express reference to the purpose for which a sign must be used in order for it to constitute a 'trade mark'; however, it is clear that the 'badge or indication of origin' concept remains as relevant under the 1994 Act as it did under the 1938 Act; the Directive states that a trade mark is

19 *Imperial Group Ltd v Philip Morris & Co Ltd*, supra.

20 See also *Concord Trade Mark* [1987] FSR 209, where it was held that the use was not bona fide because the use was only temporary and not part of a genuine attempt to establish trading under the mark.

'in particular to guarantee the trade mark as an indication of origin'. In the *Treat* case[1] Jacob J states:

> 'I think this sole purpose permeates the whole Directive and hence our 1994 Act. If there is doubt as to the meaning of any particular provision, regard should be had to this purpose.'

Accordingly, use which is inconsistent with this purpose is not likely to be considered to be 'genuine' for the purposes of the 1994 Act.

5.05 Use 'in relation to' goods or services Not only must the use of a trade mark be genuine, the trade mark must also have been used 'in relation to' the actual goods or services for which it is registered. The failure so to use a trade mark will expose its registration to revocation.

The first and easier question is one of fact, that is, whether the goods or services covered by the registration match the goods or services for which the mark has actually been used. This will be a matter of evidence which the proprietor will have to supply.[2]

The second issue is whether the phrase 'in relation to' will embrace use of a trade mark in advertisements or other media which does not involve physically affixing or applying the trade mark to the goods themselves. As the phrase 'in relation to' must be construed when referring to services as including use otherwise than physically affixing or applying the trade mark to the service, it would seem illogical to construe the phrase any differently when referring to goods. Furthermore, a narrow interpretation would appear to be inconsistent with the broad terms of ss 10(4) and 103(2).

Section 10(4) specifies certain acts or conduct which, for the purposes of infringement, will amount to the use of a sign, although that provision only applies for the purposes of s 10 itself, not s 46. It can be argued by analogy, however, that the acts and conduct specified in s 10(4) should also constitute use of a trade mark for the purposes of s 46, on the basis that it cannot be right that acts or conduct can constitute infringement of a trade mark but, when done by the proprietor (or with his consent), do not necessarily constitute use of his trade mark. On the other hand, the purpose of s 10(4) is to ensure that a wide range of acts and conduct will constitute infringement and, therefore, different considerations arguably apply

1 [1996] RPC 281 at 298.
2 Section 100.

where a proprietor is being put to proof as to what use he has made of his trade mark so as to justify maintaining the registration. On balance, it is submitted that the phrase 'in relation to' must be interpreted in s 46 in the same way as it is in the context of infringement under s 10.

Of course, the fact that a trade mark is actually physically affixed to a particular product does not necessarily mean that it is being used 'in relation to' that product. For example, the use of KODAK on T-shirts was held, in the circumstances of the case, to be use in relation to photographic film and not in relation to the T-shirts themselves, which were simply the media for conveying the trade mark.[3]

5.06 Use in relation to similar goods or services; use of an associated mark The 1938 Act enabled the proprietor in a non-use action to rely upon any use of his trade mark which was in relation to goods or services 'of the same description' as those covered by the registration.[4]

Furthermore, account could also be taken under the 1938 Act of any use by the proprietor of an associated registered trade mark.[5] As it was also possible for trade marks for goods to be associated with trade marks for related services, the association of related marks could potentially have provided a valuable defence to an attack against one or more of the associated marks based on non-use.[6]

The 1994 Act does not provide expressly for account to be taken of any use of the trade mark other than its use in relation to the actual goods or services for which it is registered, and the procedure for the association of trade marks has been abolished altogether.[7] However, use which would have been the basis of a defence on either of these grounds under the 1938 Act will, nevertheless, arguably remain relevant in the exercise of the discretion to revoke the registration.

3 *Kodak Trade Mark* [1990] FSR 49; cf *Cheetah Trade Mark* [1993] FSR 263, where the use of the mark on delivery notes and invoices was held to constitute use in relation to the goods which had been delivered.
4 1938 Act, s 26(1) proviso .
5 Ibid, s 30(1).
6 1938 Act, s 23(2).
7 Indeed, associated trade marks registered under the 1938 Act are not recorded as such on the 1994 Register: Sch 3, para 2(3).

Defences to non-use

A proprietor faced with an application (or potential/threatened application) for revocation based on non-use may be able to rely on a number of specific 'defences' which can be grouped under the following three headings:
(a) use after the five year period, as to which see paragraph 5.07;
(b) use by a third party with the proprietor's consent, as to which see paragraph 5.08; and
(c) other 'proper reasons' for non-use, as to which see paragraph 5.09;

5.07 **Use after the five year period, s 46(3)** The registration of a trade mark will not be revoked on either of the grounds of non-use if (subject to the proviso discussed below) genuine use by or with the consent of the proprietor is either commenced or resumed before the application for revocation is made. It does not matter that such use commences or resumes after the expiry of the relevant five year period because any genuine use prior to the filing of the application for revocation effectively overcomes the non-use.[8]

Proviso However, no account will be taken of any use which commences or resumes within three months prior to the making of the application for revocation, unless the proprietor began his preparations for the commencement or resumption of the use of his trade mark prior to becoming aware that the application for revocation might be made.[9]

The effect of the proviso is that someone considering applying for revocation should put the proprietor of the trade mark on notice of his intention to apply at the earliest opportunity after the five year period, so that the proprietor cannot rely on any subsequent use which he commences or resumes within three months before the making of the application for revocation. Of course, the person applying for revocation must then make his application for revocation within three months after putting the proprietor on notice, as otherwise the proprietor may be able to rely on use which commences or resumes after receiving notice of the intended application but more than three months prior to the making of the application for revocation.

8 Section 46(3).
9 Section 46(3) proviso.

Example Thus, if there has been a relevant five year period of non-use between, for example, 1 November 1992 and 31 October 1997, an application for revocation will still fail if either:

(a) the proprietor commences or resumes using his trade mark at any time on or after 1 November 1997 and provided that such use commences or resumes more than three months before the making of an application for revocation; or

(b) the proprietor commences or resumes using his trade mark on or after 1 November 1997 and even though an application for revocation is made within three months of that date but, at the time when the preparations for the commencement or resumption began, the proprietor was unaware that the application for revocation might be made.

Comment Under the 1938 Act the equivalent proviso applied to a period of only one month prior to the making of the application for revocation but it was irrelevant that the proprietor may have had no notice of the intended application. The extension of the period during which use of the trade mark is disregarded gives the parties a better opportunity to negotiate, because the party alleging non-use is not prejudiced by delaying the bringing of his application for a period of three months (at least) rather than just one month. Accordingly, the need for formal revocation proceedings may, in some instances, be avoided.[10]

One important point to bear in mind is that the effect of notifying a proprietor of a potential revocation action is that if the proprietor has commenced preparations for the commencement or resumption of the use of his mark prior to the notification, then the use by the proprietor of the mark after the notification of the proposed revocation proceedings may be taken into account even where such use commences or resumes during the three month period immediately preceding the application for revocation. In other words, if a proprietor receiving notification of revocation proceedings has, prior to the notification, commenced the preparations for the commencement or resumption of the use of his mark, that proprietor may be able to commence such use and rely upon such use to defeat a revocation action notwithstanding that such commencement/resumption occurred within the relevant three

10 It was, however, always open to the parties to agree on a without prejudice extension to the one month period under the 1938 Act.

month period prior to the filing of the revocation proceedings. Therefore, it may be advisable for a party considering revocation proceedings not to give notice of such proceedings prior to their commencement, as such notice may in itself cause the proprietor of the mark to bring forward the actual use of the trade mark and thus defeat the revocation proceedings. This will depend on whether the proprietor either has or has not commenced the necessary 'preparations', a fact which will usually be unknown to the party considering revocation and therefore the correct (better) tactics may be a matter of chance rather than planning. Clearly there can be no incentive for a party considering revocation to give notice of that fact if by doing so he may be providing the proprietor of the registration with a potential defence which, in the absence of the notification, would not be available.

5.08 Use with the proprietor's consent, s 46(1) The 1994 Act overcomes the issue which arose under the 1938 Act as to what use other than by the proprietor could be relied upon to defeat a non-use action. Strictly, the 1938 Act appeared only to permit use by the proprietor himself or a registered user to be taken into account but case law suggested, and the Registrar's practice was, that use by other persons could also be considered to be use by the proprietor for the purposes of s 26.[11]

The 1994 Act makes it clear that any genuine use with the consent of the proprietor will be sufficient. This will therefore include use by a third party even though no formal licence arrangement is in place and even though the prescribed particulars of any licence which has been entered into have not been registered in accordance with s 25, provided only that the proprietor has consented to the use. Indeed, even though the trade mark may be being used under a licence which is deemed to be 'not effective',[12] that should not of itself negate the consent necessary for the purposes of s 46(1).

5.09 Proper reasons for non-use, s 46(1) The two grounds for revocation based on non-use may be overcome if the proprietor can establish 'proper reasons' for not using his trade mark.

11 *Bostitch Trade Mark* [1963] RPC 183; use by a licensee: *Radiation Ltd's Application* (1930) 47 RPC 37; use by a subsidiary: *Molyslip Trade Mark* [1978] RPC 211.

12 ie because the licence is not in writing as required by s 28(2).

The first issue is whether the proper reasons must have related to the whole five year period of non-use or whether it is sufficient that the proper reasons existed during any part of the relevant five year period (subject, presumably, to a mere de minimis part of that period). Certainly, the proper reasons must have been the operative cause of the non-use and, therefore, the proprietor will not be able to rely on those reasons if, in any event, there would have been no use of his trade mark. This issue also arose under s 26(3) of the 1938 Act where non-use of a trade mark due to 'special circumstances in the trade . . .' could not be relied upon in support of a non-use action.

The second issue is whether the period during which the proper reasons existed will be treated as a period of actual use or whether that period will simply be disregarded for all purposes. The wording of s 46(1) does not remove the ambiguity altogether, but is more consistent with the interpretation that the party seeking revocation will not succeed if the proprietor can establish proper reasons for the non-use which relate to any period during the relevant period of non-use. Thus, any period of non-use which can be excused for proper reasons will mean that, for the purpose of calculating the relevant five year period, one will have to:

(a) stop counting as at the beginning of the period; and

(b) start counting afresh as from the end of the period,

during which the proper reasons were responsible for the non-use. It will therefore be necessary to establish a full uninterrupted five year period of non-use during which there have been no proper reasons for such non-use.

What then are 'proper reasons' for not using a trade mark? One assumes that the circumstances specified in s 26(3) of the 1938 Act would constitute proper reasons under the 1994 Act. Perhaps also the usual acts or events which constitute force majeure may constitute proper reasons if they are the proximate cause of the non-use. More complicated issues will arise where the non-use is for commercial reasons which the proprietor considers to be 'proper' on a subjective test, but which may be inconsistent with the wider public policy of not allowing statutory monopolies to subsist which are not exercised and which could therefore prevent lawful competition and the free movement of goods and services. For example, a pharmaceutical company may be delayed in putting a particular drug on the market because the necessary regulatory approval has not been forthcoming as quickly as anticipated by the company. This is a proper reason for not marketing the product, but is it a proper reason for not using the trade mark intended to be used in relation to the product?[13]

In the *Rainbow* case,[14] the Hearing Officer accepted that there were proper reasons for non-use because the mark in question belonged to a business division which the proprietor was seeking to sell. The business was, therefore, the subject of protracted negotiations with third parties which led to commercial uncertainty, which in turn meant that full scale use of the mark was not appropriate. Contrast this with the decision in *Invermont*,[15] where the Hearing Officer accepted a more stringent approach and stated that:

> 'I do not think the term "proper" was intended to cover normal situations or routine difficulties. I think it much more likely that it is intended to cover abnormal situations in the industry or the market, or even perhaps some temporary but serious disruption affecting the registered proprietor's business. Normal delays occasioned by some unavoidable regulatory requirement such as the approval of a medicine, might be acceptable but not, I think, the normal delays found in the marketing function. These are matters within the businessman's own control and I think he should plan accordingly.'

However, the Hearing Officer recognised that in the matter of acceptable excuses for non-use it may well be that s 46(1)(a) and (b) is more liberal than the corresponding s 26(3) of the 1938 Act. Under the 1938 Act, the 'special circumstances' could not be relied upon unless they related to the trade in general. Whereas, under the 1994 Act, the Hearing Officer thought that disruptive situations in which the proprietor's business alone is affected may, nonetheless, be 'proper'.

The phrase 'proper reasons' comes from Article 10 of the Directive and, although we now have the opinion of the Hearing Officer as set out above, it remains to be seen how the courts will interpret and apply these words. In the *Bali* case[16] at first instance,

13 See *Jellied Beef Trade Marks* [1993] FSR 484, a case where the ban on the product was considered to be a justification for non-use.
14 *Kaytee Products Inc's Application* (6 December 1996, unreported) (M Knight).
15 *Invermont Trade Mark* [1997] RPC 125.
16 *Bali Trade Mark* [1966] RPC 387 at 406.

Ungoed-Thomas J, referring to the 'special circumstances' exception under s 26(3) of the 1938 Act, made the point that a trade mark is a commercial asset intended to be used commercially by businessmen and special circumstances have to be understood and applied in a business sense. That statement of principle must be equally apposite today and therefore the phrase 'proper reasons' should also be construed and applied in a business sense as was done in the *Invermont* case.

5.10 Common name in the trade, s 46(1)(c) The second ground on which a registered trade mark can be revoked is that, in consequence of either the acts or inactivity of the proprietor, the trade mark has become the common name in the trade for the product or the service for which it is registered.[17]

It is well established that a mark which is generic or descriptive is the very antithesis of a registrable trade mark and a registered trade mark which becomes generic or descriptive is thus liable to revocation.

Acts or inactivity of the proprietor Section 46(1)(c) will apply only where the trade mark becomes a common name for a product or service in consequence of acts or inactivity of the proprietor. The reference to 'inactivity' will, in principle, encompass the failure by the proprietor to control effectively either the use of the trade mark by his licensee(s) and/or by a third party infringer, provided that the proprietor has notice (actual or constructive) of the infringing use by the third party. If such failure to control results in the trade mark becoming the common name in the trade for the goods or services for which it is registered, then it will be liable to revocation.

Common name in the trade It is, as yet, uncertain whether the phrase 'common name in the trade' will be interpreted differently to the phrase 'well-known and established use of the word as the name or description of the article or a substance by a person carrying on a trade therein . . .' which appeared in the proviso to s 15(1) of the 1938 Act. On its face, the phrase in the 1994 Act is simply a more compact expression of the same concept.

For a product or service for which it is registered An application for revocation under the 1994 Act on the ground that a trade mark

17 Section 46(1)(c).

has become a common name in the trade will only succeed if it has become a common name for the specific product or service for which the trade mark is registered. The 1994 Act thus overcomes the problem for proprietors which arose under the 1938 Act whereby they could lose their registration through the use of their mark (particularly by third parties, including the public) on goods or services other than those covered by the registration and in a way which the proprietor could not police.[18]

In Chapter 10 (assignments and licences) reference is made to the fact that the requirements relating to the licensing of registered trade marks have been relaxed in the 1994 Act. Nonetheless, s 46(1)(c) should always be borne in mind when licensing a trade mark, because the failure to control adequately and effectively the licensee's use of the trade mark may lead to it becoming generic or descriptive of the goods or services for which it is registered. It is ironic that this ground for revocation may arise because the product or service for which the trade mark is registered has become so successful that the public adopt the trade mark as a description of all competing products of a like nature or function. Thus, the proprietor by himself and through any licensee(s) must carefully control the manner in which he uses the trade mark so that it continues to identify and distinguish his particular products or services and not the like products or services of competitors.

Use Guidelines Some companies (particularly those who own trade marks which are in danger of becoming generic) go to considerable lengths to stress to the public that their mark is distinctive of their products and to ensure that the marks are not used in a descriptive manner. This often includes the placement of advertisements in national and trade press informing the public and warning off third parties from incorrect usage or misappropriation of the mark. For example, the proprietor of the ROLLERBLADE trade mark has published an advertisement warning the public to 'Be careful not to slip when using ROLLERBLADE skates'. The proprietor reminds readers that ROLLERBLADE is a trade mark and that references to: 'rollerblades, rollerbladers and rollerblading' are incorrect. Instead, readers are advised that the proper generic terms for the product, the athletes and the sport are, respectively: 'in-line skates, in-line skaters and in-line skating'.

18 See *Daiquiri Rum Trade Mark* [1969] RPC 600.

The placing of such advertisements will only be necessary for relatively few marks. The following guidelines are of general application for trade mark owners:

(1) The trade mark should, as far as possible, be used in the form as registered (conversely one should ensure that marks applied for cover all the intended representations of the mark).
(2) If trade marks are used in brochures or other publications, the letters TM or, in the case of a registered mark the ® symbol, should be used in conjunction with the mark and, where appropriate, wording should be included identifying the proprietor of the trade mark.
(3) Where a word mark is incorporated in text, it should be distinguished from the surrounding text, for example by the use of capitalisation or italics.
(4) Word marks should be used as adjectives and not nouns or verbs.

5.11 'Liable to mislead the public', s 46(1)(d) The third ground on which a registered trade mark can be revoked is that, in consequence of the use made of it by the proprietor or with his consent in relation to the goods or services for which it is registered, the trade mark is liable to mislead the public.[19] Particular examples of the way in which the public may be misled are cited, including as to the nature, quality, or geographical origin of the goods or services.[20]

Use made of it by the proprietor The cause of the trade mark being liable to mislead the public must be the actual use made of the mark by the proprietor or with his consent and not merely the inactivity of the proprietor.[1] Furthermore, any use of the trade mark by unauthorised third parties will not be relevant.

'Liable to mislead' The concept of misleading the public involves more than merely creating confusion. Section 11 of the 1938 Act provided a similar ground for rectification merely if the use of the trade mark was likely to cause confusion, and thus the 1994 Act imposes a stricter test. This is consistent with the shift in the emphasis in the 1994 Act from protecting the interests of the

19 Section 46(1)(d).
20 Section 46(1)(d).
1 cf s 46(1)(c).

public to being more concerned with the rights of trade mark owners.

Having said this, however, it will not be necessary for the party seeking revocation under the 1994 Act to establish that the proprietor consciously or advertently set out to mislead the public. The only requirement is that this is the result in fact (the 'consequence') of the use made of the trade mark by the proprietor or with his consent.

The goods or services for which it is registered As with s 46(1)(c), the use of the trade mark which causes it to become liable to mislead the public must be use in relation to those specific goods or services for which it is registered. Thus, any use of the trade mark on any other goods or services will be disregarded for the purposes of s 46(1)(d).

Practice and procedure – revocation

5.12 Application for revocation, s 46(4) and r 31 An application for revocation can be made by 'any person'[2] either to the Registrar or to the court.[3] However, if proceedings concerning the trade mark in question are pending in the court, then the application for revocation must be made to the court. If the application is made to the Registrar, then he can at any stage of the proceedings refer the application to the court.[4]

An application for revocation under s 46 which is made to the Registrar must be submitted together with a statement of the grounds on which the application is made.[5] The Registrar will then send a copy of the application for revocation together with the statement of grounds to the proprietor.[6] The proprietor then has three months from the date on which the Registrar sends the application to him within which to file a counter-statement, and the

2 See paragraph 4.03.
3 An application for revocation for non-use under s 46(1)(a) or (b) can be made in relation to a trade mark registered under the 1938 Act at any time after 31 October 1994: Sch 3, para 17(2); as to pending non-use applications under s 26 of the 1938 Act see paragraph 5.15.
4 Section 46(4).
5 Rule 31(1); use Form TM 26.
6 Rule 31(2).

Registrar will send a copy of the counter-statement to the applicant for revocation.[7] Where the application for revocation is based on the grounds of non-use (under s 46(1)(a) or (b)), the proprietor is obliged also to file the evidence of the use of his trade mark on which he intends to rely.[8] If the proprietor fails to file any such evidence, the Registrar is entitled to treat his defence as having been withdrawn.[9] The Registry has held that the three month filing period for submitting a counter-statement is not extensible.[10]

Thereafter, the provisions of r 13 will apply to the proceedings in the same way as if the proceedings were in respect of an opposition to the registration of a trade mark, except that an application for revocation for non-use will succeed automatically if no counter-statement is filed by the proprietor.[11]

Intervention It should also be noted that any person (other than the registered proprietor), who claims to have an interest in the revocation proceedings, can apply to the Registrar for leave to intervene.[12] The intervener must state the nature of his interest, and the Registrar may either refuse leave to intervene or grant leave upon appropriate terms or conditions as he thinks fit, which may include an undertaking as to costs.[13] As always, the parties are entitled to request a hearing in relation to the issue as to whether leave to intervene should either be refused or granted.

If the application for leave to intervene is granted, the intervener will be treated as a party for the purposes of the application for revocation, and the provisions of r 13 will apply to the intervener, subject only to any terms or conditions which the Registrar has imposed in respect of the intervention.[14]

Registrar's decision When the Registrar has made a decision in relation to the application for revocation and/or the application to intervene, he will send the applicant, the proprietor and the intervener (if any) written notice of his decision, including the

7 Use Form TM 8; r 31(3). This time period is not extensible.
8 ie pursuant to his obligation under s 100; the evidence of use must be filed within the same period as applied to the filing of the counter-statement.
9 Rule 31(3) proviso.
10 *Principles Retail Ltd's Application* (1996) 19(8) IPD 15 (M Knight).
11 Rule 31(4).
12 Using Form TM 27; r 31(5).
13 Rule 31(5).
14 Rule 31(6).

reasons for it.[15] In the event that there is any appeal from the Registrar's decision, then the date when the notice of his decision is sent to the parties will be taken to be the date of his decision.[16]

5.13 Partial revocation, s 46(5) Where grounds for revocation under s 46 exist in respect of only some of the goods or services for which the trade mark is registered, revocation will relate only to those specific goods or services.[17]

5.14 Effective date of revocation, s 46(6) Where the registration of a trade mark is revoked to any extent, the rights of the proprietor will (to the extent that it is revoked) be deemed to have ceased as from either:

(a) the date of the application for revocation; or
(b) if the Registrar or the court is satisfied that the grounds for revocation existed at an earlier date, from that earlier date.

A successful application for revocation, therefore, does not affect the validity of the original registration unless the grounds for revocation are found to have existed prior to (or at least at) the date of the application for revocation. This being so, a subsequent revocation is not necessarily a defence to a prior infringement.[18]

In the case of revocation pursuant to a counterclaim in infringement proceedings it would therefore be logical for the defendant/applicant for revocation to seek an order that the proprietor's rights should be deemed to have ceased at least immediately prior to the alleged acts of infringement. However, this must depend on the actual grounds on which revocation can be established and the facts giving rise to those grounds. For example, revocation for non-use would only, at best, date back to the end of the relevant five year period and therefore revocation on this ground would not, of itself, affect the proprietor's rights prior to or even during the five year period.

5.15 Transitional provisions, Schedule 3

Removal for non-use An application under s 26 of the 1938 Act for removal of a trade mark on the ground of non-use, which was

15 Rule 31(7).
16 Rule 31(7).
17 Section 46(5).
18 See, for example, *Second Sight Ltd v Novell UK Ltd* [1995] RPC 423.

pending as at 31 October 1994, will be dealt with under the old law and any consequent alteration will be made to the 1994 Register.[19]

Expungement for breach of a condition Under the 1938 Act the Registrar could require the proprietor to accept certain conditions relating to the registration of his mark. Pursuant to s 33 of the 1938 Act the registration of a trade mark could have been expunged or varied on the ground of any contravention of or any failure to observe such a condition. There is no equivalent provision in the 1994 Act, but proceedings which were pending under s 33 of the 1938 Act as at 31 October 1994 will continue to be dealt with under the old law and any consequent alteration will be made to the 1994 Register.[20]

Entries wrongly remaining in the 1938 Act Register An application under s 32 of the 1938 Act for the expungement or variation of an entry which was 'wrongly remaining' in the 1938 Register, and which application was pending as at 31 October 1994, is dealt with under the old law and any consequent alteration will be made to the 1994 Register.[1]

Invalidity

The first part of this chapter has been concerned with the grounds on which the registration of a trade mark can be revoked; they relate to matters which have occurred since registration. The second part of this chapter considers the grounds on which the original registration of the trade mark can be declared invalid.

5.16 Registration contrary to s 3: s 47(1) The registration of a trade mark may be declared invalid on the ground that the trade mark was registered in breach of s 3 or any of the provisions referred to in s 3.[2]

However, even where the trade mark has been registered in breach of s 3(1)(b), (c) or (d), it will still not be declared invalid if,

19 Schedule 3, para 17(1).
20 Schedule 3, para 3(1), notwithstanding that the condition will have ceased to have effect under the 1994 Act; Sch 3, para 3(1).
1 Schedule 3, para 18(1).
2 Section 47(1); see Chapter 2.

in consequence of the subsequent use which has been made of it, the trade mark has since registration acquired a distinctive character in relation to the goods or services for which it is registered.[3] The effect of this proviso was considered in the *Treat* case[4] where Jacob J confirmed that the onus in the first place rests on the party who wishes to attack the validity of the original registration. But, once it is shown that the registration was wrongly made, then it is for the proprietor to show that his mark is distinctive. As to the question of what is meant by the phrase 'distinctive character', Jacob J concluded that what the proviso really means is: 'has the mark acquired a sufficiently distinctive character that the mark has really become a trade mark'. In the case of common or apt descriptive or laudatory words, Jacob J thought that 'compelling evidence' would be needed to establish the necessary degree of distinctive character. Furthermore, he thought that mere evidence of extensive use is unlikely to be enough on its own and that it must be shown that the mark has become accepted by a 'substantial majority of persons as a trade mark' and that it 'is or is almost a household word'.[5]

5.17 Registration contrary to s 5: s 47(2) The registration of a trade mark may also be declared invalid on the ground that:

(a) there is an earlier trade mark in relation to which the conditions set out in s 5(1), (2) or (3) are satisfied;[6] or

(b) there is an earlier right in relation to which the condition set out in s 5(4) is satisfied,

unless the proprietor of the earlier trade mark or other earlier right (as the case may be) has consented to the registration.[7]

Honest concurrent use Although an applicant for registration may be able to rely on the honest concurrent use of his trade mark in order to overcome an objection to registration raised by the Registrar based on the relative grounds for refusal (ie those contained in s 5),[8] such honest concurrent use does not affect a third

3 Section 47(1) proviso; see also s 3(1) proviso.
4 *British Sugar plc v James Robertson and Sons Ltd* [1996] RPC 281 at 301-2.
5 [1996] RPC 281 at 306.
6 As to the availability of this ground for invalidity of registrations obtained under the 1938 Act, see paragraph 5.25.
7 Section 47(2).
8 See s 7 and Chapter 2, paragraph 2.28.

party application for a declaration of invalidity under s 47(2).[9] However, the fact of honest concurrent use may be relevant in the exercise of the Registrar's discretion.

5.18 Registrations obtained by agents and representatives, s 60(3) Where an application for the registration of a trade mark is made by an agent or a representative of the proprietor of the mark in a Convention country,[10] the proprietor may (if he does not oppose the agent's/representative's application) apply for a declaration of invalidity of the registration.[11] Alternatively, the proprietor can apply for rectification of the Register so as to substitute his name as the registered proprietor for that of his agent/representative.[12] This may be a more practical remedy if the proprietor uses or intends to use his trade mark in the United Kingdom.

In any event, the proprietor must make his application (whether for invalidity or rectification) within three years of becoming aware of the registration of his mark by his agent/representative.[13]

5.19 Effect of acquiescence, s 48(1)(a) In the event that the proprietor of an earlier trade mark[14] or other earlier right[15] has acquiesced for a continuous period of five years in the use of a registered trade mark in the United Kingdom, he will lose his entitlement to apply for a declaration of invalidity based on any conflict with his earlier trade mark or earlier right unless the registration was applied for in bad faith.[16]

Practice and procedure – invalidity

5.20 Application for declaration of invalidity, s 47(3) and r 31 An application for a declaration of invalidity can be made by 'any person',[17] and may be made either to the Registrar or to the

9 Section 7(4)(b); but see s 48(1)(a) and paragraph 5.19.
10 ie a country, other than the United Kingdom, which is a party to the Paris Convention; s 55(1) see Schedule 1 to this book.
11 Section 60(3)(a).
12 Section 60(3)(b); as to rectification see Chapter 3.
13 Section 60(6).
14 See s 6.
15 See s 5(4).
16 Section 48(1)(a).
17 See paragraph 4.03.

court. However, if proceedings concerning the trade mark in question are already pending in the court, then the application for the declaration must be made to the court. If the application is made to the Registrar, then he may at any stage of the proceedings refer the application to the court.[18]

In the case of an application for a declaration of invalidity on the ground that the original application for registration was made in bad faith,[19] the Registrar himself may apply directly to the court for a declaration of invalidity.[20]

An application for a declaration under s 47 which is made to the Registrar must be submitted together with a statement of the grounds on which the application is made.[1] The Registrar will then send a copy of the application together with the statement of grounds to the proprietor.[2] The proprietor then has three months from the date on which the Registrar sends the application to him within which to file a counter-statement, and the Registrar will send a copy of the counter-statement to the applicant seeking the declaration.[3]

Thereafter, the provisions of r 13 will apply to the proceedings in the same way as if the proceedings were in respect of an opposition to the registration of a trade mark.[4]

Intervention It should also be noted that any person (other than the registered proprietor) who claims to have an interest in the invalidity proceedings can apply to the Registrar for leave to intervene.[5] The intervener must state the nature of his interest and the Registrar may either refuse leave to intervene or grant leave upon appropriate terms or conditions as he thinks fit, which may include an undertaking as to costs.[6] As always, the parties are entitled to request a hearing in relation to the issue of whether leave to intervene should either be refused or granted.

If the application for leave to intervene is granted, the intervener will be treated as a party for the purposes of the application for the

18 Section 47(3).
19 ie in breach of s 3(6) and therefore pursuant to s 47(1).
20 Section 47(4).
1 Rule 31(1); use Form TM 26.
2 Rule 31(2).
3 Together with Form 8; r 31(3); this time period is not extensible.
4 Rule 31(4).
5 Using Form TM 27.
6 Rule 31(5).

declaration and the provisions of r 13 will apply to the intervener, subject only to any terms and conditions which the Registrar has imposed in respect of the intervention.[7]

Registrar's decision When the Registrar has made a decision in relation to the application for the declaration of invalidity and/or the application to intervene, he will give the applicant, the proprietor and the intervener (if any) written notice of his decision, including the reasons for it.[8] In the event that there is any appeal from the Registrar's decision, then the date when the notice of his decision is sent to the parties will be taken to be the date of his decision.[9]

5.21 Partial invalidity, s 47(5) Where grounds for invalidity exist in respect of only some of the goods or services for which the trade mark is registered, the trade mark will be declared invalid as regards only those specific goods or services.[10]

5.22 Effective date of invalidity, s 47(6) Where the registration of a trade mark is declared invalid to any extent, the registration will (to the extent that it is declared invalid) be deemed never to have been made, that is, the registration is void ab initio.[11] Although s 47(6) does not expressly state that the registration will be removed from the Register following a finding of invalidity, this would seem to be the logical conclusion.[12]

However, in order to prevent the unravelling of any dealings with the registered trade mark prior to the declaration of invalidity, the declaration will not affect any transactions which are 'past and closed', that is, transactions which are not still executory. Therefore, if the mark has been the subject of a prior assignment (or other transfer) the assignee cannot seek to recover any consideration or avoid the transaction. However, an ongoing licence, presumably, is not 'past or closed' and, therefore, the effect of a declaration of invalidity is that the proprietor/licensor may be in breach of any warranty as to title

7 Rule 31(6).
8 Rule 31(7).
9 Rule 31(7).
10 Section 46(5).
11 See also paragraph 5.25 in relation to the retrospective effect of s 47 on 1938 Act registrations.
12 Section 47(6). Jacob J refers to this issue in the *Treat* case, but expresses no final opinion other than to say that it would seem very odd to leave the mark on the Register, [1996] RPC 281 at 306.

and/or validity. Can a party previously held to have infringed the registration seek to recover any damages/costs which he has paid or to lift any injunction which may have been granted? It would seem that the answer to this question depends upon whether the earlier infringement proceedings can be characterised as a 'transaction'.

5.23 Deemed validity, s 72 There is no equivalent provision in the 1994 Act corresponding to s 13 of the 1938 Act which deemed the registration of a trade mark in Part A to be valid after seven years from the date of registration.[13] The 1994 Act does, however, state that in all legal proceedings relating to a registered trade mark (including proceedings for rectification) the registration of a person as the proprietor of a trade mark will be prima facie evidence of the validity of the original registration and of any subsequent assignment or other transmission of it.[14] The effect of this is to confirm that the party seeking the declaration of invalidity, including the Registrar himself, will have the onus of establishing that the registration is invalid on one or more of the grounds specified in s 47.

5.24 Certificate of validity, s 73 Where the validity of the registration of a trade mark is contested in any court proceedings and it is held that the trade mark is validly registered, the court can give a certificate of validity.[15] The practical/commercial value of a certificate of validity is that if in any subsequent proceedings the validity of the registration is again questioned and the proprietor again obtains a final order/judgment in his favour, then he is entitled to his costs as between solicitor and client (unless the court directs otherwise). Normally, the successful proprietor would only be entitled to his costs on a party and party basis which is a significantly lower level of assessment.[16] On a strict interpretation of this section it would appear that it does not matter that the validity of the registration in the subsequent proceedings is challenged on grounds that were not in issue in the earlier proceedings. This surely is not

13 Unless this registration was obtained by fraud or the trade mark came within s 11 of the 1938 Act.

14 Section 72.

15 Section 73; this provision mirrors s 47 of the 1938 Act, and any certificate of validity previously given under s 47 will continue to have effect as if it had been given under 1994 Act, s 73; Sch 3, para 21.

16 This does not extend to the costs of any appeal from the proceedings.

the intended purpose of this section, which is to deter unnecessary litigation, and, logically, subsequent proceedings which challenge validity on new grounds cannot be considered to be unnecessary.

5.25 Transitional provisions, Schedule 3 For the purposes of any proceedings under s 47 in relation to trade marks registered under the 1938 Act, the provisions of the 1994 Act are deemed to have been in force at all material times. Thus, a declaration of invalidity under s 47 in relation to registrations under the 1938 Act will be retrospective, that is, it will take effect as from the date of registration under the 1938 Act.[17]

However, although the 1994 Act is deemed to have been in force at all material times for the purposes of proceedings under s 47, it is not possible to challenge the validity of a registration obtained under the 1938 Act on the ground that the registration should have been refused pursuant to s 5(3) of the 1994 Act.[18] The ground for refusal of registration under s 5(3) applies in certain circumstances where there is a conflict between the mark applied for and an earlier trade mark even where the earlier trade mark in question is not protected for the goods or services in relation to which the applicant seeks the registration of his mark. This is a new ground for refusal which had no counterpart in the 1938 Act, and thus it would be inappropriate for it now to apply retrospectively.

17 Schedule 3, para 18(2).
18 Schedule 3, para 18(2).

6 Rights conferred by registration: infringement

6.01 Approach taken by the 1994 Act The registration of a trade mark under the 1994 Act confers a personal property right on the proprietor[1] which gives him exclusive rights in the trade mark, which are infringed by the unauthorised use of the trade mark in the United Kingdom.[2] However, the proprietor's exclusive rights are subject to:

(a) the qualified 'defence' provided for in s 10(6);
(b) the specific statutory limitations on the effect of registration set out in ss 11 and 12;
(c) the application of overriding competition law principles;
(d) the saving in respect of the continued use of a mark where such use did not amount to an infringement of an 'existing' registered mark under the 1938 Act; and
(e) any voluntary disclaimers or limitations relating to the registration.[3]

These limitations on the rights conferred by registration are, in effect, defences to an action for infringement and are dealt with, together with other defences which may be available, in Chapter 7.

Section 10 of the 1994 Act specifies the acts which constitute infringement of a registered trade mark and which are actionable by

1 Sections 2(1) and 22. In respect of co-proprietors, see s 23 and paragraph 6.11.
2 Section 9(1); see paragraph 6.03.
3 ie pursuant to s 13(1); disclaimers or limitations relating to registrations under the 1938 Act continue to apply: Sch 3, para 3(2).

the proprietor of the trade mark.[4] In addition to conferring rights on the proprietor, the 1994 Act also confers rights on licensees including, in certain circumstances, the right to commence proceedings in respect of acts which constitute infringement of the proprietor's registered trade mark.[5] Furthermore:

(a) s 56(2) of the 1994 Act confers a remedy on the proprietor of a 'well-known' mark[6] in circumstances which are analogous to infringement under s 10(2), notwithstanding that a well-known mark need not be registered; and
(b) s 60(4) confers a remedy on the proprietor of a mark in respect of certain acts of his agents or representatives which he has not authorised.

It is not necessary to consider either ss 56(2) or 60(4) in this chapter because neither involves establishing the infringement of a registered trade mark per se, and they are therefore dealt with in the context of remedies in Chapter 8.

Transitional provisions The 1938 Act continues to apply in relation to infringements committed before 31 October 1994, whereas ss 9–12 of the 1994 Act apply to infringements occurring after that date, including infringements of registrations obtained under the 1938 Act.[7]

6.02 Title by registration, s 2(1) The effect of s 2(1) is that the proprietor acquires his statutory rights by the registration of his trade mark. It is not a matter of the proprietor registering his existing rights.

6.03 Exclusive rights, s 9 The exclusive rights conferred by registration are not defined as such. Instead, the 1994 Act specifies the acts which, if done without the consent of the proprietor, will constitute an infringement of those exclusive rights. The proprietor's exclusive rights are, therefore, to do, and to authorise others to do,

4 Note that the 1994 Act confers no right of action for the infringement of an unregistered trade mark: s 2(2).
5 Sections 30 and 31 and see paragraph 6.10.
6 As to what constitutes a 'well-known' mark see Chapter 1.
7 Schedule 3, para 4(1); see *Road Tech Computer Systems Ltd v Unison Software (UK) Ltd* [1996] FSR 805 at 811 for a summary of the application of the transitional provisions in respect of both infringement actions and challenges to validity.

any act which if done by an unauthorised third party would amount to an infringement.[8]

The rights of the proprietor take effect from the 'date of registration', which is deemed to be the date of the filing of the application for registration.[9] However, infringement proceedings cannot be commenced before the date on which the trade mark is in fact registered.[10]

Only acts committed in the United Kingdom can amount to an infringement of the proprietor's exclusive rights.[11]

Use in a trade mark sense An issue arises as to whether the phrase 'by the use of the trade mark' in s 9(1) imports an overriding requirement that, for an infringement to incur, the defendant's use of a sign has to be 'in a trade mark sense'. The argument that this was an overriding requirement was conceded by counsel for the defendant in the *Wet Wet Wet* case[12] and this concession was accepted by Lord McCluskey. However, Jacob J in the *Treat* case[13] thought that such a concession was unnecessary and refused to limit infringement to situations where the defendant's use of a sign was use in a trade mark sense. His Lordship states:

> '. . . section 9(1) is really no more than a chatty introduction to the details set out in s 10, itself adding no more than that the acts concerned must be done without consent.'

Thus, a purely descriptive use is not excluded from falling within s 10, but such use is unlikely to constitute an infringement because of the defences available under s 11(2).

Acts of infringement The acts of infringement can be dealt with conveniently under three headings which correspond to the first three subsections of s 10. However, those subsections are substantially in the same terms as the first three subsections of s 5 which set out the relative grounds for refusal of an application. Thus, most of the issues which arise under s 10 have already been dealt with in Chapter 2 in the context of registrability, and readers should refer back to the relevant paragraphs of Chapter 2. Of course, the

8 See s 9(1).
9 Sections 9(3) and 40(3).
10 Section 9(3)(a).
11 Section 9(1).
12 *Bravado Merchandising Services Ltd v Mainstream Publishing (Edinburgh) Ltd* [1996] FSR 205.
13 *British Sugar plc v James Robertson and Sons Ltd* [1996] RPC 281 at 291–3.

terminology used in Chapter 2 is appropriate for describing the grounds on which an application for registration can be refused because of the existence of an earlier conflicting mark. Therefore, when reading Chapter 2 and applying the principles there stated on the subject of infringement:

(a) references to an 'earlier trade mark' need to be read as references to the plaintiff's registered trade mark;
(b) references to the 'applicant' need to be read as references to the defendant; and
(c) references to 'registrability' need to be read as references to infringement.

Furthermore, one important difference between s 5 and s 10 is that the onus of proof will be reversed, as to which see paragraph 6.07.

Finally, although the analysis of s 10 which follows is based on a rather clinical dissection of its individual elements, readers should bear in mind the realistic observation of Laddie J in the *Wagamama* case[14] where he said that 'whether there has been trade mark infringement is more a matter of feel than science'.

6.04 Identical marks/identical goods or services, s 10(1) It is an act of infringement for a person to use in the course of trade a sign:

(a) which is identical with a registered trade mark; and
(b) in relation to goods or services which are identical with the goods or services for which the trade mark is registered.[15]

Elements of infringement under s 10(1) A consideration of the elements required to establish infringement under s 10(1) involves looking at the following issues:

(A) the meaning of the phrase 'uses a sign';
(B) the meaning of the phrase 'in the course of trade';
(C) assessing whether the defendant's sign is identical to the proprietor's registered trade mark;
(D) the meaning of the phrase 'in relation to goods or services'; and
(E) whether the defendant's goods or services are identical to the goods or services for which the proprietor's trade mark is registered.

These issues are now discussed in turn.

14 *Wagamama Ltd v City Centre Restaurant plc* [1995] FSR 713 at 732.
15 Section 10(1).

(A) 'USES A SIGN', S 10(4) All acts of infringement involve the unauthorised use of a sign in the course of trade in the circumstances described in s 10(1), (2) or (3). For the purposes of s 10, a person is deemed to use a sign if, in particular, he:
(a) affixes the sign to goods or their packaging;
(b) offers or exposes goods for sale under the sign;
(c) puts goods on the market under the sign;
(d) stocks goods for the purpose of offering or exposing the goods for sale or to put them on the market under the sign;
(e) offers or supplies services under the sign;
(f) imports or exports goods under the sign; or
(g) uses the sign on business papers or in advertising.[16]
The use of the phrase 'in particular' in s 10(4) makes it clear that this list of examples of what constitutes use of a sign is not exhaustive. Indeed, the Directive uses the words 'inter alia' rather than 'in particular'.[17]

The concept of 'use' is clearly intended to be very broad. This is apparent from the fact that, in contrast to the 1938 Act which limited the concept of 'use of a mark' to the use of a printed or other visual representation of the mark,[18] the 1994 Act provides specifically that the use of the sign may be otherwise than by means of graphic representation.[19] This means that the oral or other non-visual use of a sign may constitute infringement if such use otherwise falls within s 10(1), (2) or (3). However, the use must be more than merely incidental or ephemeral, as to which see the comments below concerning the *Trebor Bassett* case[20] where the coincidental appearance of the proprietor's mark was held not to amount to affixing the sign to the goods in question, nor were the goods put on the market under the sign within the meaning of s 10(4)(a) and (b).

A further departure from the 1938 Act is that (as stated in paragraph 6.03 above) in order to constitute infringement it is not a requirement that the sign be used in what was referred to as 'a trade mark sense'. This issue has also been discussed in Chapter 1 in the context of the definition of a trade mark and the 1994 Act excludes, by implication, the notion of 'use in a trade mark sense' for the

16 Section 10(4).
17 Article 5(3).
18 See s 68(2) of the 1938 Act.
19 Section 103(2).
20 *Trebor Bassett Ltd v Football Association* [1997] FSR 211.

purpose of establishing infringement. This proposition derives from the fact that s 10 makes it clear that it is the use of a mere sign which constitutes infringement and Jacob J, in the *Treat* case, was clearly unwilling either to place any gloss or restriction on, or depart from, the language of s 10. Accordingly, s 10 merely requires the court to see whether the sign registered as a trade mark has been used in the course of trade and then to consider whether that use falls within one of the three defining subsections.[1]

The White Paper identified one of the objectives to be achieved by broadening the concept of use for infringement purposes as being to enable trade mark owners to prevent the use of their trade marks by third parties as business names.[2] The concern was that, under the 1938 Act, a retailer could adopt a trade mark as the name of his retail outlet selling goods for which the mark was registered and yet, by refraining from using the mark on or near the goods, avoid infringing the registration.[3] The broader definition of 'use' in ss 10(4) and 103(2) will now enable a proprietor of a registered trade mark to prevent another trader from using his trade mark as the name of a business dealing in goods or services which are identical with or similar to those for which the mark is registered.

(B) 'IN THE COURSE OF TRADE' The phrase 'in the course of trade' was used in both the definition of 'trade mark' and as one of the elements of infringement under the 1938 Act.[4] The phrase does not form part of the definition of 'trade mark' in the 1994 Act, but the phrase is adopted in s 10 which provides that the use of a sign can only constitute an infringement if the use is 'in the course of trade'.[5] It is logical that the use of a sign will not constitute an infringement if it is only being used in a domestic, social or other non-trading manner. Cases under the 1938 Act which considered the meaning of the phrase 'in the course of trade' are therefore still relevant in construing this phrase as it appears in the 1994 Act.[6]

1 Ibid at 291.
2 Paragraphs 3.26 and 3.27.
3 There was a degree of uncertainty under the 1938 Act as to whether such use would constitute an infringement: see, for example, the decision of Ploughman J in *Autodrome Trade Mark* [1969] RPC 564.
4 Sections 68(1) and 4(1) respectively.
5 'Trade' includes any business or profession and 'business' means 'a trade or profession': s 103(1).
6 For a discussion of the meaning of this phrase under the 1938 Act see Kerly, 12th edition, paragraph 2.14.

In the *One in a Million* case,[7] Sumption QC adopted a pragmatic and commercial approach to the interpretation of the phrase 'in the course of trade' and held that the use of a domain name for the purpose of making it more valuable and extracting money from the true trade mark owner constitutes use in the course of trade.

(C) COMPARING THE DEFENDANT'S SIGN WITH THE REGISTERED TRADE MARK The comparison for the purposes of s 10(1) will be governed by the same principles as those which are relevant to the comparison carried out pursuant to s 5(1) in order to determine whether there are grounds for refusing registration based on a prior conflicting identical mark. The relevant principles are discussed in Chapter 2.[8]

(D) THE MEANING OF THE PHRASE 'IN RELATION TO GOODS OR SERVICES' The requirement that the defendant must have used a sign 'in relation to goods or services' for which the proprietor's trade mark is registered is satisfied even though the defendant may not have used his sign upon the goods or services themselves and it will be sufficient if the sign has been used otherwise than by physically affixing or applying it to the goods or services. This conclusion is consistent with the interpretation of the same phrase which appeared in s 4 of the 1938 Act and is the only sensible interpretation given the wide definition of use in ss 10(4) and 103(2).

However, although there is no requirement that the sign must be physically affixed to the goods, and even though the use does not have to be 'in a trade mark sense', the phrase 'in relation to' does require the use to be other than merely incidental or ephemeral. In the *Trebor Bassett* case,[9] the proprietor's trade mark appeared on the defendant's cards because the reproduction of the photograph of an England football player on the cards necessarily incorporated the logo which appeared on the football shirts which the player was wearing. Rattee J held that it was not even arguable that such incidental use by the defendant could amount to using the plaintiff's trade mark 'in relation to' the cards.

The meaning of this phrase is also relevant to, and discussed in, the context of revocation proceedings for non-use in Chapter 5.[10]

7 *Marks & Spencer plc v One in a Million* Ch 1997 M No 5403, [1998] IPD 21016, (1997) Times, 2 December (Sumption QC).
8 See paragraph 2.18.
9 *Trebor Bassett Ltd v Football Association* [1997] FSR 211 at 216.
10 See paragraph 5.05.

(E) COMPARING THE RELEVANT GOODS OR SERVICES The final element of infringement under s 10(1) involves establishing that the defendant has used a sign in relation to goods or services which are 'identical' with those for which the proprietor's trade mark is registered. The question as to whether the goods or services are identical is a question of fact to be answered in the circumstances of each case and has been considered in the context of registrability.[11]

6.05 Identical marks/similar goods or services, s 10(2)(a); similar marks/identical goods or services; similar marks/similar goods or services, s 10(2)(b) If the defendant uses a sign which is either not identical with the proprietor's registered trade mark and/or if the sign is used in relation to goods or services which are not identical with those for which the trade mark is registered, the defendant's acts may nonetheless constitute an infringement pursuant to ss 10(2) or (3).

For the purposes of s 10(2), the proprietor's exclusive rights will be infringed by the unauthorised use in the course of trade of a sign which is either:

(a) identical with the proprietor's registered trade mark, provided that the sign is used in relation to goods or services which are similar to those covered by the registration; or

(b) similar to the proprietor's registered trade mark, provided that the sign is used in relation to goods or services which are identical with or similar to those covered by the registration; and

in either case, the proprietor can establish a likelihood of confusion on the part of the public.

This is a significant extension to the acts which constituted trade mark infringement under the 1938 Act, in that it was not an infringement under the 1938 Act to use a trade mark for goods or services not covered by the registration even if they were of the same description as the goods or services for which the mark was registered.[12]

Elements of infringement under s 10(2) A consideration of the elements required to establish infringement under s 10(2) involves looking at the following issues:

(A) the meaning of the phrase 'uses a sign';

11 See paragraph 2.18.
12 Such use may have amounted to an actionable passing off.

(B) the meaning of the phrase 'in the course of trade';
(C) whether the defendant's sign is either identical with or similar to the proprietor's registered trade mark;
(D) the meaning of the phrase 'in relation to goods or services';
(E) whether the defendant's goods or services are either identical with or similar to the goods or services for which the proprietor's trade mark is registered; and
(F) the likelihood of confusion, including the likelihood of association.

(A) 'USES A SIGN' See the discussion of the meaning of this phrase in paragraph 6.04 above.

(B) 'IN THE COURSE OF TRADE' See the discussion of the meaning of this phrase in paragraph 6.04 above.

(C) COMPARING THE DEFENDANT'S SIGN WITH THE REGISTERED TRADE MARK Section 10(2) may apply where the defendant's sign is either identical with or similar to the proprietor's registered trade mark. The question of whether a sign is identical with or similar to the registered trade mark is considered in Chapter 2 in relation to the relative grounds for refusing a registration as a result of a conflict with earlier trade mark rights.[13] The White Paper asserts that the test of similarity for the purposes of registrability and infringement is the same.[14]

(D) THE MEANING OF THE PHRASE 'IN RELATION TO GOODS OR SERVICES' See the discussion of the meaning of this phrase in paragraph 6.04 above.

(E) COMPARING THE RELEVANT GOODS OR SERVICES Section 10(2) may apply where the defendant's sign is used in relation to goods or services which are either identical with or similar to those for which the proprietor's trade mark is registered. The question of whether goods or services can be considered to be either identical with or similar to other goods or services is considered in Chapter 2 in the context of registrability.[15]

(F) ASSESSING THE LIKELIHOOD OF CONFUSION, INCLUDING THE LIKELIHOOD OF ASSOCIATION Once again this phrase has been considered in Chapter 2 in the context of registrability and, subject

13 See paragraphs 2.18 and 2.20.
14 Paragraph 3.16 of the White Paper.
15 See paragraphs 2.18 and 2.21.

to the comments in paragraph 6.07 in relation to the onus of proof, there is no reason to believe that the phrase will not be given the same meaning in s 10(2) as accorded to it in the context of s 5(2); indeed, the leading decision of the High Court in relation to the meaning of this phrase is that of Laddie J in the *Wagamama* case[16] which was an infringement case, and it is commented upon in Chapter 2 at paragraph 2.22.

6.06 Identical or similar marks/dissimilar goods or services, s 10(3) Even where a person uses a sign in the course of trade in relation to goods or services which are not similar to those for which a trade mark is registered, he may nonetheless infringe the registration of a trade mark by virtue of s 10(3). In order to establish infringement under this section the proprietor will have to establish:

(a) that the defendant has used a sign in the course of trade:
   (i) which is either identical with or similar to his registered trade mark; and
   (ii) that the defendant has used the sign in relation to goods or services which are *not* similar to those covered by his registration;
(b) that his trade mark has a 'reputation' in the United Kingdom;
(c) that the defendant has used the sign 'without due cause'; and
(d) that such use either:
   (i) takes unfair advantage of; or
   (ii) is detrimental to,

   the distinctive character or the repute of the proprietor's registered trade mark.[17]

Elements of infringement under s 10(3) A consideration of the elements required to establish infringement under s 10(3) involves looking at the following issues:

(A) the meaning of the phrase 'uses a sign';
(B) the meaning of the phrase 'in the course of trade';
(C) whether the defendant's sign is identical with or similar to the proprietor's registered trade mark;
(D) the meaning of the phrase 'in relation to goods or services';
(E) whether the registered trade mark has the necessary 'reputation' in the United Kingdom;

16 *Wagamama Ltd v City Centre Restaurants plc* [1995] FSR 713.
17 Section 10(3).

(F) the concept of what constitutes using a sign 'without due cause';
(G) the meaning of the phrases 'takes unfair advantage of' and 'detrimental to'; and
(H) the meaning of the phrase 'distinctive character or the repute' when used in relation to a trade mark.

Section 10(3) is substantially identical to s 5(3). The issues identified in (A) to (D) above have already been commented upon in this chapter in the context of s 10(1) and (2),[18] whereas the issues identified in (E) to (H) are considered in Chapter 2 in the context of registrability.[19]

6.07 Onus of proof The point has already been made that s 10 is substantially in the same terms as s 5. However, under s 5, if the Registrar is validly to refuse an application for registration, the onus is on him to establish all of the elements specified in s 5(1), (2) or (3) as the case may be.[20] In contrast, under s 10, the onus is on the plaintiff to establish the elements of infringement.

Secondary infringement

6.08 Parties to use of infringing material, s 10(5) Section 10(5) provides that a person who applies a registered trade mark to material which is intended to be used:
(a) for labelling or packaging goods;
(b) as a business paper; or
(c) for advertising goods or services,
is deemed to be a party to any use of the material which infringes the registered trade mark provided that, when he applied the mark to the material, he knew or had reason to believe that the application of the mark was not authorised by the proprietor or a licensee.

This is a new provision (for which there was no equivalent under the 1938 Act) and it extends the scope of infringement to persons who may be described as accessories or secondary infringers.

The fact that this subsection only applies to those who know or

18 See paragraphs 6.04 and 6.05 and Chapter 2.
19 See paragraph 2.23.
20 Or, in the context of an application under s 38, the onus will be on the opponent and, in the context of invalidity under s 47, the onus will be on the applicant seeking the declaration.

have reason to believe that the application of the mark was not duly authorised means that the innocent use of a trade mark for labelling, packaging etc, is not caught by this subsection. However, in relation to well-known marks (whether they be well known for the purposes of s 56(1) or otherwise), it may be more difficult for the person in question to deny actual or constructive knowledge that the application of the mark was not duly authorised by the proprietor in circumstances where he is not dealing with the proprietor or his ostensible agent or licensee. It would, therefore, be prudent for printers, publishers, packaging manufacturers and others potentially exposed to liability under this section to make reasonable enquiries and/or obtain suitable warranties and indemnities from those with whom they are dealing.

Comparative advertising

6.09 Identifying the proprietor's goods or services, s 10(6) The effect of s 10(6) is that any use of a registered trade mark which may otherwise constitute infringement under s 10 will not infringe a registration where:

(a) the use is for the purpose of identifying the goods or services as those of the proprietor or a licensee of the trade mark; and

(b) the use for that purpose is in accordance with honest practices in industrial or commercial matters.

The types of use likely to fall within this section would include the use of a registered trade mark for the purposes of comparative advertising and use in relation to the supply of spare parts or accessories. This subsection, including in particular the meaning of the phrase 'honest practices in industrial or commercial matters', is dealt with in the context of defences in Chapter 7, paragraph 7.08.

If such use of the mark is not in accordance with the relevant honest practices, then it will nonetheless be treated as infringing the registered trade mark provided that the use is:

(a) without due cause; and

(b) takes unfair advantage of, or is detrimental to, the distinctive character or repute of the trade mark.

The meaning of these phrases is considered in Chapter 2, paragraph 2.23 in the context of registrability.

Licensees

6.10 Rights of licensees The 1994 Act confers rights and remedies on licensees in relation to the infringement of registered trade marks.[1] The scope of these rights and remedies is considered in two chapters:

(a) Chapter 8, which deals specifically with the rights and remedies of licensees; and

(b) Chapter 10, which deals generally with the licensing of trade marks.

Co-proprietors

6.11 Rights of co-proprietors, s 23 Infringement proceedings may be brought by any co-proprietor of a registered trade mark. However, without the leave of the court, one co-proprietor may not proceed with an action unless each other co-proprietor is either joined as a plaintiff or added as a defendant, except in the case of an application for interlocutory relief. Where a co-proprietor is added as a defendant, he will not be liable for any costs in the action unless he takes part in the proceedings.[2]

Transitional provisions The provisions of s 23 apply as from 31 October 1994, including in relation to trade marks registered under the 1938 Act of which two or more persons were registered as joint proprietors.[3]

6.12 Infringement on the Internet The use of a sign on the Internet raises a number of interesting and difficult issues which have not yet been answered adequately by the courts. Although one could assert that the Internet should not be treated differently to any other media by which business is transacted, this approach would not take into account the problems created by the worldwide nature of the Internet and the territoriality of trade marks. The following

1 See ss 30 and 31.
2 Section 23(5); in the event that the co-proprietor has rights and obligations as a trustee or a personal representative, such rights and obligations are not affected: s 23(6).
3 Schedule 3, para 7.

issues give a flavour of the potential problems:

(1) Is a domain name a sign?

(2) Is the mere registration of a domain name sufficient to constitute 'use' of a sign? (This may depend on whether the domain name has been connected as such to the Internet and whether there is a real likelihood that the defendant will use the name.)

(3) Is the use of domain name for purely personal reasons, such as to send and receive personal e-mails, use in the 'course of trade'?

(4) Does the addition of a suffix, such as .com, result in the sign not being 'identical' to the trade mark which may be used as the main part or distinguishing element of the domain name? (If so, then the plaintiff in an infringement action will have to rely on s 10(2) or (3) – but this is unlikely to be the case given that the mark as registered is still being used in its entirety.)[4]

(5) In which jurisdiction has the sign been used in the course of trade? In theory, because the Internet is worldwide in its nature, the name will be accessible in numerous jurisdictions, but this does not necessarily mean that it has been used in the course of trade and in relation to goods or services within the jurisdiction for which the plaintiff's trade mark is registered (that is, the goods or services in question may clearly only be available for sale or supply in a jurisdiction not covered by a registration).

(6) In the context of mere domain name registrations, it may be difficult to determine in relation to which goods or services the name is being used (or is to be used), especially where the name is a mere e-mail address or bulletin board. Based on Jacob J's comments in *Avnet*[5] it is presumed that trade mark proprietors (as well as surfers on the Internet) will have to accept a certain risk of potential confusion caused by the fact that domain names are not necessarily linked to any particular goods or services and therefore a search for a particular trade mark on the Internet may result in numerous 'hits' on wrong web sites.

(7) What is the potential liability of an Internet Service Provider

4 See the comments of Jacob J in the *Treat* case [1996] RPC 281 at 293–4. See also *Avnet Inc v Isoact Ltd* [1998] FSR 16, Ch D where Jacob J dismissed the plaintiff's claim for infringement under s 10(1) because the defendant's services were not identical to the services covered by the plaintiff's registration; however, it would appear from the judgment that it was accepted (at least by his Lordship if not by the defendant) that the defendant's use of the domain name 'Avnet.co.uk' was identical to the plaintiff's registered trade mark AVNET.

5 Supra.

(ISP) as regards its customers' use of the domain name/web site? On the facts of the *Avnet* case,[6] Jacob J held that the ISP was merely making available a facility to its customers in the same way as a vendor of a plot of land merely makes available the space for whatever the purchaser may choose to build.

Harrods.com In the *Harrods.com* case,[7] these issues were all raised on the facts, but the defendants did not argue their case and the transcript of Lightman J's judgment is not available. Accordingly, although we know that his Lordship entered summary judgment against the defendants for trade mark infringement and passing off, the grounds on which he did so are unclear. Furthermore, the defendants were ordered to take all steps necessary to transfer the domain name to the plaintiff.

Use of disclaimers It may not be an infringement of a trade mark registered under the 1994 Act if the use of a sign on the Internet is in relation to goods or services which are not sold or supplied in the United Kingdom. Accordingly, the owner of a domain name/web site, which incorporates the use of a sign/trade mark which may infringe the registration of a trade mark registered under the 1994 Act, should (where it is the case) make it clear that the goods or services are not available in the United Kingdom. This should avoid infringement under the 1994 Act because the requirements of ss 9 and 10 are not satisfied in that the relevant use in the course of trade is not in the United Kingdom.

This may solve the potential problem under the 1994 Act, but it may not solve two other potential problems, namely:

(a) passing off, as to which see Chapter 18; and
(b) trade mark infringement and/or other liability in other jurisdictions arising out of the use of a name or mark on the Internet.

There is no fail safe advice as to the use of a sign or trade mark on the Internet so as to avoid all risk of infringing a third party's rights either in the United Kingdom or in other jurisdictions (which may not provide for the registration of trade marks under a system analogous to that in the United Kingdom). However, by expressly restricting the geographic availability of the goods or services sold or supplied under the sign/trade mark to customers in countries where

6 Supra.
7 *Harrods Ltd v UK Network Services Ltd* unreported (Lightman J).

the domain name/web site owner has either secured trade mark protection or has conducted appropriate clearance searches, the risk of infringement/liability is at least minimised. Strictly speaking, advice needs to be sought in relation to each relevant jurisdiction because of the territorial nature of trade marks.

Trade mark notices Another practical matter for proprietors to consider is the use of an Internet trade mark notice which provides details of all jurisdictions in which trade mark rights are claimed (whether registered or unregistered) and the goods or services sold or supplied under or by reference to those trade marks. For owners of large trade mark portfolios throughout the world this may be a time-consuming exercise unless the use of a hypertext facility is incorporated so that all trade mark rights, as well as reservations of use, can be claimed and disclaimed as required in the appropriate jurisdictions.

Threats of infringement proceedings

6.13 Groundless threats, s 21 The 1994 Act introduced for the first time into trade mark law in the United Kingdom a new cause of action in respect of groundless threats of registered trade mark infringement proceedings.[8] Accordingly, proprietors and licensees should first consider the implications of threatening someone with infringement proceedings. The elements of this cause of action and the relief available are dealt with in Chapter 9.

8 Section 21.

7 Limits on effect of registration: defences

7.01 Approach taken by the 1994 Act The proprietor's exclusive rights conferred by registration and the acts amounting to an infringement of these rights have been considered in Chapter 6. However, it is necessary to have regard to the defences which may be available before forming a final view as to whether the proprietor's rights have been infringed. It is these defences which are the subject of this chapter.

The 1994 Act does not contain any provisions which are described as defences as such. There are, however, a number of sections which, in effect, provide the basis of a defence. They can broadly be described as:

(a) the statutory limitations on the effect of registration contained in s 11;

(b) the saving in s 10(6) for the use of a registered trade mark for the purpose of identifying goods or services as those of the proprietor;

(c) statutory acquiescence, s 48;

(d) the exhaustion of rights, s 12;

(e) voluntary disclaimers and limitations, s 13; and

(f) the rights conferred on co-proprietors, s 23.

These defences all assume that an act of infringement has otherwise occurred. It will, of course, always be open to the defendant to base his defence on an assertion that one or more of the elements necessary to constitute an infringement for the purposes of s 10 is missing from the plaintiff's case, or to establish that the plaintiff's registered trade mark is liable to be declared invalid or revoked with effect from a date earlier than the alleged act of infringement.

Note that honest concurrent use of one's trade mark is not a defence per se. It is, however, relevant to the question of registrability and if a registration is secured by establishing honest concurrent use in accordance with s 7, then that registration will afford a defence under s 11(1). Furthermore, use by the defendant of his mark prior to the date of application of the plaintiff's registration may, in certain circumstances, provide a limited defence under s 11(3).[1]

Finally, the defendant may be able to establish that the exercise by the plaintiff of his exclusive statutory rights is contrary to the principles of EC and/or UK competition laws. This issue is considered in some detail in paragraphs 7.13 and 7.14.

Transitional provisions The 1938 Act will continue to apply in relation to infringements committed before 31 October 1994. The defences referred to above only apply, therefore, to infringements occurring after that date, including infringements of registrations obtained under the 1938 Act.[2]

In particular, it is not an infringement of either:

(a) a registration obtained under the 1938 Act; or
(b) a trade mark registered under the 1994 Act of which the distinctive elements are substantially the same as those of a trade mark registered under the 1938 Act and which is registered for the same goods or services,

to continue after 31 October 1994 any use of a mark which did not amount to infringement under the old law.[3]

Section 11 defences

Section 11 contains three subsections, each of which specifies quite different circumstances in which a registered trade mark is deemed not to be infringed. It is, therefore, an absolute defence to an allegation of infringement if the defendant's acts or conduct fall within one or more of these subsections. These three subsections are the subject of paragraphs 7.02 to 7.06.

1 As to which, see paragraph 7.07.
2 Schedule 3, para 4(1).
3 Schedule 3, para 4(2).

7.02 Use of a registered trade mark, s 11(1) A registered trade mark cannot be infringed by the use of another validly registered trade mark in relation to the goods or services for which the latter is registered.[4] Accordingly, both proprietors will have concurrent rights in the use of their respective trade marks notwithstanding that this may create some confusion. This provision, in effect, is substantially identical to the corresponding provision in the 1938 Act.[5]

7.03 Descriptive use, s 11(2) Section 11(2) specifies three categories of use which might otherwise constitute infringement. In broad terms they can be summarised as follows:

(a) the use of one's own name or address;
(b) the use of descriptive indications; and
(c) the use of a trade mark to indicate the intended purpose of a product or service.

Note that in each case such use may still constitute an infringement if the use 'is not in accordance with honest practices in industrial or commercial matters'. This phrase also appears in s 10(6) which provides a defence where a trade mark is used for the purpose of identifying goods or services as those of the proprietor or a licensee, and the meaning of the phrase is considered in detail in the context of that defence.[6] Apart from this phrase, specific problems of interpretation will also be raised in the context of each of the defences provided for in s 11(2).

7.04 Use of one's own name or address s 11(2)(a) A registered trade mark is not infringed by someone using their own name or address provided that the use of the name or address is in accordance with honest practices in industrial or commercial matters.[7] This provision substantially mirrors s 8(a) of the 1938 Act which required such use to be bona fide. In the *Mercury* case[8] Laddie J considered the scope of s 8(a) in considerable detail and concluded that the defence

4 Section 11(1); *Second Sight Ltd v Novell UK Ltd* [1995] RPC 423 confirms that it is registration which affords the defence and nothing before or less than registration.
5 1938 Act, s 4(4).
6 See paragraph 7.08.
7 Section 11(2)(a).
8 *Mercury Communications Ltd v Mercury Interactive (UK) Ltd* [1995] FSR 850; see also articles by Messrs Mills and Taylor [1995] 10 EIPR 503; Mr Watts and Ms Bloom in Trademark World, September 1995, p 10; and Ms Kur [1996] 4 EIPR 198.

is available where the defendant can prove that the name which it uses is the usual name by which it or its products are known in the market place, and a company can choose to omit the words 'Limited' or 'plc' from the end of its corporate title and still rely on the defence.

In the *NAD* case,[9] Ferris J stated that the words 'own name' must be the full corporate name, provided only that the omission of 'Limited' is immaterial. His judgment went on to hold that the 'own name' defence had not been established because the use of the NAD mark was not bona fide as required by s 8(a) of the 1938 Act. The defendant's lack of good faith was evidenced by the fact that after being made aware of the plaintiff's complaint, the defendant had changed the mark to make it even more like the plaintiff's mark. Although good faith is not expressly a requirement in s 11(2), as already stated, the use must be in accordance with honest practices and therefore similar considerations should apply. Thus, use will only be protected under s 11(2) if the name is 'innocently applied to the goods or used in relation to the goods without intention to mislead or confuse others or to attract another trader's goodwill'.[10]

The reference to 'honest practices in industrial or commercial matters' in the context of using one's own name or address further highlights one of the problems associated with interpreting and applying this phrase: what happens if there is no practice (honest or otherwise) of using one's own name or address in the defendant's relevant line of business? Presumably, the test will have to be applied by reference to general commercial practices.

7.05 Use of descriptive indications, s 11(2)(b) A registered trade mark is not infringed by someone using an 'indication' concerning any characteristic of the goods or services in question, including an indication of the kind, quality, quantity, intended purpose, value, geographical origin, or the time of production of the goods or the rendering of the services. Once again, however, the use of the indication must be in accordance with honest practices in industrial or commercial matters.[11]

9 *NAD Electronics Inc v NAD Computer Systems Ltd* [1997] FSR 380.

10 *George Ballantine & Sons Ltd v Ballantyne Steward & Co Ltd* [1959] RPC 47; see also *Philips Electronics NV v Remington Consumer Products* (22 December 1997, unreported) (Jacob J).

11 Section 11(2)(b); however, note the protection separately conferred on geographical indications and designations of origin by the Regulation of 14 July 1992, EEC No 2081/92.

In the *Wet Wet Wet* case,[12] Lord McCluskey held that the use by the defendant of the words 'Wet Wet Wet' in its book title 'A Sweet Little Mystery – Wet Wet Wet – the Inside Story' properly fell within the terms of s 11(2)(b). What the defendant was doing was using the plaintiff's registered trade mark as an 'indication' concerning the main characteristic of the book and so as to indicate to anyone who sees the book that it concerns the well-known musical group. His Lordship observed that:

> 'it would be a bizarre result of trade marks legislation, the primary purpose of which is "to guarantee the trade mark as an indication of origin", if it could be used to prevent publishers from using the protected name in the title of a book about the company or product.'

In the *Treat* case,[13] Jacob J considered the application of s 11(2), and the following propositions can be derived from his judgment:

(1) One must look at the whole context of the defendant's use because one cannot tell whether the use is descriptive (and hence non-infringing) from the use of the sign alone.

(2) One must distinguish between the use of the mark by way of an honest comparison and other uses. His Lordship thought that there is no reason why s 11(2) does not permit a fair and honest comparison between the defendant's goods and those of the trade mark owner (and it was acknowledged that this means that s 11(2) may overlap with s 10(6)).

(3) If a mark is used by the defendant as a trade mark for his own goods, then the trade mark is not being used as a description, thus s 11(2) does not cover the case where a descriptive word is used in a trade mark sense for the defendant's goods. (In the case in question the word 'treat' was not being used by the defendant in a trade mark sense, quite the opposite; his Lordship thought the word 'treat' would not be taken to be a badge of origin and therefore the defendant was entitled to rely on s 11(2).)

In the *European* newspaper case,[14] Rattee J came to the same conclusion via a slightly different route: he thought that for the defendant to use a sign similar to a registered trade mark, where the

12 *Bravado Merchandising Services Ltd v Mainstream Publishing (Edinburgh) Ltd* [1996] FSR 205 at 216.
13 [1996] RPC 281 at 297-300.
14 *European Ltd v Economist Newspaper Ltd* [1996] FSR 431 at 446.

relevant use by the defendant of the sign is as a trade mark for his own goods, would be inconsistent with honest commercial practices and hence the proviso to s 11(2) would not be satisfied.

7.06 Use of a trade mark to indicate intended purpose: accessories and spare parts, s 11(2)(c) A registered trade mark is not infringed by the use of that trade mark where its use is necessary to indicate the intended purpose of a product or service.

The object of this provision clearly is to enable traders in spare parts or accessories to use a registered trade mark so as to identify the goods or services for which their spare parts or accessories are to be used, although the section is not specifically limited to use in respect of accessories and spare parts.

This defence is subject to the defendant being able to establish that:

(a) his use of the registered trade mark is necessary for the purpose of indicating the intended purpose of his products or services; and
(b) such use is in accordance with honest practices in industrial or commercial matters.

By analogy with Jacob J's comments in *Philips v Remington* (in relation to the meaning of the word 'necessary' in s 3(2)(b)), it is to be assumed that a defendant will be able to rely on this defence even though, strictly speaking, there may be an alternative method of indicating the purpose of his products or services other than using the plaintiff's trade mark. The test will be whether 'in substance' the defendant has no real, practical alternative other than to use the trade mark in question.

However, a trader in spare parts or accessories may not have to rely upon s 11(2)(c). Section 11(2)(b) could instead be relied upon in so far as it also provides a defence in respect of the use of 'indications' concerning the intended purpose of goods or services. So also could s 10(6) be relied upon in that the use contemplated by s 11(2)(c) may also be for the purpose of identifying the goods or services as those of the proprietor of the mark in question.

Finally, and in any event, the defendant will have to establish that his use of the proprietor's trade mark is in accordance with honest practices in industrial or commercial matters. Apart from the issues discussed in paragraph 7.08, the requirement that the use of someone else's registered trade mark be in accordance with honest practices will involve considering the issue of whether such use can ever be honest if, in the circumstances of the case, it may involve diluting or devaluing the reputation or goodwill attaching to the registered trade mark, which may be the inevitable consequence if the spare parts or accessories are of inferior quality.

7.07 Use of an earlier right, s 11(3) The use in the course of trade of an earlier right will not infringe a registered trade mark in certain circumstances.[15] For this purpose, an 'earlier right' means either:

(a) an unregistered trade mark; or
(b) any other sign,

which has been continuously used[16] in relation to goods or services where such use commenced prior to whichever is the earlier of:

(a) the use of the registered trade mark; or
(b) the registration of that registered trade mark.

In essence, this means that someone can continue to use their unregistered trade mark or other sign where it has been used continuously since before both the use and registration of the registered trade mark without infringing that registration. However, the right to continue the use of the earlier right without infringing is restricted to use within the particular locality where the earlier right would be protected by virtue of any rule of law: in particular, the law of passing off.[17] The word 'locality' could therefore extend to the whole of the United Kingdom or any part of it.

The general principle which is reflected in ss 7 and 11(3) is that unregistered trade marks should neither be denied registration nor their use be prevented merely because they are similar to or even identical with a subsequently registered trade mark. However, it can be argued that s 11(3) is too strict, in that in order to constitute a defence it must be shown that the defendant's earlier right is protected by virtue of a 'rule of law' (the 1994 Act specifically cites the law of passing off as an example). This is more strict than either s 7 of the 1994 Act or s 7 of the 1938 Act: under s 7 of the 1994 Act, the only requirement, in order for the applicant to secure registration, is that his use must have been 'honest and concurrent';

15 Section 11(3).
16 Such use may either have been by the person claiming the right or his predecessor in title; s 11(3).
17 Section 11(3).

under s 7 of the 1938 Act, the defence based on the prior use of an unregistered trade mark was established merely by showing actual continuous use. Section 11(3) requires the defendant to establish that the prior use of his trade mark has been of such a nature and to such an extent that he would be able to protect his trade mark by means of a passing-off action or under any other rule of law. This requirement will mean that the defendant may have to adduce evidence, for example, of the reputation/goodwill that he would have to prove in a passing-off action. The expansive drafting of s 11(3), although based on Article 6(2) of the Directive, goes beyond that which could have been adopted to comply with the minimum required by the Article and it would seem that, in so limiting this defence, the 1994 Act has, to some extent, resulted in the United Kingdom becoming a 'first to register' rather than a 'first to use' system. It is, therefore, prudent to register one's mark rather than having to rely upon prior use, which may not always be sufficient to avoid infringement of a later registered trade mark.

Comparative advertising and spare parts

7.08 Use for the purpose of identifying the proprietor's goods or services, s 10(6) The use of a registered trade mark, even though the use may otherwise constitute infringement under s 10, will not infringe the registration where the use is for the purpose of identifying the goods or services as those of the proprietor (or a licensee) of the trade mark.

The proviso However, the use of another's trade mark for this purpose will nonetheless infringe the registration if the use:

(a) is otherwise than in accordance with honest practices in industrial or commercial matters; and
(b) (i) without due cause takes unfair advantage of; or
(ii) without due cause is detrimental to,
the distinctive character or repute of the trade mark.

The types of use likely to fall within s 10(6) would include the use of a registered trade mark for the purposes of comparative advertising and use in relation to the supply of spare parts or accessories. However, the proviso will disentitle a defendant from relying on this defence if his use is not in accordance with honest practices and he either derives an unfair benefit or causes detriment to the character or repute of the proprietor's trade mark. For example, he may gain an 'unfair advantage' if he is trading on the back of the reputation of the proprietor's trade mark; on the other hand, his use is likely to be 'detrimental to' the proprietor's trade mark if his goods or services are of an inferior quality and/or if the value of the proprietor's trade mark as a chose in action is in some way diminished (eg the value of the trade mark as intellectual property which is capable of being licensed).

Section 10(6) reflects government and industry feeling that comparative advertising is generally considered by the public to be an acceptable method by which to market one's product. As Lord Strathclyde stated during the debate on the Trade Marks Bill in 1994:

> 'The Government has been persuaded that there is no harm in comparative advertising . . . provided that it makes fair use of a registered mark for the purpose of informing the public. As foreshadowed in the White Paper the Bill seeks to chart a middle course; allowing comparative advertising but providing safeguards for the owner of the registered trade mark.'[18]

Despite the clear aims of those involved, the drafting of s 10(6) has left much open to interpretation. The first judicial consideration of the issues by Laddie J in the *Barclays* case[19] (in which he discussed s 10(6) in great depth) was therefore greatly welcomed.

The Barclays case Laddie J describes the first half of s 10(6) as 'home grown' and indeed it is, having no direct basis in either the Directive, the Regulation or other EC law. Both halves of the proviso, however, can be traced back to the Directive and have been adopted in, inter alia, s 11(2) and s 10(3) of the 1994 Act respectively. The Directive makes no mention of comparative advertising as such and it is therefore unclear how the two elements of the proviso, and more importantly the section as a whole, should be interpreted. Laddie J describes the drafting of the provision as 'a mess' but recognises that its meaning is clear in so far as the first half of the subsection allows comparative advertising. It is the meaning of the second half (the proviso) which is less clear. In this regard he comes to the conclusion that, although the wording of the proviso

18 Hansard, 18 January 1994, House of Lords Public Bill Committee, col 42.
19 *Barclays Bank plc v RBS Advanta* [1996] RPC 307.

does also appear (in part) in ss 11(2) and 10(3), one has to consider s 10(6) alone without deciding whether precisely the same construction of the wording used is appropriate also for the other subsections.

Briefly, the facts of the *Barclays* case were that RBS (the defendant) intended to market a new credit card and sent out 200,000 pilot samples of advertising literature. After complaints from Barclays, the literature was amended and RBS intended to use the amended literature in support of the launch of the new credit card. The amended literature comprised a leaflet setting out 15 points stating why the RBS credit card was a better credit card all round, accompanied by a brochure incorporating a comparative table including express references to BARCLAYCARD (the trade mark owned by the plaintiff). Barclays applied for an interlocutory injunction to prevent the launch of RBS's credit card and, in dismissing Barclays' claims, Laddie J held as follows:

1 The primary objective of s 10(6) is to allow comparative advertising as long as the use of a competitor's mark is 'honest'. Thus, the proviso should not be construed in a way which would effectively prohibit all comparative advertising.

2 The onus is on the plaintiff to show that the facts as indicated in the proviso exist and there will be no infringement unless the use of the registered mark is not in accordance with honest practices in industrial or commercial matters. To this end the test in s 10(6) is objective. In other words, if the use is considered honest by members of a reasonable audience, then it will not infringe. Honesty has to be gauged against what is reasonably to be expected by the relevant public of advertisements for the goods or services in issue. In applying this test the following must be taken into account:

   (a) one should ignore the fact that the advertising pokes fun at the proprietor's goods or services and emphasises the benefits of the defendant's, as this is only to be expected in comparative advertising; and

   (b) it is not to be expected that one trader will point out all the advantages of its competitor's business and failing to do so will not constitute dishonesty. Therefore, merely trade puffery, even if uncomfortable to the registered proprietor, does not bring the advertising within the scope of trade mark infringement. It was observed that the general public do recognise much advertising as hyperbole, although no doubt the nature of the products or services will affect the degree of hyperbole which is acceptable. Laddie J very much wanted to avoid this section being interpreted so as to impose on the courts an obligation to enforce, through the back door of trade mark legislation, a more puritanical standard on the advertising industry.

3 On the other hand, if a reasonable reader believes that the advertisement is not honest, for example because it is 'significantly misleading', then the protection from trade mark infringement is removed. Unfortunately, Laddie J did not elaborate on the meaning of this phrase. Each case will, therefore, have to be judged on its own merits.

4 In interpreting the words 'industrial and commercial matters', Laddie J rejected the suggestion that the courts should look at statutory or industry agreed codes of conduct in determining the relevant standard. He felt that if such codes were to be consulted it would follow that in some trades, where there was very detailed and restrictive codes of practice, it would be easier to breach the code and therefore harder to avoid infringement. By rejecting the statutory and industry codes, Laddie J has chosen to discount (although not necessarily ignore) the only real tools that may be available to a company in determining whether its comparative advertisement will be regarded as being 'honest'. However, in practice, the court's determination of 'honest practices' and the existing definitions in any codes of practice are likely to run in parallel. Accordingly, the only practical advice in these situations is that advertisers should continue to adhere to industry codes, as such adherence can only be in their favour if and when it comes to determining objectively what would be considered honest by members of a reasonable audience.

5 In respect of the final words of the proviso, Laddie J felt that they really added nothing of significance to the first part. An advertisement which makes use of a registered mark in a way which is not honest will almost always take unfair advantage of it and vice versa. Therefore, at most, he felt that these final words merely emphasised that the use of the mark must take advantage of it or be detrimental to it. In other words, the use must either give some advantage to the defendant or inflict

some harm on the character or repute of the registered mark which is above the level of de minimis. Laddie J thereby introduced an extremely low threshold of advantage/harm to be caused by the use of the mark.

6 On the facts, the leaflet and tables could not be treated as separate and the illegitimate use of a registered trade mark would not necessarily be saved by putting the registered trade mark on one document and the dishonest statements on another. If they were intended or likely to be read together, then the advertisement should be read as a whole. Laddie J felt that it was most unlikely that any reasonable reader would take the view that the advertisement was not honest and, as such, refused Barclays' application for an interlocutory injunction.

7 Finally, it is worth noting Laddie J's concluding remarks that the case was fought only on s 10(6) and not by reference to s 11(2)(b). As it happens, the defendant was successful on s 10(6) but the potential overlap with s 11 should also be borne in mind by defendants and their advisers.[20]

Vodafone case The *Barclays* case was followed later in 1996 by the decision of Jacob J in *Vodafone*.[1] Unlike the *Barclays* case, this action primarily involved the issue of malicious falsehood (otherwise known as trade libel). This case centred around the advertising slogan 'On average Orange users save £20 every month', which was expressly stated to be in comparison with Vodafone's or Cellnet's 'equivalent tariffs'. Vodafone sued for malicious falsehood and infringement of its registered trade mark VODAFONE. To succeed in a claim for malicious falsehood Vodafone had to show: (1) that the words complained of were false, (2) that they were published maliciously, and (3) that they were calculated to cause continuing damage. In terms of establishing malice, Vodafone further had to demonstrate that either Orange knew that its slogan was false or was reckless as to whether or not it was in fact false.

In determining this case, Jacob J held that the court had to decide upon a single, natural and ordinary meaning of the words used, taking into account the fact that the public expect a certain amount of hyperbole in advertising. He felt that the public expected

20 Jacob J made the same comment in the *Treat* case [1996] RPC 281 at 299.
1 *Vodafone Group Plc v Orange Personal Communications Services Ltd* [1997] FSR 34.

advertisers to highlight the good points of a product and ignore the rest. The test is whether a reasonable man would take the claim seriously and, to this end, the more precise the claim the more likely it is to be so taken. (A gloss was put on this 'reasonable man' test by Neuberger J in the *Macmillan Magazines* case[2] where he cited with approval the *Barclays* and *Vodafone* decisions. On the facts of the case he observed that, while an objective test of the reasonable man is usually appropriate, because the advertisement was contained in a specialist magazine targeted at a specialist group of people, there must be an argument for saying that one should judge the advertisement by the effect it would have on such readers and not by the effect which it would have on the general public.)

Returning to the *Vodafone* case, in respect of trade mark infringement, Jacob J followed the decision of Laddie J in the *Barclays* case. He stated that a comparative advertisement used a trade mark 'otherwise than in accordance with honest practices' if it was objectively misleading to a substantial proportion of the reasonable audience. He also said that, in most cases, the second half of the proviso to s 10(6) would add nothing of significance to the first half. The defendant's argument that even if the slogan was misleading it nonetheless did not take advantage of the distinctive character of the mark was not accepted.

In respect of trade libel, Vodafone also failed to establish any convincing evidence of malice on the part of Orange and the slogan was not found to be false. Thus the trade libel claim also failed, which is unsurprising given that the plaintiff in such an action also faces the 'freedom of speech' argument; indeed, the freedom of speech argument was relied upon by Neuberger J in the *Macmillan Magazines* case (referred to above) in refusing an interlocutory injunction for trade mark infringement.

It has been suggested that as comparative advertising will potentially increase in the more permissive era of the 1994 Act, malicious falsehood/trade libel may gain a new lease of life in an attempt to protect brand reputation. However, if the use is in accordance with honest practices (and hence not a trade mark infringement), it would be illogical if a defendant was then found liable in respect of malicious falsehood, and it may be that the courts

2 *Macmillan Magazines Ltd v RCN Publishing Co Ltd* [1997] IPD 20089 (Neuberger J).

will be unwilling to impose standards on the advertising industry by way of trade libel if there is no trade mark infringement.

The *Barclays* and *Vodafone* cases have since been considered and followed in the *BT/AT&T* case,[3] where Mr Crystal QC also made the point that a minute textual examination of an advertisement is not something on which the reasonable reader would embark and therefore neither should the court. (Readers may also wish to refer to the facts of the *Kimberly-Clark* case[4] where counsel for the plaintiff conceded that there was a sufficiently arguable defence under s 10(6) that the infringement claim was not pursued and therefore not considered at the trial.)

Comparative Advertising Directive The Comparative Advertising Directive amends the 1984 Misleading Advertising Directive[5] by including provisions relating to comparative advertising. In essence, the Comparative Advertising Directive, when implemented in the United Kingdom, will permit comparative advertising provided that the following conditions are met:

(a) the comparison is not misleading (as defined);
(b) the comparison compares goods or services meeting the same needs or intended for the same purpose;
(c) the comparison objectively compares one or more material, relevant, verifiable and representative features of those goods and services, which may include price;
(d) the comparison does not create confusion in the market place between the advertiser and a competitor or between the advertiser's trade marks, trade names, other distinguishing marks, goods or services and those of a competitor;
(e) the comparison does not discredit or denigrate the trade marks, trade names, other distinguishing marks, goods, services, activities, or circumstances of a competitor;
(f) for products with designation of origin, the comparison relates in each case to products with the same designation;

3 *British Telecommunications plc v AT & T Communications (UK) Ltd* (18 December 1996, unreported) (M Crystal QC, Deputy Judge); see the note of this decision in [1997] 5 EIPR D-134.

4 *Kimberly-Clark Ltd v Fort Sterling Ltd* [1997] FSR 877 (Laddie J); see IPD 20066.

5 Directive 97/55/EC of 6 October 1997 amending Directive 84/450/EEC concerning misleading advertising so as to include comparative advertising, published in the Official Journal on 23 October 1997 (L290/18).

(g) the comparison does not take unfair advantage of the reputation of a trade mark, trade name or other distinguishing marks of a competitor or of the designation of origin of competing products; and
(h) the comparison does not present goods or services as imitations or replicas of goods or services bearing a protected trade mark or trade name.[6]

The definition of 'comparative advertising' is very broad and will include 'any advertising which explicitly or by implication identifies a competitor or goods or services offered by a competitor'. Therefore, the advertisement does not have to be a 'comparative' advertisement as such, nor does it have to incorporate the use of a competitor's trade mark, but Article 3a only grants permission in so far as the 'comparison is concerned'. That is, not all 'comparative advertising' (as defined in Article 2) is necessarily brought within the scope of the permission granted by Article 3a.

Comparison with s 10(6) It will be interesting to see whether legislation will be required so as to amend s 10(6) of the 1994 Act in order to comply with the Comparative Advertising Directive. Clearly, Article 3a specifically identifies those requirements which must be met in order for the advertisement to come within the saving provisions, whereas s 10(6) simply refers to 'honest practices in industrial or commercial matters'. It is arguable that in order for an advertisement to fall within that broad concept of 'honest practices' it would have to meet the specific conditions of Article 3a. However, as we have seen from *Barclays* and *Vodafone*, the clear attitude of the UK courts (to date) has been to give effect to the intention of s 10(6), that is, to permit comparative advertising and not to construe the proviso (ie relating to 'honest practices') so as to frustrate this intention. Accordingly, for example, trade puffery has been held not to fall outside the concept of an 'honest practice'. But such 'puffery' may not comply with, in particular, the condition set out in Article 3a1(c) which requires the advertisement to compare objectively (inter alia) 'verifiable' features of the goods or services in question. Thus, statements such as 'probably the best lager in the world' and 'eight out of ten cats prefer Whiskers' may not comply with this requirement – although they may perhaps fall within the definition of 'comparative advertising' as, arguably, they do not sufficiently

6 Article 3a.

identify (expressly or by implication) either the competitor or the competitor's goods or services. Likewise, a statement that 'we try harder' does not identify Avis's competitors as such, but does the statement 'we try harder than the number one car rental company' sufficiently identify Hertz? If so, then Avis may be required to show that this statement is verifiable.

Implementation The United Kingdom, along with all other member states, is required to bring into force laws necessary to comply with the Comparative Advertising Directive no later than 23 April 2000 (being 30 months after the publication of the Comparative Advertising Directive in the Official Journal).

Further reading The articles referred to in the footnote below may be of interest to readers.[7]

Acquiescence

7.09 Statutory acquiescence, s 48 Statutory acquiescence applies in the situation where the proprietor of either an earlier trade mark[8] or earlier right[9] has acquiesced for a continuous period of five years in the use of a later registered trade mark in the United Kingdom. However, the proprietor will only be deemed to have acquiesced if he was aware of that use.

In these circumstances the proprietor of the earlier trade mark/earlier right will not be entitled to oppose the use of the later registered trade mark in relation to the goods or services for which it has been used[10] (except where the later registered mark was applied for in bad faith).

This section also operates as a defence for the proprietor of the earlier trade mark or earlier right because the proprietor of the later registered trade mark will not, by virtue of the earlier proprietor's acquiescence, be entitled to oppose either:

(a) the use of the earlier trade mark; or

7 Quinn [1996] 6 EIPR 368; Walsh and Watts, Trademark World, March 1996, p 26; Mills [1995] 9 EIPR 417; Willimsky [1996] 12 EIPR 649; Walsh, Trademark World, May 1995, p 33.

8 As defined in s 6.

9 As defined in s 5(4).

10 Section 48(1)(b); the proprietor also ceases to be entitled to apply for a declaration of invalidity: s 48(1)(a).

(b) the exploitation of the earlier right,

notwithstanding that the earlier proprietor may no longer be able to invoke his rights against the use of the later registered trade mark.[11]

Section 48 can therefore be relied upon by both the proprietor of an earlier trade mark/earlier right and the proprietor of a later registered trade mark for different purposes. The conditions which must be satisfied are considered below.

Proprietor of an earlier trade mark/earlier right Section 6 defines 'earlier trade mark', which includes registered trade marks and 'well-known' trade marks. Section 5(4) defines 'earlier right', which includes unregistered trade marks, copyright and design rights.

Acquiescence The proprietor of an earlier trade mark/earlier right has to have 'acquiesced'. Section 48 leaves unanswered the question as to what will constitute acquiescence . Section 48 only specifies the consequences of acquiescence. Acquiescence as a defence has been developed by the courts of equity and there are numerous cases which may, therefore, be referred to if acquiescence for the purpose of s 48 is to be interpreted consistently with the equitable defence.[12] Alternatively, it must be arguable that 'acquiescence' should be interpreted by reference to recital 11 of the Directive, Article 9 of which is the basis for s 48. Recital 11 does not use the word 'acquiescence': it uses the phrase 'knowingly tolerated', which suggests that the proprietor, in order to have acquiesced, must have had actual knowledge of the use of the registered trade mark (ie constructive knowledge will not be sufficient) and that he tolerated that use in the sense that he did nothing to prevent it. This is consistent with the phrase 'being aware of that use' in s 48. Presumably, therefore, the mere fact of registration, although constructive notice of the registration, is irrelevant in considering whether the proprietor was aware of the use of the registered trade mark.

Continuous period of five years The proprietor's acquiescence must be for a continuous period of five years, which suggests that the

11 Section 48(2).

12 See, for example, *Electrolux Ltd v Electrix Ltd* (1954) 71 RPC 23; *HP Bulmer Ltd v J Bollinger SA* [1978] RPC 79; for a more complete review of the cases see the article by Stephen James in Trademark World, May 1995, p 24.

use to which he has acquiesced must have been for at least five years, and the proprietor's awareness of the use must also be over a full five year period.

The use of a registered trade mark Statutory acquiescence only applies where the acquiescence is in relation to a later registered trade mark, but it is awareness of its use rather than its registration which is the relevant test.

Bad faith Statutory acquiescence does not apply where the registration of the later trade mark was applied for in bad faith (the meaning of which has been considered in the context of s 3(6)[13]).

Oppose the use Statutory acquiescence only precludes the entitlement of the proprietor of the earlier trade mark/earlier right to 'oppose the use' of the later registered trade mark.[14] The corollary also applies, and the proprietor of the later registered trade mark is not entitled to oppose the use of the earlier trade mark or 'oppose the exploitation' of the earlier right. A narrow interpretation of this wording would suggest that the acquiescence only prevents the earlier proprietor and/or the registered proprietor (as the case may be) from obtaining injunctive relief. Will the earlier proprietor and/or the registered proprietor also be prevented from claiming damages or other remedies if otherwise available? Surely, the narrow interpretation cannot be right, as it would lead to the absurd result that the earlier proprietor and/or the registered proprietor would be entitled to seek damages (even on-going damages) while not being able to prevent the on-going use or exploitation.

Presumably, the phrases 'oppose the use' and 'oppose the exploitation' will be interpreted so as to deny the earlier proprietor and/or registered proprietor the right to commence any proceedings in respect of the use of the registered trade mark or the earlier trade mark/earlier right.

7.10 Equitable acquiescence and consent Clearly, s 48(1) does not purport to be an exhaustive statement of the law of acquiescence and, therefore, one assumes that equitable doctrines of acquiescence, delay and consent have not been excluded. In any

13 See Chapter 2, paragraph 2.16.
14 Section 48(1)(b).

event, anything done with the consent of the proprietor of the registered trade mark will not infringe his exclusive rights.[15]

Other statutory defences

7.11 Disclaimers and limitations, s 13 It will be a defence to an action for infringement if the defendant's use of a sign falls within any disclaimer or limitation to the rights conferred by the registration.[16]

7.12 Rights of co-proprietors, s 23(3) A co-proprietor can do anything which would otherwise amount to an infringement of the registered trade mark subject only to any agreement between the co-proprietors to the contrary.[17] Thus, each co-proprietor is entitled to do any act[18] which would otherwise amount to an infringement without obtaining the consent of, or even the need to account to, his co-proprietor(s).[19]

Transitional provisions In relation to joint proprietors under the 1938 Act, whose relationship is as described in s 63 of the 1938 Act, it is deemed that there is an agreement to exclude the operation of s 23(3) of the 1994 Act and, accordingly, such co-proprietors are only able to do acts which would otherwise amount to an infringement of their registered trade mark if they have the consent of their co-proprietor(s).[20]

Competition law

The principles of EC and UK competition law should always be borne in mind, especially in the context of seeking to enforce intellectual property rights such as suing for infringement of a trade mark.

15 Section 9(1).
16 See s 13(1).
17 Section 23(3).
18 A co-proprietor does, however, need to obtain the consent of his co-proprietor(s) in respect of licensing or assigning the trade mark: s 23(4).
19 Section 23(3): he may also appoint agents to do any such acts.
20 Schedule 3, para 7.

7.13 EC competition law The 1994 Act, in particular the provisions relating to infringement (ss 9 and 10) and dealings in trade marks (ss 22 to 31), must be applied in a manner which is consistent with the principles of EC competition law. This is not simply because the 1994 Act implements the Directive: it is because all legislation in the United Kingdom must be read subject to and in light of the EC Treaty (the Treaty of Rome), which became part of English law as a result of the European Communities Act 1972. (Of course, the 1994 Act must also be interpreted and applied in a manner which is consistent with the Directive.)

EC Treaty The relevant provisions of the EC Treaty are:

(a) Article 222, which provides that the EC Treaty will in no way prejudice the rules in member states governing the system of property ownership (including the system of intellectual property ownership);

(b) Articles 30 and 34, which prohibit quantitative restrictions on imports and exports and all measures having equivalent effect (including, for example, the exercise of intellectual property rights such as trade mark rights to prevent imports and/or exports);

(c) Article 36, which states that Articles 30 and 34 (see (b) above) will *not* preclude prohibitions or restrictions on imports and exports if those prohibitions or restrictions are justified on the grounds of the protection of intellectual property (referred to as 'industrial and commercial property');

(d) The proviso to Article 36 (see (c) above), which excludes the operation of Article 36 (and therefore Articles 30 and 34 will apply), if the prohibition or restriction constitutes a means of arbitrary discrimination or a disguised restriction on trade between member states;

(e) Article 85, which prohibits agreements (etc) which may affect trade between member states and which have as their object or effect the prevention, restriction or distortion of competition within the EU. Article 85 is relevant only in the context of agreements (assignments and licences) and therefore is only considered in the context of Chapter 10; and

(f) Article 86, which prohibits abuses of a dominant position – arguably, the exercise of a quasi-monopoly such as a trade mark could expose the proprietor to the allegation that it is abusing its dominant position.[1]

Thus, in any given case, a proprietor who sues for infringement of his registered trade mark may not only be met with the defences which are provided for expressly in the 1994 Act, he may also face a defence (sometimes referred to loosely as a 'Euro-defence') based on the argument that:

(a) the exercise of his exclusive rights, conferred on him by s 9, amounts to a quantitative restriction on imports or exports, or that the exercise of his rights is a 'measure' having equivalent effect (which would therefore fall foul of Articles 30 and 34); and

(b) he is not saved by Article 36 because the exercise of his rights nonetheless constitutes a means of 'arbitrary discrimination' or a 'disguised restriction' on trade between member states (which would come within the proviso to Article 36 and therefore Article 36 would not apply);[2] and

(c) he is not saved by Article 222 (which, on first reading, purports to preserve the rules in the 1994 Act relating to intellectual property ownership), because Article 222 only preserves the *existence* of intellectual property rights, not the *exercise* of those rights.[3]

How then does the court resolve the apparent conflict between:

(1) the so-called 'freedom of movement' or 'free circulation' rules, embodied in Articles 30 and 34 and the proviso to Article 36; and

(2) the rights of intellectual property owners, including proprietors of trade marks, as recognised by Articles 36 and 222?

Existence/exercise dichotomy The first step which the ECJ took to resolve this question was to confirm that Article 222 only preserves the rules in member states relating to the *existence* of intellectual

1 Note that by virtue of the Amsterdam Treaty (which is due to be ratified in 1998) the EC Treaty will be amended with effect from 1 January 1999 and this will involve a renumbering of the Articles: Articles 30 and 36 will become 28 and 30 respectively, and Articles 85 and 86 become 81 and 82 respectively.

2 Provided that national laws are applied equally to national and foreign trade mark owners there will be no 'arbitrary' discrimination nor a 'disguised' restriction for the purposes of the proviso: see *Deutsche Renault AG v Audi AG* [1995] FSR 738

3 However, the existence of those rights may even be challenged if the national laws conferring the rights amount to an arbitrary discrimination or a disguised restriction on trade (which would therefore fall foul of the proviso to Article 36); see *Deutsche Renault AG v Audi AG* [1995] FSR 738.

property rights. Thus, the provisions relating to subsistence (ie, in particular, ss 1–7 of the 1994 Act which govern registrability and the grounds for refusal of registration) are not affected by the EC Treaty.[4] However, Article 222 does not protect the *exercise* of those intellectual property rights, and therefore one must look to Articles 30, 34 and 36 to decide whether the registered proprietor of a trade mark may be prevented from exercising his exclusive rights notwithstanding that the defendant's conduct may otherwise constitute an infringement under the terms of s 10 of the 1994 Act.

Specific subject matter of a trade mark In order to decide whether the proprietor/plaintiff, by trying to prevent the defendant's conduct, will be said to be acting in a manner which is 'anti-competitive' (ie, because he is imposing restrictions on imports or exports within Articles 30 and 34 and this is an arbitrary discrimination or a disguised restriction on trade between member states within the proviso to Article 36), the ECJ looks at the matter from first principles and asks: what is the specific subject matter of a trade mark? The specific subject matter of a trade mark is to guarantee that its owner has the exclusive right to use that trade mark for the purpose of putting products protected by it into circulation for the first time and, in this way, to protect him against competitors who would like to abuse the position and the reputation of the mark by selling products to which it has been affixed improperly.[5]

In essence, if the proprietor/plaintiff is merely exercising his trade mark rights in a manner which is consistent with its specific subject matter, then there will be no defence under the EC Treaty and the proprietor/plaintiff will not be prevented from exercising his exclusive rights.

Essential function of a trade mark The ECJ also has regard to the 'essential function' of a trade mark, which is to give the consumer a guarantee of the identity of the origin of the marked products by enabling the consumer to distinguish, without any possible confusion, the marked product from other products of a

4 *Établissement Consten SARL and Grundig-Verkaufs-GmbH v Commission* [1966] ECR 299

5 *Centrafarm BV v Winthrop BV* [1974] ECR 1183; *Hoffmann-La Roche & Co AG v Centrafarm* [1978] ECR 1139; *IHT Internationale Heiztechnik GmbH v Ideal Standard GmbH* [1994] ECR I-2789 and *Bristol-Myers Squibb v Paranova* [1997] ECR I-3457.

different origin.[6] Once again, provided that the proprietor/plaintiff is only seeking to enforce the 'essential function' of his trade mark, then he will not fall foul of competition law.

Exhaustion of rights The so-called 'exhaustion of rights' doctrine (which is embodied in s 12(1) of the 1994 Act) derives from the specific subject matter of a trade mark referred to above. If the specific subject matter of a trade mark is to give the proprietor the first right to market products bearing his trade mark, then, once the products have been put on the market by him (or with his consent), he can no longer exercise his trade mark rights so as to prevent the products from being imported from or exported to any other member state of the EU – his rights are said to be 'exhausted' (subject only to a couple of exceptions which are referred to below). The usual scenario where the exhaustion of rights doctrine may apply is where the proprietor's genuine products are put on the market in country A at a price which is lower than in country B, and a third party buys the products in country A and exports them to country B (referred to as parallel imports or 'gray goods'), thereby undercutting the retailer of the goods in country B. Although price standardisation would eliminate substantially the commercial incentive for parallel imports, such a solution may not always be available because of, for example, different safety regulations in country B which mean that the cost of manufacturing or distributing the product there is necessarily more expensive than in country A. It is not surprising that many of the cases in this area relate to the parallel importation of pharmaceutical products, which differ in price in various countries of the EU for this very reason.

Repackaging and re-labelling cases If the process of parallel importation involves repackaging or re-labelling the goods (or altering them in some other way), then it may still be legitimate for the trade mark owner to prevent such importation because, by preventing the importation of such products, he may be acting in a manner which is still consistent with the specific subject matter of his trade mark, that is, to preserve its essential function. If that is the case, then his rights will not have been exhausted: this principle is recognised and embodied in s 12(2) of the 1994 Act. There have

6 *Hoffmann-La Roche & Co AG v Centrafarm* [1978] ECR 1139; *Hag II* [1991] FSR 99; *IHT Internationale Heiztechnik GmbH v Ideal Standard GmbH* [1994] ECR I-2789 and *Bristol-Myers Squibb v Paranova* [1997] ECR I-3457.

been numerous repackaging cases in which the ECJ has had to consider whether the repackaging, re-labelling or other alteration of the products is such that the proprietor/plaintiff is entitled to rely on his exclusive rights and prevent the importation of the repackaged (but otherwise 'genuine') products. The facts of each case need to be considered, but certain 'rules' or guidelines can be discerned. The cases where the proprietor/plaintiff has been held to be acting within the specific subject matter of his trade mark rights, ie so as to preserve its essential function, include:

(a) where the repackaging affects the goods in some way, or otherwise may confuse consumers as to the origin of the goods;[7]
(b) where the use of the trade mark by the third party is liable to impair the guarantee of origin (the guarantee being that the trade marked product has not been subject at a previous stage of marketing to interference by the third party without the authorisation of the trade mark owner in such a way as to affect the original condition of the product);[8] and
(c) where the presentation of the product sold to consumers could damage the trade mark's reputation because the repackaging is defective, untidy or of poor quality – and the court is required to take into account in this regard the image (luxury or otherwise) of the products in question and their reputation in the market place.[9]

However, a trade mark proprietor will not be able to prevent parallel imports of repackaged products if:

(a) the use of his trade mark rights to prevent parallel imports will contribute to the artificial partitioning of markets between member states;
(b) the repackaging cannot adversely affect the original condition of the product; and
(c) the parallel importer complies with certain obligations as to labelling and provision of samples.

In the recent *Bristol-Myers Squibb* case,[10] the ECJ commented on

7 *Hoffmann-La Roche & Co AG v Centrafarm* [1978] ECR 1139 and *Community v Bayer AG* [1992] FSR 201.
8 *Bristol-Myers Squibb v Paranova* [1997] ECR I-3457 and affirmed and followed in *Frits Leonderslaat v George Ballantine & Son Ltd* Case C-349/95, (1997) Financial Times, 9 December, ECJ.
9 Ibid; see also *Parfums Christian Dior v Evora*, Case C-337/95 [1998] ETMR 26, ECJ.
10 Ibid.

these three requirements saying that to demonstrate 'artificial partitioning of the markets' the importer does not need to show that the trade mark owner deliberately sought to partition the markets between member states. Partitioning is artificial if the trade mark owner's reliance on his rights cannot be justified by the need to safeguard the essential function of the trade mark. This is, therefore, an objective test. In particular, where the product cannot be imported in the condition in which it has been marketed in the member state of export without repackaging (eg, because of different package sizes), reliance on trade mark rights to prevent repackaging of the product does contribute to the artificial partitioning of markets between member states. Similarly, it may be necessary to amend a label so that it complies with labelling laws in the member state of import: this may involve either deleting material which is not permissible or adding further information which is required by the laws of the importing state.[11]

Secondly, repackaging by the parallel importer is necessary and therefore justified where different package sizes are used in different member states, even if one size is common to the member states of import and export. However, the trade mark owner may oppose the use of his trade mark on the repackaged product if the repackaging is unnecessary. Repackaging is not necessary if the importer is able to achieve the same result without repackaging, for example by affixing to the external packaging a new label in the language of the member state of importation.

Thirdly, the nature of the product and the method of repackaging must be considered by the national court in order to determine whether the repackaging poses a risk that the original condition of the product inside the packaging may be affected. The hypothetical risk of isolated error (eg the risk that blisterpacks may be stored for too long before resale) will not suffice to confer on the trade mark owner the right to oppose all repackaging.

The original condition of the product may be affected indirectly (and therefore the exhaustion of rights doctrine would not apply) where, for example, the parallel importer's instructions are inaccurate or omit important information, or where the new packaging does not give the product adequate protection.

11 *Frits Leonderslaat v George Ballantine & Son Ltd* Case C-349/95 [1998] ETMR 10, ECJ.

Furthermore, and finally, the parallel importer must comply with the following obligations:

(a) he must indicate on the external packaging who repackaged the product and who manufactured the product, printed in such a way as to be understood by a person with normal eyesight exercising a normal degree of attentiveness; but
(b) he need not state that the repackaging was carried out without the authorisation of the trade mark owner; however,
(c) if the parallel importer has added an extra article to the package, he must ensure that its origin is indicated in such a way as to dispel any impression that the trade mark owner is responsible for it; and
(d) the parallel importer must give the trade mark owner advance notice of the product being put on sale, and the trade mark owner may require the importer to supply him with a specimen of the repackaged product before it goes on sale.

Re-badging cases Different considerations will apply if the importer (possibly in addition to repackaging) replaces the proprietor's trade mark, which was affixed to the goods in country A, with the proprietor's different trade mark which the proprietor uses in country B for the same goods.

In this situation, there is no exhaustion of the second/alternative trade mark rights in country B, and the proprietor can legitimately rely on his country B trade mark to prevent the importation of the re-labelled products, *unless* the courts believe that the proprietor has deliberately used different trade marks in different countries in order to partition (and hence prevent free trade within) the EU.[12]

Common origin cases In *Hag I*[13] the ECJ took the view that two proprietors who own the same mark which has a 'common origin' (ie a common original owner) cannot enforce their respective (and now divided) exclusive rights against each other. In *Hag I* the trade marks had been divided by involuntary sequestration during the war. The result was that both marks had to co-exist, and the products in respect of which they were used could be sold side-by-side bearing the same trade marks, notwithstanding that the products originated

12 *Centrafarm BV v American Home Products Corpn* [1978] ECR 1823 and *Cheetah Trade Mark* [1993] FSR 263.
13 *Van Zuylen Frères v Hag AG* [1974] ECR 731.

from two different companies. In *Hag II*,[14] however, on substantially the same facts, the ECJ reversed its decision in *Hag I*. More recently, in the *Ideal Standard* case,[15] the ECJ took the matter one step further and applied its reasoning to the fact situation where the two marks were divided by a voluntary assignment. The decision, and more importantly the reasoning, of the ECJ in *Ideal Standard* is worthy of detailed comment. Briefly, the facts were that the trade mark IDEAL STANDARD was originally owned in France and Germany by ASG (in the name of its French subsidiary and its German subsidiary respectively). The French subsidiary of ASG subsequently assigned the trade mark to SGF who later assigned it to CICh. CICh then began exporting goods bearing the trade mark IDEAL STANDARD to Germany and selling them there through its German subsidiary, namely IHT. The German subsidiary of ASG, which still owned the German registration of IDEAL STANDARD, sued IHT for trade mark infringement. IHT argued in its defence that the mark had a common origin (namely ASG) and therefore ASG's German subsidiary could not enforce its trade mark rights against IHT because, ultimately, IHT had acquired the trade mark from ASG's French subsidiary.

The court held that IHT could be prevented from using the IDEAL STANDARD trade mark in Germany notwithstanding that IHT's parent (CICh) had acquired the trade mark ultimately from the plaintiff's sister company in France. The narrow view of the judgment would be that the *Ideal Standard* case merely applies and extends the decision in *Hag II* to the situation where the trade mark in question is divided by virtue of a voluntary assignment, as opposed to the situation in *Hag II* where the trade mark was divided by compulsory sequestration.

The decision in *Hag II* was a landmark for trade mark owners in particular and a positive omen for intellectual property owners in general. This is because the court in *Hag II* specifically recognised that trade marks 'constitute an essential element of the system of undistorted competition which the Treaty aims to establish and maintain'. This passage was cited with approval in the *Ideal Standard* case and it can now be assumed with some confidence that trade marks will no longer be viewed as monopolistic icons of anti-

14 *SA CNL-Sucal NV v Hag GF AG* [1990] ECR I-3711.

15 *IHT Internationale Heiztechnik GmbH v Ideal Standard GmbH* [1994] ECR I-2789 and [1995] FSR 59.

competitive behaviour. The court in *Ideal Standard*, however, went further than *Hag II* in so far as, throughout the judgment, the court returned to and emphasised the territorial nature and independence of trade mark rights. The court focused on the fact that trade marks are the creature of national legislation and, accordingly, the proprietor's rights extend only to the national frontiers of the country in which the registration has been obtained. The court relied on this fact in holding that this feature of trade mark rights (which can also be applied to all intellectual property rights), all other things being equal, effectively means that the free movement of goods principle must take a back seat to the principle of undistorted competition. The court referred grandly to the 'principle of territoriality' and the 'principle of the independence of trade marks' emphasising (as indeed is the case) that these principles are well recognised under international law, citing Article 6*quater* of the Paris Convention and Article 9*ter* (2) of the Madrid Agreement as examples.

The defendant, IHT, had argued that the voluntary decision by ASG (in the form of its French subsidiary) to assign the trade mark in France to a third party over which it could exercise no control meant that ASG (in the form of its German subsidiary) could not now complain that the consequence of that assignment was the weakening of the uniquely identifying function of the trade mark. In essence, IHT argued that a territorially limited assignment means that the owner necessarily renounces his position as being the only person marketing goods bearing the trade mark in question in the EU. The ECJ was unequivocal in its answer:

> 'The argument must be rejected . . . it fails to take account of the fact that, since trade mark rights are territorial, the function of the trade mark is to be assessed by reference to a particular territory.'

It is this aspect of the judgment which distinguishes the court's decision from that of the opinion of the Advocate General who, after a long and very thorough analysis, had recommended that a distinction was to be drawn between voluntary assignments and compulsory sequestration. The Advocate General's opinion did not attach weight to the 'principles of territoriality and independence' and eventually came down in favour of IHT's argument that the consequence of voluntary assignment is that the proprietor loses control of his mark in the rest of the EU. The ECJ did not accept the Advocate General's opinion in this regard, saying that:

> 'Assignments and licences always relate, having regard to the territorial nature of trade mark rights, to a specified territory.'

The second argument relied on by IHT was to the effect that ASG, through its French subsidiary, had impliedly consented to the assignee putting goods into circulation in France bearing the IDEAL STANDARD trade mark and that, because of that implied consent, it should not be possible to prohibit the marketing in Germany of the same goods bearing the assigned trade mark. The court was equally dismissive of this argument, saying:

> 'that view must be rejected. The consent implicit in any assignment is not the consent required for the application of the doctrine of exhaustion of rights.'

The court was careful to limit 'exhaustion' to the circumstances where the owner of the trade mark in the importing state must, directly or indirectly, be able to determine the products to which the trade mark may be affixed in the exporting state and to control their quality. Of course, the ability is necessarily lost if, by assignment, control over the trade mark is surrendered to a third party having no economic link with the assignor. On the premises that:

(a) trade mark rights have to be considered on a territory-by-territory basis; and
(b) 'exhaustion' can only be relevant where there is the actual ability to control the party putting the goods on the market,

the court applied the reasoning in *Hag II* and confirmed that:

(a) the specific subject matter of a trade mark must be determined having regard to its essential function;
(b) the essential function of a trade mark is to give consumers a guarantee of the identity of the origin of the marked product by enabling consumers to distinguish the product from others of a different origin; and
(c) the free movement of goods principle could undermine that essential function of a trade mark and consumers would no longer be able to identify for certain the origin of the marked goods.

The importance of the *Ideal Standard* case is perhaps the fact that it arose out of circumstances which are very real and which will repeat themselves time and again, albeit each with their own 'spin'. However, before one jumps to the conclusion that *Ideal Standard* is a recipe for legalised market sharing arrangements, we should conclude this summary with the reminder that Article 85 of the EC

Treaty will still apply to strike down any such arrangements, and a trade mark assignment which implements such an arrangement will be void.

Article 86, abuse of a dominant position It has been held that the mere existence of intellectual property rights, including trade mark rights, does not amount to dominance for the purposes of Article 86 unless the proprietor has the power to impede the maintenance of effective competition over a considerable part of the relevant market (perhaps where a very well-known trade mark transcends products and territories).

However, even if a dominant position could be founded on the ownership of a trade mark, the mere enforcement of one's exclusive rights is not considered to be an 'abuse' of that dominant position.[16] An abuse of that dominant position is where the proprietor either charges excessively (deriving monopoly profits) or reduces his prices (loss leaders) in order to shut out a (usually new) competitor.[17]

References to the ECJ Because the 1994 Act implements the Directive, Article 177 of the EC Treaty should be borne in mind by trade mark owners and their advisers as being of potential relevance, not just in the context of infringement and defences to infringement, but also (in theory) in relation to any aspect of the 1994 Act.

The jurisdiction of the ECJ under Article 177 of the EC Treaty is to give preliminary rulings in relation to three matters:

1 The interpretation of the EC Treaty.
2 The validity and interpretation of the acts of the institutions of the Community and of the ECB.
3 The interpretation of the statutes of bodies established by an act of the council, where those statutes so provide.

There is a substantial body of case law relating to Article 177. However, for present purposes, broad principles can and should be stated, because it is likely that more references may be made to the ECJ under Article 177 seeking guidance from the ECJ as to:

(a) the interpretation of the Directive; and/or
(b) the consistency of the 1994 Act with the Directive.

Of course, this is not to say that the UK courts will necessarily be eager to make references under Article 177 simply because an issue

16 *Hoffmann-La Roche & Co AG v Centrafarm* [1978] ECR 1139.
17 *Imperial Chemical Industries v Berk Pharmaceuticals* [1981] FSR 1.

arises under a section of the 1994 Act which has been taken (or substantially taken) from the Directive; the more likely scenario is that the UK courts will construe the 1994 Act according to the ordinary meaning of the words used and based on their own reading and understanding of the Directive.[18] However, it should be remembered that the purpose of Article 177 is to overcome the concern that the Directive (like other EC law) may not be interpreted and applied in the same way by the national courts of the various members states. It is for this reason that paragraph 3 of Article 177 requires that courts from whose decision there is no appeal (the House of Lords and even the Court of Appeal where leave to appeal is refused) must bring the matter before the ECJ.

The following principles can be stated in relation to Article 177:

1 A reference to the ECJ may in principle be made at any stage of the proceedings pending before the national court.
2 The national court must apply the ECJ's ruling to the facts of the case before it.
3 The question referred to the ECJ may be raised either by one of the parties or by the judge of his own motion.
4 A decision on a question is considered 'necessary' for the purposes of Article 177 when the national court sees the decision as a step in its strategy for dispensing of the case, albeit not a conclusive step.
5 The jurisdiction of the ECJ covers questions concerning the interpretation of the EC Treaty as well as questions on the validity and interpretation of 'acts of the community institutions' which, for present purposes includes the Directive. This will include situations where the national court is seeking guidance from the ECJ to enable it to apply provisions of national law implemented under the Directive.
6 A reference under Article 177 is not an appeal as such: questions are referred to the ECJ, and the parties, along with the member states, the Commission and the Council, have the right to submit written and oral observations to the ECJ.
7 The ECJ does not rule on the application of its answers to the specific facts of the case – it is for the national courts to interpret the answers and to apply them to the circumstances of the case.

18 See, for example, Jacob J in the *Treat* case [1996] RPC 281 at 291-2, where he specifically looks to the Directive for guidance in interpreting the 1994 Act.

8 The national court is the sole judge of and enjoys the 'widest discretion' as to whether reference should be made under Article 177 (unless it is the court of last resort).
9 Where a question of EC law is raised, for example as to the interpretation of the Directive, in a case before a court of last resort (that is, from which there is no appeal) the court is obliged to refer the question to the ECJ.
10 A national court (including a court of last resort) may still refuse to refer a question under Article 177 to the ECJ if:
   (a) the question has already been decided by a previous decision of the ECJ; or
   (b) the answer to the question is so obvious as to leave no scope for any reasonable doubt; or
   (c) where the question arises in interlocutory proceedings, provided that the question can be raised at a later stage.
11 A ruling on interpretation given by the ECJ under Article 177 is binding on the national courts as to the interpretation of the EC law provisions in question. The referring court is under a duty to give full effect to the provisions as interpreted by the ECJ, which may mean that the national court will have to refuse to apply conflicting provisions of national law if it was adopted subsequently.
12 Finally, note that the ECJ is not bound by its previous decisions, and therefore national courts may refer questions under Article 177 even where the issue has been answered in the past – perhaps in the hope or concern that the ECJ will overturn its earlier decision (for example in *Hag II*).

7.14 UK competition law There are three sources of UK competition law which one should consider in the context of suing for infringement of a trade mark:

(a) s 12 of the 1994 Act;
(b) the Restrictive Trade Practice Act 1976 ('RTPA'); and
(c) the Competition Bill 1997.

Section 12 Section 12(1) of the 1994 Act provides that a registered trade mark will not be infringed by the use of the trade mark in relation to goods which have been put on the market in the EEA under that trade mark by the proprietor or with his consent. The proviso is that s 12(1) does not apply where there exist 'legitimate reasons' for the proprietor to oppose any further dealings in the goods. A specific example of a legitimate reason is where the condition of the goods has been 'changed or impaired' after being put on the market.[19]

Section 12 embodies, in very broad terms, the principles which have already been discussed in paragraph 7.11 and it is to be assumed that it will be applied in a manner which is consistent with the cases decided under this area of EC competition law.

RTPA The RTPA is discussed in some detail in Chapter 10 (paragraph 10.26) in the context of licensing and assigning trade marks. As far as a defence to infringement is concerned, the issue is whether a contractual restriction, made void under the RTPA, can be, in effect, 'enforced' by the proprietor of the mark suing his licensee for infringement in the situation where the licensee does something which is contrary to the contractual restriction and which also amounts to infringement. Although the contractual restriction is void under the RTPA and hence unenforceable, this does not necessarily preclude a finding of infringement.

Competition Bill 1997 The Competition Bill was introduced into Parliament on 16 October 1997. The express intention of the Bill is to bring UK competition law broadly into line with EC competition law; the key points to note are as follows:

(a) the Bill would replace the Restrictive Trade Practices Act 1976 and the Resale Prices Act 1976 with a prohibition on anti-competitive agreements, based closely on Article 85 of the EC Treaty;
(b) it would also introduce a prohibition on the abuse of a dominant position based closely on Article 86 of the EC Treaty;
(c) the Director General of Fair Trading (DGFT) will receive new powers to investigate anti-competitive behaviour; and
(d) his decisions will be published and it will be possible to appeal against those decisions to a new Competition Commission, which will replace the existing Monopolies and Mergers Commission (MMC).

It is not known when the Bill is likely to be enacted because, at the time of writing, certain provisions which will exclude its operation in specific industries are the subject of considerable debate.

19 Section 12(2).

Unfortunately, therefore, this subject remains in the category of 'watch this space'. However, even if the outstanding issues can be resolved in the near future, it was always intended that the legislation would not be enacted before summer 1998, and would not come into force for another 12 months so as to allow procedural rules and regulations to be adopted.

8 Remedies

8.01 Approach taken by the 1994 Act In Chapter 6 the acts constituting infringement under the 1994 Act were considered. This chapter now sets out the remedies which may be available to the proprietor in respect of an infringement of his registration.

An infringement of a registered trade mark[1] is actionable by the proprietor of the trade mark[2] and, upon proof of infringement, the proprietor is entitled to those remedies provided for in the 1994 Act.[3] Those remedies are:

(a) pursuant to s 14(2):
   (i) damages;
   (ii) an account of profits;
   (iii) injunctive relief; and
   (iv) any other relief which would be available in respect of the infringement of any other property right;

(b) pursuant to s 15(1), the erasure, removal or obliteration of an 'offending sign';

(c) pursuant to s 15(2), the destruction of infringing goods;

(d) pursuant to s 16, the delivery up of infringing goods, material or articles; and

1 No proceedings lie under the 1994 Act in respect of the infringement of an unregistered trade mark: s 2(2).

2 Section 14(1); or by an exclusive licensee: s 31(1) and (2) and see paragraph 8.21 et seq.

3 Section 2(1).

(e) pursuant to s 19(1), the destruction or forfeiture of infringing goods, material or articles.

The 1994 Act also provides special remedies in the case of:

(a) the importation of infringing goods, material or articles in respect of which a s 89 notice has been given to Customs and Excise;[4]

(b) the misuse of well-known trade marks;[5]

(c) an agent or representative of the proprietor of a mark making an unauthorised application for the registration of the mark;[6] and

(d) the unauthorised use of the Royal Arms etc.[7]

Each of these remedies is considered in turn in this chapter including, at the end of the chapter, in the context of the special provisions relating to co-proprietors and licensees. Many of the remedies, however, are not peculiar to the infringement of a registered trade mark and therefore readers should also refer to specialist works on the subject of remedies.

The remedies available to the proprietor can be split into two categories:

(a) general remedies, which will be available in accordance with established common law and equitable principles;[8] and

(b) statutory remedies, the availability of which is governed specifically by the 1994 Act.[9]

General remedies

8.02 Damages, s 14(2) The proprietor of a registered trade mark is entitled as of right to recover damages in respect of any infringement of his trade mark.[10]

The entitlement to and the assessment of such damages will be determined in accordance with the established principles governing any infringement of an intellectual property right. The proprietor will be entitled to recover his damages on proof of infringement and the quantum of damages recoverable will be a matter for the court to

4 Section 89(2).
5 Section 56(2).
6 Section 60.
7 Section 99(4).
8 Section 14(2).
9 Sections 15, 16, 19, 56, 60, 89 and 99.
10 Section 14(2).

determine based upon the evidence adduced.[11] Infringement of a trade mark is a statutory tort and the damages recoverable are governed by the same rules as with other torts. The elementary rules are:

(a) that the proprietor should be restored to the position in which he would have been had the infringement not occurred; and
(b) that the proprietor can recover loss which is:
  (i) foreseeable (ie not too remote); and
  (ii) caused by the infringement; and
  (iii) not excluded from recovery by public or social policy.[12]

The proprietor may, as an alternative to recovering his damages, elect to seek an account of the profits made by the defendant as a result of the defendant's infringement.[13]

Examples of calculating damages The quantum of damages is often assessed by reference to the amount of money which would constitute a reasonable licence fee or royalty for the use of the mark in question. In this context, a reasonable licence fee is the amount that objectively represents what a reasonable licensee would have been prepared to pay and what a reasonable licensor would have been prepared to accept, had a licence been negotiated in respect of the defendant's use of the proprietor's trade mark.

Alternatively, the proprietor may be able to show that the defendant's sales of infringing goods have resulted in lost sales for the proprietor and he can, in these circumstances, recover the profits which he would have made on the lost sales. Of course, the claim for lost profits is, in truth, a claim for lost income and therefore one must deduct the expenses which have not been incurred. However, it has been confirmed in the *Gerber* case[14] that if only the marginal costs of production and sale are saved by the plaintiff, then the remainder of the lost income is recoverable in full without deducting a proportion of general overheads. Furthermore, it is very unlikely that every infringing sale by the defendant will be credited to the plaintiff when assessing damages on a loss of sales basis; although, in *Gerber*, Jacob J concluded that the patentee had lost a chance of

11 Usually assessed by a Master.
12 *Gerber Garment Technology Inc v Lectra Systems Ltd* [1997] RPC 443 per Staughton LJ at 452; see also Halsbury's Laws of England, Fourth edition, vol 12, paragraphs 1128 and 1133.
13 See paragraph 8.03.
14 Supra.

making sales and went on to evaluate the lost chances as a whole rather than separately in relation to individual infringing sales.[15]

Finally, damages may also be awarded where the defendant's infringing goods are of an inferior quality to those of the proprietor. Damages are therefore awarded to compensate the proprietor for the injury to the goodwill or reputation attaching to his trade mark. Damages to compensate for injury to the goodwill of a registered trade mark will be assessed along the same lines as damages in a passing off action.[16]

Secondary loss In addition to direct loss of sales of the plaintiff's products, the plaintiff may also suffer what may be referred to as 'secondary loss', that is:

(a) the lost prospect of making follow-on sales (eg of spare parts) and servicing the goods; and
(b) the defendant may be in a better position to compete generally with the plaintiff by establishing a bridgehead or springboard to enter the market.

The question as to whether secondary loss of this nature is recoverable has been considered by the Court of Appeal in the *Gerber* case[17] in the context of patent infringement. In that case, the Court of Appeal looked at the overall objective of the Patents Act 1977 and concluded that its aim is to protect patentees from commercial loss resulting from the wrongful infringement of their rights. Accordingly, by reference to s 61 of the Patents Act 1977 and viewing the cases as a whole, the Court of Appeal held that no rule of law could be found which restricts the scope of recovery of damages by way of loss of profits to activities of the defendant which themselves constituted infringement of the patent. Thus, provided that the secondary loss is both foreseeable (ie not too remote) and is, in fact, caused by the infringement, it will be recoverable. There is no reason in principle why this aspect of the decision in *Gerber* should not be applicable to an assessment of damages in a trade mark infringement case.

Losses by a subsidiary An infringement action must necessarily be brought in the name of the registered proprietor (or by a licensee

15 See the discussion of this problem in *Dormeuil Frères SA v Feraglow Ltd* [1990] RPC 449.
16 See Chapter 18, paragraph 18.28 et seq.
17 [1997] RPC 443.

under ss 30 or 31). However, loss may in fact be suffered by another company in which the proprietor has a shareholding (eg a subsidiary or sister company). In such circumstances, the company suffering the loss may not have a cause of action against the infringer, but the proprietor/shareholder in that company can recover damages in respect of his loss (whether an income or a capital loss) by reason of the loss suffered by the other company. Damages are recoverable and calculated by reference to the reduction in the value of the shareholding in the company suffering the loss. The plaintiff (shareholder) to succeed must show that it has a personal cause of action and must prove a personal loss caused by the defendant's infringement. However, in the *Gerber* case, the Court of Appeal overruled Jacob J's decision at first instance to the effect that it was self-evident that every dollar lost to the subsidiary reduced the value of the parent's shareholding by a like amount. Instead, the Court of Appeal treated each company as a separate legal entity and required the plaintiff to prove its own financial loss to its own pocket and to quantify the loss. Thus, although a parent company will, in principle, be able to recover damages by reason of the loss suffered by its subsidiary, it is the reduction in the value of the parent's shareholding which must be quantified, not the actual loss suffered by the subsidiary as such.

8.03 Account of profits, s 14(2) An account of profits is an alternative remedy to damages. It is an equitable remedy and the order of an account will be governed by the usual equitable principles. In particular, any order will be at the discretion of the court. For example, the defendant's knowledge of the proprietor's registration may affect the making of an order for an account of profits and/or the quantum of the award. The court will also have regard to any delay by the proprietor in bringing the proceedings and/or any acquiescence to the defendant's conduct.[18]

Proprietors electing to receive an account of the defendant's profits should bear in mind the problem of defining accurately the defendant's profit. It is no secret that the use of 'creative accountancy' by the defendant may reduce the 'profit' which is attributable to his infringing acts. The proprietor may be better advised to seek to prove his damages because, notwithstanding the

18 Including statutory acquiescence: s 48; or equitable acquiescence.

difficulties associated with trying to prove what might have been, at least he is in control of the evidence upon which the calculation is to be based.

Election The proprietor must elect either to recover his damages or to receive an account of the defendant's profits at the conclusion of the hearing as to liability. The court (usually a Master) will then hear evidence either as to the proprietor's damages[19] or as to the defendant's profits, and will make an award accordingly.

Section 10(3) infringement Where the defendant has been found to have infringed under s 10(3), the proprietor's election may be governed by the finding of the court (should there be one) as to whether the defendant's use either:
(a) takes unfair advantage of; or
(b) is detrimental to,
the distinctive character or repute of the proprietor's mark. In the former case, the proprietor may prefer to seek an account of the defendant's profits, whereas, in the latter situation, the proprietor may be better advised to seek to recover damages.

Unjust enrichment The rationale for ordering an account of profits is not to punish the defendant, but to prevent unjust enrichment by the defendant. It is therefore inappropriate for the plaintiff to receive more than the profit made by the defendant which is attributable to the infringement in question. If the defendant can establish that any element of the profit is attributable to factors other than the use of the infringing mark, then this should be reflected in the account of profits awarded. It seems clear that an account of profits will not enable the plaintiff to obtain the total profit derived from the sale of the goods bearing the infringing trade mark. The onus of establishing that any element of the profit did not arise from infringement of the trade mark is, of course, borne by the defendant.

8.04 Injunctions, s 14(2) The 1994 Act refers in s 14(2) to 'injunctions', which includes both interim and final injunctions. An injunction can be obtained in addition to either an award of damages or an account of profits. Furthermore, an injunction can be

19 Referred to as an 'enquiry as to damages'.

sought prior to the commencement by the defendant of any actual acts constituting infringement, provided that there is some threat or likelihood that the infringing acts will be commenced, continued or repeated.

The grant of an injunction is also an equitable remedy and therefore, like an account of profits, will be subject to the usual equitable principles, including delay and acquiescence.[20]

Interim injunction In order to obtain an interim (or interlocutory) injunction, the proprietor must establish that he has a good arguable case and that the balance of convenience favours the grant of an injunction. That is, that the potential harm to the proprietor if the defendant's conduct is allowed to commence or continue outweighs the likely harm to the defendant if the injunction were wrongly to be granted and, subsequently at any full trial, discharged by the court. In *Series 5*,[1] Laddie J reviewed in considerable detail the 1975 House of Lords decision in *American Cyanamid*[2] and concluded that there was nothing in that decision which prevents the court from taking into account its view of the strength of each party's case. Accordingly, when deciding whether to grant interim relief the court should (according to Laddie J) bear the following matters in mind:

(a) the grant of an interim injunction is a matter of discretion and depends on all the facts of the case;
(b) there are no fixed rules;
(c) the court should rarely attempt to resolve complex issues of disputed fact or law; and
(d) major factors the court should bear in mind are:
  (i) the extent to which damages are likely to be an adequate remedy and the ability of the other party to pay;
  (ii) the balance of convenience;
  (iii) the maintenance of the status quo; and
  (iv) any clear view the court may reach as to the relative strength of the parties' cases.

A proprietor seeking an interim injunction will have to give the usual cross-undertaking as to damages, which means that, if the interim

20 Including statutory acquiescence: s 48(2); and equitable acquiescence.

1 *Series 5 Software Ltd v Philip Clarke* [1996] FSR 273; for a comment in relation to this decision see Edenborough and Tritton 'American Cyanamid Revisited' [1996] 4 EIPR 234.

2 *American Cyanamid Co v Ethicon Ltd* [1975] AC 396.

injunction is subsequently discharged, he may have to compensate the defendant in respect of any damages suffered by the defendant during the period of and arising out of the injunction. The undertaking as to damages is therefore potentially extremely onerous, as the grant of an interim injunction may have the effect of putting the defendant out of business. In some cases, the plaintiff seeking an interim injunction is required to fortify his undertaking by putting up security for the damages which the defendant may suffer.

Final injunction A final injunction will only be granted if the defendant is found to have infringed the proprietor's trade mark following the hearing of all the evidence at the full trial. Of course, the issue of balance of convenience is irrelevant in issuing a final injunction, but other relevant factors which affect the grant of equitable relief will be applicable.

Cross-border injunctions The Dutch courts have for some time taken the view that the Brussels Convention[3] gives them the jurisdiction to grant cross-border injunctions.[4] The English courts to date have not granted an injunction for trade mark infringement which has an effect outside the United Kingdom, although this would appear to be based on the exercise of the judge's discretion rather than because the court did not have the necessary jurisdiction. Aldous J in *Plastus Kreativ*[5] gave three reasons for refusing a cross-border injunction in a patent infringement case:

(a) findings of patent infringement by a foreign court are less likely to command the respect of local people;
(b) the finding that a patent is infringed implies that the patent is valid, so questions of infringement and validity should be heard together; and
(c) the local courts where the infringement has taken place are usually better placed to consider a particular act in its local context.[6]

3 Brussels Convention on Jurisdiction and the enforcement of judgments in civil and commercial matters.

4 *Applied Research Systems v Organon & Chiron*, 3 February 1994, C of A The Hague; *Chiron Corpn v Organon Tecknika Ltd* (1 December 1994, unreported), C of A The Hague; and *Murex Diagnostics Ltd v Chiron Corpn* (7 December 1995, unreported) C of A The Hague.

5 *Plastus Kreativ AB v Minnesota Mining and Manufacturing Co* [1993] RPC 438.

6 For an opinion to the effect that UK courts do have jurisdiction to grant cross-border injunctions, see Kempner and Fricker [1996] EIPR 377.

At the time of writing, this issue is the subject of a reference to the European Court of Justice, which arose out of an application to the High Court in England seeking an injunction to prevent the respondents from bringing infringement proceedings in the Dutch courts. Both Laddie J (at first instance) and the Court of Appeal considered that Articles 16(4), 19 and 24 of the Brussels Convention were capable of two interpretations.[7] Articles 16(4) and 19 are anti-forum shopping provisions where issues of registrability and/or validity are concerned. In such cases, exclusive jurisdiction is conferred on the courts of the member state where the trade mark has been applied for or in which it is registered. However, it can be argued that Article 24 operates as an exception to this principle where provisional or protective measures are being sought. That is, an interim injunction (or its equivalent) may be available from the courts of other member states (provided that they otherwise have jurisdiction) in order to do justice between the parties pending the resolution of the question of registrability/validity by the court on which exclusive jurisdiction has been conferred under Article 16(4). The Court of Appeal in *Fort Dodge* adjourned the case and has referred the issue to the ECJ for its consideration.

8.05 Any other relief, s 14(2) The 1994 Act, although expressly referring to damages, injunctions and an account of profits, does not limit the remedies available to the proprietor, and confirms that he is entitled to all such other relief as is available in respect of the infringement of any other property right.[8]

This is clearly intended to be a 'catch-all' provision, although the most frequently sought and certainly the most practical remedies are those which have already been mentioned, namely damages or an account of profits and an injunction. Indeed, other than an Anton Piller order (as to which see below), it is difficult to think of any other relief to which a proprietor would be entitled in respect of the infringement of another property right, except, of course, those expressly provided for elsewhere in the 1994 Act. These remedies are considered below.

7 *Re a petition by Fort Dodge Animal Health Ltd*, (1998) IPD 21003, (1997) Times, 24 October (Laddie J) and unreported, CA. See also *Coin Controls Ltd v Suzo International (UK) Ltd* [1997] 3 All ER 45, where Laddie J also comments in relation to Articles 16(4), 19 and 24 of the Brussels Convention.
8 Section 14(2).

Anton Piller orders An Anton Piller order,[9] in broad terms, enables the plaintiff's solicitors or representatives to enter the defendant's premises in order to search for and seize goods bearing infringing trade marks or other evidence of the alleged acts of infringement. The development of Anton Piller orders was somewhat haphazard and led to alleged abuses. Accordingly, the granting of Anton Piller orders and the manner in which they are executed has now been formalised. A specimen form of Anton Piller order appears at [1994] RPC 617 and practitioners should read the report of the Judge's Council into Anton Piller orders.[10]

The practical importance of an Anton Piller order is that the plaintiff can seek an order contemporaneously with or even before commencing proceedings for trade mark infringement. This gives the proprietor the element of surprise, because the defendant will be unaware of the making of the order until the plaintiff's solicitors appear to execute it. The defendant therefore has no opportunity to conceal infringing goods or other relevant evidence of infringement. This will be particularly useful in the case of organised counterfeiting activities; indeed, although an Anton Piller order usually identifies a specific address at which the order is to be executed, it may be possible to obtain a so called 'roving' Anton Piller order which allows the plaintiff's solicitors to carry out a search at unidentified premises, provided only that the premises are occupied by someone falling within the class of defendants specified in the order.[11]

Statutory remedies

8.06 Infringing goods, material and articles, s 17 The remedies of erasure,[12] delivery up,[13] destruction and forfeiture,[14] and

9 Named after one of the early leading cases in which such an order was granted: *Anton Piller KG v Manufacturing Processes Ltd* [1976] FSR 129.

10 Published by the Lord Chancellor's department in November 1992. For a case in which the solicitors executing an Anton Piller order were strongly criticised see *Universal Thermosensors Ltd v Hibben* [1992] FSR 361.

11 *EMI Records Ltd v Kudhail* [1985] FSR 36. See also Barron [1996] 4 EIPR 183 for a discussion of 'roving' Anton Piller orders including examples of orders granted in other jurisdictions.

12 Section 15; and see paragraph 8.07.

13 Section 16; and see paragraph 8.09.

14 Section 15; and see paragraph 8.08.

the giving of notice to Customs and Excise under s 89, are only available in respect of infringing goods, material or articles in the possession, custody or control of the defendant.[15]

Accordingly, it is necessary first to consider the meaning of each of the three terms:

(a) 'infringing goods', s 17(2);
(b) 'infringing material', s 17(4); and
(c) 'infringing articles', s 17(5).

'Infringing goods', s 17(2) Goods are 'infringing goods' if they (or their packaging) bear a sign which is identical with or similar to a registered trade mark and either:

(a) the application of the sign to the goods or to their packaging was itself an infringement of the trade mark; or
(b) the goods are proposed to be imported into the United Kingdom and the application of the sign to the goods or to their packaging would have been an infringement of the trade mark if the application had occurred in the United Kingdom;[16] or
(c) the use of the sign otherwise constitutes an infringement of the trade mark.[17]

'Infringing material', s 17(4) Material is 'infringing material' if it bears a sign which is identical with or similar to a registered trade mark and either:

(a) the material is used:
  (i) for labelling or packaging goods;
  (ii) as a business paper; or
  (iii) for advertising goods or services,

  provided that the material is used in such a way as to infringe the trade mark;[18] or
(b) the material is intended to be so used and such use would infringe the registered trade mark.[19]

15 A notice under s 89 must be in respect of goods, material or articles but they need not be in the possession, custody or control of the defendant.

16 But this will not affect the importation of goods which are lawfully imported into the UK by virtue of an enforceable Community right: s 17(3). This must be a reference to traders' rights derived from the effect of Articles 30 and 34 of the EC Treaty; as to the definition of United Kingdom see ss 107 and 108.

17 Section 17(2).

18 Section 17(4)(a).

19 Section 17(4)(b).

'Infringing articles', s 17(5) Articles are 'infringing articles' if they:

(a) are specifically designed or adapted for making copies of a sign which is identical with or similar to a registered trade mark; and
(b) are in the possession, custody or control of a person who knows or has reason to believe that such articles either have been or are to be used to produce infringing goods or material.[20]

The requirement that the article be 'specifically designed or adapted' for the purpose of making copies of a sign will be too onerous for many trade mark owners. For example, the tools of trade of a counterfeiter may have many uses other than the copying of trade marks and it may, therefore, be difficult to establish that the article was 'specifically' designed or adapted, albeit that this requirement does not mean that the article be 'exclusively' designed or adapted for the purposes of making copies of the sign.

8.07 Erasure, removal or obliteration, s 15(1)(a) Where the proprietor has established that the defendant has infringed his trade mark, the court may make an order requiring the defendant to erase, remove or obliterate the offending sign from any infringing goods, material or articles which are in the defendant's possession, custody or control.[1]

If appropriate, the court may instead order that the infringing goods, material or articles be delivered up to a person nominated by the court for that person to erase, remove or obliterate the sign. Such an order can only be made if the original order for erasure, removal or obliteration has not been complied with by the defendant, or if it appears to the court that it is likely that such an order will not be complied with by the defendant.[2]

8.08 Destruction, s 15(1)(b) If the remedy referred to above of erasure, removal or obliteration is, in the circumstances of the case, not reasonably practicable, the court may instead order the defendant to arrange for the destruction of the infringing goods, material or articles in question.[3]

Once again, where necessary, the court may instead order that the

20 Section 17(5).
1 Section 15(1)(a).
2 Section 15(2).
3 Section 15(1)(b).

infringing goods, material or articles be delivered up to another person for destruction, but only if the defendant has not complied with the original order, or if it appears to the court that the defendant is unlikely to comply with the order.[4]

This will be a useful (if not essential) remedy where the mark is integral to the goods, for example where the mark consists of the shape of the goods themselves.

8.09 Delivery up, s 16 Another alternative is for the proprietor to apply to the court for an order for the delivery up of infringing goods, material or articles.[5] However, such an order may only be granted in respect of infringing goods, material or articles which a person has in his possession, custody or control in the course of business,[6] and provided that:

(a) the proprietor's application is made before the end of the statutory limitation period specified in s 18;[7] and
(b) the court also makes or there are grounds for making an order under s 19 for the disposal of the infringing goods, material or articles.[8]

The order for delivery up can be made against someone other than the person who has infringed the proprietor's trade mark, provided only that that person has infringing goods, material or articles in his possession, custody or control in the course of a business.

Furthermore, the court may order that the delivery up be made either to the proprietor or to any other person. Such an order can, however, only be made pursuant to a specific application made by the proprietor,[9] and therefore the proprietor should consider whether it is appropriate to apply, in the alternative to an order for delivery up to himself, for an order for delivery up to 'such other person as the court may direct'. This may be appropriate if there is any reason for the court not to make an order for delivery up to the proprietor himself.

4 Section 15(2).
5 In Scotland, the application may be brought in the sheriff court; in Northern Ireland, the application may be brought in the county court: s 20.
6 Section 16(1); 'business' includes any trade or profession: s 103(1).
7 Section 16(2); and see paragraph 8.10.
8 Section 16(2); and see paragraph 8.11.
9 This follows from the fact that s 16(1) confers the right on the proprietor and does not appear to confer an inherent right on the court itself to make the order: see s 16(1) and distinguish the wording from s 15(1).

The infringing goods, material or articles which have been delivered up will become the property of the person to whom they are delivered up. That person may do with them as he likes, subject to any order of the court, and provided that he must retain them pending the making of an order for their disposal.[10]

8.10 Limitation period, s 18 Any application for an order for delivery up under s 16 must be made within the statutory limitation period, which is a period of six years calculated from a date which may vary depending on whether one is seeking the delivery up of either goods or material or articles.[11]

Goods In the case of infringing goods, the six year period commences on the date on which the trade mark was applied to the goods or their packaging.[12]

Material In the case of infringing material, the period commences on the date on which the trade mark was applied to the material.[13]

Articles In the case of infringing articles, the period commences on the date on which they were made.[14]

Exceptions In each case these dates are subject to two specific exceptions. These exceptions apply where the proprietor of the registered trade mark, during the whole or part of the limitation period, is either:

(a) under a disability;[15] or
(b) prevented from discovering the facts entitling him to apply for an order for delivery up as the result of fraud or concealment.[16]

In either of these circumstances an application for delivery up may be made at any time before the end of the six year period calculated from the date on which the proprietor:

(a) ceased to be under the disability; or

10 Section 16(3); ie an order under s 19, or pending a formal decision not to make any order under s 19; see also paragraph 8.11 in relation to orders under s 19.
11 Section 18(1).
12 Section 18(1)(a).
13 Section 18(1)(b).
14 Section 18(1)(c).
15 For the definition of 'disability' see s 18(3).
16 Section 18(2).

(b) could with reasonable diligence have discovered the facts entitling him to apply for an order for delivery up,[17]

as the case may be.

8.11 Order as to disposal of infringing goods, material or articles, s 19 Following the delivery up of infringing goods, material or articles pursuant to an order under s 16, a further application may be made to the court[18] for either:

(a) an order that they be:
   (i) destroyed; or
   (ii) forfeited to such person as the court may think fit; or

(b) a formal decision that no order as to destruction or forfeiture be made,[19] in which case the person in whose possession, custody or control the goods, material or articles were before being delivered up will be entitled to their return.[20]

Thus, the defendant can recover the goods, material or articles by making an application for a decision that no order be made for their destruction or forfeiture. In considering whether to make an order for their destruction or forfeiture, the court will have regard to whether other remedies are available which would be adequate to compensate and to protect the interests of the proprietor (and any licensee).[1]

Accordingly, if the court considers damages to be an adequate remedy, then it may decide to make no order as to destruction or forfeiture provided that the proprietor's interests are or will otherwise be protected. If so, the defendant will be entitled to the return of the goods, material or articles in question.[2]

8.12 Persons having an interest in the infringing goods, material or articles, s 19(3) The 1994 Act enables rules of court to be made to establish the procedure whereby persons having an interest[3] in the infringing goods, material or articles:

(a) must be notified of; and

17 Section 18(2).
18 In Scotland, the application may be made in the sheriff court; in Northern Ireland, the application may be made in the county court: s 20.
19 Section 19(1).
20 Section 19(5).
1 Section 19(2).
2 Section 19(5).
3 As to those persons who have such an interest see s 19(6).

(b) will be entitled to appear and to appeal in respect of,

any proceedings for an order for their destruction or forfeiture.[4] Any order under s 19 will not take effect until the end of the period within which the person interested is entitled to appeal and, if an appeal is made, the order will not take effect until the appeal is finally disposed of.[5]

If more than one person is interested in the relevant goods, material or articles, then the court will make an order as it thinks just.[6]

Section 89 notice

8.13 Importation of infringing goods, material or articles, ss 89 and 90 In order to try to stop the importation of prohibited goods into the United Kingdom, the proprietor of a registered trade mark (or his licensee) may notify the Commissioners of Customs and Excise ('Customs') in writing:

(a) that he is the proprietor (or, as the case may be, a licensee) of the trade mark; and
(b) that infringing goods, material or articles are expected to arrive in the United Kingdom either:
  (i) from outside the European Economic Area (EEA); or
  (ii) from within the EEA but not having been in free circulation in the EEA.

The notice must specify the time and place of the expected arrival in the United Kingdom of the relevant infringing goods, material or articles. Provided that the proprietor can supply all of this information he may request Customs to treat the infringing goods, material or articles as 'prohibited goods'.[7] Prohibited goods may not be imported into the United Kingdom and are liable to forfeiture.[8]

Council Regulation (EC) No 3295/94 A proprietor cannot lodge a s 89 notice with Customs where he is entitled to lodge an

4 Section 19(3).
5 Section 19(3).
6 Section 19(4).
7 Section 89(1); see also paragraph 8.14 in relation to the regulations made under s 90 relating to the form in which a s 89 notice is to be given.
8 Section 89(2); no other penalty is applicable and the prohibition does not apply to goods imported for private or domestic use.

application under Article 3(1) of the Counterfeit Goods Regulation.[9] Article 3(1) of that Regulation reads as follows:

> 'In each Member State, the holder of a right may lodge an application in writing with the competent service of the customs authority for action by the customs authorities where the goods are placed in one of the situations referred to in Article 1(1)(a) of the Counterfeit Goods Regulation, namely:
>
> . . . where goods suspected of being counterfeit or pirated are:
>
> – entered for free circulation, export or re-export,
> – found when checks are made on goods placed under a suspensive procedure within the meaning of Article 84(1)(a) of Council Regulation (EC) No 2913/92 of 12 October 1992 establishing the Community Customs Code, or re-exported subject to notification.'

8.14 Regulations, s 90 Customs have made regulations as to the giving of a s 89 notice pursuant to the power granted under s 90.[10] The regulations specify the evidence which Customs will require in support of the s 89 notice and also deal with matters such as:

(a) the fees to be paid by the proprietor for lodging the notice;[11]
(b) the giving of security by the proprietor to cover Customs' potential liability or expenses; and
(c) the giving of an indemnity by the proprietor.[12]

The Schedule to the regulations contains a form of the notice which should be used by the proprietor (or licensee) to issue a s 89 notice (and a separate form has to be used in respect of each arrival of goods). Schedule 5 hereto reproduces the Schedule to the regulation.

Well-known trade marks

The proprietor of a well-known trade mark which is registered under the 1994 Act will be entitled to the remedies which have

9 Council Regulation (EC) No 3295/94 of 22 December 1994, OJ L341, 30.12.94, p 8.
10 The Trade Marks (Customs) Regulations 1994, which came into force on 31 October 1994; SI 1994/2625.
11 £30 (plus VAT) in respect of each notice.
12 Section 90(2).

already been discussed in this chapter. However, even if the well-known mark is not registered, the 1994 Act provides additional specific remedies which are considered below.

8.15 Injunction, s 56(2) The proprietor of a well-known trade mark[13] is entitled to an injunction to restrain the use in the United Kingdom of a trade mark which, or the essential part of which:

(a) is either identical with or similar to the proprietor's well-known trade mark; and

(b) is used in respect of identical or similar goods or services to those for which the proprietor's trade mark is well known,

provided that the use by the defendant is likely to cause confusion.[14]

It is important to remember that this remedy is only available to proprietors of well-known marks who are nationals of or domiciled (etc) in a Convention country which, by virtue of the definition of 'Convention country' in s 55(1)(b), does not include the United Kingdom.

The availability of an injunction under this provision is not dependent upon establishing infringement as such, but nonetheless involves establishing conduct which would constitute infringement under s 10(1) or (2) of the 1994 Act. However, unlike an action for infringement where the sign in question is identical with the registered trade mark and is used in respect of identical goods or services,[15] the proprietor of the well-known mark must, even in such circumstances, establish that the defendant's use of the mark is likely to cause confusion. Strictly, this means that the proprietor of the well-known mark will be put to proof of the likelihood of confusion even if the defendant is using an identical mark on identical goods or services. Presumably, however, the likelihood of confusion will be more easily established (or even inferred by the court) in the case of the use of a mark which is identical with the well-known trade mark in relation to identical goods or services for which the mark is well known.

A trade mark Section 56(2) enables the proprietor of a well-known trade mark to obtain an injunction against the use in the

13 ie a mark which is entitled to protection under the Paris Convention as a well-known mark: see the definition in s 56(1); see also Chapter 1.

14 Section 56(2). Subject to any statutory acquiescence: s 48, as to which, see paragraph 8.16.

15 ie an infringement under s 10(1).

United Kingdom of 'a trade mark'. Logically, the reference to a trade mark means that the mere use of a sign is not sufficient unless that sign falls within the definition of 'trade mark' in s 1(1). Limiting the remedy under s 56(2) to the use by the defendant of a trade mark is inconsistent with s 10, which makes it an infringement of a registered trade mark to use a 'sign' in any of the circumstances provided for in s 10.

Another point of interest arises because the reference to 'trade mark' must necessarily include registered trade marks. Hence, the position must be that the proprietor of a well-known trade mark can enjoin the use of a registered trade mark if such use otherwise falls within s 56(2). This is confirmed by the proviso at the end of the subsection which provides that the right to the injunction is subject to any acquiescence by the proprietor which is caught by s 48, which only applies in relation to acquiescence in the use of a registered trade mark. However, the proprietor of the registered trade mark will not be able to rely on the defence afforded by s 11(1) because that defence is only available in an action for the infringement of a registered trade mark: an injunction under s 56(2) is not founded on such an action. This means that the proprietor of a well-known trade mark takes priority over a registered trade mark in the event that there is a conflict, and the proprietor of the registered trade mark cannot rely on his registration to defeat an application for an injunction based on a well-known trade mark. Indeed, none of the statutory defences available to a defendant in an action for infringement are available to defeat such an application, except for acquiescence and bona fide prior use.[16]

Essential part of a trade mark It is sufficient for the grant of an injunction under s 56(2) if the 'essential part' of the defendant's trade mark is either identical with or similar to the well-known trade mark.[17] Presumably, the 'essential part' of the defendant's mark will be the distinctive element(s) of the mark which distinguish the goods or services to which it is applied. It may be the case that one or more elements of the well-known trade mark can be identified as being the feature(s) which make the mark 'well known' for the purpose of comparing the well-known trade mark with the defendant's mark. If the defendant's mark contains one or more of

16 Respectively, ss 48 and 56(3).
17 Provided, of course, that the other elements are satisfied.

these elements, then it can be argued strongly that its 'essential part' is at least similar to that of the well-known trade mark.

Likely to cause confusion The wording of the requirement that the defendant's use must be 'likely to cause confusion' is similar but not identical to the requirement in s 10(2) where, in order to constitute an infringement of a registered trade mark, the use of the defendant's sign must give rise to 'a likelihood of confusion on the part of the public . . .'[18] This is because the latter phrase is derived from the Directive, whereas s 56(2) is based on Article 6*bis* of the Paris Convention. However, it is likely that the phrases will be construed and applied consistently.

Comparison with passing off Given that an injunction under s 56(2) will often be sought in conjunction with a claim in tort for passing off, it is worth contrasting the two actions. It is likely that the injunction under s 56(2) may be more readily available for two reasons:

(a) in so far as it may be easier to establish that the defendant's use is likely to cause confusion (for the purposes of s 56(2)) than it is to establish misrepresentation and deception (for the purposes of passing off); and
(b) because the plaintiff does not need to have goodwill as such in the United Kingdom in order to rely on s 56(2) – on the other hand, the plaintiff in a passing off action does not, as a matter of law, need to establish that his mark is 'well known' although the notoriety of his mark will be a factor in the case.

Exceptions The entitlement of the proprietor of a well-known trade mark to an injunction under s 56(2) is subject to two exceptions, namely:

(a) where there has been acquiescence by the proprietor of the well-known trade mark;[19] and
(b) where there has been bona fide use of the mark by the defendant prior to 31 October 1994, being the date of the commencement of s 56.[20]

These two exceptions are considered below in paragraphs 8.16 and 8.17.

18 See paragraph 2.22 in relation to this phrase which also appears in ss 10(2) and 5(2).
19 As to which, see paragraph 8.16
20 As to which, see paragraph 8.17.

8.16 Acquiescence, ss 48 and 56(2) Statutory acquiescence under s 48 applies to the proprietor of an 'earlier trade mark' which, by virtue of the definition in s 6, will include the proprietor of a well-known trade mark. Thus, the proprietor of a well-known trade mark will not be entitled to an injunction under s 56(2) to restrain the use of a registered trade mark where the proprietor:

(a) has acquiesced for a continuous period of five years to the use of the registered trade mark in the United Kingdom; and
(b) was aware of that use.

As an exception to the exception, the injunction will always be available, despite the proprietor's acquiescence, where the original registration of the trade mark was applied for in bad faith.[1]

8.17 Saving for existing bona fide use, s 56(3) An injunction will not be granted under s 56(2) to prevent the continuation of any bona fide use of a trade mark (whether registered or unregistered), provided that such use commenced prior to 31 October 1994, being the date on which s 56 came into force.[2] Section 100 makes it clear that the onus is on the proprietor of a registered trade mark to show the use to which the mark has been put and, presumably, the same onus will be on the proprietor of an unregistered trade mark who seeks to rely on the exception set out in s 56(3).

Contrast also the more appropriate requirement in s 56(3) of prior 'bona fide' use with the requirement under s 11(3) where, to constitute a defence to infringement based on the use of an earlier right, the proprietor must be able to establish that the use of his earlier right is 'protected by virtue of any rule of law (in particular, the law of passing off)'.

Agents and representatives

Another statutory remedy which is available to certain trade mark proprietors is in the situation where the proprietor's agent or representative (such as a distributor) applies for the registration of the mark without the authority of the proprietor. The remedy does

1 Section 48(1)(b); see Chapter 7 for further comments on statutory acquiescence.
2 Section 56(3).

not depend upon proof of infringement as such, and is available where the mark in question is not registered under the 1994 Act.

8.18 Unauthorised acts of agents or representatives, s 60(4)–(6) The proprietor of a trade mark in a Convention country,[3] in addition to being able to oppose an application for the registration of his trade mark made by his agent(s) or representative(s),[4] may also (where such an application has been made) obtain an injunction to restrain any unauthorised use of his trade mark in the United Kingdom. The injunction will not be granted, however, if either:

(a) the agent or representative can justify his action;[5] or
(b) the proprietor of the trade mark has acquiesced to the use of his mark in the United Kingdom for a continuous period of at least three years.[6]

Note that acquiescence for the purposes of s 60(6) is different from acquiescence under s 48:

(1) The time periods are different (three years and five years respectively).
(2) The notice must be actual notice for s 48, whereas constructive notice may be sufficient for s 60(6).
(3) Bad faith will negate the operation of s 48, but there is no express exception for bad faith in s 60(6).

The proprietor can enjoin the unauthorised use of his trade mark by any party but, curiously, the injunction can only be granted under s 60(4) once an application for registration of his trade mark has been made by either his agent(s) or representative(s).[7] Section 60 of the 1994 Act is based on and purports to implement the terms of Article 6*septies* of the Paris Convention, which also requires an unauthorised application for registration to have been made by an agent or representative before the proprietor can obtain injunctive relief.

3 A country other than the United Kingdom which is a party to the Paris Convention: s 55(1).
4 Section 60(2); the proprietor may also apply for a declaration of invalidity of any subsequent registration or, alternatively, apply for rectification so as to substitute his name as the registered proprietor for that of his agent/representative: s 60(3); see Chapter 5 as to invalidity and Chapter 3 as to rectification.
5 Section 60(5); as to which, see paragraph 8.19.
6 Section 60(6).
7 Section 60(1).

8.19 Justification, s 60(5) An injunction under s 60(4) will not be granted to the proprietor of the mark if, or to the extent that, the agent or representative justifies his action.[8]

A number of points need to be made concerning this proviso.

Justifies his action Obvious ways in which the agent or representative could seek to justify his action would be to rely on either:

(a) an express or implied authorisation, whether contractual or otherwise; or

(b) a claim to be the proprietor of the trade mark in the United Kingdom.

What is it, though, that the agent or representative must 'justify'? In the context of s 60(4), the injunction sought will be in respect of the use made of the proprietor's trade mark, and therefore the 'action' which the agent or representative must justify is his use of the trade mark. This will not be the case in the context of s 60(2) and (3) where the 'action' which the agent or representative will need to justify is the making of the application for registration.

Royal arms etc

The 1994 Act creates certain criminal offences relating to the unauthorised use, in connection with any business, of the Royal arms (or closely resembling arms) or any other device, emblem or title in such a manner as to be calculated to lead to the belief that:

(a) in the case of the Royal arms, he is authorised by Her Majesty to use the Royal arms; or

(b) in the case of other relevant devices, emblems or titles, that he is employed by or supplies goods or services to Her Majesty or other members of the Royal family.[9]

8.20 Royal arms etc, s 99(1) and(4) In addition to constituting a criminal offence, the 1994 Act also provides that the unauthorised use, in connection with any business, of the Royal arms (or closely resembling arms) may be restrained by injunction in proceedings brought by:

(a) any person who is authorised to use the arms; or

8 Section 60(5).

9 Section 99 and see Chapter 17, paragraph 17.12 et seq.

(b) any person authorised by the Lord Chamberlain to take such proceedings.[10]

8.21 Other signs denoting royal connection, s 99(2) and (4) Similarly, the unauthorised use, in connection with any business, of any device, emblem or title in such a manner as to be calculated to lead to the belief that the person using the mark is employed by, or supplies goods or services to, Her Majesty or other members of the Royal family may also be restrained by injunction in proceedings brought by:

(a) any person who is authorised to use the device, emblem or title in question; or
(b) any person authorised by the Lord Chamberlain to take such proceedings.[11]

8.22 Defence, s 99(5) Section 99(5) of the 1994 Act provides a defence to an application for an injunction made pursuant to s 99(4):

> 'Nothing in [s 99] affects any right of the proprietor of a trade mark containing any such arms, device, emblem or title to use that trade mark.'

It would seem, therefore, that as long as the defendant to such proceedings can establish that the arms etc are contained in a mark which is a 'trade mark' (as defined in s 1(1)) and that he is the proprietor of that trade mark, then his use of that trade mark cannot be enjoined pursuant to s 99(4).

Co-proprietors

8.23 Co-proprietors, s 23 Co-proprietors, subject to any agreement between them to the contrary, are entitled to an equal undivided share in the registered trade mark.[12] Accordingly, any pecuniary remedy which co-proprietors may be awarded in respect of the infringement of their trade mark will be shared equally.

It will, therefore, be advisable for a co-proprietor who brings

10 Section 99(4).
11 Section 99(4).
12 Section 23(1).

infringement proceedings by himself[13] to reach an agreement in advance with his co-proprietor(s) as to the apportionment of any pecuniary remedy which may be awarded in respect of the infringement.

Licensees

8.24 Introduction, ss 30 and 31 The position of a licensee in the context of considering his remedies for infringement will depend upon whether:

(a) the licensee is the plaintiff suing for the infringement of his licensor's registered trade mark (see paragraph 8.25); or

(b) the licensor/proprietor is the plaintiff and the licensee has suffered or is likely to suffer loss (see paragraph 8.26).

Reference should also be made to Chapter 10 on the subject of licensing in general.

8.25 Licensee as the plaintiff One further needs to distinguish between licensees generally and those exclusive licensees who have the rights and remedies of an assignee.

Licensees generally[14] Licensees generally are given a statutory entitlement (subject to the terms of the licence) to bring proceedings in their own name if the proprietor[15] refuses or fails to do so within two months of being called upon by his licensee.[16]

In these circumstances, the licensee may bring proceedings in his own name as if he were the proprietor.[17] Therefore, he will have the same rights and remedies to which the proprietor would have been entitled had the proprietor himself commenced the proceedings. This does not mean, of course, that the licensee can recover

13 ie in accordance with s 23(5).

14 Including exclusive licensees not having the rights and remedies of an assignee under s 31(1), as well as sub-licensees in the case of an exclusive licensee having the rights and remedies of an assignee: s 30(7).

15 Or an exclusive licensee who has the rights and remedies of an assignee: s 30(7)

16 Sections 30(2) and (3).

17 Section 30(3); the proprietor himself will need to be joined as a plaintiff or added as a defendant: s 30(4); but not in the case of an application for interlocutory relief which can be made by the licensee alone: s 30(4).

damages suffered by the proprietor: the licensee will only be able to recover those damages which he himself has suffered.[18]

Exclusive licensees It is necessary to consider separately the position of exclusive licensees who, pursuant to the terms of their exclusive licence,[19] have the same rights and remedies in respect of matters occurring after the grant of the licence as if the licence had been an assignment. Such exclusive licensees may bring infringement proceedings against any person (other than the proprietor) in their own name,[20] and their rights and remedies are deemed to be concurrent with those of the proprietor.[1] Some of the effects of 'concurrency' are that, in an action for infringement:

(a) the court, in assessing damages, will take into account:
   (i) the terms of the licence; and
   (ii) any pecuniary remedy already awarded or available to either the proprietor or the licensee in respect of the infringement;[2]

(b) no account of profits will be directed by the court if either:
   (i) an award of damages has been made; or
   (ii) an account of profits has been directed,

   in favour of the other of them in respect of the same infringement;[3] and

(c) the court will, if an account of profits is directed, apportion those profits between the proprietor and the exclusive licensee as the court considers just.[4]

These conditions apply to any action for infringement in respect of which the proprietor and an exclusive licensee have or had concurrent rights, regardless of whether they are both parties to the proceedings. If not, the court will make directions as it thinks fit as to how the party to the proceedings is to hold the proceeds of any pecuniary remedy on behalf of the other.

18 *Northern & Shell plc v Condé Nast and National Magazines Distributors Ltd* [1995] RPC 117.

19 For the definitions of exclusive licensee and exclusive licence see s 29(1).

20 Section 31(1); the proprietor himself will need to be joined as a plaintiff or added as a defendant: s 31(4), but not in the case of an application for interlocutory relief which can be made by the licensee alone: s 31(4).

1 Section 31(2).

2 Section 31(6)(a).

3 Section 31(6)(b).

4 Section 31(6)(c); subject to any agreement between the proprietor and the licensee: s 31(6)(c) and (8).

8.26 Proprietor as the plaintiff Once again, one must distinguish between licensees generally and those exclusive licensees who have the rights and remedies of an assignee.

Licensees generally In infringement proceedings brought by the proprietor, any loss suffered or likely to be suffered by licensees[5] will be taken into account and the court will give directions as it thinks fit as to the extent to which the proprietor is to hold the proceeds of any pecuniary remedy on behalf of licensees.[6]

Exclusive licensees The position of an exclusive licensee who has, pursuant to the terms of his licence, the rights and remedies of an assignee, is that if the proprietor and the exclusive licensee are not both parties to the proceedings, then the court will give directions as it thinks fit as to the extent to which the party to the proceedings is to hold the proceeds of any pecuniary remedy on behalf of the other.[7]

8.27 Remedy for groundless threats, s 21 The 1994 Act introduced for the first time in trade mark legislation in the United Kingdom a remedy for groundless threats of infringement proceedings. However, this is not a remedy for the infringement of a registered trade mark and therefore is dealt with separately in Chapter 9.

5 Including exclusive licensees not having the rights and remedies of an assignee under s 31(1), as well as sub-licensees in the case of an exclusive licensee having the rights and remedies of an assignee: s 30(7).
6 Section 30(6).
7 Section 31(6).

9 Groundless threats of infringement proceedings

9.01 Introduction The 1994 Act introduced a new cause of action in respect of certain (but not all) unjustifiable threats of proceedings for infringement of a registered trade mark.[1] Similar causes of action are available in respect of threats of proceedings for infringement of other intellectual property rights and the corresponding provision relating to patents[2] is in similar terms to s 21 of the 1994 Act. Useful guidance as to the interpretation and application of s 21 can therefore be found in decisions concerning unjustifiable threats of patent infringement (and notwithstanding that decisions have now been handed down under s 21).[3]

9.02 Cause of action, s 21 If someone threatens another with registered trade mark infringement proceedings, then any person aggrieved by the threat may bring proceedings for certain relief.[4]

1 Section 21(1); see also ss 52(3)(a)(i) and 54(3)(a) pursuant to which the Secretary of State may make regulations applying the provisions of s 21 to Community trade marks and international trade marks.
2 Patents Act 1977, s 70.
3 Indeed, this was the approach taken by Jacob J in *Big Smith Global Ltd v Caterpillar Inc* (unreported, see ITMA Newsletter, October 1996, p 5) and Neuberger J in *Prince plc v Prince Sports Group Inc* [1998] FSR 21. For a general commentary in relation to s 21 see Lim Heng Gee 'The "Threats" Section in the UK Trade Marks Act 1994: Can a Person still Wound without Striking?' [1995] 3 EIPR 138.
4 As to which, see paragraph 9.04.

However, no right of action exists where the alleged infringement is said to arise out of:

(a) the application of the mark to goods or their packaging;
(b) the importation of goods to which, or to the packaging of which, the mark has been applied; or
(c) the supply of services under the mark.[5]

Threat It falls to consider what will constitute a threat for the purpose of this section. It has been held in the context of a threat of patent infringement proceedings that it is enough '. . . if the language used is such as would convey to any reasonable man that the person using the language intended to bring proceedings for infringement against the person said to be threatened'.[6] The question as to whether a communication constitutes a threat will be decided objectively and in accordance with how the threat would be understood by any ordinary trader.[7] Thus, the threat may even be implied – for example, where a letter contains a threat of proceedings for passing off and at the same time notifies the recipient of details of a trade mark registration: it was held in the *Jaybeam* case[8] that the notification of the existence of a registered design, in the same letter as a threat of proceedings for copyright infringement, was an actionable threat of proceedings for infringement of the registered design.

Although communications which follow the original threat may influence the nature of any relief which may be granted under s 21, they cannot alter the fact (if it is the case) that the first communication constituted a threat.[9]

It should be noted that the mere notification that a trade mark is registered, or that an application for registration has been made, does not constitute a 'threat' 0and therefore is not actionable.[10]

5 Section 21(1).
6 *C & P Development Co (London) Ltd v Sisabro Novelty Co Ltd* (1953) 70 RPC 277 per Jenkins LJ.
7 *Brain v Ingledew Brown Bennison and Garrett (a firm) (No 3)* [1997] FSR 511. See also the decisions of Clauson J in *Luna Advertising Co Ltd v Burnham & Co* (1928) 45 RPC 258 at 260 and Aldous J in *Bowden Controls Ltd v Acco Cable Controls Ltd* [1990] RPC 427 at 431. For a useful list of what has and has not been accepted as constituting a threat under patent law, see Encyclopedia of United Kingdom and European Patent Law, paragraph 10–403.
8 *Jaybeam Ltd v Abru Aluminium Ltd* [1976] RPC 308, a case under the Registered Designs Act 1949, s 26 (3).
9 *Prince*, supra (Neuberger J).
10 Section 21(4).

On the other hand, there is no requirement that the threat be in writing, and an oral threat may therefore be actionable. Furthermore, the threat may be made from outside the United Kingdom[11] and may even be made to persons outside the United Kingdom.[12]

Recipient of the threat There is no limit to the category of persons to whom an actionable threat may be made. It is the alleged acts of infringement by the recipient of the threat which determine whether the threat is actionable.[13] The only issue is whether a 'class' threat made generally to the public or a section of the public, but not to a named individual or undertaking, is actionable. A strict reading of subs 21(1) would suggest that a general threat is not actionable because it is not made to 'another' person.[14]

Person aggrieved The cause of action is only conferred on a 'person aggrieved' by the threat of infringement proceedings. Elsewhere in the 1994 Act the right to bring proceedings is conferred on 'any person' in the case of opposition proceedings,[15] revocation proceedings,[16] and invalidity proceedings.[17] It is clearly appropriate that this new cause of action should only be available to persons actually affected by the threat.

The phrase 'person aggrieved' was the test for standing to bring proceedings under the 1938 Act for the removal of a registered trade mark on the basis of non-use[18] or for the rectification of the Register.[19] Under the 1938 Act the courts construed this phrase liberally, and it has been suggested that any person in or connected with the goods or services concerned or any allied trade or service would be likely to have sufficient standing.[20] Laddie J in *Brain v*

11 *Big Smith Global Ltd v Caterpillar Inc* unreported: see ITMA Newsletter, October 1996, p 5.

12 *Dimplex (UK) Ltd v De'Longhi Ltd* [1996] FSR 622.

13 *Cavity Trays Ltd v RMC Panel Products Ltd* [1996] RPC 361, a decision of the Court of Appeal under Patents Act 1977, s 70 per Aldous J.

14 This is consistent with the opinion of Lindley LJ in *Johnson v Edge* (1892) 9 RPC 142, where he said that the equivalent section does not prevent a patentee from issuing a general warning because it 'is not a threat against anybody in particular'.

15 Section 38(2).

16 Section 46(4).

17 Section 47(3).

18 1938 Act, s 26(1).

19 1938 Act, s 32(1).

20 Kerly, 12th edition, paragraph 11.07; see also the following cases: *KODIAK Trade Mark* [1987] RPC 269; *Ritz Hotel Ltd v Charles of the Ritz Ltd* (1988) 12 IPR 417 and *R H Macey & Co Inc v Trade Accents* (1992) 22 IPR 587.

Ingledew[1] thought that the use of the phrase was designed to exclude frivolous applications and applications by 'busybodies' who have no real personal interest in the threats. But what might the effect be of an ulterior motive on the part of the applicant? It is submitted that if the applicant is otherwise a person aggrieved it should not matter that he may also have another (or an ulterior) motive for bringing the proceedings under s 21.

Certainly, the person who is threatened must be a person aggrieved.[2] So, also, may be any manufacturer, supplier and/or distributor of the relevant goods or services. As decided in cases under earlier trade mark legislation, the courts, in considering whether a person is a 'person aggrieved' under the 1994 Act, will require that the grievance is substantial and not merely fanciful[3] or, as Laddie J states in the *Dimplex* case,[4] the person aggrieved must establish by evidence that the threats complained of had caused, or were likely to cause damage to him which was not minimal. Depending upon the facts of the case, a director, executive or even a shareholder, may be a 'person aggrieved' where the threat is made to his company; this will depend upon whether he has a sufficient personal interest in the company concerned. In the opinion of Laddie J, the courts should not be astute to find that the complainant has not been affected in his personal activities where it is clear that the purpose of the threat was to do so.[5]

In circumstances where the person claiming to be aggrieved is not the party threatened with the infringement proceedings, it will generally be necessary for that person to adduce evidence of the nature of his grievance.[6] In the *Dimplex* case,[7] Laddie J was satisfied

1 *Brain v Ingledew Brown Bennison and Garrett (a firm) (No 3)* [1997] FSR 511.
2 *John Summers & Sons Ltd v Cold Metal Process Co* (1947) 65 RPC 75 (a case under the Patents Act 1977). Although Neuberger J was prepared to accept that there could be 'exceptional circumstances' where a threat made directly to an alleged infringer would not render him a 'person aggrieved': *Prince*, supra (Neuberger J).
3 For example *Wright Crossley and Co's Trade Mark* (1898) 15 RPC 131 and at 377, CA.
4 *Dimplex (UK) Ltd v De'Longhi Ltd* [1996] FSR 622, a case under Patents Act 1977, s 70.
5 *Brain v Ingledew Brown Bennison and Garrett (a firm) (No 3)* [1997] FSR 511.
6 See *Reymes-Cole v Elite Hosiery Co Ltd* [1965] RPC 102 where the failure to adduce such evidence was held to be a fatal lacuna in the defendant's claim against the plaintiff under s 65(2) of the Patents Act 1949.
7 *Dimplex (UK) Ltd v De'Longhi Ltd* [1996] FSR 622, a case under Patents Act 1977, s 70.

that a the manufacturer was a 'person aggrieved' in respect of threatening letters sent to its customers because 'regard should be paid to the defendant's clear intention to scare off customers'.

The defendant It is clear that the cause of action will be against the person making the threat and thus proprietors and their legal advisers alike may be exposed to liability. Certainly, this has been the case under the corresponding provisions of patent legislation.

9.03 The exception or the rule? Logically, any threat of infringement proceedings must be based on an allegation that a person has infringed a registered trade mark on one or more of the grounds specified in s 10. An infringement under s 10 involves the alleged infringer using a sign (in particular, in one or more of the ways specified in s 10(4)).

The cause of action in respect of an unjustifiable threat of infringement proceedings is specifically limited to certain types of infringing activity and therefore certain threats will not be actionable. Thus, certain alleged acts of infringement can be the subject of a threat of proceedings without the risk of the alleged infringer (or other aggrieved person) being able to obtain relief under s 21(1).

In order to identify which threats are potentially actionable one needs to cross-match those uses of a mark which can constitute infringement under s 10 with those uses of a mark which are specified in the exceptions to the cause of action listed in s 21(1). The table below shows that there are some strange anomalies. For example, it is not an actionable threat under s 21 if the threatened infringement proceedings are in respect of the supply of services, but it may be actionable under s 21 to make a threat of proceedings in respect of the offer of services under the mark. The corresponding provision of the Patents Act 1977[8] has been commented upon by the Court of Appeal[9] and was considered to be 'free from ambiguity'.

Presumably, the reference in s 21(1)(a), (b) and (c) to 'the mark' must be construed as a reference to the mark, sign or indication being used by the alleged infringer. The alternative interpretation, that 'the mark' refers to the proprietor's registered trade mark, would limit the availability of the exceptions to situations where the

8 ie s 70(4).
9 *Cavity Trays Ltd v RMC Panel Products Ltd* [1996] RPC 361.

threat of infringement proceedings refers specifically to the use of the registered trade mark. This would mean that a threat of infringement proceedings in respect of the use of a sign (where the sign is not the registered trade mark) can never come within the exceptions and, hence, any such threat will be actionable under s 21(1).[10]

ACTIONABLE THREAT	NON-ACTIONABLE THREAT
Offers or exposes goods for sale	Affixes mark to goods; 21(1)(a)
Puts goods on the market	Affixes mark to packaging; 21(1)(a)
Offers services	Supplies services; 21(1)(c)
Exports goods	Imports goods; 21(1)(b)
Uses the mark on business papers	
Uses the mark in advertising	
Stocks goods for offering or exposing goods for sale	

9.04 Relief, s 21(2) A person aggrieved by an actionable threat of infringement proceedings may apply for:
(a) a declaration that the threats are unjustifiable;
(b) an injunction against the continuance of the threats; and
(c) damages in respect of any loss he has sustained by the threats.[11]
Declarations and injunctions are equitable remedies and, despite the wording of s 21(2) (which states that: 'the plaintiff is entitled to such relief'), the court still retains its discretion in respect of these equitable remedies.[12] (This is also the case under the equivalent, but differently worded, section of the Patents Act 1977.[13]) In exercising his discretion in the *Prince* case[14] Neuberger J took into account the fact that the defendant was not prepared to offer an undertaking in

10 It would have been more logical had the exceptions been drafted with reference to the use of a 'sign' rather than by reference to the use of 'the mark'.
11 Section 21(2).
12 *Prince*, supra (Neuberger J).
13 *Dimplex (UK) Ltd v De'Longhi Ltd* [1996] FSR 622, where Laddie J held that s 70 of the Patents Act 1977 did not take away from the court its discretion and, prima facie, where the tort is made out, the plaintiff is entitled to relief unless there are good reasons for deciding otherwise.
14 *Prince*, supra (Neuberger J).

lieu of the injunction sought under s 21(2)(b). Importantly, a declaration can be granted under s 21(2)(a) even though the applicant (person aggrieved) is not suffering any damages as a result of the defendant's threats.[15]

In the context of an application for damages, the applicant will need to satisfy the court that he has prima facie suffered some damage before the court will order a full inquiry as to damages.[16]

9.05 Defence, s 21 The applicant (person aggrieved) is prima facie entitled to the specified remedies unless the person making the threat establishes that the act(s) in respect of which proceedings were threatened actually constitute(s) an infringement of the registered trade mark in question.[17] It is therefore axiomatic that if the threat is made before the trade mark in question is registered, then this defence will not be available unless the mark has been registered by the time of the trial.[18]

This defence will not be made out if the applicant (person aggrieved) establishes that the registration of the trade mark relied upon is either invalid[19] or liable to be revoked[20] in a relevant respect.[1]

9.06 Comment When drafting a 'letter-before-action' threatening certain trade mark infringement proceedings it will obviously be important to bear in mind the wording of s 21, in particular, because it may be possible to draft the letter in such a way that the threat is not actionable in any event. Indeed, practitioners would be wise to heed the warning given by Laddie J in *Antec International*[2] where he said:

> 'it is quite unacceptable that professional men should make wild and unsupportable allegations of trade mark infringement [in casu, a registration where the only resemblance with the allegedly infringing mark was on a disclaimed element, the

15 *Trebor Bassett Ltd v Football Association* [1997] FSR 211.

16 *Prince*, supra: Neuberger J gave the applicant further time to adduce the necessary evidence before determining whether an inquiry should be ordered.

17 Section 21(2).

18 *Brain v Ingledew Brown Bennison and Garrett (No 2)* [1997] FSR 271, a case decided under Patents Act 1977, s 70.

19 Pursuant to s 47.

20 Pursuant to s 46.

1 Section 21(3).

2 *Antec International Ltd v South Western Chicks (Warren) Ltd* [1997] FSR 278.

> existence of the disclaimer not having been disclosed] and that they should refuse to disclose the identity of the registered trade mark on which they are threatening their client's competitors . . . it is not acceptable for those who have the status of expert professional men in the trade mark field to use the weight of their professional qualifications to make clearly unacceptable allegations of trade mark infringement against a trader.'

Similar words of warning can be found in *Prince* where Neuberger J observed that s 21 is:

> 'concerned to ensure that threats of infringement proceedings are not made casually or recklessly, because of the potential damage and concern they can cause.'

It may be argued that in certain circumstances it would be better tactics not to write a letter-before-action but merely commence proceedings to ensure that the owner of the trade mark is a plaintiff in an infringement action rather than the defendant to a 'threats' action. Of course, the cost implications of proceeding in such a manner would have to be taken into account.

9.07 Common law remedies The main remedy available under common law for unjustified threats of legal proceedings is the action for the tort of injurious falsehood. Injurious falsehood is dealt with in general terms in Chapter 19; in the specific instance where the tort relates to unjustified threats, the plaintiff will have to establish:

(a) that the threat was made;
(b) that the allegation of infringement is false;
(c) that the threat was made maliciously; and
(d) that the threat caused him special damage.[3]

3 See *Wren v Weild* (1869) LR 4 QB 730 and *Colley v Hart* (1890) 7 RPC 101.

10 Dealings in trade marks: assignments, licences and other agreements relating to trade marks

10.01 Approach taken by the 1994 Act The statutory provisions relating to the assignment and licensing of registered trade marks have become steadily less restrictive. This can be seen by comparing s 22 of the 1938 Act with s 22 of the 1905 Act and s 70 of the 1883 Act. Consistent with this more liberal attitude, the 1994 Act further simplifies the conditions and restrictions attaching to such dealings.

In particular, there are four features introduced in the 1994 Act worthy of note:

(a) it is possible under the 1994 Act to assign partially a registered trade mark in relation to a particular manner of use or in relation to a particular locality without having to seek the Registrar's approval;[1]

(b) there is no procedure under the 1994 Act for the Registrar to enter identical or similar marks on the Register as associated trade marks and thus such marks can be assigned independently of each other;[2]

(c) the assignment of a registered trade mark under the 1994 Act without the goodwill of the business in which it is used will take effect immediately, without the need to advertise the

1 Section 24(2); cf 1938 Act, s 22(6).

2 cf 1938 Act, s 23; but an assignment which renders the subsequent use of the trade mark likely to mislead the public may lead to the revocation of the registration pursuant to 1994 Act, s 46(1)(d).

assignment;[3] and

(d) it is possible under the 1994 Act to assign a pending application for the registration of a trade mark independently of another registered trade mark.[4]

These amendments reflect the new policy underlying the 1994 Act, that is, to provide a legal framework which serves the requirements of modern business and industry. Applying this policy to the assignment and licensing of trade marks has meant that the rules which sought primarily to protect the public from being misled or deceived by the fact of two or more people using the same trade mark have been relaxed. Although this policy rightly enables trade mark owners to deal more freely with their trade marks without the intervention of strict and even artificial rules, all trade mark owners will nonetheless have to be vigilant to ensure that:

(a) their dealings do not result in their trade marks becoming misleading, deceptive or even generic; and
(b) the reputation and goodwill attaching to their trade marks does not become diluted.

The 1994 Act deals with:

(a) the transmission (including the assignment) of trade marks in s 24;
(b) the licensing of trade marks in ss 28 and 29;
(c) the rights and remedies of licensees in ss 30 and 31;
(d) the entering onto the Register of prescribed particulars of registrable transactions (of which assignments and licences are examples) in s 25; and
(e) the granting of security interests in respect of trade marks in s 24(4) and (5).

This chapter deals with each of these issues; (c) above is also considered in Chapter 8 (Remedies). Furthermore:

(f) tax and stamp duty issues are considered in paragraphs 10.23 and 10.24; and
(g) the potential application of EC and UK competition law is considered in paragraphs 10.25 and 10.26,

in so far as such matters may impact on assignments and licences of trade marks.

3 cf 1938 Act, s 22(7); but the prescribed particulars of all assignments should still be registered pursuant to 1994 Act, s 25.
4 cf 1938 Act, s 22(3).

Transmissions

10.02 Assignments and other transmissions, s 24(1) A registered trade mark, or an application for the registration of a trade mark, is transmissible:

(a) by assignment;[5]
(b) by testamentary disposition; or
(c) by operation of law,

in the same way as other personal or moveable property.[6]

The transmission may be made either in connection with the goodwill of a business or independently of such goodwill.[7] This provision is similar in substance to s 22(1) of the 1938 Act,[8] except that, as already stated:

(a) there is no need to advertise an assignment which is without goodwill;[9] and
(b) applications for the registration of a trade mark may also be assigned independently of any registered trade mark.[10]

The freedom to transmit a registered trade mark or an application therefor is tempered by the risk that the subsequent use made of the mark may lead to the revocation of the registration if the use is liable to mislead the public, particularly as to the nature, quality or geographical origin of the goods or services in relation to which it is registered.[11] This risk is all the more real in practice where either:

(a) the transmission is without the goodwill of the business in which the mark has been used, because the mark may no longer be used in relation to the goods or services for which it has become known; and/or
(b) the transmission is a partial transmission to an unrelated party, because in such circumstances it is imperative to ensure, as far as possible, both in terms of the drafting of the relevant agreements and in the actual use of the mark by the parties concerned, that any deceptive or misleading use is precluded.

5 In the case of co-proprietors, subject to the consent of each: s 23(4)(b).
6 Section 24(1).
7 Section 24(1).
8 The 1938 Act will continue to apply in relation to transactions that occurred prior to 31 October 1994, while s 24 of the 1994 Act will apply to transactions occurring on or after that date: Sch 3, para 8(1).
9 ie there is no equivalent to s 22(7) of the 1938 Act.
10 Section 27(1).
11 ie pursuant to s 46(1)(d).

For example, it would be legitimate (if not prudent) for the parties concerned in their own respective interests to agree on some form of 'code of use' which, if properly followed, will at least minimise the potential for misleading the public.

Further considerations which need to be borne in mind are that:

(a) if the assignment is part of a 'market sharing' arrangement, then it may be void under competition law principles; and/or

(b) the assignor may face competition in his own territory from goods being brought into his territory bearing his former trade mark.

Both of these issues, as well as other competition law issues, are considered in more detail in paragraphs 10.25 and 10.26.

10.03 Partial assignments and other transmissions, s 24(2)

An assignment or other transmission of a registered trade mark (or of an application for the registration of a trade mark) may be partial, that is, limited so that it applies only in relation to:

(a) some but not all of the goods or services for which the trade mark is registered; and/or

(b) the use of the trade mark in a particular manner; and/or

(c) the use of the trade mark in a particular locality.[12]

The option to assign partially a registered trade mark (or an application therefor) in the manner described in (b) and (c) above extends the scope of permissible dealings which, under the 1938 Act, absent the consent of the Registrar, were limited to those specified in (a) above.[13]

10.04 Transmissions subject to licences, ss 28(3) and 29(2)

If a licence has been granted by the proprietor in respect of a registered trade mark which is subsequently assigned or otherwise transmitted, then, unless the licence otherwise provides:

(a) the licence will be binding on the successor in title to whom the mark has been assigned or otherwise transmitted;[14] and

(b) an exclusive licensee will have the same rights against the successor in title as he had against the proprietor.[15]

12 Section 24(2).

13 See 1994 Act, s 24(2) and cf 1938 Act, s 22(6).

14 Section 28(3).

15 Section 29(2); as to the rights of exclusive licensees against the proprietor, see paragraphs 10.15 and 8.22.

10.05 Requirement of writing, s 24(3) It is a mandatory requirement that an assignment (as well as an assent of a personal representative where the mark is transmitted by testamentary disposition) relating to either:

(a) a registered trade mark; or

(b) an application for the registration of a trade mark,

must be in writing and signed by or on behalf of the assignor (or, as the case may be, the personal representative).[16] The requirement of a signature may be satisfied by a body corporate affixing its seal (except in Scotland).[17]

A purported assignment or assent which does not comply with these requirements is not effective.

10.06 Operation of law, s 24(1) Apart from an assignment or a testamentary disposition, a registered trade mark (or an application therefor) is also transmissible by 'operation of law'. This phrase was not used in s 22 of the 1938 Act, but will include any order of a court or other competent authority transferring the trade mark (or the application for registration) to another person.[18] Such a transmission is a registrable transaction for the purposes of s 25(2).[19]

10.07 Assignment of unregistered trade marks, s 24(6) Nothing in the 1994 Act affects the assignment or other transmission of an unregistered trade mark as part of the goodwill of a business.[20] Thus, such an assignment will not be governed by s 24 and will stand or fall in accordance with the common law rules relating to unregistered trade marks. The fundamental common law rule relating to the assignment of unregistered trade marks is that unregistered trade marks are not items of property in their own right and, therefore, cannot be assigned independently of the goodwill of the business in which they are used. However, it has been held that the sale of the goodwill of a business will, by implication, operate as an assignment to the purchaser of the unregistered trade marks used in that business without any express

16 Section 24(3).
17 Section 24(3).
18 eg s 60(3)(b), pursuant to which the name of the proprietor can be substituted in certain circumstances.
19 As to which, see paragraph 10.18 et seq.
20 Section 24(6).

or specific assignment of the trade marks needed.[1] Accordingly, if a trade mark is neither registered nor the subject of an application, then it must be assigned in conjunction with the goodwill of the business in which it was used in order to constitute a valid assignment of the unregistered mark.

10.08 Security and charges, s 24(4) and (5) The provisions relating to the transmission of a registered trade mark apply equally to an assignment by way of security, that is, where the proprietor assigns his trade mark in order to secure a loan (usually on the condition that the trade mark is re-assigned by the proprietor on re-payment of the loan).[2]

A registered trade mark (as well as an application for the registration of a trade mark) may be the subject of a charge[3] in the same way as other personal or moveable property.[4] Thus, the proprietor of a registered trade mark (or an application for registration) can, for example, secure any loan or other debt by granting a charge over his trade mark which may be fixed or floating. As with an assignment by way of security, the charge will be discharged when the loan/debt is repaid.

Trade marks (as well as other intellectual property rights) are capable of being valued in accordance with accepted objective criteria. Furthermore, such valuations are now increasingly finding their way onto the balance sheets of many companies, despite the cynicism of certain accountants and analysts who distrust (or are at least sceptical of) these valuations because of the intangible nature of intellectual property. However, provided that the valuation of the mark is fair, trade mark owners should consider using the valuation in order to raise (or to assist in raising) capital as and when required, just as one would use any other valuable asset.

10.09 Transitional provisions, Schedule 3

Transactions occurring prior to 31 October 1994 The 1938 Act continues to apply in relation to transactions occurring prior to 31

1 *Shipwright v Clements* (1871) 19 WR 599; *W Currie & Co v Currie* (1898) 15 RPC 339; *Western Trade Mark* [1968] RPC 167 at 183.
2 Section 24(4).
3 In Scotland, the subject of security.
4 Section 24(5); in the case of co-proprietors, subject to the consent of each: s 24(3)(b).

October 1994, while s 24 of the 1994 Act applies to transactions occurring on or after that date.[5]

Assignments and transmissions registered under the 1938 Act Entries in the 1938 Register under s 25 of the 1938 Act relating to assignments and transmissions which occurred prior to 31 October 1994 were transferred to the 1994 Register on 31 October 1994 and have effect as if made under s 25 of the 1994 Act.[6]

Applications under the 1938 Act An application under s 25 of the 1938 Act for the registration of an assignment or transmission which occurred prior to 31 October 1994 is dealt with under:

(a) the 1938 Act, where the application had already been determined but not finally determined as at 31 October 1994;[7] or
(b) s 25 of the 1994 Act, where the application was pending as at 31 October 1994.[8]

Applications under the 1994 Act Where a person became entitled prior to 31 October 1994 to be recorded as the proprietor of a mark registered under the 1938 Act by virtue of an assignment or transmission, but did not register his title on or before that date, any subsequent application for the registration of his title must now be made under s 25 of the 1994 Act. Section 25(3) of the 1938 Act will, however, continue to apply as regards the consequences of his failure to register the assignment/transmission, rather than s 25(3) and (4) of the 1994 Act.[9]

Licences

10.10 Introduction A feature of the 1994 Act is that it contains no registered user provisions, although it does provide for certain particulars of registrable transactions, including licences, to be entered on the Register.[10]

5 Schedule 3, para 8(1).
6 Schedule 3, para 8(2).
7 Schedule 3, para 8(4); any subsequent registration is transferred to the 1994 Register pursuant to para 8(2).
8 Schedule 3, para 8(3); in which case the application will proceed in accordance with s 25 of the 1994 Act, except that s 25(3) of the 1938 Act will continue to apply as regards the consequences of failing to register the assignment/transmission rather than s 25(3) and (4) of the 1994 Act.
9 Schedule 3, para 8(5) and (6).

Importantly, there are no express requirements in the 1994 Act in relation to the substance of licence agreements as were found in s 28 of the 1938 Act, and the so-called 'anti-trafficking' provision has no equivalent in the 1994 Act.[11] Thus, the decision in *Holly Hobbie*[12] (as it related to s 28(6)) is no longer applicable, no doubt to the great relief of those involved in one form of merchandising or another.

As with assignments, the policy is that trade mark owners should be free to license the use of their trade marks as they see fit, and the only caveat is the proprietor's own interest in maintaining the distinctiveness and hence the value of his trade mark by, inter alia, asserting proper quality control over the goods or services for which it is licensed.

10.11 General and limited licences, s 28(1) A licence to use a registered trade mark may be general or limited.[13] A 'general' licence means that the licensee may use the trade mark throughout the United Kingdom in relation to all the goods or services for which the trade mark is registered. A 'limited' licence means that the licensee may, for example, only be allowed to use the trade mark:

(a) in relation to some but not all of the goods or services covered by the registration; and/or
(b) in a particular manner or in a particular locality.[14]

Comparison with the 1938 Act Provided that the licence otherwise complied with the requirements of s 28 of the 1938 Act, a licensee could also have been granted either a 'general' or a 'limited' licence in the same terms as provided for in s 28 of the 1994 Act. However, unlike the 1938 Act, there is no express requirement in the 1994 Act that the Registrar must first be satisfied that the use of the trade mark by the licensee would not be contrary to the public interest.[15] Of course, under the 1994 Act, if a licensee's use of the trade mark results in it becoming generic or misleading to the

10 As to registrable transactions see s 25(1) and (2).
11 ie 1938 Act, s 28(6).
12 [1984] 1 All ER 426, [1984] 1 WLR 189, [1984] RPC 329.
13 Section 28(1).
14 Section 28(1); this is not an exhaustive list of the ways in which a licence can be limited.
15 See 1938 Act, s 28(5).

public, then the registration of the trade mark may be revoked pursuant to s 46(1)(c) or (d).

10.12 Requirement of writing, s 28(2) A licence, whether general or limited, must be in writing and signed by or on behalf of the licensor.[16] The requirement of a signature may be satisfied by a body corporate affixing its seal (except in Scotland).

A purported licence which does not comply with these requirements is 'not effective'.[17] This may create a problem when read in the context of subsections 46(1)(a) or (b) which provide that a trade mark may be revoked on the grounds of non-use. However, 'use' for the purposes of these subsections will include any use of the trade mark with the 'consent' of the proprietor. What, then, is the effect in this context of a licence which is deemed to be 'not effective' because it does not comply with s 28(2)? It is assumed that the mere fact that a licence is not effective does not negate the proprietor's actual consent to the use of his trade mark by the licensee. More difficult questions may arise when a licence is deemed to be 'not effective'; for example:

(1) Can a licensor sue to enforce royalty payments?
(2) Can a licensee rely on the licence as a defence to an infringement action?
(3) What are the rights of successors in title?

Certainly, a licence which is 'not effective' is not a registrable transaction for the purposes of s 25 and therefore the licensee will not have the rights and remedies prescribed in ss 30 and 31.

10.13 Assignment and rights of licensees, ss 28(3) and 29(2) Unless the licence provides otherwise, it will be binding on any subsequent assignee (or other transferee of the licensed mark) whose title will be subject to the terms of the licence and therefore to the rights of the licensee.[18]

Furthermore, an exclusive licensee has the same rights against a subsequent proprietor/assignee, who is bound by the licence, as he (ie the exclusive licensee) has against the licensor.[19]

16 Section 28(2).
17 Section 28(2).
18 Section 28(3).
19 Section 29(2).

10.14 Sub-licences, s 28(4) The provisions of the 1994 Act relating to licences and licensees apply equally to sub-licences and to sub-licensees. However, the right to sub-license will not be implied. A licensee wishing to grant a sub-licence must obtain the express right to do so.[20]

Consequences of termination The consequences of any termination of a head licence should be considered carefully where that licence included the right to grant sub-licences. The proprietor/licensor will no doubt want to provide expressly that any sub-licence will terminate either automatically or at his election on any termination of the head licence. Whereas the sub-licensee will want to protect his rights under the sub-licence by providing expressly that the sub-licence is not conditional upon the subsistence of the head licence. Of course, the question as to whether the sub-licence survives the termination of the head licence will depend upon the intentions of the licensor and the licensee as evidenced by the terms of the head licence. The sub-licensee may therefore not be able to protect his position through the terms of the sub-licence. The sub-licensee may need to put in place some form of collateral agreement with the licensor which will be activated by any termination of the head licence.

10.15 Rights and remedies of licensees, ss 30 and 31 The rights and remedies of a licensee will depend upon whether the licensee is an exclusive licensee or a non-exclusive licensee, and upon the terms of the licence itself.

Exclusive licensees An exclusive licensee is a licensee who has been authorised to the exclusion of all other persons, including the licensor, to use a registered trade mark in the manner authorised by the terms of the licence.[1] Thus, a licensee may be an exclusive licensee even though he merely has a limited licence, provided that he is the only person who may use the trade mark in the limited manner prescribed by the licence. Any licensee not coming within the definition of an exclusive licensee must necessarily be a non-exclusive licensee.

In relation to an exclusive licensee, one must further distinguish

20 Section 28(4).
1 Section 29(1).

between exclusive licensees who have, and those who do not have, the same rights and remedies in respect of matters occurring after the grant of the licence as if the licence had been an assignment; that is, the rights and remedies of a proprietor. An exclusive licensee will only have such rights and remedies if, and to the extent that, the terms of the exclusive licence expressly so provide. If his exclusive licence does contain a provision to the effect that his rights and remedies are to be the same as if the licence had been an assignment, then his rights and remedies are governed by s 31; absent such a provision, his rights and remedies will be governed by s 30. The rights and remedies of licensees are dealt with in Chapter 8, paragraphs 8.21 and 8.22.

An exclusive licensee whose exclusive licence does contain such a provision will be treated as if he were the proprietor of the registered trade mark for the purposes of considering the rights and remedies of any sub-licensee. That is, a sub-licensee may exercise the same rights and remedies under s 30 vis-à-vis an exclusive licensee as a licensee may exercise vis-à-vis the proprietor/licensor.[2]

A decision therefore needs to be made as to whether an exclusive licence should expressly provide that the exclusive licensee is to have the rights and remedies in respect of matters occurring after the grant of the licence as if the licence were an assignment. The clear advantage for the licensee of so providing is that his rights and remedies will be concurrent with those of the proprietor.[3]

Non-exclusive licensees Non-exclusive licensees and sub-licensees (like those exclusive licensees whose rights and remedies are not governed by s 31) have the rights and remedies conferred by s 30.[4]

In the absence of any provisions in the licence to the contrary, s 30 enables the licensee to call on the proprietor to bring infringement proceedings in respect of any matter which affects the licensee's interests, but this right can be varied or even excluded by the terms of the licence. Accordingly, a proprietor who wishes to retain the sole discretion as to whether to institute infringement proceedings should exclude expressly in the licence the operation of s 30(2).

2 Sections 28(4) and 30(7).
3 Section 31(2).
4 As to which, see paragraph 8.22.

Nature of licensee's rights The fact that a person is a licensee confers no proprietary rights on that person vis-à-vis the licensed mark. The only right conferred by s 30(2) and (3) is the facility of being able to call on the proprietor to sue infringers and to sue in his own name in default by the proprietor.[5]

10.16 Drafting points The following questions need to be considered in drafting a trade mark licence under the 1994 Act.

1 *Is it intended that the licence should be exclusive?*
If so, the licence must fall within the definition of an exclusive licence: see s 29(1) and go to question 2.
If not, go to question 3.

2 (a) *Is it intended that the exclusive licensee should have the same rights and remedies in respect of matters occurring after the grant of the licence as if the licence had been an assignment, that is, is it intended that the licensee's rights and remedies should be concurrent with those of the proprietor?*
If so, the licence must expressly so provide: see s 31(1) and go to question 2(b).
If not, go to question (3).

(b) *Is it intended to vary or exclude the operation of any of subsections 31(4)–(7)?*
If so, the licence must expressly so provide: see s 31(8).
If not, no action need be taken.

3 *Is it intended that the licensee should be entitled to call upon the proprietor to bring infringement proceedings in respect of matters affecting the licensee's interests?*
If so, such an entitlement will be deemed: see s 30(2).
If not, the entitlement must be expressly varied or excluded by the terms of the licence.

4 *Is it intended that the licensee should be able to grant sub-licences?*
If so, the licence must expressly so provide: see s 28(4).
If not, the licence should simply stay silent on this issue.

10.17 Transitional provisions, Schedule 3

Licences granted prior to 31 October 1994 The 1938 Act continues to apply in relation to licences granted prior to 31 October

5 *Northern & Shell plc v Condé Nast and National Magazine Distributors Ltd* [1995] RPC 117 (Jacob J).

1994, while ss 28 and 29(2) of the 1994 Act apply to licences granted on or after that date.[6]

Registered users recorded under the 1938 Act Entries in the 1938 Register under s 28 of the 1938 Act relating to registered users were transferred to the 1994 Register on 31 October 1994 and have effect as if made under s 25 of the 1994 Act.[7]

Applications for the registration of registered users under the 1938 Act An application for the registration of a registered user is dealt with under either:

(a) the 1938 Act, where the application had already been determined but not finally determined as at 31 October 1994;[8] or
(b) s 25 of the 1994 Act, where the application was pending as at 31 October 1994.[9]

Applications for the variation or cancellation of registered users An application for the variation or cancellation of a registered user pursuant to s 28(8) or (10) of the 1938 Act which was pending as at 31 October 1994 will be dealt with under the old law, and any consequent alteration will be made to the 1994 Register.[10]

Registrable transactions

10.18 Introduction, s 25 Like the 1938 Act (and others before it), the 1994 Act provides for the registration of certain dealings affecting trade marks, referred to in the 1994 Act as 'registrable transactions'. However, the 1994 Act merely enables prescribed particulars of registrable transactions to be entered in the Register. There are no substantive requirements imposed by the 1994 Act in terms of the content of the transactions themselves, although there are certain consequences if one does not apply for the registration of the prescribed particulars.

6 Schedule 3, para 9(1).
7 Schedule 3, para 9(2).
8 Schedule 3, para 9(4); any subsequent registration will be transferred to the 1994 Register pursuant to para 9(2).
9 Schedule 3, para 9(3); in which case the application will proceed in accordance with s 25 of the 1994 Act.
10 Schedule 3, para 9(5).

10.19 Registrable transactions, s 25(2) The following are registrable transactions for the purposes of the 1994 Act:

(a) an assignment of a registered trade mark or any right in it;[11]
(b) the grant of a licence under a registered trade mark;[12]
(c) the granting of any security interest (whether fixed or floating) over a registered trade mark or any right in or under it;
(d) the making by personal representatives of an assent in relation to a registered trade mark or any right in or under it;
(e) an order of a court or other competent authority transferring a registered trade mark or any right in or under it;[13] or
(f) any of the transactions of the type specified in (a) to (e) above, in respect of an application for the registration of a trade mark.[14]

One assumes that this is an exhaustive list of registrable transactions, because ss 24 and 28 would appear to embody the provisions governing all transactions which can affect a registered trade mark, and these transactions are all included in (a) to (f) above.

10.20 Application for the registration of prescribed particulars, s 25(1) The Registrar will enter in the Register the prescribed particulars of all registrable transactions upon receiving an application from either:

(a) the person claiming to be entitled to an interest in or under a registered trade mark by virtue of a registrable transaction;[15] or
(b) any other person claiming to be 'affected' by such a transaction.[16]

In the case of registrable transactions affecting or relating to applications for the registration of a trade mark, one cannot apply to have the relevant particulars entered in the Register as such; instead, the applicant can notify the particulars to the Registrar who will enter them in the Register upon the registration of the mark.[17]

10.21 Prescribed particulars, rr 34 and 35 Rules 34 and 35 set out the prescribed particulars which must be entered in the

11 As to entries and applications for entries under s 25 of the 1938 Act relating to transactions occurring before 31 October 1994, see paragraph 10.09.
12 As to entries and applications for entries under s 28 of the 1938 Act relating to registered users, see paragraph 10.17.
13 Section 25(2).
14 Section 27(1).
15 Section 25(1)(a).
16 Section 25(1)(b); this would include a proprietor, assignor or licensor.
17 Section 27(3) and r 35(4).

Register in respect of the various registrable transactions. These are set out below.

Assignments, r 34 In the case of an assignment of a registered trade mark or any right in it, the particulars to be supplied are:
(a) the name and address of the assignee;
(b) the date of the assignment; and
(c) where the assignment is only in respect of any right in the mark,[18] a description of the right assigned.
Form TM 16 should be used.[19]

Licences, r 34 In the case of the grant of a licence under a registered trade mark, the particulars to be supplied are:
(a) the name and address of the licensee;
(b) the fact (if it is the case) that the licence is an exclusive licence;
(c) where the licence is limited, a description of the limitation; and
(d) the duration of the licence, assuming that the duration is (or is ascertainable as being) for a definite period.
Form TM 50 should be used to apply for the registration of the prescribed particulars. Form TM 51 should be used to amend or remove an entry relating to a licence granted under a registered trade mark.[20]

Security interests, r 34 In the case of the grant of any security interest over a registered trade mark or any right in or under it, the particulars to be supplied are:
(a) the name and address of the grantee;
(b) the nature of the interest (whether fixed or floating); and
(c) the extent of the security and the right in or under the mark secured.
Form TM 24 should be used.[1]

Assent, r 34 In the case of the making of any assent by a personal representative in relation to a registered trade mark or any right in or under it, the particulars to be supplied are:
(a) the name and address of the person in whom the mark (or any right) vests by virtue of the assent; and

18 ie a partial assignment pursuant to s 24(2).
19 Rule 35(1)(a).
20 Rule 35(1)(b) and (c).
1 Rule 35(1)(d).

(b) the date of the assent.

Form TM 24 should be used.[2]

Court orders, r 34 In the case of a court or other competent authority transferring a registered trade mark or any right in or under it, the particulars to be supplied are:

(a) the name and address of the transferee;
(b) the date of the order; and
(c) where the transfer is only in respect of any right in the mark, a description of the right.

Form TM 24 should be used.[3]

Applications for the registration of prescribed particulars, r 35 In each case, the prescribed particulars will only be entered in the Register if:

(a) in the case of assignments, the application is signed by or on behalf of the parties;[4] or
(b) in the case of the grant of a licence or any security interest (including any amendment or termination of same), the application is signed by the grantor of the licence or the security interest;[5] or
(c) the Registrar is otherwise satisfied with the documentary evidence of the transaction;[6] and
(d) in any event, provided that any stamp duty payable on the transaction has been paid.[7]

The date on which the entry is made is also entered in the Register.[8]

Applications for the registration of a trade mark, r 35 Section 25 provides for the registration of prescribed particulars relating to registrable transactions which affect registered trade marks. Pursuant to s 27(1) and (3) it is also possible to give notice to the Registrar of particulars of a transaction affecting an application for the registration of a trade mark.[9] Logically, the particulars of such a

2 Rule 35(1)(e).
3 Rule 35(1)(e).
4 Rule 35(2)(a).
5 Rule 35(2)(b).
6 Rule 35(2).
7 Rule 35(3).
8 Rule 34.
9 In the event that the applicant divides his original application pursuant to s 41 and r 19, then the particulars of any relevant licence or security interest will be deemed to apply to each divisional application: r 19(3).

transaction are the same particulars as are required to be given under r 34 in relation to transactions affecting registered trade marks, as otherwise the Registrar would not be able to register those particulars upon the subsequent registration of the trade mark.[10]

The same TM forms must also be used for the purpose of notifying the Registrar of transactions affecting an application for the registration of a trade mark.

10.22 Consequences of the failure to register prescribed particulars of a registrable transaction, s 25(3) and (4) There are three direct consequences of failing to register the prescribed particulars of a registrable transaction.

In the first place, until such time as an application has been made for the registration of the relevant prescribed particulars, the transaction will be ineffective against someone who acquires, in ignorance of the registrable transaction, a conflicting interest in or under the registered trade mark.[11] Does this mean that the subsequent application for the registration of the prescribed particulars will cure the omission? The wording of s 25(3) would seem to suggest that, once the application has been made for the registration of the particulars, the transaction will then become effective against a person who acquires a conflicting interest even if that interest was acquired in ignorance of the transaction. This follows from the use of the word 'until' at the beginning of the section. But was this the intention of the legislature? Surely the object was to protect the interests of third parties who acquire an interest in a trade mark without notice (either actual or constructive) of an earlier registrable transaction affecting that mark, the particulars of which had not been supplied to the Registrar?

Secondly, and in addition to the above, until such time as an application has been made for the registration of the relevant prescribed particulars, a licensee will not have the rights and remedies in relation to any infringement of the trade mark as would otherwise be available under ss 30 and 31.[12] Once again, it would seem that the licensee can cure the omission and thus become entitled to the rights and remedies conferred by ss 30 and 31 by

10 Rule 35(4).
11 Section 25(3)(a).
12 Section 25(3)(b).

applying to register the relevant particulars.

Thirdly where a person becomes either the subsequent proprietor or licensee of a registered trade mark by virtue of a registrable transaction, he will not be entitled to damages or to an account of profits in respect of any infringement of the trade mark which occurs after the date of the transaction but before the prescribed particulars of the transaction are entered in the Register, unless:

(a) an application for the registration of the prescribed particulars of the transaction is made within six months of the date of the transaction;[13] or
(b) the court is satisfied that it was not practicable for such an application to be made within six months and that an application was made as soon as practicable thereafter.[14]

The intention behind s 25 is clearly to try to ensure that the Register records as accurately as possible all interests in or under registered trade marks. The consequences of failing to register the particulars of a registrable transaction are a strong practical and commercial incentive for assignees and licensees (in particular) to treat this section as tantamount to a mandatory requirement.

Tax issues

Unlike with some other IP rights such as patents, there are virtually no provisions in the tax legislation which deal specifically with trade marks. Instead, general principles must be applied and in some instances this can make the tax treatment of any dealings in trade marks a complicated matter.

The taxes which almost always need to be considered in any dealing in a trade mark will be income tax, capital gains tax, corporation tax, VAT, stamp duty and withholding tax.[15] The paragraphs following provide an outline only of the likely tax treatment that will apply assuming both parties to the transaction are either UK individuals or companies. Issues such as the deductibility of expenses incurred by the creator or developer of the

13 Section 25(4)(a).
14 Section 25(4)(b).
15 The relevant statutes are the Income and Corporation Taxes Act 1988, the Taxation of Chargeable Gains Act 1992 and the Value Added Tax Act 1994, and various regulations made under these statutes.

trade mark from profits received have not been considered, nor have changes to the tax treatment that may arise because one of the parties to the transaction is from outside the UK. The intention is merely to make the reader aware that tax issues can be an important consideration when dealing in trade marks.

10.23 Assignments The tax treatment of any sum received under an assignment of a trade mark will depend on the capacity in which the taxpayer earns or receives the sum (for example, whether they do so in the course of a trade or profession or otherwise) and the nature of the payment itself, in particular whether it is of a revenue (that is, of an income) nature or of a capital nature.

Generally, when an assignor receives a lump sum for the assignment of a trade mark, the payment is most likely to be treated as a payment of capital rather than income. As such it will be subject to capital gains tax where the assignor is an individual, partnership or trust, or a corporation tax charge where the taxpayer is a company or unincorporated association. Should the sum be income, it will be assessed to income tax or corporation tax in the usual way.

The transfer of ownership of a trade mark by assignment will be a supply of services for the purposes of VAT.[16] If assigned to a person or company belonging in the UK by a taxable person (which by definition includes a company), the supply will be chargeable to VAT at the standard rate, which is currently 17.5 per cent. The assignor must account for the VAT so chargeable to Customs and Excise. Points to note are that if the assignment does not expressly state that the consideration is to be exclusive of VAT, then the amount payable is treated, where applicable, as VAT inclusive and on current rates $\frac{7}{47}$ of it is treated as VAT. If the transfer of the trade mark takes place as part of the transfer of the business as a whole as a going concern, the supply may be outside the scope of VAT.[17]

If executed in the UK, or executed outside the UK but relating to trade marks registered in the UK, the assignment will also be subject to stamp duty if the consideration for the assignment exceeds £60,000. The rate at which stamp duty is charged is set out in the table below. If the assignment of the trade mark is part of a global

16 Value Added Tax Act 1994, Sch 5.

17 Value Added Tax (Special Provisions) Order 1995 SI 1995/1268. Note that certain conditions must be satisfied.

transaction which also includes the assignment of other assets (which may be situated outside the UK), the stamp duty exposure will be increased (unnecessarily) if the assignment is executed in the UK (because the assignment will be stampable by reference to the entire consideration). By executing the assignment outside the UK the exposure can be limited to the value of the UK trade marks. In this connection it is always worth considering allocating a value to the UK trade marks. If the assignment is not duly stamped it is not admissible in evidence in court. More importantly, if not duly stamped the trade mark will not be able to be registered in the name of the new owner. Penalties and interest run if the document is not stamped within the requisite time limits and the document later has to be stamped. The time limits are within 30 days of first execution or, if executed outside the UK, within 30 days of the assignment having been first received in the UK.

STAMP DUTY	
Consideration (in £ sterling)	*Rate of stamp duty*
less than 250,000	1.0%
250,000–500,000	1.5%
more than 500,000	2.0%

10.24 Licences It can be even more difficult distinguishing whether a payment made under a licence is a royalty payment (that is, of an income nature) or an instalment of capital. It will depend on the facts of the case. The importance of making the distinction, however, is just as critical as it is for assignments of trade marks, as it affects which tax regime applies and what reliefs are available. If the payment is a royalty and it is received as a trade receipt, it will be taxable as trading income under Case I (receipts of a trade) or Case II (receipts of a profession) of Sch D of the Income and Corporation Taxes Act 1988. However, if the trade mark is not a trading asset but is held as an investment, the royalty may amount to pure income profit and therefore fall to be taxed under Case III of Sch D. In view of the requirements that a trade mark be used, this is likely to be rare. If the payment is to be treated as capital, a capital gains tax charge may arise where the recipient is an individual, or a corporation tax charge where the recipient is a company.

As with an assignment of a trade mark, a licence of a trade mark will be subject to VAT. The treatment is broadly the same as outlined above. Likewise, stamp duty may also be payable on a licence. The general comments made above will also apply here. However, a licence is only stampable if it is irrevocable and exclusive. Thus, a licence will not be stampable if it is revocable or if it is non-exclusive.

Where licence fees/royalties are payable to a licensor based outside the UK, an additional factor both parties should consider is the implications of the withholding tax regime in light of any double-tax treaty arrangements that may be in place between the UK and the other country.

Caveat Only the simplest of scenarios have been considered above. Trade marks are international in their application and are of considerable worth to the party exploiting them. Their protection and the taxation consequences arising from any dealings in them should be considered at an early stage and suitable advice sought.

Competition law

10.25 EC competition law

Introduction The relevant provisions of the EC Treaty have already been set out at paragraph 7.11 above. In the context of infringement (Chapter 7) the subject of competition law is relevant because the defendant in an infringement action may be able to argue that the plaintiff is not entitled to exercise his exclusive rights because of overriding principles of competition law. In the context of assigning and licensing trade marks the assignor or licensor (as the case may be) may also be restricted by similar competition law principles. The most relevant principle (in the context of assigning and licensing) is contained in Article 85 of the EC Treaty, which provides that any agreement which may affect trade between member states and which has as its object *or effect* the prevention, restriction or distortion of competition within the EU, is automatically void. Article 85 cites particular examples of such agreements as those which:

(a) directly or indirectly fix purchase or selling prices or any other trading conditions;
(b) limit or control production, markets, technical development, or investment;
(c) share markets or sources of supply;
(d) apply dissimilar conditions to equivalent transactions with other trading parties, thereby placing them at a competitive disadvantage; or
(e) make the conclusion of contracts subject to acceptance by the other parties of supplementary obligations which, by their nature or according to commercial usage, have no connection with the subject of such contracts.

The nature of many trade mark assignments and licences is such that the assignor or licensor will wish to impose certain restrictions on the assignee or licensee in terms of his use of the trade mark and such restrictions may be anti-competitive for the purposes of Article 85. (Note that Article 36, which excludes the application of Articles 30–34 where the protection of intellectual property rights is concerned, does *not* apply to Article 85.)

Examples, assignments The classic example of a trade mark assignment which will fall foul of Article 85 is one which is in fact part of a market sharing arrangement. This was confirmed in the *Ideal Standard* case;[18] thus, an assignment or a licence will be void if it is part of a scheme whereby the parties divide up or partition the European market by relying on their respective trade mark rights to prevent competition amongst the goods to which their marks are applied. The use of the word 'scheme' is not intended to imply that the arrangement necessarily involves an element of deliberate planning – the sharing of markets may simply be the result of one or more transactions when looked at as a whole. In *Pronuptia*,[19] the ECJ confirmed that clauses in a franchise agreement will infringe Article 85 if they *result* in a sharing of markets between franchisor and franchisee, or between franchisees. However, one has to distinguish such a scheme from a bona fide co-existence agreement between owners of similar marks in different member states not to use their trade marks in the other's territory. Such an agreement,

18 *IHT Internationale Heiztechnik GmbH v Ideal-Standard GmbH* [1995] FSR 59.
19 *Pronuptia de Paris GmbH v Pronuptia de Paris Irmgard Schillgalis* [1986] ECR 353.

assuming that it is designed to eliminate costly infringement proceedings, is acceptable.

Examples, licences There are many examples of terms in licence agreements which are void because the licensor has sought to impose a restriction on his licensee which is anti-competitive. It would be much easier for licensors if the reasoning of the High Court in *Ravenseft*[20] had been accepted by the European Commission. The Commission rejects the argument (that was accepted in *Ravenseft*) that the grant of a licence, albeit containing restrictions on the licensee, is nonetheless giving the licensee permission to do something which he could not otherwise have done at all. This reasoning has never been accepted by the Commission and therefore, in theory, depending on the circumstances of the case, anything less than an unfettered right to use the trade mark may be considered to be a 'restriction' for the purposes of Article 85. Thankfully, this is not the case in practice but, unfortunately, nor is it possible to state with absolute certainty that a particular restriction will not be caught by Article 85. Instead, one has to find comfort in either:

(a) a Commission Notice, which sets out the European Commission's views on the application of Article 85 to particular kinds of agreements (or particular clauses of agreements) – such 'views' are not binding as such, but they do enable the parties to proceed knowing that they have minimised their risk of infringement; and/or
(b) a block exemption, which provides for automatic exemption of certain agreements which may otherwise infringe Article 85 – unfortunately, there is no specific block exemption for trade mark agreements but one can seek to rely by analogy on block exemptions which have been issued in relation to
   (i) patent and know-how licences (now called the Technology Transfer Block Exemption);[1]
   (ii) franchising agreements;[2] and
   (iii) distribution and purchasing agreements;[3] or

20 *Ravenseft Properties Ltd's Application* [1978] QB 52, [1977] 2 WLR 432; see paragraph 10.26.
1 Technology Transfer Regulation No 240 of 1996.
2 Franchising Regulation No 4087 of 1988, OJ L 359/46, 28 December 1988.
3 Exclusive Distribution Agreements Regulation No 83 of 1983, OJ L173, 30 June 1983 and OJ L281, 13 October 1983; Exclusive Purchasing Agreements Regulation No 83 of 1984.

(c) as a last (or only) resort, one can apply to the European Commission for individual exemption from Article 85 by showing that the agreement, in reality, is not anti-competitive – the test for which is set out in Article 85(3) and requires that the trade mark assignment or licence must contribute to improving the production or distribution of goods or to promoting technical or economic progress, while allowing consumers a fair share of the resulting benefit, and provided that it does not:
   (i) impose on the parties concerned restrictions which are not indispensable to the attainment of these objectives; nor
   (ii) afford such parties the possibility of eliminating competition in respect of a substantial part of the products in question.

Application of Article 85 The difficulty for those drafting a trade mark assignment or licence is that the provisions in the agreement relating to the trade mark may only be one part of a much larger transaction. For example:

(a) a trade mark assignment may be part of the purchase and sale of a business or company; and
(b) a trade mark licence may be part of a franchise agreement, a merchandising agreement, a marketing, distribution or purchasing agreement or a joint venture.

Different considerations will apply in each case (for example, certain of the agreements referred to in (b) above are the subject of specific block exemptions) and, even if the agreement is a bare assignment or licence of a trade mark, there are still a number of grey areas in determining whether an agreement infringes Article 85, including:

(a) assessing the impact of the agreement – especially where one is trying to assess the effect on trade in the EU of a negative restriction, this being as much a question of economic theory as of law;
(b) the practice nature of the European Commission which has been to treat restrictions as prima facie falling within Article 85 and then to grant individual exemptions – rather than to grant block (or generic) exemptions; and
(c) the non-literal interpretation of EC legislation, that is, the European Commission will find an infringement of Article 85 based on the activities/conduct of the parties and even though the drafting of the agreement itself falls outside the terms of Article 85.

So, how does one go about drafting an enforceable trade mark assignment or licence which contains restrictions on the assignee or licensee and which is not void under Article 85? A complete answer to this question is beyond the scope of a user's guide to trade mark law; readers should refer to one of the specialist texts on competition law.[4] However, broad propositions can be stated.

1 Agreements entered into between parties which have, in combination, both:
   (a) a market share (as defined) in the relevant goods or services (as defined) of no more than 5 per cent; and
   (b) an aggregate annual turnover (as defined) of no more than 300 million ECU (approximately £205 million as of 31 October 1997),

   are prima facie excluded under the de minimis rule as set out in the Commission Notice on agreements of minor importance.[5]

2 The following restrictions are likely not to infringe Article 85 (although individual exemption may still be required in order to be absolutely safe):
   (a) an obligation on the licensor not to license other licensees to use the licensed trade mark in the licensed territory – ie the grant of a sole licence;
   (b) an obligation on the licensor not himself to use the licensed trade mark nor supply the licensed goods or services in the licensed territory – ie the grant of an exclusive licence;
   (c) an obligation on the licensee not to use the licensed trade mark in territories of the licensor within the EU or, more specifically, only to use the licensed trade mark in a designated territory;
   (d) an obligation on the licensee not to pursue an active policy of selling goods or supplying services in relation to which the licensed trade mark is used in territories within the EU which are licensed to other licensees – ie a restriction on 'active' sales (this obligation may specifically prohibit the licensee from advertising in those other territories and from establishing any branch or distribution depot there);
   (e) an obligation on the licensee not to supply goods or services in relation to which the licensed trade mark is used in

4 For example: *Butterworths Competition Law* (loose-leaf).
5 Commission Notice OJ C313, 29 December 1977.

territories within the EU which are licensed to other licensees, even in response to unsolicited orders – ie a restriction on 'passive' sales (the European Commission has always been hostile to attempts to divide up the European market, but the Technology Transfer Block Exemption does permit a restriction on passive sales for five years in recognition of the fact that each licensee is entitled to a certain period of 'protection' in order to justify and recoup his set-up costs);

(f) an obligation on the licensee only to use the licensor's trade mark in relation to the licensed goods or services and to identify the licensor as the owner of the licensed trade mark (provided that the licensee is not prevented from identifying himself as the manufacturer of the licensed goods);

(g) an obligation on the licensee not to divulge any associated know-how/confidential information relating to the licensed product;

(h) an obligation on the licensee not to grant sub-licences or assign the licence;

(i) an obligation on the licensee not to use the licensed trade mark after the termination of the licence;

(j) an obligation on the licensee to observe minimum quality specifications, including technical specifications, for the licensed goods or services or to procure certain goods or services from the licensor (or from a designated supplier) but only in so far as the specifications, goods or services are necessary to ensure that the licensed goods or services conform to the minimum quality specifications that are applicable to the licensor and all other licensees (care must be taken to ensure that this is not a 'tie-in' clause nor 'third-line forcing');

(k) an obligation on the licensee to inform the licensor of any infringement of the licensed trade mark and/or to take or assist the licensor in taking legal action against such infringements;

(l) a clause permitting the licensor to terminate the licence if the licensee challenges the validity of the licensed trade mark is acceptable, but a clause which purports to prohibit the licensee from making the challenge is not acceptable;

(m) an obligation on the licensee to continue paying licence fees/royalties after the term of the licence, but only where this is to facilitate payment by spreading the royalties over a reasonable extended period (great care will need to be exercised in drafting such an obligation);

(n) an obligation on the licensee to restrict his use of the licensed trade mark to one or more categories of the goods or services for which the trade mark is registered, provided that this is not a disguised means of customer sharing – it is a fine line between dividing product markets, which is acceptable, and customer sharing, which is not acceptable (again, great care will be required in drafting this restriction);

(o) an obligation on the licensee to pay a minimum royalty or to sell/supply a minimum quantity of licensed goods or services under the licensed trade mark (of course, maximum quantity restrictions are totally unacceptable, as are restrictions on minimum sale prices);

(p) an obligation on the licensor to grant the licensee more favourable terms in the future such as the licensor may grant to another licensee (ie conferring most favoured licensee status);

(q) a reservation by the licensor of the right to exercise his exclusive rights to oppose the use of the licensed trade mark by the licensee outside the licensed territory;

(r) an obligation on the licensee to use his best endeavours to market and sell the licensed goods or services (or a minimum range of licensed goods or services) and/or maintain a minimum stock of licensed goods; and

(s) a reservation by the licensor of the right to terminate the exclusivity of the licence if the licensee enters into competition within the EU with the licensor.

3 In comparison, the following restrictions are almost certainly likely to infringe Article 85 and only in exceptional circumstances would individual exemption be granted:

(a) a restriction on either party in determining the price for the licensed goods or services (ie price fixing) – a licensor may recommend prices, but Article 85 will be infringed if licensees engage in a concerted practice relating to the sale price of goods or services;

(b) a restriction on either party from competing in the EU with the other party, particularly in competing rival products (but it is not possible to define the exact boundary between acceptable and non-acceptable non-competition clauses and a case-by-case analysis is required);

(c) an obligation on either or both parties to refuse to meet orders for licensed goods from customers who would then market those goods in other territories;

(d) an obligation on either or both parties to make it difficult for customers to obtain licensed goods from other resellers within the EU;

(e) a restriction imposed on 'horizontal' competitors who, in their capacity as licensor and licensee, agree that one is restricted as to the customers he may serve – ie customer sharing or allocation by competitors;

(f) a restriction on the licensee from sourcing the licensed goods from other licensees and/or from sourcing spare parts or accessories for the licensed goods from any third party;

(g) maximum quantity restrictions relating to the licensed goods or services;

(h) an obligation on the licensee to assign back to the licensor any rights to improvements to or new applications of the licensed goods or services (licences of such improvements and applications back to the licensor are acceptable); and

(i) an obligation on the licensee to pay licence fees or royalties on the sale or supply of goods or services in relation to which the licensed trade mark is not used.

These lists are not exhaustive. Most of the obligations and restrictions referred to above are based on the Technology Transfer Block Exemption and the Franchising Block Exemption and are recast in the context of trade marks. The subject of competition law is dealt with here simply to alert readers to the very real and wide-ranging issues which need to be identified and thought through in detail. Often this will involve the application of economic theories and problems with market definition and readers should refer to specialist texts and to their legal advisers. It is probably fair to say that many trade mark agreements are drafted without proper regard to competition law principles. This may be dangerous, as the consequence of infringing Article 85 is that the provisions which infringe are automatically void, and the European Commission can impose fines on each of the parties of up to the greater of one million

ECU or 10 per cent of the party's group worldwide turnover in the preceding year (where the infringement is either deliberate or negligent).

10.26 UK competition law

Introduction There are five 'elements' which fall within the general description of UK competition law and which may be relevant when assigning or licensing trade marks. Those elements consist of four statutes and one body of common law, namely:

1 The Restrictive Trade Practices Act 1976.
2 The Resale Prices Act 1976.
3 The Competition Act 1980.
4 The Fair Trading Act 1973.
5 The common law rules relating to restraint of trade.

Restrictive Trade Practices Act 1976 ('RTPA') The RTPA applies where there is an agreement (an assignment or a licence relating to a trade mark):

(1) between two or more persons carrying on business within the United Kingdom in the supply of goods or services; and
(2) both (or more) parties accept restrictions in respect of any of the following matters:
    (a) the prices to be charged for goods supplied;
    (b) the prices to be recommended or suggested as the prices to be charged in respect of the resale of goods supplied;
    (c) the terms or conditions subject to which goods are to be supplied;
    (d) the quantities or descriptions of goods to be produced, supplied or acquired;
    (e) the process of manufacture to be applied to any goods, or the quantities or descriptions of goods to which any such process is to be applied; or
    (f) the persons or classes or persons to, for or from whom, or the areas or places in or from which, goods are to be supplied or acquired, or any such process applied.

A bare trade mark assignment or licence is therefore unlikely to fall within the RTPA, but where both parties seek to impose restrictions in relation to the matters referred to above, then the agreement may have to be registered with the Office of Fair Trading ('OFT'). (The failure to register a registrable agreement within the specified time limit will result in the restrictive provisions being void and the possibility of fines for the parties.)

Exemptions Despite the broad application of the RTPA, there are a number of in-built exemptions:

(1) A general exemption for certain types of agreements.
(2) Schedule 3 exemptions.
(3) An exemption for de minimis agreements.
(4) Agreements exempt under an EC block exemption.
(5) The parties may be able to rely on the *Ravenseft* principle.

General exemption for certain agreements The RTPA provides automatic exemption for many types of agreement. A general exemption is granted:

(a) if only one of the parties carries on business in the United Kingdom; or
(b) if the agreement contains restrictions on only one party; or
(c) if the agreement contains restrictions on both parties, but in different categories: for example, if restrictions on one party are only in relation to goods, and on the other party the restrictions are only in relation to services.

Furthermore:

(d) application may be made to the Department of Trade and Industry to exempt certain agreements that are important to the national economy; or
(e) certain agreements made by, or by members of, an agricultural, forestry or fishery association are exempted; or
(f) there is provision for obtaining approval from the relevant government department for agreements for holding down prices; or
(g) there is provision for approval by the Secretary of State of wholesale co-operative societies.

There are also specific exemptions for agreements which relate specifically either to goods or to services. In particular, in the context of assigning or licensing trade marks, it should be noted that an agreement is exempt:

(a) pursuant to s 9, if the restrictive provisions relate exclusively to the goods supplied, or to the process which is applied, in pursuance of the agreement; and
(b) again pursuant to s 9, to the extent that the restrictive provisions relate to technical standards, or the provision of customer

information, which are approved by the British Standards Institution or another body approved for this purpose by the Secretary of State; or

(c) pursuant to s 18, to the extent that the restrictions relate exclusively to the services supplied under the agreement in question; and

(d) again pursuant to s 18, to the extent that the restrictive provisions relate to technical or performance standards, or the provision of customer information, which are approved by the British Standards Institution or another body approved for this purpose by the Secretary of State.

Note the repeated use of the phrase 'to the extent' – any other restrictive provisions will not be exempted.

Schedule 3 exemptions A prima facie registrable trade mark assignment or licence may not need to be registered if it falls within one of the exempt categories set out in Sch 3 of the RTPA. There are limited exemptions for restrictions in trade mark agreements. In relation to 'ordinary' trade marks, the agreement will be exempted if the restrictions relate only to either:

(a) the description of goods bearing the mark which are to be produced or supplied, or the processes of manufacture to be applied to such goods or to goods to which the mark is to be applied; or

(b) the kinds of services in relation to which the mark is to be used which are to be made available or supplied, or the form or manner in which such services are to be made available or supplied; or

(c) the descriptions of goods which are to be produced or supplied in connection with the supply of services in relation to which the mark is to be used, or the process of manufacture to be applied to such goods.

In relation to certification trade marks and collective trade marks, the relevant regulations will contain certain restrictions relating to the use of such marks, and these restrictions are also exempted under the RTPA provided that they have been approved by the Secretary of State in accordance with either Sch 2 or 3 (as the case may be) of the 1994 Act.

De minimis An agreement is not notifiable to the OFT if the parties have an aggregate annual turnover in the United Kingdom which does not exceed £20 million as of the date of that agreement.[6]

EC block exemptions An agreement is not notifiable to the OFT if the agreement is exempted from Article 85(1) of the EC Treaty under a block exemption regulation. Unfortunately, there is no specific block exemption relating to trade mark assignments or licences. However, as stated in paragraph 10.25, certain agreements relating to or involving the assignment or licence of a trade mark are the subject of a block exemption regulation. If the agreement is exempted from Article 85, then the RTPA will not be applicable either.[7]

The Ravenseft principle Unlike the European Commission, the OFT accepts that intellectual property licences which contain restrictions may not be registrable because, in *Ravenseft*,[8] it was decided that the so-called restrictions (in a real property lease) were merely 'limitations'. That is, the tenant was being the given the right to do something which, but for the lease, he could not have done at all, and therefore the limitations on his right of occupancy could not be characterised as 'restrictions' for the purposes of the RTPA.

The OFT has since issued a statement confirming that the *Ravenseft* principle will be adopted in relation to intellectual property licences.[9] The OFT's view, therefore, is that a party to an agreement does not accept a 'restriction' within the meaning of the RTPA where:

(a) it accepts 'restrictions' on its power to grant a licence or a franchise (although any accompanying restriction on the supply of goods or services could fall within the meaning of the RTPA);
(b) it accepts a 'restriction' which simply limits rights which it would not have without the agreement (this is called the 'open door' principle); or
(c) it accepts, by way of an apparent 'restriction', any obligation which is imposed on it by law.

It should be noted for the sake of completeness that the OFT's

6 The Restrictive Trade Practices (Non-notifiable Agreements) (Turnover Threshold) Order 1996 (SI 1996/348).
7 Restrictive Trade Practices (Non-notifiable Agreements) (EC Block Exemption) Order 1996 (SI 1996/349).
8 *Ravenseft Properties Ltd's Application* [1978] QB 52, [1977] 2 WLR 432.
9 OFT Guide: 'Restrictive Trade Practices: Provisions of the RTPA' 1990 at p 16.

view does not bind the Restrictive Practices Court, nor even the OFT itself!

To register or not? The safer view is that, if in any real doubt, one should register the agreement on a fail-safe basis and seek the OFT's confirmation that the agreement is not registrable. If the agreement is registered, then it will be referred to the Restrictive Practices Court by the Director General of Fair Trading, unless he is satisfied that it is either not registrable (ie that it doesn't contain any relevant restrictions, or for some other reason), or that the restrictions fall within one of the exemptions (referred to above).

Dealing with the OFT and the practice and procedure of the RPC is a separate subject and beyond the scope of this book; readers should refer to specialist publications.[10]

Consequences of failure to register There are three important practical consequences of failing to register a registrable agreement within the specified time limits. They are:

(1) The registrable restrictions are void. If these restrictions are fundamental to the agreement then the whole agreement might become void.
(2) It is unlawful for either party to give effect to, or attempt to enforce, the registrable restrictions.
(3) An action may be brought against the parties in the RPC by the Director General of Fair Trading.

Notably, there are no fines for first 'offences', but a subsequent breach of the RTPA may result in a fine and, in theory, imprisonment for contempt of court. Furthermore, there are no fines simply for entering into a registrable agreement and failing to register it; fines are imposed only where a party has breached an undertaking or failed to comply with an Order of the RPC.

Resale Prices Act ('RPA') The RPA provides that any term or condition of a contract for the sale of goods is void in so far as it purports to establish minimum prices to be charged on the resale of such goods in the United Kingdom.[11]

The RPA may therefore be relevant where the assignment or licence of a trade mark is part of a larger transaction involving the

10 N Greene, Graham and Trotman *Commercial Agreements and Competition Law*, 2nd Edition, 1995.
11 Section 9(1).

purchase, supply, marketing or distribution of goods, or as part of a franchising agreement.

Competition Act ('CA') The CA enables the Director General of Fair Trading to investigate 'anti-competitive practices'. Clearly, market sharing agreements, even trade mark co-existence agreements, may amount to an anti-competitive practice, depending upon the circumstances of the case.

Fair Trading Act ('FTA') Monopolies and anti-competitive practices may be referred under the FTA to the Monopolies and Mergers Commission (MMC) by the Director General of Fair Trading.

It is impossible in a book of this kind to summarise the application of the FTA to trade mark assignments and licences. Usually, the FTA will only be applicable in the context of trade marks where the transfer or licence (especially an exclusive licence) would result in the assignee/licensee acquiring a dominant position (a monopoly) in the relevant market. Such a transaction will require specialist advice, including an assessment of the relevant market, which will often involve the application of economic theories as well as the provisions of the FTA.

Common law: restraint of trade Although more usually relevant in the context of employer/employee and vendor/purchaser agreements, the principle that any agreement which interferes with trade will be void, unless it is demonstrated to be reasonable as between the parties *and* in the public interest, also applies in theory to trade mark agreements. However, it is unlikely that a different result will obtain under the doctrine of restraint of trade from that under the various statutes which have been discussed above. Thus, consistent with *Ravenseft*, one would expect a condition attaching to a licensee's use of the trade mark not to be characterised as a 'restraint' for the purposes of the common law doctrine. However, an attempt by the licensor to extract licence fees in respect of sales of goods or services not covered by his registration (and outside the scope of his common law rights attaching to his goodwill) will amount to a restraint of trade at common law.

Competition Bill The Bill has not yet been enacted and it is unlikely to come into force until 1999. Readers should refer to Chapter 7, paragraph 7.26 for a brief summary of the Bill.

11 Certification marks

11.01 Introduction It has been noted on a number of occasions that a trade mark must serve to distinguish the proprietor's goods or services from those of other undertakings.[1] There are, however, two important exceptions to this rule:

(a) certification marks, which are discussed in this chapter; and

(b) collective trade marks, which are discussed in Chapter 12.

Certification marks were registrable under the 1938 Act,[2] but collective marks, although registrable in other jurisdictions for some time, are a relatively new category in the United Kingdom and became registrable for the first time under the 1994 Act.

11.02 Definition of certification mark, s 50 A certification mark is a mark which indicates that the goods or services in respect of which the mark is used have been 'certified' by the proprietor of the mark[3] to comply with certain objective standards.[4] The proprietor's certification of the goods or services may be in respect of a number of characteristics of the relevant goods or services, namely:

(a) the origin of the goods or services;

(b) the material (or composition) of the goods;

1 Section 1(1); see Chapter 1.

2 Section 37; and under s 62 of the 1905 Act.

3 Section 50(1).

4 Which must be filed as part of the regulations which accompany an application for a certification mark: see paragraph 11.08.

(c) the mode of manufacture of the goods;
(d) the performance of the services;
(e) the quality of the goods or services;
(f) the accuracy of the goods or services; or
(g) any 'other characteristics' of the goods or services.[5]

These are the same characteristics as were specified in s 37(1) of the 1938 Act.[6]

The reference to 'other characteristics' means that the list is not exhaustive. Furthermore, the proprietor of a certification mark may, if he wishes, choose only to certify one or more of these characteristics.

11.03 Application of the 1994 Act, ss 1(2), 50(2) and Schedule 2 All references in the 1994 Act to a 'trade mark' include references to a certification mark[7] but one must look to Sch 2 of the 1994 Act to ascertain the necessary adjustments which must be taken into account when applying the Act to certification marks.[8] The remainder of this chapter considers those adjustments; in all other respects the 1994 Act, the Rules (where relevant) and the other relevant chapters of this book apply equally to certification marks as they do to ordinary trade marks.

1994 Act, Schedule 2

11.04 Signs of which a certification mark may consist, paragraph 2 The definition of 'trade mark' in s 1(1) of the 1994 Act cannot be applied literally to certification marks. The second limb of the definition requires a trade mark to be 'capable of distinguishing goods or services of one undertaking from those of other undertakings'. But this is not the purpose of a certification mark, which can be applied to the goods or services of numerous undertakings. A certification mark will therefore never serve to distinguish uniquely the goods or services of one undertaking. Accordingly, the second limb of the definition must be construed,

5 Section 50(1).
6 Except for the additional reference to certifying the performance of the services, as there was no provision for certification of service marks.
7 Section 1(2).
8 Section 50(2).

for the purposes of certification marks, as a reference to distinguishing the goods or services which are certified from those which are not certified.[9]

11.05 Registrability: nature of proprietor's business, paragraph 4 A certification mark cannot be registered if the proprietor/applicant carries on a business which involves the supply of goods or services of the kind which he certifies or proposes to certify.[10]

This prohibition mirrors the proviso set out in s 68(1) of the 1938 Act. Of course, one can easily side-step para 4 by setting up two companies, one to certify and to own the certification mark and the other to carry on the business of supplying the goods or services under the trade mark.

11.06 Registrability: indications of geographical origin, paragraph 3 An absolute ground for refusing the registration of an ordinary trade mark is that it consists exclusively of a sign which indicates the geographical origin of the proprietor's goods or services.[11]

Geographical signs can be registered as certification marks.[12] The registration of a geographical sign does not, however, entitle the proprietor to prevent the use of the sign by a third party, provided that the use is in accordance with 'honest practices in industrial or commercial matters'.[13]

11.07 Grounds for refusal of registration: misleading as to character or significance, paragraph 5 In addition to the absolute grounds for refusing the registration of an ordinary trade mark,[14] a certification mark cannot be registered if the public is liable

9 Schedule 2, para 2.
10 Schedule 2, para 4.
11 Section 3(1)(c); see paragraph 2.04.
12 Schedule 2, para 3(1); subject to Council Regulation No 2081/92 on the Protection of Geographical Indications and Designations of Origin for Agricultural Products and Foodstuffs (see also Commission Regulation No 2037/93 laying down detailed rules of application of that Regulation).
13 Schedule 2, para 3(2); as to the meaning of the phrase 'honest practices in industrial or commercial matters' see paragraph 7.08 in the context of defences to infringement of a trade mark.
14 ie under s 3; see Chapter 2.

to be misled in relation to the character or significance of the mark.[15] Accordingly,the Registrar may require that a certification mark should include some indication that it is a certification mark.[16]

11.08 The regulations, paragraphs 6 and 7 Regulations governing the use of the certification mark must be filed by the applicant within nine months of the date on which the application for registration is made.[17] A failure to file the regulations on time will result in the application being treated as having been withdrawn.[18]

The regulations must include a statement as to:

(a) who is authorised to use the certification mark;
(b) the characteristics to be certified by the mark (these must be defined as precisely as their nature allows – it will not be acceptable simply to state that the goods must be of a 'good design' or that the services must be of a 'good standard', as these are matters of subjective judgment;
(c) how the certifying body is to test those characteristics and to supervise the use of the certification mark;
(d) the fees (if any) to be paid in connection with the operation of the mark; and
(e) the procedures for resolving disputes.[19]

The certification mark will not be registered unless the regulations comply with these requirements, and provided also that they are not contrary to public policy nor to accepted principles of morality.[20]

Furthermore, the Registrar is obliged to refuse the application for a certification mark if the applicant is not competent to certify the

15 Schedule 2, para 5(1); and compare this with s 3(3)(b).
16 Schedule 2, para 5(2); the Work Manual states in Chapter 12 that if the applicant objects to putting the indication (that the mark is a certification mark) within the mark itself, then it is acceptable for the regulations to establish that the nature of the mark will always be made clear in advertising and on the goods themselves.
17 Rule 22; Sch 2, para 6(1); Form TM 35 must be used and a fee will be payable; the regulations will be open to public inspection in the same way as the Register: Sch 2, para 10.
18 Schedule 2, para 7(2).
19 Schedule 2, para 6(2); the Work Manual in Chapter 12 acknowledges that the 1994 Act does not specify any particular form which the regulations must take; however, in paragraph 5.2 a suggested form is provided which groups the regulations under 16 main headings.
20 Schedule 2, para 7(1)(a).

relevant goods or services.[1] This involves the Registrar in having to assess the competence or otherwise of the applicant. In this regard, the type of information which applicants should supply to the Registrar should include at least the following:

(a) a description of the applicant (who must be able to sue and be sued in his, her or its own name);
(b) the nature of the applicant's business;
(c) what, if anything, the applicant trades in or the services provided;
(d) the applicant's competence to administer the certification scheme;
(e) the applicant's financial arrangements;
(f) an undertaking from the applicant that there will be no discrimination of any party if they meet the requirements set down in the regulations;
(g) an explanation of the mark's purpose, that is, what characteristic(s) the mark will indicate in the certified goods or in relation to the services; and
(h) how it is proposed to monitor the use of the mark in the United Kingdom.

Transitional provisions Regulations governing the use of a certification mark, the registration of which was obtained under the 1938 Act,[2] are treated as if they had been filed under para 6 of Sch 2.[3]

11.09 Approval of the regulations, paragraph 8 If the Registrar is satisfied that all the requirements for registration of a certification mark are met (including the requirements relating to the regulations), he will accept the application, and the procedure set out in s 38 will be followed as regards publication, opposition proceedings and observations.[4]

1 Schedule 2, para 7(1)(b); the Work Manual in Chapter 12 states that it is necessary for the applicant to show that he has the confidence of the trade in the goods or services to be certified and that their certification is likely to be accepted as authoritative. Clearly, competency may be more difficult to establish if an application covers multiple classes, or if the applicant is an organisation based abroad.
2 ie pursuant to s 37.
3 Schedule 3, para 19(1).
4 Schedule 2, para 8(4); see also Chapters 3 and 4.

The regulations will also be published and, again, notice of opposition can be given and observations made.[5]

If the Registrar is not satisfied that the regulations comply with para 7(1), then the procedure set out in para 8(2) and (3) will be followed. That is, the Registrar will inform the applicant of the objections and give him the opportunity:

(a) to make representations; and/or
(b) to file amended regulations,

in order to try to overcome the objections. The Registrar will refuse the application altogether if the applicant does not overcome the objections. (Note that any restrictions relating to the use of the mark which are contained in the regulations are expressly exempted from the provisions of the Restrictive Trade Practices Act 1976.)

11.10 Amendment, paragraph 11 and r 23 The regulations can only be amended in accordance with para 11 and r 23,[6] which involves the Registrar first accepting the amendments, and possibly also publishing them for opposition and/or observations if the Registrar thinks it appropriate.[7]

Transitional provisions A request for the amendment of the regulations relating to a certification mark registered under the 1938 Act which is pending as at 31 October 1994 will be dealt with under the old law.[8]

11.11 Assignment of a registered certification mark, paragraph 12 The Registrar's consent is required in order to assign or otherwise transmit a registered certification mark. Among the considerations which the Registrar will take into account is the need to ensure that the assignee has the necessary 'competence' to supervise the certification and use of the certification mark, and to ensure that the public are not misled or deceived by the use of the mark following the assignment. The matters referred to in paragraph 11.08 above are therefore relevant in order to obtain the Registrar's consent.

5 Schedule 2, para 9.
6 The application for amendment must be filed on Form TM 36.
7 See the procedure set out in r 23; any notice of opposition must be filed within three months of publication and Form TM 7 must be used; see also Chapter 4.
8 Schedule 3, para 19(2).

11.12 Rights of authorised users, paragraphs 13 and 14 An authorised user of a registered certification mark is put in a similar position to that of a licensee of an ordinary trade mark. That is, ss 10(5), 19(2) and 89 of the 1994 Act will apply for the benefit of authorised users.[9]

Any loss or potential loss suffered by authorised users will be taken into account in any infringement proceedings commenced by the proprietor of the certification mark[10] provided that the infringement was committed after 31 October 1994.[11]

11.13 Revocation and invalidity, paragraphs 15 and 16

Revocation In addition to the grounds for revocation which apply to an ordinary trade mark,[12] a registered certification mark can also be revoked on the ground that:

(a) the proprietor has begun to carry on a business involving the supply of goods or services of the kind certified;

(b) the manner in which the mark has been used by the proprietor has caused it to become liable to mislead the public as regards its character or significance;

(c) the proprietor has failed to observe, or to secure the observance of, the regulations;

(d) an amendment of the regulations has been made so that they no longer comply with the requirements of para 6(2), or such that the regulations are contrary to public policy or to accepted principles of morality; or

(e) the proprietor is no longer competent to certify the relevant goods or services.

Invalidity Furthermore, in addition to the grounds for invalidity which apply to an ordinary trade mark,[13] a registered certification mark can be declared invalid on the ground that it was registered in breach of paras 4, 5(1) or 7(1).[14]

9 Schedule 2, para 13.
10 Schedule 2, para 14.
11 Schedule 3, para 6(2).
12 ie under s 46; see also Chapter 5.
13 ie under s 47; see also Chapter 5.
14 Schedule 2, para 16.

12 Collective marks

12.01 Introduction The 1994 Act introduces for the first time in the United Kingdom the category of 'collective marks'. In Chapter 1 the requirement that a trade mark must serve to distinguish the proprietor's goods or services from those of other undertakings[1] was considered. There are, however, two important exceptions to this rule:

a) certification trade marks, which have already been discussed in Chapter 11; and
(b) collective trade marks, which are discussed in this chapter.

12.02 Definition of collective mark, s 49 A collective mark is owned by an association of members, not by a single undertaking. Thus, a collective mark is a mark which distinguishes the goods or services of the members of the association from those of other undertakings.[2]

12.03 Application of the 1994 Act, ss 1(2), 49(2) and Schedule 1 All references in the 1994 Act to a 'trade mark' include a collective mark[3] but one must look to Sch 1 of the 1994 Act to ascertain the necessary adjustments which must be taken into account when applying the Act to collective marks.[4] The remainder

1 Section 49(1).
2 Section 1(2).
3 Section 1(2).
4 Section 49(2).

of this chapter addresses those adjustments; in all other respects the 1994 Act, the Rules (where relevant) and the other relevant chapters of this book apply equally to collective marks as they do to ordinary trade marks.

1994 Act, Schedule 1

12.04 Signs of which a collective mark may consist, paragraph 2 The definition of 'trade mark' in s 1(1) of the 1994 Act cannot be applied literally to collective marks. The second limb of the definition requires a trade mark to be 'capable of distinguishing goods or services of one undertaking from those of other undertakings'. But this is not the purpose of a collective mark, which is usually applied to the goods or services of numerous 'undertakings'. A collective mark will therefore never serve to distinguish uniquely the goods or services of one undertaking. Accordingly, the second limb of the definition must be construed, for the purposes of collective marks, as a reference to distinguishing the goods or services of the members of the particular association which is the proprietor of the mark from those of other undertakings which are not members of the association.[5]

12.05 Registrability: indications of geographical origin, paragraph 3 An absolute ground for refusing the registration of an ordinary trade mark is that it consists exclusively of a sign which indicates the geographical origin of the proprietor's goods or services.[6]

Geographical signs can be registered as collective marks.[7] The registration of a geographical sign does not, however, entitle the proprietor to prevent the use of the sign by a third party, provided that the use is in accordance with 'honest practices in industrial or commercial matters'.[8]

5 Schedule 1, para 2.
6 Section 3(1)(c); see paragraph 2.04.
7 Schedule 1, para 3(1); subject to Council Regulation No 2081/92 on the Protection of Geographical Indications and Designations of Origin for Agricultural Products and Foodstuffs (see also Commission Regulation No 2037/93 laying down detailed rules of application of that Regulation).
8 Schedule 1, para 3(2); as to the meaning of the phrase 'honest practices in industrial or commercial matters', see paragraph 7.08 in the context of defences to infringement of a trade mark.

12.06 Grounds for refusal of registration: misleading as to character or significance, paragraph 4(1) In addition to the absolute grounds for refusing the registration of an ordinary trade mark,[9] a collective mark cannot be registered if the public is liable to be misled in relation to the character or significance of the mark.[10] Accordingly, the Registrar may require that certification marks include some indication that the mark is in fact a collective mark.[11]

12.07 The regulations, paragraphs 5 and 6 Regulations governing the use of the collective mark must be filed by the applicant within nine months of the date on which the application for registration is made.[12] A failure to file the regulations on time will result in the application being treated as having been withdrawn.[13]

The regulations must include a statement as to:

(a) who is authorised to use the collective mark (the proprietor must maintain, within the United Kingdom, a register of persons authorised to use the mark);
(b) the conditions of membership of the association;
(c) where they exist, the conditions of use of the collective mark, including any sanctions against misuse;[14]
(d) the procedure for taking action against misuse of the mark; and
(e) the procedure for dealing with appeals against the use of the mark.[15]

The collective mark will not be registered unless the regulations comply with these requirements and provided also that they are not contrary to public policy nor to accepted principles of morality.[16] (Note that any restrictions relating to the use of the mark which are

9 ie under s 3: see Chapter 2.
10 Paragraph 4(1); and compare this with s 3(3)(b).
11 Schedule 1, para 4(2). The Work Manual in Chapter 13 states that this requirement, in practice, means that any collective mark should include the words 'collective mark' against the mark; however, it is recognised that this requirement may alternatively be overcome by the use of the mark which in itself may indicate that it is not being used as an 'ordinary' trade mark.
12 Rule 22; Sch 1, para 5(1); Form TM 35 must be used and a fee will be payable; the regulations will be open to public inspection in the same way as the Register: Sch 1, para 9.
13 Schedule 1, para 6(2).
14 Schedule 1, para 5(2).
15 See the Work Manual, Chapter 13, paragraph 3.2.
16 Schedule 1, para 6(1).

contained in the regulations are expressly exempted from the provisions of the Restrictive Trade Practices Act 1976.)

12.08 Approval of the regulations, paragraph 7 If the Registrar is satisfied that all the requirements for registration of a collective mark are met (including the requirements relating to the regulations), he will accept the application, and the procedure set out in s 38 will be followed as regards publication, opposition proceedings and observations.[17]

The regulations will also be published and, again, notice of opposition can be given and observations made.[18]

If the Registrar is not satisfied that the regulations comply with para 6(1), then the procedure set out in para 7(2) and (3) will be followed. That is, the Registrar will inform the applicant of the objections and give him the opportunity:

(a) to make representations; and/or
(b) to file amended regulations,

in order to try to overcome the objections. The Registrar will refuse the application altogether if the applicant does not overcome the objections.

12.09 Amendment, paragraph 10 and r 23 The regulations can only be amended in accordance with para 10 and r 23,[19] which involves the Registrar first accepting the amendments and possibly also publishing them for opposition and/or observations if he thinks it appropriate.[20]

12.10 Rights of authorised users, paragraphs 11 and 12 An authorised user of a registered collective mark is put in a similar position to that of a licensee of an ordinary trade mark. That is, ss 10(5), 19(2) and 89 of the 1994 Act will apply for the benefit of authorised users.[1]

Any loss or potential loss suffered by authorised users will be

17 Schedule 1, para 7(4); see also Chapters 3 and 4.
18 Schedule 1, para 8.
19 The application for amendment must be filed on Form TM 36.
20 See the procedure set out in r 23; any notice of opposition must be filed within three months of publication; Form TM 7 should be used; see also Chapter 4.
1 Schedule 1, paras 11 and 12; see in particular para 12 in relation to the manner in which provisions corresponding to s 30 will apply to an authorised user of a registered collective mark in infringement cases.

taken into account in any infringement proceedings commenced by the proprietor of the collective mark.[2]

12.11 Revocation and invalidity, paragraphs 13 and 14

Revocation In addition to the grounds for revocation which apply to an ordinary trade mark,[3] a registered collective mark can also be revoked on the ground that:

(a) the manner in which the mark has been used by the proprietor has caused it to become liable to mislead the public as regards its character or significance;
(b) the proprietor (ie the association of members) has failed to observe, or to secure the observance of, the regulations; or
(c) an amendment to the regulations has been made such that they no longer comply with the requirements of para 5(2) or such that the regulations are contrary to public policy or to accepted principles of morality.

Invalidity Furthermore, in addition to the grounds for invalidity which apply to an ordinary trade mark,[4] a registered collective mark can be declared invalid on the ground that it was registered in breach of paras 4(1) or 6(1).[5]

2 Schedule 1, para 12(6).
3 ie under s 46; see also Chapter 5.
4 ie under s 47; see also Chapter 5.
5 Schedule 1, para 14.

13 The Community trade mark

13.01 Introduction Section 52 of the 1994 Act confers upon the Secretary of State the power to make provision in connection with the implementation of the Community Trade Mark Regulation ('the Regulation').[1] Pursuant to this power, the Community Trade Mark Regulations 1996 were made on 23 July 1996 and came into force on 14 August 1996. The background to all this begins on 20 December 1993 when the European Council issued the Regulation which was then published in the Official Journal on 14 January 1994 and came into force on 15 March 1994. The Regulation is a free-standing supranational instrument which is legally and directly binding in all member states of the European Union ('EU').[2] As of 1 February 1998, the EU comprised the following countries: Austria, Belgium, Denmark, Finland, France, Germany, Greece, Ireland (Republic of), Italy, Luxembourg, the Netherlands, Portugal, Sweden, Spain and the United Kingdom. Although there are 15 countries within the EU, there are only 13 jurisdictions, because Belgium, the Netherlands and Luxembourg constitute, for trade mark purposes at least, a single jurisdiction, namely Benelux. There are a number of other 'associated countries' from Central and Eastern Europe which have signed an Association Agreement but are not full members of the EU.

1 Regulation No 40/94 on the Community Trade Mark. The Regulation has been amended in order to incorporate the Agreement establishing the World Trade Organisation: Regulation 3288/94.
2 EC Treaty, Article 189.

The Regulation establishes the Office for Harmonisation in the Internal Market ('OHIM'),[3] known colloquially to trade mark practitioners, and referred to hereafter, as the Community Trade Mark Office ('CTMO'). The CTMO is located in Alicante, Spain and it opened for business on 1 April 1996. However, applications for Community Trade Marks ('CTMs') filed on or after 1 January 1996 and prior to 1 April 1996 were deemed to have been filed on 1 April 1996. As of 1 November 1997 in excess of 63,000 applications for the registration of a CTM had been filed with the CTMO. It was also possible to claim Paris Convention priority of an earlier filed application, thus effectively securing a filing date prior to the opening date of the CTMO; for example, a CTM application filed on 1 April 1996 could have claimed priority based on an earlier national application filed on or after 1 October 1995.[4]

The Regulation needs to be read in conjunction with:

(a) Commission Regulation (EC) No 2868/95 of 13 December 1995, which implements the Regulation, and which is generally known and is referred to hereafter as the Implementing Regulation; and

(b) Commission Regulation (EC) No 2869/95 of 13 December 1995, which specifies the fees payable to the CTMO in respect of those matters designated in the Regulation and/or the Implementing Regulation. This Regulation is generally known and is referred to hereafter as the Fees Regulation.

The Regulation does not replace national trade mark law nor the national systems for the registration of trade marks. Rather, it provides an alternative system.

An applicant seeking to protect a trade mark in the EU may have several options:

(a) to file a national application in any one or more member states of the EU; or

(b) to file a single CTM application (either at the CTMO or with an individual member state's national trade mark registry, which will then transmit the application to the CTMO); or

(c) to file an application under the Madrid Systems (Agreement or Protocol); or

(d) to do any combination of (a), (b) and (c).

3 Article 2.

4 See paragraph 13.07 as to priority claims.

The purpose of this chapter on the CTM is:
(a) to introduce the reader to the CTM system;
(b) to compare and contrast the major features of the CTM system with the alternative national systems and the system for the international registration of trade marks under the Madrid Systems; and
(c) to highlight the most important considerations in choosing amongst the alternative trade mark systems.

Readers will need to refer to more comprehensive texts in order to gain an in-depth analysis of the Regulation and the practice and procedure in the CTMO.[5] However, this chapter should provide trade mark owners and their advisers with a working understanding of the Regulation and the issues which arise in formulating a trade mark registration and protection strategy in the EU.

References in this chapter to Articles are to the Articles of the Regulation.

13.02 Community Trade Mark Office

Representation, Articles 88 and 89 The general rule is that no person is compelled to be represented before the CTMO. However, both natural and legal persons who do not have either their domicile or their principal place of business or a real and effective industrial or commercial establishment in the EU must be represented in all proceedings before the CTMO. The only exception is in relation to the actual filing of an application for a CTM.[6] Representation of natural or legal persons before the CTMO may only be undertaken by:
(a) a legal practitioner qualified in one of the member states and having his place of business within the EU – to the extent that he is entitled to act as a representative in trade mark matters; or
(b) a professional representative whose name appears on the list maintained by the CTMO.[7]

In addition to deciding whether to accept applications for the

5 For example 'The Community Trade Mark', INTA 1996–7, edited by Julian Gyngell and Allan Poulter.
6 Article 88(1) and (2).
7 Article 89(1): representatives acting before the CTMO must file with the CTMO a signed authorisation for insertion on the CTMO's files. Article 89(2) specifies the conditions which must be satisfied by any natural person before his name is entered on the list of professional representatives.

registration of a CTM, the CTMO handles revocation and invalidation actions. Oppositions are also filed with the CTMO. Thus, the CTMO considers questions of distinctiveness, descriptiveness, deceptiveness, non-use and conflicts with earlier trade mark rights.

The Register, Article 83 The CTMO maintains a Register which is known as the Register of Community trade marks ('the Register'), which contains all the particulars of registrations which are provided for by the Regulation or in the Implementing Regulation. The Register is open to public inspection.[8]

Publications, Article 85 The CTMO publishes two periodic documents:

(a) the Community Trade Marks Bulletin, which contains entries made in the Register as well as all other particulars prescribed by the Regulation or the Implementing Regulation; and
(b) the Official Journal, which contains notices and information of a general nature issued by the President of the CTMO, as well as any other information relevant to this Regulation.[9]

These publications can be obtained either individually or by subscription from various distributors around the world.

Languages, Article 115 The languages of the CTMO are English, French, German, Italian and Spanish.[10] However, applications for the registration of a CTM may be filed in any one of the official languages of the EU,[11] but the applicant must also indicate a second language, which must be one of the languages of the CTMO.[12] (Note that a word mark will appear and be registered in the language that it is applied for: for example, an English applicant may apply for the registration of a French word – the application itself will be in the language chosen by the applicant, but the mark itself will appear and be registered in French.) Subject to any contrary agreement between the parties, this second language may become the language of proceedings for oppositions, revocation or invalidity in the event that the language in which the application was filed is not one of the

8 Article 83.
9 Article 85.
10 Article 115(2).
11 Article 115(1). The 11 official languages are: Danish, Dutch, English, Finnish, French, German, Greek, Italian, Portuguese, Spanish, and Swedish.
12 Article 115(3).

languages of the CTMO.[13]

Where the applicant for a CTM is the only party to proceedings before the CTMO, the language of the proceedings will be the language used for filing the application. However, if the application was made in a language other than one of the languages of the CTMO, then the CTMO may choose to communicate in the second language indicated by the applicant.[14]

All notices of opposition and all applications for revocation or invalidity must be filed in one of the languages of the CTMO.[15]

All information published under the Regulation including all entries in the Register of CTMs will be made in all the official languages of the EU.[16]

Officers, Articles 119 and 120 The CTMO is managed by the President, who is assisted by Vice-Presidents. The President is appointed by the European Council for a period not exceeding five years.[17]

Oral proceedings, Article 75 There is provision for oral proceedings before the CTMO, but such proceedings will only take place if the CTMO considers this to be expedient; and it is clear that the CTMO intends to minimise the use of oral proceedings wherever possible. However, Article 75(1) provides that oral proceedings must be held if so requested by either party to the proceedings.

Taking of evidence, Article 76 The means of giving or obtaining evidence before the CTMO may include any of the following:
(a) hearing the parties;
(b) requests for information;
(c) the production of documents and items of evidence;
(d) hearing witnesses;
(e) opinions of experts; and
(f) sworn or affirmed statements in writing.[18]

13 Article 115(6) and (7). See paragraph 13.07 for a discussion on the tactical issues in selecting an appropriate language.
14 Article 115(4).
15 Article 115(5); the opponent/applicant may be required to provide a translation in certain circumstances: see Article 115(6).
16 Article 116(1) and (2).
17 Articles 119(1) and 120(1) and (2).
18 Article 76(1).

The CTMO has the power to issue a summons to a person concerned to appear before it.[19]

Natural justice, Articles 73 and 77 The CTMO must, as a matter of course, notify those concerned of decisions and summonses and of any notice or other communication.[20]

Decisions of the CTMO must state the reasons on which they are based. Furthermore, the decisions must be based only on reasons or evidence on which the parties concerned have had an opportunity to present their comments.[1]

Appeals, Articles 57 to 63 Decisions of departments of the CTMO may be appealed.[2] Notice of appeal must be filed with the CTMO within two months of the date of the decision the subject of the appeal[3] and referred to the particular department where the application was made. If the decision is not then rectified by the relevant department within one month, the appeal must be remitted to the Board of Appeal.[4] Finally, an appeal from the Board of Appeal may be brought before the Court of First Instance ('CFI') of the European Court of Justice ('ECJ') within two months of the decision of the Board of Appeal.[5]

13.03 Unitary nature of the CTM, Article 1(2) The registration of a mark as a CTM results in that mark having equal effect throughout the entire EU. This means that a CTM can only be:

(a) registered;
(b) transferred;
(c) surrendered; or
(d) revoked or declared invalid,

in respect of the whole of the EU.[6]

The application for a CTM must therefore stand or fall for the

19 Article 76(3).
20 Article 77.
1 Article 73.
2 Article 57.
3 Article 59.
4 Article 60; see also Commission Regulation (EC) No 216/96 of 5 February 1996 which lays down the rules of procedure of the Boards of Appeal of the CTMO; for a commentary on the procedure and function of the Boards of Appeal see Fabio Angelini 'The Community Trade Mark: Procedure and Function of the Boards of Appeal' Trademark World, June/July 1996.
5 Article 63(1) and (5).
6 Article 1(2).

entire EU. Thus, for example, if a successful opposition is encountered on the basis of an earlier trade mark in a single EU country, the CTM application will be rejected in toto. Also, once a CTM registration is obtained, the registration as a whole will be revoked if it is attacked successfully on the basis of an earlier trade mark in a single member state. However, if a CTM registration or application is revoked or is rejected for this reason, the CTM may be converted into a series of individual national trade mark applications.[7] This will result in the loss of the original CTM filing fees, which will not be refunded. A conversion fee will be payable to the CTMO in respect of each converted application, but the fee is only payable once to the CTMO, regardless of the number of national filings into which the CTM application is converted.[8] However, in addition, each national Registry may also require the payment of the appropriate national application fees.[9]

The unitary nature of a CTM raises a question as to how this unitary nature will survive or be adapted following any enlargement of the membership of the EU. That is, will CTMs already in force before a new country joins the EU automatically extend to and retain their unitary character in the new member state? The Regulation does not make provision regarding any future expansion of the membership of the EU, and therefore this remains a moot issue for the Commission to deal with.[10]

13.04 Who can own a CTM registration, Article 5 Nationals (which includes natural or legal persons) of member states may apply for a CTM;[11] so also may non-EU nationals provided that they are nationals of countries which are party to the Paris Convention or to the World Trade Organisation Agreement.[12] Furthermore, nationals domiciled in or which have their seat or which have a real and effective industrial or commercial establishment within either the EU or a state which is a party to the Paris Convention can own CTMs.[13]

7 See paragraph 13.11 below; Articles 108–110.
8 Article 109(1). See r 45(2) of the Implementing Regulation and Article 2(20) of Commission Regulation (EC) No 2869/95.
9 Article 110(3); a translation may also be required.
10 For a more complete discussion of this issue see Bojan Pretnar 'Is the Future Enlargement of the EU an Immediate Issue for the CTM System' [1997] 4 EIPR 185.
11 Article 5(1)(a).
12 Article 5(1)(b), as amended by Article 1(1) Regulation 3288/94.
13 Article 5(1)(c).

In addition, other trade mark owners not falling within the above categories are able to obtain a CTM registration on the basis that such owners are nationals of countries which accord reciprocal protection to all EU nationals.[14]

13.05 Definition of a CTM, Article 4 The key definition in the Regulation as to what constitutes a 'Community trade mark' is found in Article 4, which provides that a CTM may consist of any 'sign' which is both:
(a) capable of being represented graphically; and
(b) capable of distinguishing the goods or services of one undertaking from those of other undertakings.
Readers will recognise that this is the same definition as is used in the 1994 Act and therefore reference should be made to the matters and issues discussed in Chapter 1. Of course, decisions of the Registry and the UK national courts under the 1994 Act are not binding on the CTMO, the Boards of Appeal and/or the CTM Courts and therefore, despite the aim of harmonisation, one may encounter divergence. Ultimately such divergence may need to be cured or at least minimised through appeals and references to the European Court of Justice, pursuant to Article 177 of the EC Treaty.

13.06 Registrable CTMs, Articles 7 and 8 The Regulation stipulates only those trade marks which *cannot* be registered rather than setting down mandatory criteria for registrability. Accordingly, all trade marks are prima facie registrable as CTMs unless there are express grounds for refusal. The grounds for refusal fall under two headings:
(a) the absolute grounds for refusal: Article 7; and
(b) the relative grounds for refusal: Article 8.
Furthermore, any failure to comply with the formalities associated with the application procedure (discussed in paragraph 13.07 below) will result in the application being refused.

It is worth noting at this point that it is important to distinguish between the two main grounds for refusal for at least two reasons:
(a) at the application/examination stage the CTMO may only raise objections to registration on the basis of the absolute grounds

14 Article 5(1)(d), as amended by Article 1(2) Regulation 3288/94. See also Article 5(3).

for refusal or the failure to comply with the formalities of the application procedure, and it is for a proprietor of an earlier conflicting mark or earlier right in opposition proceedings to raise any relative grounds for refusal; whereas
(b) after registration of a CTM, a party challenging its validity may rely on either the absolute or relative grounds for refusal.

Absolute grounds for refusal, Article 7 The absolute grounds for refusing the registration of a CTM are matters which, in essence, are deemed to be necessarily inconsistent with the requirement of distinctiveness or are otherwise contrary to the conferral of monopoly rights. The exhaustive list of absolute grounds for refusal is as follows:
(a) signs which do not conform to the requirements of Article 4, that is, signs which cannot be represented graphically and/or are not capable of distinguishing the goods or services of one undertaking from those of other undertakings;
(b) trade marks which (subject to the proviso below) are devoid of any distinctive character;
(c) trade marks which (subject to the proviso below) consist exclusively of signs or indications which may serve, in trade, to designate the kind, quality, quantity, intended purpose, value, geographical origin or the time of production of the goods or of rendering of the service, or other characteristics of the goods or service;
(d) trade marks which (subject to the proviso below) consist exclusively of signs or indications which have become customary in the current language or in the bona fide and established practices of the trade (ie generic marks are excluded);
(e) signs which consist exclusively of;
  (i) the shape which results from the nature of the goods themselves; or
  (ii) the shape of goods which is necessary to obtain a technical result; or
  (iii) the shape which gives substantial value to the goods;
(f) trade marks which are contrary to public policy or to accepted principles of morality;
(g) trade marks which are of such a nature as to deceive the public, for instance as to the nature, quality or geographical origin of the goods or service;

(h) trade marks which are to be refused pursuant to Article 6*ter* of the Paris Convention (and the use of which has not been authorised by the appropriate authority);
(i) trade marks which include badges, emblems or escutcheons (other than those covered by Article 6*ter*) and which are of 'particular public interest' (and the use of which has not been authorised by the appropriate authorities); or
(j) trade marks for wines which contain or consist of a geographical indication identifying wines or for spirits which contain or consist of a geographical indication identifying spirits with respect to such wines or spirits not having that origin.[15]

Note that these absolute grounds for refusal will apply notwithstanding that the grounds exist only in one part of the EU.[16] For example, under (d) above, as a necessary incidence of the unitary nature of a CTM, this ground for refusal will apply if the mark has become customary in any language of the EU and/or in the practices of the trade in any country of the EU. Likewise, under (f) above, a trade mark will not be registrable if it is contrary to the public policy of any one country in the EU. This apart, readers will recognise that the absolute grounds for refusal set out in Article 7 closely reflect those set out in s 3 of the 1994 Act and reference should therefore be made to Chapter 2.

Proviso, Article 7(3) Importantly, however, the absolute grounds for refusal set out in (b), (c) and (d) above will not apply if the trade mark has in fact become distinctive in relation to the goods or services for which registration is requested in consequence of the use which has been made of it. This represents a fundamental departure from trade mark jurisprudence in much of the EU, where distinctiveness in fact was not necessarily sufficient to obtain registration. However, under the Regulation, if an applicant can establish that the mark applied for has become distinctive as a result of the use made of the mark, then the mark will proceed to registration as long as it is not otherwise caught by any of the other grounds for refusal which are not subject to the proviso. The proviso embodies the now accepted proposition that a trade mark which is

15 Article 7(1), as amended by Article 1(3) Regulation 3288/94.
16 Article 7(2).

in fact recognised as designating the origin of goods or services should not be denied registration.

Relative grounds for refusal, Article 8 The relative grounds for refusal (unlike the absolute grounds for refusal) are only triggered when the proprietor of an 'earlier trade mark' opposes the registration of the subsequent mark. It is therefore necessary first to consider the meaning of the phrase 'earlier trade mark'. Article 8(2) provides that:

'"Earlier trade mark" means:

(a) Trade marks of the following kinds with a date of application for registration which is earlier than the date of application for registration of the CTM, taking account, where appropriate, of the priorities claimed in respect of those trade marks:
   (i) CTMs;
   (ii) trade marks registered in a Member State (including at the Benelux Trade Mark Office); and
   (iii) trade marks registered under international arrangements which have effect in a Member State;
(b) applications for the trade marks referred to in paragraph 1 (subject to their registration); and
(c) trade marks which, on the date of application for registration of the CTM, or, where appropriate, of the priority claimed in respect of the application for registration of the CTM, are well known in a Member State, (in the sense in which the words 'well known' are used in Article 6*bis* of the Paris Convention).'

Article 8(1) provides that, upon such opposition, the trade mark applied for shall not be registered:

(a) if it is identical with the earlier trade mark and the goods or services for which registration is applied for are identical with the goods or services for which the earlier trade mark is protected; or
(b) if because of its identity with or similarity to the earlier trade mark and the identity or similarity of the goods or services covered by the trade marks there exists a likelihood of confusion on the part of the public in the territory in which the earlier trade mark is protected (the 'likelihood of confusion' specifically includes the 'likelihood of association' with the earlier trade mark).

Other specified conflicting rights, Article 8(4) The proprietor of an unregistered trade mark[17] may also oppose and prevent the registration of a trade mark based on his rights to that mark which were acquired prior to the date of application for registration of the CTM and provided that the law of the relevant member state confers on its proprietor the right to prohibit the use of the CTM in question.[18]

In addition, the proprietor of an earlier trade mark may also oppose the registration of the trade mark applied for where it is identical with or similar to the earlier trade mark and is to be registered for goods or services even though they are *not* similar to those for which the earlier trade mark is registered, but provided that the earlier trade mark has a 'reputation' in the EU, and where the use of the mark applied for without due cause would take unfair advantage of or be detrimental to the distinctive character or the repute of the earlier trade mark.[19]

Agents and representatives, Article 8(3) In addition to the general right of all proprietors of earlier trade marks to oppose the registration of subsequent identical/similar marks, the Regulation also confers a specific right in the case of agents and representatives who seek to register their principal's trade mark.

A trade mark will not be registered where an agent or representative of the proprietor of the trade mark applies for registration of his principal's mark in his own name without the principal's consent – unless the agent or representative can justify his action.[20] This will be particularly apposite in the case of a distributor 'poaching' his supplier's trade mark(s).

Word marks An issue arises as to whether a mark which consists of a word or words in one language will be considered to be identical with or similar to an earlier trade mark simply because the subsequent trade mark has the same meaning as (ie is a translation of) the earlier trade mark. Although the two marks may be quite different visually and phonetically, they may have an identical

17 Including the proprietor of a sign which is used in the course of trade and which has 'more than mere local significance'.
18 Article 8(4).
19 Article 8(5).
20 Article 8(3), provided that the principal opposes the registration.

meaning. This issue will be particularly relevant given the increasing knowledge of foreign languages amongst members of the public in the EU. The CTMO's view is that a word is not identical or similar to another word simply because it has an identical or similar meaning when translated. Certainly, the CTMO does not require applicants to file translations of their word marks.

13.07 Applying for CTMs, Articles 25 to 28

Filing of applications, Article 25 Applications for the registration of a CTM must be filed either at:

(a) the CTMO; or
(b) the Trade Mark Registry of a member state of the EU.[1]

There is no mandatory requirement for an applicant to appoint a representative in order to file an application but, following the filing of an application, all applicants must be represented by Professional Representatives (as defined in Article 89) in all proceedings established by the Regulation.[2]

Note that the application forms are available free of charge on diskettes and the CTMO will accept applications filed on these diskettes (but not via e-mail).[3]

Conditions, Article 26 An application for a CTM must contain the following:

(a) a request for the registration of the CTM;
(b) information identifying the applicant;
(c) a list of the goods or services in respect of which the registration is requested;
(d) a representation of the trade mark;[4]
(e) the name and address of the applicant's representative (where applicable);
(f) a declaration setting out the details of any previous application in respect of which priority is claimed pursuant to Article 30 of the Regulation;
(g) a declaration setting out the details of any exhibition priority claim pursuant to Article 33 of the Regulation;

1 Article 25(1); including the Benelux Trade Mark Office.
2 Article 88(2).
3 Rule 82 Implementing Regulation.
4 Article 26(1).

(h) a declaration setting out the details of any claim to seniority pursuant to Article 34 of the Regulation;
(i) where applicable, a statement that the application is for the registration of a Community collective mark pursuant to Article 64 of the Regulation;
(j) a specification of the language in which the application has been filed, and of the second language pursuant to Article 115(3) of the Regulation; and
(k) the signature of the applicant or the applicant's representative.[5]

As one would expect, the application is subject to the payment of a fee and, where appropriate, one or more class fees.[6] However, the CTMO will issue a formal filing date provided only that the application contains the matters set out in (a)–(d) above; the application fee must be paid within one month after lodging the application.[7]

Statement of use Note that it is not required to file or make a statement of use in relation to the mark applied for. The only sanctions for non-use arise if the mark is not in fact used within five years of registration and/or if use is suspended during any uninterrupted period of five years.[8]

Languages Applicants should give serious thought as to the language in which the application should be filed. As already stated in paragraph 13.02, applications for the registration of a CTM may be filed in any one of the official languages of the EU, but the applicant must also indicate a second language, which must be one of the languages of the CTMO.[9] A tactical question arises when considering which language would be more appropriate in the event that the application is opposed by a third party. This is because all oppositions must be in one of the languages of the CTMO. Thus, for example, if the applicant wanted to guarantee that any opposition should be conducted in English, then he should consider filing the application in one of the official languages of the EU but not being one of the languages of the CTMO. He should then indicate English as his second language, being one of the languages

5 See r 1 Implementing Regulation.
6 Article 26(2); see Appendix IV for a list of the relevant fees.
7 Article 27.
8 Article 15.
9 Article 115(3).

of the CTMO. In these circumstances, the opposition would have to be conducted in English. Note, however, that the application itself and the subsequent certificate would be issued in the language chosen by the applicant for his application. This may be particularly relevant if the applicant has any cause to suspect an opposition from a particular (foreign) source: the applicant should take such steps as he can in order to avoid giving the potential opponent the opportunity to conduct the opposition in the opponent's own language.

Classification, Article 28 and r 2 Goods and services in respect of which CTMs are applied for are divided into 42 classes (34 goods classes and 8 service classes) in accordance with the Nice Convention, which is well known to trade mark owners and practitioners around the world.[10]

Priority, Articles 29 to 32 In accordance with the Paris Convention, priority can be claimed based on prior national filings in countries which are signatories to the Convention. This means that CTM applications can be backdated (up to six months) to the date of the relevant national filing.

A claim for priority can be based on a relevant prior national application which was filed within the six month period prior to the filing of the CTM application. Note that, unlike the position under the 1994 Act, a priority claim can also be made within two months of filing the CTM application.[11]

There is a further provision for claiming priority based on the case of a trade mark on goods or services displayed at international exhibitions.[12]

13.08 Examination and searches, Articles 36 to 39

Examination, Articles 36 to 38 The CTMO checks that the application complies with the Regulation and that the appropriate fees have been paid. The applicant is given a chance to remedy any deficiencies. Unlike the examination procedure adopted in some EU countries (for example in the United Kingdom Registry under the 1994 Act), the CTMO will only examine:

10 Article 28.
11 Rule 6(2) Implementing Regulation.
12 Article 33 and see r 7 Implementing Regulation.

(a) whether the applicant is entitled to be a proprietor of a CTM under Article 5;[13] and
(b) whether there are absolute grounds for refusal of registration under Article 7.[14]

The CTMO does not examine whether there are relative grounds for refusal, but a search for possible conflicting marks is carried out. The Guidelines by reference to which the examination is carried out are now available from the CTMO.[15]

Search, Article 39 Once official examination is completed, the CTMO will draw up a search report identifying any prior conflicting CTM registrations or applications (but not any prior conflicting national registrations or applications). (Note that all CTM applications filed between 1 January 1996 and 31 March 1996 were given a filing date of 1 April 1996 and therefore will not conflict with each other and will not be raised in the CTMO's search report.) The CTMO does not conduct an official search covering the national Registers. National Registries may search their own records for conflicting national registrations and applications but they are not obliged to do so. However, if a national Registry does conduct a search, then it is obliged to send the results of the search to the CTMO.[16]

Results of searches of the CTM Register and of any national Registers will be sent by the CTMO to the applicant, who must then decide whether or not to proceed with his application, but the CTMO itself will not raise an objection based on the search report. The owner of an earlier CTM registration or application is likewise informed of the application upon publication, thus alerting him to the subsequent application and giving him the opportunity to oppose the registration if necessary and appropriate.[17] As France, Germany and Italy do not conduct searches as part of the national trade mark registration process, none of these three countries provides searches for the CTMO. However, each of the other member states do provide national search reports, and the presentation and quality of the reports varies considerably from country to country.

13 Article 37.
14 Article 38.
15 Tel: 0034 6 5139333; Fax: 0034 6 5139173.
16 Article 39(3).
17 Article 39(5) and (6).

The fact that the CTMO only examines whether there are absolute grounds for refusal will mean that more applications are likely to be accepted than would be the case if examination also extended to the relative grounds for refusal. However, the result in practice will be that more oppositions will be commenced by third party proprietors. This reflects the policy that the CTMO should not, at the examination stage, become involved in the possibly academic and/or nugatory exercise of resolving disputes between proprietors of potentially conflicting marks. Proprietors of earlier marks therefore need to be vigilant in monitoring applications for CTMs to ensure that they become aware of any application for a subsequent conflicting mark and are therefore able to file a notice of opposition in order to protect their rights. The most efficient way of monitoring the large number of applications is to instruct attorneys to maintain a regular 'watching brief' or to subscribe to a watching service. Of course, the fact that the CTMO will not examine as to whether there are relative grounds for refusal does not mean that an applicant for a CTM should not consider first carrying out an availability search himself prior to filing the application. It must still be advisable to consider carrying out such a search (especially in France, Germany, and Italy where searches are not carried out) in order to avoid incurring filing and prosecution fees, which may be thrown away if a third party subsequently successfully opposes the registration of the applicant's mark. Against this must be weighed the potential cost and effectiveness of the search, as well as the desirability of securing the earliest possible filing date which may be crucial in certain cases.

13.09 Observations and oppositions, Articles 41 to 43 After a search of the CTM Register and any search conducted by national Registries, the CTM application is then published (to the extent that it has not been refused).[18]

Observations, Article 41 Following the publication of a CTM application, third parties may submit written observations to the CTMO stating the grounds on which the mark applied for should not be registered (in particular, the absolute grounds, but Article 41 does not expressly exclude observations on relative or other grounds).

18 Article 40.

Such third parties will not be parties to the proceedings before the CTMO, but observations will be communicated to the applicant who may comment upon them.[19]

Oppositions, Article 42 Not more than three months following publication, a proprietor of, or his authorised licensee under, an earlier trade mark[20] (and other specified persons with interests in marks[1]) can give notice of opposition to the CTM application. Unlike a CTM application, notice of opposition can only be filed at the CTMO in Alicante, Spain and not at any of the national offices of the member states. An opposition may be brought on the basis of any or all of the relative grounds for refusal referred to above,[2] but not on the absolute grounds for refusal under Article 7, which are matters for the CTMO.

The examination of an opposition is dealt with in Article 43(1) which requires the parties to file observations (ie arguments) in support of their respective positions. Rules 15 to 22 of the Implementing Regulation provide for:

(a) the contents of the Notice of Opposition;
(b) the facts, evidence and arguments presented in support of and against the opposition (cf the case of languages in opposition proceedings); and
(c) the examination of the opposition on its merits.

The Guidelines setting out the procedure for oppositions are now available from the CTMO.[3]

Cooling off period Following receipt of a Notice of Opposition the CTMO will first satisfy itself that the Notice complies with the requirements of Article 42. Provided that it does so, the CTMO will communicate the opposition to the applicant for registration and will invite the applicant to file his observations within a period which will be specified by the CTMO. However, in effect, there is a cooling off period because the CTMO will draw the applicant's attention to the fact that the opposition proceedings will only be deemed to commence two months after the applicant has been

19 Article 41.
20 As defined in Article 8(2).
1 As provided for in Article 8(3) or (4).
2 Article 42; Article 8 for the relative grounds for refusal and paragraph 13.06 above.
3 Tel: 0034 6 5139333; Fax: 0034 6 5139173.

informed of the opposition. Within that two month period the applicant for registration has the opportunity to inform the CTMO that he withdraws his application or restricts the application to goods or services (as the case may be) against which the opposition is not directed.[4] This two month cooling off period may be extended by the CTMO pursuant to a request by both parties.[5] In the event that the application is withdrawn or restricted within the two month cooling off period (or any extended period), the CTMO will so inform the opposing party and will refund the opposition fee.[6]

Costs The award of costs in opposition proceedings is governed by Article 81; the usual order will be that the losing party will bear the fees incurred by the other party as well as all costs essential to the proceedings, including travel and subsistence and the remuneration of an agent, adviser or advocate, within the limits of the scales laid down in the Implementing Regulation.[7]

Defence, Article 43(2) Another important feature of the CTM use requirement is that non-use can be raised by the applicant as a defence to an opposition.[8] The proprietor of an earlier CTM who is opposing an application is obliged, at the request of the applicant, to provide proof of genuine use of his mark in the last five years, or proper reasons for non-use, or else the opposition will fail.

13.10 Registration, Articles 45 to 47 Where an application meets the requirements of the Regulation, and where no Notice of Opposition has been given, or where the opposition has been rejected, the trade mark will be registered as a CTM – subject only to the payment of the fee within two months of the receipt by the applicant of the request for payment.[9]

4 Rule 19 Implementing Regulation.
5 Rule 19(2) Implementing Regulation.
6 Rule 19(3) Implementing Regulation.
7 See r 94(6) and (7), which sets out maximum rates for travel expenses, subsistence expenses, costs entailed in the taking of evidence and the cost of representation.
8 Article 43(2); as to which see paragraph 13.09 above.
9 Article 45; See Appendix III for a list of the relevant fees. The time for payment can be extended by up to two months but there is a penalty for late payment (r 23(2) and (3)).

Duration of registration, Article 46 CTMs are registered for a period of ten years from the date of filing of the application; registration can be renewed indefinitely for further periods of ten years.[10]

Renewal, Article 47 CTMs can be renewed at the request of the proprietor, provided that the requisite renewal fees have been paid.[11] There is no requirement to certify or prove use of the mark in order to renew the registration.

The CTMO will inform proprietors (and any recorded licensees) of the impending expiry of the registration of the CTM at least six months before the expiry.[12]

A request by the applicant for renewal must be submitted within a period of six months ending on the last day of the month in which protection would otherwise expire.[13]

13.11 Conversion into a national application, Article 108

An application for a CTM which is refused, or a CTM which ceases to have effect, can be converted into one or more national trade mark applications.[14] A CTM cannot be converted in a particular member state if it is cancelled for non-use or if the specific grounds for revocation or invalidity apply in that member state.[15] An example of where such grounds apply (and where conversion would not therefore be allowed) in a particular country is where there exists a conflict between a prior national registration and the CTM in question.

The term 'conversion' as used in the Regulation means that a CTM application or registration is transformed into a national trade mark application (or series of applications). It will enjoy the same date of filing and priority as the CTM application or (where appropriate) the same seniority as the registered CTM.[16] Requests for

10 Article 46.
11 Article 47.
12 Rule 29, but note that the failure by the CTMO to inform proprietors of the impending expiry will not affect the expiry of the registration: thus the onus is on proprietors to manage the renewal of their registrations.
13 Article 47(3); there is provision for late renewal on payment of an additional fee (Article 47(3)).
14 Article 108(1); so also may CTM applications which are withdrawn or deemed to be withdrawn.
15 Article 108(2).
16 Article 108(3).

conversion must be made with the payment of a conversion fee at the CTMO.[17] If the conditions are satisfied, the request will then be sent to the relevant national Registries which will examine the converted CTM application or registration as a national application.[18]

CTM applications and registrations which are converted to national applications are not subjected to any formal requirements (as opposed to substantive requirements) of national law which are different from, or in addition to, those provided by the Regulation.[19] However, the national Registry can request the payment of an official national fee, the submission of a translation of the converted application, an indication of an address for service, and representations of the mark.[20]

13.12 Seniority based on a national registration, Articles 34 and 35 Applicants for the registration of a CTM may already own national registrations within a member state of the identical mark for the identical goods or services. In order to avoid duplication of registrations, but so as to avoid losing the earlier national registration date, the applicant will be able to claim the 'seniority' of his earlier national trade mark registration for the purpose of his later CTM registration in respect of the member state in, or for which, the national registration has been obtained.[1] Note that seniority can be claimed based on an earlier national registration which is not wholly co-extensive with the later CTM application, but the seniority will be limited to those goods and/or services covered by the national registration: this is referred to as 'partial' seniority. The proprietor of the earlier national registration may choose either to maintain that registration or he may surrender it or allow it to lapse and rely on his new CTM. Where the proprietor surrenders his national trade mark registration or allows it to lapse he will continue to have the same rights as he would have had if his earlier national registration had been retained.[2] But the seniority will

17 Article 109(1); and within the timescales specified in Article 108(4)–(6); see Appendix IV for a list of the relevant fees.
18 Articles 109 and 110(1).
19 Article 110(2).
20 Article 110(3); this may involve supplying a translation of the mark itself (where appropriate) which will be recorded in accordance with the requirements and practices of the national Registry.
1 Article 34(1).
2 Article 34(2).

lapse if the earlier national trade mark is revoked or invalidated or if it is surrendered prior to the registration of the CTM.[3]

A practical issue arises, however, because (at least in the UK Registry) the details of the abandoned national registration will not be maintained. Therefore, the UK Registrar will not cite the earlier national (but now abandoned) registration against subsequent national applications. The proprietor of the CTM registration who has abandoned his national registration will have to rely on the Registrar picking up his CTM registration and/or on self-help remedies (ie opposition proceedings against the subsequent national application).

The claim to seniority based on a national registration may be made either in the application for the CTM[4] or within two months of the filing of the application,[5] or even after the registration of the CTM in accordance with Article 35. However, if the claim to seniority is delayed until after registration (ie it is made pursuant to Article 35) then the claim will only be valid if there is identity between the goods or services of the national registration and the CTM registration. That is, one cannot make a claim for partial seniority after the date of registration of the CTM.[6]

13.13 Rights conferred by registration: infringement, Article 9 The registration of a CTM confers a personal property right on the proprietor, which gives him exclusive rights in the trade mark which are infringed by the unauthorised use of the trade mark in any part of the EU.[7]

Article 9 of the Regulation specifies the acts which constitute infringement of a registered CTM and which are actionable by the proprietor of the trade mark.

The exclusive rights conferred by registration are not defined as such. Instead, the Regulation specifies the acts which, if done without the consent of the proprietor, will constitute an infringement of those exclusive rights. The proprietor's exclusive rights are, therefore, to do and to authorise others to do, any act

3 Article 34(3).
4 See r 8(1) Implementing Regulation.
5 See r 8(2) Implementing Regulation.
6 For a more complete treatment of the subject of seniority see Section V, 'The Community Trade Mark', INTA 1996–8, supra.
7 Article 9(1).

which, if done by an unauthorised third party, would amount to an infringement.

The acts of infringement can be dealt with conveniently under three headings which correspond to the three paragraphs of Article 9(1). Those paragraphs are substantially in the same terms as Article 8(1) and (5): the relative grounds for refusal of registration. (Of course, the important difference between Article 8 and Article 9 is that the onus of proof will be reversed. Under Article 9 the onus is on the proprietor to prove infringement.)

The following acts constitute infringement:

(a) the use in the course of trade of any sign which is identical with the CTM in relation to goods or services which are identical with those for which the CTM is registered; or
(b) the use in the course of trade of any sign where, because of its identity with or similarity to the CTM and the identity or similarity of the goods or services covered by the CTM and the sign, there exists a likelihood of confusion on the part of the public (the 'likelihood of confusion' specifically includes the 'likelihood of association' between the sign and the trade mark); or
(c) the use in the course of trade of any sign which is identical with or similar to the CTM in relation to goods or services which are *not* similar to those for which the CTM is registered, but provided that the latter has a reputation in the Community and where use of that sign without due cause takes unfair advantage of, or is detrimental to, the distinctive character or the repute of the CTM.

It should be noted that (b) and (c) above are not free of ambiguity. The phrase 'likelihood of confusion' and its interpretation, given that it is deemed to include the 'likelihood of association', has already attracted conflicting opinions of the Courts of Benelux and England and Wales. This issue has already been discussed in Chapter 2.

Use in the course of trade, Article 9(2) Article 9(2) contains a non-exclusive list of those acts which can be considered to be use of a trade mark in the course of trade. The list is identical to s 10(4) of the 1994 Act. Thus, the following acts may amount to infringement:

(a) affixing a sign to the goods or to the packaging thereof;
(b) offering the goods, putting them on the market or stocking them

for these purposes under a sign, or offering or supplying services thereunder;
(c) importing or exporting the goods under a sign; or
(d) using the sign on business papers and in advertising.[8]

Agents and representatives, Articles 11 and 18 The Regulation contains specific provisions covering the situation where an agent or representative wrongly uses his principal's trade mark. Thus, where a CTM is registered in the name of an agent or representative of the person who is the proprietor of that trade mark, the proprietor is entitled to oppose the use of his mark by his agent or a representative provided that he has not authorised the use in question and provided that the agent or representative cannot justify his action.[9]

Furthermore, in such circumstances, the proprietor is entitled to demand that the agent or representative assign the CTM to him.[10]

Word marks The issue as to whether a word mark which is a translation of a registered mark is by reason thereof identical or similar to the registered mark has been considered in the context of registrability, see paragraph 13.06 above.

13.14 Limitations on the effects of registration, Articles 12 and 106 The registration of a CTM does not entitle the proprietor to prohibit others from using, in the course of trade:
(a) his own name or address; or
(b) indications concerning the kind, quality, quantity, intended purpose, value, geographical origin, the time of production of the goods or of rendering of the service, or other characteristics of the goods or service; or
(c) a trade mark where it is necessary to indicate the intended purpose of a product or service, in particular as accessories or spare parts,

provided in each case that such use is in accordance with honest practices in industrial or commercial matters.[11]

National registrations, Article 106(1) In many jurisdictions it is an absolute defence to infringement for the defendant to prove that

8 Article 9(2).
9 Article 11.
10 Article 18.
11 Article 12; this is the same as s 11(2) of the 1994 Act, as to which, see Chapter 7.

he was using a registered trade mark, that is, he can rely on his registration as a complete defence. However, Article 106(1) provides that the Regulation will not affect the right existing under the laws of the member states to invoke claims for infringement of earlier rights. Thus, it is no defence for the defendant to aver that he was using a registered CTM when faced with an allegation of infringement of an earlier national right.

Acquiescence The general rule stated above is, however, subject to an important proviso. A claim for infringement of an earlier national right cannot be invoked if the proprietor of the earlier right is not in a position to apply for a declaration that the CTM registration is invalid pursuant to Article 53(2). That is, if the proprietor of the earlier right has acquiesced (as defined in Article 53(2)) then the owner of the later CTM will be able to rely on his registration as a defence.[12]

13.15 Exhaustion of rights, Article 13 The registration of a CTM does not entitle the proprietor to prohibit the use of that trade mark in relation to goods which have been put on the market in the EU under that trade mark by the proprietor or with his consent. Article 13 limits the doctrine of exhaustion to goods put on the market in the EU; this means that the proprietor of a CTM may be able to prevent parallel imports originating from outside the EU. In short, there is no express provision for international exhaustion, only EU exhaustion of rights.

However, the exhaustion principle stated above does not apply where there exist legitimate reasons for the proprietor to oppose further commercialisation of the goods – especially where the condition of the goods is changed or impaired after they have been put on the market.[13] This issue has been considered in more detail in Chapter 7.

13.16 Jurisdiction, Articles 91 to 94 Subject to any express or deemed submission by the parties to a particular jurisdiction,[14] an infringement action is brought in the member state where the defendant has his domicile or, if he has no such domicile, where he

12 Article 106(1).
13 Article 13.
14 Article 93(4).

has an establishment.[15] If he has neither, the action is to be brought in the country of the plaintiff's domicile or establishment.[16] If neither the plaintiff nor the defendant has such a domicile or establishment, the action is to be brought in the courts of Spain, being the country where the CTMO has its seat.[17] In each case, the court[18] has exclusive jurisdiction regardless of where the infringement occurred. Of course, an infringement action can always be brought in the member state in which the infringement has been committed or threatened[19] (although the extent of the court's jurisdiction is limited accordingly: see below). These exhaustive rules as to jurisdiction will in many cases limit the plaintiff's scope for forum shopping (certainly if a pan-European injunction is considered desirable).[20]

A decision in a particular member state involving a CTM will have effect throughout the whole EU. The exception to this is where an infringement action is brought in the member state where the infringement occurred and the only basis of the court's jurisdiction is that the infringement was committed in that member state. In these circumstances, the court's jurisdiction is only in respect of acts committed or threatened within the territory of that member state,[1] that is, the remedies available to the proprietor will only extend to acts committed or threatened in that member state.

Putting this in perspective, if the two parties are non-EU undertakings, then the plaintiff (absent an agreement with the defendant) can either:

(a) bring the proceedings in Spain, in which case the procedure and language of the Spanish courts as well as all remedies provided for under the Regulation will be available; or
(b) bring the proceedings in the member state(s) where the infringement occurred, but in so doing he must accept that the

15 Article 93(1); this Article also applies to actions for a declaration of non-infringement and counterclaims for revocation, or for a declaration of invalidity under Article 96.
16 Article 93(2).
17 Article 93(3).
18 Definition, see Article 91.
19 Article 93(5).
20 For a more complete discussion of the potential for forum shopping see Neil Jenkins 'Forum Shopping under the Community Trade Mark Regulation' Trademark World, February 1996.
1 Article 94(2).

remedies available will be limited to that member state only (hence a pan-EU injunction would necessarily not be within the jurisdiction of the court).

No special courts are established to handle infringement cases involving a CTM. Each member state is to designate a limited number of existing national courts to handle CTM cases. The High Court has been designated by the UK and the Court of Appeal has been designated to hear appeals from decisions of the High Court. All these courts are called 'Community trade mark courts' although they remain national courts.[2]

CTM Courts have exclusive jurisdiction for certain CTM actions: in essence, for infringement and validity actions and for counterclaims for revocation or for a declaration of invalidity.[3] Such counterclaims may be based on non-use, generic use, the assertion of earlier trade mark rights or other earlier rights, or allegations that a mark was wrongly registered because, for example, it is descriptive or generic. Thus, national courts (sitting as CTM Courts) will rule on a very large number of issues involving the Regulation.

Applicable law The CTM Courts will apply the provisions of the Regulation; where the Regulation is silent (including as to procedure), the courts will apply their own national law.[4] The Regulation is quite rightly directed at 'pure' trade mark law; it does not purport to deal with the many incidental areas of national law which will arise during trade mark proceedings, such as the Rules of Court, evidence (rules of hearsay etc) and, more importantly, the entitlement to special remedies which are available under the laws of certain member states. Accordingly, in respect of these matters, the CTM Courts will apply their own national law.

Appeals, Article 101 Article 101 provides that an appeal is available from judgments in respect of actions and claims brought pursuant to Article 92 (ie actions in relation to infringement and validity). Thus, an appeal lies to the CTM Courts of Second Instance from judgments of CTM Courts of First Instance in respect of all such proceedings.

However, the conditions under which such an appeal may be

2 Article 91.
3 Article 92.
4 Article 97.

lodged with a CTM Court of Second Instance are to be found in the national law of the particular member state in which the CTM Court of Second Instance is located. Likewise, the national laws concerning any further appeal are also applicable in respect of judgments of CTM Courts of Second Instance.[5] The availability of, and the procedure for, such appeals may therefore vary in different member states, and local advice will be required. In the UK, the nominated CTM Court of First Instance is the High Court and any and all appeals will be to the Court of Appeal (the nominated CTM Court of Second Instance). Thereafter an appeal lies to the House of Lords in accordance with the UK's national rules governing all appeals from the Court of Appeal.

13.17 Remedies, Articles 14 and 98 While the effects of CTMs are governed solely by the provisions of the Regulation, in other respects, infringement of a CTM is governed by the national law relating to infringement of a national trade mark.[6] Accordingly, the remedies available in an infringement action will be those remedies which are available to the proprietor of a national trade mark under national trade mark law. However, there is limited scope for forum shopping because of the rules relating to jurisdiction: see paragraph 13.16 above.

Article 98 also specifies certain sanctions which are available in an infringement case. CTM Courts are expressly directed, in circumstances where the defendant has infringed or threatened to infringe a CTM, to issue an Order prohibiting the defendant from proceeding with the infringing acts and the court must also take such additional measures in accordance with its national laws as are aimed at ensuring that the prohibition is complied with.[7]

13.18 Relation of national law to CTMs, Articles 106 and 107 The Regulation will co-exist with national trade mark laws. This has several consequences. The Regulation does not affect the rights of owners of prior national trade marks to prevent under national law the use of a CTM.[8]

5 Article 101(2) and (3).
6 Article 14(1), and see the Regulation: Title X – Jurisdiction and Procedure in Legal Actions Relating to CTMs.
7 Article 98(1).
8 Articles 106 and 107.

In a particular country, the same proprietor may own both CTM and national trade mark registrations. He may commence simultaneously an infringement action on the basis of national and CTM rights. (There may in certain circumstances be advantages in commencing dual actions: the scope of the protection afforded by each registration may differ in terms of the acts which constitute infringement, and the goods or services covered by the registration may vary, as may the remedies available; while, on the other hand, certain counterclaims may not be available in respect of either the national or CTM registration.) However, where successive actions involving identical marks for identical goods or services are commenced in different countries, the court where the later action is commenced may decline jurisdiction in favour of the court where the first proceedings were commenced, or stay the proceedings if jurisdiction is contested.[9]

Also, a court hearing an infringement case brought on the basis of a CTM must dismiss the action if there is a final decision on the merits regarding the same cause of action between the same parties on the basis of an identical national trade mark in force for identical goods or services. Similarly, a court hearing an infringement action based on a national trade mark must dismiss the case if such a decision has already been made on the basis of an identical CTM valid for identical goods or services.[10] These Rules are intended to avoid contradictory decisions, but do not apply to interlocutory proceedings.[11]

13.19 Transfer and assignments, Article 17[12] Since a CTM registration stands or falls for the whole EU, a CTM cannot be assigned for individual member states.[13]

Assignments need not include the goodwill of the assignor.[14] However, an important safeguard is that the assignment must not be likely to mislead the public.[15] The onus thus falls on the parties to ensure that the practical effect of any assignment is not such as to mislead the public.

9 Article 105(1)(a); see Article 105(1)(b) as to similar goods or services.
10 Article 105(2) and (3).
11 Article 105(4).
12 These provisions apply to both applications for and registrations of CTMs; Article 24.
13 Article 16(1).
14 Article 17(1).
15 Article 17(4).

All assignments must be made in writing and signed by all parties (except where it is the result of a judgment), otherwise the assignment is void.[16]

It is vital that the assignee/transferee should ensure that the transfer is entered in the Register; until this happens he may not invoke the rights arising from registration (ie he cannot sue for infringement) and third parties without knowledge of the transfer will not be affected until entry in the Register.[17]

Procedure, r 31 The procedure for filing an application for the registration of a transfer is governed by r 31 which requires the applicant to set out particulars of the CTM in question and of the new proprietor. Note that a single application for registration of a transfer may be submitted for two or more marks, provided that the registered proprietor and the successor in title are the same in each case. The applicable fee is set out in the Fees Regulation.

13.20 Licensing, Article 22[18] A CTM may be licensed for some or all of the goods or services for which it is registered and for the whole or just a part of the EU (but licences should be drafted with care in order to avoid contravention of the competition laws).

A licence may be either exclusive or non-exclusive.[19]

Rights of licensees Subject to the terms of the licence, a licensee may bring proceedings for infringement of a CTM only if the proprietor consents to such proceedings. However, an exclusive licensee may bring such proceedings if the proprietor of the trade mark, after formal notice, does not himself bring infringement proceedings within an appropriate period (the 'appropriate period' is not specified in the Regulation).[20] An exclusive licensee is therefore able to protect his interest in the licensed mark more effectively than a non-exclusive licensee (unless the non-exclusive licensee obtains equivalent rights under the terms of the licence). The implication is that a licensee bringing proceedings for

16 Article 17(3).
17 Article 17(6); see also Article 23(1).
18 These provisions apply to both applications for and registrations of CTMs; Article 24.
19 Article 22.
20 Article 22(3).

infringement may do so as though he were the proprietor and is entitled to the same remedies.

Furthermore, a licensee has, for the purpose of obtaining compensation for himself, the right to intervene in infringement proceedings which have been brought by the proprietor of the CTM.[1]

The CTMO will make no inquiry as to the practical effect of the grant of the licence: the onus is once again with the parties to ensure that the use of the trade mark by the licensee does not mislead the public, as this may result in revocation.[2]

It is important (in particular for the licensee) that the licence is recorded in the Register; until this happens third parties will not be affected unless they have actual notice of the licence.[3]

Procedure, rr 33 and 34 Rule 33 provides that r 31 (which governs the procedure for filing an application for the registration of a transfer of a CTM) will apply mutatis mutandis to the registration of the grant or transfer of a licence.

There are also special provisions for the registration of a licence where the licence is either an exclusive licence, a sub-licence or a limited licence (either as to the goods or services, the territory covered by the licence or the duration of the licence).[4]

The fees payable for the registration of a licence are set out in the Fees Regulation. There is a standard form for applying for the registration of a licence.

13.21 Revocation, Article 50 The rights of the proprietor of a CTM can be declared to be revoked on the application of a third party (including on the basis of a counterclaim in infringement proceedings), in the following circumstances:

(a) for non-use (as to which, see 'Use requirements' below) within a continuous period of five years, and where there are no proper reasons for non-use and provided that genuine use of the trade mark has not been started or resumed (however, any use within a period of three months preceding the filing of the application or counterclaim will be disregarded where preparations for the

1 Article 22(4).
2 See Article 50 and paragraph 13.21 below.
3 Article 23(1).
4 See r 34.

commencement or resumption occurred only after the proprietor became aware that the application or counterclaim may be filed); or

(b) if, in consequence of acts or inactivity of the proprietor, the trade mark has become the common name in the trade for a product or service in respect of which it is registered (ie if it has become generic); or

(c) if, in consequence of the use made of it by the proprietor or with his consent in respect of the goods or services for which it is registered, the trade mark is liable to mislead the public, particularly as to the nature, quality or geographical origin of those goods or services; or

(d) if the proprietor of the trade mark no longer satisfies the conditions laid down by Article 5.[5]

Use requirements, Article 15 Rights to a CTM can be lost for non-use during any continuous five year period following registration.[6] The use required must be 'genuine use', which should eliminate token use, and includes affixing the CTM to goods or packaging in the EU solely for export purposes.[7]

The genuine use must be in the EU, and thus use in only a single member state will be sufficient. This is a significant advantage of the CTM system over both the national trade mark and Madrid Systems. Under existing national systems, if a mark is registered in several member states as a national mark but is used in only one of those states, it may be revoked in the others due to non-use.

Another important feature of the CTM use requirement is that non-use can be raised by the applicant as a defence to an opposition.[8] The proprietor of an earlier CTM who is opposing an application is obliged, at the request of the applicant, to provide proof of genuine use of his mark in the last five years, or proper reasons for non-use, or else the opposition will fail.

Importantly, it is not necessary formally to record licences in order for permitted use by the licensee to accrue to the benefit of the licensor.[9]

5 Article 50(1)(a)–(d).
6 Article 15.
7 Article 15(2)(b).
8 Article 43(2); as to which, see paragraph 13.09 above.
9 This being the effect of Article 15(3).

Procedure, Articles 55 and 56 An application for revocation may be submitted to the CTMO; alternatively, the application, if part of a defence to an infringement action, will be heard by the relevant CTM Court hearing the action. The examination of the application is governed by Article 56.

13.22 Invalidity, Articles 51 and 52 A CTM is deemed to be valid unless its validity is put in issue by a defendant.[10]

The registration of a CTM may be declared invalid on the ground that it should not have been registered, that is, where:

(a) the proprietor is not entitled to a CTM registration under Article 5;
(b) absolute grounds for refusal existed at the time of registration; or
(c) the applicant was acting in bad faith when he filed the application for the CTM.[11]

The Regulation refers to such grounds as 'absolute grounds for invalidity'. However, a mark may not be declared invalid under (b) above if, in consequence of the use made of it, it has after registration acquired a distinctive character in relation to the goods or services for which it is registered.[12]

The registration of a CTM may also be declared invalid because the mark conflicts with earlier rights of third parties.[13] The Regulation refers to such grounds as 'relative grounds for invalidity'. However, if the proprietor of a CTM or national registration has acquiesced for five years to the use of a later CTM, the owner of that earlier CTM or national mark is barred from applying for a declaration that the later CTM is invalid and from opposing the use of the later CTM in respect of goods or services for which it is being used (unless the registration of the later CTM was applied for in bad faith).[14]

Earlier rights, Article 52(2) A CTM may also be declared invalid on application to the CTMO (or on the basis of a counterclaim in infringement proceedings) where the use of the trade mark may be prohibited pursuant to the national law governing the protection of

10 Article 95(1).
11 Article 51(1).
12 Article 51(2).
13 Article 51(1).
14 Article 53.

'any other earlier right'. Article 52(2) sets out a non-exclusive list of such 'other earlier rights', including:

(a) a right to a name;
(b) a right of personal portrayal;
(c) a copyright; and
(d) an industrial property right.

Importantly, these 'earlier rights' may be based upon signs or indications which would neither qualify as CTMs nor even as trade marks as commonly understood by the lay person. This provision will almost certainly be interpreted in different ways in the different jurisdictions of the EU. One may (at least initially) encounter inconsistencies which may be irreconcilable as a result of the different legal systems (common law and civil law) and which, despite the harmonisation (of substantive trade mark law) throughout the EU, are still widely disparate in certain member states – not least in defining what is an 'industrial property right'. Subject to the rules relating to jurisdiction (see paragraph 13.16 above), Article 52(2) may be the incentive for forum shopping to identify the member state which has the broadest interpretation of the concepts/rights set out above.

Locus standi There is no express requirement that the applicant should have any particular interest in having a particular CTM declared invalid. However, given the likely costs involved, it is considered highly unlikely that there will be a glut of philanthropic actions.

Procedure, Articles 55 and 56 An application for a declaration of invalidity may be submitted to the CTMO; alternatively, the application, if part of a defence to an infringement action, will be heard by the relevant CTM Court hearing the action. The examination of the application is governed by Article 56.

13.23 Consequences of revocation or invalidity, Article 54

Revocation Where a CTM is revoked, the CTM is deemed not to have had, as from the date of application for revocation or of the relevant counterclaim, the effects specified in the Regulation (to the extent that the rights have been revoked).

Invalidity Where a CTM has been declared invalid, it is deemed not to have had, as from the outset, the effects specified in the

Regulation (to the extent that the trade mark has been declared invalid).[15]

However, the retroactive effect of revocation or invalidity of the trade mark shall not affect:

(a) any decision on infringement which has acquired the authority of a final decision and has been enforced prior to the revocation or invalidity decision; or

(b) any contract concluded prior to the revocation or invalidity decision, in so far as it has been performed before that decision.[16]

13.24 Community collective marks, Articles 64 to 72 A collective mark is owned by an association of members, not by a single undertaking. Thus, a Community collective mark is a mark which distinguishes the goods or services of the members of the association from those of other undertakings.[17]

The provisions relating to Community collective marks are found in Articles 64–72. (The Regulation does not provide for nor recognise the concept of a Community 'certification' mark.) In essence the Regulation applies equally to Community collective marks as it does to 'ordinary' CTMs unless Articles 65–72 provide otherwise.

13.25 Rules – implementing provisions, Article 140 The Rules implementing the Regulation have been adopted in the Implementing Regulation. It is not easy to find one's way around the Implementing Regulation, in particular because there is no index. In broad terms, the Implementing Regulation consists of 101 Rules which are arranged under numerous 'Titles' and 'Parts'. The Rules set out the procedural aspects which are not dealt with in detail in the Regulation itself.[18]

13.26 Factors to be taken into account before deciding whether to file an application for a CTM The CTM system will not be suitable for all trade mark owners who wish to secure registered

15 Article 54(2).
16 Article 54(3). However, repayment, to an extent justified by the circumstances, of sums paid under the relevant contract, may be claimed on grounds of equity: Article 54(3)(b).
17 Article 64(1).
18 See 'The Community Trade Mark' INTA 1996–7, supra, Appendices II and III which set out the structure of the Implementing Regulation and provide a cross-reference to the Regulation.

trade mark protection within the EU. In certain circumstances it may be preferable to use the alternative methods of securing registration in EU countries such as the Madrid Systems (Agreement and Protocol), separate national filings or, indeed, a combination of the various filing systems. The answer to this question depends upon a consideration of the individual circumstances of the trade mark owner. The factors which need to be considered include:

(a) which of the various registration systems are available (see paragraph 13.27 below);
(b) in which countries is protection required (or likely to be required) – this will involve assessing the owner's present and future marketing strategies (see paragraph 13.28 below);
(c) the pros and cons of the various registration systems (particularly in terms of the level of protection conferred, the remedies available and any specific limitations or caveats) (see paragraphs13.29 and 13.30 below);
(d) the timescale for obtaining registration under each system; and
(e) the cost of filing applications and maintaining registrations under each system.

13.27 Which systems are available to the applicant? It may be the case that not all of the alternative systems will be available to a potential applicant.

To use the Madrid Agreement or Madrid Protocol filing systems, it is necessary for the applicant to be a national of or domiciled (or to have a real and effective place of business) within a member country of the relevant system. In the absence of such a connection with a relevant country, the choice will be between filing separate national applications in the particular countries of interest or a CTM application.

In contrast to the Madrid Systems, there are very few exceptions as to who may use the CTM system. The CTM system is open to nationals of member states, nationals of countries which are party to the Paris Convention or the World Trade Organisation Agreement, companies with an establishment in the EU, and nationals of countries which accord reciprocal protection to all EU members.

Where the applicant is able to take advantage of the Madrid Agreement filing system[19] (but not the Protocol) a separate national

19 For a list of those countries which are party to the Madrid Agreement, see Schedule 2.

application would have to be filed in those EU countries which are not signatories to the Madrid Agreement, namely: United Kingdom, Ireland, Denmark, Finland, Sweden and Greece. Similarly, the availability of the Madrid Protocol system will depend upon which countries eventually ratify the Protocol.[20]

13.28 In which countries is protection required? If, for whatever reason, a registration is only required in a small number of EU countries, the national filing route may be more cost-effective. Indeed, cost will often be the determining factor in deciding which filing route to follow.

Where protection is required in all of the EU countries, the cost factor, coupled with the need to instruct only one agent to file one application, will make the CTM system the obvious choice. (Of course, if all the EU countries – or the EC itself, as appears likely – eventually ratify the Madrid Protocol, an applicant using this system will also only need to instruct one agent and may benefit from cost savings.) In theory, the proprietor of multiple national registrations covering each EU country will obtain the same (or at least substantially similar) rights as the proprietor of a CTM: this is because the member states of the EU are bound by the Directive, which is substantially similar to the Regulation (in terms of the substantive law). However, the proprietor of the multiple national registrations will need to obtain advice in each jurisdiction in respect of each act of infringement, whereas the proprietor of the CTM will only need to obtain the advice of a single legal adviser – regardless of the place of infringement.

Between these two extreme situations it will be necessary to balance carefully the merits of the alternative methods of filing and the nature of the registrations secured (as to which see paragraphs 13.29 and 13.30 below).

Undoubtedly, the Madrid Systems provide a cheap way of filing applications in member countries. Aside from the question of costs, however, it is necessary to look at other features of the Madrid Systems and the CTM system before deciding which route to follow.

13.29 Arguments in favour of the CTM system Many of the arguments in favour of the CTM system arise from the unitary

20 For a list of those countries which have ratified the Protocol, see Schedule 2.

nature of the registration secured. Perhaps the most attractive attribute of a CTM, from a commercial viewpoint, is the fact that the genuine, commercial use of the mark in any one of the member states will constitute use of the mark throughout the EU. The CTM would, therefore, appear to be ideally suited to those applicants who currently use their mark in only part of the EU but who envisage gradual expansion throughout the EU.

This may be contrasted with the registration secured via the national filing or Madrid routes (which is a collection of separate national registrations) that could become vulnerable to attack if use of the mark in each country is not made within any period specified by the national trade mark legislation (usually five years).

As previously stated, the application procedure is simplified in that it is only necessary to instruct one agent (representative or attorney) in any one of the EU countries to file the application. Assuming the application is ultimately successful, this will produce a single registration and, therefore, a single renewal fee. This will result in a reduction in the cost of maintaining a European trade mark portfolio as well as simplifying its administration.

Unlike applications filed under the Madrid Systems, it is not a requirement of the CTM system that the application is based on an existing national registration or application. The CTM application will not, therefore, be limited to the scope of protection afforded by an earlier registration or be delayed (in the case of the Madrid Agreement system) until a registration has been secured.

Applications may be filed in the applicant's choice of any of the official languages of the EU and subsequent proceedings may be conducted in the applicant's first or second choice of language. Translation fees will thus be kept to a minimum and, in many cases, be avoided altogether.

The proprietor of a CTM will benefit from the knowledge that the enforcement of his rights will be governed by a single law throughout the EU and that any oppositions to an application for a CTM will, again, be governed by one set of rules and be determined uniformly under the provisions of the Regulation. Therefore, an applicant will not be faced with the (theoretical) possibility of several separate oppositions being fought in separate jurisdictions pursuant to different laws in numerous languages with different results.

Of course, the divergence of the national laws of EU countries has, to a certain extent, been reduced due to the implementation of new legislation in most EU countries reflecting the Directive. However, the determination of disputes at the CTMO and in CTM Courts will eventually enable a proprietor of a CTM registration to be advised with greater certainty, and at a lower cost, as to his rights and remedies throughout the EU.

A CTM is a single registration having equal effect in all 13 EU jurisdictions. There are no geographical limitations within the concept of the CTM. It is, therefore, open to any CTM Court to grant an injunction which will be pan-European in effect (subject to the exception where the jurisdiction of the CTM Court is based only on the fact that the infringement occurred within the member state of the court concerned). In contrast, trade marks registered through the Madrid Systems can only be enforced at the national level. This is because the registration secured is a package of national rights which only the respective national courts are competent to enforce.

Only the proprietors of existing applications/registrations will be notified by the CTMO of subsequently filed conflicting applications. Therefore, proprietors who do not apply for a CTM will have to rely upon watching services to ensure that they are notified when potentially conflicting marks are the subject of a CTM application.

Finally, a practical advantage of obtaining a CTM registration is that a single certificate can therefore be used for filing with the Customs Authorities of the EU countries in order to activate the Customs Monitoring System under the Counterfeit Goods Regulation. Furthermore, any action having to do or concerned with seizures at Customs based on a CTM certificate or registration under the Counterfeit Goods Regulation will be decided by a CTM Court rather than a national court in the port of entry.

13.30 Arguments against the CTM system Of course, there are certain potential 'downsides' of the unitary nature of a CTM.

Perhaps the most often repeated criticism of the CTM system is that it will be difficult to secure registration, on the basis that there will be very few marks which will be available for registration and use throughout the EU. Early indications are that there are likely to be numerous opposition proceedings, with up to 20 per cent of all published applications being the subject of opposition proceedings as at November 1997. This problem should not be underestimated, but in many cases potential conflicts with third parties' rights may be capable of resolution either prior to the filing of an application (where searches have previously been conducted or where there is a particular problem known to the applicant) or during the prosecution of the application. Of course, there is always the option, should an application meet with an opposition which is incapable of successful resolution, of the CTM application being converted into a series of national applications in the remainder of the countries where no conflict exists. Because of the two month 'cooling off' period following the filing of a notice of opposition, the applicant will be able to convert to national applications without incurring any liability for the opponent's costs (provided that the conversion is during the two month period).

Potential opponents may, however, be dissuaded from filing an opposition to an application for a CTM if they have not used their earlier conflicting registration within the previous five years. An applicant for a CTM which is the subject of an opposition may request the opponent to show that he has made genuine use of his earlier registered CTM or national mark within the five year period preceding the date of the publication of the CTM application.

Many potential applicants may, initially, be put off from applying for a CTM because they already have registrations in one or more of the EU countries and do not wish to duplicate their protection or, to avoid such duplication, abandon an existing registration which may have been on the national register for many years. The CTM system provides for this situation by enabling the proprietor of a CTM to claim the seniority of existing registrations of the identical mark. This, in effect, backdates the registration in that particular country to the date of the earlier registration. However, if the specification of goods or services of the CTM registration is broader than those of the national registration in respect of which seniority is claimed, the seniority will only pertain to the more limited specification of the national registration.

The claiming of seniority will, therefore, allow the proprietor of CTMs eventually to abandon certain national registrations if they so choose (subject to the caveat, referred to in paragraph 13.12 above, concerning the practice by national registries of maintaining records of 'abandoned' national registrations).

The CTM system may be less suitable for an applicant who proposes to use variations of a mark (or indeed different marks) in separate countries of the EU. This may arise as a result of the non-suitability of the mark within a particular territory (for example, the mark may have undesirable connotations in a particular country) or where the product or service in question has already secured a reputation under separate marks in the separate countries of the EU. A further possibility would be that an existing agreement with a third party would preclude the proprietor from using a particular mark in certain countries of the EU. In these situations the national filing route may have to be adopted – subject to the alternative view that it may still be desirable to protect one's trade mark throughout the EU under a CTM registration to enable the proprietor to prevent the registration and/or use of his trade mark (or similar mark) even in countries of the EU where he does not in fact use nor propose to use his mark (ie using a CTM as a defensive tactic).

Finally, it is not possible to assign the registration in respect of only part of the EU. However, it is always open to the proprietor of a registration to convert a CTM registration to a series of national applications or, indeed, to license the use of the mark in part only of the EU. The inability to assign a CTM for part only of the EU is, in truth, a disadvantage because, since the decision in *Ideal Standard*,[1] it is possible for a trade mark proprietor to assign his national trade mark in one or more countries of the EU, and this will not necessarily expose him to parallel imports of goods bearing 'his mark' (ie his former mark) which are no longer being manufactured under his control. In that case the ECJ recognised and applied what it called the 'principle of territoriality' of national marks, but this will not apply to CTMs. For a further discussion of the *Ideal-Standard* case, see Chapter 7.

Combination of systems In certain circumstances it may be possible for an applicant to take advantage of a combination of the Madrid and CTM systems. The Madrid Protocol provides for the nomination of the CTM system in a Protocol application, and it would, therefore, be possible for an applicant who is entitled to take advantage of the Protocol system to file a single application at WIPO in Geneva, which could cover any of the countries that has ratified the Protocol and, once the EU ratifies, an application for a CTM. Such an application would, however, have to be based on an existing registration or application in one of the Protocol countries, which

1 *IHT International Heiztechnik GmbH v Ideal-Standard GmbH* [1995] FSR 59.

may unnecessarily restrict or delay the specification covered by the application subsequently filed in the other nominated countries and at the CTMO.

Conclusion There can be no 'conclusion' as such, because it is impossible to state categorically that any one of the systems of obtaining trade mark registration within the EU should be used on any or every occasion. The requirements of each applicant will have to be considered individually, as will the availability of the alternative systems.

14 The Madrid Protocol

14.01 Introduction Section 54 of the 1994 Act conferred on the Secretary of State the power to make provision to give effect in the United Kingdom to the provisions of the Madrid Protocol relating to 'international registrations'. Pursuant to this power the Trade Marks (International Registration) Order 1996[1] was made on 11 March 1996 and came into force on 1 April 1996. This Order gives effect in the United Kingdom to the Madrid Protocol which, therefore, became effective in the United Kingdom on 1 April, 1996.

14.02 The Madrid Agreement Since the end of the nineteenth century a system has been in place whereby a so-called 'international registration' of a trade mark can be secured covering all or any of the Contracting States to the Madrid Agreement.[2] There are notable exceptions from the current list of contracting states, including the United States of America, Japan, the United Kingdom, and three other EU countries: namely, Ireland, Denmark and Greece.

The phrase 'international registration' is perhaps something of a misnomer, as it tends to suggest that there is a single registration which has equal effect in each of the countries covered by the registration. It is more accurate to describe the procedure as an

1 SI 1996/714.
2 Madrid Agreement Concerning the International Registration of Marks, of 14 April 1891; see Schedule 2 of this book for a list of Contracting States as at 1 January 1998.

international application which leads to separate registrations within the nominated countries.

Who may apply Under the Madrid Agreement, only the owner of a national registration in a contracting state (in which the owner has a real and effective place of business) can apply for an international registration. Therefore, although the United Kingdom is not a contracting state, this does not necessarily preclude a United Kingdom based company from applying for such a registration if it can show that it has a real and effective industrial or commercial establishment in one of the contracting states.

Requirement of home national registration It is necessary for an application for an international registration to be based upon an existing national registration in the applicant's country. The goods to be covered by an application for an international registration must be goods which fall within the national registration.

Scope of registration An international registration does not extend to the country of origin, as the mark is protected in that country by virtue of the national registration. The protection afforded by an international registration extends only to those countries nominated in the application or to which an extension is subsequently sought.

Procedure An application for an international registration is filed with the national registry of the country of the applicant. The details of the application are then forwarded to the International Bureau of the World Intellectual Property Organisation (WIPO) in Geneva. The International Bureau must satisfy itself that the mark is recorded in the national register in the name of the applicant company and that such national registration covers all the goods or services for which the international registration is being sought. When the International Bureau is in receipt of an application which complies with the requirements of the Agreement, it assigns a serial number to the application and publishes the mark in its bulletin 'Les Marques Internationales'. The acceptance of the application is notified to the registries of the nominated countries.

Each national registry has a period of 12 months within which to accept or refuse registration of the mark in its country. In the absence of notification by a registry of refusal within the one year period, registration is deemed to have been accepted in that country.

In some contracting states a mark which has been accepted by the International Bureau is subjected to a national administrative examination and, in certain cases, may be refused. Such refusal may be provisional (which may be overcome by argument) or final.

Duration of registration The initial duration of an international registration under the Madrid Agreement is 20 years, renewable indefinitely thereafter for further 20 year terms.

Dependency on national registration The registration within each of the nominated contracting states remains dependent upon the validity of the original national registration for a period of five years. Therefore, if the national registration is attacked and declared invalid or allowed to lapse within this five year period, the registration in each relevant contracting state is automatically invalidated. It is, therefore, important to ensure that proper commercial use of the mark in the applicant's home country is made within the relevant period. On the expiration of the five year period the international registration becomes independent in each of the nominated contracting states where registration was accepted and is, therefore, no longer susceptible to central attack.

14.03 Limitations of the Madrid Agreement The Madrid Agreement in its original form is very well suited to those countries where there is little or no examination of a trade mark application prior to registration. The registration procedure in countries where there is a substantive examination will inevitably take longer, and the requirement of a home national registration would place companies based in such countries at a disadvantage when seeking to benefit from the international registration system.

Other perceived deficiencies of the Madrid Agreement (in so far as a United Kingdom company and the United Kingdom Registry is concerned) include having French as the only official language and a fixed low-fee structure which again unfairly prejudices those countries where, through substantive examination procedures, official fees are maintained at a higher level. Many of the countries refusing to join the Madrid Agreement were also concerned that the principle of central attack resulting in the invalidity of the registration in each country is unduly harsh.

14.04 Madrid Protocol The International Bureau established a Protocol relating to the Madrid Agreement[3] with a view to overcoming the limitations of the Agreement, and in an attempt to attract other countries to become contracting states to the Protocol. The main advantages of the Protocol are set out below.

1 The Protocol provides that an application for an international registration can be based not only on a national registration but also on a national application. This addresses to some degree the concern that countries with long application procedures are unfairly disadvantaged under the Agreement.

2 The time limit within which each national registry may notify the International Bureau of refusal may be extended to 18 months, again in recognition of the concerns voiced by some countries that the period of 12 months was considered too short. The Order implementing the Protocol in the United Kingdom has adopted the 18 month time limit.[4]

3 In response to the strong objection to the central attack possibility, the Protocol provides for the conversion of an international registration or application into a series of national registrations or applications in any of the nominated contracting states in the event that the home national registration or application ceases to have effect within five years[5] or is cancelled. The original priority date of the international registration will, however, be maintained.[6]

4 In addition to French, the Protocol also nominates English as an official language.

5 The Protocol also provides for inter-governmental organisations to become a party to the Protocol, and the Community trade mark system will shortly be linked into the international registration system.

6 Registration of a mark at the International Bureau is effected for ten years, renewable thereafter for further ten year periods.[7]

14.05 Current status of the Protocol As at 15 January 1998, there are 28 countries which are party to the Protocol (or which will

3 Protocol relating to the Madrid Agreement Concerning the International Registration of Marks of 28 June 1989.
4 The Trade Marks (International Registration) Order 1996/714, Article 11.
5 See Article 6(3) of the Protocol.
6 Article 9*quinquies*.
7 Articles 6(1) and 7(1).

become parties by April 1998).[8] There are thus a sufficient number of Protocol countries for applicants now to consider using the Madrid system when contemplating overseas filings.

14.06 Registrability The registrability of a mark applied for under the Protocol is determined by reference to the respective national laws of the countries nominated in the application.

14.07 Priority Priority under the Paris Convention can be claimed in the usual way. In addition, where the mark which is the subject of the international registration is also the subject of a national registration in the office of a contracting party and where both registrations stand in the name of the same person, the international registration is deemed to replace the national registration,[9] provided that:

(a) the protection resulting from the international registration extends to the said contracting party under Article 3*ter* (1) or (2);
(b) all the goods and services listed in the national or regional registration are also listed in the international registration in respect of the said contracting party; and
(c) such extension takes effect after the date of the national or regional registration.

14.08 Registration procedure An international application is filed at the 'office of origin' (in the case of a UK based applicant, the UK Patent Office) using the prescribed form. The office of origin receiving the application will check that the particulars appearing in the application correspond to the particulars appearing in the application or registration upon which the international application is based. The office of origin will certify that the particulars are correct and also indicate the application date and number of the basic application or registration and, where the application is based on a registration, the date of registration.

The applicant must also state the goods and services in respect of which protection is sought and also, if possible, the corresponding class or classes according to the Nice classification.

8 See Schedule 2 of this book for a list of countries which have either signed or ratified the Protocol as at 15 January 1998.
9 Article 4*bis* of the Protocol.

Once the office of origin is satisfied that the application conforms to these requirements, it is then forwarded to WIPO which, in the absence of any formal objections, registers the mark and publishes the details of the registration. WIPO also sends details of the registration to the national offices of the designated countries, which then have a period of 12 months (or up to 18 months where the relevant country has extended the term) within which to notify WIPO of any objections they may have to the registration within that country. In examining the application the national offices apply their own national laws. An objection may result from the mark being opposed by a third party in accordance with the national opposition procedures. If the national office fails to notify WIPO of its refusal of an application within the relevant period, then the application is deemed to have been accepted.[10]

14.09 Extension of territories A request for territorial extension may be made subsequently to the securing of an international registration.[11] An application for extension is recorded by the International Bureau, which then notifies the relevant national offices. The recordal of the extension is published in the gazette of the International Bureau. The territorial extension takes effect from the date on which it is recorded in the International Register.

14.10 Transfers and licences A transfer of an international registration can be effected in respect of some or all of the countries covered by the registration. However, such a transfer can only be made to a person who is entitled to own an international registration.[12] Details of the change of ownership are recorded in the International Register.[13]

Although it is possible to licence an international registration in respect of some or all of the countries covered by the registration, there is no provision in the Protocol for the recordal of licence agreements on the International Register. Where appropriate, licences should be recorded in the national offices.

10 For a more detailed consideration of the application procedure see the 'Notes for Guidance' published by The Patent Office and issued as a supplement to the Trade Marks Journal of 27 March 1996.
11 Article 3*ter* of the Protocol.
12 Article 9 of the Protocol.
13 Article 9*bis*.

14.11 Infringement Questions of infringement are determined under the laws of the relevant country by the national courts of that country.

14.12 Revocation, cancellation or invalidation Any revocation, cancellation or invalidation of the international registration in respect of all or some of the countries covered by the registration shall be recorded in the International Register.[14] However, it is for the national offices or courts to determine such matters.

14.13 Fees The fees to be paid in respect of any matter in connection with the Madrid Protocol are specified in the Schedule to the Trade Marks (International) (Fees) Rules 1996.[15]

14.14 Comment Companies based in the United Kingdom now have the choice of filing either:
(a) national applications in countries of interest;
(b) an international application pursuant to the Madrid Protocol;
(c) an application for a Community trade mark;[16] or
(d) a combination of the above.
The decision at the end of the day will require careful consideration, and the factors that will determine which route is preferable in each instance will include the nature and importance of the mark, the countries for which registration is required, and the cost. For a more complete consideration of the pros and cons of the various systems see Chapter 13, paragraphs 13.27–13.30.

14 Article 9*bis* of the Protocol.
15 SI 1996/715, which came into force on 1 April 1996.
16 See Chapter 13.

15 Emblems

15.01 Introduction The 1994 Act contains specific provisions which will prevent a trade mark from being registered if it consists of or contains either:

(a) the Royal arms (etc): s 4(1), and as to which see paragraph 15.03;

(b) certain national flags: s 4(2), and as to which see paragraph 15.04;

(c) certain national emblems: ss 4(3) and 57, and as to which see paragraph 15.05;

(d) certain emblems of international organisations: ss 4(3) and 58, and as to which see paragraph 15.07; and

(e) arms to which a person is entitled by virtue of a grant of arms from the Crown: s 4(4) and r 9, and as to which see paragraph 15.09.

In addition to these provisions of the 1994 Act, the Olympic Symbol etc (Protection) Act 1995 creates a right known as the 'Olympics Association Right', which confers exclusive rights in relation to the use of the 'Olympic Symbol', the 'Olympic Motto' and so-called 'protected words'. Section 13 of this Act provides for an amendment to s 4 of the 1994 Act, and a summary of the relevant provisions is set out in paragraph 15.10 below.

15.02 Specially protected emblems By virtue of s 3(5) of the 1994 Act, it is an absolute ground for refusal of registration if the applicant's trade mark consists of or contains one or more of the various emblems, arms or flags which are specified in s 4.

Special remedies are also conferred for the benefit of the owners of protected emblems, arms and flags and these remedies are also considered in this chapter.

The 1938 Act contained an express provision proscribing the use of the Royal Arms (etc)[1] but did not specifically refer to other protected emblems. It was a part of the Registrar's general discretion under the 1938 Act to be able to refuse registration on the ground that the applicant's mark contained or consisted of a specially protected emblem. As the Registrar retains no general discretion under the 1994 Act, it has been necessary to codify the grounds for refusal of registration based on conflicts with such emblems.

15.03 Royal arms, s 4(1) The applicant's trade mark will be refused registration if it consists of or contains either:

(a) the Royal arms,[2] or any insignia or device which so nearly resembles the Royal arms as to be likely to be mistaken for them or it;[3]
(b) a representation of the Royal crown or any of the Royal flags;[4]
(c) a representation of Her Majesty or any member of the Royal family, or any colourable imitation thereof;[5] or
(d) words, letters or devices likely to lead people to think that the applicant either has or recently has had Royal patronage or authorisation,[6]

unless the consent of Her Majesty or the relevant member of the Royal family has been obtained by the applicant.

15.04 National flags, s 4(2) A trade mark which consists of or contains a representation of either:

(a) the Union Jack;[7] or
(b) the flag of England, Wales, Scotland, Northern Ireland or the Isle of Man,[8]

can be refused registration, but only if it appears to the Registrar that

1 Section 61 1938 Act; see also the 1986 Rules.
2 Including any of the principal armorial bearings of the Royal arms.
3 Section 4(1)(a).
4 Section 4(1)(b).
5 Section 4(1)(c).
6 Section 4(1)(d).
7 Section 4(2)(a).
8 Section 4(2)(b).

the use of the applicant's trade mark would be misleading or grossly offensive.

For example, it can easily be imagined that the use of national flags could imply an official status or endorsement which may not exist. However, if the use of the flag merely indicates the nationality or domicile of the applicant, or the origin of the applicant's goods or services, then that should not of itself cause the trade mark to be refused registration under this section.

15.05 Emblems of Convention countries, ss 4(3), 57 and 59

A trade mark which consists of or contains either:

(a) the flag;
(b) the armorial bearings or any other state emblem; or
(c) an official sign or hallmark,

of, or adopted by, a Convention country[9] will not be registered unless certain conditions are satisfied. The relevant conditions for registration differ slightly in each case and are set out below.

Flags, s 57(1) In relation to the flags of a Convention country, a trade mark which consists of or contains such a flag will only be registered with the authorisation of the competent authorities of the relevant country, unless it appears to the Registrar that the applicant's use of the flag is permitted without any authorisation.[10]

Armorial bearings and state emblems, s 57(2) In relation to the armorial bearings or any other state emblem of a Convention country which are protected under the Paris Convention,[11] a trade mark

9 'A Convention country' means a country, other than the United Kingdom, which is a party to the Paris Convention: s 55(1).

10 Section 57(1).

11 An emblem, official sign or hallmark is regarded as protected under the Paris Convention only if, or to the extent that:
(a) the country in question has notified the United Kingdom in accordance with Article 6*ter*(3) of the Convention that it desires to protect that emblem, sign or hallmark;
(b) the notification remains in force; and
(c) the United Kingdom has not objected to it in accordance with Article 6*ter*(4) or any such objection has been withdrawn: s 59(1). Note also that notification under Article 6*ter*(3) of the Convention shall have effect only in relation to applications for registration made more than two months after the receipt of the notification: s 59(3). The Registrar keeps and makes available for public inspection a list of emblems, signs and hallmarks which are for the time being protected under the Convention by virtue of notification under Article 6*ter*(3): s 59(4)(a).

which consists of or contains such bearings or such an emblem will only be registered with the authorisation of the competent authorities of the relevant country, and there is no exception to this condition.[12]

Signs and hallmarks, s 57(3) In relation to official signs or hallmarks adopted by a Convention country which indicate control and warranty and which are protected under the Paris Convention,[13] trade marks which consist of such signs or hallmarks will not be registered where the applicant seeks registration in relation to goods or services of the same, or a similar kind, as those in relation to which the sign or hallmark indicates control and warranty. Registration can only be obtained with the authorisation of the competent authorities of the country concerned.[14]

Imitations, s 57(4) It should also be noted that the ground for refusal of registration relating to national flags, armorial bearings and other state emblems and official signs or hallmarks applies equally to anything which, from a heraldic point of view, is an imitation of any such flags, bearings or other state emblems or signs or hallmarks.[15]

Authorised use, s 57(5) The grounds for refusal of registration under s 57 do not apply to applications lodged by a national of a country who is authorised to make use of the emblem, sign or hallmark of that country, and notwithstanding that it may be similar to that of another country.[16]

15.06 Injunction, s 57(6) Section 57(6) provides a remedy for the authorities of a Convention country to restrain by injunction any use of a mark in the United Kingdom which could not be registered without their consent by reason of s 57.

15.07 Emblems of international organisations, ss 4(3), 58 and 59 A trade mark will be refused registration if it consists of or contains either:

(a) an armorial bearing, flag or other emblem; or
(b) the abbreviation or name,

12 Section 57(2).
13 See note 11.
14 Section 57(3).
15 Section 57(4).
16 Section 57(5).

of an international intergovernmental organisation of which one or more Convention countries[17] are members and which are protected under the Paris Convention.[18]

Authorisation, s 58(2) Where the applicant's trade mark consists of or contains any such emblem, abbreviation or name which is protected under the Paris Convention, it may still be registered provided that the authorisation of the international organisation concerned is first obtained. Furthermore, the trade mark may yet be registered even without such authorisation if the Registrar is satisfied that the applicant's proposed use of the emblem, abbreviation or name:

(a) is not such as to suggest to the public that a connection exists between the organisation concerned and the applicant's trade mark; or
(b) is not likely to mislead the public as to the existence of a connection between the use and the organisation concerned.[19]

Imitations, s 58(3) It should also be noted that the ground for refusal of registration in relation to armorial bearings, flags and other emblems of an international organisation applies equally to anything which, from a heraldic point of view, is an imitation of any such emblem.[20]

Bona fide use, s 58(5) The ground for refusal of registration under s 58 does not affect the rights of a person whose bona fide use of the trade mark in question began before 4 January 1962.[1]

17 See paragraph 15.05, note 9.
18 Emblems, abbreviations and names of an international organisation are regarded as protected under the Paris Convention only if, or to the extent that:
(a) the organisation in question has notified the United Kingdom in accordance with Article 6*ter*(3) of the Convention that it desires to protect that emblem, abbreviation or name;
(b) the notification remains in force; and
(c) the United Kingdom has not objected to it in accordance with Article 6*ter*(4) or any such objection has been withdrawn: s 59(2). Note also that notification under Article 6*ter*(3) of the Convention shall have effect only in relation to applications for registration made more than two months after the receipt of the notification: s 59(3). The Registrar keeps and makes available for public inspection a list of emblems, abbreviations and names of international organisations which are for the time being protected under the Convention by virtue of notification under Article 6*ter*(3): s 59(4)(b).
19 Section 58(2).
20 Section 58(3).
1 Being the date on which the relevant provisions of the Paris Convention entered into force in relation to the United Kingdom: s 58(5).

15.08 Injunction, s 58(4) Section 58(4) confers upon international organisations the right to restrain by injunction any use of a trade mark in the United Kingdom which could not be registered without their authorisation by reason of s 58.

15.09 Grant of arms, s 4(4) and r 9 Pursuant to s 4(4), r 9 prohibits the registration of a trade mark which consists of or contains either:

(a) arms to which a person is entitled by virtue of a grant of arms by the Crown; or

(b) insignia so nearly resembling such arms as to be likely to be mistaken for them,

unless it appears to the Registrar that the person entitled to the arms has given his consent to the registration (and not merely to the use of the arms).

In any event, where such a mark is registered, neither its registration nor anything else in the 1994 Act can be relied upon as authorising the use of that mark, which would be contrary to the laws of arms.[2]

15.10 Olympics Association Right The Olympic Symbol etc (Protection) Act 1995 ('the Olympic Symbol Act') creates a right known as the 'Olympics Association Right' which confers exclusive rights in relation to the use of the 'Olympic Symbol', the 'Olympic Motto' and certain 'protected words'.[3]

The Olympic Symbol means the symbol of the International Olympic Committee consisting of five interlocking rings. The Olympic Motto means the motto of the International Olympic Committee being the phrase 'citius altius fortius' (meaning fastest, highest, strongest). The protected words are: OLYMPIAD, OLYMPIADS, OLYMPIAN, OLYMPIANS, OLYMPIC and OLYMPICS. The Olympic Symbol Act protects not only these words, the motto and the symbol, but anything else which is sufficiently similar as to be likely to create in the mind of the public an association with the motto or words in any language.

Infringement The Olympics Association Right is infringed if a person in the course of trade uses a controlled representation of the

2 As to which, see Halsbury's Volume 48, pp 6 and 95.
3 Section 2.

words, motto or symbol. Infringing use is defined as being when the defendant either:

(a) affixes the controlled representation to goods or the packaging thereof;
(b) incorporates it in a flag or banner;
(c) offers or exposes for sale, puts on the market or stocks for those purposes goods which bear it or whose packaging bears it;
(d) imports or exports goods which bear it or whose packaging bears it;
(e) offers or supplies services under a sign which consists of or contains it; or
(f) uses it on business papers or in advertising.

This is subject to the proviso that there will be no infringement if the use of the controlled representation is in accordance with honest practices in industrial or commercial matters, and provided that the user did not intend the word to be used in relation to goods or services in circumstances which will involve an infringement of the Olympics Association Right. Nor will infringement take place if the use of the controlled representation is in a literary work, a musical work, an artistic work, a sound recording, a film broadcast or cable programme.

Super trade mark The Olympics Association Right has been described as a 'super' trade mark, because the monopoly conferred by the legislation is not limited to specific goods and services.[4]

1994 Act Section 13 of the Olympic Symbol Act amends s 4 of the 1994 Act by inserting a new s 4(5) which reads as follows:

> 'A trade mark which consists of or contains a controlled representation within the meaning of the Olympic Symbol etc (Protection) Act 1995 shall not be registered unless it appears to the Registrar:
> (a) that the application is made by the person for the time being appointed under section 1(2) of the Olympic Symbol etc (Protection) Act 1995; or
> (b) that consent has been given by or on behalf of the person mentioned in paragraph (a) above.'

4 Viscount Ascot (the Parliamentary Under Secretary of State, Department of National Heritage), a statement made during the passage of the Trade Marks Bill through Parliament.

16 Trade mark agents

16.01 Approach taken by the 1994 Act The 1994 Act contains several specific provisions relating to trade mark agents. These are found in ss 82–88 as supplemented by rr 46 and 47.

These provisions deal with the following matters:

(a) the recognition of agents, ss 82 and 88;
(b) the register of trade mark agents, s 83;
(c) the regulation of 'registered trade mark agents', s 83;
(d) proscribing unregistered persons from calling themselves 'registered trade mark agents', ss 84 and 85;
(e) the use of the term 'trade mark attorney', s 86; and
(f) privilege in relation to communications with a trade mark agent, s 87.

16.02 Recognition of agents, ss 82 and 88 Section 82 of the 1994 Act substantially reproduces s 65 of the 1938 Act. Thus, subject to the provisions referred to below, an agent may, on behalf of his principal, do any act which is required or authorised by the 1994 Act to be done by the principal in connection with the registration of a trade mark or any procedure relating to a trade mark. Similarly, any act which is required or authorised by the 1994 Act to be done to the principal may be done to the agent.[1] In this regard, the agent may be authorised by his principal either orally or

1 Section 82.

in writing.[2] It should be noted that the reference to an agent is not restricted to a 'registered trade mark agent' as defined in s 83. Therefore, any person may act as an agent for the purposes of, inter alia, filing and prosecuting trade mark applications on behalf of an applicant. However, communications with an agent who is not a registered trade mark agent will not be the subject of privilege under s 87; similarly, neither can an agent who is not a registered trade mark agent call himself a trade mark attorney pursuant to s 86.

There are circumstances in which an agent's capacity to act on behalf of his principal may not be recognised by the Registrar. These circumstances arise under rules made pursuant to ss 82 and 88.

Rule 46(2), made pursuant to s 82, is purely procedural and applies where a person has become a party to proceedings before the Registrar, and thereafter he either appoints an agent for the first time or substitutes one agent for another. In either case, the agent must file Form TM 33, and until he does so he may not act on behalf of his principal.

Rule 47, made pursuant to s 88(1), is substantive and enables the Registrar to refuse to recognise certain agents on the grounds that:

(a) the person has been convicted of an offence under s 84 (that is to say, a person who wrongly uses the description of 'registered trade mark agent');
(b) the person is an individual whose name is currently removed from the register of trade mark agents on the grounds of misconduct;
(c) the person, whose name has not been in the register of trade mark agents, has been guilty of such conduct as would have rendered him liable to have had his name erased from the register on the grounds of misconduct; or
(d) in the case of a partnership or body corporate, one of the partners or directors is a person whom the Registrar could refuse to recognise by virtue of either (a), (b) or (c) above.

Furthermore, the Registrar may refuse to recognise an agent on the grounds specified in r 14(5) of the Trade Marks and Service Marks Rules 1986 as amended.[3] Rule 14(5) operates in parallel with r 47 of the Rules pursuant to para 22(2) of Sch 3.

2 Section 82; the Registrar may require the personal signature or presence of either the agent or his principal: r 46(1); and the Registrar may, by notice in writing sent to the agent, require him to produce evidence of authority: r 46(3).
3 See SI 1990/1459.

Additional rules can be made under s 88(2) prescribing the circumstances in which a person is to be taken to have been guilty of misconduct. As at 1 November 1997, no rules had been made pursuant to s 88(2).

16.03 The register of trade mark agents, s 83 Section 83(1) of the 1994 Act enables the Secretary of State to make rules in relation to the keeping of a register of persons who act as trade mark agents.[4] Anyone whose name is entered in the register is entitled to be referred to as a 'registered trade mark agent'.[5]

As at 1 November 1997, no rules had been made pursuant to s 83. In due course, however, such rules may be made which contain provisions regulating the registration of trade mark agents.[6] In the meantime, the transitional provisions set out in Schedule 3 of the 1994 Act apply. Thus, the Register of Trade Mark Agents Rules 1990,[7] which were made pursuant to s 282 of the Copyright, Designs and Patents Act 1988, will continue in force and have effect as if they had been made under s 83 of the 1994 Act.[8]

16.04 Registered trade mark agents, ss 84 and 85 The permissible use of the term 'registered trade mark agent' has to be considered in the separate context of an individual, a partnership and a body corporate.

Individuals Only an individual who is a registered trade mark agent may:

(a) carry on a business (otherwise than in partnership) under any name or other description which contains the words 'registered trade mark agent'; or

(b) in the course of business otherwise describe or hold himself out, or permit himself to be described or held out, as a 'registered trade mark agent'.[9]

4 Section 83(1); the rules may delegate the keeping of the register to another person: s 83(3).

5 Section 83(1).

6 Section 83(2).

7 SI 1990/1458.

8 Schedule 3, para 22(1); notwithstanding that s 282 is repealed by the 1994 Act: Sch 5.

9 Section 84(1).

Partnerships A partnership is only entitled:

(a) to carry on a business under any name or other description which contains the words 'registered trade mark agent'; or
(b) in the course of a business otherwise to describe or hold itself out, or permit itself to be described or held out, as a firm of registered trade mark agents;

provided that either:

(a) all the partners are registered trade mark agents; or
(b) the partnership satisfies the conditions as may be prescribed for the purposes of s 84.[10]

Bodies corporate A body corporate is only entitled:

(a) to carry on a business (otherwise than in partnership) under any name or other description which contains the words 'registered trade mark agent'; or
(b) in the course of a business otherwise to describe or hold itself out, or permit itself to be described or held out, as a registered trade mark agent;

provided that either:

(a) all the directors of the body corporate are registered trade mark agents; or
(b) the body satisfies the conditions as may be prescribed for the purposes of s 84.[11]

16.05 Mixed partnerships and bodies corporate, s 85 As already stated, partnerships and bodies corporate may only make use of the words 'registered trade mark agent' if all the partners or all the directors as the case may be are either:

(a) registered trade mark agents; or
(b) members of a partnership or body corporate satisfying conditions prescribed in rules to be made pursuant to s 85.

Although s 85 enables the Secretary of State to make rules prescribing these conditions, no such rules had been made as at 1 November 1997. Accordingly, pursuant to the transitional provisions in Sch 3 of the 1994 Act, the Registered Trade Mark Agents (Mixed Partnerships and Bodies Corporate) Rules 1994,[12] which were made under

10 Section 84(2); the conditions will be prescribed in rules to be made pursuant to s 85.
11 Section 84(3); conditions shall be prescribed in rules to be made pursuant to s 85.
12 SI 1994/363.

s 283 of the Copyright, Designs and Patents Act 1988 governing those persons entitled to describe themselves as registered trade mark agents, will continue in force and will have effect as if they had been made under s 85 of the 1994 Act.[13]

16.06 Offences, s 84(4) It is an offence for a person (including a partnership or body corporate) to use the words 'registered trade mark agent' contrary to the provisions of s 84. On summary conviction an offender is liable to a fine not exceeding level 5 on the standard scale.[14] It will also be an offence to contravene any requirement imposed by any rules which may be made pursuant to s 85(1).[15] As stated above (in paragraph 16.05), as at 1 November 1997 there have been no rules made under s 85(1) and, therefore, in the meantime it will continue to be an offence to contravene the Registered Trade Mark Agents (Mixed Partnerships and Bodies Corporate) Rules 1994.

16.07 Trade mark attorney, s 86 Prior to the implementation of s 86 it was an offence under s 21 of the Solicitor's Act 1974,[16] in certain circumstances, for any person not qualified to act as a solicitor to use the term 'attorney'. Section 86 now provides that it will not be an offence to use the term 'trade mark attorney' in reference to a registered trade mark agent. This section removes the inconsistency in the use of the term 'attorney' by patent agents and some overseas trade mark agents, who already describe themselves as patent attorneys and trade mark attorneys respectively.

16.08 Privilege, s 87 Section 87 of the 1994 Act governs privilege attaching to certain communications with registered trade mark agents. This section substantially reproduces s 284 of the Copyright, Designs and Patents Act 1988, which is repealed by the 1994 Act.[17]

13 Schedule 3, para 22(1): s 85 of the 1994 Act substantially reproduces s 283 of the Copyright, Designs and Patents Act, 1988, which is repealed by the 1994 Act.

14 Section 84(4): proceedings for such an offence must be commenced within a year from the date of the offence; in Scotland, see the supplementary provisions as to summary proceedings: s 96.

15 Section 85(3).

16 In Scotland: Solicitors (Scotland) Act 1980, s 31; in Northern Ireland: Solicitors (Northern Ireland) Order 1976, Article 22.

17 Schedule 5 of the 1994 Act.

Scope of the communication Privilege will attach to any communication:

(a) between a person and his trade mark agent;[18] or

(b) for the purpose of obtaining, or in response to a request for, information which a person is seeking for the purpose of instructing his trade mark agent,

provided that the communication relates to any matter involving the protection of any design or trade mark or involving passing-off.[19]

The word 'protection' must include the prosecution of a trade mark application as well as matters concerning the infringement of registered trade mark rights. Arguably, it may also encompass many circumstances in relation to dealings with trade marks, including, in particular, the assignment and licensing of trade marks. For example, a communication between a trade mark agent and his client relating to the quality control provisions to be incorporated in a trade mark licence should be privileged on the basis that such advice relates to the protection of the validity of the trade mark. However, communications which relate to other aspects of a deal involving trade marks may not be privileged if they do not relate to the 'protection' of the trade marks as such. Of course, such communications may be confidential, but confidentiality is not the same as privilege.[20]

Section 87(2)(b) will confer privilege upon relevant communications between parties other than the applicant and/or his trade mark agent provided that they relate to the obtaining of information required by the applicant for the purpose of instructing his trade mark agent.

Scope of the privilege Communications which fall within the scope of s 87(1) and (2) are privileged from[1] disclosure in legal proceedings in the same way as a communication would be if it had been made between a person and his solicitor or, as the case may be, for the purpose of instructing his solicitor.[2]

18 As to the meaning of 'trade mark agent' see s 87(3), the effect of which is that registered trade mark agents, partnerships and bodies corporate entitled to describe themselves as registered trade mark agents under ss 84 and 85 are 'trade mark agents' for the purpose of privilege.
19 Section 87(1) and (2).
20 Confidential communications in writing would still be discoverable, whereas privileged communications in writing are not.
1 In Scotland: 'protected against'.
2 Section 87(2).

16.09 Duty of trade mark agent to client As with all professional advisers a trade mark agent has a duty of care towards his client. The standard of care that can be expected is judged objectively, namely that which may reasonably be expected from a trade mark agent. Jacob J has recently commented upon the duty owed to a client by a trade mark agent as follows:

> '. . . where a trade mark agent undertakes to pursue a trade mark application for a client, then his duties to that client extend to advising in relation to all legal pitfalls reasonably connected with that application. The trade mark agent is not under a duty to give commercial advice as such, but he is under a duty to keep his client informed of the legal problems which may arise, and his duty extends to warning his client to consider any commercial problems which may arise as a result of the legal problems which he, as a trade mark agent, should reasonably discern. His duty also extends to informing his client of any matter in relation to which he needs instructions on the facts to give proper advice. If, of course, the client fails to give any instructions, despite being asked, then the trade mark agent has fulfilled his duty. But if he fails to ask the client a question which he, as a trade mark agent, ought to see was important, it is not open to him to say later "the client never told me". The reason that this is so is because the client may not have the expertise to know what facts matter and what do not. The client is entitled to expect his agent to ask for the information necessary to give proper advice.'[3]

3 *Halifax Building Society v Urquhart-Dykes and Lord* [1997] RPC 55.

17 Offences

17.01 Approach taken by the 1994 Act The 1994 Act sets out certain criminal offences specifically relating to trade marks. These are:

(a) the unauthorised use of a trade mark, s 92;[1]
(b) the falsification of the Register and related offences, s 94;[2]
(c) the making of false representations that a trade mark is registered, s 95;[3] and
(d) the unauthorised use of the Royal arms, s 99(1) and (3).[4]

The 1994 Act also lays down the penalties in respect of these offences and provides for the forfeiture of counterfeit goods.[5]

This chapter describes these offences in turn, together with the relevant penalties and the availability of any defences specifically provided for in the 1994 Act.

Unauthorised use of a trade mark

17.02 Elements of the offence, s 92(1)–(4) It is an offence for a person who with a view to gain for himself or another, or with

1 See paragraph 17.02.
2 See paragraph 17.06.
3 See paragraph 17.09.
4 See paragraph 17.12.
5 In England, Wales or Northern Ireland see s 97; in Scotland see s 98.

intent to cause loss to another, and without the consent of the proprietor:

(a) applies to goods or their packaging a sign identical to, or likely to be mistaken for, a registered trade mark;[6]

(b) sells or lets for hire, offers or exposes for sale or hire or distributes goods which bear, or the packaging of which bears, such a sign;[7]

(c) has in his possession, custody or control in the course of a business any such goods with a view to the doing of anything, by himself or another, which would be an offence under paragraph (b);[8]

(d) applies a sign identical to, or likely to be mistaken for, a registered trade mark to material intended to be used:

  (i) for labelling or packaging goods;

  (ii) as a business paper in relation to goods; or

  (iii) for advertising goods;[9]

(e) uses in the course of a business material bearing such a sign for labelling or packaging goods, as a business paper in relation to goods, or for advertising goods;[10]

(f) has in his possession, custody or control in the course of a business any such material with a view to the doing of anything, by himself or another, which would be an offence under paragraph (e);[11]

(g) makes an article specifically designed or adapted for making copies of a sign identical to, or likely to be mistaken for, a registered trade mark;[12] or

(h) has such an article specified in (g) above in his possession, custody or control in the course of a business.[13]

In the case of (g) and (h), the offence is only committed if the offender knew or had reason to believe that the article has been, or is to be, used:

  (i) to produce goods; or

  (ii) to produce material for labelling or packaging goods; or

6 Section 92(1)(a).
7 Section 92(1)(b).
8 Section 92(1)(c).
9 Section 92(2)(a).
10 Section 92(2)(b).
11 Section 92(2)(c).
12 Section 92(3)(a).
13 Section 92(3)(b).

(iii) as a business paper in relation to goods; or
(iv) for advertising goods.

In the case of all offences referred to in (a)–(h), the offence is only committed under s 92 if:

(i) the relevant goods are goods in respect of which the trade mark is registered; or
(ii) the trade mark has a reputation in the United Kingdom and the use of the sign takes or would take unfair advantage of, or is or would be detrimental to, the distinctive character or the repute of the trade mark.[14]

In any event, no offence under s 92 is committed by anything done before the date of publication of the registration.[15]

17.03 Defence, s 92(5) It will be a complete defence for a person charged with an offence under s 92 to show that he believed on reasonable grounds that the use of the sign in the manner in which it was used, or was to be used, was not an infringement of the registered trade mark.[16] Two cases in which reliance has been placed by the defendant on this statutory defence are *R v Gookey*[17] and *R v Johnstone*.[18] In the former case the accused was acquitted, while in the latter case, although on apparently similar facts, the defendant was successfully prosecuted.

17.04 Enforcement, s 93 All local weights and measures authorities have a statutory duty to enforce, within their respective area, the provisions of s 92.[19] For this purpose certain provisions of the Trade Descriptions Act 1968, namely ss 27, 28, 29 and 33 will apply in relation to the enforcement of s 92.[20]

Furthermore, the Trade Descriptions Act 1968 applies as if s 92 of the 1994 Act were contained within it for the purposes of any

14 Section 92(4); the requirement in s 92(4)(b) also appears in s 10(3): see comments in paragraph 6.06
15 Section 9(3)(b).
16 Section 92(5); as to the question of infringement see Chapter 6.
17 (25 April 1996, unreported); judgment of Rivlia J.
18 Unreported; judgment of Kingston Crown Court.
19 Section 93(1); in Northern Ireland it is the duty of the Department of Economic Development to enforce s 92: s 93(3).
20 Section 93(2); in Northern Ireland references in the Trade Descriptions Act 1968 to a local weight and measures authority and any officer of such an authority must be read as references to the Department of Economic Development and any of its officers: s 93(2).

other Act which authorises the disclosure of information to facilitate the enforcement of the Trade Descriptions Act 1968.[1]

17.05 Penalties, s 92(6) A person guilty of an offence under s 92 is liable:

(a) on summary conviction, to imprisonment for a term not exceeding six months or a fine not exceeding the statutory maximum, or both; or
(b) on conviction on indictment, to a fine or imprisonment for a term not exceeding ten years, or both.[2]

In the case of *R v Robinson*[3] the defendant pleaded guilty to the charges under s 92 and was sentenced to ten weeks in prison. His offence related to the mass production of counterfeit copies of video films and he was prosecuted not only under s 92 but also under the Copyright, Designs and Patents Act 1988. In *R v Muzafar Din*[4] the accused was convicted under s 92 following the seizure from his shop in Petticoat Lane of allegedly the largest haul of counterfeit brand name watches. The defendant was sentenced to 18 months in prison and fined £16,500.

Falsification of the Register and related offences

17.06 Elements of the offence, s 94(1) and (2) Section 94 creates various offences relating to the Register.

In the first place, it is an offence to make, or cause to be made, a false entry in the Register knowing or having reason to believe that it is false.[5]

Secondly, it is also an offence to:

(a) make or cause to be made anything falsely purporting to be a copy of an entry in the Register; or
(b) to produce or tender or cause to be produced or tendered in evidence any such thing, knowing or having reason to believe that it is false.[6]

1 Section 93(4).
2 Section 92(6); in Scotland see the supplementary provisions as to summary proceedings: s 96.
3 Unreported; noted in 19 IPN No 5, May 1996, p 6.
4 Unreported; noted in ITMA News (September 1996).
5 Section 94(1).
6 Section 94(2).

17.07 Defences There are no statutory defences to an offence under s 94.

17.08 Penalties, s 94(3) A person guilty of an offence under s 94(3) is liable:

(a) on summary conviction, to imprisonment for a term not exceeding six months or a fine not exceeding the statutory maximum, or both; or

(b) on conviction on indictment, to imprisonment for a term not exceeding two years or a fine, or both.[7]

False representations

17.09 Elements of the offence, s 95 It is an offence for a person:

(a) falsely to represent that a mark is a registered trade mark; or

(b) to make a false representation as to the goods or services for which a trade mark is registered,

knowing or having reason to believe that the representation is false.

The use in the United Kingdom of the word 'registered', or any other word or symbol (presumably including the symbol ®) importing an express or implied reference to registration in relation to a trade mark, is deemed to be a representation as to registration under the 1994 Act.[8]

17.10 Defences, s 95(2) A defence will be available where the defendant can show that the use of the word or symbol is a reference to registration in a country other than in the United Kingdom and that, in fact, the trade mark is registered in that other country for the goods or services in question.[9] This raises the question whether the reference required, in order for this defence to succeed, is an indication on the face of the materials that the registration is not in the United Kingdom, or is it sufficient that the reference is in fact consistent with a registration outside the United Kingdom. In *Second Sight v Novell*[10] Lightman J held that it is sufficient that the

7 Section 94(3); in Scotland, see the supplementary provisions as to summary proceedings: s 96.

8 Section 95(2).

9 Section 95(2).

10 *Second Sight Ltd v Novell UK Ltd* [1995] RPC 423.

reference is consistent with a registration outside the United Kingdom and that this registration does in fact exist.[11]

17.11 Penalty, s 95(3) A person guilty of an offence under s 95 is liable on summary conviction to a fine not exceeding level 3 on the standard scale.[12]

Unauthorised use of Royal arms etc

17.12 Elements of the offence, s 99(1) or (3) It is an offence for a person, without the authority of Her Majesty, to use in connection with any business the Royal arms (or arms so closely resembling the Royal arms as to the calculated to deceive) in such manner as to be calculated to lead to the belief that he is duly authorised to use the Royal arms.

17.13 Defences There are no statutory defences to an offence under s 99(1). However, s 99(5) provides that nothing in s 99 affects any right of the proprietor of a trade mark containing any such arms to use that trade mark.

17.14 Penalties, s 99(3) A person guilty of an offence under s 99(1) is liable on summary conviction to a fine not exceeding level 2 on the standard scale.

Forfeiture

17.15 Introduction The 1994 Act provides for an application to be made for an order for the forfeiture of goods, material or articles. Section 97 deals with the making of an application for forfeiture in England, Wales and Northern Ireland, while s 98 deals with the position in Scotland. The substantive provisions relating to forfeiture in Scotland are similar to those in England, Wales and Northern Ireland. Accordingly, this chapter sets out the forfeiture provisions as

11 This construction accords with a ruling of the European Court of Justice in Case C-238/89 *Pall Corpn v PJ Dahlhausen & Co* [1990] ECR I-4827.

12 Section 95(3): at the time of writing, a maximum of £1,000; in Scotland see the supplementary provisions as to summary proceedings: s 96.

they apply in England, Wales and Northern Ireland with appropriate footnote references to the corresponding provisions which apply in Scotland.

17.16 Application for forfeiture, s 97(1)–(4) An application may be made for an order for the forfeiture of relevant goods, material or articles which have come into the possession of any person in connection with the investigation or prosecution of a relevant offence. A 'relevant offence'[13] is:

(a) an offence under s 92 of the 1994 Act;
(b) an offence under the Trade Descriptions Act 1968; or
(c) any offence involving dishonesty or deception.

The relevant goods, material or articles are respectively:

(a) goods which, or the packaging of which, bears a sign identical to or likely to be mistaken for a registered trade mark;
(b) material bearing such a sign and intended to be used for labelling or packaging goods, as a business paper in relation to goods, or for advertising goods; and
(c) articles specifically designed or adapted for making copies of such a sign.[14]

Where proceedings have been brought in any court for a relevant offence relating to some or all of the goods, material or articles, the application for forfeiture should be made to that court. However, where no such proceedings have been brought, the application for forfeiture should be made by way of complaint to a magistrates' court.[15]

The court will only make an order for forfeiture of any goods, material or articles if it is satisfied that a relevant offence has been committed in relation to relevant goods, material or articles.[16] However, a court may infer that such an offence has been committed if it is satisfied that such an offence has been committed in relation to goods, material or articles which are representative of them (which may be by reason of their being of the same design or part of the same consignment or batch, or otherwise).[17]

13 Section 97(8); in Scotland: s 98(14).
14 Section 97(1); in Scotland: s 98(1).
15 Section 97(2); in Scotland: s 98(2); as to 'the court' in Scotland, see s 98(14).
16 Section 97(3); in Scotland: s 98(3).
17 Section 97(4); in Scotland: s 98(4).

17.17 Appeals, s 97(5) Any person who is aggrieved by:

(a) an order for forfeiture made under s 97 by a magistrates' court; or

(b) a decision of a magistrates' court not to make an order for forfeiture,

may appeal against the order or the decision (as the case may be). The appeal in England and Wales is to the Crown Court and in Northern Ireland to the County Court.[18]

Any order made by a magistrate under s 97 may provide that the order will not come into force pending the making and determination of any appeal.[19]

17.18 Destruction or release, s 97(6) and (7) Any goods, material or articles which are forfeited pursuant to an order under s 97 will be destroyed in accordance with the directions of the court.[20] However, at the discretion of the court it may instead order that the goods, material or articles be released to a person specified by the court on condition that the person to whom they are released:

(a) causes the offending sign to be erased, removed or obliterated; and

(b) complies with any order to pay costs which has been made against him in the proceedings for the order for forfeiture.[1]

18 Section 97(5); appeal includes an application under s 111 of the Magistrates' Courts Act 1980 or Article 146 of the Magistrates' Courts (Northern Ireland) Order 1981 (statement of case); in Scotland see the procedure for any person interested appearing at the hearing of the application for forfeiture: s 98(5), (6), (7), (8) and (9).

19 Section 97(5); in Scotland: s 98(10) and (11).

20 Section 97(6); in Scotland: s 98(12).

1 Section 97(7); in Scotland: s 98(13).

Part 2 Common law: passing off and trade libel

In Part 1 of this book we have considered the law relating to trade marks under the 1994 Act. Of course, the 1994 Act is only the most recent legislation relating to trade marks: the first was the Trade Marks Act 1875. However, prior to 1875, and since then, in parallel with the legislation, the common law has also provided protection for traders against certain tortious (wrongful) activities of third parties. These activities will sometimes include the wrongful use of a trade mark. The rights and remedies conferred by the common law in respect of such activities, namely:

(a) passing off, as to which see Chapter 18; and
(b) trade libel (also known as malicious or injurious falsehood), as to which see Chapter19,

are the subject of Part 2.

18 Passing off

18.01 Introduction As a business expands its operations, it is likely (and certainly it will be the intention of the business) that customers will gradually become loyal to the particular products or services of that business and that customers will choose those products or services in preference to those of a competitor. It may therefore be tempting for competitors (especially), instead of offering better products and/or providing a better service, to hold out or dress up their own products or services in such a way as to mislead customers into thinking that they are purchasing the products or services of the first business. The common law tort known as 'passing off' was developed to prevent one business from misrepresenting its goods or services to be the goods or services of another business (where the two businesses are usually, but not always, in competition). Lord Halsbury stated the basic principle of the tort of passing off as follows:

> 'for myself, I believe the principle of law may be very plainly stated, and that is that nobody has any right to represent his goods as the goods of somebody else. How far the use of particular words, signs, or pictures does or does not come up to the proposition . . . must always be a question of evidence.'[1]

The first sentence of this quotation encapsulates the simple way in which the tort may be stated while the second sentence identifies the

1 *Frank Reddaway & Co Ltd v George Banham & Co Ltd* (1896) 13 RPC 218 at 224; described by Jacob J as 'the classic exposition' of the tort: [1995] FSR 169 at 175.

very difficult (if not insoluble) problem of defining the boundaries of passing off which, from time to time, appear to expand and contract as each judge applies the same basic principle to the different facts before him in the context of the changing commercial climate in which the facts take place. In the *Fortnum & Mason* case,[2] Harman J sums up the situation as follows:

> '. . . in the end the trouble with passing off cases is that they all turn upon their curiosities of individual fact. The principles may be clear enough . . . But the application of those principles to the facts of individual cases is extremely anxious for those judges who have to try and decide them.'

Before turning to consider the law of passing off, there is merit in following the approach of Jacob J in the *Roho* case[3] and identifying what is *not* the law. In that case, Jacob J reminds us that:

- there is no tort of copying a product or idea;
- there is no tort of taking a man's market or customers;
- neither the market nor the customers are the plaintiff's to own;
- there is no tort of making use of another's goodwill as such;
- there is no tort of competition.

Thus, the mere fact that a competitor copies some aspect of the plaintiff's business, the mere fact that he may profit from a market created and established by the plaintiff, and the mere fact that he may take the plaintiff's customers does not necessarily amount to passing off. At the heart of passing off lies deception or its likelihood, deception of the ultimate consumer in particular and, as we shall see, such deception can only occur where the plaintiff has established the necessary goodwill and where the defendant's conduct amounts to a misrepresentation.

The rationale behind the common law tort of passing off is two-fold:

(a) to protect the goodwill of a business; and
(b) to prevent a competitor from unjustly benefiting from that goodwill.

Although it is very often the case that the act of passing off will involve the defendant using the plaintiff's trade mark (whether registered or unregistered), the tort of passing off does not seek to protect trade marks as a right of property. The common law does

2 *Fortnum & Mason plc v Fortnam Ltd* [1994] FSR 438 at 443.
3 *Hodgkinson and Corby Ltd v Wards Mobility Services Ltd* [1995] FSR 169.

not recognise any proprietary rights in a trade mark which are breached or infringed as is the case under the 1994 Act. However, the tort of passing off is, in some respects, potentially wider than an action for trade mark infringement under the 1994 Act. An infringement action can only be brought if the plaintiff owns a trade mark which has been registered under the 1994 Act, whereas a passing off action can be brought on the basis of any misrepresentation by the defendant to the effect that his goods or services are those of the plaintiff. As stated, it is likely that the misrepresentation will take the form of the defendant using the plaintiff's trade mark, but the tort of passing off is not limited to the wrongful use of trade marks, and certainly the concept of what constitutes a trade mark for passing off purposes is, in theory, unlimited. Thus, where the use by one person of any sign or other feature (or, indeed, any mark of trade) amounts to a misrepresentation by that person that his goods or services are those of another, this may be the basis of a passing off action.

This chapter will focus on passing off by the wrongful use of a trade mark where the term 'trade mark' will be used in a very broad sense to embrace any sign, name (business name, brand name or Internet domain name), get-up, slogan, visual image or other feature of the plaintiff's business, goods or services (and regardless of whether or not the trade mark is registered, or would be registrable, under the 1994 Act).[4] Note also that a passing off action can only be brought by the person (or class of persons) whose goodwill is being injured, not by the general public who may be deceived by the wrongful use of the trade mark; however, the indirect effect of a successful passing off action is that the public will, in practice, be protected from being deceived as to the origin of goods or services or as to their quality.

There is an enormous body of case law which has defined and refined the scope and requirements of the tort of passing off over the

4 This approach is consistent with the comment of Lord Scarman in the *Pub Squash* case:

> 'The tort is no longer anchored, as in its nineteenth century formulation, to the name or trade mark of a product or business. It is wide enough to encompass other descriptive material, such as slogans or visual images, which radio, television or newspaper advertising campaigns can lead the market to associate with a plaintiff's product, provided always that such descriptive material has become part of the goodwill of the product' [1981] RPC 429 at 490.

years. Many of these cases were decided very much on their own particular facts and are merely illustrative of the numerous ways in which the courts have applied the generally accepted principles. Furthermore, many of the decisions were made in the course of an application for an interim injunction, and therefore the value of such decisions, even on the particular facts, is sometimes somewhat limited (except in terms of what will suffice for the grant of such an injunction). It is not within the scope of a user's guide to review the historical development of the tort of passing off; instead, this chapter simply describes the scope and requirements of the tort as they appear to us to exist as at the end of November 1997.[5]

18.02 Elements of the tort of passing off The necessary ingredients in passing off are authoritatively stated in two passages in the *Advocaat* case.[6] The two passages (cited below) need to be read together since the first concentrates primarily on what the *plaintiff* in a passing off action needs to show as a prerequisite, while the second concentrates on what the *defendant* must be shown to have done. The passage concentrating on the plaintiff's position is in Lord Fraser's speech, where he said:

> 'It is essential for the plaintiff in a passing off action to show at least the following facts:
> (1) that his business consists of, or includes, selling in England a class of goods to which the particular trade name is applied;
> (2) that the class of goods is clearly defined, and that in the minds of the public, or a section of the public, in England, the trade name distinguishes that class from other similar goods;
> (3) that because of the reputation of the goods, there is goodwill attached to the name;
> (4) that he, the plaintiff, as a member of the class of those who sell the goods, is the owner of goodwill in England which is of substantial value;
> (5) that he has suffered, or is *really likely* to suffer, substantial damage to his property in the goodwill by reason of the

5 For a history of the tort of passing off, see *Singer Machine Manufacturers v Wilson* (1876) 2 Ch D 434 at 452; *GE Trade Mark* [1973] RPC 297 at 325–7 and *Harrods Ltd v Harrodian School Ltd* [1996] RPC 697 at 706–9 and 712–15.

6 *Erven Warnink BV v J Townend & Sons (Hull) Ltd* [1979] AC 731.

> defendants selling goods which are falsely described by the trade name to which the goodwill is attached.'[7]

The passage concentrating on the defendant's activities is in Lord Diplock's speech, where he said that, for there to be a valid cause of action for passing off, five characteristics must be present:

> '(1) a misrepresentation
> (2) made by a trader in the course of trade,
> (3) to prospective customers of his or ultimate consumers of goods or services supplied by him,
> (4) which is calculated to injure the business or goodwill of another trader (in the sense that this is a reasonably foreseeable consequence) and
> (5) which causes actual damage to the business or goodwill of the trader by whom the action is brought or (in a *quia timet* action) will probably do so . . .'[8]

Other judges have also stated their own formulation of the law. In the *Jif Lemon* case, Lord Oliver and Lord Jauncey each identified three elements of a passing off action. Lord Oliver expressed them in these terms:

> 'First, he must establish a goodwill or reputation attached to the goods or services which he supplies in the mind of the purchasing public by association with the identifying "get-up" (whether it consists simply as a brand name or a trade description, or the individual features of labelling or packaging) under which his particular goods or services are offered to the public, such that the get-up is recognised by the public as distinctive specifically of the plaintiff's goods or services. Secondly, he must demonstrate a misrepresentation by the defendant to the public (whether or not intentional) leading or likely to lead the public to believe that goods or services offered by him are the goods or services of the plaintiff. Whether the public is aware of the plaintiff's identity as manufacturer or supplier of the goods or services is immaterial, as long as they are identified with a particular source which is in fact the plaintiff . . . Thirdly, he must demonstrate that he suffers, or in a *quia timet* action, that he is likely to suffer damage by reason of the erroneous belief engendered by the defendant's misrepresentation that the source

7 Ibid, at 755.
8 Ibid, at 742.

of the defendant's goods or services is the same as the source of those offered by the plaintiff.'[9]

Lord Jauncey also identified three elements in the tort of passing off:

'It is a prerequisite of any successful passing off action that the plaintiff's goods have acquired a reputation in the market and are known by some distinguishing feature. It is also a prerequisite that the misrepresentation has deceived or is likely to deceive and that the plaintiff is likely to suffer damage by such deception. Mere confusion which does not lead to a sale is not sufficient.

. . .

In a case such as the present where what is in issue is whether the goods of A are likely to be passed off as those of B, a plaintiff to succeed, must establish (1) that his goods have acquired a particular reputation among the public; (2) that persons wishing to buy his goods are likely to be misled into buying the goods of the defendant; and (3) that he is likely to suffer damage thereby.'[10]

However one expresses or defines the elements or characteristics of a passing off action, there is no avoiding the fact that the outcome of passing off cases depends very much on the quality of the evidence put to the court. The plaintiff in each case will have to establish the following matters (described by Nourse LJ in the *Parma Ham* case[11] as the 'classical trinity'):

(a) a sufficient goodwill associated with the plaintiff's business, goods or services;

(b) that the actual use by the defendant of a trade mark amounts to a misrepresentation to the defendant's customers (or potential customers), which deceives those customers into believing that the defendant's business or his goods or services are those of, or connected in a relevant way with, the plaintiff;[12] and

9 *Reckitt & Coleman Products Ltd v Borden Inc* [1990] RPC 341 at 406.

10 Ibid at 417.

11 *Consorzio del Prosciutto di Parma v Marks & Spencer plc* [1991] RPC 351.

12 This is the 'classic' misrepresentation as to the true origin of the goods or services in question. There is also the so-called 'reverse' passing off action where the misrepresentation by the defendant is to the effect that the goods in question are of a higher or different quality than is in fact the case. For example, where the defendant uses the plaintiff's trade mark which is associated with high quality goods on lower quality goods, albeit that the lower quality goods are in fact the plaintiff's: *AG Spalding & Bros v A W Gamage Ltd* (1915) 32 RPC 273 at 283.

(c) that the misrepresentation causes or is likely to cause damage to the plaintiff's business or goodwill.

What is likely to give rise to a 'sufficient goodwill' for the purposes of (a) above will be a combination of several factors, including:

(i) the inherent distinctiveness (or otherwise) of the trade mark used by the plaintiff;
(ii) the quality of the plaintiff's goods or services in question;
(iii) the nature and extent of the use of the trade mark by the plaintiff, in terms of the period of use, the geographic extent of such use and the quantity, volume or value of sales of the goods or services in relation to which the mark has been used; and
(iv) the nature and extent of the advertising and other promotion of the goods or services in question.

The question as to whether the defendant's use of the plaintiff's trade mark constitutes a misrepresentation of the kind referred to in (b) above will also depend upon a combination of several factors, including:

(i) the origin of the goods or services;
(ii) the nature of the market place, the trade channels used for putting the goods or services on the market, the activities of competitors and their use of their own trade marks and other signs;
(iii) the nature of the goods or services themselves;
(iv) the nature of the customers in question; and
(v) the use by the defendant of any distinguishing features (or 'disavowals') which, when looked at as a whole, may negate the operative effect of what may otherwise have been a misrepresentation.

For the purposes of (c) above, the plaintiff may suffer damage directly or indirectly in the following ways:

(i) loss of sales;
(ii) a diminution of the value of the goodwill associated with his products or services, ie the dilution of his reputation amongst his customers and potential customers;
(iii) a diminution in the value of his trade mark as a licensable asset; and
(iv) loss of opportunity to expand one's business into other (usually related) goods or services, ie a limitation or restriction on his ability to exploit and develop his brand.

18.03 Structure of this chapter Although it is relatively easy to state the law of passing off as a collection of three (or even five) elements, the difficulty lies in trying to state with confidence whether any particular activity falls within those elements. As already stated, the decided cases provide examples, and the remaining paragraphs of this chapter are an attempt to bring together some of those cases in a way which will enable the reader to appreciate the scope and requirements of a passing off action.[13] This involves a consideration of the following issues:

(a) the nature of the requisite goodwill which the plaintiff must have built up and established;
(b) the range of trade marks, signs, get-up, images and other features of the plaintiff's business or of his goods or services in which the goodwill may be embodied;
(c) the subject matter of an operative misrepresentation;
(d) factors which may negate what may otherwise have been a misrepresentation;
(e) the relevance of a common field of activity as between the plaintiff's and the defendant's business;
(f) the type of damage or loss which may be suffered by the plaintiff;
(g) the evidence which the plaintiff may need to present to the court, and the ways of obtaining that evidence;
(h) remedies for passing off; and
(i) practical matters for trade mark owners and practitioners alike.

Nature of goodwill

The first issue to consider is the nature of the goodwill which the plaintiff must have built up, because without sufficient and relevant goodwill there may be no operative misrepresentation and/or no damage or loss suffered (or likely to be suffered) by the plaintiff.

18.04 Definition of goodwill The concept of goodwill is very broad. Lord MacNaughten is credited with the classic definition of goodwill when he said that it is:

13 For a more complete treatment of the law of passing off readers should refer to Drysdale and Silverleaf *Passing Off Law and Practice*, 2nd Edition, Butterworths 1995; David Young QC *Passing Off*, 3rd Edition, Longman 1994; and Wadlow *Passing Off*, 2nd Edition, Sweet & Maxwell 1995.

'. . . the benefit and advantage of the good name, reputation and connection of a business. It is the attractive force which brings in custom.'[14]

The 'attractive force' normally derives from the quality of the goods or services in question, where 'quality' is judged by reference to all the relevant circumstances, including functionality, aesthetic appearance, value for money, performance, reliability, inherent quality, the purpose for which the product is intended to be used, and any other relevant feature of the goods or services which causes customers to choose one product or service in preference to another. Over time, of course, customers will come to associate a particular trade mark (to use that word broadly) as representing a particular quality (again, in the broad sense defined above) and thus the trade mark itself is representative of and is identified as being synonymous with that particular quality (ultimately, the trade mark itself becomes the attractive force which brings in the custom). It is this attractive force, however it manifests itself in relation to the particular goods or services in question, that the common law seeks to protect.

18.05 Proprietor of the goodwill There is no requirement that customers should necessarily know the identity of the actual person or entity who manufactures or supplies the goods or services in question. Very often the customer will only know or recognise the trade mark which is used in relation to the particular goods or services and for this reason the goodwill (or attractive force) is embodied in that trade mark. It is, therefore, sufficient that the goodwill attaches to the trade mark and not necessarily to the identity of the manufacturer or supplier, provided that customers understand the trade mark to indicate a particular (albeit unidentified) origin.[15]

In the *Penguin/Puffin* case[16] it was confirmed that to establish passing off it was unnecessary to prove that the customer knew or cared about the name of the manufacturer who owned the goodwill, provided that that customer knew that there was such a person and cared that the goods which he bought were made by

14 *IRC v Muller & Co's Margarine Ltd* [1901] AC 217 at 223.
15 There are numerous authorities for this proposition, see for example: *T Oertli AG v E J Bowman (London) Ltd* [1959] RPC 1, per Lord Simmons at 4.
16 *United Biscuits (UK) Ltd v Asda Stores Ltd* [1997] RPC 513 at 533.

that person. In that case, Walker J was satisfied that although the majority of customers would not know who manufactured Penguin biscuits as such, they would be concerned about the taste, quality and cost of the product which the PENGUIN trade mark had come to represent. This finding of fact may be contrasted with the *Spice Girls* case,[17] where Lightman J thought that the defendants, in supplying a sticker collection featuring the Spice Girls, were doing no more than catering for a popular demand for 'effigies and quotes of today's idols' and that that popular demand was not concerned about the origin of the goods in question, that is, customers would not know who manufactured the sticker collection and would not care whether the collection was being published either with or without the consent of the Spice Girls.

18.06 Scope and extent of goodwill It will always be very important to identify the scope and extent of the relevant goodwill. Initially, the goodwill is likely to be co-extensive with the plaintiff's actual business and will only relate to the actual goods or services sold or supplied by the plaintiff. However, over time, the use by a third party of the plaintiff's trade mark (which embodies that goodwill) in relation to other goods or services may nonetheless constitute a misrepresentation, even though those particular goods or services are not sold or supplied by the plaintiff. Thus, although it is very important for the plaintiff to establish the scope of his business and the range of goods and services which he sells or supplies, the evidence in relation to these matters does not necessarily predefine or limit the nature of the business or the goods or services sold or supplied by the defendant which may be passed off as those of the plaintiff.

One must therefore distinguish the enquiry which relates to the scope and the extent of the plaintiff's actual business from the separate enquiry as to whether the defendant has made a misrepresentation to his customers. In paragraphs 18.26 and 18.27 below, we examine the issue of the relevance of the fields of activity of the plaintiff and the defendant and the extent to which a lack of a common field of activity may either negate the existence of an

17 *Halliwell v Panini* (6 June 1997, unreported) (Lightman J); see also *Elvis Presley Trade Marks* [1997] RPC 543.

operative misrepresentation and/or result in the representation causing no damage to the plaintiff.

18.07 Time of assessment The relevant time at which to assess the plaintiff's goodwill is the time of the first actual or threatened passing off.[18]

18.08 Class actions (or 'extended' passing off) The requisite goodwill may not be exclusive to one particular business, but may vest in a class of persons or businesses such as:

(a) producers who carry on business in a particular geographic area, such as the champagne producers in the Champagne district of France,[19] the sherry producers in the Jerez district of Spain,[20] the whisky producers in Scotland,[1] and chocolate manufacturers in Switzerland;[2]

(b) producers who manufacture goods to a common and defined specification or standard such as in accordance with the recipe for Advocaat,[3] or in accordance with industry standards and regulations;[4] or

(c) suppliers of services who operate under a code of practice or in accordance with rules or guidelines.

In such cases the action may be brought either by the relevant association established to represent its members and/or by one or more individual members of the relevant class. For a recent review of this category of passing off cases see Laddie J's decision in *Chocosuisse*,[5] where he describes this cause of action as 'extended' passing off, which protects the accuracy and exclusivity of the descriptive (in that case geographical) term. Importantly, it should be noted that the proprietors currently using a descriptive term

18 *Cadbury-Schweppes Pty Ltd v Pub Squash Co Ltd* [1981] RPC 429; *J C Penney Inc v Penneys Ltd* [1975] FSR 367, and see also the recent case of *Barnsley Brewery Co Ltd v RBNB* [1997] FSR 462 at 470.

19 *J Bollinger v Costa Brava Wine Co Ltd* [1960] RPC 16 and [1961] RPC 116 and *Taittinger SA v Allbev Ltd* [1993] FSR 641 and Court of Appeal at 659.

20 *Vine Products Ltd v MacKenzie & Co Ltd* [1969] RPC 1.

1 *John Walker & Sons Ltd v Henry Ost & Co Ltd* [1970] RPC 489.

2 *Chocosuisse Union Des Fabricants Suisses de Chocolat v Cadbury Ltd*, 29 (1997) Times, 25 November (Laddie J).

3 *Erven Warnink BV v J Townend & Sons (Hull) Ltd* [1980] RPC 85.

4 *Hodge Clemco Ltd v Airblast Ltd* [1995] FSR 806.

5 *Chocosuisse Union des Fabricants Suisses de Chocolat v Cadbury Ltd*, 29 (1997) Times, 25 November (Laddie J).

(such as champagne or Swiss chocolate) cannot prevent a new competitor from manufacturing and selling goods to which the term can accurately be applied. (The difficulty for new competitors will be to identify those features of the goods which must be present in order for the term to be applied accurately.)

18.09 Geographic nexus of the goodwill Care needs to be taken to distinguish between reputation and goodwill. A trader may have a reputation in the United Kingdom because of his advertising overseas and/or his sales to UK customers who have travelled abroad, but he may have no goodwill as such in the United Kingdom because he does not trade or carry on business in this country. In such a case the reputation alone is not sufficient to establish a passing off action. Although business or trading activity in the United Kingdom is necessary in order to establish the requisite goodwill (the attractive force), it is not necessary that the plaintiff should have an actual place of business in the United Kingdom, provided that he does business in the United Kingdom. Examples of decisions based on different fact situations are:

- in the *Sheraton* case,[6] the court found that goodwill had been established in the United Kingdom, as the plaintiff received bookings at an office in the United Kingdom for its hotels, albeit that the hotels themselves were located in the United States;
- whereas, in the *Crazy Horse* case,[7] a different conclusion was reached: the court ruled against the owner of the Crazy Horse Saloon in Paris and allowed the defendant to set up a bar/club in London of the same name because the plaintiff could only establish a mere reputation in this country (through advertising and patronage of the Crazy Horse Saloon in Paris by British tourists), but could not establish any actual sales or bookings (or other business) in the United Kingdom;
- similarly, in the *Budweiser* case,[8] the Court of Appeal held that reputation 'spilling over' into the United Kingdom from advertising in American magazines was insufficient and that the

6 *Sheraton Corpn of America v Sheraton Motels Ltd* [1964] RPC 202; see also *Anciens Établissements Panhard et Levassor SA v Panhard-Levassor Motor Co Ltd* [1901] 2 Ch 513, where the importation of cars from France into England was sufficient notwithstanding that the plaintiff did not have a place of business or an agent here.

7 *Alain Bernardin et Cie v Pavilion Properties Ltd* [1967] RPC 581.

8 *Anheuser-Busch Inc v Budejovicky Budvar NP* [1984] FSR 413.

availability of the American Budweiser beer to American servicemen on American military bases in the United Kingdom did not constitute goodwill in this country; and

- more recently, Knox J has confirmed, after considering the history of the case law on this subject, that if a plaintiff has no customers in this jurisdiction he will not succeed in attempting to restrain passing off.[9]

It is arguable that the comments of Sir Nicolas Browne-Wilkinson V-C (as he then was) may be regarded as better reflecting modern trading conditions: recognising the international nature of trade and telecommunications, he clearly wanted to extend passing off to 'meet the challenge thrown up by trading patterns which cross national and jurisdictional boundaries'.[10] Unfortunately, the Vice-Chancellor felt unable to extend passing off in this way because of binding authority to the contrary. It may also be noted that courts in other common law jurisdictions have recognised and protected international reputation without local goodwill.[11] It is submitted that there should be no rule as such which necessarily limits the scope of the passing off action to fact situations where the plaintiff carries on business in this country, provided that the elements of passing off are otherwise established, and albeit that in the absence of carrying on business it may be more difficult for him to establish an operative misrepresentation and/or damage to his business.The logical consequence of the proposition that goodwill depends upon local trade is that, absent such trade, a third party can commence business in the United Kingdom and acquire its own goodwill in this country. This was described in the *NASA* case[12] as the acquisition of goodwill 'somewhat parasitically', that is, by virtue of and derived from the pre-existing reputation which existed in the United Kingdom. In these circumstances, the local trader may eventually itself build up sufficient goodwill to be in a position to bring a passing off action in its own name against a defendant, who may even be the licensee of the 'original' overseas proprietor of the goodwill (as was the case in *NASA*).

9 *Jian Tools for Sales Inc v Roderick Manhattan Group Ltd* [1995] FSR 924 at 935–7.
10 *Pete Waterman Ltd v CBS United Kingdom Ltd* [1993] EMLR 27.
11 In Hong Kong: *Tan-Ichi Co v Jancar Ltd* [1990] FSR 151; in India: *Calvin Klein Inc v International Apparel Syndicate* [1995] FSR 515; in Australia: *Fletcher Challenge v Fletcher Challenge Pty Ltd* [1982] FSR 1; in Ireland: *C&A Modes v C&A (Waterford) Ltd* [1978] FSR 126.
12 *Nice and Safe Attitude Ltd v Piers Flook (T/A 'Slaam Clothing Co')* [1997] FSR 14.

1994 Act, s 56(2) In the absence of actual goodwill in the United Kingdom, the proprietor of a trade mark may still have a remedy if his mark is sufficiently 'well known' for the purposes of s 56(2) of the 1994 Act. An injunction is available under s 56(2) to protect marks which are either registered or unregistered, provided that they are, in fact, well known.[13]

1994 Act, s 60 Furthermore, or in the alternative, in the absence of goodwill in the United Kingdom, the proprietor of a trade mark may have a remedy if his mark is the subject of an application for registration made by his agent or representative in the United Kingdom. In such circumstances, an injunction may be available under s 60(4) to restrain any unauthorised use of that mark (including use by the agent or representative or any other third party).[14]

18.10 'Anticipatory' goodwill Goodwill is normally built up over the medium to long term and will result from, in broad terms:

(a) substantial sales of the goods or services in question; and
(b) substantial advertising/marketing of the goods or services.

However, there are cases where sufficient goodwill has been established literally overnight and even prior to the commencement of actual trade. The two important cases are:

- *Fletcher Challenge*,[15] an Australian case, where advance publicity of the merger of two companies to form a new company was sufficient to establish sufficient goodwill in the name of the newly merged company; and
- *Glaxo Wellcome*, a recent decision of the High Court on similar facts to *Fletcher Challenge*, where the court accepted that the plaintiff owned the goodwill in the name GLAXO WELLCOME notwithstanding that it had only very recently been formed as a result of the merger between Glaxo plc and Wellcome plc.[16]

13 See Chapter 1 for the definition of 'well known' and Chapter 8 for a commentary on the injunction available under s 56(2).

14 See Chapter 8 for a commentary on the injunction available under s 60(4).

15 *Fletcher Challenge v Fletcher Challenge Pty Ltd* [1982] FSR 1.

16 *Glaxo plc and Wellcome plc v GlaxoWellcome Ltd* [1996] FSR 388; this case may be contrasted with the *Ben & Jerry's* case (19 January 1995, IPD 18051) where the well-known manufacturer of BEN & JERRY ice cream was not granted an injunction against Ben & Jerry's Ice Cream Ltd because the defendant had not traded and had stated positively that it had no present intention to do so. Ferris J held that the plaintiff had to show more than the mere existence of the defendant company bearing its corporate name.

18.11 Residual goodwill What is the situation where a trader ceases or suspends the use of a particular trade mark and/or trade or business altogether? The two issues are:

1 What effect has such a cessation/suspension on the existence of any previously established goodwill?
2 Even if there is a residual goodwill which survives after the cessation/suspension, will the plaintiff suffer any damage if he has ceased/suspended the relevant trade?

The answer is that residual goodwill may subsist for a considerable period of time after the plaintiff has ceased or suspended carrying on business, and particularly where the plaintiff has taken steps to keep the goodwill alive and such goodwill may found a passing off action. Examples of cases are:

- the *Ad Lib* case,[17] where four years suspended use did not negate the plaintiff's residual goodwill because there was advance publicity concerning the plaintiff's return to business; and
- the *Thermawear* case,[18] where the plaintiff's residual goodwill lasted for five years after the cessation of business.

Embodiment of goodwill

From the paragraphs which follow it will be seen that, depending on the circumstances of the case, there is no limit to the category of trade marks which may embody the plaintiff's goodwill, the use of which by a third party may constitute an actionable misrepresentation.

18.12 Inherently distinctive trade marks As already stated, the plaintiff must establish a sufficient goodwill relating to his goods or services or business. Goodwill is normally embodied in or attaches to a trade mark, particularly where the trade mark is inherently distinctive of the plaintiff or his goods or services. The courts have referred to inherently distinctive trade marks as 'fancy' or 'newly coined' because they have no meaning when originally applied to the plaintiff's goods or services or, at most, merely contain an indirect reference or skilful allusion to some character or quality of the plaintiff's goods or services. In such cases, the courts

17 *Ad-Lib Club Ltd v Granville* [1972] RPC 673.
18 *Thermawear Ltd v Vedonis Ltd* [1982] RPC 44.

will readily assume that there can be no conceivable legitimate use of such trade marks by another person and that, in employing such a mark in connection with his own goods or services, the defendant is likely to deceive customers (or potential customers). In the *Penguin/Puffin* case,[19] Walker J stated that:

> 'There is a good deal of authority for the proposition that long use of a particularly distinctive get-up does (without creating a monopoly) place on a new competitor (minded to use a similar get-up) a special obligation to avoid confusion.'

Of course, it must be stressed that what is inherently distinctive for one category of goods or services may not be distinctive if used in relation to another category, and the defendant's use of the plaintiff's inherently distinctive trade mark may nonetheless not constitute an actionable misrepresentation if, for example, in the circumstances of the case:

(a) the defendant's use is in relation to dissimilar goods or services; and/or
(b) the defendant otherwise distinguishes his goods or services,

so as to negate any misrepresentation which may otherwise be caused from the use of the trade mark.

18.13 Other signs, get-up, images and features In addition to inherently distinctive trade marks, any other trade mark (using that word broadly, to include any sign, feature, indication, image or get-up) may embody the plaintiff's goodwill, and may therefore be the basis of a passing off action if that trade mark is used by the defendant in such a way as to constitute an operative misrepresentation. This is because the concept of goodwill and the category of trade marks which may embody the requisite goodwill is very broad and not closed. Examples of trade marks which embody (if not constitute) the necessary goodwill capable of protection, are as follows:

(a) the distinctive packaging or get-up of the goods, such as the lemon-shaped, lemon-coloured and lemon-sized container in the *Jif Lemon* case;[20]
(b) slogans;
(c) visual images;

19 *United Biscuits (UK) Ltd v Asda Stores Ltd* [1997] RPC 513.
20 *Reckitt & Coleman Products Ltd v Borden Inc* [1990] RPC 341.

(d) a radio, TV or newspaper advertising campaign;[1]
(e) a trading style;
(f) names of businesses, companies and unincorporated associations;[2] and
(g) any other sign which enables a customer to distinguish one proprietor's goods or services from competing goods or services, or (in the words of Lord Jauncey in the *Jif Lemon* case) any sign which 'is the badge of the plaintiff's goodwill, that which associates the goods with the plaintiff in the mind of the public'.

In the *Roho* cushion case,[3] Jacob J had to consider whether the distinctive appearance of a cushion could be 'passed off'. In that case the defendant used a different name for its cushion and, on all the facts, it was held that, by virtue of the way in which the goods were sold and reached customers, the likelihood of actual deception was non-existent. However, the judgment is instructive in that Jacob J reviews numerous cases and makes it clear that there is no difference in law whether a misrepresentation arises by the defendant's use of a trade mark or sign, or whether it results from the very appearance of the goods themselves. The appearance of goods can therefore itself embody or represent the requisite goodwill for passing off purposes – indeed this was recognised and anticipated by Lord Herschell over one hundred years ago in the *Camel Hair Belting* case[4] when he said:

> 'It is a fundamental rule which governs all cases, whatever be the particular mode adopted by any man for putting off his goods as those of a rival trader, whether it is done by the use of mark which become his Trade Mark, or in *any other way* . . .'

The relevant question identified by Jacob J was whether the plaintiff had proved that the shape of its cushion was the 'crucial point of reference' for those who wanted specifically a ROHO cushion. In general terms, the plaintiff in a passing off action has to show that customers are 'moved to buy by source' and, if that is the case, the plaintiff will have to identify the feature or features of its goods by which the public identify the source of the goods in question. Thus,

1 The features of the 'pub squash man', a fictional character developed by the plaintiff to advertise its product: *Cadbury-Schweppes Pty Ltd v Pub Squash Co Ltd* [1981] 1 WLR 193.
2 *Law Society of England and Wales v Society of Lawyers* [1996] FSR 739.
3 *Hodgkinson and Corby Ltd v Wards Mobility Services Ltd* [1995] FSR 169.
4 *Frank Reddaway & Co Ltd v George Banham & Co Ltd* (1896) 13 RPC 218 at 231; see also *Singer Manufacturing Co v Loog* (1880) 18 Ch D 395 per James LJ at 412.

there is no limit to the category of potentially distinguishing features of a particular business or of particular goods or services which may embody goodwill, and the use of which by a third party may constitute passing off.

However, although there is no such limit imposed by the law itself, the plaintiff's problem when he relies on a feature which is not a trade mark in the traditional sense is that he may have difficulty in establishing that the public are 'moved to buy' by reference to the feature, no matter how well recognised the feature may be. If the feature is not regarded as a trade mark, ie it is not regarded by customers as a badge of trade origin, then the use of that feature by a third party will not amount to a misrepresentation because customers will not be deceived. Put another way, if customers are likely to buy the article in question because of what it is, and not in reliance upon any belief that the feature indicates any particular trade origin, then the plaintiff will have failed to establish any, or insufficient, goodwill in the feature because it does not operate as an 'attractive force' which brings in custom. One therefore has to draw a fine distinction between:

(a) features which merely make the product attractive to customers (eg its aesthetic appeal or its functionality), but which do not, of themselves, represent goodwill for a passing off action; and
(b) features which also indicate a particular trade origin or source such that customers are moved to buy the article because of its source and not just because they like the look of it or like what it does.

The hurdle for the plaintiff to overcome was described by Learned Hand J in an American case concerning the physical appearance of an adjustable wrench as follows:

> 'The plaintiff [must] show that the appearance of his wares has in fact come to mean that some particular person . . . makes them, and the public cares who does make them, and not merely for their appearance and structure.'[5]

18.14 Descriptive names – secondary meaning Obviously it will be easier to establish that the plaintiff has acquired the necessary goodwill in a particular trade mark if the trade mark in question is, of itself, inherently distinctive. A non-distinctive mark or sign which merely describes the goods, services or business of

5 *Crescent Tool Co v Kilborn & Bishop Co* 247 F 299 (1917).

the plaintiff will usually not be sufficient because such a mark or sign does not have any attractive force of itself to bring in customers and/or to distinguish the plaintiff's goods or services from those of his competitors. There is also the very real reluctance of the courts to afford quasi-monopolistic protection to an ordinary English word.[6] However, even a mark or sign which would appear to be non-distinctive/descriptive at first sight may nonetheless be shown by evidence of use and recognition in the marketplace to have acquired a 'secondary meaning', that is, a second distinctive meaning apart from its primary descriptive meaning. Examples of marks and signs which, at first sight, would appear to be wholly descriptive and non-distinctive but which have been held to have acquired the requisite 'secondary meaning' include the following:

- the words 'camel hair belting', the term used to describe belting made of camel hair, was nonetheless held to have acquired a secondary meaning;[7] and
- the lemon-coloured, lemon-sized, lemon-shaped container for JIF lemon juice was held to have acquired a secondary distinctive meaning signifying to customers not just any lemon juice but the plaintiff's particular lemon juice.[8]

On the other hand, the following are examples of cases where a descriptive/non-distinctive mark was held not to have acquired the requisite secondary meaning:

- the term 'slip-on', the term used by the plaintiff to describe its shoes and held by the court not to have acquired a secondary meaning;[9] and
- the name 'office cleaning services', the inherent descriptiveness of this name meant that the plaintiff had to accept the risk of confusion.[10]

6 As to which, see *William Stephens Ltd v Cassell* (1913) 30 RPC 199, where Neville J spoke of protecting '. . . all His Majesty's subjects in their right to use the King's English . . .'

7 *Frank Reddaway & Co Ltd v George Banham & Co Ltd* (1896) 13 RPC 218.

8 Notwithstanding the apparent descriptiveness of the container, the court held that the evidence showed that the container had acquired a secondary meaning which was distinctive of the plaintiff's product: *Reckitt & Coleman Products Ltd v Borden Inc* [1990] RPC 341.

9 *Burberrys v Cording & Co Ltd* (1909) 26 RPC 693; but see the discussion of the issues by Parker J at 701.

10 *Office Cleaning Services Ltd v Westminster Office Cleaning Association* (1946) 63 RPC 39; see also *British Diabetic Association v Diabetic Society* [1996] FSR 1.

That the distinction may be difficult to define has always been recognised. Lord Scarman in the *Pub Squash* case, delivering the opinion of the Privy Council, stated that the tort of passing off:

> '. . . is wide enough to encompass other descriptive material such as slogans or visual images . . . provided always that such descriptive material has become part of the goodwill of the product. And the test is whether the product has derived from the advertising a distinctive character which the market recognises.'[11]

The final analysis is the same as that which must take place in cases of passing off where the plaintiff relies not on a trade mark (in the traditional sense) but on features such as the appearance of his goods (see paragraph 18.13 above). The plaintiff will, therefore, have to show that a descriptive name is not merely well known but has become associated in the mind of the public with the plaintiff as manufacturer or as the source of the product, and that the defendant's use of the name will cause the public to believe that the defendant's goods have come from the plaintiff and will buy, at least in part, because of that deception. Once again, the test adopted by Jacob J is whether the public is moved to buy by source and, if so, what are the features of the plaintiff's product which enable the public to identify his product? It will be a matter of evidence whether a common or descriptive name has acquired the necessary 'secondary meaning' such that customers believe that that name indicates a particular source and that customers want the goods or services from that source.

The misrepresentation: subject matter

In broad terms, any misrepresentation which deceives (and not merely confuses) customers as to the origin of the goods or services in question, may amount to passing off. A misrepresentation as to origin is the so-called 'classic' case of passing off, but the cases show that the misrepresentation may take a number of forms.

18.15 Misrepresentation as to origin It is so well established that a misrepresentation by the defendant that his goods or services

11 *Cadbury-Schweppes Pty Ltd v Pub Squash Co Ltd* [1981] 1 WLR 193.

are those of the plaintiff amounts to passing off that one can proceed immediately to look at the variations of and extensions to this statement.

18.16 Misrepresentation as to association, sponsorship, approval or other trade connection In many cases the alleged misrepresentation is said to arise out of a suggestion or implication of some form of association, sponsorship, approval or other trade connection with the plaintiff which does not exist. Issues arise here because:

(a) passing off does not protect the plaintiff's trade mark per se: it protects the plaintiff's goodwill which the trade mark may come to represent and embody and, as we have seen, the goodwill may be limited to a particular category of goods or services; and

(b) the use of the plaintiff's likeness or image may not in fact amount to a representation of any association, sponsorship, approval or other connection with the plaintiff.

The cases show that the facts vary enormously and that the reasoning of the courts has not been consistent in this area:

- In *Kojak*,[12] the defendant's use of the name KOJAKPOPS for its lollipops, although drawing inspiration from and clearly referring to the then well-known television character Kojak, was held not to amount to passing off (despite the fact that a feature of the television character was his habit of sucking lollipops).
- In the *Teenage Mutant Hero Turtles* case,[13] the Vice-Chancellor took passing off in the United Kingdom to its highest point and held that the defendant's similar cartoon characters were being passed off as those of the plaintiff because it was accepted that a substantial percentage of the buying public now expect and know that where a famous cartoon or television character is reproduced on goods, that reproduction is a result of a licence granted by the owner of the intellectual property rights (or other rights) in the character.
- In the *Spice Girls* case,[14] the use of images of the pop group was

12 *Tavener Rutledge Ltd v Trexapalm Ltd* [1977] RPC 275, see also *Wombles Ltd v Womble Skips Ltd* [1977] RPC 99 and *Lyngstad v Anabas Products Ltd* [1977] FSR 62 ('the Abba case').

13 *Mirage Studios v Counter-Feat Clothing Co Ltd* [1991] FSR 145.

14 *Halliwell v Panini*, 6 June 1997, unreported (Lightman J); see also similar comments by Laddie J in *Elvis Presley Trade Marks* [1997] RPC 543.

held not to amount to a misrepresentation because Walker J thought that the public would not take the use of their images in a sticker collection as amounting to a representation that they were responsible for licensing, endorsing, approving or in any other way associating themselves with the stickers; instead, the defendant was simply supplying a demand by the public for 'effigies and quotes of today's idols', a demand which took no account of the origin or provenance of the goods themselves.

- In *Harrods*,[15] the judges in the Court of Appeal were agreed on the essential ingredients of the tort of passing off, but there were different opinions as to what misrepresentations are relevant to the tort: Millet LJ (with Beldam LJ concurring) thought that the relevant connection or association with the plaintiffs which was being suggested or alluded to by the defendant had to be one where the plaintiffs would be taken by the public to have made themselves responsible for the quality of the defendant's goods or services, and that a belief that the plaintiffs had sponsored or given financial support to the defendant would not suffice. Sir Michael Kerr (delivering a dissenting judgment) was satisfied that a trader might be injured if the defendant misrepresented that he was simply 'connected' with the defendant or 'in some way mixed up with' the plaintiff (citing and adopting the words of Cozens-Hardy MR in the *Buttercup* case).[16]
- In the *Law Society* case,[17] Rimer J was satisfied that there was an arguable case that the use of the defendant's name ('Society of Lawyers') involved misrepresenting to the public the status of those to whom it issued its certificates and would mislead the public into believing that the defendant's members had legal qualifications or were solicitors.
- In *Penguin/Puffin*,[18] Walker J thought that is was sufficient for the general public to be led to suppose, or assume, or to guess that the plaintiff was in some way responsible for the defendant's goods or services. In that case, although the defendant's PUFFIN packaging was considered to be sufficiently different from the plaintiff's PENGUIN packaging that it was unlikely

15 *Harrods Ltd v Harrodian School Ltd* [1996] RPC 697.
16 *Ewing (t/a Buttercup Dairy Co) v Buttercup Margarine Co Ltd* (1917) 34 RPC 232.
17 *Law Society of England and Wales v Society of Lawyers* [1996] FSR 739.
18 *United Biscuits (UK) Ltd v Asda Stores Ltd* [1997] RPC 513.

that a significant proportion of shoppers would fail to distinguish the two products, it was nonetheless thought that the public would suppose, assume or guess that there was a 'connection' between the PUFFIN biscuit and the PENGUIN biscuit, in that the two biscuits were made by the same manufacturer, when in fact they were not. (It is worth noting that Walker J expressly cites and relies upon the *Buttercup* case, which was also relied upon by Sir Michael Kerr in his dissenting judgment in the *Harrods* case.)

- In the *Polo* case[19] in the Court of Appeal, Aldous LJ drew a fine but important distinction between a representation by the defendant which could lead members of the public to 'make an association' with the plaintiff's product, and a representation that the plaintiff is actually associated with/the manufacturer of the defendant's product. His Lordship thought that the former type of association would not amount to a misrepresentation because, at most, it would be a representation as to the shape and taste of the defendant's LIFESAVER sweets and that they were the same type of sweets as POLOS. An 'association' with the plaintiff's product in this way was not sufficient to establish passing off, because it did not amount to a misrepresentation that the defendant's LIFESAVERS were in fact POLOS or that they came from the plaintiff.
- Similarly, the clear allusion to (even parody of) the well-known BAYWATCH television series by the producers of the adult satellite programme BABEWATCH was held not to amount to passing off. The similarity of the names, and even of the subject matter of the two programmes (beach scenes, red swimming costumes and red floats etc), was not sufficient to amount to any form of operative misrepresentation because of the distinguishing features in terms of the mode of transmission, mode of reception and content.[20]

Although the *Baywatch* and the *Polo* cases are based on entirely different fact situations, it is clear that the tort of passing off is not established by the defendant selling a similar (even competing) product in such a way that customers make some form of mere association with the plaintiff's product in the sense that the

19 *Nestlé (UK) Ltd v Trustin the Food Finders Ltd* (22 August 1996, unreported), CA.
20 *Baywatch Productions Co Inc v Home Video Channel* [1997] FSR 22.

plaintiff's product might be called to the mind of the customer – the association must be far more precise, that is, that the plaintiff is actually associated or connected in a relevant way with the defendant's goods.

18.17 Other misrepresentations: the test of deception Other examples of an operative misrepresentation for the purposes of passing off show that: 'at the heart of passing off lies deception or its likelihood, deception of the ultimate consumer in particular'.[1] Thus, from the classic case of the defendant selling his goods as and for those of the plaintiff, the tort of passing off now covers other heads of misrepresentation. For example:

- Representing that the defendant's goods are the same as those of the plaintiff (in terms of quality, performance or functionality), when they are not.[2]
- Representing that the defendant's goods are the same as goods sold by a class of persons of which the plaintiff is a member, when they are not.[3]
- In another case involving The Law Society,[4] Aldous J (as he then was) granted an interlocutory injunction against the defendant because, by selecting a telephone number confusingly similar to the plaintiff's, the defendant may well have represented that he is the plaintiff, either by saying so or by failing to take steps to disabuse anyone mistakenly calling his number (ie misrepresentation by silence).
- At 'the outer limits' of the tort of passing off is a misrepresentation to the effect that the defendant's goods would 'suit' the plaintiff's goods: in *Hodge Clemco v Airblast*,[5] although the

1 Per Jacob J in *Hodgkinson and Corby Ltd v Wards Mobility Services Ltd* [1995] FSR 169 at 175; cited by Walker J in the *NASA* case where he states that: 'it is deception, and nothing else, that lies at the heart of passing off'. [1997] FSR 14 at 20.
2 *Combe International Ltd v Scholl (UK) Ltd* [1980] RPC 1.
3 *Erven Warnink BV v J Townend & Sons (Hull) Ltd* [1980] RPC 31.
4 *Law Society of England and Wales v Griffiths* [1995] RPC 16.
5 *Hodge Clemco Ltd v Airblast Ltd* [1995] FSR 806, and see also *LEEC Ltd v Morquip Ltd* (unreported, noted in [1996] 6 EIPR D-176) where Laddie J held that the use by the defendant of photographs or other illustrations of the plaintiff's products, to demonstrate that his products were equivalent to or a substitute for the plaintiff's, was not passing off per se unless the plaintiff could prove some actual deception (ie a misrepresentation) through such use (on the evidence there was none).

defendant's lenses would have fitted into the plaintiff's helmets, the helmets when fitted with the defendant's lenses would not have complied with the relevant safety regulations.

- Alternatively, there is the so-called situation of reverse passing off when the defendant makes a misrepresentation, not as to his own goods, but as to the plaintiff's goods; for example, by selling the plaintiff's lower quality goods as those of the plaintiff's higher quality goods.[6]
- Finally, the defendant may be committing a tort of enabling others to pass off, that is, putting the means of passing off into the hands of another person: for example, a manufacturer who supplies goods to a retailer may be liable in passing off even though it is the retailer who actually makes the misrepresentation to the ultimate customers.[7] In such a case the court will look to see whether the manufacturer has supplied a 'badge of fraud' to its retailer so as to effect the passing off.[8] In the *One in a Million* case,[9] it was held that the mere creation of an 'instrument of deception' (such as the registration of a deceptive company or Internet domain name), without either using it or putting it into the hands of someone else to do so, is not passing off per se; however, a quia timet injunction is available where the defendant's conduct amounts to a threat of passing off or is calculated to infringe the plaintiff's rights.

18.18 Who must be deceived by the misrepresentation The misrepresentation must be made to the plaintiff's actual or potential customers, as otherwise the plaintiff's goodwill will not be injured. However, the judges in the Court of Appeal in *Harrods*[10] were divided in terms of the application of this statement. Millett LJ took a narrow view, stating that the misrepresentation must be made to the common customers of the parties (that is, affluent members of the middle class who live in London, shop at Harrods and wish to send their children to a fee-paying school). Sir Michael Kerr on the other hand was prepared to consider the effect of the misrepresentation on

6 *AG Spalding & Bros v AW Gamage Ltd* (1915) 32 RPC 273.
7 *Sykes v Sykes* (1824) 3 B & C 541.
8 *Cadbury Ltd v Ulmer GmbH* [1988] FSR 385.
9 *Marks & Spencer plc v One in a Million* Ch 1997 M No 5403, [1998] IPD 21016, (1997) Times, 2 December (Sumption QC).
10 *Harrods Ltd v Harrodian School Ltd* [1996] RPC 697.

anyone who was aware of the well-known retailer and who was at least a potential customer of the plaintiff, but who may never have heard of the defendant's school. Such people are potentially relevant because, when they do hear of the defendant's school, the relevant question will be whether they are deceived into thinking that the school is connected or associated in a material sense with the retailer.

Factors which may negate the misrepresentations

There are a number of ways in which the defendant may be able to avoid making, or negate what would otherwise be, a misrepresentation. This is because, in general terms, the courts will always look at all the relevant evidence in order to decide the case. Having said that, the first issue of 'intent' considered under this heading does not in fact negate any misrepresentation.

18.19 Intent It is well established that intent, let alone malice, is not a requirement in order to establish passing off. Thus, it is no defence for the defendant to say that he did not intend to pass off his goods or services nor to injure the plaintiff. Nonetheless, the question why the defendant chose to adopt a particular name or get-up is always highly relevant. It is 'a question which falls to be asked and answered',[11] and where there is clear evidence to suggest that the defendant's conduct was undertaken with a view to diverting business from the plaintiff, then the court will be likely to conclude that the defendant will succeed in its aim.[12] In *Penguin/Puffin*,[13] Walker J clearly thought that the defendants were, under advice, seeking to make only such changes to their packaging as were needed to avoid what they judged to be an unacceptable risk of being sued. In the circumstances, the defendants were said to be 'taking a conscious decision to live dangerously' and that was not a

11 Kerr LJ in *Sodastream Ltd v Thorn Cascade Co Ltd* [1982] RPC 459.

12 See the comment to this effect by Aldous J (as he then was) in *Law Society of England and Wales v Griffiths* [1995] RPC 16 at 21; and see also Lindley LJ in *Slazenger & Sons v Feltham & Co* (1889) 6 RPC 531, whose comments were cited by both Millett LJ in *Harrods Ltd v Harrodian School Ltd* [1996] RPC 697 at 706, and Walker J in *United Biscuits (UK) Ltd v Asda Stores Ltd* [1997] RPC 513.

13 *United Biscuits (UK) Ltd v Asda Stores Ltd*, supra.

matter which the court could disregard. Similarly, in the *One in a Million* case,[14] Sumption QC observed that, where the defendant deliberately registers a domain name on account of its similarity to the name, brand name or trade mark of an unconnected business, the defendant must expect to find himself on the receiving end of an injunction to restrain the threat of passing off.

Furthermore, the fact of 'innocence' (ie the lack of an intent to pass off) does not mean that the plaintiff is only entitled to an injunction – he may also recover his damages.[15]

18.20 Use of own name It has been suggested that, provided the defendant is using his own name honestly, then he must be allowed to trade in his own name and, if some confusion results, that is considered to be a lesser evil than depriving him of his 'natural and inherent right'.[16]

However, it is also clear that this natural and inherent right will not be applied broadly, and the court will look carefully to see whether, in fact, the defendant is indeed passing off his business, goods or services:

- Where the defendant deliberately adopts a name to benefit from the plaintiff's goodwill, an injunction will be granted.[17]
- Sometimes a qualified injunction will be granted not to use a surname without clearly distinguishing the defendant's business in other ways.[18]
- In some cases a distinction that is difficult to apply has been drawn between the defendant carrying on business under his own name and, on the other hand, using the name in respect of his goods. As a business name will often become the brand name itself, this may be a distinction without a difference.[19]
- It would appear that the exception (in so far as there is an

14 *Marks & Spencer plc v One in a Million*, supra.

15 *Gillette UK Ltd v Edenwest Ltd* [1994] RPC 279 at 291–4 (where Blackburne J reviews the conflicting (sometimes obiter) decisions on this point and concludes that the relief available where passing off is established should not be governed by considerations which may have been applicable to the cause of action at an earlier stage of its development).

16 *Marengo v Daily Sketch and Sunday Graphic Ltd* (1948) 65 RPC 242 per Lord Simonds at 251.

17 *Joseph Rodgers & Sons v W N Rodgers & Co* (1924) 41 RPC 277.

18 *Wright, Layman & Umney Ltd v Wright* (1949) 66 RPC 149.

19 The distinction was made by Romer J in the *Rodgers v Rodgers* case, supra.

exception) does not extend to the use of one's first name or a nickname.[20]

- Ultimately, where the defendant is in fact representing his goods as those of the plaintiff, it is no defence to say that he is doing so only by using his own name.[1]

18.21 Acts outside the United Kingdom The relevant trade for the purpose of passing off is the plaintiff's trade within this jurisdiction and not any trade carried on overseas. For example:

- In the *Fortnum & Mason* case,[2] the well-known English retailer was unable to prevent the defendant from using the name FORTNAM because the plaintiff's trade was in high class merchandise in England, whereas the defendants sold cheap, wholesale goods abroad. Accordingly, Harman J could find no basis on which to conclude that any customer of the defendant would buy the defendant's goods in the belief that he was acquiring the goods of the plaintiff.
- However, the situation will be different where the defendant's activities will necessarily stray into the jurisdiction (by design or, presumably, even by accident): in the *Internet World* case,[3] Jacob J restrained the German defendant from passing off its INTERNET WORLD trade show and exhibitions which were intended to be held in Germany but which were advertised in the United Kingdom through the Internet (albeit from a web site on a server in Germany).

18.22 Descriptive use of terms or names The defendant will often assert that he is merely using a term or name to describe some aspect of the nature, quality, composition, geographic origin or purpose of his business, goods or services. Such a defence is not based so much on negating a misrepresentation as on asserting that there is no misrepresentation in the first place. The cases and issues discussed in paragraph 18.14 above are relevant in this context. It will be a question of fact whether a descriptive term or name used by the defendant has acquired a 'secondary meaning' which has become distinctive of the plaintiff's business, goods or services and,

20 *Biba Group Ltd v Biba Boutique* [1980] RPC 413.
1 *NAD Electronics Inc v NAD Computer Systems Ltd* [1997] FSR 380.
2 *Fortnum & Mason plc v Fortnam Ltd* [1994] FSR 438.
3 *Mecklermedia Corpn v D C Congress GmbH* [1998] Ch 40.

if so, the defendant may still be passing off through the use of that term or name.

The circumstances in which a plaintiff can succeed in a passing off action based on a descriptive name, and the significance of the length of use of that name, have been considered in numerous cases over the last twenty years.[4]

The starting principle, however, is that the courts will not readily assume that the use by the defendant as part of his trade name of descriptive words which are already used by the plaintiff as part of his trade name is likely to cause confusion, and the courts will accept small differences as adequate to avoid such confusion.

The cases again suggest (as stated above in the context of the use of one's own name) that there may be a distinction to be drawn where the descriptive term or name is used in relation to the actual article or product, rather than as the name of a business. In the latter case, the nature of the business, its goods or services and the way in which the business is carried on may either negate or add to the likelihood of deception.

18.23 Use of other distinguishing material, including disclaimers As is often stated, all the circumstances of the case will be looked at to determine whether the defendant's activities amount to an operative misrepresentation. It is not sufficient for the plaintiff simply to show that the defendant is using a similar (or even identical) trade mark, as would be the case to prove trade mark infringement under the 1994 Act. This is because, unlike the 1994 Act, the tort of passing off does not seek to protect trade marks as such and therefore, despite certain similarities with the plaintiff's business, goods or services, the overall features of the defendant's business, goods or services may mean that there is no operative misrepresentation. For example:

- In the *Polo* case,[5] despite the similarity of the shape of the defendant's LIFESAVERS sweets with the plaintiff's POLO mints,

4 The important cases are: *McCain International v Country Fayre Foods* [1981] RPC 69 (especially at 73/80); *My Kinda Town Ltd v Soll and Grunts Investments* [1983] RPC 407 (especially at 415 and 424–6); *Reckitt & Coleman Products Ltd v Borden Inc* [1990] RPC 341 (especially at 412); and *County Sound plc v Ocean Sound Ltd* [1991] FSR 367 (especially at 373–6).

5 *Nestlé (UK) Ltd v Trustin the Food Finders Ltd* (19 August 1996, unreported) (Walker J) (22 August 1996, unreported), CA.

both Walker J and Aldous LJ (on appeal affirming the decision of Walker J) thought that the packaging as a whole of the defendant's product and the fact that it bore the trade mark LIFESAVERS meant that consumers would not be led to believe that LIFESAVERS were the product of the plaintiff. Aldous LJ observed that the situation may have been different if LIFESAVERS were to be marketed in an unmarked plastic bag, because in such circumstances the representation to consumers conveyed by the shape of LIFESAVERS alone may have been such as to suggest that they were either POLOS or manufactured by the plaintiff.

- In the *Fortnum & Mason* case,[6] the similarity of the defendant's name alone (FORTNAM) was insufficient to establish passing off because of:
  - (a) the differing nature of the trade channels – the plaintiff being a retailer and the defendant a wholesaler; and
  - (b) the differing quality and cost of the goods and hence the nature of the ultimate consumer – the plaintiff selling high class, relatively expensive goods and the defendant selling relatively cheap goods.
- On the other hand, in the *Penguin/Puffin* case,[7] Walker J thought that although the PENGUIN trade mark was not infringed by the defendant's PUFFIN sign, nonetheless, when looked at as a whole, the PUFFIN packaging would cause a substantial number of customers to suppose that there was a connection between the PUFFIN biscuit and the plaintiff. Thus, the misrepresentation conveyed by the similar packaging as a whole was not negated by the use of a different trade mark.
- In the *Roho* case,[8] Jacob J thought that the near-identical shape and appearance of the defendant's cushions did not amount to a misrepresentation because the shape itself was not a feature by reference to which customers bought the cushion. In effect, the shape and appearance of the parties' respective cushions conveyed no representation as to the origin of the goods and, instead, other features of the two products clearly distinguished them, such as:
  - (a) the manner in which they were bought (ie because they were expensive, they were not bought casually);
  - (b) the process of supply, which inevitably involved health care

6 *Fortnum & Mason plc v Fortnam Ltd* [1994] FSR 438.
7 *United Biscuits (UK) Ltd v Asda Stores Ltd* [1997] RPC 513.
8 *Hodgkinson & Corby Ltd v Wards Mobility Ltd* [1995] FSR 169.

professionals (who were described as caring and careful people);

(c) the process of ordering the goods by reference to a precise model number; and

(d) the use by the defendant of a dissimilar trade mark.

- In the *Blu-Tack* case,[9] the misrepresentation (if any) was made too late, that is, the feature of the defendant's product which was alleged to convey the misrepresentation (the blue colour of the adhesive) was not visible at the point of sale because the adhesive itself was packaged inside a wallet which was not in any way to be confused with the wallet in which the plaintiff's BLU-TACK was sold.
- Compare the facts of the *Blu-Tack* case with the *Sodastream* case,[10] where the defendant's fizzy drink cylinders were substantially identical to the plaintiff's cylinders, except only for an attached label which did not sufficiently distinguish the two products and therefore did not negate the misrepresentation conveyed by the substantially identical features.
- Similarly, in the *Jif Lemon* case,[11] the fact that the defendant used distinguishing labels attached to the neck of its lemon-shaped containers did not negate the misrepresentation (caused by the similarity of the containers themselves), because the trial judge found that those purchasing lemon juice did not read the labels and simply assumed that all lemon-shaped containers must contain JIF lemon juice.

Notwithstanding these last two cases, it is clear that it is not impossible to adopt certain features of a competitor's product, even if those features are distinctive of the competitor, provided that some other aspect of one's business, goods or services sufficiently distinguishes them from those of the competitor. One needs to tread carefully however: Walker J in *Penguin/Puffin* was clearly influenced by the fact that the defendant had chosen to live dangerously by adopting as much as it thought it could of the PENGUIN packaging.

18.24 Honest concurrent use The defendant's honest and concurrent use of a trade mark similar to that of the plaintiff will be a good defence where the defendant's use of the mark does not convey

9 *Bostik Ltd v Sellotape GB Ltd* [1994] RPC 556.
10 *Sodastream Ltd v Thorn Cascade Co Ltd* [1982] RPC 459.
11 *Reckitt & Coleman Products Ltd v Borden Inc* [1990] RPC 341.

a misrepresentation to the plaintiff's customers. The mere fact of honest and concurrent use is not, therefore, an absolute defence because, notwithstanding that the use is honest and concurrent, such use may still convey a misrepresentation. Once again, it will be a question of fact as to whether the plaintiff's mark identifies the plaintiff's business, goods or services alone, or whether the goodwill is shared between the plaintiff and defendant such that neither party can be said to be guilty of any misrepresentation.

- In the *Habib Bank* case,[12] the Court of Appeal confirmed that the fact that two or more persons may be entitled to rely on honest concurrent user of a mark (so as to secure registration of the mark) leaves unaffected the separate question of whether one may be entitled to sue the other for passing off. Oliver LJ (with whom the other members of the Court of Appeal agreed) was careful not to elevate the concept of honest concurrent use to a 'doctrine', and described such use as merely 'a facet of Lord Diplock's first essential ingredient of misrepresentation'. On the facts of this case it was held that there was a shared reputation and that there was no exclusive goodwill subsisting in the plaintiff.

18.25 Comparative advertising, spares and accessories The use of the plaintiff's trade mark or name in a comparative advertisement will not amount to passing off because, provided that is all that the defendant is doing, there is no misrepresentation as such: quite the opposite – the defendant is representing his goods or services to be different from those of the plaintiff by comparing them in some way.

Similarly, a statement by the defendant that his goods are spares or accessories for the plaintiff's goods conveys no relevant misrepresentation for passing off purposes. The law of malicious falsehood/trade libel may, however, be relevant: as to which, see Chapter 19.

Common field of activity

There has been much written about the relevance of a 'common field of activity' as between the plaintiff's and the defendant's business. The issue is whether there must be, as a matter of law, a

12 *Habib Bank Ltd v Habib Bank AG Zurich* [1982] RPC 1.

'common field of activity' in order to establish passing off and that, absent such a common field, the plaintiff's claim must fail. In the *Harrods* case,[13] Millett LJ reviews the history of this issue, commencing with the *Uncle Mac* case in which Wynn-Parry J coined the phrase and dismissed the plaintiff's claim for want of a common field of activity.[14] Suffice it to say that it is now well settled that there is no threshold requirement for there to be a common field of activity, but the respective fields of activity of the parties remains a relevant (but not determinative) consideration in assessing the likelihood of deception and the likelihood of damage.

18.26 Deception and likelihood of deception The proximity of the defendant's field of activity to that of the plaintiff's is a factor to be taken into account when deciding whether the defendant's conduct will (or is likely to) deceive the relevant public.

It is clearly possible to conceive of a situation where the defendant's use of even a very well-known trade mark will convey no misrepresentation to the relevant customers because the defendant's business, goods or services are wholly different from those sold or supplied by the plaintiff. The following cases are indicative of the issues:

- In *Stringfellows*,[15] the nature of the plaintiff's business (a nightclub) was so divorced from the defendant's products (oven chips) that the Court of Appeal refused to grant an injunction to the plaintiff notwithstanding that the defendant was clearly making use of the plaintiff's reputation in its advertising. However, such use did not amount to passing off because there was no suggestion that customers would be deceived into thinking that the plaintiff had anything to do with the manufacture and/or supply of the oven chips.
- In *Harrods*,[16] the Court of Appeal was dealing with the famous Harrods department store and Millett LJ recognised that, where the plaintiff's business name is a household name, the degree of

13 *Harrods Ltd v Harrodian School Ltd* [1996] RPC 697.
14 *McCulloch v Lewis A May (Produce Distributors) Ltd* (1948) 65 RPC 58. In the *Abba* case [1977] FSR 62 at 67 Oliver J explains that Wynn-Parry J was not adding a new element to the tort of passing off: instead, the expression 'common field of activity' he says is merely a convenient shorthand term for the need for a real possibility of confusion.
15 *Stringfellow v McCain Foods (GB) Ltd* [1984] RPC 501.
16 Supra.

overlap between the fields of activity of the parties' respective businesses may be a less important consideration in assessing whether there is likely to be deception. However, it remains a consideration and, on the facts of the case, the Court of Appeal (by a majority of two to one) held that parents would not send their children to the Harrodian School wrongly thinking that it was connected or associated with the Harrods department store.

- In another case involving a famous English retailer, Harman J held in the *Fortnum & Mason* case[17] that despite the plaintiff's very great goodwill in the name FORTNUMS which was 'long established and beyond question in its particular field', the defendant's use of FORTNAMS did not amount to passing off, having regard to the nature of the goods in which the respective parties dealt and the nature of their respective trade channels. Although Harman J cites the *Stringfellows* case (and others involving the common field of activity issue), it is clear that his decision is based not on the lack of a common field of activity per se, but on the fact that, having looked at all of the evidence, there was no real likelihood of deception.
- Contrast these cases with the *Lego* case,[18] where the plaintiff manufacturer of children's plastic building blocks succeeded in its passing off action against the manufacturer of plastic irrigation equipment (the fact that both products, although not in competition with each other, were made out of plastic may have been influential in this decision).
- In the *Turtles* case,[19] Sir Nicholas Browne-Wilkinson V-C specifically refused to follow the narrow common field of activity cases in England (namely: the *Wombles* case,[20] the *Kojak* case,[1] and the *Abba* case[2]) and, instead, approved the broader statements of the law in this area in two Australian cases (namely, the *Muppets* case,[3] and the *Fido Dido* case[4]). The fact that there was no common field of activity as such between the first plaintiff

17 Supra.
18 *Lego System A/S v Lego M Lemelstritch Ltd* [1983] FSR 155.
19 *Mirage Studios v Counter-Feat Clothing Co Ltd* [1991] FSR 145.
20 *Wombles Ltd v Womble Skips Ltd* [1977] RPC 99.
1 *Tavener Rutledge Ltd v Trexapalm Ltd* [1977] RPC 275.
2 *Lyngstad v Anabas Products Ltd* [1977] FSR 62.
3 *Children's Television Workshop Inc v Woolworths (NSW) Ltd* [1981] 1 NSWLR 273.
4 *Fido Dido Inc v Venture Stores (Retailers) Pty Ltd* (1988) 16 IPR 365.

(the proprietor of four cartoon characters known as Teenage Mutant Ninja Turtles) and the defendants (distributors of goods in relation to which an image of similar characters was used) was irrelevant, because the public would still be deceived, not into thinking that the plaintiffs were in fact the manufacturers or suppliers of the goods, but into believing or expecting that the plaintiffs had granted a licence to the defendants to sell the goods. The misrepresentation was found to arise based on the evidence that showed that the public believed that the Turtle characters would not appear on a product without the licence of the plaintiff and, in the absence of such a licence, the public is therefore deceived into a wrongful belief. It may be that the *Turtles* case will only be relevant in the context of character merchandising; indeed, the Vice-Chancellor based his decision on the premise that 'the buying public now expects and knows that where a *famous cartoon or television character* is reproduced on goods, that reproduction is a result of a licence . . .' (emphasis added); however, even in the field of character merchandising it cannot be taken for granted that the buying public will necessarily assume there is a relevant trade connection; indeed, in the *Spice Girls* case[5] Lightman J came to the opposite conclusion. It may be that the *Turtles* case (an interlocutory decision) will be limited to its own facts, where the evidence before the court of the substantial media coverage of the official merchandising activities of the plaintiff enabled his Lordship to reach his conclusion as to the public expectation of a licensing programme.

- However, in the *Nike* case,[6] the manufacturers of the well-known NIKE sports clothing succeeded in a passing off action where the defendant's were engaged in the distribution of toiletries and cosmetics. Jacob J accepted the evidence which showed that the marketing and sale of the defendant's goods would lead to actual deception, notwithstanding that the parties traded in entirely different fields of activity and even though the plaintiff had no present intention to move into toiletries/cosmetics.
- More recently, however, in the *NASA* case,[7] Walker J cites and

5 Supra.
6 *Nike (Ireland) Ltd v Network Management Ltd* (22 July 1994, unreported) (Jacob J).
7 *Nice and Safe Attitude Ltd v Piers Flook* [1997] FSR 14.

appears to rely on the *Kojak* and the *Abba* cases[8] in concluding that a trader can, in effect, appropriate another's name and reputation in some other field, making it distinctive of his own goods, and thereby acquire the exclusive goodwill in that trader's own field of activity (and albeit that Walker J described the acquisition of goodwill in this way as 'somewhat parasitical'). Walker J went on to observe that the *Lego* and *Turtles* cases illustrate a 'relaxation' of the common field of activity concept, but do not mark its extinction.

- Another factor to bear in mind is the ever-changing nature of the marketplace; in *NAD*,[9] Ferris J noted that the fields of audio hi-fi and computers were converging and were no longer sufficiently distinct to prevent confusion.

It is also worth noting that, while a lack of a common field of activity will not necessarily deprive the plaintiff of a remedy, the existence of a common field of activity does not necessarily guarantee a finding of passing off. For example:

- In the *Roho* case,[10] despite the defendant copying certain features of the plaintiff's cushion which was sold in direct competition with the defendant's cushion, there was no passing off because, on the facts, the features in question were not indicative of the plaintiff (see the summary of this case in paragraph 18.13 above).

18.27 Damage or loss to the plaintiff In addition to the issue as to whether a lack of a common field of activity will prevent deception is the question whether a lack of a common field of activity must necessarily mean that the plaintiff will suffer no damage or loss if he is not competing with the defendant.

For instance, suppose that customers do in fact buy a product in the mistaken belief that it is the plaintiff's, or that the plaintiff has licensed its manufacture, or is in some relevant way connected or associated with the product. The customer is certainly deceived in those circumstances but, if the plaintiff does not trade in the particular product, how is he injured when he has not 'lost' a sale of one of his own products? The answer may be that he suffers no damage in these circumstances. For example, in the *Stringfellows*

8 Supra.
9 *NAD Electronics Inc v NAD Computer Systems Ltd* [1997] FSR 380.
10 Supra.

case,[11] Slade LJ cautioned that even if there is a risk of confusion, the court should not readily go on to infer the likelihood of any resulting damage to the plaintiff and that, in such a case, a heavy onus falls on the plaintiff to show that damage to his business is in truth likely to ensue and to cause him more than minimal loss.

However, it is not only 'lost' sales which may damage or injure a plaintiff and there are a number of cases which show that, even where the parties are not in competition with each other, the plaintiff's goodwill may still be damaged. An analysis of the various types of damage which the plaintiff may suffer as a result of passing off follows in the next section.

Damage to or loss of goodwill

Ultimately, the misrepresentation must cause (or be likely to cause) damage or injury to the plaintiff's goodwill. As stated in the introduction to this chapter, there is no tort of merely making use of another's goodwill: the goodwill must be damaged. The following paragraphs explore the nature of that damage.

18.28 Loss of sales, damage by substitution In the classic case of passing off, where the defendant represents his business, goods or services as those of the plaintiff, there is an obvious risk of damage to the plaintiff's business by substitution. Customers and potential customers will be lost by the plaintiff if they transfer their custom to the defendant in the erroneous belief that they are dealing with the plaintiff.

18.29 Dilution of the value of the goodwill Where the parties are not in direct competition with each other there will be no sales which are 'lost' by the plaintiff to the defendant. However, a number of cases have identified other ways in which the plaintiff's goodwill can be damaged:

- In the *Lego* case,[12] it was accepted that a customer who was dissatisfied with the defendant's LEGO plastic irrigation equipment might be dissuaded from buying one of the plaintiff's

11 Supra.
12 *Lego System A/S v Lego M Lemelstrich Ltd* [1983] FSR 155.

LEGO plastic toy construction kits if he believed that it was made by the defendant.

- Furthermore, again in the *Lego* case, Falconer J recognised that one way of commercialising one's goodwill is to license or franchise another trader to use one's trade mark and its attractive force (ie its goodwill) in another field of activity. The effect, therefore, of the defendant continuing to use LEGO in relation to their irrigation equipment was to negate the plaintiff's opportunity to commercialise its goodwill in the market for such equipment and this was held to damage that goodwill.
- Compare *Lego* with the *Stringfellows* case,[13] where the evidence did not support a finding that the defendant's sales of STRINGFELLOWS oven chips had deprived the plaintiff of an opportunity to merchandise his name in relation to other products (let alone oven chips), nor did the court accept that the plaintiff's nightclub would suffer a fall in membership or attendance.
- In the *Elderflower Champagne* case,[14] the Court of Appeal accepted as relevant damage the 'blurring or erosion of the uniqueness' that attaches to the mark CHAMPAGNE, and this was said to 'debase' the exclusive reputation of the Champagne houses.
- The *Elderflower Champagne* case, however, needs to be read in light of the decision in *Harrods*,[15] where Millett LJ accepts that the application of the plaintiff's trade mark to inferior goods is likely to injure the plaintiff's goodwill if customers assume the inferior goods to be those of the plaintiff, but he confesses to an 'intellectual difficulty' in accepting the concept that the law could recognise a head of damage (for the purposes of passing off) which does not depend on confusion. Millet LJ draws a distinction between mere damage to reputation and damage to goodwill; the former is not actionable because it does not involve deception, whereas the latter is actionable because damage to goodwill results from deception. In commercial terms, this means that Millet LJ would not accept as an actionable head of damage the effects of dilution caused by the

13 Supra.
14 *Taittinger SA v Allbev Ltd* [1993] FSR 641.
15 Supra.

mark CHAMPAGNE gradually becoming generic of any kind of sparkling wine.[16]

- On the other hand, Sir Michael Kerr, dissenting in the *Harrods* case, was far more liberal in identifying potential relevant damage for a passing off action. Relying on the *Elderflower Champagne* case, he thought that loss of distinctiveness and dilution were actionable and clearly he was seeking to prevent the defendant's from 'riding on the back' (ie appropriating the benefit) of the plaintiff's reputation.
- Consistent with Sir Michael Kerr, Laddie J in *Chocosuisse* takes the view that the plaintiff inevitably will suffer actionable damages if the exclusivity of the designation 'Swiss chocolate' is diminished. Quoting the Master of the Rolls in the *Elderflower Champagne* case, he describes the damage as 'insidious'.

It will be a fine line, which has yet to be drawn clearly by the courts, between:

(a) merely making use of another's goodwill (which Jacob J says quite clearly is not passing off);

(b) making use of another's goodwill in circumstances which may harm the reputation of the plaintiff, but which does not involve a misrepresentation or deception (which is not actionable, according to Millet LJ);

(c) making use of another's goodwill in circumstances where the defendant derives a benefit, ie cashes in on or appropriates for his benefit the reputation of the plaintiff (which is actionable, according to Sir Michael Kerr in *Harrods* and the Court of Appeal in *Elderflower Champagne*);

(d) making use of another's goodwill in circumstances where this dilutes the distinctiveness of the plaintiff's trade mark in the sense that the plaintiff's trade mark may become generic of the goods in relation to which it is used (which is actionable, according to Sir Michael Kerr in *Harrods*, the Court of Appeal in *Elderflower Champagne* and Laddie J in *Chocosuisse*, but not actionable, according to Millet LJ); and

(e) making use of another's goodwill in circumstances where this dilutes the reputation of the plaintiff's trade mark as being representative of high quality products, for example by using the

16 For further commentary on this issue, see Carty 'Passing Off at the Crossroads' [1996] 11 EIPR 629.

trade mark in relation to inferior quality goods (which appears to be actionable, according to each of the judges, because this form of dilution results in the plaintiff losing control over his own reputation and, consequently, the loss of sales of his goods).

Evidence

We have stated on numerous occasions that the outcome of many passing off cases will depend on the court's findings of fact which, in turn, depend on the quality of the evidence submitted to the court by the parties. The type of material, the information, the statistics and the way in which this evidence can be obtained will depend on the plaintiff's and the defendant's respective businesses, goods or services and the way in which the defendant is alleged to be making the relevant misrepresentation. Furthermore, different types of evidence will be required in establishing the three elements of the 'classical trinity' of passing off: goodwill, misrepresentation and damage. The following paragraphs examine in broad terms the type of evidence required in order to establish each of these elements and the ways in which that evidence might be obtained.

18.30 Evidence of reputation/goodwill The plaintiff needs to establish, in the first place, sufficient goodwill in the United Kingdom. The following evidence is therefore likely to be relevant:

1 The length of time that the plaintiff has been in business and, more specifically, the length of time that the plaintiff has sold or supplied the goods or services in question.
2 The turnover of the plaintiff's business and, in particular, the turnover in the goods or services in question.
3 The nature and extent of the plaintiff's activities in advertising/marketing his business, goods or services.
4 The independent individual and collective awareness and opinions of members of the relevant trade, business or profession.
5 The independent individual and collective awareness and opinions of members of the relevant sector of the public, ie the likely consumers/customers of the goods or services in question.

The purpose of this evidence is to establish, in the words of Jacob J in the *Roho* case,[17] that customers are 'moved to buy by source'. That is, the trade mark of the plaintiff's product must have acquired a sufficient goodwill (or 'attractive force') such that customers will want the goods of that particular brand rather than the goods of any brand. If consumers do not know of the trade mark or brand, or do not realise that it indicates the source of the goods or services in question, then the plaintiff will not have established a sufficient goodwill. In marketing terms, the plaintiff must establish 'brand loyalty', that is, that the customer wanted brand A but mistakenly bought brand B – it is not sufficient if the customer simply bought brand B not caring whether he was buying brand A or B.

18.31 Evidence of misrepresentation The second element of the 'classical trinity' will be established by showing that people are at least confused, if not deceived, by the defendant's conduct. That is, one proves a misrepresentation by submitting evidence of confusion or deception. Accordingly, the most relevant evidence will be:

(a) the independent individual and collective awareness and opinions of members of the relevant trade, business or profession; and
(b) the independent individual and collective awareness and opinions of members of the relevant sector of the public, ie the likely consumers/customers of the goods or services in question.

However, the ultimate decision is one for the judge. In *Spalding v Gamage*,[18] Lord Parker made it clear that the question whether the defendant's conduct amounts to a misrepresentation is 'a matter for the judge, who, looking at the documents and evidence before him, comes to his own conclusion'.

The exception, acknowledged by Lord Parker, is where the goods in question are of a kind not normally sold to the general public but in a specialised market. In such cases, evidence of persons accustomed to dealing in that specialised market as to the likelihood of deception or confusion will be essential:

- In the *Sodastream* case,[19] the judge was particularly welcoming of evidence from the relevant trade, saying that 'it is perfectly proper and admissible for someone in the trade to express

17 *Hodgkinson and Corby Ltd v Wards Mobility Services Ltd* [1995] FSR 169.
18 *A G Spalding & Bros v A W Gamage Ltd* (1915) 32 RPC 273.
19 *Sodastream Ltd v Thorn Cascade Co Ltd* [1982] RPC 459.

opinions about the likely reaction of others in relation to matters which are within his or her sphere of work'.

Furthermore, judges, despite the words of Lord Parker, will sometimes accept the evidence of the public in preference to or in substitution for their own subjective views:

- In the *Jif Lemon* case,[20] Lord Bridge in the House of Lords, although he felt surprised by the finding that a lemon-coloured, lemon-shaped container had become distinctive of the plaintiff's goods, agreed (reluctantly) that the trial judge was right as a matter of law to find in favour of the plaintiff.
- In the *Chocosuisse* case,[1] Laddie J confessed that he would not have taken the defendant's SWISS CHALET to be Swiss chocolate, but he was concerned not to allow his personal view to influence his decision for two reasons:
  (a) because he thought that it would not be right to assume automatically that his view would be shared even by a substantial minority of the public at large; and
  (b) especially, because he only came to hear of the defendant's product knowing that it was the subject of passing off proceedings, in which case it was therefore difficult to assess what his reaction might have been in a genuine point of sale situation.

This must be right, because the test is not whether any one individual is or is not confused or deceived (even if that individual is a judge); the test is whether a relevant section of the public is confused or deceived (or likely to be confused or deceived). The point is clearly made in:

- *Chocosuisse*,[2] where Laddie J found on the evidence that the majority of consumers would not be confused or deceived into thinking that the defendant's SWISS CHALET chocolate came from Switzerland. However, nonetheless, he was satisfied that 'a substantial number of the public' would be confused as to whether SWISS CHALET is Swiss chocolate or not. Accordingly, he held that the defendant's use of the trade mark SWISS CHALET did amount to passing off.

In contrast, the courts will reject the evidence of the now famous

20 *Reckitt & Coleman Products Ltd v Borden Inc* [1990] RPC 341.
1 *Chocosuisse Union des Fabricants Suisses de Chocolat v Cadbury Ltd* (1997) Times, 25 November (Laddie J).
2 Supra.

'moron in a hurry', that is, the member of the public who is confused or deceived simply because he does not pay reasonable attention to protect his own interests.[3]

Quia timet actions Many passing off cases are commenced before the defendant has begun trading or, at least, before he has undertaken the activities of which the plaintiff complains. In such cases, it is impossible to obtain evidence of actual confusion or deception, but this is not of itself a concern:

- In the *Sodastream* case,[4] Kerr LJ stated that, in interlocutory proceedings, it is not a justifiable criticism of the evidence to say that no evidence concerning the likelihood of confusion has been adduced from the general public, especially where the product with which the plaintiff alleges the likelihood of confusion is not yet on the market. Thus, evidence of the likely reactions of customers to the proposed activities of the defendant was admitted.
- In the *One in a Million* case,[5] Sumption QC issued a final injunction quia timet in the absence of proof of damage, on the basis that the defendant's conduct was calculated to infringe the plaintiff's rights.

Defendant in trade Where the defendant has already commenced selling or supplying the goods or services in question, then the lack of any evidence of actual confusion or deception may prove fatal to the plaintiff's case. This is because the courts are entitled to infer that, notwithstanding any apparent similarities of the defendant's goods or services with those of the plaintiffs, the relevant section of the public is nonetheless not confused or deceived, and therefore the similarities convey no misrepresentation. The inference will be drawn all the more readily where the parties have been trading for some time, for example:

- In *City Link v Lakin*,[6] the parties had been trading side by side for a number of years and, in that time, despite both using CITY LINK as part of their business name, the only evidence of confusion was a few misdirected cheques or invoices.
- In the *Fortnum & Mason* case,[7] Harman J thought that, in

3 *Star Industrial Co Ltd v Yap Kwee Kor* [1976] FSR 256.
4 Supra.
5 *Marks & Spencer plc v One in a Million*, supra.
6 *City Link Travel Holdings Ltd v Lakin* [1979] FSR 653.
7 *Fortnum & Mason plc v Fortnam Ltd* [1994] FSR 438.

March 1993, the fact that the defendant had been trading under the name FORTNAM since 1988 without anybody at any time bringing its existence to the notice of the plaintiff went 'some way' to supporting his conclusion that people were not likely to confuse the two businesses.

- In the *Harrods* case,[8] Millett LJ (with Beldam LJ concurring) thought that the lapse of time between the publication of the defendant's brochure and the trial was such that, had confusion really existed, the plaintiff would have been in a position to call evidence that some of its customers had at least asked for a brochure of the school, or enquired about whether the store supplied the school's uniforms or that its customers had otherwise 'manifested an impression that the school was connected with the store'.

Sometimes the plaintiff may have difficulty in getting members of the public to 'admit' to being confused or deceived because they may feel foolish. Instead, the plaintiff may be able to rely on the hallmarks of people being confused or deceived (which may be more persuasive than a witness testifying to being confused or deceived and certainly may be of greater probative value than surveys and questionnaires). For example:

(a) evidence of complaints or enquiries intended to be directed to or about the plaintiff, which have in fact been made to or about the defendant (or vice versa), such as in the *Neutrogena* case,[9] where Jacob J (affirmed on appeal by the Court of Appeal) accepted the likelihood of deception and confusion based on evidence of letters of complaint about NEUTROGENA which were sent to the Independent Television Commission concerning an advertisement on television which was in fact for the defendant's product NEUTRALIA; and

(b) likewise, evidence of misdirected orders, invoices, returned goods for refund, replacement or repair.

Furthermore, the circumstances may be such that it is inherently unlikely that the plaintiff will ever hear of the confusion or deception, even where it is widespread:

- In the *Andrex/Nouvelle* comparative advertising case,[10] Laddie J

8 *Harrods Ltd v Harrodian School Ltd* [1996] RPC 697.
9 *Neutrogena Corpn v Golden Ltd* [1996] RPC 473, CA.
10 *Kimberly-Clark Ltd v Fort Sterling Ltd* [1997] FSR 877 (Laddie J).

accepted that this was the case, because nappies are low cost items and the customers themselves may either never realise that they have been deceived or not complain even if they do realise.

18.32 Evidence of damage to goodwill The relevant evidence of damage or injury to goodwill will depend on the nature of the damage/injury alleged by the plaintiff. We have already seen that the defendant's misrepresentation may cause different types of damage/injury to the plaintiff, including:

(a) lost sales;

(b) loss of the opportunity to license/franchise/merchandise his goods or services to a third party in another field of activity; and

(c) loss of the exclusivity attached to the trade mark.

Many plaintiffs will consider seeking an injunction, which ideally prevents or, at least, brings the defendant's conduct to a halt, as the most relevant remedy. However, damages can be substantial and the court will order an inquiry as to damages, except only where it appears that the plaintiff has suffered no damage or only nominal damage.

At the inquiry, which will be conducted by a Master, the object is not so much to carry out a precise calculation based on a minute examination of the evidence, but to award a sum to the plaintiff which fairly compensates him for the damage/injury to his goodwill which, being intangible of its nature, can never be the subject of precise calculation. The general statement of principle is that the plaintiff is entitled to recover the damages which are the natural and direct consequence of the unlawful acts of the defendant including:

> '. . . any loss of trade actually suffered by the plaintiffs, either directly from the acts complained of, or properly attributable to injury to the plaintiff's reputation, business, goodwill and trade and business connection caused by the acts complained of; in other words, such damages as flow directly and in the usual course of things, from the wrongful acts, excluding any speculative and unproven damage.'[11]

Translating that general statement into a few specific examples reveals that, as always, each case depends on its own facts:

- Evidence of sales made by the defendant will be relevant and perhaps indicative of lost sales by the plaintiff. However, in

11 *A G Spalding & Bros v A W Gamage Ltd* (1918) 35 RPC 101, per Swinfen Eady LJ at 117.

some cases, not all sales by the defendant will result from the misrepresentation but from some other aspect of the goods or from some other specific requirement of the individual customer.[12]

- Actual evidence of the effects of dilution (loss of exclusivity and reputation) will always be difficult to obtain, and the Master will usually have to form an opinion based on:
  (a) the degree of the plaintiff's goodwill and his reputation in the marketplace; and
  (b) the quality (or level of inferiority) of the defendant's goods or services,

so as to assess to what extent the plaintiff's reputation has been depreciated or debased.

- In the recent *Chocosuisse* case,[13] Laddie J accepted as a general proposition, without the need for specific evidence on the subject (which was not argued by the defendant), that in the champagne-type cases, if there is likely to be confusion, then it must follow that the exclusivity of the designation 'Swiss chocolate' must suffer and that will damage the plaintiffs and those whom they represent. As the Master of the Rolls said in *Elderflower Champagne*, that damage must be 'insidious'.
- Likewise, actual evidence of the plaintiff's capacity himself to expand into or to license (franchise/merchandise) third parties in another market sector will be difficult to come by (let alone evidence of the actual damage caused by the defendant in limiting or negating that capacity). In *Lego*,[14] the court accepted that the capacity existed for the manufacturer of LEGO children's plastic building blocks to expand, either itself or by licensing third parties, to manufacture plastic irrigation equipment and sell it under the trade mark LEGO. The court accepted this proposition based on:
  (a) the overwhelming evidence of the strength (and hence

12 See for example *Dormeuil Frères v Feraglow Ltd* [1990] RPC 449, where Knox J refused to award damages on a royalty basis for each sale by the defendant.

13 *Chocosuisse Union des Fabricants Suisses de Chocolat v Cadbury Ltd* (1997) Times, 25 November (Laddie J).

14 *Lego System A/S v Lego M Lemelstritch Ltd* [1983] FSR 155. Falconer J in *Lego* relies in particular on the Australian case of *Henderson v Radio Corpn Pty Ltd* [1969] RPC 218 where the Supreme Court of New South Wales equated the appropriation of another's reputation as an injury no less than the appropriation of goods or money.

value) of the goodwill attaching to the mark LEGO such that it was a 'household word'; and

(b) the testimony of a marketing expert, in whose opinion the plaintiff had a clear opportunity for licensing or franchising the mark LEGO in other fields, particularly the 'plastics area' and garden implements would have been an 'ideal market'.

Conversely, in *Stringfellows*,[15] the court was not prepared to accept, in the absence of any evidence, that the owner of a nightclub had the capacity to expand into making oven chips, and therefore there was no misrepresentation and no damage to the plaintiff's business.

18.33 Obtaining evidence The plaintiff will be able to adduce evidence relating to his own business, but he may also need to obtain evidence from:

(a) the public in general, or from the relevant section of the public;
(b) members of the trade;
(c) the defendant, in relation to his business; and
(d) the opinions of experts.

Witness collection programmes The plaintiff should consider undertaking a witness collection programme whereby ordinary, independent members of the public are approached randomly and asked various relevant questions relating to the goods or services in question. These witness collection programmes can be used for a number of reasons:

(a) to obtain individual affidavits from those who are willing to participate; and/or
(b) as the basis of a survey which can then be the subject of expert opinion from the person responsible for the survey as to the likely or actual state of mind of the relevant section of the public as a whole; and/or
(c) as the basis of a survey which can then be used to establish or support a wider conclusion.

These programmes can therefore be useful in establishing either the reputation of the plaintiff and/or the likelihood of confusion or deception (for the purposes of proving a misrepresentation).

Having conducted the witness collection programme, however,

15 *Stringfellow v McCain Foods (GB) Ltd* [1984] RPC 501.

one should have regard to the observations of Jacob J in *Neutrogena*[16] to the effect that surveys or witness collection programmes of the type in which questionnaires are filled in and the results subjected to statistical analysis are unnecessarily elaborate. Further, pure questionnaire evidence he described as 'seldom helpful'. Instead, he thought that 'the best evidence is the oral evidence of those alleged to have been deceived or confused', that is, by such persons giving their evidence in chief by direct oral examination rather than simply confirming their witness statements.

Survey evidence There have been many cases in which 'survey evidence' has been obtained by the plaintiff (and by the defendant). In some cases, it has been admitted and relied upon, in others it has been wholly rejected as being either irrelevant or because of the way in which the survey was conducted. Whitford J has stated the requirements which, in his opinion, are necessary in order for survey evidence to be both admissible and of probative value:

(i) the survey must be done fairly and by a method such that a relevant cross-section of the public is interviewed;
(ii) it must be of a sufficient size to produce a statistically significant result;
(iii) where several surveys are carried out, full disclosure must be given to the other side of their number, the methodology and the numbers of persons involved;
(iv) the totality of all answers given to all surveys must be disclosed and made available to the other side;
(v) the questions should neither be leading, nor should they direct the interviewee into a field of speculation upon which he would never otherwise have embarked;
(vi) the exact answers must be recorded, not an abbreviation or digest;
(vii) the instructions given to those carrying out the interviews, and to those who subsequently code the answers if computer coding is used, must be disclosed.[17]

Survey evidence has been rejected (or at least given little weight) in certain cases for various reasons, including:

1 Because, ultimately, the issue as to the likelihood of confusion

16 *Neutrogena Corpn v Golden Ltd*, supra.
17 *Imperial Group v Philip Morris* [1984] RPC 293 at 302–3.

or deception is one for the courts to decide. Dillon LJ in *Mothercare*[18] was dismissive of surveys, saying that they were not helpful (but it should always be remembered that the question is not whether the judge is likely to be confused or deceived, but whether the judge is satisfied that a relevant section of the public would be confused or deceived).

2 Because of the methodology used to conduct the survey.[19]

3 Because the questions asked were not in surroundings similar to a point of sale; for example, in the *Polo* case[20] the plaintiff adduced evidence of customers' reactions on seeing the defendant's sweets contained loose in a plastic bag, whereas they were in fact to be sold wrapped in distinctive packaging with a different trade mark/brand name. Compare this with the *Chocosuisse* case,[1] where the plaintiff's solicitors set up a display stand which reproduced an actual in-store confectionary display.

4 Because the witness was asked to speculate about an issue which would not normally arise in his or her mind at point of sale; for example, the simple question 'What does this trade mark mean to you?' may be a leading question because the trade mark may not 'mean' anything until the person is asked to speculate. Again, in the *Chocosuisse* case,[2] the members of the public were never asked 'What does the trade mark SWISS CHALET mean to you?' Instead, they were asked to choose the cheapest Swiss chocolate from a wide selection of confectionary – the fact that certain people then chose the defendant's SWISS CHALET chocolate was accepted as evidence that that trade mark conveyed a misrepresentation that the product was Swiss chocolate.

Despite the mixed success of surveys, and the inevitable criticisms which will be made by each party against the other's survey, the use of survey evidence will continue to be an important part of

18 *Mothercare UK Ltd v Penguin Books Ltd* [1988] RPC 113; see also *Parker-Knoll Ltd v Knoll International Ltd* [1962] RPC 265, per Lord Hodson, and *Financial Times Ltd v Evening Standard Ltd* [1991] FSR 7, per Aldous J.

19 See *Nationwide Building Society v Nationwide Estate Agents* [1987] FSR 579 at 588.

20 *Nestlé (UK) Ltd v Trustin The Food Finders Ltd* (19 August 1996, unreported) (Walker J) (22 August 1996, unreported), CA.

1 *Chocosuisse Union des Fabricants Suisses de Chocolat v Cadbury Ltd* (1997) Times, 25 November (Laddie J).

2 Ibid.

(especially) the plaintiff's case and, in particular, in interlocutory proceedings. Perhaps this is because the plaintiff has the easier task of simply having to establish that only a significant/substantial number (but not necessarily all) of the public are likely to be confused or deceived (and, in interlocutory proceedings, that there is a serious issue to be tried in this regard):

- In the comparative advertising case of ANDREX nappies and NOUVELLE nappies,[3] Laddie J (as he was later to do in *Chocosuisse*) accepted that the plaintiff's survey evidence had qualitative value and, even though it did not prove that all interviewees would have been deceived had they seen the defendant's packaging, the evidence was consistent with a 'considerable number' of them being so deceived.
- In the *Pot Noodle* case,[4] even though Blackburne J thought that the affidavit evidence obtained from a survey of members of the public was open to criticism (in relation to the way in which it was obtained and the pro forma nature of the affidavits), such evidence could not be disregarded, and he held that there was therefore a serious issue to be tried.
- The Court of Appeal in *Neutrogena*,[5] although presented with evidence from numerous sources, including survey evidence, was not able to extrapolate from that evidence so as to arrive at any quantitative or qualitative measure of the confusion caused by the defendant's use of NEUTRALIA, but, nonetheless, Morritt LJ (with whom Kennedy and Ward LJJ agreed) was still able to conclude that the confusion was 'substantial' and that the effect on the goodwill of NEUTROGENA was 'real'.

The defendant has a much more difficult task because simply to bring along witnesses to say that they were not confused or deceived does not, of itself, overcome or negate the evidence of the plaintiff's witnesses to say that they were confused or deceived.

Expert opinion Expert evidence may be put forward for a number of reasons:

(a) as to the superiority/inferiority of the goods or services in question – which will be admissible;

(b) to prove the circumstances and the places in which the goods

3 *Kimberly-Clark Ltd v Fort Sterling Ltd* [1997] FSR 877 (Laddie J).
4 *Dalgety Spillers Foods Ltd v Food Brokers Ltd* [1994] FSR 504.
5 *Neutrogena Corpn v Golden Ltd* [1996] RPC 473.

are sold, the kind of persons who bought them, and the manner in which the public were accustomed to ask for those goods – which is always admissible (see, for example, the *Pot Noodle* case[6]);

(c) as the opinion of a marketing expert as to whether the relevant section of the public would be confused or deceived – which will be inadmissible where the experience of the judge as an ordinary shopper or consumer will enable him, just as well as any other, to assess the likelihood of confusion;[7] and

(d) as the opinion of a statistician, based on a market survey, as to what the survey 'proves' in terms of whether the statistics obtained can be extrapolated and used to come to a finding that a substantial number of the relevant section of the public are likely to be confused or deceived.

Trap orders As an alternative (or, of course, in addition) to a survey, the plaintiff may seek to obtain evidence by placing 'trap orders', that is, the plaintiff (or someone on his behalf) places a dummy order on the defendant for the plaintiff's goods in the expectation that the defendant will substitute his goods for those of the plaintiff. There are a number of general propositions which can be stated in relation to trap orders. They must be:

(a) clear and unambiguous;
(b) fair, in the sense of not calculated to induce the defendant to fall into the trap;
(c) carried out in circumstances analogous to the conditions under which a 'genuine' order would be placed, and such as to avoid the defendant simply making a bona fide mistake;[8] and
(d) once carried out, the defendant should be advised without delay.[9]

6 Supra.

7 See, for example, the *Pot Noodle* case, supra, where it was acknowledged that if the goods in question were for public consumption or domestic use, then evidence of persons accustomed to dealing in those goods as to the likelihood of deception or confusion *may be* admissible, whereas, if the goods were of a kind not normally sold to the general public, then evidence of persons accustomed to deal in the relevant specialist market *was* admissible.

8 See the warnings to this effect of Roxburgh J in *Procea Products Ltd v Evans & Sons Ltd* (1951) 68 RPC 210 at 211.

9 Harman J held a trap order to be unsatisfactory in *Cellular Clothing Co Ltd v G White & Co Ltd* (1952) 70 RPC 9 at 14, because no notice was given to the defendant.

Remedies

Passing off is a tort, and therefore the common law principles apply as they do to all other torts. In broad terms, the remedies available for passing off are the same as those which are available for the infringement of a registered trade mark (as to which, see Chapter 8). Thus, the remedies fall under the following headings:

(a) damages; or
(b) an account of profit;
(c) an injunction;
(d) delivery up; and
(e) a mandatory order requiring the defendant to change its name (including its corporate, business or domain name).

As stated, the principles set out in Chapter 8 are directly applicable, and therefore the comments which follow merely address the issues which are peculiar to passing off cases.

18.34 Damages The successful plaintiff may elect on receiving judgment after the trial either to have an enquiry as to his own damages or an account of the profits made by the defendant. The general principle in passing off cases for the award of damages is to compensate the plaintiff for the natural and direct consequences of the unlawful acts of the defendant. The specific heads of damage which are recoverable in a passing off action have already been discussed in paragraph 18.28 and 18.29 above because, unlike trade mark infringement, the type of damage caused to the plaintiff is an issue to be considered in the context of whether the cause of action for passing off has been established.

Innocent passing off It is also worth noting that Blackburne J has recently considered the position of an 'innocent' defendant. In the *Gillette* case,[10] his Lordship (after reviewing the cases) concluded that innocent passing off should be treated in the same way as innocent trade mark infringement and, therefore, damages are recoverable for innocent passing off.

18.35 Account of profits As with trade mark infringement, it is important to identify those profits made by the defendant which

10 *Gillette UK Ltd v Edenwest Ltd* [1994] RPC 279 at 291.

were actually attributable to the operative misrepresentation. In *My Kinda Town*,[11] Slade J refused to order the defendant to account to the plaintiff for all its profits. He stated that:

> 'it is necessary to ascertain how much of the profits made by the defendants over the relevant period are properly attributable to the use of the name Chicago Pizza Co. Clearly, profits made by the defendants by the sale of meals to customers who are *not* confused by this name are not attributable to this use'.

Obviously, this calculation cannot be carried out with scientific or mathematical precision, and therefore the Master will have to come to a reasonable apportionment based on the evidence at the trial.

Innocent passing off The innocence of the defendant does not affect the plaintiff's entitlement to damages (see paragraph 18.34 above) but, as an account of profits is an equitable remedy, the innocence of the defendant will be a matter relevant to the exercise of the judge's discretion as to whether he orders an account (this proposition was not doubted by Blackburne J in the *Gillette* case cited in paragraph 18.34 above). Thus, for obvious reasons, the plaintiff should elect to have an enquiry as to his damages rather than an account of the defendant's profits, if the judge finds that the defendant's passing off was innocent.

18.36 Injunctions An injunction is an equitable remedy, and therefore general equitable principles will apply. This can work both ways for the plaintiff:

(a) on the one hand, the terms of the injunction can be tailored to do that which is necessary to do justice in the particular circumstances of the case; but

(b) on the other hand, an injunction may not be awarded because of other acts of the plaintiff, such as his delay, acquiescence or unclean hands.

Interim injunctions The following issues are likely to be relevant when seeking an interim injunction in passing off cases (the list is not exhaustive – indeed, there is no such thing as an exhaustive list of such issues, because the facts of each case will usually put a different 'spin' on where the equities lie between the parties):

1 The fundamental principle which the courts are seeking to

11 *My Kinda Town v Soll and Grunts Investments* [1983] RPC 15.

achieve in granting or refusing to grant an interim injunction is to take whichever course of action appears to carry the lower risk of injustice if it should turn out to be 'wrong' (in the sense that, at the full trial, the decision goes the other way).[12] This usually involves comparing the detriment likely to be suffered by the plaintiff if the injunction is not granted as compared with the detriment likely to be suffered by the defendant if the injunction is granted.

2 The *American Cyanamid* principles[13] as developed in *Series 5*,[14] will apply.[15]

3 In *Antec International*,[16] Laddie J applied his own decision in *Series 5* (a confidential information case) to a passing off case, and stated that it was correct to assess the parties' respective prospects of success at the interlocutory stage and that this was 'particularly so' in a passing off case, where the strength of a party's case also affects the likelihood of damage, which is a factor to be taken into account in assessing the balance of convenience.

4 The adequacy of damages – an interim injunction will not usually be granted if the plaintiff can adequately be compensated for the injury to his goodwill by the defendant paying the plaintiff's damages.

5 The ability of the defendant to pay the plaintiff's damages – clearly, even if damages are considered to be an adequate remedy for the plaintiff, the defendant must be able to satisfy any subsequent award of damages.

6 The ability of the plaintiff to satisfy his undertaking as to damages (that is, the undertaking which must be given by the plaintiff before an interim injunction is awarded, in order to compensate the defendant for his damages if the plaintiff ultimately is unsuccessful at the full trial).

7 The desirability of maintaining the status quo existing immediately preceding the issue of the writ (or immediately preceding the motion, if there was unreasonable delay following the issue of the writ),[17] especially where the defendant has not

12 *Films Rover International Ltd v Cannon Film Sales Ltd* [1987] 1 WLR 670 at 680.
13 *American Cyanamid Co v Ethicon Ltd* [1975] AC 396.
14 *Series 5 Software Ltd v Philip Clarke* [1996] FSR 273.
15 As to which, see Chapter 8.
16 *Antec International Ltd v South Western Chicks (Warren) Ltd* [1997] FSR 278.
17 *Garden Cottage Foods Ltd v Milk Marketing Board* [1984] AC 130.

yet commenced trading – but this may be irrelevant if neither party has commenced significant trading activities, as was the case in *Barnsley Brewery*.[18]

8 Any delay by the plaintiff in bringing the proceedings which has resulted in the defendant incurring additional expenditure; for example, in the *Pot Noodles* case, the defendant had written to the plaintiff one year before the launch of its product in the United Kingdom, and the fact that the plaintiff chose to ignore the warning, and in the meantime the defendant had expended time, trouble and expense in launching its product, was a factor which 'weighed heavily' in Blackburne J refusing to grant an injunction.[19]

9 The unclean hands of the plaintiff, for example where the plaintiff himself has used the trade mark or name in a way which is deceptive. In the *Chocosuisse* case,[20] Laddie J considered this issue and concluded that a plaintiff should only fail in the action in those cases where the court concludes that, in all the circumstances of the case, it is unconscionable for him to be given the relief he would otherwise be entitled to.

10 The failure by the plaintiff to take all reasonable steps to police the use of his trade marks by third parties and, generally, to secure the continued exclusive connotation of the trade mark as a 'badge of origin.' Again, in *Chocosuisse*, Laddie J considered this issue and rejected it, saying that the exclusivity of the connotation is a question of fact, and if that exclusivity exists, then the plaintiff's contribution (positive or negative) is irrelevant. Conversely, the fact that the plaintiff has taken all reasonable steps to police the use of his trade mark does not help his case if, in fact, the exclusivity has been lost.

11 The fact that an interim injunction may, in practice, be decisive of the outcome of the case (in the sense that, if an interim injunction is granted, the defendant will often not bother to contest a final hearing) will be a factor when applying *American Cyanamid*, because the fact that it may be decisive will go to assessing the risk of injustice.[1]

18 *Barnsley Brewery Co Ltd v RBNB* [1997] FSR 462.
19 *Dalgety Spillers Foods Ltd v Food Brokers Ltd* [1994] FSR 504.
20 *Chocosuisse Union des Fabricants Suisses de Chocolat v Cadbury Ltd* (1997) Times, 25 November (Laddie J).
1 *Barnsley Brewery Co Ltd v RBNB* [1997] FSR 462.

18.37 Comment Lord Diplock in the House of Lords in *American Cyanamid* noted that it would be unwise to attempt even to list the various matters which may need to be taken into consideration in deciding where the balance of convenience lies, let alone to suggest the relative weight to be attached to these matters, as this will vary from case to case. This is undoubtedly a correct statement. A list derived from cases decided during the 1990s would alone take up many pages. This increases the difficulty for trade mark practitioners when advising their clients as to their prospects of success because the balance of convenience issue will need to be considered in almost every passing off case in which the plaintiff seeks an interim injunction, if only because there will normally be doubt as to the adequacy of damages. (Some cases have suggested that damages cannot be adequate simply because the loss or injury suffered by the plaintiff is, of its nature, not capable of precise arithmetical calculation.) Therefore, the consideration of the factors relevant to the balance of convenience is often the major task of the court in such cases.

Finally, the successful plaintiff who is awarded an interim injunction should also consider making an application for an immediate lump sum order for his costs to be paid by the defendant. For an example of a case where this was considered to be appropriate, see the *Direct Line* case (where the defendant chose to represent himself in court).[2]

Final injunction There is nothing to add to what is said in Chapter 8 in relation to the grant of a final injunction in trade mark infringement cases.

18.38 Delivery up A practical remedy for a plaintiff to consider is an order requiring the defendant to deliver up to the plaintiff, or to destroy, the offending goods. Such an order will only be made, however, if the goods cannot be rendered benign in passing off terms, that is, by the removal or obliteration of an offending trade mark, or by repackaging the goods, or otherwise through the use of disclaimers and the like.

18.39 Order to change name Another practical remedy for a plaintiff to consider is to seek a mandatory injunction requiring the

2 *Direct Line Group Ltd v Direct Line Estate Agency Ltd* [1997] FSR 374 at 377–9.

defendant to change its own corporate, business or Internet domain name. See for example:

- the *Glaxo* case;[3]
- the *Law Society* case;[4] and
- the *Harrods* and *One in a Million* domain name cases.[5]

In the *One in a Million* case, Sumption QC likened the order to an order for the delivery up of infringing goods.

Practical matters

18.40 Pre-emptive measures to consider Given the importance of the evidence in passing off cases, trade mark proprietors should strongly consider taking pre-emptive measures so that they are in the best position possible to submit the best evidence to the court in support of an application for an interim injunction. The following steps can assist in preparing for any future dispute (which may be won without the need to go to court):

- Keeping records of sales and turnover.
- Keeping records of advertising and marketing expenditure.
- Establishing a system to record incidents of actual confusion, such as enquiries, complaints, letters, invoices, phone calls etc being directed to the proprietor when they were intended for the other party.
- Subscribing to a trade mark watching service and, generally, maintaining market awareness, including by educating one's employees and agents as to the issues and importance of maintaining the exclusivity of one's trade marks.
- Policing the use by licensees of one's trade marks to ensure that quality control mechanisms are in place and enforced.
- Adhering to the best practice guidelines relating to the use of one's trade marks (as to which, see Chapter 5, paragraph 5.10 above).
- Keeping copies of letters of recommendation, gratitude or endorsement.
- Keeping copies of articles and other publications (in print or

3 *Glaxo plc v GlaxoWellcome Ltd* [1996] FSR 388.
4 *Law Society of England and Wales v Society of Lawyers* [1996] FSR 739.
5 *Harrods Ltd v UK Network Services Ltd*, Ch 1996 No 5453, unreported; *Marks & Spencer plc v One in a Million* C 1997 M No 5403, [1998] IPD 21016, (1997) Times, 2 December (Sumption QC).

other media) written or broadcast by independent third parties concerning one's business, goods or services.
- Ultimately, taking swift action, upon advice, against third parties who are considered to be passing off.

The quality of the information/evidence which a client can provide by adopting, as far as possible, these measures will be invaluable in enabling his legal adviser to form a considered view of his prospects of success and also maximising those prospects of success in any subsequent proceedings. Of course, certain additional information/ evidence will also be required which can only be obtained once the activities of the other party have commenced (or have been threatened), namely:

(a) evidence of actual confusion or deception (or evidence of the likelihood of confusion or deception); and
(b) the relevant facts relating to the other party itself, its business, goods or services, such as the length of time that they have been on the market and the other party's advertising and marketing expenditure etc,

all of which will also be relevant in assessing whether the elements of passing off can be established.

18.41 Other matters A potential plaintiff would also be well advised to seek professional advice because the possibility of seeking appropriate ex parte orders from the court should always be considered: eg an Anton Piller order and/or Mareva injunction may assist in protecting the plaintiff's position, which may otherwise be prejudiced.

Readers should also have regard to Chapter 9, relating to groundless threats of trade mark infringement proceedings, which may be relevant in so far as a threat of passing off proceedings, in conjunction with notifying the other party of the existence of a registered trade mark, may constitute such a groundless threat for the purposes of s 21 of the 1994 Act.

19 Trade libel

19.01 Introduction Trade libel is a common law cause of action which encompasses numerous tortious acts which are variously referred to as malicious falsehood, injurious falsehood, slander of title and slander of goods.

In general terms, the classic definition of trade libel is that formulated by Lord Davey:

> 'To support such an action it is necessary for the plaintiff to prove (1) that the statements complained of were untrue; (2) that they were made maliciously, that is to say, without just cause or excuse; (3) that the plaintiffs have suffered special damage thereby.'[1]

The third requirement of special damage has since been relaxed by the Defamation Act 1952 (as to which see paragraph 19.07), but the requirement remains that the statement must have been calculated to cause the plaintiff pecuniary damage.[2]

In the context of trade marks, trade libel may therefore be a relevant cause of action to consider in at least the following circumstances:

(1) acts which constitute reverse passing off;
(2) a groundless threat of trade mark infringement proceedings; and
(3) a comparative advertisement that does not come within the defence set out in s 10(6),

1 *Royal Baking Powder Co v Wright, Crossley & Co* (1900) 18 RPC 95 at 99.
2 *Vodafone Group plc v Orange Personal Communications Services Ltd* [1997] FSR 34.

provided that, in each case, the three ingredients identified by Lord Davey are present.

19.02 Malice Malice means some dishonest or improper motive of the defendant in making the misrepresentation. It has been said that a bona fide assertion, even if mistaken and even if made in one's own interest, is not malicious per se.[3] On the other hand, Stable J in the *Wilts Dairies* case[4] stated that a misrepresentation will be made maliciously in the following circumstances:

(a) where it is false in fact and published with the intention of injuring the plaintiff and notwithstanding that the defendant thought it to be true; and
(b) where it is false in fact and known by the defendant to be so and notwithstanding that the defendant did not intend to injure the plaintiff.

19.03 Comparison with passing off The torts of passing off and trade libel are each aimed at redressing the damaging effects of a misrepresentation by the defendant. However:

(a) in the case of passing off, the misrepresentation relates to the *defendant's* own business, goods or services (ie that they are those of, or connected in a relevant way with, the plaintiff); whereas
(b) in the case of trade libel, the misrepresentation relates to some aspect of the *plaintiff's* business, goods or services.

A trade libel may therefore be made by the direct use of the plaintiff's trade mark (eg the reference to the plaintiff's business, goods or services may be made by using the plaintiff's trade mark); alternatively, the plaintiff's trade mark may only be incidental or wholly absent.

19.04 Comparison with reverse passing off It appears that there are two distinct situations which are described as 'reverse' passing off, both involving misrepresentations in relation to the plaintiff's business, goods or services:

(a) where the defendant misrepresents the plaintiff's goods or services to be his own business, goods or services;[5] and

3 *Balden v Shorter* [1933] 1 Ch 427 at 430.
4 *Wilts United Dairy Ltd v Thomas Robinson Sons & Co Ltd* [1957] RPC 220.
5 *Bristol Conservatories Ltd v Conservatories Custom Built Ltd* [1989] RPC 455.

(b) where the defendant misrepresents the plaintiff's goods of a lower relative quality to be those of the plaintiff, but of a higher relative quality.[6]

The phrase 'passing off' is apt to describe both situations, and the adjective 'reverse' is also apt in that it distinguishes these two situations from so-called 'classic' passing off where the defendant misrepresents *his* business, goods or services to be those of, or connected in a relevant way with, the plaintiff. In truth, the first type of misrepresentation described in (a) above is usually the initial stage of a 'classic' passing off as the defendant, having misled the customer into believing that the plaintiff's goods are his goods, will then sell the customer his real goods having, in effect, misrepresented his real goods to be those of the plaintiff.

Each of these cases of reverse passing off may, however, also constitute trade libel if malice is proven, for example:

- In the *Wilts Dairies* case,[7] where the defendant held out the plaintiff's old stock of condensed milk as being the plaintiff's new stock and Stable J held that this was both reverse passing off and trade libel.

19.05 Comparative advertising: overlap with s 10(6) One area of business in which trade libel may arise is in the context of a comparative advertisement in which the defendant trumpets the virtues of his products in comparison with those of the plaintiff. Where the advertisement involves the use of the plaintiff's registered trade mark, then the defendant may also infringe the registration, unless the defence under s 10(6) (and possibly s 11(2)) is available. Readers should refer to Chapter 7, paragraph 7.08 which contains a summary of a number of cases, some of which considered trade libel in the context of a comparative advertisement.

19.06 Puffing There is a fine line between, on the one hand, merely puffing one's own goods or services at the expense of a competitor and, on the other hand, disparaging the competitor's goods or services.

In relation to the former, the courts have always been lenient, if only because judges expect the public to be sufficiently cynical and worldly

6 *AG Spalding & Bros v AW Gamage Ltd* (1915) 32 RPC 273.
7 Supra.

to ignore 'puffs' as mere hyperbole. However, the line between puffing and disparagement always turns on the circumstances of the case. For example:

- Aldous J (as he then was) indicated in the *Ciba-Geigy* case[8] that one should focus on the nature of the goods being advertised; in the case of a pharmaceutical product (for example) it would be more likely that the test would be applied strictly because one would expect representations in relation to such products to be absolutely truthful. Whereas, in the case of a benign domestic product, the courts would be likely to apply a different, lower standard.
- In *Vodafone v Orange*,[9] it was noted that, although the public expect a certain amount of hyperbole in advertising, the more precise and specific the claim, the more likely it was that the public would take it seriously: the more general or fuzzy, the less so.

19.07 Defamation Act 1952 Section 3(1) of the Defamation Act removes the need to prove 'special damage' for the purposes of trade libel if the statement in question:

(a) was calculated to cause pecuniary damage to the plaintiff and was published in writing or other permanent form; or

(b) was calculated to cause pecuniary damage to the plaintiff in respect of any office, profession, calling, trade or business held or carried on by him at the time of publication.

19.08 Freedom of speech The courts have always sought to protect the common law right of freedom of speech. This can be seen in the recent decisions under s 10(6) of the 1994 Act:

- In the *BT/AT & T* case,[10] Mr Crystal QC acknowledged that the right to free speech was no defence to infringement as such, but considered it to be a factor when assessing the balance of convenience in interlocutory proceedings.
- In *MacMillan Magazines*,[11] Neuberger J was unable to determine

8 *Ciba-Geigy plc v Parke Davis & Co Ltd* [1994] FSR 8.

9 *Vodafone Group plc v Orange Personal Communications Services Ltd* [1997] FSR 34.

10 *British Telecommunications plc v AT & T Communications (UK) Ltd* (18 December 1996, unreported) (Crystal QC): see [1997] 5 EIPR D-134.

11 *MacMillan Magazines Ltd v RCN Publishing Co Ltd* [1997] IPD 20089 (Neuberger J).

where the balance of convenience would lie and, in refusing to grant an injunction, fell back on the principle of allowing free speech.

The courts will strike a balance between the two conflicting principles, namely freedom of speech and the principle that one trader is not entitled to make false and malicious statements or other misrepresentations in relation to a competitor's business, goods or services.

19.09 One meaning rule In libel cases it appears well settled that the jury is required to identify 'the natural and ordinary meaning' of the words in question. The natural and ordinary meaning is that which the words 'would convey to the mind of the ordinary, reasonable, fair minded reader'. Of course, it is recognised that certain words may have more than one meaning but, in a libel case, the jury is required to base its verdict and any award of damages on the assumption that the 'natural and ordinary meaning' was the *one* sense in which *all* readers would have understood the words.[12] In *Vodafone*,[13] Jacob J admitted to being a 'comparative stranger' to libel law but commented that the 'one meaning rule' was 'strange, particularly for malicious falsehood'. By analogy with passing off, and distinguishing the special requirements of a jury trial, his Lordship thought that:

> 'it would be enough [for the purposes of malicious falsehood] to satisfy the criterion of falsity for the plaintiff to prove that the defendant made a statement which was false to a substantial number of people . . . even if not most of them.'

However, it was apparently common ground between the parties that the one meaning rule did apply, and therefore Jacob J's comments are strictly obiter (until next time, no doubt).

12 *Charleston v News Group Newspapers Ltd* [1995] 2 All ER 313, per Lord Bridge at 317.

13 *Vodafone Group plc v Orange Personal Communications Services Ltd* [1997] FSR 34.

Appendix

Index to appendix

The Trade Marks Act 1994

1994 CHAPTER 26

An Act to make new provision for registered trade marks, implementing Council Directive No 89/104/EEC of 21 December 1988 to approximate the laws of the Member States relating to trade marks; to make provision in connection with Council Regulation (EC) No 40/94 of 20 December 1993 on the Community trade mark; to give effect to the Madrid Protocol Relating to the International Registration of Marks of 27 June 1989, and to certain provisions of the Paris Convention for the Protection of Industrial Property of 20 March 1883, as revised and amended; and for connected purposes.

Annotations

Council Directive No 89/104/EEC: OJ No L40, 11.2.89, p 1.

Council Regulation (EC) No 40/94: OJ No L11, 14.1.94, p 1.

[21 July 1994]

BE IT ENACTED by the Queen's most Excellent Majesty, by and with the advice and consent of the Lords Spiritual and Temporal, and Commons, in this present Parliament assembled, and by the authority of the same, as follows: –

Part I
Registered Trade Marks

Introductory

1 Trade marks

(1) In this Act a 'trade mark' means any sign capable of being represented graphically which is capable of distinguishing goods or services of one undertaking from those of other undertakings.

A trade mark may, in particular, consist of words (including personal names), designs, letters, numerals or the shape of goods or their packaging.

(2) References in this Act to a trade mark include, unless the context otherwise requires, references to a collective mark (see section 49) or certification mark (see section 50).

Annotations

Date in force: 31 October 1994.

Commencement order: SI 1994 No 2550.

2 Registered trade marks

(1) A registered trade mark is a property right obtained by the registration of the trade mark under this Act and the proprietor of a registered

trade mark has the rights and remedies provided by this Act.

(2) No proceedings lie to prevent or recover damages for the infringement of an unregistered trade mark as such; but nothing in this Act affects the law relating to passing off.

Annotations

Date in force: 31 October 1994.

Commencement order: SI 1994 No 2550.

Grounds for refusal of registration

3 Absolute grounds for refusal of registration

(1) The following shall not be registered –

(a) signs which do not satisfy the requirements of section 1(1),

(b) trade marks which are devoid of any distinctive character,

(c) trade marks which consist exclusively of signs or indications which may serve, in trade, to designate the kind, quality, quantity, intended purpose, value, geographical origin, the time of production of goods or of rendering of services, or other characteristics of goods or services,

(d) trade marks which consist exclusively of signs or indications which have become customary in the current language or in the bona fide and established practices of the trade:

Provided that, a trade mark shall not be refused registration by virtue of paragraph (b), (c) or (d) above if, before the date of application for registration, it has in fact acquired a distinctive character as a result of the use made of it.

(2) A sign shall not be registered as a trade mark if it consists exclusively of –

(a) the shape which results from the nature of the goods themselves,

(b) the shape of goods which is necessary to obtain a technical result, or

(c) the shape which gives substantial value to the goods.

(3) A trade mark shall not be registered if it is –

(a) contrary to public policy or to accepted principles of morality, or

(b) of such a nature as to deceive the public (for instance as to the nature, quality or geographical origin of the goods or service).

(4) A trade mark shall not be registered if or to the extent that its use is prohibited in the United Kingdom by any enactment or rule of law or by any provision of Community law.

(5) A trade mark shall not be registered in the cases specified, or referred to, in section 4 (specially protected emblems).

(6) A trade mark shall not be registered if or to the extent that the application is made in bad faith.

Annotations

Date in force: 31 October 1994.

Commencement order: SI 1994 No 2550.

4 Specially protected emblems

(1) A trade mark which consists of or contains –
  (a) the Royal arms, or any of the principal armorial bearings of the Royal arms, or any insignia or device so nearly resembling the Royal arms or any such armorial bearing as to be likely to be mistaken for them or it,
  (b) a representation of the Royal crown or any of the Royal flags,
  (c) a representation of Her Majesty or any member of the Royal family, or any colourable imitation thereof, or
  (d) words, letters or devices likely to lead persons to think that the applicant either has or recently has had Royal patronage or authorisation,

shall not be registered unless it appears to the registrar that consent has been given by or on behalf of Her Majesty or, as the case may be, the relevant member of the Royal family.

(2) A trade mark which consists of or contains a representation of –
  (a) the national flag of the United Kingdom (commonly known as the Union Jack), or
  (b) the flag of England, Wales, Scotland, Northern Ireland or the Isle of Man,

shall not be registered if it appears to the registrar that the use of the trade mark would be misleading or grossly offensive.

Provision may be made by rules identifying the flags to which paragraph (b) applies.

(3) A trade mark shall not be registered in the cases specified in –
  section 57 (national emblems, etc of Convention countries), or
  section 58 (emblems, etc of certain international organisations).

(4) Provision may be made by rules prohibiting in such cases as may be prescribed the registration of a trade mark which consists of or contains –
  (a) arms to which a person is entitled by virtue of a grant of arms by the Crown, or
  (b) insignia so nearly resembling such arms as to be likely to be mistaken for them,

unless it appears to the registrar that consent has been given by or on behalf of that person.

Where such a mark is registered, nothing in this Act shall be construed as authorising its use in any way contrary to the laws of arms.

(5) A trade mark which consists of or contains a controlled representation within the meaning of the Olympic Symbol etc (Protection) Act 1995 shall not be registered unless it appears to the registrar
  (a) that the application is made by the person for the time being appointed under section 1(2) of the Olympic Symbol etc (Protection) Act 1995 (power of Secretary of State to appoint a person as the proprietor of the Olympics association right), or

(b) that consent has been given by or on behalf of the person mentioned in paragraph (a) above.

Annotations

Date in force: 20 September 1995 (sub-s (5)); 31 October 1994 (sub-ss (1)(3), sub-s (4) certain purposes); 29 September 1994 (sub-s (4), remaining purposes).

Commencement order: SI 1994 No 2550.

Sub-s (5): added, in relation to applications for registration made on or after 20 September 1995, by the Olympic Symbol etc (Protection) Act 1995, s 13(2), (3).

5 Relative grounds for refusal of registration

(1) A trade mark shall not be registered if it is identical with an earlier trade mark and the goods or services for which the trade mark is applied for are identical with the goods or services for which the earlier trade mark is protected.

(2) A trade mark shall not be registered if because –

(a) it is identical with an earlier trade mark and is to be registered for goods or services similar to those for which the earlier trade mark is protected, or

(b) it is similar to an earlier trade mark and is to be registered for goods or services identical with or similar to those for which the earlier trade mark is protected,

there exists a likelihood of confusion on the part of the public, which includes the likelihood of association with the earlier trade mark.

(3) A trade mark which –

(a) is identical with or similar to an earlier trade mark, and

(b) is to be registered for goods or services which are not similar to those for which the earlier trade mark is protected,

shall not be registered if, or to the extent that, the earlier trade mark has a reputation in the United Kingdom (or, in the case of a Community trade mark, in the European Community) and the use of the later mark without due cause would take unfair advantage of, or be detrimental to, the distinctive character or the repute of the earlier trade mark.

(4) A trade mark shall not be registered if, or to the extent that, its use in the United Kingdom is liable to be prevented –

(a) by virtue of any rule of law (in particular, the law of passing off) protecting an unregistered trade mark or other sign used in the course of trade, or

(b) by virtue of an earlier right other than those referred to in subsections (1) to (3) or paragraph (a) above, in particular by virtue of the law of copyright, design right or registered designs.

A person thus entitled to prevent the use of a trade mark is referred to in this Act as the proprietor of an 'earlier right' in relation to the trade mark.

(5) Nothing in this section prevents the registration of a trade mark where the proprietor of the earlier trade mark or other earlier right consents to the registration.

Annotations

Date in force: 31 October 1994.

Commencement order: SI 1994 No 2550.

6 Meaning of 'earlier trade mark'

(1) In this Act an 'earlier trade mark' means –
   (a) a registered trade mark, international trade mark (UK) or Community trade mark which has a date of application for registration earlier than that of the trade mark in question, taking account (where appropriate) of the priorities claimed in respect of the trade marks,
   (b) a Community trade mark which has a valid claim to seniority from an earlier registered trade mark or international trade mark (UK), or
   (c) a trade mark which, at the date of application for registration of the trade mark in question or (where appropriate) of the priority claimed in respect of the application, was entitled to protection under the Paris Convention as a well known trade mark.

(2) References in this Act to an earlier trade mark include a trade mark in respect of which an application for registration has been made and which, if registered, would be an earlier trade mark by virtue of subsection 1(a) or (b), subject to its being so registered.

(3) A trade mark within subsection (1)(a) or (b) whose registration expires shall continue to be taken into account in determining the registrability of a later mark for a period of one year after the expiry unless the registrar is satisfied that there was no bona fide use of the mark during the two years immediately preceding the expiry.

Annotations

Date in force: 31 October 1994.

Commencement order: SI 1994 No 2550.

7 Raising of relative grounds in case of honest concurrent use

(1) This section applies where on an application for the registration of a trade mark it appears to the registrar –
   (a) that there is an earlier trade mark in relation to which the conditions set out in section 5(1), (2) or (3) obtain, or
   (b) that there is an earlier right in relation to which the condition set out in section 5(4) is satisfied,

   but the applicant shows to the satisfaction of the registrar that there has been honest concurrent use of the trade mark for which registration is sought.

(2) In that case the registrar shall not refuse the application by reason of the earlier trade mark or other earlier right unless objection on that ground is raised in opposition proceedings by the proprietor of that earlier trade mark or other earlier right.

(3) For the purposes of this section 'honest concurrent use' means such use in

the United Kingdom, by the applicant or with his consent, as would formerly have amounted to honest concurrent use for the purposes of section 12(2) of the Trade Marks Act 1938.

(4) Nothing in this section affects –
(a) the refusal of registration on the grounds mentioned in section 3 (absolute grounds for refusal), or
(b) the making of an application for a declaration of invalidity under section 47(2) (application on relative grounds where no consent to registration).

(5) This section does not apply when there is an order in force under section 8 below.

Annotations

Date in force: 31 October 1994.

Commencement order: SI 1994 No 2550.

8 Power to require that relative grounds be raised in opposition proceedings

(1) The Secretary of State may by order provide that in any case a trade mark shall not be refused registration on a ground mentioned in section 5 (relative grounds for refusal) unless objection on that ground is raised in opposition proceedings by the proprietor of the earlier trade mark or other earlier right.

(2) The order may make such consequential provision as appears to the Secretary of State appropriate –
(a) with respect to the carrying out by the registrar of searches of earlier trade marks, and
(b) as to the persons by whom an application for a declaration of invalidity may be made on the grounds specified in section 47(2) (relative grounds).

(3) An order making such provision as is mentioned in subsection (2)(a) may direct that so much of section 37 (examination of application) as requires a search to be carried out shall cease to have effect.

(4) An order making such provision as is mentioned in subsection (2)(b) may provide that so much of section 47(3) as provides that any person may make an application for a declaration of invalidity shall have effect subject to the provisions of the order.

(5) An order under this section shall be made by statutory instrument, and no order shall be made unless a draft of it has been laid before and approved by a resolution of each House of Parliament.

No such draft of an order making such provision as is mentioned in subsection (1) shall be laid before Parliament until after the end of the period of ten years beginning with the day on which applications for Community trade marks may first be filed in pursuance of the Community Trade Mark Regulation.

(6) An order under this section may contain such transitional provisions as appear to the Secretary of State to be appropriate.

Annotations

Date in force: 31 October 1994.

Commencement order: SI 1994 No 2550.

Effects of registered trade mark

9 Rights conferred by registered trade mark

(1) The proprietor of a registered trade mark has exclusive rights in the trade mark which are infringed by use of the trade mark in the United Kingdom without his consent.

The acts amounting to infringement, if done without the consent of the proprietor, are specified in section 10.

(2) References in this Act to the infringement of a registered trade mark are to any such infringement of the rights of the proprietor.

(3) The rights of the proprietor have effect from the date of registration (which in accordance with section 40(3) is the date of filing of the application for registration):

Provided that –

(a) no infringement proceedings may be begun before the date on which the trade mark is in fact registered; and

(b) no offence under section 92 (unauthorised use of trade mark, etc in relation to goods) is committed by anything done before the date of publication of the registration.

Annotations

Date in force: 31 October 1994.

Commencement order: SI 1994 No 2550.

10 Infringement of registered trade mark

(1) A person infringes a registered trade mark if he uses in the course of trade a sign which is identical with the trade mark in relation to goods or services which are identical with those for which it is registered.

(2) A person infringes a registered trade mark if he uses in the course of trade a sign where because –

(a) the sign is identical with the trade mark and is used in relation to goods or services similar to those for which the trade mark is registered, or

(b) the sign is similar to the trade mark and is used in relation to goods or services identical with or similar to those for which the trade mark is registered,

there exists a likelihood of confusion on the part of the public, which includes the likelihood of association with the trade mark.

(3) A person infringes a registered trade mark if he uses in the course of trade a sign which –

(a) is identical with or similar to the trade mark, and

(b) is used in relation to goods or services which are not similar to those for which the trade mark is registered,

where the trade mark has a reputation in the United Kingdom and the use of the sign, being without due cause, takes unfair advantage of, or is detrimental to, the distinctive character or the repute of the trade mark.

(4) For the purposes of this section a person uses a sign if, in particular, he –
   (a) affixes it to goods or the packaging thereof;
   (b) offers or exposes goods for sale, puts them on the market or stocks them for those purposes under the sign, or offers or supplies services under the sign;
   (c) imports or exports goods under the sign; or
   (d) uses the sign on business papers or in advertising.

(5) A person who applies a registered trade mark to material intended to be used for labelling or packaging goods, as a business paper, or for advertising goods or services, shall be treated as a party to any use of the material which infringes the registered trade mark if when he applied the mark he knew or had reason to believe that the application of the mark was not duly authorised by the proprietor or a licensee.

(6) Nothing in the preceding provisions of this section shall be construed as preventing the use of a registered trade mark by any person for the purpose of identifying goods or services as those of the proprietor or a licensee.

But any such use otherwise than in accordance with honest practices in industrial or commercial matters shall be treated as infringing the registered trade mark if the use without due cause takes unfair advantage of, or is detrimental to, the distinctive character or repute of the trade mark.

Annotations

Date in force: 31 October 1994.

Commencement order: SI 1994 No 2550.

11 Limits on effect of registered trade mark

(1) A registered trade mark is not infringed by the use of another registered trade mark in relation to goods or services for which the latter is registered (but see section 47(6) (effect of declaration of invalidity of registration)).

(2) A registered trade mark is not infringed by –
   (a) the use by a person of his own name or address,
   (b) the use of indications concerning the kind, quality, quantity, intended purpose, value, geographical origin, the time of production of goods or of rendering of services, or other characteristics of goods or services, or
   (c) the use of the trade mark where it is necessary to indicate the intended purpose of a product or service (in particular, as accessories or spare parts),

provided the use is in accordance with honest practices in industrial or commercial matters.

(3) A registered trade mark is not infringed by the use in the course of trade in a particular locality of an earlier right which applies only in that locality.

For this purpose an 'earlier right' means an unregistered trade mark or other sign continuously used in relation to goods or services by a person or a predecessor in title of his from a date prior to whichever is the earlier of –

(a) the use of the first-mentioned trade mark in relation to those goods or services by the proprietor or a predecessor in title of his, or

(b) the registration of the first-mentioned trade mark in respect of those goods or services in the name of the proprietor or a predecessor in title of his;

and an earlier right shall be regarded as applying in a locality if, or to the extent that, its use in that locality is protected by virtue of any rule of law (in particular, the law of passing off).

Annotations

Date in force: 31 October 1994.

Commencement order: SI 1994 No 2550.

12 Exhaustion of rights conferred by registered trade mark

(1) A registered trade mark is not infringed by the use of the trade mark in relation to goods which have been put on the market in the European Economic Area under that trade mark by the proprietor or with his consent.

(2) Subsection (1) does not apply where there exist legitimate reasons for the proprietor to oppose further dealings in the goods (in particular, where the condition of the goods has been changed or impaired after they have been put on the market).

Annotations

Date in force: 31 October 1994.

Commencement order: SI 1994 No 2550.

13 Registration subject to disclaimer or limitation

(1) An applicant for registration of a trade mark, or the proprietor of a registered trade mark, may –

(a) disclaim any right to the exclusive use of any specified element of the trade mark, or

(b) agree that the rights conferred by the registration shall be subject to a specified territorial or other limitation;

and where the registration of a trade mark is subject to a disclaimer or limitation, the rights conferred by section 9 (rights conferred by registered trade mark) are restricted accordingly.

(2) Provision shall be made by rules as to the publication and entry in the register of a disclaimer or limitation.

Annotations
Date in force: 31 October 1994 (sub-s (1), sub-s (2) certain purposes); 29 September 1994 (sub-s (2), remaining purposes).
Commencement order: SI 1994 No 2550.

Infringement proceedings

14 Action for infringement

(1) An infringement of a registered trade mark is actionable by the proprietor of the trade mark.
(2) In an action for infringement all such relief by way of damages, injunctions, accounts or otherwise is available to him as is available in respect of the infringement of any other property right.

Annotations
Date in force: 31 October 1994.
Commencement order: SI 1994 No 2550.

15 Order for erasure, etc of offending sign

(1) Where a person is found to have infringed a registered trade mark, the court may make an order requiring him –
   (a) to cause the offending sign to be erased, removed or obliterated from any infringing goods, material or articles in his possession, custody or control, or
   (b) if it is not reasonably practicable for the offending sign to be erased, removed or obliterated, to secure the destruction of the infringing goods, material or articles in question.
(2) If an order under subsection (1) is not complied with, or it appears to the court likely that such an order would not be complied with, the court may order that the infringing goods, material or articles be delivered to such person as the court may direct for erasure, removal or obliteration of the sign, or for destruction, as the case may be.

Annotations
Date in force: 31 October 1994.
Commencement order: SI 1994 No 2550.

16 Order for delivery up of infringing goods, material or articles

(1) The proprietor of a registered trade mark may apply to the court for an order for the delivery up to him, or such other person as the court may direct, of any infringing goods, material or articles which a person has in his possession, custody or control in the course of a business.
(2) An application shall not be made after the end of the period specified in section 18 (period after which remedy of delivery up not available);

and no order shall be made unless the court also makes, or it appears to the court that there are grounds for making, an order under section 19 (order as to disposal of infringing goods, etc).

(3) A person to whom any infringing goods, material or articles are delivered up in pursuance of an order under this section shall, if an order under section 19 is not made, retain them pending the making of an order, or the decision not to make an order, under that section.

(4) Nothing in this section affects any other power of the court.

Annotations

Date in force: 31 October 1994.

Commencement order: SI 1994 No 2550.

17 Meaning of 'infringing goods, material or articles'

(1) In this Act the expressions 'infringing goods', 'infringing material' and 'infringing articles' shall be construed as follows.

(2) Goods are 'infringing goods', in relation to a registered trade mark, if they or their packaging bear a sign identical or similar to that mark and –

- (a) the application of the sign to the goods or their packaging was an infringement of the registered trade mark, or
- (b) the goods are proposed to be imported into the United Kingdom and the application of the sign in the United Kingdom to them or their packaging would be an infringement of the registered trade mark, or
- (c) the sign has otherwise been used in relation to the goods in such a way as to infringe the registered trade mark.

(3) Nothing in subsection (2) shall be construed as affecting the importation of goods which may lawfully be imported into the United Kingdom by virtue of an enforceable Community right.

(4) Material is 'infringing material', in relation to a registered trade mark, if it bears a sign identical or similar to that mark and either –

- (a) it is used for labelling or packaging goods, as a business paper, or for advertising goods or services, in such a way as to infringe the registered trade mark, or
- (b) it is intended to be so used and such use would infringe the registered trade mark.

(5) 'Infringing articles', in relation to a registered trade mark, means articles –

- (a) which are specifically designed or adapted for making copies of a sign identical or similar to that mark, and
- (b) which a person has in his possession, custody or control, knowing or having reason to believe that they have been or are to be used to produce infringing goods or material.

Annotations

Date in force: 31 October 1994.

Commencement order: SI 1994 No 2550.

18 Period after which remedy of delivery up not available

(1) An application for an order under section 16 (order for delivery up of infringing goods, material or articles) may not be made after the end of the period of six years from –
(a) in the case of infringing goods, the date on which the trade mark was applied to the goods or their packaging,
(b) in the case of infringing material, the date on which the trade mark was applied to the material, or
(c) in the case of infringing articles, the date on which they were made,
except as mentioned in the following provisions.

(2) If during the whole or part of that period the proprietor of the registered trade mark –
(a) is under a disability, or
(b) is prevented by fraud or concealment from discovering the facts entitling him to apply for an order,
an application may be made at any time before the end of the period of six years from the date on which he ceased to be under a disability or, as the case may be, could with reasonable diligence have discovered those facts.

(3) In subsection (2) 'disability' –
(a) in England and Wales, has the same meaning as in the Limitation Act 1980;
(b) in Scotland, means legal disability within the meaning of the Prescription and Limitation (Scotland) Act 1973;
(c) in Northern Ireland, has the same meaning as in the Limitation (Northern Ireland) Order 1989.

Annotations

Date in force: 31 October 1994.
Commencement order: SI 1994 No 2550.

19 Order as to disposal of infringing goods, material or articles

(1) Where infringing goods, material or articles have been delivered up in pursuance of an order under section 16, an application may be made to the court –
(a) for an order that they be destroyed or forfeited to such person as the court may think fit, or
(b) for a decision that no such order should be made.

(2) In considering what order (if any) should be made, the court shall consider whether other remedies available in an action for infringement of the registered trade mark would be adequate to compensate the proprietor and any licensee and protect their interests.

(3) Provision shall be made by rules of court as to the service of notice on persons having an interest in the goods, material or articles, and any such person is entitled –
(a) to appear in proceedings for an order under this section, whether or not he was served with notice, and

(b) to appeal against any order made, whether or not he appeared;
and an order shall not take effect until the end of the period within which notice of an appeal may be given or, if before the end of that period notice of appeal is duly given, until the final determination or abandonment of the proceedings on the appeal.

(4) Where there is more than one person interested in the goods, material or articles, the court shall make such order as it thinks just.

(5) If the court decides that no order should be made under this section, the person in whose possession, custody or control the goods, material or articles were before being delivered up is entitled to their return.

(6) References in this section to a person having an interest in goods, material or articles include any person in whose favour an order could be made under this section or under section 114, 204 or 231 of the Copyright, Designs and Patents Act 1988 (which make similar provision in relation to infringement of copyright, rights in performances and design right).

Annotations

Date in force: 31 October 1994.

Commencement order: SI 1994 No 2550.

20 Jurisdiction of sheriff court or county court in Northern Ireland

Proceedings for an order under section 16 (order for delivery up of infringing goods, material or articles) or section 19 (order as to disposal of infringing goods, etc) may be brought –

(a) in the sheriff court in Scotland, or

(b) in a county court in Northern Ireland.

This does not affect the jurisdiction of the Court of Session or the High Court in Northern Ireland.

Annotations

Date in force: 31 October 1994.

Commencement order: SI 1994 No 2550.

21 Remedy for groundless threats of infringement proceedings

(1) Where a person threatens another with proceedings for infringement of a registered trade mark other than –

  (a) the application of the mark to goods or their packaging,

  (b) the importation of goods to which, or to the packaging of which, the mark has been applied, or

  (c) the supply of services under the mark,

any person aggrieved may bring proceedings for relief under this section.

(2) The relief which may be applied for is any of the following –

  (a) a declaration that the threats are unjustifiable,

  (b) an injunction against the continuance of the threats,

  (c) damages in respect of any loss he has sustained by the threats;

and the plaintiff is entitled to such relief unless the defendant shows that the acts in respect of which proceedings were threatened constitute (or if done would constitute) an infringement of the registered trade mark concerned.

(3) If that is shown by the defendant, the plaintiff is nevertheless entitled to relief if he shows that the registration of the trade mark is invalid or liable to be revoked in a relevant respect.

(4) The mere notification that a trade mark is registered, or that an application for registration has been made, does not constitute a threat of proceedings for the purposes of this section.

Annotations

Date in force: 31 October 1994.

Commencement order: SI 1994 No 2550.

Registered trade mark as object of property

22 Nature of registered trade mark

A registered trade mark is personal property (in Scotland, incorporeal moveable property).

Annotations

Date in force: 31 October 1994.

Commencement order: SI 1994 No 2550.

23 Co-ownership of registered trade mark

(1) Where a registered trade mark is granted to two or more persons jointly, each of them is entitled, subject to any agreement to the contrary, to an equal undivided share in the registered trade mark.

(2) The following provisions apply where two or more persons are co-proprietors of a registered trade mark, by virtue of subsection (1) or otherwise.

(3) Subject to any agreement to the contrary, each co-proprietor is entitled, by himself or his agents, to do for his own benefit and without the consent of or the need to account to the other or others, any act which would otherwise amount to an infringement of the registered trade mark.

(4) One co-proprietor may not without the consent of the other or others –

(a) grant a licence to use the registered trade mark, or

(b) assign or charge his share in the registered trade mark (or, in Scotland, cause or permit security to be granted over it).

(5) Infringement proceedings may be brought by any co-proprietor, but he may not, without the leave of the court, proceed with the action unless the other, or each of the others, is either joined as a plaintiff or added as a defendant.

A co-proprietor who is thus added as a defendant shall not be made liable for any costs in the action unless he takes part in the proceedings.

Nothing in this subsection affects the granting of interlocutory relief on the application of a single co-proprietor.

(6) Nothing in this section affects the mutual rights and obligations of trustees or personal representatives, or their rights and obligations as such.

Annotations

Date in force: 31 October 1994.

Commencement order: SI 1994 No 2550.

24 Assignment, etc of registered trade mark

(1) A registered trade mark is transmissible by assignment, testamentary disposition or operation of law in the same way as other personal or moveable property.

It is so transmissible either in connection with the goodwill of a business or independently.

(2) An assignment or other transmission of a registered trade mark may be partial, that is, limited so as to apply –
   (a) in relation to some but not all of the goods or services for which the trade mark is registered, or
   (b) in relation to use of the trade mark in a particular manner or a particular locality.

(3) An assignment of a registered trade mark, or an assent relating to a registered trade mark, is not effective unless it is in writing signed by or on behalf of the assignor or, as the case may be, a personal representative.

Except in Scotland, this requirement may be satisfied in a case where the assignor or personal representative is a body corporate by the affixing of its seal.

(4) The above provisions apply to assignment by way of security as in relation to any other assignment.

(5) A registered trade mark may be the subject of a charge (in Scotland, security) in the same way as other personal or moveable property.

(6) Nothing in this Act shall be construed as affecting the assignment or other transmission of an unregistered trade mark as part of the goodwill of a business.

Annotations

Date in force: 31 October 1994.

Commencement order: SI 1994 No 2550.

25 Registration of transactions affecting registered trade mark

(1) On application being made to the registrar by –
   (a) a person claiming to be entitled to an interest in or under a registered trade mark by virtue of a registrable transaction, or
   (b) any other person claiming to be affected by such a transaction,

the prescribed particulars of the transaction shall be entered in the register.

(2) The following are registrable transactions –
(a) an assignment of a registered trade mark or any right in it;
(b) the grant of a licence under a registered trade mark;
(c) the granting of any security interest (whether fixed or floating) over a registered trade mark or any right in or under it;
(d) the making by personal representatives of an assent in relation to a registered trade mark or any right in or under it;
(e) an order of a court or other competent authority transferring a registered trade mark or any right in or under it.

(3) Until an application has been made for registration of the prescribed particulars of a registrable transaction –
(a) the transaction is ineffective as against a person acquiring a conflicting interest in or under the registered trade mark in ignorance of it, and
(b) a person claiming to be a licensee by virtue of the transaction does not have the protection of section 30 or 31 (rights and remedies of licensee in relation to infringement).

(4) Where a person becomes the proprietor or a licensee of a registered trade mark by virtue of a registrable transaction, then unless –
(a) an application for registration of the prescribed particulars of the transaction is made before the end of the period of six months beginning with its date, or
(b) the court is satisfied that it was not practicable for such an application to be made before the end of that period and that an application was made as soon as practicable thereafter,

he is not entitled to damages or an account of profits in respect of any infringement of the registered trade mark occurring after the date of the transaction and before the prescribed particulars of the transaction are registered.

(5) Provision may be made by rules as to –
(a) the amendment of registered particulars relating to a licence so as to reflect any alteration of the terms of the licence, and
(b) the removal of such particulars from the register –
(i) where it appears from the registered particulars that the licence was granted for a fixed period and that period has expired, or
(ii) where no such period is indicated and, after such period as may be prescribed, the registrar has notified the parties of his intention to remove the particulars from the register.

(6) Provision may also be made by rules as to the amendment or removal from the register of particulars relating to a security interest on the application of, or with the consent of, the person entitled to the benefit of that interest.

Annotations

Date in force: 31 October 1994 (sub-ss (1), (5), (6) certain purposes, sub-ss (2)–(4)); 29 September 1994 (sub-ss (1), (5), (6), remaining purposes).

Commencement order: SI 1994 No 2550.

26 Trusts and equities

(1) No notice of any trust (express, implied or constructive) shall be entered in the register; and the registrar shall not be affected by any such notice.

(2) Subject to the provisions of this Act, equities (in Scotland, rights) in respect of a registered trade mark may be enforced in like manner as in respect of other personal or moveable property.

Annotations

Date in force: 31 October 1994.

Commencement order: SI 1994 No 2550.

27 Application for registration of trade mark as an object of property

(1) The provisions of sections 22 to 26 (which relate to a registered trade mark as an object of property) apply, with the necessary modifications, in relation to an application for the registration of a trade mark as in relation to a registered trade mark.

(2) In section 23 (co-ownership of registered trade mark) as it applies in relation to an application for registration, the reference in subsection (1) to the granting of the registration shall be construed as a reference to the making of the application.

(3) In section 25 (registration of transactions affecting registered trade marks) as it applies in relation to a transaction affecting an application for the registration of a trade mark, the references to the entry of particulars in the register, and to the making of an application to register particulars, shall be construed as references to the giving of notice to the registrar of those particulars.

Annotations

Date in force: 31 October 1994.

Commencement order: SI 1994 No 2550.

Licensing

28 Licensing of registered trade mark

(1) A licence to use a registered trade mark may be general or limited.

A limited licence may, in particular, apply –

(a) in relation to some but not all of the goods or services for which the trade mark is registered, or

(b) in relation to use of the trade mark in a particular manner or a particular locality.

(2) A licence is not effective unless it is in writing signed by or on behalf of the grantor.

Except in Scotland, this requirement may be satisfied in a case where the grantor is a body corporate by the affixing of its seal.

(3) Unless the licence provides otherwise, it is binding on a successor in title to the grantor's interest.
References in this Act to doing anything with, or without, the consent of the proprietor of a registered trade mark shall be construed accordingly.
(4) Where the licence so provides, a sub-licence may be granted by the licensee; and references in this Act to a licence or licensee include a sub-licence or sub-licensee.

Annotations
Date in force: 31 October 1994.
Commencement order: SI 1994 No 2550.

29 Exclusive licensees

(1) In this Act an 'exclusive licence' means a licence (whether general or limited) authorising the licensee to the exclusion of all other persons, including the person granting the licence, to use a registered trade mark in the manner authorised by the licence.
The expression 'exclusive licensee' shall be construed accordingly.
(2) An exclusive licensee has the same rights against a successor in title who is bound by the licence as he has against the person granting the licence.

Annotations
Date in force: 31 October 1994.
Commencement order: SI 1994 No 2550.

30 General provisions as to rights of licensees in case of infringement

(1) This section has effect with respect to the rights of a licensee in relation to infringement of a registered trade mark.
The provisions of this section do not apply where or to the extent that, by virtue of section 31(1) below (exclusive licensee having rights and remedies of assignee), the licensee has a right to bring proceedings in his own name.
(2) A licensee is entitled, unless his licence, or any licence through which his interest is derived, provides otherwise, to call on the proprietor of the registered trade mark to take infringement proceedings in respect of any matter which affects his interests.
(3) If the proprietor –
(a) refuses to do so, or
(b) fails to do so within two months after being called upon,
the licensee may bring the proceedings in his own name as if he were the proprietor.
(4) Where infringement proceedings are brought by a licensee by virtue of this section, the licensee may not, without the leave of the court, proceed with the action unless the proprietor is either joined as a plaintiff or added as a defendant.

This does not affect the granting of interlocutory relief on an application by a licensee alone.

(5) A proprietor who is added as a defendant as mentioned in subsection (4) shall not be made liable for any costs in the action unless he takes part in the proceedings.

(6) In infringement proceedings brought by the proprietor of a registered trade mark any loss suffered or likely to be suffered by licensees shall be taken into account; and the court may give such directions as it thinks fit as to the extent to which the plaintiff is to hold the proceeds of any pecuniary remedy on behalf of licensees.

(7) The provisions of this section apply in relation to an exclusive licensee if or to the extent that he has, by virtue of section 31(1), the rights and remedies of an assignee as if he were the proprietor of the registered trade mark.

Annotations

Date in force: 31 October 1994.

Commencement order: SI 1994 No 2550.

31 Exclusive licensee having rights and remedies of assignee

(1) An exclusive licence may provide that the licensee shall have, to such extent as may be provided by the licence, the same rights and remedies in respect of matters occurring after the grant of the licence as if the licence had been an assignment.

Where or to the extent that such provision is made, the licensee is entitled, subject to the provisions of the licence and to the following provisions of this section, to bring infringement proceedings, against any person other than the proprietor, in his own name.

(2) Any such rights and remedies of an exclusive licensee are concurrent with those of the proprietor of the registered trade mark; and references to the proprietor of a registered trade mark in the provisions of this Act relating to infringement shall be construed accordingly.

(3) In an action brought by an exclusive licensee by virtue of this section a defendant may avail himself of any defence which would have been available to him if the action had been brought by the proprietor of the registered trade mark.

(4) Where proceedings for infringement of a registered trade mark brought by the proprietor or an exclusive licensee relate wholly or partly to an infringement in respect of which they have concurrent rights of action, the proprietor or, as the case may be, the exclusive licensee may not, without the leave of the court, proceed with the action unless the other is either joined as a plaintiff or added as a defendant.

This does not affect the granting of interlocutory relief on an application by a proprietor or exclusive licensee alone.

(5) A person who is added as a defendant as mentioned in subsection (4) shall not be made liable for any costs in the action unless he takes part in the proceedings.

(6) Where an action for infringement of a registered trade mark is brought which relates wholly or partly to an infringement in respect of which the proprietor and an exclusive licensee have or had concurrent rights of action –
   (a) the court shall in assessing damages take into account –
      (i) the terms of the licence, and
      (ii) any pecuniary remedy already awarded or available to either of them in respect of the infringement;
   (b) no account of profits shall be directed if an award of damages has been made, or an account of profits has been directed, in favour of the other of them in respect of the infringement; and
   (c) the court shall if an account of profits is directed apportion the profits between them as the court considers just, subject to any agreement between them.

The provisions of this subsection apply whether or not the proprietor and the exclusive licensee are both parties to the action; and if they are not both parties the court may give such directions as it thinks fit as to the extent to which the party to the proceedings is to hold the proceeds of any pecuniary remedy on behalf of the other.

(7) The proprietor of a registered trade mark shall notify any exclusive licensee who has a concurrent right of action before applying for an order under section 16 (order for delivery up); and the court may on the application of the licensee make such order under that section as it thinks fit having regard to the terms of the licence.

(8) The provisions of subsections (4) to (7) above have effect subject to any agreement to the contrary between the exclusive licensee and the proprietor.

Annotations
Date in force: 31 October 1994.
Commencement order: SI 1994 No 2550.

Application for registered trade mark

32 Application for registration

(1) An application for registration of a trade mark shall be made to the registrar.

(2) The application shall contain –
   (a) a request for registration of a trade mark,
   (b) the name and address of the applicant,
   (c) a statement of the goods or services in relation to which it is sought to register the trade mark, and
   (d) a representation of the trade mark.

(3) The application shall state that the trade mark is being used, by the applicant or with his consent, in relation to those goods or services, or that he has a *bona fide* intention that it should be so used.

(4) The application shall be subject to the payment of the application fee and such class fees as may be appropriate.

Annotations

Date in force: 31 October 1994.

Commencement order: SI 1994 No 2550.

33 Date of filing

(1) The date of filing of an application for registration of a trade mark is the date on which documents containing everything required by section 32(2) are furnished to the registrar by the applicant.

If the documents are furnished on different days, the date of filing is the last of those days.

(2) References in this Act to the date of application for registration are to the date of filing of the application.

Annotations

Date in force: 31 October 1994.

Commencement order: SI 1994 No 2550.

34 Classification of trade marks

(1) Goods and services shall be classified for the purposes of the registration of trade marks according to a prescribed system of classification.

(2) Any question arising as to the class within which any goods or services fall shall be determined by the registrar, whose decision shall be final.

Annotations

Date in force: 31 October 1994 (sub-s (1) certain purposes, sub-s (2)); 29 September 1994 (sub-s (1), remaining purposes).

Commencement order: SI 1994 No 2550.

Priority

35 Claim to priority of Convention application

(1) A person who has duly filed an application for protection of a trade mark in a Convention country (a 'Convention application'), or his successor in title, has a right to priority, for the purposes of registering the same trade mark under this Act for some or all of the same goods or services, for a period of six months from the date of filing of the first such application.

(2) If the application for registration under this Act is made within that six-month period –

(a) the relevant date for the purposes of establishing which rights take precedence shall be the date of filing of the first Convention application, and

(b) the registrability of the trade mark shall not be affected by any use of the mark in the United Kingdom in the period between that date and the date of the application under this Act.

(3) Any filing which in a Convention country is equivalent to a regular national filing, under its domestic legislation or an international agreement, shall be treated as giving rise to the right of priority.

A 'regular national filing' means a filing which is adequate to establish the date on which the application was filed in that country, whatever may be the subsequent fate of the application.

(4) A subsequent application concerning the same subject as the first Convention application, filed in the same Convention country, shall be considered the first Convention application (of which the filing date is the starting date of the period of priority), if at the time of the subsequent application –

(a) the previous application has been withdrawn, abandoned or refused, without having been laid open to public inspection and without leaving any rights outstanding, and

(b) it has not yet served as a basis for claiming a right of priority.

The previous application may not thereafter serve as a basis for claiming a right of priority.

(5) Provision may be made by rules as to the manner of claiming a right to priority on the basis of a Convention application.

(6) A right to priority arising as a result of a Convention application may be assigned or otherwise transmitted, either with the application or independently.

The reference in subsection (1) to the applicant's successor in title shall be construed accordingly.

Annotations

Date in force: 31 October 1994 (sub-ss (1)–(4), (6), sub-s (5) certain purposes); 29 September 1994 (sub-s (5), remaining purposes).

Commencement order: SI 1994 No 2550.

36 Claim to priority from other relevant overseas application

(1) Her Majesty may by Order in Council make provision for conferring on a person who has duly filed an application for protection of a trade mark in –

(a) any of the Channel Islands or a colony, or

(b) a country or territory in relation to which Her Majesty's Government in the United Kingdom have entered into a treaty, convention, arrangement or engagement for the reciprocal protection of trade marks,

a right to priority, for the purpose of registering the same trade mark under this Act for some or all of the same goods or services, for a specified period from the date of filing of that application.

(2) An Order in Council under this section may make provision corresponding to that made by section 35 in relation to Convention countries or such other provision as appears to Her Majesty to be appropriate.

(3) A statutory instrument containing an Order in Council under this

section shall be subject to annulment in pursuance of a resolution of either House of Parliament.

Annotations

Date in force: 31 October 1994.

Commencement order: SI 1994 No 2550.

Registration procedure

37 Examination of application

(1) The registrar shall examine whether an application for registration of a trade mark satisfies the requirements of this Act (including any requirements imposed by rules).

(2) For that purpose he shall carry out a search, to such extent as he considers necessary, of earlier trade marks.

(3) If it appears to the registrar that the requirements for registration are not met, he shall inform the applicant and give him an opportunity, within such period as the registrar may specify, to make representations or to amend the application.

(4) If the applicant fails to satisfy the registrar that those requirements are met, or to amend the application so as to meet them, or fails to respond before the end of the specified period, the registrar shall refuse to accept the application.

(5) If it appears to the registrar that the requirements for registration are met, he shall accept the application.

Annotations

Date in force: 31 October 1994.

Commencement order: SI 1994 No 2550.

38 Publication, opposition proceedings and observations

(1) When an application for registration has been accepted, the registrar shall cause the application to be published in the prescribed manner.

(2) Any person may, within the prescribed time from the date of the publication of the application, give notice to the registrar of opposition to the registration.

The notice shall be given in writing in the prescribed manner, and shall include a statement of the grounds of opposition.

(3) Where an application has been published, any person may, at any time before the registration of the trade mark, make observations in writing to the registrar as to whether the trade mark should be registered; and the registrar shall inform the applicant of any such observations.

A person who makes observations does not thereby become a party to the proceedings on the application.

Annotations

Date in force: 31 October 1994 (sub-ss (1), (2) certain purposes, sub-s (3)); 29 September 1994 (sub-ss (1), (2), remaining purposes).

Commencement order: SI 1994 No 2550.

39 Withdrawal, restriction or amendment of application

(1) The applicant may at any time withdraw his application or restrict the goods or services covered by the application.

If the application has been published, the withdrawal or restriction shall also be published.

(2) In other respects, an application may be amended, at the request of the applicant, only by correcting –

(a) the name or address of the applicant,

(b) errors of wording or of copying, or

(c) obvious mistakes,

and then only where the correction does not substantially affect the identity of the trade mark or extend the goods or services covered by the application.

(3) Provision shall be made by rules for the publication of any amendment which affects the representation of the trade mark, or the goods or services covered by the application, and for the making of objections by any person claiming to be affected by it.

Annotations

Date in force: 31 October 1994 (sub-ss (1), (2), sub-s (3) certain purposes); 29 September 1994 (sub-s (3), remaining purposes).

Commencement order: SI 1994 No 2550.

40 Registration

(1) Where an application has been accepted and –

(a) no notice of opposition is given within the period referred to in section 38(2), or

(b) all opposition proceedings are withdrawn or decided in favour of the applicant,

the registrar shall register the trade mark, unless it appears to him having regard to matters coming to his notice since he accepted the application that it was accepted in error.

(2) A trade mark shall not be registered unless any fee prescribed for the registration is paid within the prescribed period.

If the fee is not paid within that period, the application shall be deemed to be withdrawn.

(3) A trade mark when registered shall be registered as of the date of filing of the application for registration; and that date shall be deemed for the purposes of this Act to be the date of registration.

(4) On the registration of a trade mark the registrar shall publish the registration in the prescribed manner and issue to the applicant a certificate of registration.

Annotations

Date in force: 31 October 1994 (sub-ss (1)–(3), sub-s (4) certain purposes); 29 September 1994 (sub-s (4), remaining purposes).

Commencement order: SI 1994 No 2550.

41 Registration: supplementary provisions

(1) Provision may be made by rules as to –
  (a) the division of an application for the registration of a trade mark into several applications;
  (b) the merging of separate applications or registrations;
  (c) the registration of a series of trade marks.

(2) A series of trade marks means a number of trade marks which resemble each other as to their material particulars and differ only as to matters of a non-distinctive character not substantially affecting the identity of the trade mark.

(3) Rules under this section may include provision as to –
  (a) the circumstances in which, and conditions subject to which, division, merger or registration of a series is permitted, and
  (b) the purposes for which an application to which the rules apply is to be treated as a single application and those for which it is to be treated as a number of separate applications.

Annotations

Date in force: 31 October 1994 (sub-ss (1), (3) certain purposes, sub-s (2)); 29 September 1994 (sub-ss (1), (3) remaining purposes).

Commencement order: SI 1994 No 2550.

Duration, renewal and alteration of registered trade mark

42 Duration of registration

(1) A trade mark shall be registered for a period of ten years from the date of registration.

(2) Registration may be renewed in accordance with section 43 for further periods of ten years.

Annotations

Date in force: 31 October 1994.

Commencement order: SI 1994 No 2550.

43 Renewal of registration

(1) The registration of a trade mark may be renewed at the request of the proprietor, subject to payment of a renewal fee.

(2) Provision shall be made by rules for the registrar to inform the proprietor of a registered trade mark, before the expiry of the registration, of the date of expiry and the manner in which the registration may be renewed.

(3) A request for renewal must be made, and the renewal fee paid, before the expiry of the registration.

Failing this, the request may be made and the fee paid within such further period (of not less than six months) as may be prescribed, in which case an additional renewal fee must also be paid within that period.

(4) Renewal shall take effect from the expiry of the previous registration.

(5) If the registration is not renewed in accordance with the above provisions, the registrar shall remove the trade mark from the register.

Provision may be made by rules for the restoration of the registration of a trade mark which has been removed from the register, subject to such conditions (if any) as may be prescribed.

(6) The renewal or restoration of the registration of a trade mark shall be published in the prescribed manner.

Annotations

Date in force: 31 October 1994 (sub-ss (1), (4), sub-ss (2), (3), (5), (6) certain purposes); 29 September 1994 (sub-ss (2), (3), (5), (6), remaining purposes).

Commencement order: SI 1994 No 2550.

44 Alteration of registered trade mark

(1) A registered trade mark shall not be altered in the register, during the period of registration or on renewal.

(2) Nevertheless, the registrar may, at the request of the proprietor, allow the alteration of a registered trade mark where the mark includes the proprietor's name or address and the alteration is limited to alteration of that name or address and does not substantially affect the identity of the mark.

(3) Provision shall be made by rules for the publication of any such alteration and the making of objections by any person claiming to be affected by it.

Annotations

Date in force: 31 October 1994 (sub-ss (1), (2), sub-s (3) certain purposes); 29 September 1994 (sub-s (3), remaining purposes).

Commencement order: SI 1994 No 2550.

Surrender, revocation and invalidity

45 Surrender of registered trade mark

(1) A registered trade mark may be surrendered by the proprietor in respect of some or all of the goods or services for which it is registered.

(2) Provision may be made by rules –

(a) as to the manner and effect of a surrender, and

(b) for protecting the interests of other persons having a right in the registered trade mark.

Annotations

Date in force: 31 October 1994 (sub-s (1), sub-s (2) certain purposes); 29 September 1994 (sub-s (2), remaining purposes).

Commencement order: SI 1994 No 2550.

46 Revocation of registration

(1) The registration of a trade mark may be revoked on any of the following grounds –

(a) that within the period of five years following the date of completion of the registration procedure it has not been put to genuine use in the United Kingdom, by the proprietor or with his consent, in relation to the goods or services for which it is registered, and there are no proper reasons for non-use;

(b) that such use has been suspended for an uninterrupted period of five years, and there are no proper reasons for non-use;

(c) that, in consequence of acts or inactivity of the proprietor, it has become the common name in the trade for a product or service for which it is registered;

(d) that in consequence of the use made of it by the proprietor or with his consent in relation to the goods or services for which it is registered, it is liable to mislead the public, particularly as to the nature, quality or geographical origin of those goods or services.

(2) For the purposes of subsection (1) use of a trade mark includes use in a form differing in elements which do not alter the distinctive character of the mark in the form in which it was registered, and use in the United Kingdom includes affixing the trade mark to goods or to the packaging of goods in the United Kingdom solely for export purposes.

(3) The registration of a trade mark shall not be revoked on the ground mentioned in subsection (1)(a) or (b) if such use as is referred to in that paragraph is commenced or resumed after the expiry of the five year period and before the application for revocation is made:

Provided that, any such commencement or resumption of use after the expiry of the five year period but within the period of three months before the making of the application shall be disregarded unless preparations for the commencement or resumption began before the proprietor became aware that the application might be made.

(4) An application for revocation may be made by any person, and may be made either to the registrar or to the court, except that –

(a) if proceedings concerning the trade mark in question are pending in the court, the application must be made to the court; and

(b) if in any other case the application is made to the registrar, he may at any stage of the proceedings refer the application to the court.

(5) Where grounds for revocation exist in respect of only some of the goods or services for which the trade mark is registered, revocation shall relate to those goods or services only.

(6) Where the registration of a trade mark is revoked to any extent, the rights of the proprietor shall be deemed to have ceased to that extent as from –

(a) the date of the application for revocation, or

(b) if the registrar or court is satisfied that the grounds for revocation existed at an earlier date, that date.

Annotations

Date in force: 31 October 1994.

Commencement order: SI 1994 No 2550.

47 Grounds for invalidity of registration

(1) The registration of a trade mark may be declared invalid on the ground that the trade mark was registered in breach of section 3 or any of the provisions referred to in that section (absolute grounds for refusal of registration).

Where the trade mark was registered in breach of subsection (1)(b), (c) or (d) of that section, it shall not be declared invalid if, in consequence of the use which has been made of it, it has after registration acquired a distinctive character in relation to the goods or services for which it is registered.

(2) The registration of a trade mark may be declared invalid on the ground –

(a) that there is an earlier trade mark in relation to which the conditions set out in section 5(1), (2) or (3) obtain, or

(b) that there is an earlier right in relation to which the condition set out in section 5(4) is satisfied,

unless the proprietor of that earlier trade mark or other earlier right has consented to the registration.

(3) An application for a declaration of invalidity may be made by any person, and may be made either to the registrar or to the court, except that –

(a) if proceedings concerning the trade mark in question are pending in the court, the application must be made to the court; and

(b) if in any other case the application is made to the registrar, he may at any stage of the proceedings refer the application to the court.

(4) In the case of bad faith in the registration of a trade mark, the registrar himself may apply to the court for a declaration of the invalidity of the registration.

(5) Where the grounds of invalidity exist in respect of only some of the goods or services for which the trade mark is registered, the trade mark shall be declared invalid as regards those goods or services only.

(6) Where the registration of a trade mark is declared invalid to any extent, the registration shall to that extent be deemed never to have been made:

Provided that this shall not affect transactions past and closed.

Annotations

Date in force: 31 October 1994.

Commencement order: SI 1994 No 2550.

48 Effect of acquiescence

(1) Where the proprietor of an earlier trade mark or other earlier right has acquiesced for a continuous period of five years in the use of a registered trade mark in the United Kingdom, being aware of that use, there shall cease to be any entitlement on the basis of that earlier trade mark or other right –

(a) to apply for a declaration that the registration of the later trade mark is invalid, or

(b) to oppose the use of the later trade mark in relation to the goods or services in relation to which it has been so used,

unless the registration of the later trade mark was applied for in bad faith.

(2) Where subsection (1) applies, the proprietor of the later trade mark is not entitled to oppose the use of the earlier trade mark or, as the case may be, the exploitation of the earlier right, notwithstanding that the earlier trade mark or right may no longer be invoked against his later trade mark.

Annotations

Date in force: 31 October 1994.

Commencement order: SI 1994 No 2550.

Collective marks

49 Collective marks

(1) A collective mark is a mark distinguishing the goods or services of members of the association which is the proprietor of the mark from those of other undertakings.

(2) The provisions of this Act apply to collective marks subject to the provisions of Schedule 1.

Annotations

Date in force: 31 October 1994 (sub-s (1), sub-s (2) certain purposes); 29 September 1994 (sub-s (2), remaining purposes).

Commencement order: SI 1994 No 2550.

Certification marks

50 Certification marks

(1) A certification mark is a mark indicating that the goods or services in connection with which it is used are certified by the proprietor of the mark in respect of origin, material, mode of manufacture of goods or performance of services, quality, accuracy or other characteristics.

(2) The provisions of this Act apply to certification marks subject to the provisions of Schedule 2.

Annotations

Date in force: 31 October 1994 (sub-s (1), sub-s (2) certain purposes); 29 September 1994 (sub-s (2), remaining purposes).

Commencement order: SI 1994 No 2550.

Part II
Community Trade Marks and International Matters

Community trade marks

51 Meaning of 'Community trade mark'

In this Act –

'Community trade mark' has the meaning given by Article 1(1) of the Community Trade Mark Regulation; and

'the Community Trade Mark Regulation' means Council Regulation (EC) No 40/94 of 20 December 1993 on the Community trade mark.

Annotations

Date in force: 31 October 1994.

Commencement order: SI 1994 No 2550.

Council Regulation (EC) No 40/94: OJ No L11, 14.1.94, p 1.

52 Power to make provision in connection with Community Trade Mark Regulation

(1) The Secretary of State may by regulations make such provision as he considers appropriate in connection with the operation of the Community Trade Mark Regulation.

(2) Provision may, in particular, be made with respect to –

(a) the making of applications for Community trade marks by way of the Patent Office;

(b) the procedures for determining *a posteriori* the invalidity, or liability to revocation, of the registration of a trade mark from which a Community trade mark claims seniority;

(c) the conversion of a Community trade mark, or an application for a Community trade mark, into an application for registration under this Act;

(d) the designation of courts in the United Kingdom having jurisdiction over proceedings arising out of the Community Trade Mark Regulation.

(3) Without prejudice to the generality of subsection (1), provision may be made by regulations under this section –

(a) applying in relation to a Community trade mark the provisions of –

(i) section 21 (remedy for groundless threats of infringement proceedings);

(ii) sections 89 to 91 (importation of infringing goods, material or articles); and

(iii) sections 92, 93, 95 and 96 (offences); and

(b) making in relation to the list of professional representatives maintained in pursuance of Article 89 of the Community Trade Mark Regulation, and persons on that list, provision corresponding to that made by, or capable of being made under, sections 84 to 88 in relation to the register of trade mark agents and registered trade mark agents.

(4) Regulations under this section shall be made by statutory instrument which shall be subject to annulment in pursuance of a resolution of either House of Parliament.

Annotations

Date in force: 31 October 1994.

Commencement order: SI 1994 No 2550.

The Madrid Protocol

International registration

53 The Madrid Protocol

In this Act –

'the Madrid Protocol' means the Protocol relating to the Madrid Agreement concerning the International Registration of Marks, adopted at Madrid on 27 June 1989;

'the International Bureau' has the meaning given by Article 2(1) of that Protocol; and

'international trade mark (UK)' means a trade mark which is entitled to protection in the United Kingdom under that Protocol.

Annotations

Date in force: 31 October 1994.

Commencement order: SI 1994 No 2550.

54 Power to make provision giving effect to Madrid Protocol

(1) The Secretary of State may by order make such provision as he thinks fit for giving effect in the United Kingdom to the provisions of the Madrid Protocol.

(2) Provision may, in particular, be made with respect to –

(a) the making of applications for international registrations by way of the Patent Office as office of origin;

(b) the procedures to be followed where the basic United Kingdom application or registration fails or ceases to be in force;

(c) the procedures to be followed where the Patent Office receives from the International Bureau a request for extension of protection to the United Kingdom;

(d) the effects of a successful request for extension of protection to the United Kingdom;

(e) the transformation of an application for an international registration, or an international registration, into a national application for registration;

(f) the communication of information to the International Bureau;

(g) the payment of fees and amounts prescribed in respect of applications for international registrations, extensions of protection and renewals.

(3) Without prejudice to the generality of subsection (1), provision may be made by regulations under this section applying in relation to an international trade mark (UK) the provisions of –

(a) section 21 (remedy for groundless threats of infringement proceedings);

(b) sections 89 to 91 (importation of infringing goods, material or articles); and

(c) sections 92, 93, 95 and 96 (offences).

(4) An order under this section shall be made by statutory instrument which shall be subject to annulment in pursuance of a resolution of either House of Parliament.

Annotations

Date in force: 31 October 1994.
Commencement order: SI 1994 No 2550.

The Paris Convention

Supplementary provisions

55 The Paris Convention

(1) In this Act –

(a) 'the Paris Convention' means the Paris Convention for the Protection of Industrial Property of 20 March 1883, as revised or amended from time to time, and

(b) a 'Convention country' means a country, other than the United Kingdom, which is a party to that Convention.

(2) The Secretary of State may by order make such amendments of this Act, and rules made under this Act, as appear to him appropriate in consequence of any revision or amendment of the Paris Convention after the passing of this Act.

(3) Any such order shall be made by statutory instrument which shall be subject to annulment in pursuance of a resolution of either House of Parliament.

Annotations

Date in force: 31 October 1994.
Commencement order: SI 1994 No 2550.

56 Protection of well-known trade marks: Article 6*bis*

(1) References in this Act to a trade mark which is entitled to protection under the Paris Convention as a well-known trade mark are to a mark which is well known in the United Kingdom as being the mark of a person who –

(a) is a national of a Convention country, or

(b) is domiciled in, or has a real and effective industrial or commercial establishment in, a Convention country,

whether or not that person carries on business, or has any goodwill, in the United Kingdom.

References to the proprietor of such a mark shall be construed accordingly.

(2) The proprietor of a trade mark which is entitled to protection under the Paris Convention as a well-known trade mark is entitled to restrain by injunction the use in the United Kingdom of a trade mark which, or the essential part of which, is identical or similar to his mark, in relation to identical or similar goods or services, where the use is likely to cause confusion.

This right is subject to section 48 (effect of acquiescence by proprietor of earlier trade mark).

(3) Nothing in subsection (2) affects the continuation of any *bona fide* use of a trade mark begun before the commencement of this section.

Annotations

Date in force: 31 October 1994.

Commencement order: SI 1994 No 2550.

57 National emblems, etc of Convention countries: Article 6*ter*

(1) A trade mark which consists of or contains the flag of a Convention country shall not be registered without the authorisation of the competent authorities of that country, unless it appears to the registrar that use of the flag in the manner proposed is permitted without such authorisation.

(2) A trade mark which consists of or contains the armorial bearings or any other state emblem of a Convention country which is protected under the Paris Convention shall not be registered without the authorisation of the competent authorities of that country.

(3) A trade mark which consists of or contains an official sign or hallmark adopted by a Convention country and indicating control and warranty shall not, where the sign or hallmark is protected under the Paris Convention, be registered in relation to goods or services of the same, or a similar kind, as those in relation to which it indicates control and warranty, without the authorisation of the competent authorities of the country concerned.

(4) The provisions of this section as to national flags and other state emblems, and official signs or hallmarks, apply equally to anything which from a heraldic point of view imitates any such flag or other emblem, or sign or hallmark.

(5) Nothing in this section prevents the registration of a trade mark on the application of a national of a country who is authorised to make use of a state emblem, or official sign or hallmark, of that country, notwithstanding that it is similar to that of another country.

(6) Where by virtue of this section the authorisation of the competent authorities of a Convention country is or would be required for the registration of a trade mark, those authorities are entitled to restrain by

injunction any use of the mark in the United Kingdom without their authorisation.

Annotations

Date in force: 31 October 1994.

Commencement order: SI 1994 No 2550.

58 Emblems, etc of certain international organisations: Article 6*ter*

(1) This section applies to –

(a) the armorial bearings, flags or other emblems, and

(b) the abbreviations and names,

of international intergovernmental organisations of which one or more Convention countries are members.

(2) A trade mark which consists of or contains any such emblem, abbreviation or name which is protected under the Paris Convention shall not be registered without the authorisation of the international organisation concerned, unless it appears to the registrar that the use of the emblem, abbreviation or name in the manner proposed –

(a) is not such as to suggest to the public that a connection exists between the organisation and the trade mark, or

(b) is not likely to mislead the public as to the existence of a connection between the user and the organisation.

(3) The provisions of this section as to emblems of an international organisation apply equally to anything which from a heraldic point of view imitates any such emblem.

(4) Where by virtue of this section the authorisation of an international organisation is or would be required for the registration of a trade mark, that organisation is entitled to restrain by injunction any use of the mark in the United Kingdom without its authorisation.

(5) Nothing in this section affects the rights of a person whose *bona fide* use of the trade mark in question began before 4 January 1962 (when the relevant provisions of the Paris Convention entered into force in relation to the United Kingdom).

Annotations

Date in force: 31 October 1994.

Commencement order: SI 1994 No 2550.

59 Notification under Article 6*ter* of the Convention

(1) For the purposes of section 57 state emblems of a Convention country (other than the national flag), and official signs or hallmarks, shall be regarded as protected under the Paris Convention only if, or to the extent that –

(a) the country in question has notified the United Kingdom in accordance with Article 6*ter*(3) of the Convention that it desires to protect that emblem, sign or hallmark,

(b) the notification remains in force, and

(c) the United Kingdom has not objected to it in accordance with

Article 6*ter*(4) or any such objection has been withdrawn.

(2) For the purposes of section 58 the emblems, abbreviations and names of an international organisation shall be regarded as protected under the Paris Convention only if, or to the extent that –
  (a) the organisation in question has notified the United Kingdom in accordance with Article 6*ter*(3) of the Convention that it desires to protect that emblem, abbreviation or name,
  (b) the notification remains in force, and
  (c) the United Kingdom has not objected to it in accordance with Article 6*ter*(4) or any such objection has been withdrawn.

(3) Notification under Article 6*ter*(3) of the Paris Convention shall have effect only in relation to applications for registration made more than two months after the receipt of the notification.

(4) The registrar shall keep and make available for public inspection by any person, at all reasonable hours and free of charge, a list of –
  (a) the state emblems and official signs or hallmarks, and
  (b) the emblems, abbreviations and names of international organisations,

which are for the time being protected under the Paris Convention by virtue of notification under Article 6*ter*(3).

Annotations

Date in force: 31 October 1994.

Commencement order: SI 1994 No 2550.

60 Acts of agent or representative: Article 6*septies*

(1) The following provisions apply where an application for registration of a trade mark is made by a person who is an agent or representative of a person who is the proprietor of the mark in a Convention country.

(2) If the proprietor opposes the application, registration shall be refused.

(3) If the application (not being so opposed) is granted, the proprietor may –
  (a) apply for a declaration of the invalidity of the registration, or
  (b) apply for the rectification of the register so as to substitute his name as the proprietor of the registered trade mark.

(4) The proprietor may (notwithstanding the rights conferred by this Act in relation to a registered trade mark) by injunction restrain any use of the trade mark in the United Kingdom which is not authorised by him.

(5) Subsections (2), (3) and (4) do not apply if, or to the extent that, the agent or representative justifies his action.

(6) An application under subsection (3)(a) or (b) must be made within three years of the proprietor becoming aware of the registration; and no injunction shall be granted under subsection (4) in respect of a use in which the proprietor has acquiesced for a continuous period of three years or more.

Annotations

Date in force: 31 October 1994.

Commencement order: SI 1994 No 2550.

Miscellaneous

61 Stamp duty

Stamp duty shall not be chargeable on an instrument relating to a Community trade mark or an international trade mark (UK), or an application for any such mark, by reason only of the fact that such a mark has legal effect in the United Kingdom.

Annotations

Date in force: 31 October 1994.

Commencement order: SI 1994 No 2550.

Part III
Administrative and other Supplementary Provisions

The registrar

62 The registrar

In this Act 'the registrar' means the Comptroller-General of Patents, Designs and Trade Marks.

Annotations

Date in force: 31 October 1994.

Commencement order: SI 1994 No 2550.

The register

63 The register

(1) The registrar shall maintain a register of trade marks.

References in this Act to 'the register' are to that register; and references to registration (in particular, in the expression 'registered trade mark') are, unless the context otherwise requires, to registration in that register.

(2) There shall be entered in the register in accordance with this Act –
- (a) registered trade marks,
- (b) such particulars as may be prescribed of registrable transactions affecting a registered trade mark, and
- (c) such other matters relating to registered trade marks as may be prescribed.

(3) The register shall be kept in such manner as may be prescribed, and provision shall in particular be made for –
- (a) public inspection of the register, and
- (b) the supply of certified or uncertified copies, or extracts, of entries in the register.

Annotations

Date in force: 31 October 1994 (sub-s (1), sub-ss (2), (3) certain purposes); 29 September 1994 (sub-ss (2), (3), remaining purposes).

Commencement order: SI 1994 No 2550.

64 Rectification or correction of the register

(1) Any person having a sufficient interest may apply for the rectification of an error or omission in the register:

Provided that an application for rectification may not be made in respect of a matter affecting the validity of the registration of a trade mark.

(2) An application for rectification may be made either to the registrar or to the court, except that –

(a) if proceedings concerning the trade mark in question are pending in the court, the application must be made to the court; and

(b) if in any other case the application is made to the registrar, he may at any stage of the proceedings refer the application to the court.

(3) Except where the registrar or the court directs otherwise the effect of rectification of the register is that the error or omission in question shall be deemed never to have been made.

(4) The registrar may, on request made in the prescribed manner by the proprietor of a registered trade mark, or a licensee, enter any change in his name or address as recorded in the register.

(5) The registrar may remove from the register matter appearing to him to have ceased to have effect.

Annotations

Date in force: 31 October 1994 (sub-ss (1)–(3), (5), sub-s (4) certain purposes); 29 September 1994 (sub-s (4), remaining purposes).

Commencement order: SI 1994 No 2550.

65 Adaptation of entries to new classification

(1) Provision may be made by rules empowering the registrar to do such things as he considers necessary to implement any amended or substituted classification of goods or services for the purposes of the registration of trade marks.

(2) Provision may in particular be made for the amendment of existing entries on the register so as to accord with the new classification.

(3) Any such power of amendment shall not be exercised so as to extend the rights conferred by the registration, except where it appears to the registrar that compliance with this requirement would involve undue complexity and that any extension would not be substantial and would not adversely affect the rights of any person.

(4) The rules may empower the registrar –

(a) to require the proprietor of a registered trade mark, within such time as may be prescribed, to file a proposal for amendment of the register, and

(b) to cancel or refuse to renew the registration of the trade mark in the event of his failing to do so.

(5) Any such proposal shall be advertised, and may be opposed, in such manner as may be prescribed.

Annotations

Date in force: 31 October 1994 (sub-ss (1), (3)–(5) certain purposes, sub-s (2)); 29 September 1994 (sub-ss (1), (3)–(5), remaining purposes).

Commencement order: SI 1994 No 2550.

Powers and duties of the registrar

66 Power to require use of forms

(1) The registrar may require the use of such forms as he may direct for any purpose relating to the registration of a trade mark or any other proceeding before him under this Act.

(2) The forms, and any directions of the registrar with respect to their use, shall be published in the prescribed manner.

Annotations

Date in force: 31 October 1994 (certain purposes); 29 September 1994 (remaining purposes).

Commencement order: SI 1994 No 2550.

67 Information about applications and registered trade marks

(1) After publication of an application for registration of a trade mark, the registrar shall on request provide a person with such information and permit him to inspect such documents relating to the application, or to any registered trade mark resulting from it, as may be specified in the request, subject, however, to any prescribed restrictions.

Any request must be made in the prescribed manner and be accompanied by the appropriate fee (if any).

(2) Before publication of an application for registration of a trade mark, documents or information constituting or relating to the application shall not be published by the registrar or communicated by him to any person except –

(a) in such cases and to such extent as may be prescribed, or

(b) with the consent of the applicant,

but subject as follows.

(3) Where a person has been notified that an application for registration of a trade mark has been made, and that the applicant will if the application is granted bring proceedings against him in respect of acts done after publication of the application, he may make a request under subsection (1) notwithstanding that the application has not been published and that subsection shall apply accordingly.

Annotations

Date in force: 31 October 1994 (sub-ss (1), (2) certain purposes, sub-s (3)); 29 September 1994 (sub-ss (1), (2), remaining purposes).

Commencement order: SI 1994 No 2550.

68 Costs and security for costs

(1) Provision may be made by rules empowering the registrar, in any proceedings before him under this Act –

(a) to award any party such costs as he may consider reasonable, and

(b) to direct how and by what parties they are to be paid.

(2) Any such order of the registrar may be enforced –

(a) in England and Wales or Northern Ireland, in the same way as an order of the High Court;

(b) in Scotland, in the same way as a decree for expenses granted by the Court of Session.

(3) Provision may be made by rules empowering the registrar, in such cases as may be prescribed, to require a party to proceedings before him to give security for costs, in relation to those proceedings or to proceedings on appeal, and as to the consequences if security is not given.

Annotations

Date in force: 31 October 1994 (sub-ss (1), (3) certain purposes, sub-s (2)); 29 September 1994 (sub-ss (1), (3), remaining purposes).

Commencement order: SI 1994 No 2550.

69 Evidence before registrar

Provision may be made by rules –

(a) as to the giving of evidence in proceedings before the registrar under this Act by affidavit or statutory declaration;

(b) conferring on the registrar the powers of an official referee of the Supreme Court as regards the examination of witnesses on oath and the discovery and production of documents; and

(c) applying in relation to the attendance of witnesses in proceedings before the registrar the rules applicable to the attendance of witnesses before such a referee.

Annotations

Date in force: 31 October 1994 (certain purposes); 29 September 1994 (remaining purposes).

Commencement order: SI 1994 No 2550.

70 Exclusion of liability in respect of official acts

(1) The registrar shall not be taken to warrant the validity of the registration of a trade mark under this Act or under any treaty, convention, arrangement or engagement to which the United Kingdom is a party.

(2) The registrar is not subject to any liability by reason of, or in connection with, any examination required or authorised by this Act, or any such treaty, convention, arrangement or engagement, or any report or other proceedings consequent on such examination.

(3) No proceedings lie against an officer of the registrar in respect of any matter for which, by virtue of this section, the registrar is not liable.

Annotations

Date in force: 31 October 1994.

Commencement order: SI 1994 No 2550.

71 Registrar's annual report

(1) The Comptroller-General of Patents, Designs and Trade Marks shall in his annual report under section 121 of the Patents Act 1977, include

a report on the execution of this Act, including the discharge of his functions under the Madrid Protocol.

(2) The report shall include an account of all money received and paid by him under or by virtue of this Act.

Annotations

Date in force: 31 October 1994.

Commencement order: SI 1994 No 2550.

Legal proceedings and appeals

72 Registration to be prima facie evidence of validity

In all legal proceedings relating to a registered trade mark (including proceedings for rectification of the register) the registration of a person as proprietor of a trade mark shall be prima facie evidence of the validity of the original registration and of any subsequent assignment or other transmission of it.

Annotations

Date in force: 31 October 1994.

Commencement order: SI 1994 No 2550.

73 Certificate of validity of contested registration

(1) If in proceedings before the court the validity of the registration of a trade mark is contested and it is found by the court that the trade mark is validly registered, the court may give a certificate to that effect.

(2) If the court gives such a certificate and in subsequent proceedings –

(a) the validity of the registration is again questioned, and

(b) the proprietor obtains a final order or judgment in his favour,

he is entitled to his costs as between solicitor and client unless the court directs otherwise.

This subsection does not extend to the costs of an appeal in any such proceedings.

Annotations

Date in force: 31 October 1994.

Commencement order: SI 1994 No 2550.

74 Registrar's appearance in proceedings involving the register

(1) In proceedings before the court involving an application for –

(a) the revocation of the registration of a trade mark,

(b) a declaration of the invalidity of the registration of a trade mark, or

(c) the rectification of the register,

the registrar is entitled to appear and be heard, and shall appear if so directed by the court.

(2) Unless otherwise directed by the court, the registrar may instead of appearing submit to the court a statement in writing signed by him, giving particulars of –
   (a) any proceedings before him in relation to the matter in issue,
   (b) the grounds of any decision given by him affecting it,
   (c) the practice of the Patent Office in like cases, or
   (d) such matters relevant to the issues and within his knowledge as registrar as he thinks fit;

   and the statement shall be deemed to form part of the evidence in the proceedings.

(3) Anything which the registrar is or may be authorised or required to do under this section may be done on his behalf by a duly authorised officer.

Annotations

Date in force: 31 October 1994.

Commencement order: SI 1994 No 2550.

75 The court

In this Act, unless the context otherwise requires, 'the court' means –
   (a) in England and Wales and Northern Ireland, the High Court, and
   (b) in Scotland, the Court of Session.

Annotations

Date in force: 31 October 1994.

Commencement order: SI 1994 No 2550.

76 Appeals from the registrar

(1) An appeal lies from any decision of the registrar under this Act, except as otherwise expressly provided by rules.

   For this purpose 'decision' includes any act of the registrar in exercise of a discretion vested in him by or under this Act.

(2) Any such appeal may be brought either to an appointed person or to the court.

(3) Where an appeal is made to an appointed person, he may refer the appeal to the court if –
   (a) it appears to him that a point of general legal importance is involved,
   (b) the registrar requests that it be so referred, or
   (c) such a request is made by any party to the proceedings before the registrar in which the decision appealed against was made.

   Before doing so the appointed person shall give the appellant and any other party to the appeal an opportunity to make representations as to whether the appeal should be referred to the court.

(4) Where an appeal is made to an appointed person and he does not refer it to the court, he shall hear and determine the appeal and his decision shall be final.

(5) The provisions of sections 68 and 69 (costs and security for costs;

evidence) apply in relation to proceedings before an appointed person as in relation to proceedings before the registrar.

Annotations

Date in force: 31 October 1994 (sub-s (1) certain purposes, sub-ss (2)–(5)); 29 September 1994 (sub-s (1), remaining purposes).

Commencement order: SI 1994 No 2550.

77 Persons appointed to hear and determine appeals

(1) For the purposes of section 76 an 'appointed person' means a person appointed by the Lord Chancellor to hear and decide appeals under this Act.

(2) A person is not eligible for such appointment unless –
- (a) he has a 7 year general qualification, within the meaning of section 71 of the Courts and Legal Services Act 1990;
- (b) he is an advocate or solicitor in Scotland of at least 7 years' standing;
- (c) he is a member of the Bar of Northern Ireland or solicitor of the Supreme Court of Northern Ireland of at least 7 years' standing; or
- (d) he has held judicial office.

(3) An appointed person shall hold and vacate office in accordance with his terms of appointment, subject to the following provisions –
- (a) there shall be paid to him such remuneration (whether by way of salary or fees), and such allowances, as the Secretary of State with the approval of the Treasury may determine;
- (b) he may resign his office by notice in writing to the Lord Chancellor;
- (c) the Lord Chancellor may by notice in writing remove him from office if –
  - (i) he has become bankrupt or made an arrangement with his creditors or, in Scotland, his estate has been sequestrated or he has executed a trust deed for his creditors or entered into a composition contract, or
  - (ii) he is incapacitated by physical or mental illness,

  or if he is in the opinion of the Lord Chancellor otherwise unable or unfit to perform his duties as an appointed person.

(4) The Lord Chancellor shall consult the Lord Advocate before exercising his powers under this section.

Annotations

Date in force: 31 October 1994.

Commencement order: SI 1994 No 2550.

Rules, fees, hours of business, etc

78 Power of Secretary of State to make rules

(1) The Secretary of State may make rules –
- (a) for the purposes of any provision of this Act authorising the making of rules with respect to any matter, and
- (b) for prescribing anything authorised or required by any provision of this Act to be prescribed,

and generally for regulating practice and procedure under this Act.

(2) Provision may, in particular, be made –

(a) as to the manner of filing of applications and other documents;

(b) requiring and regulating the translation of documents and the filing and authentication of any translation;

(c) as to the service of documents;

(d) authorising the rectification of irregularities of procedure;

(e) prescribing time limits for anything required to be done in connection with any proceeding under this Act;

(f) providing for the extension of any time limit so prescribed, or specified by the registrar, whether or not it has already expired.

(3) Rules under this Act shall be made by statutory instrument which shall be subject to annulment in pursuance of a resolution of either House of Parliament.

Annotations

Date in force: 31 October 1994 (certain purposes); 29 September 1994 (remaining purposes).

Commencement order: SI 1994 No 2550.

79 Fees

(1) There shall be paid in respect of applications and registration and other matters under this Act such fees as may be prescribed.

(2) Provision may be made by rules as to –

(a) the payment of a single fee in respect of two or more matters, and

(b) the circumstances (if any) in which a fee may be repaid or remitted.

Annotations

Date in force: 31 October 1994 (certain purposes); 29 September 1994 (remaining purposes).

Commencement order: SI 1994 No 2550.

80 Hours of business and business days

(1) The registrar may give directions specifying the hours of business of the Patent Office for the purpose of the transaction by the public of business under this Act, and the days which are business days for that purpose.

(2) Business done on any day after the specified hours of business, or on a day which is not a business day, shall be deemed to have been done on the next business day; and where the time for doing anything under this Act expires on a day which is not a business day, that time shall be extended to the next business day.

(3) Directions under this section may make different provision for different classes of business and shall be published in the prescribed manner.

Annotations

Date in force: 31 October 1994 (sub-ss (1), (3) certain purposes, sub-s (2)); 29 September 1994 (sub-ss (1), (3), remaining purposes).

Commencement order: SI 1994 No 2550.

81 The trade marks journal

Provision shall be made by rules for the publication by the registrar of a journal containing particulars of any application for the registration of a trade mark (including a representation of the mark) and such other information relating to trade marks as the registrar thinks fit.

Annotations

Date in force: 31 October 1994 (certain purposes); 29 September 1994 (remaining purposes).

Commencement order: SI 1994 No 2550.

Trade mark agents

82 Recognition of agents

Except as otherwise provided by rules, any act required or authorised by this Act to be done by or to a person in connection with the registration of a trade mark, or any procedure relating to a registered trade mark, may be done by or to an agent authorised by that person orally or in writing.

Annotations

Date in force: 31 October 1994 (certain purposes); 29 September 1994 (remaining purposes).

Commencement order: SI 1994 No 2550.

83 The register of trade mark agents

(1) The Secretary of State may make rules requiring the keeping of a register of persons who act as agent for others for the purpose of applying for or obtaining the registration of trade marks; and in this Act a registered trade mark agent means a person whose name is entered in the register kept under this section.

(2) The rules may contain such provision as the Secretary of State thinks fit regulating the registration of persons, and may in particular –
  (a) require the payment of such fees as may be prescribed, and
  (b) authorise in prescribed cases the erasure from the register of the name of any person registered in it, or the suspension of a person's registration.

(3) The rules may delegate the keeping of the register to another person, and may confer on that person –
  (a) power to make regulations –
    (i) with respect to the payment of fees, in the cases and subject to the limits prescribed by the rules, and
    (ii) with respect to any other matter which could be regulated by the rules, and
  (b) such other functions, including disciplinary functions, as may be prescribed by the rules.

Annotations

Date in force: 31 October 1994.

Commencement order: SI 1994 No 2550.

84 Unregistered persons not to be described as registered trade mark agents

(1) An individual who is not a registered trade mark agent shall not –
  (a) carry on a business (otherwise than in partnership) under any name or other description which contains the words 'registered trade mark agent'; or
  (b) in the course of a business otherwise describe or hold himself out, or permit himself to be described or held out, as a registered trade mark agent.

(2) A partnership shall not –
  (a) carry on a business under any name or other description which contains the words 'registered trade mark agent'; or
  (b) in the course of a business otherwise describe or hold itself out, or permit itself to be described or held out, as a firm of registered trade mark agents,

unless all the partners are registered trade mark agents or the partnership satisfies such conditions as may be prescribed for the purposes of this section.

(3) A body corporate shall not –
  (a) carry on a business (otherwise than in partnership) under any name or other description which contains the words 'registered trade mark agent'; or
  (b) in the course of a business otherwise describe or hold itself out, or permit itself to be described or held out, as a registered trade mark agent,

unless all the directors of the body corporate are registered trade mark agents or the body satisfies such conditions as may be prescribed for the purposes of this section.

(4) A person who contravenes this section commits an offence and is liable on summary conviction to a fine not exceeding level 5 on the standard scale; and proceedings for such an offence may be begun at any time within a year from the date of the offence.

Annotations

Date in force: 31 October 1994.

Commencement order: SI 1994 No 2550.

85 Power to prescribe conditions, etc for mixed partnerships and bodies corporate

(1) The Secretary of State may make rules prescribing the conditions to be satisfied for the purposes of section 84 (persons entitled to be described as registered trade mark agents) –
  (a) in relation to a partnership where not all the partners are qualified persons, or
  (b) in relation to a body corporate where not all the directors are qualified persons,

and imposing requirements to be complied with by such partnerships or bodies corporate.

(2) The rules may, in particular –
  (a) prescribe conditions as to the number or proportion of partners or directors who must be qualified persons;
  (b) impose requirements as to –
    (i) the identification of qualified and unqualified persons in professional advertisements, circulars or letters issued by or with the consent of the partnership or body corporate and which relate to its business, and
    (ii) the manner in which a partnership or body corporate is to organise its affairs so as to secure that qualified persons exercise a sufficient degree of control over the activities of unqualified persons.

(3) Contravention of a requirement imposed by the rules is an offence for which a person is liable on summary conviction to a fine not exceeding level 5 on the standard scale.

(4) In this section qualified person means a registered trade mark agent.

Annotations

Date in force: 31 October 1994.

Commencement order: SI 1994 No 2550.

86 Use of the term 'trade mark attorney'

(1) No offence is committed under the enactments restricting the use of certain expressions in reference to persons not qualified to act as solicitors by the use of the term 'trade mark attorney' in reference to a registered trade mark agent.

(2) The enactments referred to in subsection (1) are section 21 of the Solicitors Act 1974, section 31 of the Solicitors (Scotland) Act 1980 and Article 22 of the Solicitors (Northern Ireland) Order 1976.

Annotations

Date in force: 31 October 1994.

Commencement order: SI 1994 No 2550.

87 Privilege for communications with registered trade mark agents

(1) This section applies to communications as to any matter relating to the protection of any design or trade mark, or as to any matter involving passing off.

(2) Any such communication –
  (a) between a person and his trade mark agent, or
  (b) for the purpose of obtaining, or in response to a request for, information which a person is seeking for the purpose of instructing his trade mark agent,

is privileged from, or in Scotland protected against, disclosure in legal proceedings in the same way as a communication between a person and his solicitor or, as the case may be, a communication for the purpose of obtaining, or in response to a request for, information which a person is seeking for the purpose of instructing his solicitor.

(3) In subsection (2) 'trade mark agent' means –
  (a) a registered trade mark agent, or
  (b) a partnership entitled to describe itself as a firm of registered trade mark agents, or
  (c) a body corporate entitled to describe itself as a registered trade mark agent.

Annotations

Date in force: 31 October 1994.

Commencement order: SI 1994 No 2550.

88 Power of registrar to refuse to deal with certain agents

(1) The Secretary of State may make rules authorising the registrar to refuse to recognise as agent in respect of any business under this Act –
  (a) a person who has been convicted of an offence under section 84 (unregistered persons describing themselves as registered trade mark agents);
  (b) an individual whose name has been erased from and not restored to, or who is suspended from, the register of trade mark agents on the ground of misconduct;
  (c) a person who is found by the Secretary of State to have been guilty of such conduct as would, in the case of an individual registered in the register of trade mark agents, render him liable to have his name erased from the register on the ground of misconduct;
  (d) a partnership or body corporate of which one of the partners or directors is a person whom the registrar could refuse to recognise under paragraph (a), (b) or (c) above.

(2) The rules may contain such incidental and supplementary provisions as appear to the Secretary of State to be appropriate and may, in particular, prescribe circumstances in which a person is or is not to be taken to have been guilty of misconduct.

Annotations

Date in force: 31 October 1994 (certain purposes); 29 September 1994 (remaining purposes).

Commencement order: SI 1994 No 2550.

Importation of infringing goods, material or articles

89 Infringing goods, material or articles may be treated as prohibited goods

(1) The proprietor of a registered trade mark, or a licensee, may give notice in writing to the Commissioners of Customs and Excise –
  (a) that he is the proprietor or, as the case may be, a licensee of the registered trade mark,
  (b) that, at a time and place specified in the notice, goods which are, in relation to that registered trade mark, infringing goods, material

or articles are expected to arrive in the United Kingdom –
(i) from outside the European Economic Area, or
(ii) from within that Area but not having been entered for free circulation, and
(c) that he requests the Commissioners to treat them as prohibited goods.

(2) When a notice is in force under this section the importation of the goods to which the notice relates, otherwise than by a person for his private and domestic use, is prohibited; but a person is not by reason of the prohibition liable to any penalty other than forfeiture of the goods.

(3) This section does not apply to goods entered, or expected to be entered, for free circulation, export, re-export or for a suspensive procedure in respect of which an application may be made under Article 3(1) of Council Regulation (EC) No 3295/94 laying down measures to prohibit the release for free circulation, export, re-export or entry for a suspensive procedure of counterfeit and pirated goods.

Annotations

Date in force: 31 October 1994.

Commencement order: SI 1994 No 2550.

Sub-s (3): substituted by the Trade Marks (EC Measures Relating to Counterfeit Goods) Regulations 1995, SI 1995 No 1444, reg 2.

Council Regulation (EEC) No 3842/86: OJ No L357, 18.12.86, p 1.

90 Power of Commissioners of Customs and Excise to make regulations

(1) The Commissioners of Customs and Excise may make regulations prescribing the form in which notice is to be given under section 89 and requiring a person giving notice –
(a) to furnish the Commissioners with such evidence as may be specified in the regulations, either on giving notice or when the goods are imported, or at both those times, and
(b) to comply with such other conditions as may be specified in the regulations.

(2) The regulations may, in particular, require a person giving such a notice –
(a) to pay such fees in respect of the notice as may be specified by the regulations;
(b) to give such security as may be so specified in respect of any liability or expense which the Commissioners may incur in consequence of the notice by reason of the detention of any goods or anything done to goods detained;
(c) to indemnify the Commissioners against any such liability or expense, whether security has been given or not.

(3) The regulations may make different provision as respects different classes of case to which they apply and may include such incidental and supplementary provisions as the Commissioners consider expedient.

(4) Regulations under this section shall be made by statutory instrument

which shall be subject to annulment in pursuance of a resolution of either House of Parliament.

(5) Section 17 of the Customs and Excise Management Act 1979 (general provisions as to Commissioners receipts) applies to fees paid in pursuance of regulations under this section as to receipts under the enactments relating to customs and excise.

Annotations

Date in force: 31 October 1994 (certain purposes); 29 September 1994 (remaining purposes).

Commencement order: SI 1994 No 2550.

91 Power of Commissioners of Customs and Excise to disclose information

Where information relating to infringing goods, material or articles has been obtained by the Commissioners of Customs and Excise for the purposes of, or in connection with, the exercise of their functions in relation to imported goods, the Commissioners may authorise the disclosure of that information for the purpose of facilitating the exercise by any person of any function in connection with the investigation or prosecution of an offence under section 92 below (unauthorised use of trade mark, etc in relation to goods) or under the Trade Descriptions Act 1968.

Annotations

Date in force: 31 October 1994.

Commencement order: SI 1994 No 2550.

Offences

92 Unauthorised use of trade mark, etc in relation to goods

(1) A person commits an offence who with a view to gain for himself or another, or with intent to cause loss to another, and without the consent of the proprietor –

- (a) applies to goods or their packaging a sign identical to, or likely to be mistaken for, a registered trade mark, or
- (b) sells or lets for hire, offers or exposes for sale or hire or distributes goods which bear, or the packaging of which bears, such a sign, or
- (c) has in his possession, custody or control in the course of a business any such goods with a view to the doing of anything, by himself or another, which would be an offence under paragraph (b).

(2) A person commits an offence who with a view to gain for himself or another, or with intent to cause loss to another, and without the consent of the proprietor –

- (a) applies a sign identical to, or likely to be mistaken for, a registered trade mark to material intended to be used –
  - (i) for labelling or packaging goods,

(ii) as a business paper in relation to goods, or
(iii) for advertising goods, or

(b) uses in the course of a business material bearing such a sign for labelling or packaging goods, as a business paper in relation to goods, or for advertising goods, or
(c) has in his possession, custody or control in the course of a business any such material with a view to the doing of anything, by himself or another, which would be an offence under paragraph (b).

(3) A person commits an offence who with a view to gain for himself or another, or with intent to cause loss to another, and without the consent of the proprietor –
(a) makes an article specifically designed or adapted for making copies of a sign identical to, or likely to be mistaken for, a registered trade mark, or
(b) has such an article in his possession, custody or control in the course of a business,

knowing or having reason to believe that it has been, or is to be, used to produce goods, or material for labelling or packaging goods, as a business paper in relation to goods, or for advertising goods.

(4) A person does not commit an offence under this section unless –
(a) the goods are goods in respect of which the trade mark is registered, or
(b) the trade mark has a reputation in the United Kingdom and the use of the sign takes or would take unfair advantage of, or is or would be detrimental to, the distinctive character or the repute of the trade mark.

(5) It is a defence for a person charged with an offence under this section to show that he believed on reasonable grounds that the use of the sign in the manner in which it was used, or was to be used, was not an infringement of the registered trade mark.

(6) A person guilty of an offence under this section is liable –
(a) on summary conviction to imprisonment for a term not exceeding six months or a fine not exceeding the statutory maximum, or both;
(b) on conviction on indictment to a fine or imprisonment for a term not exceeding ten years, or both.

Annotations

Date in force: 31 October 1994.

Commencement order: SI 1994 No 2550.

93 Enforcement function of local weights and measures authority

(1) It is the duty of every local weights and measures authority to enforce within their area the provisions of section 92 (unauthorised use of trade mark, etc in relation to goods).

(2) The following provisions of the Trade Descriptions Act 1968 apply in

relation to the enforcement of that section as in relation to the enforcement of that Act –

section 27 (power to make test purchases),

section 28 (power to enter premises and inspect and seize goods and documents),

section 29 (obstruction of authorised officers), and

section 33 (compensation for loss, etc of goods seized).

(3) Subsection (1) above does not apply in relation to the enforcement of section 92 in Northern Ireland, but it is the duty of the Department of Economic Development to enforce that section in Northern Ireland.

For that purpose the provisions of the Trade Descriptions Act 1968 specified in subsection (2) apply as if for the references to a local weights and measures authority and any officer of such an authority there were substituted references to that Department and any of its officers.

(4) Any enactment which authorises the disclosure of information for the purpose of facilitating the enforcement of the Trade Descriptions Act 1968 shall apply as if section 92 above were contained in that Act and as if the functions of any person in relation to the enforcement of that section were functions under that Act.

(5) Nothing in this section shall be construed as authorising a local weights and measures authority to bring proceedings in Scotland for an offence.

Annotations

Date in force: 31 October 1994.

Commencement order: SI 1994 No 2550.

94 Falsification of register, etc

(1) It is an offence for a person to make, or cause to be made, a false entry in the register of trade marks, knowing or having reason to believe that it is false.

(2) It is an offence for a person –

(a) to make or cause to be made anything falsely purporting to be a copy of an entry in the register, or

(b) to produce or tender or cause to be produced or tendered in evidence any such thing,

knowing or having reason to believe that it is false.

(3) A person guilty of an offence under this section is liable –

(a) on conviction on indictment, to imprisonment for a term not exceeding two years or a fine, or both;

(b) on summary conviction, to imprisonment for a term not exceeding six months or a fine not exceeding the statutory maximum, or both.

Annotations

Date in force: 31 October 1994.

Commencement order: SI 1994 No 2550.

95 Falsely representing trade mark as registered

(1) It is an offence for a person –
(a) falsely to represent that a mark is a registered trade mark, or
(b) to make a false representation as to the goods or services for which a trade mark is registered
knowing or having reason to believe that the representation is false.
(2) For the purposes of this section, the use in the United Kingdom in relation to a trade mark –
(a) of the word registered, or
(b) of any other word or symbol importing a reference (express or implied) to registration,
shall be deemed to be a representation as to registration under this Act unless it is shown that the reference is to registration elsewhere than in the United Kingdom and that the trade mark is in fact so registered for the goods or services in question.
(3) A person guilty of an offence under this section is liable on summary conviction to a fine not exceeding level 3 on the standard scale.

Annotations

Date in force: 31 October 1994.

Commencement order: SI 1994 No 2550.

96 Supplementary provisions as to summary proceedings in Scotland

(1) Notwithstanding anything in [section 136 of the Criminal Procedure (Scotland) Act 1995], summary proceedings in Scotland for an offence under this Act may be begun at any time within six months after the date on which evidence sufficient in the Lord Advocate's opinion to justify the proceedings came to his knowledge.
For this purpose a certificate of the Lord Advocate as to the date on which such evidence came to his knowledge is conclusive evidence.
(2) For the purposes of subsection (1) and of any other provision of this Act as to the time within which summary proceedings for an offence may be brought, proceedings in Scotland shall be deemed to be begun on the date on which a warrant to apprehend or to cite the accused is granted, if such warrant is executed without undue delay.

Annotations

Date in force: 31 October 1994.

Commencement order: SI 1994 No 2550.

Sub-s (1): words in square brackets substituted by the Criminal Procedure (Consequential Provisions) (Scotland) Act 1995, s 5, Sch 4, para 92(2).

Forfeiture of counterfeit goods, etc

97 Forfeiture: England and Wales or Northern Ireland

(1) In England and Wales or Northern Ireland where there has come into the possession of any person in connection with the investigation or

prosecution of a relevant offence –

(a) goods which, or the packaging of which, bears a sign identical to or likely to be mistaken for a registered trade mark,

(b) material bearing such a sign and intended to be used for labelling or packaging goods, as a business paper in relation to goods, or for advertising goods, or

(c) articles specifically designed or adapted for making copies of such a sign,

that person may apply under this section for an order for the forfeiture of the goods, material or articles.

(2) An application under this section may be made –

(a) where proceedings have been brought in any court for a relevant offence relating to some or all of the goods, material or articles, to that court;

(b) where no application for the forfeiture of the goods, material or articles has been made under paragraph (a), by way of complaint to a magistrates' court.

(3) On an application under this section the court shall make an order for the forfeiture of any goods, material or articles only if it is satisfied that a relevant offence has been committed in relation to the goods, material or articles.

(4) A court may infer for the purposes of this section that such an offence has been committed in relation to any goods, material or articles if it is satisfied that such an offence has been committed in relation to goods, material or articles which are representative of them (whether by reason of being of the same design or part of the same consignment or batch or otherwise).

(5) Any person aggrieved by an order made under this section by a magistrates' court, or by a decision of such a court not to make such an order, may appeal against that order or decision –

(a) in England and Wales, to the Crown Court;

(b) in Northern Ireland, to the county court;

and an order so made may contain such provision as appears to the court to be appropriate for delaying the coming into force of the order pending the making and determination of any appeal (including any application under section 111 of the Magistrates' Courts Act 1980 or Article 146 of the Magistrates' Courts (Northern Ireland) Order 1981 (statement of case)).

(6) Subject to subsection (7), where any goods, material or articles are forfeited under this section they shall be destroyed in accordance with such directions as the court may give.

(7) On making an order under this section the court may, if it considers it appropriate to do so, direct that the goods, material or articles to which the order relates shall (instead of being destroyed) be released, to such person as the court may specify, on condition that that person –

(a) causes the offending sign to be erased, removed or obliterated; and

(b) complies with any order to pay costs which has been made against him in the proceedings for the order for forfeiture.

(8) For the purposes of this section a 'relevant offence' means an offence

under section 92 above (unauthorised use of trade mark, etc in relation to goods) or under the Trade Descriptions Act 1968 or any offence involving dishonesty or deception.

Annotations

Date in force: 31 October 1994.

Commencement order: SI 1994 No 2550.

Modified, in relation to representations of the Olympic symbol, motto or protected word, by the Olympic Symbol etc (Protection) Act 1995, s 11.

98 Forfeiture: Scotland

(1) In Scotland the court may make an order for the forfeiture of any –
  (a) goods which bear, or the packaging of which bears, a sign identical to or likely to be mistaken for a registered trade mark,
  (b) material bearing such a sign and intended to be used for labelling or packaging goods, as a business paper in relation to goods, or for advertising goods, or
  (c) articles specifically designed or adapted for making copies of such a sign.

(2) An order under this section may be made –
  (a) on an application by the procurator-fiscal made in the manner specified in [section 134 of the Criminal Procedure (Scotland) Act 1995], or
  (b) where a person is convicted of a relevant offence, in addition to any other penalty which the court may impose.

(3) On an application under subsection (2)(a), the court shall make an order for the forfeiture of any goods, material or articles only if it is satisfied that a relevant offence has been committed in relation to the goods, material or articles.

(4) The court may infer for the purposes of this section that such an offence has been committed in relation to any goods, material or articles if it is satisfied that such an offence has been committed in relation to goods, material or articles which are representative of them (whether by reason of being of the same design or part of the same consignment or batch or otherwise).

(5) The procurator-fiscal making the application under subsection (2)(a) shall serve on any person appearing to him to be the owner of, or otherwise to have an interest in, the goods, material or articles to which the application relates a copy of the application, together with a notice giving him the opportunity to appear at the hearing of the application to show cause why the goods, material or articles should not be forfeited.

(6) Service under subsection (5) shall be carried out, and such service may be proved, in the manner specified for citation of an accused in summary proceedings under the [Criminal Procedure (Scotland) Act 1995].

(7) Any person upon whom notice is served under subsection (5) and any other person claiming to be the owner of, or otherwise to have an

interest in, goods, material or articles to which an application under this section relates shall be entitled to appear at the hearing of the application to show cause why the goods, material or articles should not be forfeited.

(8) The court shall not make an order following an application under subsection (2)(a) –
- (a) if any person on whom notice is served under subsection (5) does not appear, unless service of the notice on that person is proved; or
- (b) if no notice under subsection (5) has been served, unless the court is satisfied that in the circumstances it was reasonable not to serve such notice.

(9) Where an order for the forfeiture of any goods, material or articles is made following an application under subsection (2)(a), any person who appeared, or was entitled to appear, to show cause why goods, material or articles should not be forfeited may, within 21 days of the making of the order, appeal to the High Court by Bill of Suspension; and [section 182(5)(a) to (e) of the Criminal Procedure (Scotland) Act 1995] shall apply to an appeal under this subsection as it applies to a stated case under Part II of that Act.

(10) An order following an application under subsection (2)(a) shall not take effect –
- (a) until the end of the period of 21 days beginning with the day after the day on which the order is made; or
- (b) if an appeal is made under subsection (9) above within that period, until the appeal is determined or abandoned.

(11) An order under subsection (2)(b) shall not take effect –
- (a) until the end of the period within which an appeal against the order could be brought under the [Criminal Procedure (Scotland) Act 1995]; or
- (b) if an appeal is made within that period, until the appeal is determined or abandoned.

(12) Subject to subsection (13), goods, material or articles forfeited under this section shall be destroyed in accordance with such directions as the court may give.

(13) On making an order under this section the court may if it considers it appropriate to do so, direct that the goods, material or articles to which the order relates shall (instead of being destroyed) be released, to such person as the court may specify, on condition that that person causes the offending sign to be erased, removed or obliterated.

(14) For the purposes of this section –

'relevant offence' means an offence under section 92 (unauthorised use of trade mark, etc in relation to goods) or under the Trade Descriptions Act 1968 or any offence involving dishonesty or deception,

'the court' means –
- (a) in relation to an order made on an application under subsection (2)(a), the sheriff, and

(b) in relation to an order made under subsection (2)(b), the court which imposed the penalty.

Annotations

Date in force: 31 October 1994.

Commencement order: SI 1994 No 2550.

Sub-ss (2), (6), (9), (11): words in square brackets substituted by the Criminal Procedure (Consequential Provisions) (Scotland) Act 1995, s 5, Sch 4, para 92(3).

Modified, in relation to representations of the Olympic symbol, motto or protected word, by the Olympic Symbol etc (Protection) Act 1995, s 12.

Part IV
Miscellaneous and General Provisions

Miscellaneous

99 Unauthorised use of Royal arms, etc

(1) A person shall not without the authority of Her Majesty use in connection with any business the Royal arms (or arms so closely resembling the Royal arms as to be calculated to deceive) in such manner as to be calculated to lead to the belief that he is duly authorised to use the Royal arms.

(2) A person shall not without the authority of Her Majesty or of a member of the Royal family use in connection with any business any device, emblem or title in such a manner as to be calculated to lead to the belief that he is employed by, or supplies goods or services to, Her Majesty or that member of the Royal family.

(3) A person who contravenes subsection (1) commits an offence and is liable on summary conviction to a fine not exceeding level 2 on the standard scale.

(4) Contravention of subsection (1) or (2) may be restrained by injunction in proceedings brought by –
- (a) any person who is authorised to use the arms, device, emblem or title in question, or
- (b) any person authorised by the Lord Chamberlain to take such proceedings.

(5) Nothing in this section affects any right of the proprietor of a trade mark containing any such arms, device, emblem or title to use that trade mark.

Annotations

Date in force: 31 October 1994.

Commencement order: SI 1994 No 2550.

100 Burden of proving use of trade mark

If in any civil proceedings under this Act a question arises as to the use to which a registered trade mark has been put, it is for the proprietor to show what use has been made of it.

Annotations

Date in force: 31 October 1994.

Commencement order: SI 1994 No 2550.

101 Offences committed by partnerships and bodies corporate

(1) Proceedings for an offence under this Act alleged to have been committed by a partnership shall be brought against the partnership in the name of the firm and not in that of the partners; but without prejudice to any liability of the partners under subsection (4) below.

(2) The following provisions apply for the purposes of such proceedings as in relation to a body corporate –

(a) any rules of court relating to the service of documents;

(b) in England and Wales or Northern Ireland, Schedule 3 to the Magistrates' Courts Act 1980 or Schedule 4 to the Magistrates' Courts (Northern Ireland) Order 1981 (procedure on charge of offence).

(3) A fine imposed on a partnership on its conviction in such proceedings shall be paid out of the partnership assets.

(4) Where a partnership is guilty of an offence under this Act, every partner, other than a partner who is proved to have been ignorant of or to have attempted to prevent the commission of the offence, is also guilty of the offence and liable to be proceeded against and punished accordingly.

(5) Where an offence under this Act committed by a body corporate is proved to have been committed with the consent or connivance of a director, manager, secretary or other similar officer of the body, or a person purporting to act in any such capacity, he as well as the body corporate is guilty of the offence and liable to be proceeded against and punished accordingly.

Annotations

Date in force: 31 October 1994.

Commencement order: SI 1994 No 2550.

Interpretation

102 Adaptation of expressions for Scotland

In the application of this Act to Scotland –

'account of profits' means accounting and payment of profits;
'accounts' means count, reckoning and payment;
'assignment' means assignation;
'costs' means expenses;
'declaration' means declarator;
'defendant' means defender;
'delivery up' means delivery;
'injunction' means interdict;

'interlocutory relief' means interim remedy; and
'plaintiff' means pursuer.

Annotations

Date in force: 31 October 1994.
Commencement order: SI 1994 No 2550.

103 Minor definitions

(1) In this Act –
'business' includes a trade or profession;
'director', in relation to a body corporate whose affairs are managed by its members, means any member of the body;
'infringement proceedings', in relation to a registered trade mark, includes proceedings under section 16 (order for delivery up of infringing goods, etc);
'publish' means make available to the public, and references to publication –
(a) in relation to an application for registration, are to publication under section 38(1), and
(b) in relation to registration, are to publication under section 40(4);
'statutory provisions' includes provisions of subordinate legislation within the meaning of the Interpretation Act 1978;
'trade' includes any business or profession.

(2) References in this Act to use (or any particular description of use) of a trade mark, or of a sign identical with, similar to, or likely to be mistaken for a trade mark, include use (or that description of use) otherwise than by means of a graphic representation.

(3) References in this Act to a Community instrument include references to any instrument amending or replacing that instrument.

Annotations

Date in force: 31 October 1994.
Commencement order: SI 1994 No 2550.

104 Index of defined expressions

In this Act the expressions listed below are defined by or otherwise fall to be construed in accordance with the provisions indicated –

account of profits and accounts (in Scotland)	section 102
appointed person (for purposes of section 76)	section 77
assignment (in Scotland)	section 102
business	section 103(1)
certification mark	section 50(1)
collective mark	section 49(1)
commencement (of this Act)	section 109(2)
Community trade mark	section 51
Community Trade Mark Regulation	section 51

Convention country	section 55(1)(b)
costs (in Scotland)	section 102
the court	section 75
date of application	section 33(2)
date of filing	section 33(1)
date of registration	section 40(3)
defendant (in Scotland)	section 102
delivery up (in Scotland)	section 102
director	section 103(1)
earlier right	section 5(4)
earlier trade mark	section 6
exclusive licence and licensee	section 29(1)
infringement (of registered trade mark)	sections 9(1) and (2) and 10
infringement proceedings	section 103(1)
infringing articles	section 17
infringing goods	section 17
infringing material	section 17
injunction (in Scotland)	section 102
interlocutory relief (in Scotland)	section 102
the International Bureau	section 53
international trade mark (UK)	section 53
Madrid Protocol	section 53
Paris Convention	section 55(1)(a)
plaintiff (in Scotland)	section 102
prescribed	section 78(1)(b)
protected under the Paris Convention	
– well-known trade marks	section 56(1)
– state emblems and official signs or hallmarks	section 57(1)
– emblems, etc of international organisations	section 58(2)
publish and references to publication	section 103(1)
register, registered (and related expressions)	section 63(1)
registered trade mark agent	section 83(1)
registrable transaction	section 25(2)
the registrar	section 62
rules	section 78
statutory provisions	section 103(1)
trade	section 103(1)
trade mark	
– generally	section 1(1)
– includes collective mark or certification mark	section 1(2)
United Kingdom (references include Isle of Man)	section 108(2)
use (of trade mark or sign)	section 103(2)
well-known trade mark (under Paris Convention)	section 56(1)

Annotations

Date in force: 31 October 1994.

Commencement order: SI 1994 No 2550.

Other general provisions

105 Transitional provisions

The provisions of Schedule 3 have effect with respect to transitional matters, including the treatment of marks registered under the Trade Marks Act 1938, and applications for registration and other proceedings pending under that Act, on the commencement of this Act.

Annotations

Date in force: 31 October 1994 (certain purposes); 29 September 1994 (remaining purposes).

Commencement order: SI 1994 No 2550.

106 Consequential amendments and repeals

(1) The enactments specified in Schedule 4 are amended in accordance with that Schedule, the amendments being consequential on the provisions of this Act.

(2) The enactments specified in Schedule 5 are repealed to the extent specified.

Annotations

Date in force: 31 October 1994.

Commencement order: SI 1994 No 2550.

107 Territorial waters and the continental shelf

(1) For the purposes of this Act the territorial waters of the United Kingdom shall be treated as part of the United Kingdom.

(2) This Act applies to things done in the United Kingdom sector of the continental shelf on a structure or vessel which is present there for purposes directly connected with the exploration of the sea bed or subsoil or the exploitation of their natural resources as it applies to things done in the United Kingdom.

(3) The United Kingdom sector of the continental shelf means the areas designated by order under section 1(7) of the Continental Shelf Act 1964.

Annotations

Date in force: 31 October 1994.

Commencement order: SI 1994 No 2550.

108 Extent

(1) This Act extends to England and Wales, Scotland and Northern Ireland.

(2) This Act also extends to the Isle of Man, subject to such exceptions and modifications as Her Majesty may specify by Order in Council; and subject to any such Order references in this Act to the United Kingdom shall be construed as including the Isle of Man.

Annotations

Date in force: 31 October 1994.

Commencement order: SI 1994 No 2550.

109 Commencement

(1) The provisions of this Act come into force on such day as the Secretary of State may appoint by order made by statutory instrument.

Different days may be appointed for different provisions and different purposes.

(2) The references to the commencement of this Act in Schedules 3 and 4 (transitional provisions and consequential amendments) are to the commencement of the main substantive provisions of Parts I and III of this Act and the consequential repeal of the Trade Marks Act 1938.

Provision may be made by order under this section identifying the date of that commencement.

Annotations

Date in force: 31 October 1994.

Commencement order: SI 1994 No 2550.

110 Short title

This Act may be cited as the Trade Marks Act 1994.

Annotations

Date in force: 31 October 1994 (certain purposes); 29 September 1994 (remaining purposes).

Commencement order: SI 1994 No 2550.

SCHEDULE 1
Collective Marks

Section 49

General

1

The provisions of this Act apply to collective marks subject to the following provisions.

Signs of which a collective mark may consist

2

In relation to a collective mark the reference in section 1(1) (signs of which a trade mark may consist) to distinguishing goods or services of one undertaking from those of other undertakings shall be construed as a reference to distinguishing goods or services of members of the association which is the proprietor of the mark from those of other undertakings.

Indication of geographical origin

3

(1) Notwithstanding section 3(1)(c), a collective mark may be registered which consists of signs or indications which may serve, in trade, to designate the geographical origin of the goods or services.

(2) However, the proprietor of such a mark is not entitled to prohibit the use of the signs or indications in accordance with honest practices in industrial or commercial matters (in particular, by a person who is entitled to use a geographical name).

Mark not to be misleading as to character or significance

4

(1) A collective mark shall not be registered if the public is liable to be misled as regards the character or significance of the mark, in particular if it is likely to be taken to be something other than a collective mark.

(2) The registrar may accordingly require that a mark in respect of which application is made for registration include some indication that it is a collective mark.

Notwithstanding section 39(2), an application may be amended so as to comply with any such requirement.

Regulations governing use of collective mark

5

(1) An applicant for registration of a collective mark must file with the registrar regulations governing the use of the mark.

(2) The regulations must specify the persons authorised to use the mark, the conditions of membership of the association and, where they exist, the conditions of use of the mark, including any sanctions against misuse.

Further requirements with which the regulations have to comply may be imposed by rules.

Approval of regulations by registrar

6

(1) A collective mark shall not be registered unless the regulations governing the use of the mark –

(a) comply with paragraph 5(2) and any further requirements imposed by rules, and

(b) are not contrary to public policy or to accepted principles of morality.

(2) Before the end of the prescribed period after the date of the application for registration of a collective mark, the applicant must file the regulations with the registrar and pay the prescribed fee.

If he does not do so, the application shall be deemed to be withdrawn.

7

(1) The registrar shall consider whether the requirements mentioned in paragraph 6(1) are met.

(2) If it appears to the registrar that those requirements are not met, he shall inform the applicant and give him an opportunity, within such period as the registrar may specify, to make representations or to file amended regulations.

(3) If the applicant fails to satisfy the registrar that those requirements are met, or to file regulations amended so as to meet them, or fails to respond before the end of the specified period, the registrar shall refuse the application.

(4) If it appears to the registrar that those requirements, and the other requirements for registration, are met, he shall accept the application and shall proceed in accordance with section 38 (publication, opposition proceedings and observations).

8

The regulations shall be published and notice of opposition may be given, and observations may be made, relating to the matters mentioned in paragraph 6(1).

This is in addition to any other grounds on which the application may be opposed or observations made.

Regulations to be open to inspection

9

The regulations governing the use of a registered collective mark shall be open to public inspection in the same way as the register.

Amendment of regulations

10

(1) An amendment of the regulations governing the use of a registered collective mark is not effective unless and until the amended regulations are filed with the registrar and accepted by him.

(2) Before accepting any amended regulations the registrar may in any

case where it appears to him expedient to do so cause them to be published.

(3) If he does so, notice of opposition may be given, and observations may be made, relating to the matters mentioned in paragraph 6(1).

Infringement: rights of authorised users

11

The following provisions apply in relation to an authorised user of a registered collective mark as in relation to a licensee of a trade mark –

(a) section 10(5) (definition of infringement: unauthorised application of mark to certain material);

(b) section 19(2) (order as to disposal of infringing goods, material or articles: adequacy of other remedies);

(c) section 89 (prohibition of importation of infringing goods, material or articles: request to Commissioners of Customs and Excise).

12

(1) The following provisions (which correspond to the provisions of section 30 (general provisions as to rights of licensees in case of infringement)) have effect as regards the rights of an authorised user in relation to infringement of a registered collective mark.

(2) An authorised user is entitled, subject to any agreement to the contrary between him and the proprietor, to call on the proprietor to take infringement proceedings in respect of any matter which affects his interests.

(3) If the proprietor –
  (a) refuses to do so, or
  (b) fails to do so within two months after being called upon,
the authorised user may bring the proceedings in his own name as if he were the proprietor.

(4) Where infringement proceedings are brought by virtue of this paragraph, the authorised user may not, without the leave of the court, proceed with the action unless the proprietor is either joined as a plaintiff or added as a defendant.

This does not affect the granting of interlocutory relief on an application by an authorised user alone.

(5) A proprietor who is added as a defendant as mentioned in sub-paragraph (4) shall not be made liable for any costs in the action unless he takes part in the proceedings.

(6) In infringement proceedings brought by the proprietor of a registered collective mark any loss suffered or likely to be suffered by authorised users shall be taken into account; and the court may give such directions as it thinks fit as to the extent to which the plaintiff is to hold the proceeds of any pecuniary remedy on behalf of such users.

Grounds for revocation of registration

13

Apart from the grounds of revocation provided for in section 46, the registration of a collective mark may be revoked on the ground –

(a) that the manner in which the mark has been used by the proprietor has caused it to become liable to mislead the public in the manner referred to in paragraph 4(1), or

(b) that the proprietor has failed to observe, or to secure the observance of, the regulations governing the use of the mark, or

(c) that an amendment of the regulations has been made so that the regulations –

  (i) no longer comply with paragraph 5(2) and any further conditions imposed by rules, or

  (ii) are contrary to public policy or to accepted principles of morality.

Grounds for invalidity of registration

14

Apart from the grounds of invalidity provided for in section 47, the registration of a collective mark may be declared invalid on the ground that the mark was registered in breach of the provisions of paragraph 4(1) or 6(1).

Annotations

Date in force: 31 October 1994 (paras 1–5, 7–14, para 6 in part); 29 September 1994 (remainder).

Commencement order: SI 1994 No 2550.

SCHEDULE 2
Certification Marks

Section 50

General

1

The provisions of this Act apply to certification marks subject to the following provisions.

Signs of which a certification mark may consist

2

In relation to a certification mark the reference in section 1(1) (signs of which a trade mark may consist) to distinguishing goods or services of one undertaking from those of other undertakings shall be construed as a reference to distinguishing goods or services which are certified from those which are not.

Indication of geographical origin

3

(1) Notwithstanding section 3(1)(c), a certification mark may be registered which consists of signs or indications which may serve, in trade, to designate the geographical origin of the goods or services.

(2) However, the proprietor of such a mark is not entitled to prohibit the use of the signs or indications in accordance with honest practices in industrial or commercial matters (in particular, by a person who is entitled to use a geographical name).

Nature of proprietor's business

4

A certification mark shall not be registered if the proprietor carries on a business involving the supply of goods or services of the kind certified.

Mark not to be misleading as to character or significance

5

(1) A certification mark shall not be registered if the public is liable to be misled as regards the character or significance of the mark, in particular if it is likely to be taken to be something other than a certification mark.

(2) The registrar may accordingly require that a mark in respect of which application is made for registration include some indication that it is a certification mark.

Notwithstanding section 39(2), an application may be amended so as to comply with any such requirement.

Regulations governing use of certification mark

6

(1) An applicant for registration of a certification mark must file with the registrar regulations governing the use of the mark.

(2) The regulations must indicate who is authorised to use the mark, the characteristics to be certified by the mark, how the certifying body is to

test those characteristics and to supervise the use of the mark, the fees (if any) to be paid in connection with the operation of the mark and the procedures for resolving disputes.

Further requirements with which the regulations have to comply may be imposed by rules.

Approval of regulations, etc

7

(1) A certification mark shall not be registered unless –
   (a) the regulations governing the use of the mark –
      (i) comply with paragraph 6(2) and any further requirements imposed by rules, and
      (ii) are not contrary to public policy or to accepted principles of morality, and
   (b) the applicant is competent to certify the goods or services for which the mark is to be registered.

(2) Before the end of the prescribed period after the date of the application for registration of a certification mark, the applicant must file the regulations with the registrar and pay the prescribed fee.

If he does not do so, the application shall be deemed to be withdrawn.

8

(1) The registrar shall consider whether the requirements mentioned in paragraph 7(1) are met.

(2) If it appears to the registrar that those requirements are not met, he shall inform the applicant and give him an opportunity, within such period as the registrar may specify, to make representations or to file amended regulations.

(3) If the applicant fails to satisfy the registrar that those requirements are met, or to file regulations amended so as to meet them, or fails to respond before the end of the specified period, the registrar shall refuse the application.

(4) If it appears to the registrar that those requirements, and the other requirements for registration, are met, he shall accept the application and shall proceed in accordance with section 38 (publication, opposition proceedings and observations).

9

The regulations shall be published and notice of opposition may be given, and observations may be made, relating to the matters mentioned in paragraph 7(1).

This is in addition to any other grounds on which the application may be opposed or observations made.

Regulations to be open to inspection

10

The regulations governing the use of a registered certification mark shall be open to public inspection in the same way as the register.

Amendment of regulations

11

(1) An amendment of the regulations governing the use of a registered certification mark is not effective unless and until the amended regulations are filed with the registrar and accepted by him.
(2) Before accepting any amended regulations the registrar may in any case where it appears to him expedient to do so cause them to be published.
(3) If he does so, notice of opposition may be given, and observations may be made, relating to the matters mentioned in paragraph 7(1).

Consent to assignment of registered certification mark

12

The assignment or other transmission of a registered certification mark is not effective without the consent of the registrar.

Infringement: rights of authorised users

13

The following provisions apply in relation to an authorised user of a registered certification mark as in relation to a licensee of a trade mark –
(a) section 10(5) (definition of infringement: unauthorised application of mark to certain material);
(b) section 19(2) (order as to disposal of infringing goods, material or articles: adequacy of other remedies);
(c) section 89 (prohibition of importation of infringing goods, material or articles: request to Commissioners of Customs and Excise).

14

In infringement proceedings brought by the proprietor of a registered certification mark any loss suffered or likely to be suffered by authorised users shall be taken into account; and the court may give such directions as it thinks fit as to the extent to which the plaintiff is to hold the proceeds of any pecuniary remedy on behalf of such users.

Grounds for revocation of registration

15

Apart from the grounds of revocation provided for in section 46, the registration of a certification mark may be revoked on the ground –

(a) that the proprietor has begun to carry on such a business as is mentioned in paragraph 4,

(b) that the manner in which the mark has been used by the proprietor has caused it to become liable to mislead the public in the manner referred to in paragraph 5(1),

(c) that the proprietor has failed to observe, or to secure the observance of, the regulations governing the use of the mark,

(d) that an amendment of the regulations has been made so that the regulations –

  (i) no longer comply with paragraph 6(2) and any further conditions imposed by rules, or

  (ii) are contrary to public policy or to accepted principles of morality, or

(e) that the proprietor is no longer competent to certify the goods or services for which the mark is registered.

Grounds for invalidity of registration

16

Apart from the grounds of invalidity provided for in section 47, the registration of a certification mark may be declared invalid on the ground that the mark was registered in breach of the provisions of paragraph 4, 5(1) or 7(1).

Annotations

Date in force: 31 October 1994 (paras 1–6, 8–16, para 7 in part); 29 September 1994 (remainder).

Commencement order: SI 1994 No 2550.

SCHEDULE 3
Transitional Provisions

Section 105

Introductory

1

(1) In this Schedule –

'existing registered mark' means a trade mark, certification trade mark or service mark registered under the 1938 Act immediately before the commencement of this Act;

'the 1938 Act' means the Trade Marks Act 1938; and

'the old law' means that Act and any other enactment or rule of law applying to existing registered marks immediately before the commencement of this Act.

(2) For the purposes of this Schedule –

(a) an application shall be treated as pending on the commencement of this Act if it was made but not finally determined before commencement, and

(b) the date on which it was made shall be taken to be the date of filing under the 1938 Act.

Existing registered marks

2

(1) Existing registered marks (whether registered in Part A or B of the register kept under the 1938 Act) shall be transferred on the commencement of this Act to the register kept under this Act and have effect, subject to the provisions of this Schedule, as if registered under this Act.

(2) Existing registered marks registered as a series under section 21(2) of the 1938 Act shall be similarly registered in the new register.

Provision may be made by rules for putting such entries in the same form as is required for entries under this Act.

(3) In any other case notes indicating that existing registered marks are associated with other marks shall cease to have effect on the commencement of this Act.

3

(1) A condition entered on the former register in relation to an existing registered mark immediately before the commencement of this Act shall cease to have effect on commencement.

Proceedings under section 33 of the 1938 Act (application to expunge or vary registration for breach of condition) which are pending on the commencement of this Act shall be dealt with under the old law and any necessary alteration made to the new register.

(2) A disclaimer or limitation entered on the former register in relation to an existing registered mark immediately before the commencement of this Act shall be transferred to the new register and have effect as if entered on the register in pursuance of section 13 of this Act.

Effects of registration: infringement

4

(1) Sections 9 to 12 of this Act (effects of registration) apply in relation to an existing registered mark as from the commencement of this Act and

section 14 of this Act (action for infringement) applies in relation to infringement of an existing registered mark committed after the commencement of this Act, subject to sub-paragraph (2) below.

The old law continues to apply in relation to infringements committed before commencement.

(2) It is not an infringement of –

(a) an existing registered mark, or

(b) a registered trade mark of which the distinctive elements are the same or substantially the same as those of an existing registered mark and which is registered for the same goods or services,

to continue after commencement any use which did not amount to infringement of the existing registered mark under the old law.

Infringing goods, material or articles

5

Section 16 of this Act (order for delivery up of infringing goods, material or articles) applies to infringing goods, material or articles whether made before or after the commencement of this Act.

Rights and remedies of licensee or authorised user

6

(1) Section 30 (general provisions as to rights of licensees in case of infringement) of this Act applies to licences granted before the commencement of this Act, but only in relation to infringements committed after commencement.

(2) Paragraph 14 of Schedule 2 of this Act (court to take into account loss suffered by authorised users, etc) applies only in relation to infringements committed after commencement.

Co-ownership of registered mark

7

The provisions of section 23 of this Act (co-ownership of registered mark) apply as from the commencement of this Act to an existing registered mark of which two or more persons were immediately before commencement registered as joint proprietors.

But so long as the relations between the joint proprietors remain such as are described in section 63 of the 1938 Act (joint ownership) there shall be taken to be an agreement to exclude the operation of subsections (1) and (3) of section 23 of this Act (ownership in undivided shares and right of co-proprietor to make separate use of the mark).

Assignment, etc of registered mark

8

(1) Section 24 of this Act (assignment or other transmission of registered mark) applies to transactions and events occurring after the commencement of this Act in relation to an existing registered mark; and the old law continues to apply in relation to transactions and events occurring before commencement.

(2) Existing entries under section 25 of the 1938 Act (registration of assignments and transmissions) shall be transferred on the commencement of this Act to the register kept under this Act and have effect as if made under section 25 of this Act.

Provision may be made by rules for putting such entries in the same form as is required for entries made under this Act.

(3) An application for registration under section 25 of the 1938 Act which is pending before the registrar on the commencement of this Act shall be treated as an application for registration under section 25 of this Act and shall proceed accordingly.

The registrar may require the applicant to amend his application so as to conform with the requirements of this Act.

(4) An application for registration under section 25 of the 1938 Act which has been determined by the registrar but not finally determined before the commencement of this Act shall be dealt with under the old law; and sub-paragraph (2) above shall apply in relation to any resulting entry in the register.

(5) Where before the commencement of this Act a person has become entitled by assignment or transmission to an existing registered mark but has not registered his title, any application for registration after commencement shall be made under section 25 of this Act.

(6) In cases to which sub-paragraph (3) or (5) applies section 25(3) of the 1938 Act continues to apply (and section 25(3) and (4) of this Act do not apply) as regards the consequences of failing to register.

Licensing of registered mark

9

(1) Sections 28 and 29(2) of this Act (licensing of registered trade mark; rights of exclusive licensee against grantor's successor in title) apply only in relation to licences granted after the commencement of this Act; and the old law continues to apply in relation to licences granted before commencement.

(2) Existing entries under section 28 of the 1938 Act (registered users) shall be transferred on the commencement of this Act to the register kept under this Act and have effect as if made under section 25 of this Act.

Provision may be made by rules for putting such entries in the same form as is required for entries made under this Act.

(3) An application for registration as a registered user which is pending

before the registrar on the commencement of this Act shall be treated as an application for registration of a licence under section 25(1) of this Act and shall proceed accordingly.

The registrar may require the applicant to amend his application so as to conform with the requirements of this Act.

(4) An application for registration as a registered user which has been determined by the registrar but not finally determined before the commencement of this Act shall be dealt with under the old law; and sub-paragraph (2) above shall apply in relation to any resulting entry in the register.

(5) Any proceedings pending on the commencement of this Act under section 28(8) or (10) of the 1938 Act (variation or cancellation of registration of registered user) shall be dealt with under the old law and any necessary alteration made to the new register.

Pending applications for registration

10

(1) An application for registration of a mark under the 1938 Act which is pending on the commencement of this Act shall be dealt with under the old law, subject as mentioned below, and if registered the mark shall be treated for the purposes of this Schedule as an existing registered mark.

(2) The power of the Secretary of State under section 78 of this Act to make rules regulating practice and procedure, and as to the matters mentioned in subsection (2) of that section, is exercisable in relation to such an application; and different provision may be made for such applications from that made for other applications.

(3) Section 23 of the 1938 Act (provisions as to associated trade marks) shall be disregarded in dealing after the commencement of this Act with an application for registration.

Conversion of pending application

11

(1) In the case of a pending application for registration which has not been advertised under section 18 of the 1938 Act before the commencement of this Act, the applicant may give notice to the registrar claiming to have the registrability of the mark determined in accordance with the provisions of this Act.

(2) The notice must be in the prescribed form, be accompanied by the appropriate fee and be given no later than six months after the commencement of this Act.

(3) Notice duly given is irrevocable and has the effect that the application shall be treated as if made immediately after the commencement of this Act.

Trade marks registered according to old classification

12

The registrar may exercise the powers conferred by rules under section 65 of this Act (adaptation of entries to new classification) to secure that any existing registered marks which do not conform to the system of classification prescribed under section 34 of this Act are brought to conformity with that system.

This applies, in particular, to existing registered marks classified according to the pre-1938 classification set out in Schedule 3 to the Trade Marks Rules 1986.

Claim to priority from overseas application

13

Section 35 of this Act (claim to priority of Convention application) applies to an application for registration under this Act made after the commencement of this Act notwithstanding that the Convention application was made before commencement.

14

(1) Where before the commencement of this Act a person has duly filed an application for protection of a trade mark in a relevant country within the meaning of section 39A of the 1938 Act which is not a Convention country (a 'relevant overseas application'), he, or his successor in title, has a right to priority, for the purposes of registering the same trade mark under this Act for some or all of the same goods or services, for a period of six months from the date of filing of the relevant overseas application.

(2) If the application for registration under this Act is made within that six-month period –

(a) the relevant date for the purposes of establishing which rights take precedence shall be the date of filing of the relevant overseas application, and

(b) the registrability of the trade mark shall not be affected by any use of the mark in the United Kingdom in the period between that date and the date of the application under this Act.

(3) Any filing which in a relevant country is equivalent to a regular national filing, under its domestic legislation or an international agreement, shall be treated as giving rise to the right of priority.

A 'regular national filing' means a filing which is adequate to establish the date on which the application was filed in that country, whatever may be the subsequent fate of the application.

(4) A subsequent application concerning the same subject as the relevant overseas application, filed in the same country, shall be considered the relevant overseas application (of which the filing date

is the starting date of the period of priority), if at the time of the subsequent application –

(a) the previous application has been withdrawn, abandoned or refused, without having been laid open to public inspection and without leaving any rights outstanding, and

(b) it has not yet served as a basis for claiming a right of priority.

The previous application may not thereafter serve as a basis for claiming a right of priority.

(5) Provision may be made by rules as to the manner of claiming a right to priority on the basis of a relevant overseas application.

(6) A right to priority arising as a result of a relevant overseas application may be assigned or otherwise transmitted, either with the application or independently.

The reference in sub-paragraph (1) to the applicant's 'successor in title' shall be construed accordingly.

(7) Nothing in this paragraph affects proceedings on an application for registration under the 1938 Act made before the commencement of this Act (see paragraph 10 above).

Duration and renewal of registration

15

(1) Section 42(1) of this Act (duration of original period of registration) applies in relation to the registration of a mark in pursuance of an application made after the commencement of this Act; and the old law applies in any other case.

(2) Sections 42(2) and 43 of this Act (renewal) apply where the renewal falls due on or after the commencement of this Act; and the old law continues to apply in any other case.

(3) In either case it is immaterial when the fee is paid.

Pending application for alteration of registered mark

16

An application under section 35 of the 1938 Act (alteration of registered trade mark) which is pending on the commencement of this Act shall be dealt with under the old law and any necessary alteration made to the new register.

Revocation for non-use

17

(1) An application under section 26 of the 1938 Act (removal from register or imposition of limitation on ground of non-use) which is pending on the commencement of this Act shall be dealt with under

the old law and any necessary alteration made to the new register.

(2) An application under section 46(1)(a) or (b) of this Act (revocation for non-use) may be made in relation to an existing registered mark at any time after the commencement of this Act.

Provided that no such application for the revocation of the registration of an existing registered mark registered by virtue of section 27 of the 1938 Act (defensive registration of well-known trade marks) may be made until more than five years after the commencement of this Act.

Application for rectification, etc

18

(1) An application under section 32 or 34 of the 1938 Act (rectification or correction of the register) which is pending on the commencement of this Act shall be dealt with under the old law and any necessary alteration made to the new register.

(2) For the purposes of proceedings under section 47 of this Act (grounds for invalidity of registration) as it applies in relation to an existing registered mark, the provisions of this Act shall be deemed to have been in force at all material times.

Provided that no objection to the validity of the registration of an existing registered mark may be taken on the ground specified in subsection (3) of section 5 of this Act (relative grounds for refusal of registration: conflict with earlier mark registered for different goods or services).

Regulations as to use of certification mark

19

(1) Regulations governing the use of an existing registered certification mark deposited at the Patent Office in pursuance of section 37 of the 1938 Act shall be treated after the commencement of this Act as if filed under paragraph 6 of Schedule 2 to this Act.

(2) Any request for amendment of the regulations which was pending on the commencement of this Act shall be dealt with under the old law.

Sheffield marks

20

(1) For the purposes of this Schedule the Sheffield register kept under Schedule 2 to the 1938 Act shall be treated as part of the register of trade marks kept under that Act.

(2) Applications made to the Cutlers' Company in accordance with that

Schedule which are pending on the commencement of this Act shall proceed after commencement as if they had been made to the registrar.

Certificate of validity of contested registration

21

A certificate given before the commencement of this Act under section 47 of the 1938 Act (certificate of validity of contested registration) shall have effect as if given under section 73(1) of this Act.

Trade mark agents

22

(1) Rules in force immediately before the commencement of this Act under section 282 or 283 of the Copyright, Designs and Patents Act 1988 (register of trade mark agents; persons entitled to describe themselves as registered) shall continue in force and have effect as if made under section 83 or 85 of this Act.

(2) Rules in force immediately before the commencement of this Act under section 40 of the 1938 Act as to the persons whom the registrar may refuse to recognise as agents for the purposes of business under that Act shall continue in force and have effect as if made under section 88 of this Act.

(3) Rules continued in force under this paragraph may be varied or revoked by further rules made under the relevant provisions of this Act.

Annotations

Date in force: 31 October 1994 (paras 1–9, 13, 15–22, paras 10–12, 14 in part); 29 September 1994 (remainder).

Commencement order: SI 1994 No 2550.

SCHEDULE 4
Consequential Amendments

Section 106(1)

General adaptation of existing references

1

(1) References in statutory provisions passed or made before the commencement of this Act to trade marks or registered trade marks within the meaning of the Trade Marks Act 1938 shall, unless the

context otherwise requires, be construed after the commencement of this Act as references to trade marks or registered trade marks within the meaning of this Act.

(2) Sub-paragraph (1) applies, in particular, to the references in the following provisions –

Industrial Organisation and Development Act 1947	Schedule 1, paragraph 7.
Crown Proceedings Act 1947	section 3(1)(b).
Horticulture Act 1960	section 15(1)(b).
Printer's Imprint Act 1961	section 1(1)(b).
Plant Varieties and Seeds Act 1964	section 5A(4).
Northern Ireland Constitution Act 1973	Schedule 3, paragraph 17.
Patents Act 1977	section 19(2); section 27(4); section 123(7).
Unfair Contract Terms Act 1977	Schedule 1, paragraph 1(c).
Judicature (Northern Ireland) Act 1978	section 94A(5).
State Immunity Act 1978	section 7(a) and (b).
Supreme Court Act 1981	section 72(5); Schedule 1, paragraph 1(i).
Civil Jurisdiction and Judgments Act 1982	Schedule 5, paragraph 2; Schedule 8, paragraphs 2(14) and 4(2).
Value Added Tax Act 1983	Schedule 3, paragraph 1.
Companies Act 1985	section 396(3A)(a) or (as substituted by the Companies Act 1989) section 396(2)(d)(i); section 410(4)(c)(v); Schedule 4, Part I, Balance Sheet Formats 1 and 2 and Note (2); Schedule 9, Part I, paragraphs 5(2)(d) and 10(2).
Law Reform (Miscellaneous Provisions) (Scotland) Act 1985	section 15(5).
Atomic Energy Authority Act 1986	section 8(2).
Companies (Northern Ireland) Order 1986	article 403(3A)(a) or (as substituted by the Companies (No 2) (Northern Ireland) Order 1990) article 403(2)(d)(i); Schedule 4, Part I, Balance Sheet Formats 1 and 2 and Note (2);

Companies (Northern Ireland) Order 1986 - *contd*	Schedule 9, Part I, paragraphs 5(2)(d) and 10(2).
Consumer Protection Act 1987	section 2(2)(b).
Consumer Protection (Northern Ireland) Order 1987	article 5(2)(b).
Income and Corporation Taxes Act 1988	section 83(a).
Taxation of Chargeable Gains Act 1992	section 275(h).
Tribunals and Inquiries Act 1992	Schedule 1, paragraph 34.

Patents and Designs Act 1907 (c 29)

2

(1)–(3) (. . .)

(4) The repeal by the Patents Act 1949 and the Registered Designs Act 1949 of the whole of the 1907 Act, except certain provisions, shall be deemed not to have extended to the long title, date of enactment or enacting words or to so much of section 99 as provides the Act with its short title.

3–9

(. . .)

Annotations

Date in force: 31 October 1994.

Commencement order: SI 1994 No 2550.

Para 2: sub-paras (1)–(3) amend the Patents and Designs Act 1907, ss 62, 63.

Paras 3–9: amend the Patents, Designs, Copyright and Trade Marks (Emergency) Act 1939, ss 4(1)(c), 6(1), 7(1)(a), 10(1), the Trade Descriptions Act 1968, s 34, the Solicitors Act 1974, s 22(2), (3A), the House of Commons Disqualification Act 1975, Sch 1, Part III, the Copyright, Designs and Patents Act 1988, ss 114(6), 204(6), 231(6), 280(1) and the Tribunals and Inquiries Act 1992, Sch 1, Part I, and substitute the Patents, Designs, Copyright and Trade Marks (Emergency) Act 1939, s 3 and the Restrictive Trade Practices Act 1976, Sch 3, para 4.

SCHEDULE 5
Repeals and Revocations

Section 106(2)

Chapter or number	Short title	Extent of repeal or revocation
1891 c 50.	Commissioners for Oaths Act 1891.	In section 1, the words 'or the Patents, Designs and Trade Marks Acts, 1883 to 1888,'.

Chapter or number	Short title	Extent of repeal or revocation
1907 c 29.	Patents and Designs Act 1907.	In section 63(2), the words from 'and those salaries' to the end.
1938 c 22.	Trade Marks Act 1938.	The whole Act.
1947 c 44.	Crown Proceedings Act 1947.	In section 3(1)(b), the words 'or registered service mark'.
1949 c 87.	Patents Act 1949.	Section 92(2).
1964 c 14.	Plant Varieties and Seeds Act 1964.	In section 5A(4), the words 'under the Trade Marks Act 1938'.
1967 c 80.	Criminal Justice Act 1967.	In Schedule 3, in Parts I and IV, the entries relating to the Trade Marks Act 1938.
1978 c 23.	Judicature (Northern Ireland) Act 1978.	In Schedule 5, in Part II, the paragraphs amending the Trade Marks Act 1938.
1984 c 19.	Trade Marks (Amendment) Act 1984.	The whole Act.
1985 c 6.	Companies Act 1985.	In section 396 – (a) in subsection (3A)(a), and (b) in subsection (2)(d)(i) as inserted by the Companies Act 1989, the words 'service mark,'.
1986 c 12.	Statute Law (Repeals) Act 1986.	In Schedule 2, paragraph 2.
1986 c 39.	Patents, Designs and Marks Act 1986.	Section 2; section 4(4); in Schedule 1, paragraphs 1 and 2; Schedule 2.
SI 1986/1032 (NI 6).	Companies (Northern Ireland) Order 1986.	In article 403 – (a) in paragraph (3A)(a), and (b) in paragraph (2)(d)(i) as inserted by the Companies (No 2) (Northern Ireland) Order 1990, the words 'service mark,'.
1987 c 43.	Consumer Protection Act 1987.	In section 45 – (a) in subsection (1), the definition of 'mark' and 'trade mark'; (b) subsection (4).

Chapter or number	Short title	Extent of repeal or revocation
SI 1987/2049.	Consumer Protection (Northern Ireland) Order 1987.	In article 2 – (a) in paragraph (2), the definitions of 'mark' and 'trade mark'; (b) paragraph (3).
1988 c 1.	Income and Corporation Taxes Act 1988.	In section 83, the words from 'References in this section' to the end.
1988 c 48.	Copyright, Designs and Patents Act 1988.	Sections 282 to 284; in section 286, the definition of 'registered trade mark agent'; Section 300.
1992 c 12.	Taxation of Chargeable Gains Act 1992.	In section 275(h), the words 'service marks' and 'service mark'.

Annotations

Date in force: 31 October 1994.

Commencement order: SI 1994 No 2550.

The Trade Marks Rules 1994

1994 No 2583

Made - - - 5 October 1994.

The Secretary of State, in exercise of the powers conferred upon him by sections 4(4), 13(2), 25(1), (5) and (6), 34(1), 35(5), 38(1) and (2), 39(3), 40(4), 41(1) and (3), 43(2), (3), (5) and (6), 44(3), 45(2), 63(2) and (3), 64(4), 65, 66(2), 67(1) and (2), 68(1) and (3), 69, 76(1), 78, 80(3), 81, 82 and 88 of, paragraph 6(2) of Schedule 1 to, paragraph 7(2) of Schedule 2 to, and paragraphs 10(2), 11(2), 12 and 14(5) of Schedule 3 to, the Trade Marks Act 1994, after consultation with the Council on Tribunals pursuant to section 8(1) of the Tribunals and Inquiries Act 1992, hereby makes the following Rules: –

Preliminary

1 Citation and commencement

These Rules may be cited as the Trade Marks Rules 1994 and shall come into force on 31 October 1994.

Annotations

Date in force: 31 October 1994.

2 Interpretation

(1) In these Rules, unless the context otherwise requires –

'the Act' means the Trade Marks Act 1994;

'the Journal' means the Trade Marks Journal published in accordance with rule 65 below;

'the Office' means the Patent Office;

'old law' means the Trade Marks Act 1938 (as amended) and any rules made thereunder existing immediately before the commencement of the Act;

'proprietor' means the person registered as the proprietor of the trade mark;

'publish' means publish in the Journal;

'send' includes give;

'specification' means the statement of goods or services in respect of which a trade mark is registered or proposed to be registered;

'United Kingdom' includes the Isle of Man.

(2) In these Rules, except where otherwise indicated, a reference to a section is a reference to that section in the Act, a reference to a rule is a reference to that rule in these Rules, a reference to a Schedule is a reference to that Schedule to these Rules and a reference to a form is a reference to that form as published by the registrar under rule 3 below.

(3) In these Rules references to the filing of any application, notice or other

document are to be construed as references to its being sent or delivered to the registrar at the Office.

Annotations

Date in force: 31 October 1994.

3 Forms and directions of the registrar under s 66

(1) Any forms required by the registrar to be used for the purpose of registration of a trade mark or any other proceedings before him under the Act pursuant to section 66 and any directions with respect to their use shall be published and any amendment or modification of a form or of the directions with respect to its use shall be published.

(2) A requirement under this rule to use a form as published is satisfied by the use either of a replica of that form or of a form which is acceptable to the registrar and contains the information required by the form as published and complies with any directions as to the use of such a form.

Annotations

Date in force: 31 October 1994.

The Act: Trade Marks Act 1994.

4 Requirement as to fees

(1) The fees to be paid in respect of any application, registration or any other matter under the Act and these Rules shall be those (if any) prescribed in relation to such matter by rules under section 79 (fees).

(2) Any form required to be filed with the registrar in respect of any specified matter shall be subject to the payment of the fee (if any) prescribed in respect of that matter by those rules.

Annotations

Date in force: 31 October 1994.

The Act: Trade Marks Act 1994.

Application for registration

5 Applications for registration; s 32 (Form TM3)

An application for the registration of a trade mark shall be filed on Form TM3 and shall be subject to the payment of the application fee and such class fees as may be appropriate.

Annotations

Date in force: 31 October 1994.

Section 32: Trade Marks Act 1994, s 32.

6 Claim to priority; ss 35 & 36

(1) Where a right to priority is claimed by reason of an application for protection of a trade mark duly filed in a Convention country under

section 35 or in another country or territory in respect of which provision corresponding to that made by section 35 is made under section 36, particulars of that claim shall be included in the application for registration under rule 5 above and, where no certificate as is referred to in paragraph (2) below is filed with the application, such particulars shall include the country or countries and the date or dates of filing.

(2) Unless it has been filed at the time of the filing of the application for registration, there shall be filed, within three months of the filing of the application under rule 5, a certificate by the registering or other competent authority of that country certifying, or verifying to the satisfaction of the registrar, the date of the filing of the application, the country or registering or competent authority, the representation of the mark, and the goods or services covered by the application.

Annotations

Date in force: 31 October 1994.

Sections 35, 36: Trade Marks Act 1994, ss 35, 36.

7 Classification of goods and services; s 34

(1) For the purposes of trade mark registrations in respect of goods dated before 27 July 1938, goods are classified in accordance with Schedule 3 to these Rules, except where a specification has been converted, whether under the old law or under rule 40 below, to Schedule 4.

(2) For the purposes of trade mark registrations in respect of goods dated on or after 27 July 1938 and for the purposes of any registrations dated before that date in respect of which the specifications were converted under the old law, and for the purposes of trade mark registrations in respect of services, goods and services are classified in accordance with Schedule 4, which sets out the current version of the classes of the International Classification of Goods and Services.

Annotations

Date in force: 31 October 1994.

Section 34: Trade Marks Act 1994, s 34.

8 Application may relate to more than one class and shall specify the class (Form TM3A)

(1) An application may be made for registration in more than one class of Schedule 4.

(2) Every application shall specify the class in Schedule 4 to which it relates; and if the application relates to more than one class in that Schedule the specification contained in it shall set out the classes in consecutive numerical order and list under each class the goods or services appropriate to that class.

(3) If the specification contained in the application lists items by reference to a class in Schedule 4 in which they do not fall, the applicant may request, by filing Form TM3A, that his application be amended to

include the appropriate class for those items, and upon the payment of such class fee as may be appropriate the registrar shall amend his application accordingly.

Annotations

Date in force: 31 October 1994.

9 Prohibition on registration of mark consisting of arms; s 4

Where a representation of any arms or insignia as is referred to in section 4(4) appears on a mark, the registrar shall refuse to accept an application for the registration of the mark unless satisfied that the consent of the person entitled to the arms has been obtained.

Annotations

Date in force: 31 October 1994.

Section 4: Trade Marks Act 1994, s 4.

10 Address for service (Form TM33)

(1) For the purposes of any proceedings before the registrar under these Rules or any appeal from a decision of the registrar under the Act or these Rules, an address for service in the United Kingdom shall be filed by –

(a) every applicant for the registration of a trade mark;

(b) every person opposing an application for registration of a trade mark;

(c) every applicant applying to the registrar under section 46 for the revocation of the registration of a trade mark, under section 47 for the invalidation of the registration of a trade mark, or under section 64 for the rectification of the register;

(d) every person granted leave to intervene under rule 31(5) (the intervener); and

(e) every proprietor of a registered trade mark which is the subject of an application to the registrar for the revocation, invalidation or rectification of the registration of the mark.

(2) The address for service of an applicant for registration of a trade mark shall upon registration of the mark be deemed to be the address for service of the registered proprietor, subject to any filing to the contrary under paragraph (1) above or rule 38(2) below.

(3) In any case in which an address for service is filed at the same time as the filing of a form required by the registrar under rule 3 which requires the furnishing of an address for service, the address shall be filed on that form and in any other case it shall be filed on Form TM33.

(4) Anything sent to any applicant, opponent, intervener or registered proprietor at his address for service shall be deemed to be properly sent; and the registrar may, where no address for service is filed, treat as the address for service of the person concerned his trade or business address in the United Kingdom, if any.

(5) An address for service in the United Kingdom may be filed at any time

by the proprietor of a registered trade mark and by any person having an interest in or charge on a registered trade mark which has been registered under rule 34.

(6) Where an address for service is not filed as required by paragraph (1) above, the registrar shall send the person concerned notice to file an address for service within two months of the date of the notice and if that person fails to do so –

(a) in the case of an applicant as is referred to in sub-paragraph (a) or (c), the application shall be treated as abandoned;

(b) in the case of a person as is referred to in sub-paragraph (b) or (d), he shall be deemed to have withdrawn from the proceedings; and

(c) in the case of the proprietor referred to in sub-paragraph (e), he shall not be permitted to take part in any proceedings.

Annotations

Date in force: 31 October 1994.

The Act: Trade Marks Act 1994.

11 Deficiencies in application; s 32

Where an application for registration of a trade mark does not satisfy the requirements of section 32(2), (3) or (4) or rule 5 or 8(2), the registrar shall send notice thereof to the applicant to remedy the deficiencies or, in the case of section 32(4), the default of payment and if within two months of the date of the notice the applicant –

(a) fails to remedy any deficiency notified to him in respect of section 32(2), the application shall be deemed never to have been made; or

(b) fails to remedy any deficiency notified to him in respect of section 32(3) or rule 5 or 8(2) or fails to make payment as required by section 32(4), the application shall be treated as abandoned.

Annotations

Date in force: 31 October 1994.

Section 32: Trade Marks Act 1994, s 32.

Publication, observations, oppositions and registration

12 Publication of application for registration; s 38(1)

An application which has been accepted for registration shall be published.

Annotations

Date in force: 31 October 1994.

Section 38(1): Trade Marks Act 1994, s 38(1).

13 Opposition proceedings; s 38(2) (Forms TM7 & TM8)

(1) Notice of opposition to the registration of a trade mark shall be sent to the registrar on Form TM7 within three months of the date on which the application was published under rule 12, and shall include a

statement of the grounds of opposition; the registrar shall send a copy of the notice and the statement to the applicant.

(2) Within three months of the date on which a copy of the statement is sent by the registrar to the applicant the applicant may file, in conjunction with notice of the same on Form TM8, a counter-statement; the registrar shall send a copy of the Form TM8 and the counter-statement to the person opposing the application.

(3) Within three months of the date on which a copy of the counter-statement is sent by the registrar to the person opposing the registration, that person shall file such evidence by way of statutory declaration or affidavit as he may consider necessary to adduce in support of his opposition and shall send a copy thereof to the applicant.

(4) If the person opposing the registration files no evidence under paragraph (3) above, he shall, unless the registrar otherwise directs, be deemed to have abandoned his opposition.

(5) If the person opposing the registration files evidence under paragraph (3) above or the registrar otherwise directs under paragraph (4) above, the applicant shall, within three months of the date on which either a copy of the evidence or a copy of the direction is sent to the applicant, file such evidence by way of statutory declaration or affidavit as he may consider necessary to adduce in support of his application, and shall send a copy thereof to the person opposing the application.

(6) Within three months of the date on which a copy of the applicant's evidence is sent to him, the person opposing the application may file evidence in reply by statutory declaration or affidavit which shall be confined to matters strictly in reply to the applicant's evidence, and shall send a copy thereof to the applicant.

(7) No further evidence may be filed, except that, in relation to any proceedings before him, the registrar may at any time if he thinks fit give leave to either party to file evidence upon such terms as he may think fit.

(8) Upon completion of the evidence the registrar shall, if a hearing is requested by any party to the proceedings, send to the parties notice of a date for the hearing.

Annotations

Date in force: 31 October 1994.
Section 38(2): Trade Marks Act 1994, s 38(2).

14 Decision of registrar in opposition proceedings

(1) When the registrar has made a decision on the acceptability of an application for registration following the procedure under rule 13, he shall send the applicant and the person opposing the application written notice of it, stating the reasons for his decision.

(2) For the purpose of any appeal against the registrar's decision the date of the decision shall be the date when notice of the decision is sent under paragraph (1) above.

Annotations

Date in force: 31 October 1994.

15 Observations on application to be sent to applicant; s 38(3)

The registrar shall send to the applicant a copy of any documents containing observations made under section 38(3).

Annotations

Date in force: 31 October 1994.

Section 38(3): Trade Marks Act 1994, s 38(3).

16 Publication of registration; s 40

On the registration of the trade mark the registrar shall publish the registration, specifying the date upon which the trade mark was entered in the register.

Annotations

Date in force: 31 October 1994.

Section 40: Trade Marks Act 1994, s 40.

Amendment of application

17 Amendment of application; s 39 (Form TM21)

A request for an amendment of an application to correct an error or to change the name or address of the applicant or in respect of any amendment requested after publication of the application shall be made on Form TM21.

Annotations

Date in force: 31 October 1994.

Section 39: Trade Marks Act 1994, s 39.

18 Amendment of application after publication; s 39

(1) Where, pursuant to section 39, a request is made for amendment of an application which has been published and the amendment affects the representation of the trade mark or the goods or services covered by the application, the amendment or a statement of the effect of the amendment shall also be published.

(2) Notice of opposition to the amendment shall be sent to the registrar on Form TM7 within one month of the date on which the application as amended was published under paragraph (1) above, and shall include a statement of the grounds of objection and, in particular, how the amendments would be contrary to section 39(2).

(3) The provisions of rule 13 shall apply to proceedings relating to the opposition to the amendment of the application as they apply to proceedings relating to opposition to the registration of a trade mark.

Annotations

Date in force: 31 October 1994.

Section 39: Trade Marks Act 1994, s 39.

Division, merger and series of marks

19 Division of application; s 41 (Form TM12)

(1) At any time before registration an applicant may send to the registrar a request on Form TM12 for a division of his application for registration (the original application) into two or more separate applications (divisional applications), indicating for each division the specification of goods or services; each divisional application shall be treated as a separate application for registration with the same filing date as the original application.

(2) Where the request to divide an application is sent after publication of the application, any objections in respect of, or opposition to, the original application shall be taken to apply to each divisional application and shall be proceeded with accordingly.

(3) Upon division of an original application in respect of which notice has been given to the registrar of particulars relating to the grant of a licence, or a security interest or any right in or under it, the notice and the particulars shall be deemed to apply in relation to each of the applications into which the original application has been divided.

Annotations

Date in force: 31 October 1994.

Section 41: Trade Marks Act 1994, s 41.

20 Merger of separate applications or registrations; s 41 (Form TM17)

(1) An applicant who has made separate applications for registration of a mark may, at any time before preparations for the publication of any of the applications have been completed by the Office, request the registrar on Form TM17 to merge the separate applications into a single application.

(2) The registrar shall, if satisfied that all the applications which are the subject of the request for merger –

(a) are in respect of the same trade mark,

(b) bear the same date of application, and

(c) are, at the time of the request, in the name of the same person,

merge them into a single application.

(3) The proprietor of two or more registrations of a trade mark may request the registrar on Form TM17 to merge them into a single registration; and the registrar shall, if satisfied that the registrations are in respect of the same trade mark, merge them into a single registration.

(4) Where any registration of a trade mark to be merged under paragraph (3) above is subject to a disclaimer or limitation, the merged registration shall also be restricted accordingly.

(5) Where any registration of a trade mark to be merged under paragraph (3) above has had registered in relation to it particulars relating to the grant of a licence or a security interest or any right in or under it, or of any memorandum or statement of the effect of a memorandum, the

registrar shall enter in the register the same particulars in relation to the merged registration.

(6) The date of registration of the merged registration shall, where the separate registrations bear different dates, be the latest of those dates.

Annotations

Date in force: 31 October 1994.

Section 41: Trade Marks Act 1994, s 41.

21 Registration of a series of trade marks; s 41 (Form TM12)

(1) The proprietor of a series of trade marks may apply to the registrar on Form TM3 for their registration as a series in a single registration and there shall be included in such application a representation of each mark claimed to be in the series; and the registrar shall, if satisfied that the marks constitute a series, accept the application.

(2) At any time before preparations of publication of the application have been completed by the Office, the applicant under paragraph (1) above may request on Form TM12 the division of the application into separate applications in respect of one or more marks in that series and the registrar shall, if he is satisfied that the division requested conforms with section 41(2), divide the application accordingly.

(3) At any time the applicant for registration of a series of trade marks or the proprietor of a registered series of trade marks may request the deletion of a mark in that series, and the registrar shall delete the mark accordingly.

(4) The division of an application into one or more applications under paragraph (2) above shall be subject to the payment of a divisional fee and such application and class fees as are appropriate.

Annotations

Date in force: 31 October 1994.

Section 41: Trade Marks Act 1994, s 41.

Collective and certification marks

22 Filing of regulations for collective and certification marks; Schs 1 & 2 (Form TM35)

Within nine months of the date of the application for the registration of a collective or certification mark, the applicant shall file Form TM35 accompanied by a copy of the regulations governing the use of the mark.

Annotations

Date in force: 31 October 1994.

23 Amendment of regulations of collective and certification marks; Sch 1 para 10 and Sch 2 para 11 (Forms TM36 & TM7)

(1) An application for the amendment of the regulations governing the use of a registered collective or certification mark shall be filed on Form TM36.

(2) Where it appears expedient to the registrar that the amended regulations should be made available to the public he shall publish a notice indicating where copies of the amended regulations may be inspected.

(3) Any person may, within three months of the date of publication of the notice under paragraph (2) above, make observations to the registrar on the amendments relating to the matters referred to in paragraph 6(1) of Schedule 1 in relation to a collective mark, or, paragraph 7(1) of Schedule 2 in relation to a certification mark; the registrar shall send a copy thereof to the proprietor.

(4) Any person may, within three months of the date of publication of the notice, file notice on Form TM7 to the registrar of opposition to the amendment, accompanied by a statement of the grounds of opposition, indicating why the amended regulations do not comply with the requirements of paragraph 6(1) of Schedule 1 or, as the case may be, paragraph 7(1) of Schedule 2.

(5) The registrar shall send a copy of the notice and the statement to the proprietor and thereafter the procedure in rule 13(2)–(8) shall apply to the proceedings as they apply to proceedings relating to opposition to an application for registration.

Annotations

Date in force: 31 October 1994.

Disclaimers, limitations and alteration or surrender of registered trade mark

24 Registration subject to disclaimer or limitation; s 13

Where the applicant for registration of a trade mark or the proprietor by notice in writing sent to the registrar –

(a) disclaims any right to the exclusive use of any specified element of the trade mark, or

(b) agrees that the rights conferred by the registration shall be subject to a specified territorial or other limitation,

the registrar shall make the appropriate entry in the register and publish such disclaimer or limitation.

Annotations

Date in force: 31 October 1994.

Section 13: Trade Marks Act 1994, s 13.

25 Alteration of registered trade marks; s 44 (Forms TM25 & TM7)

(1) The proprietor may request the registrar on Form TM25 for such alteration of his registered mark as is permitted under section 44; and the registrar may require such evidence by statutory declaration or otherwise as to the circumstances in which the application is made.

(2) Where, upon the request of the proprietor, the registrar proposes to allow such alteration, he shall publish the mark as altered.

(3) Any person claiming to be affected by the alteration may within three months of the date of publication of the alteration under paragraph (2) send a notice on Form TM7 to the registrar of opposition to the alteration and shall include a statement of the grounds of opposition; the registrar shall send a copy of the notice and the statement to the proprietor and thereafter the procedure in rule 13(2)–(8) shall apply to the proceedings as they apply to proceedings relating to opposition to an application for registration.

Annotations

Date in force: 31 October 1994.

Section 44: Trade Marks Act 1994, s 44.

26 Surrender of registered trade mark; s 45 (Forms TM22 & TM23)

(1) Subject to paragraph (2) below, the proprietor may surrender a registered trade mark, by sending notice to the registrar –
  - (a) on Form TM22 in respect of all the goods or services for which it is registered; or
  - (b) on Form TM23, in respect only of those goods or services specified by him in the notice.

(2) A notice under paragraph (1) above shall be of no effect unless the proprietor in that notice –
  - (a) gives the name and address of any person having a registered interest in the mark, and
  - (b) certifies that any such person –
    - (i) has been sent not less than three months' notice of the proprietor's intention to surrender the mark, or
    - (ii) is not affected or if affected consents thereto.

(3) The registrar shall, upon the surrender taking effect, make the appropriate entry in the register and publish the same.

Annotations

Date in force: 31 October 1994.

Section 45: Trade Marks Act 1994, s 45.

Renewal and restoration

27 Reminder of renewal of registration; s 43

At any time not earlier than six months nor later than one month before the expiration of the last registration of a trade mark, the registrar shall (except where renewal has already been effected under rule 28 below) send to the registered proprietor notice of the approaching expiration and inform him at the same time that the registration may be renewed in the manner described in rule 28 below.

Annotations

Date in force: 31 October 1994.

Section 43: Trade Marks Act 1994, s 43.

28 Renewal of registration; s 43 (Form TM11)

Renewal of registration shall be effected by filing a request for renewal on Form TM11 at any time within the period of six months ending on the date of the expiration of the registration.

Annotations

Date in force: 31 October 1994.

Section 43: Trade Marks Act 1994, s 43.

29 Delayed renewal and removal of registration; s 43 (Form TM11)

(1) If on the expiration of the last registration of a trade mark, the renewal fee has not been paid, the registrar shall publish that fact; and if, within six months from the date of the expiration of the last registration, the request for renewal is filed on Form TM11 accompanied by the appropriate renewal fee and additional renewal fee, the registrar shall renew the registration without removing the mark from the register.

(2) Where no request for renewal is filed as aforesaid, the registrar shall, subject to rule 30 below, remove the mark from the register.

(3) Where, in the case of a mark the registration of which (by reference to the date of application for registration) becomes due for renewal, the mark is registered at any time within six months before the date on which renewal is due, the registration may be renewed by the payment of –

- (a) the renewal fee within six months after the actual date of registration; or
- (b) the renewal fee and additional renewal fee within the period commencing on the date six months after the actual date of registration (that is to say, at the end of the period referred to in paragraph (a)) and ending on the date six months after the due date of renewal;

and, where the fees referred to in paragraph (b) are not paid within the period specified in that paragraph the registrar shall, subject to rule 30 below, remove the mark from the register.

(4) Where, in the case of a mark the registration of which (by reference to the date of application for registration) becomes due for renewal, the mark is registered after the date of renewal, the registration may be renewed by the payment of the renewal fee within six months of the actual date of registration; and where the renewal fee is not paid within

that period the registrar shall, subject to rule 30 below, remove the mark from the register.

(5) The removal of the registration of a trade mark shall be published.

Annotations

Date in force: 31 October 1994.

Section 43: Trade Marks Act 1994, s 43.

30 Restoration of registration; s 43 (Form TM13)

(1) Where the registrar has removed the mark from the register for failure to renew its registration in accordance with rule 29 above, he may, upon a request filed on Form TM13 within six months of the date of the removal of the mark accompanied by the appropriate renewal fee and appropriate restoration fee, restore the mark to the register and renew its registration if, having regard to the circumstances of the failure to renew, he is satisfied that it is just to do so.

(2) The restoration of the registration shall be published, with the date of restoration shown.

Annotations

Date in force: 31 October 1994.

Section 43: Trade Marks Act 1994, s 43.

Revocation, invalidation and rectification

31 Procedure on application for revocation, declaration of invalidity and rectification of the register; ss 46, 47 & 64 (Forms TM26 & TM27)

(1) An application to the registrar for revocation under section 46 or declaration of invalidity under section 47 of the registration of a trade mark or for the rectification of an error or omission in the register under section 64 shall be made on Form TM26 together with a statement of the grounds on which the application is made.

(2) Where any application is made under paragraph (1) by a person other than the proprietor of the registered trade mark, the registrar shall send a copy of the application and the statement to the proprietor.

(3) Within three months of the date on which the registrar sends a copy of the application and the statement to the proprietor, the proprietor may file a counter-statement together with Form TM8 and the registrar shall send a copy thereof to the applicant:

Provided that where an application for revocation is based on the ground of non-use under section 46(1)(a) or (b), the proprietor shall file (within the period allowed for the filing of any counter-statement) evidence of the use by him of the mark; and if he fails so to file evidence the registrar may treat his opposition to the application as having been withdrawn.

(4) Subject to paragraph (2) above and paragraphs (6) and (7) below, the

provisions of rule 13 shall apply to proceedings relating to the application as they apply to opposition proceedings for the registration of a trade mark, save that, in the case of an application for revocation on the grounds of non-use under section 46(1)(a) or (b), the application shall be granted where no counter-statement is filed.

(5) Any person, other than the registered proprietor, claiming to have an interest in proceedings on an application under this rule may file an application to the registrar on From TM27 for leave to intervene, stating the nature of his interest and the registrar may, after hearing the parties concerned if so required, refuse such leave or grant leave upon such terms or conditions (including any undertaking as to costs) as he thinks fit.

(6) Any person granted leave to intervene (the intervener) shall, subject to the terms and conditions imposed in respect of the intervention, be treated as a party for the purposes of the application of the provisions of rule 13 to the proceedings on an application under this rule.

(7) When the registrar has made a decision on the application following any opposition, intervention or proceedings held in accordance with this rule, he shall send the applicant, the person opposing the application and the intervener (if any) written notice of it, stating the reasons for his decision; and for the purposes of any appeal against the registrar's decision the date when the notice of the decision is sent shall be taken to be the date of the decision.

Annotations

Date in force: 31 October 1994.

Sections 46, 47, 64: Trade Marks Act 1994, ss 46, 47, 64.

The register

32 Form of register; s 63(1)

The register required to be maintained by the registrar under section 63(1) need not be kept in documentary form.

Annotations

Date in force: 31 October 1994.

Section 63(1): Trade Marks Act 1994, s 63(1).

33 Entry in register of particulars of registered trade marks; s 63(2) (Form TM24)

In addition to the entries in the register of registered trade marks required to be made by section 63(2)(a), there shall be entered in the register in respect of each trade mark registered therein the following particulars –

(a) the date of registration as determined in accordance with section 40(3) (that is to say, the date of the filing of the application for registration);

(b) the actual date of registration (that is to say, the date of the entry in the register);

(c) the priority date (if any) to be accorded pursuant to a claim to a right to priority made under section 35 or 36;
(d) the name and address of the proprietor;
(e) the address for service (if any) as furnished pursuant to rule 10 above;
(f) any disclaimer or limitation of rights under section 13(1)(a) or (b);
(g) any memorandum or statement of the effect of any memorandum relating to a trade mark of which the registrar has been notified on Form TM24;
(h) the goods or services in respect of which the mark is registered;
(i) where the mark is a collective or certification mark, that fact; and
(j) where the mark is registered pursuant to section 5(5) with the consent of the proprietor of an earlier trade mark or other earlier right, that fact.

Annotations

Date in force: 31 October 1994.

Sections 5(5), 13(1), 35, 36, 40(3), 63(2): Trade Marks Act 1994, ss 5(5), 13(1), 35, 36, 40(3), 63(2).

34 Entry in register of particulars of registrable transactions; s 25

Upon application made to the registrar by such person as is mentioned in section 25(1)(a) or (b) there shall be entered in the register the following particulars of registrable transactions, that is to say –

(a) in the case of an assignment of a registered trade mark or any right in it –
  (i) the name and address of the assignee,
  (ii) the date of the assignment, and
  (iii) where the assignment is in respect of any right in the mark, a description of the right assigned;
(b) in the case of the grant of a licence under a registered trade mark –
  (i) the name and address of the licensee,
  (ii) where the licence is an exclusive licence, that fact,
  (iii) where the licence is limited, a description of the limitation, and
  (iv) the duration of the licence if the same is or is ascertainable as a definite period;
(c) in the case of the grant of any security interest over a registered trade mark or any right in or under it –
  (i) the name and address of the grantee,
  (ii) the nature of the interest (whether fixed or floating), and
  (iii) the extent of the security and the right in or under the mark secured;
(d) in the case of the making by personal representatives of an assent in relation to a registered trade mark or any right in or under it –
  (i) the name and address of the person in whom the mark or any right in or under it vests by virtue of the assent, and
  (ii) the date of the assent; and
(e) in the case of a court or other competent authority transferring a registered trade mark or any right in or under it –
  (i) the name and address of the transferee,
  (ii) the date of the order, and

(iii) where the transfer is in respect of a right in the mark, a description of the right transferred;

and, in each case, there shall be entered the date on which the entry is made.

Annotations

Date in force: 31 October 1994.

Section 25: Trade Marks Act 1994, s 25.

35 Application to register or give notice of transaction; ss 25 & 27(3) (Forms TM16, TM24, TM50 & TM51)

(1) An application to register particulars of a transaction to which section 25 applies or to give notice to the registrar of particulars of a transaction to which section 27(3) applies shall be made, subject to paragraph (2) below,

(a) relating to an assignment or transaction other than a transaction referred to in sub-paragraphs (b) to (d) below, on form TM16;

(b) relating to a grant of a licence, on form TM50;

(c) relating to an amendment to, or termination of a licence, on form TM51;

(d) relating to the grant, amendment or termination of any security interest, on form TM24; and

(e) relating to the making by personal representatives of an assent or to an order of a court or other competent authority, on form TM24.

(2) An application under paragraph (1) above shall –

(a) where the transaction is an assignment, be signed by or on behalf of the parties to the assignment;

(b) where the transaction falls within sub-paragraphs (b), (c) or (d) of paragraph (1) above, be signed by or on behalf of the grantor of the licence or security interest;

or be accompanied by such documentary evidence as suffices to establish the transaction.

(3) Where the transaction is effected by an instrument chargeable with duty, the application shall be subject to the registrar being satisfied that the instrument has been duly stamped.

(4) Where an application to give notice to the registrar has been made of particulars relating to an application for registration of a trade mark, upon registration of the trade mark, the registrar shall enter those particulars in the register.

Annotations

Date in force: 31 October 1994.

Sections 25, 27(3): Trade Marks Act 1994, ss 25, 27(3).

36 Public inspection of register; s 63(3)

(1) The register shall be open for public inspection at the Office during the hours of business of the Office as published in accordance with rule 64 below.

(2) Where any portion of the register is kept otherwise than in documentary form, the right of inspection is a right to inspect the material on the register.

Annotations

Date in force: 31 October 1994.

Section 63(3): Trade Marks Act 1994, s 63(3).

37 Supply of certified copies etc; s 63(3) (Form TM31R)

The registrar shall supply a certified copy or extract or uncertified copy or extract, as requested on Form TM31R, of any entry in the register.

Annotations

Date in force: 31 October 1994.

Section 63(3): Trade Marks Act 1994, s 63(3).

38 Request for change of name or address in register; s 64(4) (Forms TM21 & TM33)

(1) The registrar shall, on a request made on Form TM21 by the proprietor of a registered trade mark or a licensee or any person having an interest in or charge on a registered trade mark which has been registered under rule 34, enter any change in his name or address as recorded in the register.

(2) The registrar may at any time, on a request made on Form TM33 by any person who has furnished an address for service under rule 10 above, if the address is recorded in the register, change it.

Annotations

Date in force: 31 October 1994.

Section 64(4): Trade Marks Act 1994, s 64(4).

39 Removal of matter from register; s 64(5) (Form TM7)

(1) Where it appears to the registrar that any matter in the register has ceased to have effect, before removing it from the register –
- (a) he may, where he considers it appropriate, publish his intention to remove that matter, and
- (b) where any person appears to him to be affected by the removal, he shall send notice of his intention to that person.

(2) Within three months of the date on which his intention to remove the matter is published, or notice of his intention is sent, as the case may be –
- (a) any person may file notice of opposition to the removal on form TM7; and
- (b) the person to whom a notice is sent under paragraph (1)(b) above may file, in writing –
  - (i) his objections, if any, to the removal, or
  - (ii) a request to have his objections heard orally;

and where such opposition or objections are made, rule 47 shall apply.

(3) If the registrar is satisfied after considering any objections or opposition to the removal that the matter has not ceased to have effect, he shall not remove it.

(4) Where there has been no response to the registrar's notice he may remove the matter; where representations objecting to the removal of the entry have been made (whether in writing or orally) the registrar may, if he is of the view after considering the objections that the entry or any part thereof has ceased to have effect, remove it or, as appropriate, the part thereof.

Annotations

Date in force: 31 October 1994.

Section 64(5): Trade Marks Act 1994, s 64(5).

Change of classification

40 Change of classification; ss 65(2) & 76(1)

(1) Subject to section 65(3), the registrar may –

(a) in order to reclassify the specification of a registered trade mark founded on Schedule 3 to one founded on Schedule 4, or

(b) consequent upon an amendment of the International Classification of Goods and Services referred to in rule 7(2) above,

make such amendments to entries on the register as he considers necessary for the purposes of reclassifying the specification of the registered trade mark.

(2) Before making any amendment to the register under paragraph (1) above the registrar shall give the proprietor of the mark written notice of his proposals for amendment and shall at the same time advise him that –

(a) he may make written objections to the proposals, within three months of the date of the notice, stating the grounds of his objections, and

(b) if no written objections are received within the period specified the registrar will publish the proposals and he will not be entitled to make any objections thereto upon such publication.

(3) If the proprietor makes no written objections within the period specified in paragraph (2)(a) above or at any time before the expiration of that period gives the registrar written notice of his intention not to make any objections, the registrar shall as soon as practicable after the expiration of that period or upon receipt of the notice publish the proposals.

(4) Where the proprietor makes written objections within the period specified in paragraph (2)(a) above, the registrar shall, as soon as practicable after he has considered the objections, publish the proposals or, where he has amended the proposals, publish the

proposals as amended; and his decision shall be final and not subject to appeal.

Annotations

Date in force: 31 October 1994.

Sections 65, 76(1): Trade Marks Act 1994, ss 65, 76(1).

41 Opposition to proposals; ss 65(3) & 76(1)

(1) Notice of any opposition shall be filed on Form TM7 within three months of the date of publication of the proposals under rule 40 above and there shall be stated in the notice the grounds of opposition and, in particular, how the proposed amendments would be contrary to section 65(3).

(2) The registrar may require or admit evidence directed to the questions in issue and if so requested by any person opposing the proposal give that person the opportunity to be heard thereon before deciding the matter.

(3) If no notice of opposition under paragraph (1) above is filed within the time specified, or where any opposition has been determined, the registrar shall make the amendments as proposed and shall enter in the register the date when they were made; and his decision shall be final and not subject to appeal.

Annotations

Date in force: 31 October 1994.

Sections 65(3), 76(1): Trade Marks Act 1994, ss 65(3), 76(1).

Request for information, inspection of documents and confidentiality

42 Request for information; s 67(1) (Form TM31C)

A request for information relating to an application for registration or to a registered trade mark shall be made on Form TM31C.

Annotations

Date in force: 31 October 1994.

Section 67(1): Trade Marks Act 1994, s 67(1).

43 Information available before publication; s 67(2)

Before publication of an application for registration the registrar shall make available for inspection by the public the application and any amendments made to it and any particulars contained in a notice given to the registrar under rule 35.

Annotations

Date in force: 31 October 1994.

Section 67(2): Trade Marks Act 1994, s 67(2).

44 Inspection of documents; ss 67 & 76(1)

(1) Subject to paragraphs (2) and (3) below, the registrar shall permit all documents filed or kept at the Office in relation to a registered mark or, where an application for the registration of a trade mark has been published, in relation to that application, to be inspected.

(2) The registrar shall not be obliged to permit the inspection of any such document as is mentioned in paragraph (1) above until he has completed any procedure, or the stage in the procedure which is relevant to the document in question, which he is required or permitted to carry out under the Act or these Rules.

(3) The right of inspection under paragraph (1) above does not apply to –
- (a) any document until fourteen days after it has been filed at the Office;
- (b) any document prepared in the Office solely for use therein;
- (c) any document sent to the Office, whether at its request or otherwise, for inspection and subsequent return to the sender;
- (d) any request for information under rule 42 above;
- (e) any document issued by the Office which the registrar considers should be treated as confidential;
- (f) any document in respect of which the registrar issues directions under rule 45 below that it be treated as confidential.

(4) Nothing in paragraph (1) shall be construed as imposing on the registrar any duty of making available for public inspection –
- (a) any document or part of a document which in his opinion disparages any person in a way likely to damage him; or
- (b) any document filed with or sent to the Office before 31 October 1994.

(5) No appeal shall lie from a decision of the registrar under paragraph (4) above not to make any document or part of a document available for public inspection.

Annotations

Date in force: 31 October 1994.

Sections 67, 76(1): Trade Marks Act 1994, ss 67, 76(1).

45 Confidential documents

(1) Where a document other than a form required by the registrar and published in accordance with rule 3 above is filed at the Office and the person filing it requests, at the time of filing or within fourteen days of the filing, that it or a specified part of it be treated as confidential, giving his reasons, the registrar may direct that it or part of it, as the case may be, be treated as confidential, and the document shall not be open to public inspection while the matter is being determined by the registrar.

(2) Where such direction has been given and not withdrawn, nothing in this rule shall be taken to authorise or require any person to be allowed to inspect the document or part of it to which the direction relates except by leave of the registrar.

(3) The registrar shall not withdraw any direction given under this rule without prior consultation with the person at whose request the direction was given, unless the registrar is satisfied that such prior consultation is not reasonably practical.

(4) The registrar may where he considers that any document issued by the Office should be treated as confidential so direct, and upon such direction that document shall not be open to public inspection except by leave of the registrar.

(5) Where a direction is given under this rule for a document to be treated as confidential a record of the fact shall be filed with the document.

Annotations

Date in force: 31 October 1994.

Agents

46 Proof of authorisation of agent may be required; s 82 (Form TM33)

(1) Where an agent has been authorised under section 82, the registrar may in any particular case require the personal signature or presence of the agent or the person authorising him to act as agent.

(2) Where after a person has become a party to proceedings before the registrar, he appoints an agent for the first time or appoints one agent in substitution for another, the newly appointed agent shall file Form TM33, and any act required or authorised by the Act in connection with the registration of a trade mark or any procedure relating to a trade mark may not be done by or to the newly appointed agent until on or after the date on which he files that form.

(3) The registrar may by notice in writing sent to an agent require him to produce evidence of his authority.

Annotations

Date in force: 31 October 1994.

The Act: Trade Marks Act 1994.

47 Registrar may refuse to deal with certain agents; s 88

The registrar may refuse to recognise as agent in respect of any business under the Act –

(a) a person who has been convicted of an offence under section 84;

(b) an individual whose name has been erased from and not restored to, or who is suspended from, the register of trade mark agents on the ground of misconduct;

(c) a person who is found by the Secretary of State to have been guilty of such conduct as would, in the case of an individual registered in that register, render him liable to have his name erased from it on the ground of misconduct;

(d) a partnership or body corporate of which one of the partners or directors is a person whom the registrar could refuse to recognise under paragraph (a), (b) or (c) above.

Annotations
Date in force: 31 October 1994.
The Act: Trade Marks Act 1994.

Decision of registrar, evidence and costs

48 Decisions of registrar to be taken after hearing

(1) Without prejudice to any provisions of the Act or these Rules requiring the registrar to hear any party to proceedings under the Act or these Rules, or to give such party an opportunity to be heard, the registrar shall, before taking any decision on any matter under the Act or these Rules which is or may be adverse to any party to any proceedings before him, give that party an opportunity to be heard.
(2) The registrar shall give that party at least fourteen days' notice of the time when he may be heard unless that party consents to shorter notice.

Annotations
Date in force: 31 October 1994.
The Act: Trade Marks Act 1994.

49 Evidence in proceedings before registrar; s 69

(1) Where under these Rules evidence may be admitted by the registrar in any proceedings before him, it shall be by the filing of a statutory declaration or affidavit.
(2) The registrar may in any particular case take oral evidence in lieu of or in addition to such evidence and shall, unless he otherwise directs, allow any witness to be cross-examined on his statutory declaration, affidavit or oral evidence.

Annotations
Date in force: 31 October 1994.
Section 69: Trade Marks Act 1994, s 69.

50 Making and subscription of statutory declaration or affidavit

(1) Any statutory declaration or affidavit filed under the Act or these Rules shall be made and subscribed as follows –
  (a) in the United Kingdom, before any justice of the peace or any commissioner or other officer authorised by law in any part of the United Kingdom to administer an oath for the purpose of any legal proceedings;
  (b) in any other part of Her Majesty's dominions or in the Republic of

Ireland, before any court, judge, justice of the peace or any officer authorised by law to administer an oath there for the purpose of any legal proceedings; and

(c) elsewhere, before a commissioner for oaths, notary public, judge or magistrate.

(2) Any document purporting to have affixed, impressed or subscribed thereto or thereon the seal or signature of any person authorised by paragraph (1) above to take a declaration may be admitted by the registrar without proof of the genuineness of the seal or signature, or of the official character of the person or his authority to take the declaration.

Annotations

Date in force: 31 October 1994.

The Act: Trade Marks Act 1994.

51 Registrar's power to require documents, information or evidence

At any stage of any proceedings before the registrar, he may direct that such documents, information or evidence as he may reasonably require shall be filed within such period as he may specify.

Annotations

Date in force: 31 October 1994.

52 Registrar to have power of an official referee; s 69

(1) The registrar shall in relation to the examination of witnesses on oath and the discovery and production of documents have all the powers of an official referee of the Supreme Court.

(2) The rules applicable to the attendance of witnesses before such a referee shall apply in relation to the attendance of witnesses in proceedings before the registrar.

Annotations

Date in force: 31 October 1994.

Section 69: Trade Marks Act 1994, s 69.

53 Hearings before registrar to be in public

(1) The hearing before the registrar of any dispute between two or more parties relating to any matter in connection with an application for the registration of a mark or a registered mark shall be in public unless the registrar, after consultation with those parties who appear in person or are represented at the hearing, otherwise directs.

(2) Nothing in this rule shall prevent a member of the Council on Tribunals or of its Scottish Committee from attending a hearing in his capacity as such.

Annotations

Date in force: 31 October 1994.

54 Costs of proceedings; s 68

The registrar may, in any proceedings before him under the Act or these Rules, by order award to any party such costs as he may consider reasonable, and direct how and by what parties they are to be paid.

Annotations

Date in force: 31 October 1994.

The Act: Trade Marks Act 1994.

55 Security for costs; s 68

(1) The registrar may require any person who is a party in any proceedings before him under the Act or these Rules to give security for costs in relation to those proceedings; and he may require security for the costs of any appeal from his decision.

(2) In default of such security being given, the registrar, in the case of the proceedings before him, or, in the case of an appeal, the person appointed under section 76 may treat the party in default as having withdrawn his application, opposition, objection or intervention, as the case may be.

Annotations

Date in force: 31 October 1994.

The Act: Trade Marks Act 1994.

56 Decision of registrar (Form TM5)

(1) When, in any proceedings before him, the registrar has made a decision following a hearing or, if a hearing has not been requested, after considering any submission in writing, he shall send notice of his decision in writing to each party to the proceedings, and for the purpose of any appeal against the registrar's decision, subject to paragraph (2) below, the date of the decision shall be the date when the notice is sent.

(2) Where a statement of the reasons for the decision is not included in the notice sent under paragraph (1) above, any party may, within one month of the date on which the notice was sent to him, request the registrar on form TM5 to send him a statement of the reasons for the decision and upon such request the registrar shall send such a statement; and the date on which that statement is sent shall be deemed to be the date of the registrar's decision for the purpose of any appeal against it.

Annotations

Date in force: 31 October 1994.

Appeals

57 Appeal to person appointed; s 76

(1) Notice of appeal to the person appointed under section 76 shall be sent to the registrar within one month of the date of the registrar's decision

which is the subject of the appeal accompanied by a statement in writing of the appellant's grounds of appeal and of his case in support of the appeal.

(2) The registrar shall send the notice and the statement to the person appointed.

(3) Where any person other than the appellant was a party to the proceedings before the registrar in which the decision appealed against was made, the registrar shall send to that person a copy of the notice and the statement.

Annotations

Date in force: 31 October 1994.

Section 76: Trade Marks Act 1994, s 76.

58 Determination whether appeal should be referred to court; s 76(3)

(1) Within one month of the date on which the notice of appeal is sent by the registrar under rule 57(3) above;

- (a) the registrar, or
- (b) any person who was a party to the proceedings in which the decision appealed against was made,

may request that the person appointed refer the appeal to the court.

(2) Where the registrar requests that the appeal be referred to the court, he shall send a copy of the request to each party to the proceedings.

(3) A request under paragraph (1)(b) above shall be sent to the registrar; the registrar shall send it to the person appointed and shall send a copy of the request to any other party to the proceedings.

(4) Within one month of the date on which a copy of a request is sent by the registrar under paragraph (2) or (3) above, the person to whom it is sent may make representations as to whether the appeal should be referred to the court.

(5) In any case where it appears to the person appointed that a point of general legal importance is involved in the appeal, he shall send to the registrar and to every party to the proceedings in which the decision appealed against was made, notice thereof.

(6) Within one month of the date on which a notice is sent under paragraph (5) above, the person to whom it was sent may make representations as to whether the appeal should be referred to the court.

Annotations

Date in force: 31 October 1994.

Section 76(3): Trade Marks Act 1994, s 76(3).

59 Hearing of appeal; s 76(4)

(1) Where the person appointed does not refer the appeal to the court, he shall send notice of the time and place appointed for the hearing of the appeal –

- (a) where no person other than the appellant was a party to the

proceedings in which the decision appealed against was made, to the registrar and to the appellant, and
(b) in any other case, to the registrar and to each person who was a party to those proceedings.
(2) The provisions of rule 48(2) and rules 49 to 55 shall apply to the person appointed and to proceedings before the person appointed as they apply to the registrar and to proceedings before the registrar.
(3) The person appointed shall send a copy of his decision, with a statement of his reasons therefor, to the registrar and to each person who was a party to the proceedings before him.

Annotations
Date in force: 31 October 1994.
Section 76(4): Trade Marks Act 1994, s 76(4).

Correction of irregularities, calculation and extension of time

60 Correction of irregularities of procedure

(1) Any irregularity in procedure in or before the Office or the registrar may be rectified, subject to paragraph (2) below, on such terms as he may direct.
(2) In the case of an irregularity or prospective irregularity –
(a) which consists of a failure to comply with any limitation as to times or periods specified in the Act, these Rules or the old law as that law continues to apply and which has occurred or appears to the registrar as likely to occur in the absence of a direction under this rule, and
(b) which is attributable wholly or in part to an error, default or omission on the part of the Office or the registrar and which it appears to him should be rectified,
he may direct that the time or period in question shall be altered in such manner as he may specify.
(3) Paragraph (2) above is without prejudice to the registrar's power to extend any time or periods under rule 62 below.

Annotations
Date in force: 31 October 1994.
The Act: Trade Marks Act 1994.

61 Calculation of times and periods

(1) Where, on any day, there is –
(a) a general interruption or subsequent dislocation in the postal services of the United Kingdom, or
(b) an event or circumstances causing an interruption in the normal operation of the Office,
the registrar may certify the day as being one on which there is an

'interruption' and, where any period of time specified in the Act or these Rules for the giving, making or filing of any notice, application or other document expires on a day so certified the period shall be extended to the first day next following (not being an excluded day) which is not so certified.

(2) Any certificate of the registrar given pursuant to this rule shall be posted in the Office.

(3) If in any particular case the registrar is satisfied that the failure to give, make or file any notice, application or other document within any period of time specified in the Act or these Rules for such giving, making or filing was wholly or mainly attributable to a failure or undue delay in the postal services in the United Kingdom, the registrar may, if he thinks fit, extend the period so that it ends on the day of the receipt by the addressee of the notice, application or other document (or, if the day of such receipt is an excluded day, on the first following day which is not an excluded day), upon such notice to other parties and upon such terms as he may direct.

(4) In this rule 'excluded day' means a day which is not a business day of the Office under the registrar's direction pursuant to section 80, as published in accordance with rule 64 below.

Annotations

Date in force: 31 October 1994.

The Act: Trade Marks Act 1994.

62 Alteration of time limits (Form TM9)

(1) The time or periods –

(a) prescribed by these Rules, other than the times or periods prescribed by the rules mentioned in paragraph (3) below, or

(b) specified by the registrar for doing any act or taking any proceedings,

may, at the request of the person or party concerned, be extended by the registrar as he thinks fit, upon such notice to any other person or party affected and upon such terms as he may direct.

(2) A request for the extension of a period prescribed by these Rules which is filed after the application has been published under rule 12 above shall be on Form TM9 and shall in any other case be on that form if the registrar so directs.

(3) The rules excepted from paragraph (1) above are rule 10(6) (failure to file address for service), rule 11 (deficiencies in application), rule 13(1) (time for filing opposition), rule 13(2) (time for filing counter-statement), rule 29 (delayed renewal) and rule 30 (restoration of registration).

(4) Subject to paragraph (5) below, a request for extension under paragraph (1) above shall be made before the time or period in question has expired.

(5) Where the request for extension is made after the time or period has expired, the registrar may, at his discretion, extend the period or time if

he is satisfied with the explanation for the delay in requesting the extension and it appears to him that any extension would not disadvantage any other person or party affected by it.

(6) Where the period within which any party to any proceedings before the registrar may file evidence under these Rules is to begin upon the expiry of any period in which any other party may file evidence and that other party notifies the registrar that he does not wish to file any, or any further, evidence the registrar may direct that the period within which the first mentioned party may file evidence shall begin on such date as may be specified in the direction and shall notify all parties to the dispute of that date.

Annotations

Date in force: 31 October 1994.

Filing of documents, hours of business, Trade Marks Journal and translations

63 Filing of documents by electronic means

The registrar may, at his discretion, permit as an alternative to the sending by post or delivery of the application, notice or other document in legible form the filing of the application, notice or other document by electronic means subject to such terms or conditions as he may specify either generally by published notice or in any particular case by written notice to the person desiring to file any such documents by such means.

Annotations

Date in force: 31 October 1994.

64 Directions on hours of business; s 80

Any directions given by the registrar under section 80 specifying the hours of business of the Office and business days of the Office shall be published and posted in the Office.

Annotations

Date in force: 31 October 1994.

Section 80: Trade Marks Act 1994, s 80.

65 Trade Marks Journal; s 81

The registrar shall publish a journal, entitled 'The Trade Marks Journal', containing particulars of any application for the registration of a trade mark (including a representation of the mark), such information as is required to be published under these Rules and such other information as the registrar thinks fit.

Annotations

Date in force: 31 October 1994.

Section 81: Trade Marks Act 1994, s 81.

66 Translations

(1) Where any document or part thereof which is in a language other than English is filed or sent to the registrar in pursuance of the Act or these Rules, the registrar may require that there be furnished a translation into English of the document or that part, verified to the satisfaction of the registrar as corresponding to the original text.

(2) The registrar may refuse to accept any translation which is in his opinion inaccurate and thereupon another translation of the document in question verified as aforesaid shall be furnished.

Annotations

Date in force: 31 October 1994.

The Act: Trade Marks Act 1994.

Transitional provisions and revocations

67 Pending applications for registration; Sch 3, para 10(2)

Where an application for registration of a mark made under the old law is advertised on or after 31 October 1994, the period within which notice of opposition may be filed shall be three months from the date of advertisement, and such period shall not be extendible.

Annotations

Date in force: 31 October 1994.

Sch 3, para 10(2): Trade Marks Act 1994, Sch 3, para 10(2).

68 Form for conversions of pending application; Sch 3, para 11(2)

A notice to the registrar under paragraph 11(2) of Schedule 3 to the Act, claiming to have the registrability of the mark determined in accordance with the provisions of the Act, shall be in the form set out in Schedule 2 to these Rules.

Annotations

Date in force: 31 October 1994.

The Act: Trade Marks Act 1994.

69 Revocation of previous Rules

(1) The Rules specified in Schedule 1 are hereby revoked.

(2) Except as provided by rule 67 above, where –

(a) immediately before these Rules come into force, any time or period prescribed by the Rules hereby revoked has effect in relation to any act or proceeding and has not expired, and

(b) the corresponding time or period prescribed by these Rules would have expired or would expire earlier,

the time or period prescribed by those Rules and not by these Rules shall apply to that act or proceeding.

Annotations

Date in force: 31 October 1994.

SCHEDULE 1
Revocations

Rule 69

Rules revoked	**Reference**
The Trade Marks and Service Marks Rules 1986	SI 1986/1319
The Trade Marks and Service Marks (Amendment) Rules 1988	SI 1988/1112
The Trade Marks and Service Marks (Amendment) Rules 1989	SI 1989/1117
The Trade Marks and Service Marks (Amendment) Rules 1990	SI 1990/1459
The Trade Marks and Service Marks (Amendment) (No 2) Rules 1990	SI 1990/1799
The Trade Marks and Service Marks (Amendment) Rules 1991	SI 1991/1431
The Trade Marks and Service Marks (Amendment) Rules 1994	SI 1994/2549

Annotations

Date in force: 31 October 1994.

SCHEDULE 2

Rule 68

Form TM15

Notice under Schedule 3, paragraph 11 of the Act: claim to have registrability of a mark applied for before 31 October 1994 determined under the Act (Conversion of application)

1

Your reference

2

Give details of the application you made under the Trade Marks Act 1938

Number Class

3

Full name, address and postcode of the applicant

Trade Marks ADP number (if you know it)

4

Name of agent (if appropriate) address for service in the United Kingdom which all correspondence should be sent to (including postcode)

Trade Marks ADP number (if you know it)

I claim to have the registrability of the mark determined in accordance with the provisions of the Trade Marks Act 1994. I acknowledge that this notice is irrevocable.

Signature

Name (block capitals)

Date

Name and daytime telephone number of person we should contact

State the number of any sheets attached to this form

Reminder

You cannot amend a mark under the 1994 Act. If you want to amend the mark you must file form TM21 before or with this form.

The new filing date of your converted application will be the 31st October 1994, which is the commencement date of the 1994 Act.

Form TM15

Annotations

Date in force: 31 October 1994.

The Act: Trade Marks Act 1994.

SCHEDULE 3
Classification of Goods (Pre-1938)

Rule 7(1)

Class 1	Chemical substances used in manufactures, photography, or philosophical research, and anti-corrosives.
Class 2	Chemical substances used for agricultural, horticultural, veterinary and sanitary purposes.
Class 3	Chemical substances prepared for use in medicine and pharmacy.
Class 4	Raw, or partly prepared, vegetable, animal, and mineral substances used in manufactures, not included in other Classes.
Class 5	Unwrought and partly wrought metals used in manufacture.
Class 6	Machinery of all kinds, and parts of machinery, except agricultural and horticultural machines and their parts included in Class 7.

Class 7	Agricultural and horticultural machinery, and parts of such machinery.
Class 8	Philosophical instruments, scientific instruments, and apparatus for useful purposes; instruments and apparatus for teaching.
Class 9	Musical instruments.
Class 10	Horological instruments.
Class 11	Instruments, apparatus, and contrivances, not medicated, for surgical or curative purposes, or in relation to the health of men or animals.
Class 12	Cutlery and edge tools.
Class 13	Metal goods, not included in other Classes.
Class 14	Goods of precious metals and jewellery, and imitations of such goods and jewellery.
Class 15	Glass.
Class 16	Porcelain and earthenware.
Class 17	Manufactures from mineral and other substances for building or decoration.
Class 18	Engineering, architectural, and building contrivances.
Class 19	Arms, ammunition, and stores, not included in Class 20.
Class 20	Explosive substances.
Class 21	Naval architectural contrivances and naval equipments not included in other Classes.
Class 22	Carriages.
Class 23	(a) Cotton yarn; (b) Sewing cotton.
Class 24	Cotton piece goods.
Class 25	Cotton goods not included in other Classes.
Class 26	Linen and hemp yarn and thread.
Class 27	Linen and hemp piece goods.
Class 28	Linen and hemp goods not included in other Classes.
Class 29	Jute yarns and tissues, and other articles made of jute, not included in other Classes.
Class 30	Silk, spun, thrown, or sewing.
Class 31	Silk piece goods.
Class 32	Silk goods not included in other Classes.
Class 33	Yarns of wool, worsted, or hair.
Class 34	Cloths and stuffs of wool, worsted, or hair.
Class 35	Woollen and worsted and hair goods, not included in other Classes.
Class 36	Carpets, floor-cloth, and oil-cloth.
Class 37	Leather, skins unwrought and wrought, and articles made of leather not included in other Classes.
Class 38	Articles of clothing.
Class 39	Paper (except paper hangings), stationery, and book-binding.
Class 40	Goods manufactured from india-rubber and gutta- percha not included in other Classes.
Class 41	Furniture and upholstery.
Class 42	Substances used as food or as ingredients in food.

Class 43 Fermented liquors and spirits.

Class 44 Mineral and aerated waters, natural and artificial, including ginger beer.

Class 45 Tobacco, whether manufactured or unmanufactured.

Class 46 Seeds for agricultural and horticultural purposes.

Class 47 Candles, common soap, detergents; illuminating, heating, or lubricating oils; matches; and starch, blue, and other preparations for laundry purposes.

Class 48 Perfumery (including toilet articles, preparations for the teeth and hair, and perfumed soap).

Class 49 Games of all kinds and sporting articles not included in other Classes.

Class 50 Miscellaneous –

(1) Goods manufactured from ivory, bone or wood, not included in other Classes.
(2) Goods manufactured from straw or grass, not included in other Classes.
(3) Goods manufactured from animal and vegetable substances, not included in other Classes.
(4) Tobacco pipes.
(5) Umbrellas, walking sticks, brushes and combs for the hair.
(6) Furniture cream, plate powder.
(7) Tarpaulins, tents, rick-cloths, rope (jute or hemp), twine.
(8) Buttons of all kinds other than of precious metal or imitations thereof.
(9) Packing and hose.
(10) Other goods not included in the foregoing Classes.

Annotations

Date in force: 31 October 1994.

SCHEDULE 4
Classification of Goods and Services

Rule 7(2)

Goods

Class 1 Chemicals used in industry, science and photography, as well as in agriculture, horticulture and forestry; unprocessed artificial resins, unprocessed plastics; manures; fire extinguishing compositions; tempering and soldering preparations; chemical substances for preserving foodstuffs; tanning substances; adhesives used in industry.

Class 2 Paints, varnishes, lacquers; preservatives against rust and against deterioration of wood; colorants; mordants; raw natural resins; metals in foil and powder form for painters, decorators, printers and artists.

Class 3 Bleaching preparations and other substances for laundry use; cleaning, polishing, scouring and abrasive preparations; soaps; perfumery, essential oils, cosmetics, hair lotions; dentifrices.

Class 4 Industrial oils and greases; lubricants; dust absorbing, wetting and binding compositions; fuels (including motor spirit) and illuminants; candles, wicks.

Class 5 Pharmaceutical, veterinary and sanitary preparations; dietetic substances adapted for medical use, food for babies; plasters, materials for dressings; material for stopping teeth, dental wax; disinfectants; preparations for destroying vermin; fungicides, herbicides.

Class 6 Common metals and their alloys; metal building materials; transportable buildings of metal; materials of metal for railway tracks; non-electric cables and wires of common metal; ironmongery, small items of metal hardware; pipes and tubes of metal; safes; goods of common metal not included in other classes; ores.

Class 7 Machines and machine tools; motors and engines (except for land vehicles); machine coupling and transmission components (except for land vehicles); agricultural implements; incubators for eggs.

Class 8 Hand tools and implements (hand operated); cutlery; side arms; razors.

Class 9 Scientific, nautical, surveying, electric, photographic, cinematographic, optical, weighing, measuring, signalling, checking (supervision), life-saving and teaching apparatus and instruments; apparatus for recording, transmission or reproduction of sound or images; magnetic data carriers, recording discs; automatic vending machines and mechanisms for coin-operated apparatus; cash registers, calculating machines, data processing equipment and computers; fire-extinguishing apparatus.

Class 10 Surgical, medical, dental and veterinary apparatus and instruments, artificial limbs, eyes and teeth; orthopaedic articles; suture materials.

Class 11 Apparatus for lighting, heating, steam generating, cooking, refrigerating, drying, ventilating, water supply and sanitary purposes.

Class 12 Vehicles; apparatus for locomotion by land, air or water.

Class 13 Firearms; ammunition and projectiles; explosives; fireworks.

Class 14 Precious metals and their alloys and goods in precious metals or coated therewith, not included in other classes; jewellery, precious stones; horological and chronometric instruments.

Class 15 Musical instruments.

Class 16 Paper, cardboard and goods made from these materials, not included in other classes; printed matter; bookbinding material;

photographs; stationery; adhesives for stationery or household purposes; artists' materials; paint brushes; typewriters and office requisites (except furniture); instructional and teaching material (except apparatus); plastic materials for packaging (not included in other classes); playing cards; printers' type; printing blocks.

Class 17 Rubber, gutta-percha, gum, asbestos, mica and goods made from these materials and not included in other classes; plastics in extruded form for use in manufacture; packing, stopping and insulating materials; flexible pipes, not of metal.

Class 18 Leather and imitations of leather, and goods made of these materials and not included in other classes; animal skins, hides; trunks and travelling bags; umbrellas, parasols and walking sticks; whips, harness and saddlery.

Class 19 Building materials (non-metallic); non-metallic rigid pipes for building; asphalt, pitch and bitumen; non-metallic transportable buildings; monuments, not of metal.

Class 20 Furniture, mirrors, picture frames; goods (not included in other classes) of wood, cork, reed, cane, wicker, horn, bone, ivory, whalebone, shell, amber, mother-of-pearl, meerschaum and substitutes for all these materials, or of plastics.

Class 21 Household or kitchen utensils and containers (not of precious metal or coated therewith); combs and sponges; brushes (except paint brushes); brush-making materials; articles for cleaning purposes; steel wool; unworked or semi-worked glass (except glass used in building); glassware, porcelain and earthenware not included in other classes.

Class 22 Ropes, string, nets, tents, awnings, tarpaulins, sails, sacks and bags (not included in other classes); padding and stuffing materials (except of rubber or plastics); raw fibrous textile materials.

Class 23 Yarns and threads, for textile use.

Class 24 Textiles and textile goods, not included in other classes; bed and table covers.

Class 25 Clothing, footwear, headgear.

Class 26 Lace and embroidery, ribbons and braid; buttons, hooks and eyes, pins and needles; artificial flowers.

Class 27 Carpets, rugs, mats and matting, linoleum and other materials for covering existing floors; wall hangings (non-textile).

Class 28 Games and playthings; gymnastic and sporting articles not included in other classes; decorations for Christmas trees.

Class 29 Meat, fish, poultry and game; meat extracts; preserved, dried and cooked fruits and vegetables; jellies, jams, fruit sauces; eggs, milk and milk products; edible oils and fats.

Class 30 Coffee, tea, cocoa, sugar, rice, tapioca, sago, artificial coffee; flour and preparations made from cereals, bread, pastry and confectionery, ices; honey, treacle; yeast, baking-powder; salt, mustard; vinegar, sauces (condiments); spices; ice.

Class 31 Agricultural, horticultural and forestry products and grains not included in other classes; live animals; fresh fruits and vegetables; seeds, natural plants and flowers; foodstuffs for animals, malt.

Class 32 Beers; mineral and aerated waters and other non-alcoholic drinks; fruit drinks and fruit juices; syrups and other preparations for making beverages.

Class 33 Alcoholic beverages (except beers).

Class 34 Tobacco; smokers' articles; matches.

Services

Class 35 Advertising; business management; business administration; office functions.

Class 36 Insurance; financial affairs; monetary affairs; real estate affairs.

Class 37 Building construction; repair; installation services.

Class 38 Telecommunications.

Class 39 Transport; packaging and storage of goods; travel arrangement.

Class 40 Treatment of materials.

Class 41 Education; providing of training; entertainment; sporting and cultural activities.

Class 42 Providing of food and drink; temporary accommodation; medical, hygienic and beauty care; veterinary and agricultural services; legal services; scientific and industrial research; computer programming; services that cannot be placed in other classes.

Annotations

Date in force: 31 October 1994.

Comparison between the 1938 Act and the 1994 Act

Summarised below are the key differences between the 1938 Act and the 1994 Act

Subject	1938 Act	1994 Act
The Register	Divided into Parts A and B	Unified register
Trade Marks Definition 1	Marks used for the purpose of indicating a connection in the course of trade	Signs capable of distinguishing the applicant's goods or services
Trade Marks Definition 2	Something applied to or attached to the goods	A sign may consist of the goods themselves
Registrability Definition 1	Onus on proprietor to establish registrability	Onus on registrar to establish grounds for refusal of registration
Registrability Definition 2	Test of inherently capable of distinguishing in fact and in law	Distinctiveness in fact only required
Registrar's discretion	Overriding discretion to refuse registration	No discretion to refuse registration
Multi-class applications/ registrations	Not available	Available
Assignment of applications	Not permitted	Permitted

Subject	1938 Act	1994 Act
Amendment of an application	More liberal, s 17(7)	More limited, s 39(2)
Divisional applications	Not available	Available
Merger of applications and registrations	Not available	Available
Advertisement prior to acceptance	Available pursuant to s 18(1)	Not available
Observations after acceptance	Not available	Available under s 38(3)
Extensions of time: opposition	Allowed	Not allowed: three months maximum
Registrability: effect of consent	Registrar retained overriding discretion to refuse	Overcomes relative grounds for refusal: s 5(5)
Compulsory disclaimers	May have been imposed by the registrar	Not applicable. Voluntary disclaimers and limitations only
Conditions of registration	May have been imposed by the registrar	Not applicable. Existing conditions will be removed
Association of trade marks	Available under s 23	Not available
Alteration of a registered trade mark	More liberal, s 35	More limited, s 44
Restoration of a removed registration	No time limit	Six month time limit

Subject	1938 Act	1994 Act
Conflicts with earlier trade marks	Prior registered marks in the United Kingdom only relevant	United Kingdom, Community and international registrations as well as well-known marks are now all relevant
Infringement	Limited to use on goods or services within the specification	Similar goods or services also protected as well as goods and services which are not similar under s 10(3)
Comparative advertising	Often led to infringement: s 4(1)(b)	No infringement if in accordance with honest practices in industrial or commercial matters: s 10(6)
Use of a trade mark Definition 1	Printed or other visual representation, s 68(2)	Not restricted to graphic representation, s 103(2)
Use of a trade mark Definition 2	Use on goods or services of the same description was sufficient to avoid non-use, s 26	Use must be on the actual goods or services for which the mark is registered, s 49
Use of a trade mark Definition 3	Use by registered users deemed to be use by proprietor	Use by any third party with proprietor's consent sufficient to overcome non-use action, s 46(1)
Non-use	Onus on applicant for expungement to establish non-use	Onus on proprietor to show use
Registered users/licensees	Licensees registered as registered users on substantive examination	Prescribed particulars of licences only recorded. No examination: s 25

Subject	1938 Act	1994 Act
Trafficking	Recording as registered users prohibited: s 28(6)	No express prohibition
Well-known trade marks	Defensive registration for invented words only	Wide protection and remedies even if unregistered
Defensive registrations	Available	Not available: see well-known trade marks
Collective marks	Not recognised	Available for registration: s 49 and Schedule 1
Invalidity: distinctiveness acquired since registration	Not relevant	Good defence to application for declaration of invalidity: s 47(1) proviso
Deemed validity	Section 13: after 7 years for Part A marks	Prima facie evidence of validity, s 72; no deemed validity
Duration of registration	7+14 (etc) years	10+10 (etc) years

Schedule 1: Paris Convention for the Protection of Industrial Property

Status on 10 December 1997

State	Date on which State became party to the Convention	Latest Act[1] of the Convention to which State is party and date on which State became party to that Act	
Albania	4 October 1995	Stockholm:	4 October 1995
Algeria	1 March 1966	Stockholm:	20 April 1975[2]
Argentina	10 February 1967	Lisbon:	10 February 1967
		Stockholm:	Articles 13 to 30: 8 October 1980
Armenia	25 December 1991	Stockholm:	25 December 1991[2]
Australia	10 October 1925	Stockholm:	Articles 1 to 12: 27 September 1975
		Stockholm:	Articles 13 to 30: 25 August 1972
Austria	1 January 1909	Stockholm:	18 August 1973
Azerbaijan	25 December 1995	Stockholm:	25 December 1995
Bahamas	10 July 1973	Lisbon:	10 July 1973
		Stockholm:	Articles 13 to 30: 10 March 1977
Bahrain	29 October 1997	Stockholm:	29 October 1997
Bangladesh	3 March 1991	Stockholm:	3 March 1991[2]
Barbados	12 March 1985	Stockholm:	12 March 1985
Belarus	25 December 1991	Stockholm:	25 December 1991[2]
Belgium	7 July 1884	Stockholm:	12 February 1975
Benin	10 January 1967	Stockholm:	12 March 1975
Bolivia	4 November 1993	Stockholm:	4 November 1993
Bosnia and Herzegovina	1 March 1992	Stockholm:	1 March 1992
Brazil	7 July 1884	Stockholm:	Articles 1 to 12: 24 November 1992
		Stockholm:	Articles 13 to 30: 24 March 1975[2]

1 'Stockholm' means the Paris Convention for the Protection of Industrial Property as revised at Stockholm on 14 July 1967 (Stockholm Act); 'Lisbon' means the Paris Convention as revised at Lisbon on 31 October 1958 (Lisbon Act); 'London' means the Paris Convention as revised at London on 2 June 1934 (London Act); 'The Hague' means the Paris Convention as revised at The Hague on 6 November 1925 (Hague Act).

2 With the declaration provided for in Article 28(2) of the Stockholm Act relating to the International Court of Justice.

State	Date on which State became party to the Convention	Latest Act[1] of the Convention to which State is party and date on which State became party to that Act
Bulgaria	13 June 1921	Stockholm: Articles 1 to 12: 19 or 27 May 1970[3] Stockholm: Articles 13 to 30: 27 May 1970
Burkina Faso	19 November 1963	Stockholm: 2 September 1975
Burundi	3 September 1977	Stockholm: 3 September 1977
Cameroon	10 May 1964	Stockholm: 20 April 1975
Canada	12 June 1925	Stockholm: Articles 1 to 12: 26 May 1996 Stockholm: Articles 13 to 30: 7 July 1970
Central African Republic	19 November 1963	Stockholm: 5 September 1978
Chad	19 November 1963	Stockholm: 26 September 1970
Chile	14 June 1991	Stockholm: 14 June 1991
China[4]	19 March 1985	Stockholm: 19 March 1985[2]
Colombia	3 September 1996	Stockholm: 3 September 1996
Congo	2 September 1963	Stockholm: 5 December 1975
Costa Rica	31 October 1995	Stockholm: 31 October 1995
Côte d'Ivoire	23 October 1963	Stockholm: 4 May 1974
Croatia	8 October 1991	Stockholm: 8 October 1991
Cuba	17 November 1904	Stockholm: 8 April 1975[2]
Cyprus	17 January 1966	Stockholm: 3 April 1984
Czech Republic	1 January 1993	Stockholm: 1 January 1993
Democratic People's Republic of Korea	10 June 1980	Stockholm: 10 June 1980
Democratic Republic of the Congo	31 January 1975	Stockholm: 31 January 1975
Denmark[5]	1 October 1894	Stockholm: Articles 1 to 12: 26 April or 19 May 1970[3] Stockholm: Articles 13 to 30: 26 April 1970

3 These are the alternative dates of entry into force which the Director General of WIPO communicated to the states concerned.

4 The Stockholm Act applies also to the Hong Kong Special Administrative Region with effect from 1 July 1997.

5 Denmark extended the application of the Stockholm Act to the Faroe Islands with effect from 6 August 1971.

State	Date on which State became party to the Convention	Latest Act[1] of the Convention to which State is party and date on which State became party to that Act	
Dominican Republic	11 July 1890	The Hague:	6 April 1951
Egypt	1 July 1951	Stockholm:	6 March 1975[2]
El Salvador	19 February 1994	Stockholm:	19 February 1994
Equatorial Guinea	26 June 1997	Stockholm:	26 June 1997
Estonia	24 August 1994[6]	Stockholm:	24 August 1994
Finland	20 September 1921	Stockholm:	Articles 1 to 12: 21 October 1975
		Stockholm:	Articles 13 to 30: 15 September 1970
France[7]	7 July 1884	Stockholm:	12 August 1975
Gabon	29 February 1964	Stockholm:	10 June 1975
Gambia	21 January 1992	Stockholm:	21 January 1992
Georgia	25 December 1991	Stockholm:	25 December 1991[2]
Germany	1 May 1903	Stockholm:	19 September 1970
Ghana	28 September 1976	Stockholm:	28 September 1976
Greece	2 October 1924	Stockholm:	15 July 1976
Guinea	5 February 1982	Stockholm:	5 February 1982
Guinea-Bissau	28 June 1988	Stockholm:	28 June 1988
Guyana	25 October 1994	Stockholm:	25 October 1994
Haiti	1 July 1958	Stockholm:	3 November 1983
Holy See	29 September 1960	Stockholm:	24 April 1975
Honduras	4 February 1994	Stockholm:	4 February 1994
Hungary	1 January 1909	Stockholm:	Articles 1 to 12: 26 April or 19 May 1970[3]
		Stockholm:	Articles 13 to 30: 26 April 1970[2]
Iceland	5 May 1962	Stockholm:	Articles 1 to 12: 9 April 1995
		Stockholm:	Articles 13 to 30: 28 December 1984
Indonesia	24 December 1950	London:	24 December 1950
		Stockholm:	Articles 1 to 12: 5 September 1997
		Stockholm:	Articles 13 to 30: 20 December 1979[2]

6 Estonia acceded to the Paris Convention (Washington Act 1911) with effect from 12 February 1924. It lost its independence on 6 August 1940 and regained it on 20 August 1991.

7 Including all Overseas Departments and Territories.

State	Date on which State became party to the Convention	Latest Act[1] of the Convention to which State is party and date on which State became party to that Act	
Iran (Islamic Republic of)	16 December 1959	Lisbon:	4 January 1962
Iraq	24 January 1976	Stockholm:	24 January 1976[2]
Ireland	4 December 1925	Stockholm:	Articles 1 to 12: 26 April or 19 May 1970[3]
		Stockholm:	Articles 13 to 30: 26 April 1970
Israel	24 March 1950	Stockholm:	Articles 1 to 12: 26 April or 19 May 1970[3]
		Stockholm:	Articles 13 to 30: 26 April 1970
Italy	7 July 1884	Stockholm:	24 April 1977
Japan	15 July 1899	Stockholm:	Articles 1 to 12: 1 October 1975
		Stockholm:	Articles 13 to 30: 24 April 1975
Jordan	17 July 1972	Stockholm:	17 July 1972
Kazakhstan	25 December 1991	Stockholm:	25 December 1991[2]
Kenya	14 June 1965	Stockholm:	26 October 1971
Kyrgyzstan	25 December 1991	Stockholm:	25 December 1991[2]
Latvia	7 September 1993[8]	Stockholm:	7 September 1993
Lebanon	1 September 1924	London:	30 September 1947
		Stockholm:	Articles 13 to 30: 30 December 1986[2]
Lesotho	28 September 1989	Stockholm:	28 September 1989[2]
Liberia	27 August 1994	Stockholm:	27 August 1994
Libya	28 September 1976	Stockholm:	28 September 1976[2]
Liechtenstein	14 July 1933	Stockholm:	25 May 1972
Lithuania	22 May 1994	Stockholm:	22 May 1994
Luxembourg	30 June 1922	Stockholm:	24 March 1975
Macedonia, Republic of	8 September 1991	Stockholm:	8 September 1991
Madagascar	21 December 1963	Stockholm:	10 April 1972
Malawi	6 July 1964	Stockholm:	25 June 1970
Malaysia	1 January 1989	Stockholm:	1 January 1989
Mali	1 March 1983	Stockholm:	1 March 1983

8 Latvia acceded to the Paris Convention (Washington Act 1911) with effect from 20 August 1925. It lost its independence on 21 July 1940 and regained it on 21 August 1991.

State	Date on which State became party to the Convention	Latest Act[1] of the Convention to which State is party and date on which State became party to that Act	
Malta	20 October 1967	Lisbon:	20 October 1967
		Stockholm:	Articles 13 to 30: 12 December 1977[2]
Mauritania	11 April 1965	Stockholm:	21 September 1976
Mauritius	24 September 1976	Stockholm:	24 September 1976
Mexico	7 September 1903	Stockholm:	26 July 1976
Monaco	29 April 1956	Stockholm:	4 October 1975
Mongolia	21 April 1985	Stockholm:	21 April 1985[2]
Morocco	30 July 1917	Stockholm:	6 August 1971
Netherlands[9]	7 July 1884	Stockholm:	10 January 1975
New Zealand[10]	29 July 1931	London:	14 July 1946
		Stockholm:	Articles 13 to 30: 20 June 1984
Nicaragua	3 July 1996	Stockholm:	3 July 1996[2]
Niger	5 July 1964	Stockholm:	6 March 1975
Nigeria	2 September 1963	Lisbon:	2 September 1963
Norway	1 July 1885	Stockholm:	13 June 1974
Panama	19 October 1996	Stockholm:	19 October 1996
Paraguay	28 May 1994	Stockholm:	28 May 1994
Peru	11 April 1995	Stockholm:	11 April 1995
Philippines	27 September 1965	Lisbon:	27 September 1965
		Stockholm:	Articles 13 to 30: 16 July 1980
Poland	10 November 1919	Stockholm:	24 March 1975
Portugal	7 July 1884	Stockholm:	30 April 1975
Republic of Korea	4 May 1980	Stockholm:	4 May 1980
Republic of Moldova	25 December 1991	Stockholm:	25 December 1991[2]
Romania	6 October 1920	Stockholm:	Articles 1 to 12: 26 April or 19 May 1970[3]
		Stockholm:	Articles 13 to 30: 26 April 1970[2]
Russian Federation	1 July 1965[11]	Stockholm:	Articles 1 to 12: 26 April or 19 May 1970[3,11]
		Stockholm:	Articles 13 to 30: 26 April 1970[2,11]

9 Ratification for the Kingdom in Europe, the Netherlands Antilles and Aruba.

10 The accession of New Zealand to the Stockholm Act, with the exception of Articles 1 to 12 extends to the Cook Islands, Niue and Tokelau.

11 Date of adherence of the Soviet Union, continued by the Russian Federation as from 25 December 1991.

State	Date on which State became party to the Convention	Latest Act[1] of the Convention to which State is party and date on which State became party to that Act
Rwanda	1 March 1984	Stockholm: 1 March 1984
Saint Kitts and Nevis	9 April 1995	Stockholm 9 April 1995
Saint Lucia	9 June 1995	Stockholm: 9 June 1995[2]
Saint Vincent and the Grenadines	29 August 1995	Stockholm: 29 August 1995
San Marino	4 March 1960	Stockholm: 26 June 1991
Senegal	21 December 1963	Stockholm: Articles 1 to 12: 26 April or 19 May 1970[3] Stockholm: Articles 13 to 30: 26 April 1970
Sierra Leone	17 June 1997	Stockholm: 17 June 1997
Singapore	23 February 1995	Stockholm: 23 February 1995
Slovakia	1 January 1993	Stockholm: 1 January 1993
Slovenia	25 June 1991	Stockholm: 25 June 1991
South Africa	1 December 1947	Stockholm: 24 March 1975[2]
Spain	7 July 1884	Stockholm: 14 April 1972
Sri Lanka	29 December 1952	London: 29 December 1952 Stockholm: Articles 13 to 30: 23 September 1978
Sudan	16 April 1984	Stockholm: 16 April 1984
Suriname	25 November 1975	Stockholm: 25 November 1975
Swaziland	12 May 1991	Stockholm: 12 May 1991
Sweden	1 July 1885	Stockholm: Articles 1 to 12: 9 October 1970 Stockholm: Articles 13 to 30: 26 April 1970
Switzerland	7 July 1884	Stockholm: Articles 1 to 12: 26 April or 19 May 1970[3] Stockholm: Articles 13 to 30: 26 April 1970
Syria	1 September 1924	London: 30 September 1947
Tajikistan	25 December 1991	Stockholm: 25 December 1991[2]
Togo	10 September 1967	Stockholm: 30 April 1975
Trinidad and Tobago	1 August 1964	Stockholm: 16 August 1988
Tunisia	7 July 1884	Stockholm: 12 April 1976[2]
Turkey	10 October 1925	Stockholm: Articles 1 to 12: 1 February 1995 Stockholm: Articles 13 to 30: 16 May 1976

State	Date on which State became party to the Convention	Latest Act[1] of the Convention to which State is party and date on which State became party to that Act	
Turkmenistan	25 December 1991	Stockholm:	25 December 1991[2]
Uganda	14 June 1965	Stockholm:	20 October 1973
Ukraine	25 December 1991	Stockholm:	25 December 1991[2]
United Arab Emirates	19 September 1996	Stockholm:	19 September 1996
United Kingdom[12]	7 July 1884	Stockholm:	Articles 1 to 12: 26 April or 19 May 1970[3]
		Stockholm:	Articles 13 to 30: 26 April 1970
United Republic of Tanzania	16 June 1963	Lisbon:	16 June 1963
		Stockholm:	Articles 13 to 30: 30 December 1983
United States of America[13]	30 May 1887	Stockholm:	Articles 1 to 12: 25 August 1973
		Stockholm:	Articles 13 to 30: 5 September 1970
Uruguay	18 March 1967	Stockholm:	28 December 1979
Uzbekistan	25 December 1991	Stockholm:	25 December 1991[2]
Venezuela	12 September 1995	Stockholm:	12 September 1995
Vietnam	8 March 1949	Stockholm:	2 July 1976[2]
Yugoslavia	26 February 1921	Stockholm:	16 October 1973
Zambia	6 April 1965	Lisbon:	6 April 1965
		Stockholm:	Articles 13 to 30: 14 May 1977
Zimbabwe	18 April 1980	Stockholm:	30 December 1981

(Total: 143 States)

12 The United Kingdom extended the application of the Stockholm Act to the Isle of Man with effect from 29 October 1983.

13 The United States of America extended the application of the Stockholm Act to all territories and possessions of the United States of America, including the Commonwealth of Puerto Rico, as from 25 August 1973.

Schedule 2: Madrid Agreement and Protocol Relating To the Madrid Agreement concerning the International Registration of Marks

Status on 15 January 1998

State	Date on which State became party to the Agreement	Date on which State became party to the Madrid Protocol (1989)
Albania	4 October 1995	–
Algeria	5 July 1972	–
Armenia	25 December 1991	–
Austria	1 January 1909	–
Azerbaijan	25 December 1995	–
Belarus	25 December 1991	–
Belgium	15 July 1892	1 April 1998,[1,3]
Bosnia and Herzegovina	1 March 1992	–
Bulgaria	1 August 1985	–
China	4 October 1989	1 December 1995,[2,3]
Croatia	8 October 1991	–
Cuba	6 December 1989	26 December 1995
Czech Republic	1 January 1993	25 September 1996
Democratic People's Republic of Korea	10 June 1980	3 October 1996
Denmark	–	13 February 1996[2,3,4]
Egypt	1 July 1952	–
Finland	–	1 April 1996[2,3]
France	15 July 1892	7 November 1997[5]

1 The territories of Belgium, Luxembourg and the Netherlands are to be deemed a single country, for the application of the Madrid Agreement as from 1 January 1971 and for the application of the Protocol as from 1 April 1998.

2 In accordance with Article 5(2)(b) and (c) of the Protocol, this Contracting Party has declared that the time limit to notify a refusal of protection shall be 18 months and that, where a refusal of protection results from an opposition to the granting of protection, such refusal may be notified after the expiry of the 18-month time limit.

3 In accordance with Article 8(7)(a) of the Protocol, this Contracting Party has declared that, in connection with each request for territorial extension to it of the protection of an international registration and the renewal of any such international registration, it wants to receive, instead of a share in the revenue produced by the supplementary and complementary fee, an individual fee.

4 Not applicable to the Faroe Islands and to Greenland.

5 Including all Overseas Departments and Territories.

State	Date on which State became party to the Agreement	Date on which State became party to the Madrid Protocol (1989)
Germany	1 December 1922	20 March 1996
Hungary	1 January 1909	3 October 1997[6]
Iceland	–	15 April 1997[3,7]
Italy	15 October 1894	–
Kazakhstan	25 December 1991	–
Kyrgyzstan	25 December 1991	–
Latvia	1 January 1995	–
Liberia	25 December 1995	–
Liechtenstein	14 July 1933	17 March 1998
Lithuania	–	15 November 1997[2]
Luxembourg	1 September 1924	1 April 1998[1,3]
Macedonia, Republic of	8 September 1991	–
Monaco	29 April 1956	27 September 1996
Mongolia	21 April 1985	–
Morocco	30 July 1917	–
Netherlands	1 March 1893	1 April 1998[1,3,8]
Norway	–	29 March 1996[2,3]
Poland	18 March 1991	4 March 1997[8]
Portugal	31 October 1893	20 March 1997
Republic of Moldova	25 December 1991	1 December 1997
Romania	6 October 1920	–
Russian Federation	1 July 1976[9]	10 June 1997
San Marino	25 September 1960	–
Sierra Leone	17 June 1997	–
Slovakia	1 January 1993	13 September 1997[8]
Slovenia	25 June 1991	12 March 1998
Spain	15 July 1892	1 December 1995
Sudan	16 May 1984	–
Sweden	–	1 December 1995[2,3]
Switzerland	15 July 1892	1 May 1997[3,7]
Tajikistan	25 December 1991	–

6 In accordance with Article 14(5) of the Protocol, this Contracting Party has declared that the protection resulting from any international registration effected under this Protocol before the date of entry into force of this Protocol with respect to it cannot be extended to it.

7 In accordance with Article 5(2)(b) of the Protocol, this Contracting Party has declared that the time limit to notify a refusal of protection shall be 18 months.

8 The instrument of ratification of the Stockholm Act and the instrument of acceptance of the Protocol were deposited for the Kingdom in Europe.

9 Date of accession by the Soviet Union, continued by the Russian Federation as from 25 December 1991.

State	Date on which State became party to the Agreement	Date on which State became party to the Madrid Protocol (1989)
Ukraine	25 December 1991	–
United Kingdom	–	1 December 1995[2, 3, 10]
Uzbekistan	25 December 1991	–
Vietnam	8 March 1949	–
Yugoslavia	26 February 1921	17 February 1998
(Total: 54 States)		**(28)**

10 Ratification in respect of the United Kingdom and the Isle of Man.

Schedule 3: Trade Marks Registry Forms

Status on 1 February 1998

Form Number	Title	Fee
TM3	Application to register a trade mark (including certification and collective marks)	£225
TM3A	Application for additional class	£50 (per class)
TM5	Request to Registrar for a statement of grounds of decision	£100
TM7	Notice of opposition	£200
TM8	Form for counterstatement	FREE
TM9	Request for an extension of time on an application	£50
TM11	Renewal of trade mark registration	£250 £200 (per class) £50 (late)
TM12	Request to divide an application	£100
TM13	Request for the restoration and renewal of a registration removed from the register because of non-payment of the renewal fee	£100
TM16	Application to register a change of Proprietor	£50
TM17	Request to merge either applications or registrations	£100
TM21	Request to change the details of an application or registration	FREE
TM22	Notice to surrender a registration	FREE
TM23	Notice of a partial surrender of the specification of goods or services for which the mark is registered	£50
TM24	Application to record or cancel a registrable transaction or memoranda relating to a trade mark, but not an assignment or licence	£50
TM25	Request for alteration of a registered trademark	FREE

Form Number	Title	Fee
TM26	Application for the revocation or rectification of a registration or for it to be declared invalid	£200
TM27	Application to intervene in proceedings for revocation or rectification of a registration	FREE
TM31C	Request for information about applications or registered marks	£20
TM31M	Request for information in relation to an international trade mark	£20
TM31R	Request for Registrar's General certificate	£20
TM33	Request to appoint an agent or to enter or change an address for service	FREE
TM35	Filing of regulations governing the use of a certification or collective mark	£200
TM36	Application to amend the regulations governing the use of a certification or collective mark	£100
TM50	Application for the registration of a licensee for a registered trade mark	£50
TM51	Application to remove or amend a licence	FREE

Schedule 4: Statutory declarations

The United Kingdom

The United Kingdom covers England, Scotland, Wales and Northern Ireland, but not the Isle of Man or the Channel Islands. The declaration should be witnessed by a solicitor, justice of the peace, commissioner for oaths or an officer authorised by law to administer oaths.

A statutory declaration should begin:

'I (name) of (address) hereby solemnly and sincerely declare that . . .'

and end

'and I make this declaration conscientiously believing the same to be true and by virtue of the Statutory Declarations Act 1835.'

Outside of the United Kingdom but within Her Majesty's dominions

The declaration or affidavit must be witnessed by a competent authority, eg a declaration made in Canada would be as follows:

'I (name) of (address) hereby solemnly and sincerely declare that . . .'

and end

'and I make this solemn declaration conscientiously believing it to be true and knowing that it is of the same force and effect as if made under oath and by virtue of the Canadian Evidence Act. Declared in Toronto before a Notary Public by a United Kingdom citizen resident in Canada.'

Outside of the United Kingdom and Her Majesty's dominions

The declaration may be made under local national law.

Before a Notary Public

If made before a Notary Public the declaration should contain an assertion that the deponent

'solemnly and sincerely testifies that the content of the document is true'.

Before a British Minister or Consul

If made before a British Minister or the British Consul, the declaration must be made by virtue of the Statutory Declarations Act 1835, eg a declaration made before a British Pro-Consul, by a French citizen, could be worded as follows:

'I (name) a French citizen, solemnly and sincerely declare that I am familiar with the English language,'

and end

'and I make the above solemn declaration conscientiously believing the same to be true by virtue of the Statutory Declarations Act 1835.'

A declaration made by an American citizen could be worded to end:

'and I make this solemn declaration conscientiously believing the same to be true by virtue of the provision of Section 1778 of the revised statutes of the USA approved on the 22nd day of June 1874.'

Declarations made by non-English speakers

Unless the person making the declaration has a good command of the English language they will be unable to testify in English. In such cases, the declaration may be filed in his mother tongue accompanied by a certified translation prepared by a competent translator. This translator should prepare their own statutory declaration or affidavit stating that they are (at least) familiar with the English and the other language. As an exhibit to his declaration the translator should file copies of the foreign declaration and his translation.

Schedule 5: Notice under Trade Marks Act 1994 s 89 requesting infringing goods, material or articles to be treated as prohibited goods

NOTES

1 This notice may only be given by the proprietor of a registered trade mark, or a licensee. A separate notice must be given in respect of each consignment.
2 Please note that in Part 3 it is not mandatory to provide details other than the time and place of expected arrival of infringing goods but it will greatly increase the prospect of intercepting the consignment concerned if all the details requested are given.
3 A fee of £30 (plus VAT) is payable for each notice given. Please enclose a cheque for the required amount, made payable to 'Commissioners of Customs and Excise'.
4 A copy of the certificate of registration for the trade mark, as well as the certificate of renewal (where applicable), is to be enclosed with the notice, or submitted when the goods are imported.
5 The person who has given notice shall keep the Commissioners of Customs and Excise indemnified against any liability or expense which they may incur in consequence of the notice by reason of the detention of any goods or anything done to goods detained. The person giving the notice may be required to provide a security to cover this indemnity.

1 Person giving notice

. . . .

(Name of signatory in BLOCK LETTERS)

give notice to the Commissioners of Customs and Excise that

. . . .

. . . .

(Name and address of proprietor or licensee in BLOCK LETTERS)

is the *proprietor/licensee of a trade mark registered in the United Kingdom and that infringing goods, material or articles are expected to arrive in the United Kingdom, and *I/we request that they be treated as prohibited goods.

*Delete as necessary

2 Details of infringing goods, material or articles

Trade mark . . . .

Infringing goods,
material or articles . . . .

Quantity ....

Commodity
Code(s) ....

3 Details of expected importation

Place of
importation ....

Method of
importation ....
(Please include details of ship, aircraft or vehicle, where known)

Expected date
of arrival ....

Country of
origin ....

Country of
consignment ....

Importer's
details ....
(Please include VAT number, if known)

Consignor's
details ....

4 Declaration

I declare that the information given by me in this notice is true.

Signature ....
(*Sole Proprietor/Partner/Director/Company Secretary/Duly
Authorised Person)

Date ....

*Delete as necessary

5 Submission of notice

Please send the completed notice, fee and copies of relevant certificates to:

HM Customs and Excise
CD3A
New King's Beam House
22 Upper Ground
London
SE1 9PJ

Index